DATE DUE

UPI 261-2505 G   PRINTED IN U.S.A.

United Nations System

INTERNATIONAL ORGANIZATIONS SERIES

General Editors:

Robert G. Neville (Executive Editor)

John J. Horton

Robert A. Myers   John Paxton

Ian Wallace   Hans H. Wellisch

John J. Horton is Deputy Librarian of the University of Bradford and currently Chairman of its Academic Board of Studies in Social Sciences. He has maintained a longstanding interest in the discipline of area studies and its associated bibliographical problems, with special reference to European Studies. In particular he has published in the field of Icelandic and of Yugoslav studies, including the two relevant volumes in the World Bibliographical Series.

Robert A. Myers is Associate Professor of Anthropology in the Division of Social Sciences and Director of Study Abroad Programs at Alfred University, Alfred, New York. He has studied post-colonial island nations of the Caribbean and has spent two years in Nigeria on a Fulbright Lectureship. His interests include international public health, historical anthropology and developing societies. In addition to Amerindians of the Lesser Antilles: a bibliography (1981), A Resource Guide to Dominica, 1493-1986 (1987) and numerous articles, he has compiled the World Bibliographical Series volumes on Dominica (1987), Nigeria (1989) and Ghana (1991).

John Paxton was the editor of The Statesman's Year-Book from 1969 to 1990. His published works include The Developing Common Market, The Dictionary of the European Communities (which was commended by the McColvin Medal Committee of the British Library Association), The Penguin Dictionary of Abbreviations, The Penguin Dictionary of Proper Names (with G. Paton), Companion to Russian History, Companion to the French Revolution, and The Statesman's Year-Book Gazetteer. He was also chief consultant editor of the New Illustrated Everyman's Encyclopaedia.

Ian Wallace is Professor of German at the University of Bath. A graduate of Oxford in French and German, he also studied in Tübingen, Heidelberg and Lausanne before taking teaching posts at universities in the USA, Scotland and England. He specializes in contemporary German affairs, especially literature and culture, on which he has published numerous articles and books. In 1979 he founded the journal GDR Monitor, which he continues to edit under its new title German Monitor.

Hans H. Wellisch is Professor emeritus at the College of Library and Information Services, University of Maryland. He was President of the American Society of Indexers and was a member of the International Federation for Documentation. He is the author of numerous articles and several books on indexing and abstracting, and has published The Conversion of Scripts and Indexing and Abstracting: an International Bibliography, and Indexing from A to Z. He also contributes frequently to Journal of the American Society for Information Science, The Indexer and other professional journals.

VOLUME 10

United Nations System

Joseph Preston Baratta

CLIO PRESS

OXFORD, ENGLAND

British Library of Cataloguing in Publication Data

Baratta, Joseph Preston.
United Nations System.—(International
Organizations Series; Vol. 10)
I. Title.   II. Series
341.23

ISBN 1-85109-224-2

ABC-CLIO Ltd.,
35A Great Clarendon Street,
Oxford OX2 6AT, England.

Typeset by Columns Design and Production Services Ltd., Reading, England.

INTERNATIONAL ORGANIZATIONS SERIES

Each volume in the International Organizations Series is either devoted to one specific organization, or to a number of different organizations operating in a particular region, or engaged in a specific field of activity. The scope of the series is wide-ranging and includes intergovernmental organizations, international non-governmental organizations, and national bodies dealing with international issues. The series is aimed mainly at the English-speaker and each volume provides a selective, annotated, critical bibliography of the organization, or organizations, concerned. The bibliographies cover books, articles, pamphlets, directories, databases and theses and, wherever possible, attention is focused on material about the organizations rather than on the organizations' own publications. Notwithstanding this, the most important official publications, and guides to those publications, will be included. The views expressed in individual volumes, however, are not necessarily those of the publishers.

VOLUMES IN THE SERIES

TITLES IN PREPARATION

For Virginia, beloved wife

Contents

Contents

Contents

Introduction

Historical reflection will immediately show why we have the United Nations and what the U.N. has achieved. International organization arose in the nineteenth century to help states solve certain common technical problems, such as linking national telegraph systems or delivering mail from one country to another. After the general breakdown of the state system of balance of power in the Great War of 1914-18, it was a logical extension of ideas for Woodrow Wilson to propose, in his famous fourteenth point on a peace settlement, the establishment of a 'general association of nations' to provide 'mutual guarantees of political independence and territorial integrity to great and small states alike'. But the League of Nations was too weak to revise the Versailles Treaty or to stop the aggressions of Japan, Italy, and Germany once their leaders decided once again, in accordance with long usage, to pursue their national policies by the use of force.

Led by Franklin D. Roosevelt, who accepted the internationalism of Woodrow Wilson, the United States, Great Britain, Soviet Union, and China agreed in 1943, in the midst of the Second World War, to establish a 'general international organization . . . for the maintenance of international peace and security'. In 1945, the United Nations Organization, designed 'to save succeeding generations from the scourge of war', was duly established. Organized on the assumption of great power unanimity in the Security Council, the U.N. could not withstand the breakup of the Grand Alliance over making the peace, and within two years the Cold War between the Western liberal capitalist democracies and the communist bloc replaced the U.N. as the fundamental reality of international relations. Nevertheless, the United Nations did not die within twenty years, as the League did, for moderate statesmen, dutiful international civil servants, resourceful activists, patient scholars, and immense majorities of people, determined never again to have to fight another general war, struggled to save what had been so painfully won.

Introduction

In the next forty years, the United Nations provided the multilateral diplomatic setting for many achievements that had been barely begun under the League: the practical development of peaceful means for the resolution of disputes; the enlarged use of peacekeeping observers, and the creation of peacekeeping forces; the launching of the movement to define and observe human rights; the peaceful dismantling of the European empires in a rapid process of decolonization; the admission of many new self-governing states into the family of nations; the beginnings of disinterested economic development aid; even the negotiation of six multilateral arms control treaties in the midst of a headlong nuclear and conventional arms race. The U.N also entered new areas of international relations for which there was virtually no precedent under the League: peacekeeping is the best example, but so are preventive diplomacy, majority rule in all the organs (even the Security Council, though qualified by unanimity of the permanent members), and a declared renunciation of the threat and use of force (Article 2(4)).

But surely the trend of history was toward another breakdown of the balance of power – now called deterrence – when an accident or an 'irrational' national leader would precipitate a general, ultimately nuclear war. It is to the credit of Soviet statesman Mikhail Gorbachev and his circle of advisers that they summoned the courage to undertake unilateral measures to break the vicious circle and end the Cold War. By 1990, when, at a conference on the Conventional Forces in Europe Treaty, George Bush of the United States said the words, 'The Cold War is over', a great historic opportunity to put international relations on a new foundation, like that from about 1943 to 1950, opened up again.

The end of the Cold War, said U.N. Secretary-General Boutros Boutros-Ghali in his daring report to the Security Council, *An agenda for peace*, has given nation-states and their peoples a 'second chance to create the world of our Charter' (see item no. 121). Not only is the United Nations beginning to work as it was designed, but there is general acknowledgement, supported by the Secretary-General, of the necessity for U.N. reform as the Organization approaches its fiftieth anniversary in 1995 (item no. 11). The U.N. clearly has far to go to end the scourge of war.

How will humanity respond to the historic opportunity opened up by the end of the Cold War? The idea of U.N. reform is in the air, and there is no lack of imaginative and informed proposals for 'strengthening the United Nations'. Yet states and peoples seem to lack the will to make the U.N. work in accordance with its Charter, or to interpret or amend that Charter in order to give the U.N. the powers necessary to achieve its declared purposes. Along with *hope* in the U.N. (at least through the Persian Gulf War of 1990-91), there remains a large measure of *disenchantment*, marked, as Mr. Boutros-Ghali says in his 1993 *Report on the work of the organization* (item no. 11), by the continual financial crisis 'as the demands of Member States on the Organization are not matched by the resources provided'.

The problems of the United Nations are first of all problems of *will*. States, other international organizations, businesses, associations of individuals, and broad publics in the many states-members lack confidence in the U.N. as it attempts to fulfil its primary purpose to maintain international peace and security, or its second, to develop friendly relations among nations (items 18, 521, 603). To some extent, confidence in an institution can be developed by a string of small, then larger, successes, but often, especially at the beginning, there is no escaping taking a risk; as C. Wilfred Jenks argued, risk has been necessary for every major step in the progress of humanity, from the elimination of private vengeance to the formal renunciation of war as an instrument of national policy (item no. 489).

In this bibliography, we take *will* to mean the recognition of the necessity and usefulness of the United Nations and the free and courageous act to risk exercising its processes in order to build international peace. We are not awaiting another 'failure' of international organization, which, like that of the League, can be blamed on the states-members, while humanity is again chastened by bitter experience (item no. 403). Every work cited here has been chosen to build such a will.

To seize the opportunity opened by the end of the Cold War, states and other actors on the world stage will need, in addition to political will, a shared purpose or at least an agreement about the general direction of their efforts. It is not enough to know that we are living through a time of transition – we must decide or discern where the transition will end.

There are, it appears from the literature, three general directions for the United Nations, analogous to the three fundamental bases of international life – balance of power, collective security, and rule of law (item no. 58):

- Cautious development of the state system, utilizing the U.N. as at present only when bilateral diplomacy must avail itself of the services of multilateral diplomacy.

- A non-hierarchical system of perhaps one hundred international organizations, including a much more effective United Nations empowered to achieve the purposes in its Charter.

- A world federal government, preserving the nation-states but providing a higher level of legislative, executive, and judicial authority, probably on the model of the emerging European Union.

Different assessments of international reality lead to different choices of such alternatives. The literature covered in this bibliography tends to focus on a non-hierarchical system (the second alternative), though works upholding absolute state sovereignty or world federation have been included for completeness. That is, realism and idealism here generally make way for practical international organization and international law, whose recent developments are often astonishing.

Any scheme of U.N. reform must accommodate such new facts of international life as these:

- U.S. hegemony since 1973, like British hegemony after 1918, has been declining (items 29, 179).

- The absolute sovereignty of states, enshrined in the U.N. Charter's Article 2(7), no longer preserves states from war, economic disruption, or, now, humanitarian intervention (items 304, 607, 616).

- Interdependence is now more of a reality than independence, as the world is knit ever closer by modern industry and democracy (items 137, 735, 739, 745).

- International war is decreasing in incidence, while domestic and ethnic conflict affecting international peace and security is increasing. The U.N., which was designed to stop Hitlerite aggression across borders, is now increasingly charged with maintaining the peace among individuals, as if it were a world state (item no. 401).

- Common security is supplanting national security as the first interest of states (items 135, 219), and economic power is increasingly recognized as more of a reality than military power (items 124, 134, 208, 699).

- Nuclear weapons, which their most optimistic champions claimed undermined *Realpolitik*, are unusable (items 49, 728, 733). Disarmament, even in a decentralized world political system, has made sudden progress in reducing both nuclear and conventional arms, though dangers are not to be discounted (items 647, 666, 681).

- The 'effective international control' that since 1961 has been recognized as necessary to fill the security vacuum produced by general disarmament continues to be affirmed at the United Nations (items 666, 674).

- Despite a public posture of ignoring or criticizing the U.N., the U.S. government in particular recognizes the need for a general security system (items 189, 209, 212, 721); and, since the Persian Gulf War, many states have applauded the U.N.'s acquisition of greater enforcement powers (items 563, 610, 617).

- Newer techniques of conflict resolution and more traditional means for the peaceful settlement of international disputes are combining and progressing rapidly – to the point where John Burton argues that they offer a universal ideology in place of liberalism and communism, mutually exhausted in the struggles of the Cold War (items 390, 397). Preventive diplomacy and all devices to prevent conflict, rather than contain or stop it, are held to be the elements of a mature international system (items 410, 417, 462, 469, 566).

- Although there is general agreement that the states, cultures, and peoples of the world are, in sociological terms, at most a 'society' (*Gesellschaft*), and not yet a 'community' – so that international cooperation and not the rule of law is the most that can be expected of it as a goal for common action – everyone speaks of the 'world community'. They seem to do so either as an aspiration (as in 'European Union') or as an unconscious recognition of the changed reality of the planet (items 95, 98, 118, 256, 269, 542).

- The world is 'governable', as Georgi Shakhnazarov wrote in 1988, for a strengthened United Nations no longer threatens to take sides in the struggle between East and West (items 134, 218, 223, 739, 742).

- Since the great influx of new states from Asia and Africa into the U.N., the Third World has had the lead in projects of U.N. reform, notably in the proposed New International Economic Order (items 356, 365, 1195). But economic power has proven decisive in this contest, and now there is real potential for the West, allied with the new independent states and market economies of the former communist bloc and with Japan, to return to the lead (items 25, 139, 182). The First World, after all, established the U.N. and led the negotiations over the Universal Declaration of Human Rights.

- An 'economic United Nations' on the model of the European Community, as has been proposed by Maurice Bertrand, would give more weight to the North (items 127, 152, 156, 163, 164). Only the new standards of human rights (political and civil, economic, social, and cultural) will protect the South (items 171, 618).

- Yet a future focus on economic development will not preclude continued primary focus on the U.N.'s main function to maintain international peace and security, as the bulk of this bibliography attests.

- Much can be expected of non-Western peoples and states as the world becomes increasingly one (items 97, 275, 346, 518). The new states already reject customary international law as the law of European imperialism; the prospect, then, is for a truly universal international law, already being called 'world law' (items 89, 388, 524).

- A global *problematique* of common problems beyond the powers of any one national state to solve for the protection of its people – ranging from defence against attack and cooperation for international financial and commercial interests to protection and promotion of human rights and preservation of the environment – requires common action by the U.N. (items 38, 59, 137, 141, 298).

- The General Assembly, even as presently constituted, has a quasi-legislative competence, which would be increased if a second chamber, representative of peoples like the European Parliament, were established (items 128, 271, 275).

- Increasingly, consensus, rather than consent of every state willing to be bound, is recognized as the basis of international obligation laid down in the recommendations, or enactments, of the General Assembly (items 276, 279).

- Groups of states, like the G-7 or the G-77, are already being described as nascent transnational political parties (items 69, 329), as are international associations of individuals in the non-governmental organizations (NGOs) dedicated to peace, economic development, human rights, or protection of the environment (items 47, 48, 144, 374, 377).

- The individual is being recognized as a 'subject' of international law, particularly under the Nuremberg principles and now under some ninety-five human rights instruments (items 633, 636).

- Equity – arbitrators' sense of what is equitable and fair – is beginning to join treaty, custom, principles, and teachings as sources of international law (items 349, 476).

When the individual is protected by international human rights law, has a role in the making of treaties and the hardening of customs, and has standing before world courts and tribunals, have we not crossed the line from an association of sovereign states to a government of peoples and states? 'We are living through the birth pangs of a world community', said C. Wilfred Jenks in 1969 (item no. 261). We are immersed in the 'emerging constitutionalism of world order', said Edward McWhinney in 1987 (item no. 342). Judging by the works cited in this bibliography, humanity is in search for some more stable, more peaceful world order – hence the interest in what the Americans call 'governance' and the British 'government' – but very few are ready to plunge into a world federal state (items 175, 177) in order to escape the fundamental flaw, found in the U.N. Charter, of attempting to legislate for states or governments in their collective capacities, as distinguished from the individuals of which they consist, as Alexander Hamilton argued in *The Federalist,* No. 15.

Everyone seems to prefer a decentralized United Nations system of international organizations. People fear any new coercive state power. They would strengthen the U.N. Organization itself only to the minimal degree necessary to maintain international peace and security or perhaps to assist in the more equitable economic development of the poorer states (items 63, 72, 73, 91, 314, 401, 506, 517, 745).

Scholars of world politics – especially the 'realists' – have long maintained that there can be international *order* without a strong central authority. That is, they did so at least until the functionalists, transnationalists, and internationalists made deep inroads into their numbers in recent years. Even Hans Morgenthau abandoned 'realism' for Louis Sohn's reformed U.N. authority in 1978 on the grounds that balance of power in a nuclearly armed world was leading inexorably toward a general war (items 79, 187). Similarly, international legal scholars have long claimed that there can be an international *law* without a central legislature or an independent judiciary (items 90, 91, 94). And the leading advocate of meaningful U.N. reform, Maurice Bertrand, whose analyses and prescriptions have been the inspiration for this book, speaks with only a certain irony of over one hundred legally independent organizations, offices, programmes, and the like in the U.N. system (item no. 164).

Introduction

These one hundred entities provide an image of the many nuclei of a safe yet secure international system. In a world so much more diverse than any national community yet united under a federal system, the necessary world political system of the future will probably look as different from any of the seventeen historical federations as the United States federal government looked from the confederation that preceded it. 'Unity and diversity' remain the watchwords for the future (item no. 219).

Humanity is in the midst of the danger and the opportunity of a world constitutional crisis. Anyone who thinks that the state system is eternal, or the United Nations expendable, need only reflect on the world in A.D. 2050, if present trends continue: a world population of 9,000 million – two-thirds of whom will be poor, hungry, and young; the world divided again into two, this time into industrially developed and underdeveloped; massive emigration from the South, or totalitarian controls in the North to keep out the masses and to guard against terrorism; an environment denuded of its natural variety and abundance; no superpowers, but instead an multipolar system of fearful and hostile states; and nuclear proliferation. This is a future prospect of war, famine, disease, and death.

Perhaps, as it took the First World War to convince statesmen and national peoples of the necesssity of establishing the League of Nations, and the Second World War to establish the United Nations, so it will take some third general disaster to substantially reform the U.N. or establish a superior successor organization. Arnold Toynbee feared such an event in the mottoes he chose for *A study of history*: 'Man must learn by suffering' (Aeschylus, *Agamemnon* l. 177). 'Whom the Lord loveth, he chasteneth' (Epistle to the Hebrews, 12: 6).

We take the view that the disaster is foreseeable and hence, if we are wise, avoidable. To quote that optimistic and quintessential American, Benjamin Franklin, 'Experience keeps a dear school, but fools will learn in no other.' This book is based on a faith that the United Nations system represents a stage on humanity's search for a world constitutional order. Every work here cited has some connection to the U.N., though some, particularly on world politics, nearly pass over it; they have been included in order to warn the reader of a peculiar blindness in the reigning school of thought on international relations ('realism') and to try to contribute to a wiser study of the emerging world community in the future ('interdependence'). Critical works especially have been sought, and, as said before, those on U.N. reform are central. The new work by Erskine Childers and Brian Urquhart, *Renewing the United Nations system* (item no. 157), is typical of the most recent, visionary, and practical proposals of U.N. reform.

No diagram of the United Nations system quite makes sense to this compiler, since the relation of the U.N. Organization itself to the specialized agencies or indeed to all the one hundred legally independent nuclei is not one of administrative direction. Moreover, the states-members are actually supreme. The U.N. is not a world government, as its brochures say, but an organization of sovereign states. The 'system' is not like the solar system or the system of blood and nerves in the human body. Hence, the most meaningful display of the U.N. system that can be taken in at a glance is probably a table of organizations. The following is updated and adapted from one given by Maurice Bertrand in his 1985 report, *Some reflections on the reform of the United Nations.*

Table 1

Budget Appropriations and Personnel, 1992-93 Biennium

Organization	Budget (US$)	Personnel
United Nations Organization		
Overall policy making	34,621,700	
Political affairs (e.g., peacekeeping)	168,996,500	
International justice and law (ICJ, LOS)	50,296,100	
International cooperation for development	326,386,700	
Regional cooperation for development	282,545,600	
Human rights and humanitarian affairs	100,500,500	
Public information	103,006,000	
Support services (conferences)	853,139,700	
Special expenses	47,661,700	
Capital expenditures (buildings)	98,850,200	
Staff assessment	402,034,500	
Professionals		3,945 P
General Staff		9,017 GS
Project Experts		921 EX
Total, U.N.O.	2,468,039,200	13,883
U.N. Peacekeeping Operations (13 in 1992)	2,800,000,000*	93,821**
(projected in 1993)	4,300,000,000	

Notes: * Regular and voluntary funding.
        ** Soldiers, police, and civilians.
Sources: Revised budget appropriations for the biennium, 1992-93
         A/Res/47/220A, 23 December 1992;
         Yearbook of the United Nations, 1992, p.1031-32;
         United Nations peacekeeping (1993).

Introduction

Table 2

Selected Juridically Independent Centres, Institutes, Funds, etc. within the U.N.O.

Administrative Tribunal of the U.N.
Committee against Torture
Committee on the Elimination of Discrimination against Women (CEDAW)
Committee on the Peaceful Uses of Outer Space (COPUOS)
Consultative Committee on Administrative Questions
Conference on Disarmament (CD)
European Centre for Social Welfare Policy and Research
Intergovernmental Oceanographic Commission
International Civil Service Commission
International Law Commission (ILC)
Joint Inspection Unit (JIU)
Special Committee on the Charter of the United Nations and on the Strengthening of the Role of the Organization
U.N. Centre against Apartheid
U.N. Centre for Human Rights
U.N. Centre for Regional Development
U.N. Centre for Science and Technology for Development
U.N. Commission on Human Settlements
U.N. Commission on International Trade Law (UNCITRAL)
U.N. Commission on Narcotic Drugs
U.N. Committee on the Development and Utilization of New and Renewable Sources of Energy
U.N. Committee on the Exercise of the Inalienable Rights of the Palestinian People
U.N. Committee for Programme and Coordination
U.N. Development Fund for Women (UNIFEM)
U.N. Interregional Crime and Justice Research Institute
U.N. Population Commisssion
U.N. Preparatory Commission on the International Sea-Bed Authority and for the International Tribunal for the Law of the Sea (LOS PrepCom)
U.N. Regional Commissions, New York Office
U.N. Special Committee against Apartheid
U.N. Special Committee on Enhancing the Effectiveness of the Principle of the Non-Use of Force in International Relations
U.N. Special Committee on Peacekeeping Operations
U.N. Special Committee on . . . the Granting of Independence to Colonial Countries and Peoples
U.N. Voluntary Fund for Victims of Torture
U.N. World Disarmament Campaign
World Commission on Environment and Development

Source: *Yearbook of international organizations, 1991-92.*

Table 3

Other Selected Juridically Independent Entities within the U.N.O. (regular and voluntary funding, 1992-93 biennium)

Organization	Budget (US$)	Personnel
World Food Programme (WFP, Rome)	2,190,000,000	Shared w/FAO & UNDP
U.N. High Commissioner for Refugees (UNHCR, Geneva)	2,186,200,000	749 P 1,377 GS
U.N. Development Programme (UNDP, New York)	2,128,000,000	1,571 P 5,033 GS
U.N. Children's Fund (UNICEF, New York)	1,036,000,000	1,126 P 2,840 GS
U.N. Relief and Works Agency for Palestine Refugees (UNRWA, Vienna, Beirut)	480,000,000	135 P 18,000 GS
U.N. Fund for Population Activities (UNFPA, New York)	460,000,000	299 P 395 GS
U.N. Fund for Drug Abuse Control (UNFDAC, Vienna)	138,600,000	
U.N. Conference on Trade and Development (UNCTAD, New York)	92,514,000	400 P&GS
U.N. Environment Programme (UNEP, Nairobi)	12,832,100	500 P&GS
U.N. Centre for Human Settlements (Habitat, Nairobi)	12,029,900	126 P 1,250 GS
U.N. International Research and Training Institute for the Advancement of Women (INSTRAW)	3,100,000	42 P
U.N. Disaster Relief Office (UNDRO, Geneva)	2,010,600	
U.N. Institute for Disarmament Research (UNIDIR, Geneva)	2,000,000	10 P
U.N. Institute for Training and Research (UNITAR, New York)	725,518	10 P 9 GS
U.N. Social Defence Research Institute (Rome)		
U.N. Research Institute for Social Development (Geneva)		
U.N. University (UNU, Tokyo)	Endowment	36 P 65 GS

Sources: Bertrand, *Some reflections on the reform of the U.N.*, A/40/988, (1985); Childers and Urquhart, *Renewing the United Nations system* (1994); Yearbook of international organizations, 1991-92; *Image and reality: questions and answers* (1993)

Introduction

Table 4

Specialized Agencies of the U.N. System (1992-93 biennium)

Organization	Budget (US$)	Personnel
World Health Organization (WHO)	734,936,000	1,584 P
		3,075 GS
Food and Agricultural Organization (FAO)	645,600,000	2,180 P
		3,750 GS
U.N. Educational, Scientific, and Cultural Organization (UNESCO)	444,704,000	956 P
		1,585 GS
International Labour Organization (ILO)	405,690,000	1,330 P
		1,933 GS
International Atomic Energy Agency (IAEA)	359,730,800	798 P
		1,337 GS
World Bank (IBRD)	Self-financed	3,893 P
		2,153 GS
International Development Association (IDA)	Self-financed	Same as IBRD
International Monetary Fund (IMF)	Self-financed	2,167 P&GS
International Finance Corporation (IFC)	Self-financed	732 P&GS
International Telecommunications Union (ITU)	197,694,800	590 P
		139 GS
U.N. Industrial Development Organization (UNIDO)	181,013,400	437 P
		922 GS
World Intellectual Property Organization (WIPO)	151,800,000	126 P
		276 GS
General Agreement on Tariffs and Trade (GATT)	119,400,000	168 P
		242 GS
International Fund for Agricultural Development (IFAD)	104,800,000	106 P
		152 GS
International Civil Aviation Organization (ICAO)	96,146,000	303 P
		459 GS
International Maritime Organization (IMO)	78,008,700	115 P
		182 GS
World Meteorological Organization (WMO)	77,784,000	134 P
		159 GS
Universal Postal Union (UPU)	35,641,600	58 P
		88 GS

Note: The specialized agencies also include legally independent entities, like WHO's Onchocercosis Fund.

Sources: Budget appropriations for 1992-93, A/Res/47/220A, 23 December 1992; *Yearbook of the United Nations, 1992;* *Yearbook of international organizations, 1991-92.*

Table 5

Grand totals, 1992-93 biennium

Organization	Budget (US$)	Personnel
U.N. Organization		13,883
Regular budget (assessments)	2,467,458,200	
Extrabudget (voluntary contributions)	3,718,026,200	
Peacekeeping	7,100,000,000	93,821
Total, U.N.O., 1992-93	13,285,484,400	
Specialized agencies	3,632,949,300	32,129
Total, U.N. system, 1992-93	16,918,433,700	148,623

Note: Arrearages to regular budget: $500,607,665
       To peacekeeping budget (31/12/92): $664,300,000
Source: Proposed programme budget for the biennium 1994-95,
       A/48/6 (Part 1/Corr. 1), 16 August 1993.

Acknowledgements

Several people have been particularly helpful in producing this bibliography. Dr. Robert G. Neville, Director of Clio Press, saw it through from the first letter of invitation to the last editorial correction. Professor Saul Mendlovitz, Co-director of the World Order Models Project, reviewed a draft still lacking an index. Ms. Tahani El-Erian, Head Librarian of the Dag Hammarskjöld Library at the United Nations, made many helpful suggestions about items overlooked. Professor Louis B. Sohn, one of the world's greatest living teachers of international law, from time to time has guided me. M. Maurice Bertrand, whose works on U.N. reform have been an inspiration, is always in the background and between the lines.

I also wish to thank Professor Gary B. Ostrower, historian at Alfred University; Professor Robert Myers, cultural anthropologist there; Professor Lawrence S. Wittner (SUNY Albany), who has recently written a history of disarmament; Professor (Emeritus) Robert F. Meagher of the Fletcher School of Law and Diplomacy; Professor Winston Langley of the University of Massachusetts at Boston; Ambassador John W. McDonald, Chairman of the Institute for Multi-track Diplomacy in Washington; and Ms. Charlotte Waterlow, M.B.E., of Great Britain, who put me in touch with Ms. Susan J. Sayde, Librarian of the Royal Institute of International Affairs.

Deserving special thanks for their patience and resourcefulness are the unsung librarians of Boston University's School of Law, the Boston Public Library's Research Library, M.I.T.'s Dewey Library, Tufts' Edwin Ginn Library, and the libraries of Suffolk University, Boston College School of Law, and Northeastern University.

No one mentioned above reviewed the annotations. I am responsible for any errors, omissions, or superfluous inclusions.

How to use this book

The concerned citizen, student, teacher, scholar, international lawyer, national policy-maker, and international civil servant are assumed to be the audience for this book.

Readers in search of a particular topic may prefer to turn directly to the subject index. Entries are numbered, so references are to entry items, not pages. Authors may be found in the author index. Subjects of biographies are listed in both subject and author indexes.

The bibliography is organized in the 'synthetic' order – from the more general to the more specific – through the sections on the United Nations *Organization*. Thus, works are arranged in descending order of interest, context, or controversy, as in sections on the United Nations in general, world politics, international law, and the like. The heart of the work, which has informed the whole and is most significant for the future, is the section on U.N. reform. The General Assembly, as the universal deliberative body, is treated before the Security Council, whose membership is more limited. Peaceful settlement of international disputes, which is much more often employed in pursuit of the U.N.'s primary function to maintain international peace and security, is treated before enforcement of decisions. The sequence of subjects within the primary function follows the list given in Article 33 of the U.N. Charter.

Thereafter, in the sections on the specialized agencies or *organizations* of the U.N. *system*, the bibliography is organized in the order of declining international consensus on ends and means for the management of global problems. Thus regulation of the international mails and humanitarian activities, on which the world already acts virtually as one without fear of infringements on national sovereignty, are placed very near the top, followed by technical functions like the regulation of international aviation and sea transport, and so on. International economic development and the regulation of international trade and commerce come farther down the list. Such issues as protection of human rights and of the environment, though they are currently subjects of the greatest interest and may revolutionize the system, are near the end, for there is as yet little international consensus about them. The United Nations was established primarily to keep the peace, and secondarily to advance the cause of justice. A glance at the table of contents should make this order clear.

Items are described following British usage. If a work is published by the United Nations, its sales number (of the form E.90.I.2) and, where appropriate, its document symbol (A/40/988) are also given. U.S. publications are also identified by the Superintendant of Documents Number (SuDoc No.). Every effort has been made to help the researcher positively identify the work in a library.

Works have been chosen that were published since the end of the Cold War (officially, when President George Bush said the words, in 1990), or in anticipation of it, going back through the 1980s or even earlier. The compiler has not hesitated to include classic and historical works, sometimes going back to the founding of the United Nations, if these would illuminate the human predicament at another period of historic opportunity. The aim has not been to exhaust the field (a whole library would not be sufficient for that), but to choose representative works from every area of concern about the U.N. in order to help readers find their way into a vast literature. Hence, the notation, 'bibliog.', after the publication data of any entry should alert the reader to further works on a subject. But 'bibliog.' is used only if the work has a separate bibliography in the back matter or after chapters. Even if the notation is absent, however, the works included here usually have scholarly footnotes, which also will guide the reader into the literature.

The annotations have been designed to inform, interest, and provoke. Because of the compiler's conviction that the idea of a federal government of the world provides perspective on the immense issues of international organization, he has particularly noted authors' mention of supranational innovations during the present transition toward some more effective international organization. If the annotations inspire others to open the literature on the United Nations, the bibliography will have proved a success.

'To understand is what is hard', said Sun Yat-sen, the founder of the Chinese republic. 'Once one understands, action is easy.' The works identified here should help the reader to understand the great issues of organizing the world to achieve lasting peace and justice.

Acronyms and Abbreviations

ABM	Anti-ballistic missile
ACABQ	Advisory Committee on Administrative and Budgetary Questions
ACC	Administrative Committee on Coordination
ASEAN	Association of Southeast Asian Nations
BBC	British Broadcasting Corporation
CD	Conference on Disarmament (Geneva)
CFE	Conventional Forces in Europe (treaty)
C.I.S.	Commonwealth of Independent States (successor to U.S.S.R.)
CSD	Commission on Sustainable Development
CTB	Comprehensive Test Ban (treaty)
CTC	Centre on Transnational Corporations
CSCE	Conference on Security and Cooperation in Europe
DIESA	Department of International Economic and Social Affairs (U.N.)
E.C.	European Community (now European Union)
ECA	Economic Commission for Asia
ECE	Economic Commission for Europe
Ecosoc	Economic and Social Council (not an acronym)
E.E.C.	European Economic Community
Enmod	Environmental Modification (convention)
ECLA	Economic Commission for Latin America
ECWA	Economic Commission for Western Asia
ESCAP	Economic and Social Commission for Asia and the Pacific
FAO	Food and Agricultural Organization
FRG	Federal Republic of Germany
G-7	Group of 7 (developed industrialized countries)
G-77	Group of 77 (now 124 developing countries)
GATT	General Agreement on Tariffs and Trade
GNP	Gross National Product

Acronyms and Abbreviations

GWP	Gross World Product
IAEA	International Atomic Energy Agency
IBRD	International Bank for Reconstruction and Development (World Bank)
ICAO	International Civil Aviation Organization
ICC	International Chamber of Commerce (Paris)
ICJ	International Court of Justice
ICRC	International Committee of the Red Cross
ICSID	International Centre for the Settlement of Investment Disputes
IDA	International Development Association
IEA	International Energy Agency (of OECD)
IFAD	International Fund for Agricultural Development
IFC	International Finance Corporation
IGO	Inter-governmental organization
ILC	International Law Commission
ILO	International Labour Organization
IMF	International Monetary Fund
IMO	International Maritime Organization
INF	Intermediate-range Nuclear Forces (treaty)
INGO	International non-governmental organization
IO	International organization
ITO	International trade organization (proposed in 1948)
ITU	International Telecommunications Union
LDCs	Least or less developed countries
MFO	Multilateral Force and Observers (Sinai)
MIGA	Multilateral Investment Guarantee Agency
MIRVs	Multiple, independently targetable, re-entry vehicles
MNCs	Multinational corporations
MNF	Multinational Force (Beirut)
NAM	Non-aligned Movement
NATO	North Atlantic Treaty Organization
NGO	Non-governmental organization
NICs	Newly industrialized countries
NIEO	New International Economic Order
NPT	Non-proliferation Treaty
NWICO	New World Information and Communication Order (UNESCO)
O.A.S.	Organization of American States
O.A.U.	Organization of African Unity
ODA	Official Development Aid
OECD	Organization for Economic Cooperation and Development (successor to the Marshall Plan)

ONUC	Opération des Nations Unies au Congo
OPEC	Organization of Petroleum Exporting Countries
PCIJ	Permanent Court of International Justice (succeeded by ICJ)
PLO	Palestine Liberation Organization
R&D	Research and development
SAARC	South Asian Association for Regional Cooperation
SALT I	Strategic Arms Limitation Treaty I (1972)
SALT II	Strategic Arms Limitation Treaty II (1979)
SDI	Strategic Defence Initiative (Star Wars)
SDRs	Special Drawing Rights
SIPRI	Stockholm International Peace Research Institute
START	Strategic Arms Reduction Treaty (1991)
TNCs	Transnational corporations U.K. United Kingdom
U.N.	United Nations (organization or system)
UNA	United Nations Association (an NGO)
UNCED	U.N. Conference on the Environment and Development (Rio)
UNCITRAL	U.N. Commission on International Trade Law
UNCTAD	U.N. Conference on Trade and Development
UNDOF	U.N. Disengagement Observer Force (Golan Heights)
UNDP	U.N. Development Programme
UNDRO	U.N. Disaster Relief Office
UNEF I	U.N. Emergency Force I (Sinai)
UNEF II	U.N. Emergency Force II (Sinai)
UNEP	U.N. Environmental Programme
UNESCO	U.N. Educational, Scientific, and Cultural Organization
UNFICYP	U.N. Force in Cyprus
UNHCR	U.N. High Commissioner for Refugees
UNICEF	U.N. Children's Fund
UNIDIR	U.N. Institute for Disarmament Research (Geneva)
UNIDO	U.N. Industrial Development Organization
UNIFIL	U.N. Interim Force in Lebanon
UNIIMOG	U.N. Iran-Iraq Military Observer Group
UNIKOM	U.N. Iraq-Kuwait Observer Mission
UNIPOM	U.N. India-Pakistan Observer Mission (Kashmir)
UNITAR	U.N. Institute for Training and Research (New York)
UNMOGIP	U.N. Military Observer Group in India and Pakistan (Kashmir)
U.N.O.	United Nations Organization
UNOGIL	U.N. Observer Group in Lebanon
UNSCOB	U.N. Special Commission on the Balkans

Acronyms and Abbreviations

UNRRA	U.N. Relief and Rehabilitation Administration (1946-47)
UNRWA	U.N. Relief and Works Agency (Palestine)
UNSF	U.N. Security Force (West Irian)
UNTAC	U.N. Transitional Authority in Cambodia
UNTAG	U.N. Transition Assistance Group (Namibia)
UNTEA	U.N. Temporary Executive Authority (West Irian)
UNTSO	U.N. Truce Supervision Organization (Palestine)
UNU	United Nations University
UNYOM	U.N. Yemen Observer Mission
UPU	Universal Postal Union
U.S.A.	United States of America
U.S.S.R.	Union of Soviet Socialist Republics (dissolved 1991)
WEU	Western European Union (defence alliance similar to NATO)
WFC	World Food Council WHO World Health Organization
WMO	World Meteorological Organization
WIPO	World Intellectual Property Organization
WTO	World Trade Organization (1994)

United Nations

General works

1 **Basic facts about the United Nations.**
U.N. Department of Public Information.   New York: United Nations,
1992 (regularly updated). 291p. bibliog. (E.93.I.2).
The United Nations is an association of sovereign states, yet it cannot function
without the support of the peoples of the world. This official guide is aimed at the
general public. Here the reader can begin to learn the impartial language so painfully
devised for a united world. Topics include: brief history of the U.N., its structure,
peacekeeping operations (which since 1989 have greatly expanded), economic and
social development programmes, human rights, decolonization (a major success),
international law, and specialized or intergovernmental agencies within the system.
The book is recommended for everyone.

2 **Charter of the United Nations and Statute of the International Court
of Justice.**
United Nations.   New York: United Nations, 1993. 108p. (DPI/1398).
No one should pretend to understand the United Nations without reading the Charter –
at least through Chapter VII, 'Action with respect to threats to the peace, breaches of
the peace, and acts of aggression'. The U.N. Charter offers an education to everyone
about the meaning of international legal agreements, which often defy the usual course
of international relations.

3 **The contemporary role of the United Nations.**
Evan Luard.   In: *United Nations, divided world*. Edited by Adam
Roberts and Benedict Kingsbury.   Oxford: Oxford University Press,
1988, p.209-30.
The author briefly surveys the political history of the U.N. culminating with general
disillusionment that the organization can 'significantly affect' the 'reality of warfare'.
He reviews and disputes the criticisms that the U.N. is biased against the U.S., is
financially irresponsible, is a mere talking shop, has a voting system with no relation

to effective power, and is ineffective in fulfilling its primary mission to maintain world peace. Member-states are failing the U.N., as they failed the League of Nations, Luard implies. 'Only a belief that the "United Nations" has an existence independent of nations makes it possible to shift responsibility for its actions from states themselves to the joint undertaking of which they form a part. . . . It will inevitably be difficult to build up the authority of the organization in the way that its critics demand so long as its leading members reserve for themselves the right to defy it when they believe their own national interests dictate this.' Luard discusses a range of reforms that seem acceptable to sovereign states, including increased use by the Security Council of Chapter VI, more vigour by the Secretary-General in using Article 99, greater fact-finding resources, more private meetings of the Security Council, more codes of conduct, increased peacekeeping, a powerful budgetary committee, creation of a high commissioner for human rights, improved coordination of the deliberately decentralized specialized economic and social agencies (as Maurice Bertrand recommends), and a new commitment by all state members to make their U.N. system work.

4   **The encyclopedia of the United Nations and international agreements.**
Edmund Jan Osmańczyk.   Philadelphia and London: Taylor & Francis, 1985; 2nd ed., 1990. 1,220p. bibliog.

This is a comprehensive reference work on the U.N. system, including its organs, specialized agencies, intergovernmental organizations, the League of Nations, European Community and other regional organizations, and related international agreements (like the Geneva Conventions). Technical terms are defined (air piracy to zoology), and texts of the most important treaties are printed in full, with brief historical details and references. Coverage begins in the 19th century. Some statistics are included. This is the finest reference book available, a must for every library.

5   **Everyone's United Nations: a complete handbook of the activities and evolution of the United Nations.**
Office of Public Information.   New York: United Nations, 10th ed., 1985. 484p. (E.85.I.16).

This is an older, official history and guide to the United Nations (first edition in 1948). It is more detailed than the subsequent *Basic facts about the United Nations* (see item no. 1) and hence is still valuable as a general reference. The book was written and updated in times when faith in the U.N. was less clouded by charges of 'anti-Western bias', 'politicization', and 'mismanagement'. Topics include: U.N. Charter, organs, political and security questions (disarmament, early peacekeeping), economic and social questions (development decades, technical cooperation), human rights, trusteeship over former colonies, international law, finance, and specialized agencies. Many students will benefit by beginning their research here.

6   **Image and reality: questions and answers about the United Nations; how it works and who pays for it.**
United Nations.   New York: United Nations, 1993. 104p. (DPI/1288).

This is an invaluable little booklet, answering today's most insistent questions. Yes, the U.S. is the largest financial contributor to the U.N. system ($1,272 million), followed by Japan, Germany, Sweden, and U.S.S.R. (1990). But in *per capita* terms, the largest are Norway ($64.81), Sweden, Denmark, etc. (U.S., $5.10; U.K., $4.90). In easy-to-understand terms, answers are given to questions like, Why is the U.N. necessary? Is there a 'tyranny of the majority' in the General Assembly? How effective have U.N. peacekeeping operations been? What has happened to the representation of the former Soviet Union? Is the IMF telling countries to cut social programmes? How is the U.N. budget determined? How can I get involved in the U.N.? The booklet is the perfect answer to the Heritage Foundation.

7 International organizations: principles and issues.
A. Leroy Bennett. New York: Prentice Hall, 5th ed., 1991. 480p. bibliog.

This is an up-to-date, excellent textbook on the United Nations, its predecessor the League of Nations, and the specialized agencies. Primary focus is on intergovernmental organizations (IGOs); secondary focus on non-governmental organizations (NGOs). In 1980, there were 380 IGOs and 4,700 NGOs. 'The author', Bennett writes, 'is normatively committed to the indispensability of global and regional international and transnational organizations in an age when people and nation-states must adapt to a shrinking and increasingly interdependent globe.' Topics include: brief history of the idea of international organization, the failure of the League, the origins of the United Nations, its principles and organization, basic issues, peaceful settlement of disputes, collective security (enforcement), search for justice under law, disarmament and arms control, international economic development, social progress (human rights, health, food, labour, child welfare, drugs, refugees), conference diplomacy, decolonization (self-government), regional organization, U.N. administration, and transnational corporations. For the future, the author is careful to set out the difficulties and dangers, but he is hopeful that humanity has the capacity to develop both its nation-states and international organizations, or, if disaster comes, to make 'revolutionary modifications in the international system'.

8 Issues before the 47th General Assembly of the United Nations.
Edited by John Tessitore and Susan Woolfsen. New York: United Nations Association–United States of America, 1993. 257p.

An annual volume, this is the best source to start with in order to follow the annual debate in detail. Organization of contents is correlated with the General Assembly's six committees: dispute settlement and decolonization, arms control and disarmament, economics and development, global resource management, human rights and social issues, legal issues, administration and budget. Sections are rewritten yearly by individual experts, are precise and well documented.

9 A life in peace and war.
Brian Urquhart. New York: Harper & Row, 1987. 390p.

The U.N. official who, after Dag Hammarskjöld, did most to develop the concept and practice of peacekeeping, provides here an illuminating autobiography. 'The weapons of peacekeeping,' he writes, 'are presence, consensus, the defusing of tension, and non-violence.' Urquhart's career extends from the founding of the U.N. in 1945 to its fortieth anniversary in 1985, when he admitted feeling that 'only an invasion from outer space would be a sufficiently non-controversial disaster to bring the Council back to the great power unanimity that the Charter required to make the United Nations effective'. At the time, the implications of Mikhail Gorbachev's coming to

3

power in the Soviet Union could barely be imagined. Because of its personal interest, this is one of the best books on the political nature of the U.N. – soon to undergo a renaissance, thanks in large part to creative international civil servants like Urquhart.

10   **My testament to the U.N.: a contribution to the 50th anniversary of the United Nations, 1995.**
Robert Muller.   Anacortes, WA: World Happiness and Cooperation, 1992. 249p. bibliog.

The author, a former Assistant-Secretary-General and now Chancellor of the University for Peace in Costa Rica, has long been popular with young people and older ones for a spiritual approach to the United Nations. 'What the world needs most', he writes in the chapter on the U.N. and spirituality, 'is architects of the Planet of God.' This book, like Dag Hammarskjöld's *Markings*, is a collection of musings and aphorisms, followed by appendixes of basic information about the U.N. Those who imagine a world organization of peoples on a planet at peace will find this book useful.

11   **Report of the Secretary-General on the work of the organization.**
Boutros Boutros-Ghali.   New York: United Nations, September 1993. 197p. (A/48/1).

'A year ago the United Nations, its Member States, and the peoples of the world recognized that a new opportunity had presented itself. The cold war being over, the United Nations could play the pivotal role in establishing world order and progress that had been assigned to it by the drafters of the Charter.' In a much longer report than usual, the new Secretary-General sets out the achievements of the U.N. and continuing challenges to it. The latter includes the 'comprehensive nature' of global problems, the 'indispensability' but weakness of the United Nations, and the financial crisis 'as the demands of Member States on the Organization are not matched by the resources provided'. He discusses the comprehensive global challenges under the heads of peace, development, and democracy. Peacekeeping and peacemaking cannot grow rapidly enough to meet the need, an acceptable and useful concept of economic development still eludes us, and the participation of people everywhere in their states – and the protection of their human rights – is slowly being recognized as a necessity for their development. 'Cooperative global integration', he argues, 'is now an inescapable fact and requirement for all the world's peoples.' This short book is an invaluable introduction to the United Nations as it approaches its 50th anniversary.

12   **Report of the Secretary-General on the work of the organization.**
Javier Pérez de Cuéllar.   New York: United Nations, 1982. 11p. (A/37/1).

At a time of renewed threat of nuclear war and of a retreat from multilateralism, the Secretary-General in 1982 boldly defended the U.N. Charter. 'It seems to me that our most urgent goal is to reconstruct the Charter concept of collective action for peace and security so as to render the United Nations more capable of carrying out its primary function.' He made a number of proposals for increasing state recourse to the Security Council, including greater civility and responsibilty among the permanent members, restraint in use of the veto, less reliance on mere resolutions, assistance to the Secretary-General's exercise of good offices, and improved fact-finding. Years later, Pérez de Cuéllar's leadership was bearing fruit in the revival of the U.N. These annual September reports are invaluable for the student and the concerned citizen to understand realistically what the U.N. is doing.

13 **U.N. Chronicle.**
U.N. Department of Public Information.   New York: United Nations, 1964- . quarterly.
For thirty years, this semi-official magazine of the United Nations has been for many the first entry point into the daily work of the organization. The issue of December 1993, for instance, is devoted to 'the road to reform', followed by news of developments in the Middle East, South Africa, Cambodia and other areas where peacekeeping observers or forces are deployed, news of progress in human rights, a conference on protection of fisheries, and the like.

14 **The United Nations: a handbook on the United Nations, its structure, history, purposes, activities, and agencies.**
Edited by Moshe Y. Sachs.   New York: Worldmark, 1977. 246p. bibliog.
This is a detailed reference to the structure and functioning of the United Nations and its affiliated specialized agencies. Functions include: maintaining peace and security, disarmament, peaceful use of outer space and of the seabed, economic development through the regional economic commissions, the development decades, U.N. Development Programme (UNDP), drug control, environmental protection, protection of children, human rights, advancement of knowledge, refugee relief, decolonization, international law. The volume is particularly informative on the specialized agencies. Principal intergovernmental organizations (IGOs) and non-governmental organizations (NGOs) are listed. The editor regarded the Cold War as a fact of international life (explaining the U.N.'s 'ineffectuality') but was hopeful for the future.

15 **The United Nations and a just world order.**
Edited by Richard A. Falk, Samuel S. Kim, and Saul H. Mendlovitz. Boulder, CO: Westview, 1991. 589p. bibliog.
This is a valuable reader, especially for students of all ages, on the world situation as the Cold War was coming to an end. Mikhail Gorbachev's 'Realities and guarantees for a secure world' is here, as is his adviser Georgi Shakhnazarov's 'The world community is amenable to government'. The United Nations is interpreted in accordance with the World Order school's 'preferred values': international peace and security, economic abundance, social justice, and ecological balance. Certain classics of U.N. reform are conveniently collected here: Marc Nerfin's 'The future of the United Nations system', UNA–USA's 'A successor vision', Silviu Brucan's 'The establishment of a world authority', Richard Falk's 'Openings for peace and justice', and Saul Mendlovitz's 'Struggles for a just world peace'. The editors have contributed plainspoken and judicious introductions. 'Our main concern is with the enhancement of the power and authority of the United Nations to meet the challenges of international political life in the 1990s and beyond.'

16   **The United Nations and the maintenance of international peace and security.**
United Nations Institute for Training and Research.   Dordrecht,
The Netherlands: M. Nijhoff, 1987. 431p.
This is a series of articles by experts from the First, Second, and Third Worlds on the
U.N.'s performance in its primary mission, the maintenance of international peace
and security. The book is the fruit of a collaborative meeting with Columbia
University's School of International and Public Affairs in order to commemorate the
International Year of Peace in 1986. Topics include: the historical record of collective
management of international conflict (by Ernst B. Haas), the developing international
law against the use of force, the Secretary-General's expanding role in quiet
diplomacy, international peacekeeping, disarmament, and meeting the challenge of
terrorism. No author undertakes to explore the maintenance of peace and security as a
whole. The implication remains, however, as UNITAR Executive Director M.D.
Kingué writes, 'that the United Nations has the potential further to develop its role
and to be a more readily utilized instrument for managing and resolving conflicts'.

17   **The United Nations and the maintenance of international peace and security.**
Leland M. Goodrich and Anne P. Simons.   Washington, DC:
Brookings Institute, 1955. 709p.
This study reflects serious American liberal and internationalist opinion on the United
Nations in anticipation of a U.N. Charter review conference in 1955. (Hence its value
for a similar conference in 1995.) The founding of the U.N. and the coming of the
Cold War are treated in a realistic, responsible spirit: the inability of the Security
Council to maintain international peace and security meant that many members turned
to regional arrangements like NATO and the Warsaw Pact. Then the existing
procedures for the peaceful resolution of disputes (Chapter VI), enforcement (Chapter
VII), and regulation of armaments (Article 26) are carefully examined for their
effectiveness in the conditions of 1955. The authors conclude that, to strengthen the
U.N., neither world government was practical, nor eviction of the Soviet Union likely
to retain the membership of the new non-aligned nations. Hence, the wise course was
'to allow a little more time for improvement in the political atmosphere'.

18   **The United Nations: an inside view.**
C.V. Narasimham.   New Delhi: Vikas for UNITAR, 1988. 385p.
(E.88.III.K.ST/23).
The author is an experienced Indian member of the Secretariat. The book may be read
– perhaps against the intentions of its author – as a view from the Third World. The
U.N. Conference on Trade and Development (UNCTAD) is reported very favourably,
and even an international trade organization (ITO) to supplement GATT is
recommended as in the original conception of 1948. 'What are the reasons for the
relative ineffectiveness of the United Nations in the political field?' Narasimham
asks. 'The fact of the matter is that the United Nations mirrors a divided world.' The
group system (G-77 etc.) is treated very favourably as a counterfoil to the Cold War
division of the world into two. The author, like the immense majority of U.N.
officials, delegates, and governments, opposes U.N Charter amendments. His
preferred course is to make the Charter work, if the requisite 'political will' can be
aroused.

19   **The United Nations as a political institution.**
Herbert G. Nicholas.   London: Oxford University Press, 1959; 5th ed.,
1975. 263p. bibliog.
This is a political guide, repeatedly updated, on the U.N. system by a British scholar
with an acute sense of history. The origins of the United Nations out of the ashes of
the League are particularly well covered. The author declares his purpose as being
neither 'for' nor 'against' the U.N., but to answer the questions, 'What is it like?' and
'How does it work?' By the last edition (1975), Nicholas carries the story to the verge
of U.S. disenchantment with the U.N., when China and East and West Germany had
been finally admitted, but the Third World had not yet produced its 'Zionism is
racism' resolution. Readers will be reminded that before 1975 the worst U.N.
financial crisis was caused by *Soviet* refusal to pay its assessments. In many ways, the
situation has now turned full circle, with the Americans playing the part of reluctant
partners. Nicholas, in his final chapter, does not offer any prescriptions for U.N.
reform beyond incremental improvements in international cooperation.

20   **The United Nations: a short political guide.**
Sydney D. Bailey.   New York: Praeger, 1963. 141p. bibliog.
The political essentials of the United Nations have not changed since this
enlightening little book was written. The U.N. is based on the principle of 'sovereign
equality', yet, by joining, member-states necessarily accept limitations on their
freedom of action. The one-nation-one-vote rule is producing an increasingly absurd
situation in which a two-thirds majority in the General Assembly paying but 3 per
cent of the budget can outvote one-third paying 97 per cent, yet weighted voting is
not an easy solution. 'Wisdom is not a monopoly of states with large populations or
abundant resources; irresponsibility is not the prerogative of states paying small
budgetary assessments.' For the beginning student, this book still lives up ito its title.
Topics include; the purpose of the U.N., its structure, the group system (budding
transnational parties), peacekeeping, disarmament, decolonization, refugees, and U.N.
reform. Comparisons are made to national politics, not so that readers see the defects
of the U.N., but so they appreciate the historical experiment of forming a political
union of the whole world.

21   **The United Nations at forty: a foundation to build on.**
United Nations.   New York: United Nations, 1985. 199p. (E.85.I.24.)
This is a clear, intelligible, comprehensive account of the United Nations system,
prepared when the U.N. was under severe attack by the Heritage Foundation and
when even the Secretary-General warned of a 'retreat from internationalism'. Hence,
this official account is less dry and more engaged politically than *Everyone's United
Nations* (see item no. 5). It contains a brief historical overview; gives accounts of the
working of the General Assembly, Security Council, International Court of Justice,
and Secretary-General; and then discusses global issues such as decolonization,
disarmament, peacekeeping, peacemaking, apartheid and racial discrimination, human
rights, international law, economic and social development, and humanitarian
assistance. The U.N. is a 'foundation to build on'.

22 **United Nations, divided world.**
Edited by Adam Roberts and Benedict Kingsbury.   Oxford: Oxford
University Press, 1988. 287p.

This is one of the most objective and measured assessments of the U.N. system near
the end of the Cold War. It contains critical yet supportive political judgements on the
U.N. in today's divided world, on international security, economic development, good
offices, protection of human rights, development of international law, and U.N.
reform. 'The picture which emerges from the various chapters is of a U.N. which,
while operating in an evolving world, is not itself fundamentally concerned to
restructure or replace the system of sovereign states so such as to ameliorate the
problems spawned by its imperfections, and to manage the rapid changes in many
distinct fields.'

23 **United Nations handbook, 1993.**
New Zealand Ministry of Foreign Affairs.   Wellington: Ministry of
Foreign Affairs, 1961- . annual. 305p.

This is a standard, quick reference guide to the U.N. system, designed for use by busy
official delegates who must know the facts instantly. It covers the six main organs
(General Assembly, etc.); their committees, subsidiary bodies (32 pages alone),
peacekeeping forces, related programmes (e.g. UNDP), treaty bodies (like the Human
Rights Committee) special bodies (UNITAR), the intergovernmental specialized
agencies (FAO, etc.), and the budget. It contains minimal histories, mandates, and
names of personnel.

24 **The United Nations: international organization and world politics.**
Robert E. Riggs and Jack C. Plano.   Belmont, CA: Wadsworth, 1988;
2nd ed., 1994. 364p. bibliog.

This is a new text on the U.N. written by two leading American political scientists.
They give special attention to the actual influence of the U.N. on states within the
context of world politics. They state clearly the promises in the Charter and the
procedures accepted for the settlement of international disputes and for the promotion
of economic and social advancement; they discuss the disappointments and
complexities of international cooperation, maintain a historical perspective, and close
with a positive evaluation and a vision of future world order. 'More than a hundred
years of experience with functional international organizations, now greatly
augmented by the growth of the U.N. system, has not produced a global political
community. It has, however, produced a practical approach to international
cooperation.' This is an excellent place for the student to begin.

25 **The United Nations' role in world affairs.**
Edited by Donald Altschiller.   New York: H.W. Wilson,
The Reference Shelf, 1993. 218p. bibliog.

This is a collection of recent articles, reflecting current interest in the U.N., its reform,
U.S. and other nations' policies toward it, and its critics, written for the general
public. Gene Lyons's comprehensive article, 'Reforming the United Nations', may be
taken as typical. He is doubtful that the U.N. can be reformed along the lines of a
centralized organization and inclines to the possibilities of decentralized 'free-
standing organizations' in addition to traditional diplomacy and regional defence

organizations like NATO. U.N. reform, like dispute settlement within the U.N., depends on consensus. 'The North needs a rule-bound world of greater certainty and stability to protect its wealth and power. The South needs an open world in which it can more effectively participate in world politics. But the stakes are different and can only serve to create a new consensus if the two sides have something to offer each other on the issues that have divided them so sharply.'

26   **We the peoples: a citizen's guide to the United Nations.**
United Nations Association–U.S.A.   New York: UNA–USA, 1992.
20p. bibliog.
This fact-filled booklet on the U.N. will be of interest to beginner or expert. It includes history, an account of the structure of the organization, a survey of the specialized agencies in the system, and a bibliography.

27   **A world fit for people: Thinkers from many countries address the political, economic, and social problems of our time.**
Edited by Üner Kirdar and Leonard Silk. Foreword by Boutros Boutros-Ghali.   New York: New York University Press for U.N. Development Programme, 1994. 481p. (E.93.III.B.2).
'The end of the Cold War and the collapse of bipolarity have transformed the international scene', writes the Secretary-General in his foreword. 'There are great opportunities for a new start in international cooperation.' This book contains contributions from more than fifty writers from around the globe on the new opportunities. It is not limited to even the most visionary of American or British thinkers. The editors say, 'We want to make the world fit for ordinary people hoping for a better life for themselves and their children.' The papers included are all policy proposals, divided into four categories: political reconstruction, economic development, strengthening human and ecological values, and helping countries in transition to overcome the legacy of the old order, enter the world economy, and find both freedom and order in their governments. The editors conclude in their introduction to the fourth part: 'The goals of political freedom and protection of human rights cannot be treated as secondary to, or separable from, the goal of economic freedom and progress. Ultimately, these goals are joined together.' They follow with ten specific conclusions for the Eastern European and former Soviet republics in 'transition'. This is a book that thoughtful persons, who have some knowledge of state and international institutions and who wish to transform their dreams into reality, will not want to ignore.

28   **Yearbook of the United Nations, 1992.**
Department of Public Information.   New York: United Nations, 1946-47, annual; vol. 46, 1992. 1,277p. (E.93.I.1).
This is the principal reference book on the U.N. system. It is the place to go for exact and authoritative information about the U.N.'s work in international peace and security, disarmament, peaceful uses of outer space, regions (Africa, America, Asia, Europe, Middle East), regional economic and social cooperation, international economic development, disasters and relief, trade and transport, international finance, transnational corporations, natural resources, energy, science and technology, environment, population, human settlements, human rights, health, food and nutrition, social and cultural development, women, children, refugees, abused drugs, statistics,

9

restructuring, decolonization, trusteeship, adjudication and arbitration (International Court of Justice), international law, law of the sea, U.N. financing, budget, staff, administration and management, and the eighteen specialized agencies. The work contains full texts of important resolutions, votes, dollar amounts, names of key personnel, and up-to-date references. The Secretary-General's 'Report on the work of the organization' – always a plain-spoken and enlightening political document – introduces the work.

See also International organizations p.259ff.

World politics

29 **After hegemony: cooperation and discord in the world political economy.**
Robert O. Keohane. Princeton, NJ: Princeton University Press, 1984. 290p. bibliog.
This is an influential study of international cooperation – contrasted with discord – in an anarchic but interdependent system of sovereign states. Keohane concentrates on cooperation in the political economy of the industrialized 'West' since World War II, where there were sufficient 'common interests' to permit cooperation in the absence of a shared Atlantic or European government. He does not explore how common interests have been or could be forged, nor how political and economic ideals influence state behaviour. But he hopes that a clear exposition of West–West cooperation will admit an extension to East–West and North–South relations. He continues his challenge to 'realist' theories of world politics (state conflict over power), and he inclines to a 'functionalist' one (international institutions assisting national policies of cooperation). He sees international institutions as the necessary setting for cooperation. But by *institutions* he does not mean the U.N. system (apart from the IMF and GATT) but international 'regimes' (ad hoc rules, principles, and procedures) such as the international trade and political regimes under U.S. 'hegemony' (leadership) after World War II. Here the reader will find full exposition of these concepts devised to explain the facts of world politics, where the United Nations, on balance, has very marginal influence on sovereign state conduct. Since U.S. hegemony began to decline with the abandonment of the gold standard (1971) and the first oil crisis (1973), Keohane is at pains to explain how international cooperation is still possible without a hegemon. Yet he does not call, even in his normative last chapter, for stronger common international organizations. The book is typical of recent political science.

30 **The Algiers declaration on the rights of peoples and the struggle for human rights.**
Richard A. Falk. In: *U.N. law/fundamental rights.* Edited by Antonio Cassese. Alphen aan den Rijn, The Netherlands: Sijthoff & Noordhoff, 1979, p.225-35.
Writing in the aftermath of the Vietnam War, Falk provides a highly political account of the setbacks in the progress of human rights. He accepts the view in the (private)

Algiers Declaration on the Rights of Peoples (1976) that 'imperialist tactics and structure are the root cause of human misery', and he boldly finds that the 'United States is the organizing, ideological center of this new form of imperialism. . . .' Even President Carter's then new human rights policy Falk treats as a hypocritical play for domestic audiences. Readers fifteen years later may find this overwrought – the end of the Cold War, then, would mean the complete victory of U.S. imperialism – but Falk's views always have the virtue of making us think about global political processes. He is particularly clear about the significance of the Algiers Declaration. Against the notion that binding human rights conventions derive their legitimacy from the consent of states, or at least from their consensus, Falk declares: 'The Algiers Declaration is itself an assertion of popular sovereignty, asserting that it is the peoples of the world that are the fundamental source of authority with respect to governing process.'

31   **The anarchical society: a study of order in world politics.**
Hedley Bull.   London: Macmillan, 1977. 335p. bibliog.
This is the leading British study of international relations from a 'realist' point of view. The author admits that the subject could as well be *disorder*, but he maintains that, within the international 'anarchy', there exists some order, even without international law or international organization. Much of the book is a running dispute with Richard A. Falk's idea of *world order*, achieved, if not by world government, then by new institutions of global governance evolving out of the decentralized U.N. system. Bull's chapter on alternatives to the contemporary states system surveys, with a certain contempt not unusual among mainstream scholars and state officials, such ideas as general and complete disarmament, a working cooperative organization like the U.N., acceptable nuclear proliferation, ideological homogeneity under world capitalism or communism, a world of small self-sufficient states, world government, world religion like medieval Christendom, or some other 'non-historical' successor to the state system. Bull maintains throughout the realist's equanimity toward war as a normal concomitant of the adjustment of the balance of power. He concludes that the state system is not in decline and that efforts to deliberately reform it are misguided.

32   **Approaches to peace: an intellectual map.**
Edited by W. Scott Thompson and Kenneth M. Jensen.   Washington, DC: U.S. Institute of Peace, 1991. 413p.
This is a major survey of the literature and conceptual approaches to the resolution of international conflict by the new (1986) U.S. Institute of Peace. The United Nations is but one of a larger set of national, international, non-governmental and individual institutions and actors contributing to peace. Typology: traditional approaches (defence, deterrence, collective security, diplomacy, negotiation, arms control); international law (treaties, custom, principles of law, teachings of qualified publicists, U.N. system, other inter-state organizations, third-party dispute settlement); new approaches (transformation, game theory, conflict resolution); political systems approaches (Gandhian pacifism, Marxism, liberalism, world federalism, world order).

33   **Beyond sovereignty: the challenge of global policy.**
Marvin S. Soroos.   Columbia, SC: University of South Carolina Press, 1986, 388p. bibliog.
World politics is usually studied as power politics, in accordance with the 'realist' paradigm of a struggle for power among the sovereign nations of the earth. It can also

be studied as 'policy-oriented politics', focusing on the more cooperative efforts of the decentralized international community to address problems of global scope. The author of this broadly informative text, written with care for clarity of terms and aptness of historical examples, surveys such alternative paradigms as international organization, functionalism, integration, transnationalism, interdependence, dependence, ecology, regimes, peace, and world order. He chooses to focus on *global policies*, which are internationally agreed courses of action to solve problems common to all states and peoples, or at least to representatives of each of the principal types of states and geographical regions of the planet. Six such global policies are examined in detail: nuclear non-proliferation, economic development, human rights, the law of the sea, protection of the environment, and world telecommunications. Soroos plainly thinks that 'power politics has become counter-productive in the modern, interdependent world', and he presents the alternative so reasonably that all students will find light and hope in the book. National governments 'persist in pursuing self-help strategies, failing to consider that the welfare of their societies in an interdependent world may be better served by sacrificing some of the prerogatives of state sovereignty in order to play a more constructive role in tackling the problems of the larger community'.

34 Beyond the nation state. functionalism and international organization.
Ernst B. Haas.   Stanford, CA: Stanford University Press, 1964. 595p. bibliog.

This is a classic of neofunctionalism, a fundamental alternative to the 'realist' theory of world politics as a struggle for power. Haas takes up David Mitrany's argument that, at humanity's stage of development in the mid-twentieth century, a constitutional world union to establish peace is impossible, but functional cooperation in technical and 'non-political' sectors like health and labour standards could lead to restraints on national users of power and to shifting loyalties toward world institutions. 'The end product is a world federation emerging from an indefinite number of task-oriented agencies that overlie the sovereign state and detach man's loyalty to it.' Haas answers criticism by leading realist scholars, then turns to a close examination of the International Labour Organization for signs of progress toward 'world integration'. (Hence the book is a daring interpretation of this functional organization, which at its founding in 1919 admitted representation from governments, business, and labour unions.) He predicts a 'continued drift toward supranationality', mostly in the areas of international economic planning, peacekeeping (new in 1964), and ad hoc disarmament. 'Common concerns' will slowly prevail over the chaos of national confrontation.

35 Contending approaches to world order.
Richard A. Falk.   *Journal of International Affairs* (New York), vol. 31 (Fall-Winter 1977), p.171-98.

Professor Falk here presents a concentrated defence of world order studies in the context of international relations theory. It is his answer to critics of the 'world order' school's advocacy of values (like peace), its link to the world federalist movement, its excessive rationality, superficial pre-emption by mainstream political leaders (Carter on world order), and paradoxically, both idealism and realism. Falk defines *world order*, with Raymond Aron, as 'the minimum conditions for coexistence'; and world order *studies*, with Saul Mendlovitz and Thomas Weiss, as 'the study of international relations . . . that focuses on the manner in which mankind can significantly reduce the likelihood of international violence and create minimum acceptable conditions of worldwide economic well-being, social justice, ecological stability, and participation in decision-making'. Falk sees world order studies moving away from traditional 'Machiavellian' states to the 'present world situation'. The main focus is on system-transforming approaches, especially the need for global political leadership, transnational social solidarity, human rights mobilizations, synthesizing knowledge, enlarging education, and developing planetary citizenship.

36 **Contending theories of international relations: a comprehensive survey.**
James E. Dougherty and Robert L. Pfaltzgraff, Jr. New York: Harper & Row, 1971; 3rd ed., 1990. 607p. bibliog.
This is a standard text on the various theories of international relations – most generally divided into 'traditional' (balance of power, realism) and 'behaviorist' (quantitative method, social science). The theories are in flux and the authors admit that no single theory is widely accepted. But here the student will find mature discussion of such theories as balance of power, geopolitics, utopianism and realism, systems theory, causes of war, economic theories of war, biological aggression, sociological theories (anarchy, domestic conflict, war as a distraction), nuclear deterrence, arms control, international integration, bureaucratic decision-making, and game theory. The U.N. has a small place in such theorizing, being a development of balance of power (collective security) with implications for integration (international organization as a step toward world community or world government).

37 **On the creation of a just world order: preferred worlds for the 1990s.**
Edited by Saul Mendlovitz. New York: Free Press, 1975. 302p.
This is the lead volume of the World Order Models Project. Participants from the principal regions of the Earth – North America, Latin America, Europe, Africa, and Asia – prepared openly normative social science studies on a reformed international system (a 'relevant utopia', a 'preferred world'), and on the transition steps to it by the 1990s, when it was anticipated, correctly, that the Cold War would have wound down. Contributors aimed to solve the deeper global problems, neglected by preoccupation with the Cold War, of war in general, poverty, social injustice, environmental decay, and personal alienation. 'It is my considered judgment', Mendlovitz writes, 'that there is no longer a question of whether or not there will be world government by the year 2000. As I see it, the questions we should be addressing to ourselves are: how will it come into being – by cataclysm, drift, more or less rational design – and whether it will be totalitarian, benignly elitist, or participatory (the probabilities being in that order).'

38 **The crisis of world order and the problem of international organization in the 1980s.**
Robert Cox. *International Journal*, vol. 35 (Spring 1980), p.370-95.
This is the last article in a dedicated issue on the 'U.N. galaxy'. Cox surveys the accumulating global problems, the lack of international consensus on the principles and norms for construction of corrective programmes, the split between the First and Third Worlds over preferred fora for addressing common problems (UNCTAD *vs.*

IBRD and IMF), and withdrawal by the U.S. from effective leadership. He finds an historical analogy to the present crisis in the decline of Pax Britannica after World War I. Meanwhile, the 'internationalization of production' is producing its own 'emerging structure'. Three realistic versions contend for the mastery of such a process: a 'reconstructed political directorate for the world economy' as championed by the Trilateral Commission; an anarchic division of the international economy into blocs, 'each following protectionist neo-mercantilist policies'; or continued anarchy at the national state level, without Group of Seven domination or bloc leadership, as in the apparent Third World vision. Cox does not regard U.N. reform as wise when the political bases are so unsettled. For the 1980s, he recommended only the education of public opinion about the difficulties of diplomacy aiming at a 'new world order'.

39 Diplomacy at the United Nations.
Edited by G.R. Berridge and A. Jennings.   New York: St. Martin's, 1985. 227p.

The U.N. was given in 1945 a limited role in world power politics – 'to graft a cutting of collective security onto the wild briar of the balance of power'. The authors clarify and evaluate diplomacy at the U.N.: third-party diplomacy (Security Council and Secretary-General, notably in the Falklands/Malvinas crisis), multilateral (conference) diplomacy, and bilateral (traditional) diplomacy. 'Quiet diplomacy' is here treated as a branch of third-party diplomacy; 'corridor diplomacy', as bilateral; and 'parliamentary diplomacy' in the General Assembly as 'really propaganda' since it does not (immediately) produce agreements in international law. This British book does not lose sight of the realities of state power, but a few authors see potential in international cooperation within the U.N. system.

40 The functional theory of politics.
David Mitrany.   London: Martin Robertson for the London School of Economics and Political Science, 1975. 294p. bibliog.

This retrospective volume includes an autobiographical memoir and illuminating notes of Mitrany's career and the origins and influence of his functional theory; substantial excerpts of writings leading up to *A working peace system* (1943); and extracts from subsequent writings, notably on international technical assistance and the U.N. in historical perspective. The *functional* approach to international organization – gradually expanding the field of economic and defensive cooperation – is contrasted with the *constitutional* – establishing legal structures and rules, which occur at rare historical opportunities. 'When ten or twenty national authorities, each of which had performed a certain task [like setting the terms of trade] for itself, can be induced to perform that task jointly, they will to that end quite naturally pool their sovereign authority in so far as the good performance of the task demands it.'

41 The globalization of politics: the changed focus of political action in the modern world.
Evan Luard.   New York: New York University Press, 1990. 195p.

In a world shrinking by modern communications and transportation, national politics is no longer 'significant' or 'relevant' to solve the problems confronting states and their people; 'the only type of political action which is significant is international action'. The author, a leading scholar of the United Nations, develops this thesis carefully and systematically with respect to social welfare, the environment, human rights, and economic power. Each chapter on these topics is clearly set out, beginning with the national approach to, say, security; progressing through international approaches to date; then concluding with 'transnational' or 'global' political efforts now in progress or imaginable in the short term. Hence the book is particularly valuable to students and concerned citizens trying to orient their minds to serious international political action. The final two chapters contain a stunning but constructive critique of the U.N.'s 'functional system' and a realistic but bold set of proposals for U.N. reform. To Luard, U.N. politics today resembles British politics in the 18th century, before factionalism was overcome by disciplined political parties. The U.N.'s lack of *authority*, which would lead to realistic solutions of global problems and to willing implementation of decisions, he sees as rooted in its lack of popularly representative institutions; but a world parliament, directly representative of peoples rather than states, he admits 'would take a transformation of both state institutions and international bodies more fundamental than any that can now be foreseen'.

42 Global goals and the crisis of political will.
Ervin Laszlo. *Journal of International Affairs*, vol. 31 (1977), p.199-214.

Following his Club of Rome report, *Goals for mankind*, Laszlo summarized its findings in this brief article. 'The issue deciding the fate of our species is not the finitude of the planet, and not even the number of humans inhabiting it. It is the will of the present and the next generation, and the wisdom from which it springs.' Along with environmentalist Garrett Hardin, Laszlo emphasizes the importance of *acting locally*, but *thinking globally* about the problematique of world security, food, energy, resources, and balanced socio-economic development. The last half of the article is devoted to a survey of the goals and preoccupations of leading states, the regions of the world, and international organizations, including the U.N. 'People are intent', he concludes, 'on their immediate material benefits, leaders play games of power and wealth, while the clouds of doom gather overhead.'

43 Global order: values and power in international politics.
Lynn H. Miller. Boulder, CO: Westview, 1985. 226p.

This is an introduction to the study of international relations, written from a 'world order' point of view shortly before the Soviet initiatives and positive American response that ended the Cold War. 'A basic thesis of this book is that the fundamental reason for our frequent failures to make the right kind of policy choices in the world today stems from our continued refusal to see the planetary system as a whole.' After a fair exposition of the Westphalian system of sovereign states, the author discusses new global challenges to it: nuclear weapons, the erasure of the distinctions between domestic and international affairs, the finiteness of the Earth's environment, demands for human rights and self-determination, the rise of international non-governmental organizations (INGOs) and transnational corporations (TNCs). Miller shows that government is lacking at the world level – and with it the familiar rule of law and democratic participation by individuals. The last half of the book is devoted to finding precedents, like the European Community, for solving, on a basis of both realism and idealism, the largest global problems: international peace and security, economic well-being, human dignity and rights, and preservation of the natural environment.

44 Global outlook 2000: an economic, social and environmental perspective. Report [of the Secretary-General to the General Assembly].
United Nations. New York: United Nations, 1990. 340p. (E.90.II.C.3).

The prospects for long-term global economic development are here presented quantitatively, with an abundance of tables and graphs. Projections are based on present national policies (to 1989) and alternative policies (if the end of the Cold War permits reallocation of investment from military to civilian use). By 2000, the world economy will probably be in 'fundamental disequilibrium' (worsened income distribution, environmental degradation), but there will also be improvements in some countries, classes and sectors. Topics include: environment, energy, agriculture, technology, structural change, population, urbanization, education, health, social policy. The conclusion discusses eight 'surprises' that could radically affect future socio-economic developments. Recommended for policy-makers, NGOs, students, and scholars.

45 Global peace and security: trends and challenges.
Edited by Wolfram F. Hanrieder. Boulder, CO: Westview, 1987. 223p.

This volume of public lectures, given as part of the Program on Global Peace and Security at the University of California at Santa Barbara, contains ten wide-ranging and provocative essays designed to guide students to exercising their responsibilities as citizens in the world after the Cold War. Elise Boulding sets the tone with an essay on 'learning peace'. Richard Falk warns against easy escapes into utopias like world government, which is usually proposed without attending to the hard political work of the transition, or into mysticism, of the Maharishi or newer Californian types. What is needed, he argues, is 'a new surge of democratization of political life'. Other authors survey the main sectors of future concern: the globalization of capitalism, the 'Fourth World' of very poor states, European union, the Soviet bloc (then crumbling), and 'Star Wars'. There is very little on the United Nations as humanity's beginning in world political organization.

46 Governance without government: order and change in world politics.
Edited by James N. Rozenan and Ernst-Otto Czempiel. New York: Cambridge University Press, 1992. 311p.

Here is another leading work of recent political science reflecting the unravelling of the 'realist' (state power) paradigm for understanding international relations. Hegemons (superpowers) are declining, borders disappearing, military alliances decaying, migrants mixing massively with homogeneous national populations, and citizens everywhere challenging their national authorities over new issues of world politics like human rights and environmental protection. The authors, understandably, find no government at the world level, yet they are convinced there is a degree of 'governance' or 'order' at that level, much as international lawyers find law without a world legislature. Governance, like international law, is a 'system of rule that works only if it is accepted by the majority (or at least by the most powerful of those it affects)'. Global governance is wider than technical regimes like the whaling regime or non-proliferation regime. Topics include: an historical case of governance without government (the concept of Europe), decay of the state system into transnationalism, Third World political convergence, slightly increasing effectiveness of international organizations like the U.N., international regulation of terrorism and the drug trade, European integration, democratization as a basis for world peace, and the role of individual national citizens to bring about a better world.

47   Gramsci, hegemony and international relations: an essay in method.
Robert Cox. *Millennium: Journal of International Studies*, vol. 12 (Summer 1983), p.162-75.

This is a daring essay on the undermining of great power hegemony by international organizations. It will not come about, Cox argues, by a 'war of movement at the international level through which radicals would seize control of international institutions'. Rather, it will be the result of a 'war of position by a new 'historic bloc' of a 'broad alliance of the disadvantaged against the sectors of capital and labour which find common ground in international production and the monopoly-liberal world order'. That is, a new transnational social class, analogous to the revolutionary working class, would have to form within existing anarchic international society until a 'popular political base' was prepared to seize the 'revolutionary opportunity'.

48   On humane governance.
Rajni Kothari. *Alternatives*, vol. 12 (1987), p.277-90.

'Governance has been usurped by governments.' The 'good life', the author argues, has been replaced by 'economism' as the principle for organization of both state and society; popular self-government for the protection of society and nature replaced by the 'immoral' free market and its associated corporate, technocratic, and military elites. The result is a 'homogeneous world' in which most people are reduced to 'victims of oppression'. Kothari urges that current interest in governance should turn, not to national government, but to a 'return to humane governance' led by social movements devoted to restoring power to the people, as in Gandhi's non-violent resistance movement to British imperial rule of India. At the world level, he warns that the United Nations is 'unreservably committed to the preservation of a stable status quo' – that is, to a technological world order in which 70 percent of humanity is 'dispensable'. Hence, the struggle for humane world governance has to proceed from 'non-state, relatively non-monetized spaces' in the Third World, the ecology movement, feminist movement, and especially the modern 'knowledge system'. Intellectuals must formulate a new vision of the world in place of the 19th century one of the progress of industrialization and democracy. Like Gandhi, they must see themselves identified with the 'victims of history'.

49   International ethics in the nuclear age.
Edited by Robert Myers, Jr. New York: Carnegie Council on Ethics and International Affairs, 1987. 369p.

The authors here are doubtful that moral standards are easily translated into principles of national foreign policy, but they reject the 'dogmatic realist position' that moral goals and rules of action should be excluded from policy discussions, which then can be conducted on grounds of expediency and calculations of selfish interest. The book is typical of recent American thinking on a more sophisticated approach to a moral or ideal U.S. foreign policy that would not repeat the wishful thinking of the period of

1920-41 nor the excesses of the Vietnam War. Nuclear weapons, Robert Jervis and Ernst B. Haas argue, have changed all the old verities of *Realpolitik.* Topics include: nuclear and conventional armed deterrence, the role of scientists, arms control negotations, economic development, immigration, and American nationalism.

50 **Internationalism under siege.**
Shridath S. Ramphal. *Journal of Development Planning,* vol. 17 (1987), p.227-31.
The author is Secretary-General of the Commonwealth. Ramphal provides an eloquent defence of internationalism when the U.N. was under American attack for mismanagement of budget and inefficiency of programmes. 'The essential case for internationalism, for cooperation between nations on as global a scale as possible, rests ultimately on its being the only feasible way in the long term – not to mention the only human and enlightened way – to advance the common and mutual interests of all nations.' Ramphal warns that democracies themselves are turning from international cooperation, world democracy, and interdependence – symbolized by the U.S. and U.K. withdrawals from UNESCO and by the collapse of the North–South dialogue over the new international economic order (NIEO) – and are turning back to the disastrous nationalism of the years before 1939. 'We have to lift internationalism to the level of a national ethic and reach the point where leaders are in no doubt that their people will not support policies that turn the clock back on internationalism.'

51 **International regimes.**
Edited by Stephen D. Krasner.   Ithaca, NY: Cornell University Press, 1983. 372p. bibliog.
By the 1970s, American students of world politics were generally divided between 'realists', who focused on the struggle for power of sovereign states, and 'liberals' (here also called 'Grotians' respectful of the reality and potential of international law), who argued that, in addition to states, transnational coalitions, parties, corporations, and individuals contributed to events. The most innovative concept of the Grotians was that of a 'regime' – a set of newly customary 'rules of the game' of international relations (principles, norms, rules, and decision-making procedures) – which was transitional to a legal organization or even a government. The United Nations, to these scholars, was not even yet a regime, for mere membership did not constrain state decision-making. A better example is the ocean regime, or the non-proliferation regime, or the regime of international finance. This important volume virtually settled the debate in favour of structural realist theory, for regimes were shown to be hardly autonomous from states, and state sovereignty remains the 'constitutive principle' of the present international system. The editor is at a loss to predict the future in a world where there are so few limitations on sovereign state conduct, but he concludes that thinking about regimes has enlarged the 'mechanism' of knowledge and understanding in the national calculation of interests and power. The book is a must for all theorists of international relations.

52 **Negotiating world order: the artisanship and architecture of global diplomacy.**
Edited by Alan K. Henrikson.   Wilmington, DE: Scholarly Resources, 1986. 265p. bibliog.
The study of international relations is divided between two modes of thinking: 'world order' theorists and 'negotiators' of actual working agreements between sovereign states. This fine, well-integrated collection of essays aims to bring together the 'architects' and the 'artisans' of global polity. The focus is on negotiation the process of transition to a better world. The authors examine problems that require multilateral action, are the results of new challenges, and have potential for solution by an improved norm-setting or rule-making system or regime. These problems are: food, acid rain, law of the sea, communications, collective security, arms control, non-proliferation, regional order (CSCE, NATO, O.A.S., ASEAN), international trade, debt, and finance (UNCTAD, GATT, IMF). Henrikson's final essay concludes that the building of international *consensus* is the 'central idea and principal finding of the entire volume'.

53 **New dimensions in international security.**
International Institute for Strategic Studies (London).
Adelphi Papers, No. 265 (Winter 1991-92). 92p.
Zbigniew Brzezinski here comments on the end of the Cold War; and Brian Urquhart, on the evolution of U.N. peacekeeping into an effective system of collective security. The former U.S. National Security Advisor sees the end of the Cold War as the 'third grand transformation of world politics' (after World Wars I and II) into a 'functionally pragmatic transnationalism'. But he warns of great dangers: no counterbalance to the single 'victorious' superpower, regional conflicts decoupled from superpower rivalry, a public distracted by issues of 'global well-being' like underdevelopment, the future of Europe. The former U.N. Under-Secretary-General for peacekeeping treats the Persian Gulf War as a 'prototype' of collective international response to new challenges of domestic disorder that threatens international peace and security, of deep economic inequalities aggravated by instantaneous world communications, of natural and ecological disasters. What is needed in the U.N. is not a safety net, he argues, but 'a *system* for peace and security'. Urquhart outlines this in terms of vigilance, preventive action, collective action, and sanctions. He would go so far as to implement Articles 43 and 47 of the Charter. 'What is certainly true', he concludes, 'is that the world now faces a series of urgent global problems. . . . To tackle those problems effectively will require international co-operation and understanding, resources, and leadership on a scale unknown in the past.'

54 **Peace and war: a theory of international relations.**
Raymond Aron. Translated from the French by R. Howard and A.B. Fox.   Garden City, N.Y.: Doubleday, 1966; abridged ed., 1973. 820p., 468p.
This is the best recent 'traditionalist' account of international society, by a leading French political scientist. It is comprehensive at levels of theory, sociology, history, and praxis. As the economic problem is scarcity, so, to Aron, the problem of international relations is war. The U.N. figures little in his view, since it seems 'obvious' to him (as to most people) that 'the United Nations has not exercised a

major influence on the course of international relations'. Hence, he finds peace rooted in diplomacy, preparedness for war, and the strategy of deterrence. His final chapters, 'Beyond power politics', may be of most interest to readers after the Cold War, for he treats there of the perfection of international law, a delegation of sovereignty to a world federation. The probability in 1966, however, was that the Russian communists would seek a military empire, against which the West needed a 'rational strategy'.

55 Politics in the United Nations system.

Edited by Lawrence S. Finkelstein. Foreword by Javier Pérez de Cuéllar.   Durham, NC: Duke University Press, 1988. 503p.

Written just before the end of the Cold War (officially 1990), this book of authoritative essays on the U.N. system maintains the thesis that the U.N. is moving away from a diplomatic system of sovereign states, requiring individual state consent for effective action (a 'unit-veto' system), to a *political* system of powerful states, blocs, groups, NGOs, and a few influential individual persons, based on voting under majority rule, consensus, and some executive policy-making (a 'hierarchical' system). 'The hypothesis of this book . . . is that the predominant movement on the spectrum has been from required consent toward majority procedures.' *Politics* is defined as the 'allocation of values', where 'values' include, very broadly: power, authority (majority rule), legitimacy (consent, consensus), principles (like human rights or self-determination), rules (of procedure, of voting, especially by amendment processes), technical assistance, terms of trade, development loans, financial aid, and other tangible benefits. The book is realistic, yet animated by a spirit of hope in the 'centralized authority' of the United Nations. 'It may not be too far-fetched to speculate that the widespread rule that decisions should be made by majority votes might in the long run deal a mortal blow to sovereignty as the basis of the international order.' There are excellent essays on international law, the veto, economic cooperation, GATT's deterioration, North–South conflict, environment, human rights, refugees, nuclear non-proliferation, UNESCO, and the U.N. system as a whole.

56 The politics of interdependence.

Edward L. Morse.   *International Organization*, vol. 23 (Spring 1969), p.311-26.

Here is early doctrine on interdependence. 'High politics', which aims at preservation of the state or security, is distinguished from 'low politics', which aims at humanitarian assistance. (By the 1990s, high politics could be thought of as world statesmanship aimed at creating effective international institutions, while low is the usual national power politics aimed at self-defined national interest.)

57 Power and interdependence: world politics in transition.

Robert O. Keohane and Joseph S. Nye.   Boston: Little, Brown, 1977. 273p. bibliog.

This is a continued critique of the 'realist' theory of world politics begun in the authors' *Transnational relations* (q.v.). The alternative theory of 'interdependence' is here developed in polemical style. Interdependence means *mutual* dependence – not mere interconnectedness. There must be 'reciprocal costly effects of transactions'. Keohane and Nye do not predict a 'brave new world of cooperation', but they do focus on interim 'governing arrangements' called *international regimes*, like the regime (norms, rules and procedures) of international monetary policy or the ocean regime. The U.N. is understood as one international organization among many, useful in building temporary coalitions of states in an interdependent world, but not an 'incipient world government'. 'Leadership will not come from international organizations, nor will effective power', they argue not unreasonably. Their focus is on the immediate alternatives of U.S. foreign policy – not the global policy of the decentralized international community, nor the unorganized demands of all humanity.

58   **Power and international relations.**
      Inis L. Claude, Jr.   New York: Random House, 1962. 310p. bibliog.
This is a classic exposition of the fundamental alternatives for ordering the international systems: balance of power, collective security, world government. The three differ most fundamentally in the degree of centralization of power and authority implied: the first leaves the nation-states least unified, the second partially centralizes power, and the third would create a centralized 'monopoly of power' as in organized states. *Power* is understood as 'essentially military capability', and *management* of power is taken as the practical objective in international organization, since the elimination of power is unrealistic. Because modern weapons threaten all civilization, 'the management of power in international relations looms as the central issue of our time'.

59   **On the problems of 'the global problematique': what roles for international organizations?**
      John G. Ruggie.   *Alternatives*, vol. 5 (1979-80), p.517-50.
The 'global problematique', a complex of processes and problems engaging the entire world, is defined in terms of a long list of demands for food, energy, and materials; shortages of fuel, fresh water, arable soils, and wholesome air; ecological degradation; urban shortages of housing, medical facilities, and schools; high inflation; recessions; political repression; pollution; soil erosion, deforestation, and desertification; epidemic and new diseases. Generally, the problematique can be studied under the heads of overpopulation, no limits to economic growth, and destructive international division of labour. Ruggie surveys the response of international organizations, particularly (1) to expand the collective knowledge base (UNESCO's Man and Biosphere research programme and INFOTERRA data bank, UNEP's GEMS monitoring project), and (2) to pursue collective policies (conference diplomacy, alternative development, 'counter-hegemonic' symposia and seminars on the fringes of the intergovernmental system). He expects 'rule-governed change' (where states set the rules), not 'transformation of the intergovernmental political system'. That is, world governance, not world government.

60   **Regime decay: conflict management and international organizations, 1945-1991.**
      Ernst B. Haas.   *International Organization*, vol. 37 (Spring 1983), p.189-235.
The general failure of the United Nations to achieve its primary purpose – the maintenance of international peace and security – is here proven by quantitative demonstration. But the author argues that to blame the U.N. for 'failure' is to mistake it for an autonomous superstate, 'set up to coerce or cajole states into substituting cooperation for conflict'. He regards the U.N. as a 'regime', or temporary association

of states, who have established it to moderate, not eliminate, conflict ('conflict is, after all, almost a synonym for politics'). Haas admits only that the U.N. regime has 'decayed'. He examines such causes as the decline of U.S. hegemony or the increase in the number of voting blocs in the General Assembly with respect to 282 international disputes from 1945 to 1981. He finds, quantitatively, that U.N. 'success' declines steadily after 1970; since then, the international community has 'tolerated' much more conflict.

61 **The revolution in statecraft: intervention in an age of interdependence.**
Andrew M. Scott.   Durham, NC: Duke Press Policy Studies Paperbacks, 1965; 2nd rev. ed., 1982. 214p.

The first edition was devoted to 'informal contact' (people-to-people and state-to-people) among nations. Such contacts include propaganda designed to reach an enemy's population, economic aid to influence other states through benefits to their citizens, covert military operations, subversion, use of international organizations to intervene in foreign countries – all forms of 'Cold Warfare'. Scott treats the U.N. cynically, but not unrealistically, as an instrument of U.S. or other national policy. 'An international organization does not have a mind or soul to guide it along a consistent path. There is no general will determining the actions of the United Nations for instance. Calling an organization "international" does nothing to remove its decision making processes from the political arena.' The second edition (1982) added two chapters on direct military intervention by great powers into weak states and on non-intervention in accordance with international law and the U.N. Charter's Article 2(7). The book needs to be read in conjunction with works of international law on humanitarian intervention. Scott writes in the tradition of 'realist' political science and is contemptuous of non-intervention, though he supports a U.N. code to limit it. The book marks another decline in sovereign independence of states.

62 **Some aspects of power sharing in international organizations.**
Lawrence S. Finkelstein.   In: *Shared power: What is it? How does it work? How can we make it work better?* Edited by John M. Bryson and Robert C. Einsweiler.   Lanham, MD: University Press of America, 1991, p.309-39.

'Power in international arenas is ordinarily shared', writes the author, an American political scientist. Finkelstein describes four ways by which power is shared (granted by states): by delegation in the U.N. Charter, by distribution in the charters of the functional specialized agencies, by *de facto* shifts from universal to regional organizations (NATO), and by internal allocations between the organs within one organization. He traces the shifting grants and assumptions of power due to changing historical circumstances, including the 'processes of struggle over the authority to allocate values in international arenas'. He finds power-sharing in practice to occupy an intermediate zone between 'centralized majority decisions' (world government) and 'decentralized unit vetoes' (anarchy). U.N. reform, for instance, has not moved toward centralized economic functions, as the Group of 77 last attempted (1974-79), but remains stuck in the intermediate zone.

63　**States and the global system: politics, law, and organization.**
　　Inis L. Claude, Jr.　New York: St. Martin's, 1988. 205p.

A leading American political scientist here presents a late volume of his mature essays on international politics, the last of which was written in 1986 and hence before the end of the Cold War. Claude finds that the 'system' of sovereign states is generally orderly, though prone to sudden and disastrous disorder, as in war. 'The fundamental question is whether, in a multistate system, the peril of disorder is so great that states cannot be expected to succeed in upholding the values that justify their existence.' He reluctantly concludes that only balance of power is available and effective as an approach to world order, for collective security as in the U.N. 'has never moved significantly past the design stage', and world government, while the 'ideally correct solution', has not attracted a mass movement able to establish it as in the establishment of republican states. The reality is that 'states constitute both the problem of world order and the only available resources for its solution'. This is an excellent source on U.N. reform, American ambivalence toward international organization, the growth despite state resistance of international institutions, and world 'community'.

64　**A strategy for peace: human values and the threat of war.**
　　Sissela Bok.　New York: Pantheon, 1989. 202p.

Written before the end of the Cold War, this sophisticated book in the tradition of the moral conduct of foreign policy is addressed to the problem of building *trust* in a world armed with nuclear and conventional weapons of mass destruction. International cooperation, Bok argues, cannot replace deterrence 'without renewed attention to the fundamental human values that have traditionally promoted the cohesion and survival of communities under stress'. Her arguments are addressed primarily to national citizens and their leaders, but the international and personal context is also brought into account. The United Nations is regarded as playing the 'central role' in her 'strategy for peace', if governments will not misuse its fora for debate and negotiation. This book will answer many anxious questions about the transition.

65　**Systems in crisis: new imperatives of high politics at century's end.**
　　Charles F. Doran.　Cambridge: Cambridge University Press, 1991.
　　294p. bibliog. (Cambridge Studies in International Relations, 16).

This is a timely work of political science on the international 'system change' after the Cold War, written especially for the strategist, policy-maker, and concerned citizen. 'As bipolarity yields in the coming decades to some as yet undetermined new international system, world order and the other imperatives of high politics will increasingly have to face this uncertainty and its psychological and behavioral underpinnings. The inescapable reality of systems transformation is that statesmen must navigate these unexplored waters.' Doran develops an analysis of 'power cycles' over the 19th and 20th centuries with almost mathematical precision, and he tries to illuminate the present with historical 'critical points' when foreign policy expectations went awry. Unhappily, these were usually periods of 'transformative' war, though the burden of this book is that war can be avoided in another round of change in the balance of power. Doran's cyclic theory is rather opposed to the observed decline in Paul Kennedy's *Rise and fall of the great powers* (1987). The U.N. hardly figures in Doran's view, which is entirely focused on the currently still predominant state actors. An uncomfortable, intensely practical book on the global dangers ahead.

66   **Toward a just world order.**
Edited by Richard A. Falk, Samuel S. Kim and Saul H. Mendlovitz.
Boulder, CO: Westview, 1982, 652p. bibliog.

Here is a collection of expert articles on international relations in 'Stage III' of world order studies, after earlier concentrations on (I) war prevention and then (II) on the positive values of peace, economic well-being, social justice, and ecological balance. By Stage III, concentration was on the *transition*, particularly on identification with the 'struggle of the oppressed'. Most of these essays were written in the 1970s, when hopes for 'some dramatic discontinuity in political behavior by way of catastrophic or spiritual conversion' had not yet been realized by the rise of Gorbachev. With the end of the Cold War, the readings have renewed significance.

67   **Toward a new world order: modest methods and drastic visions.**
Richard A. Falk.   In: *On the creation of a just world order*. Edited by Saul Mendlovitz.   New York: Free Press, 1975, p.211-58.

Here is an attempt to provide an 'ideology' for a 'global movement for world order reform'. Common values, shared by all cultures and serving to guide the reform, are said to be: peace, economic well-being, social justice, and ecological balance. The transition steps: 1970s Decade of Consciousness raising; 1980s Decade of Mobilization; 1990s Decade of Transformation. Falk sets out the existing or approaching world systems in clear diagrams, then cites precedents and examples for action during the coming decades. For fuller exposition, see his book, *A study of future worlds* (1975).

68   **Traditions of international ethics.**
Edited by Terry Nardin and David R. Mapel.   Cambridge: Cambridge University Press, 1992. 326p. bibliog.

These are well-integrated essays on the major traditions of international ethics: customary international law, declaratory international law (including treaties), realism, natural law, Kant's cosmopolitanism aiming at a world federation of free republics ('deontology'), utilitarianism, social contract theory, liberalism (including the world order school), Marxism, human rights, and Jewish and Christian influences on international conduct. (Only Islamic, Chinese and other non-Western traditions are omitted.) Each chapter explores the relations among the ideas of the individual good, common good, state, and international 'community' of states, the relation of principles to consequences, the validity of principles, and the nature of international relations. The United Nations occupies a rather small place in ethical traditions, as it does in theories of world politics – reflecting its nature as a mere consequence of certain innovations in the traditions of realism or international law.

69   **Transnational parties: organizing the world's precincts.**
Edited by Ralph M. Goldman.   Lanham, MD: University Press of America, 1983. 374p. bibliog.

If the General Assembly will be made even indirectly representative of peoples (a second chamber, elected by national parliaments), then 'transnational political parties' will surely become important actors in the nascent world political community. Current transnational parties include: the World Communist Movement (the Cominform is defunct), the Socialist International, the Christian Democratic International, liberal parties allied in spirit around the world, and European parties devoted to integration and unity especially in the European Parliament. The authors take a broad historical view and conclude with a chapter on U.S. interests in transnational parties, especially to promote genuine democracy in many of the oligarchic and authoritarian states of the world. (The end of the Cold War should increase this interest.) The editor in his conclusion answers objections that transnational parties are not real political parties, are undesirable or un-American, or generate civil strife and war. He expressly sees the United Nations as an 'incipient world government' for which 'transnationals are pregovernmental parties'.

70   **Transnational relations and world politics.**
Edited by Robert O. Keohane and Joseph S. Nye, Jr.   Cambridge, MA: Harvard University Press, 1971. 428p. bibliog.

This is a fundamental book on 'transnationalism'. The editors argue that the 'state-centric paradigm' for international relations is now anachronistic and deserves to be replaced by the 'world politics paradigm'. The latter includes interstate interactions – both traditional foreign relations and international organizations in the U.N. system and elsewhere – but also 'transnational' interactions such as global economic and financial activity, the business of multinational corporations, the public outreach of international non-governmental organizations, the grants of philanthropic foundations, the missions of churches, the exchanges of international science, world tourism, and so on. The authors explore questions of 'loss of control' by national state governments and of implications for international organizations, but reach no definite answers. Well before the Third World made its demands for a new international economic order, they warned that the U.N. is in danger of becoming 'simply an arena for harangues over intergovernmental aid and an administrator of technical assistance'. Hence, the volume marks a broadening of realist assumptions in which the U.N. still has a small role in world politics.

71   **Types of international society.**
Evan Luard.   New York: Free Press, 1976. 389p.

The author looks on international relations as neither a 'system', like the self-regulating solar system or circulatory system, nor a 'community', like the neighbourhood community of face-to-face contacts or the scholarly community of those sharing common values and assumptions. The world is at most a 'society' (*Gesellschaft*), an association of states and peoples linked by trade and intercourse, not always peaceful, but possessed of some common institutions short of a government. Luard provides an approach of 'international sociology' to world society – which must be contrasted with the theories of systems, games, bargaining, decision-making, and communications analysis that dominate the field of study. He analyses international society in terms of ideology, elites, motives, means, stratification, structure, roles, norms, and institutions. Each factor is traced through successive historical ages, such as the age of sovereignty (1648-1789), age of nationalism (1789-1914), and age of ideology (1914-74). He concludes with a view of future international societies, particularly the transnational (with few governing institutions), the international (with mature international organizations but not an oppressive world government), spheres of influence (dominated by great powers), a world of regions (integrated states as in the E.C.), and a world divided into rich and poor (as in the North–South conflict). International society is held together not by common values nor by coercion but by a minimal *mechanism for the adjustment of interests.* Luard favours, therefore, improvements in both the principles (norms of conduct) and procedures for resolution of conflicts, as in the U.N. This is a clear book of basic thinking about the world at the end of the age of ideology.

72 The United Nations: how it works and what it does.
Evan Luard. New York: St. Martin's, 1979. 187p. bibliog.

This is one of the most luminous, sensible, and friendly studies of the U.N. in the period of détente before the last worsening of the Cold War and a 'victory' for the United States (if not, as Gorbachev said, a mutual defeat for both the U.S. and U.S.S.R.). Luard discusses frankly the general public impression that the U.N. has failed to keep the world's peace. He explains its place in world politics, its history and changing role, its organization, finance, fundamental problems, and potential for reform. He recognizes that the fundamental political problem of the U.N. is the uncertainty that states and peoples feel about the degree of centralization of authority necessary or desirable in the world organization. Hence, his proposed reforms are limited to promoting negotiations instead of merely passing resolutions in the General Assembly, providing for more private meetings of the Security Council, providing the Secretariat with an anticipatory global intelligence service, providing for better Great Power representation in semi-permanent membership in the Security Council, granting only associate membership to new mini-states, regularizing peacekeeping, restoring the Secretary-General's administration of an independent international civil service, coordinating the specialized agencies, and solving the U.N.'s endemic financial problem. Fifteen years later, these are still realistic and achievable ideas. He concludes that humanity will be engaged in improving the U.N. structure for another century. Compare his companion volume, *The emerging framework of inter-dependence*.

73 The United Nations in a turbulent world.
James N. Rosenau. Boulder, CO: Lynne Rienner for International Policy Association, 1992. 87p.

The world is being transformed by the proliferation of states, organizations, influential individuals, technology, the global economy, interdependence, and the weakening of loyalties to the state. How are the transformations affecting the U.N.? Some say the state system is fundamentally unchanged and the U.N. remains 'ephemeral'. Others, that the changes are deep, but the U.N. as a creature of the states is unable to influence events. A third group say that the global transformations are creating opportunities for the U.N. that it can fill as an agent as well as a product of change. Rosenau, a political scientist, inclines to the third view. The U.N., he argues, will be 'enlarged, not engulfed'. Worldwide public education has produced a world citizenry who aim to govern themselves, and everywhere authority is being relocated away from its centres in states, big business, labour unions, and churches, until by the 1990s a kind of grand, 'bifurcated' choice is being presented to humanity – a choice between a 'state-centric world' and a 'multi-centric world'. The U.N. could be a beneficiary of bifurcation as the principle of sovereignty erodes and the locus of authority shifts from states to people. Rosenau does not revert to the 18th-century language of the 'sovereignty of the people', but he does make six recommendations to enhance the role of the U.N. in such a period of devolution. One is to 'enhance the authority' of the U.N. by granting the Secretary-General his request made since 1949 to establish U.N. embassies in critical countries in order to discover incipient conflicts when they can be resolved by rather small but timely efforts.

74 **The United Nations: meeting the challenges of the post-Cold War world.**
Edwin M. Smith, Keith R. Krause, and Brian Urquhart. *American Society of International Law Proceedings*, vol. 87 (1993), p.268-99.
The challenges include eroding sovereignty due to secession movements in the name of self-determination and to humanitarian intervention in the name of human rights. They also include a return to the 'common security' concept as the permanent members of the Security Council find themselves less divided. Smith argues that continued deference to the sovereign state, as in Boutros-Ghali's *An agenda for peace* (item no. 121), ignores the new reality of non-state actors and the norms of a new world order. No paradigms of international relations seem to fit the current scene – not multipolar balance of power ('realism'), nor 'international institutions relying on broad values and international law' (Wilsonian internationalism), nor 'multi-level interdependence' (Joseph Nye), nor 'unipolar' hegemony (Charles Krauthammer). Krause argues that the end of the Cold War is part of a deeper historical transformation of the Westphalian state system toward 'the vision of world politics articulated by Immanuel Kant in *Perpetual peace*'. U.N. reform proposals tend to fall into two camps: either they seek to preserve the status quo by technical or administrative devices, or they aim to transform the U.N. into a democratic world authority empowered to maintain the rule of law and protect and promote human rights. He proposes a third alternative, linked to existing popular consensus, which is something like Maurice Bertrand's forum for the negotiation of consensus – a 'site for contestation'. Without collective legitimation, reform is likely to continue ineffective. Urquhart warns that U.N. reform ought not to destroy what was so painfully won at the end of World War II, but he accepts that the *world of sovereign states* is in process of transformation to a *world community*. He concludes with a question: 'Do the major powers in the world really want a consistently strong and effective international organization?'

75 **Visions of a better world: a peace messenger initiative dedicated to the United Nations.**
Brahma Kumaris. Foreword by Sir Peter Ustinov. London: Brahma Kumaris World Spiritual University, 1992. 216p.
This book is a report on the international non-governmental organization Brahma Kumaris's Global Cooperation Programme, which involved the general public and leaders throughout the world in formulating a 'vision of a better world'. It is, without any political pretensions, a kind of plebiscite of the body politic of all humanity on the kind of world they want after the Cold War. It began with the Million Minutes of Peace project in 1986, designed to invite people to meditate on peace for at least one minute until one million 'minutes' were collected from each country. In four weeks, 1,231,975,713 minutes were gathered from 88 countries! That led to the Global Cooperation project carefully designed to gather full statements on peace by representative individuals from some 120 countries. There is a summary 'Global Vision Statement' plus hundreds of actual quotations. 'In a better world, all people celebrate the joy of life', begins the summary statement. It affirms human rights, freedom of expression, open communications, tolerance, secure family life, liberal education, social and economic justice, ecological balance, sustainable development, equal opportunity, science and technology at the service of humanity, the rule of law, self-government, and international cooperation. Peter Ustinov contributes a vision of world federalism. 'At long last, there seems to be a growing realization that

interdependence is the best guarantee of independence. Federalism is . . . a generally accepted legal method of guaranteeing independence.'

76 **A working peace system: an argument for the functional development of international organization.**
David Mitrany. London: Royal Institute of International Affairs, 1943. 60p.
This is the classic on the political approach effectively taken by the new United Nations Organization. Mitrany rejected schemes to enact world constitutions or to merge national sovereignties. He supported continuation of specialized agencies like the International Labour Organization or of wartime agencies that coordinated supply, food distribution, and the like, and he also supported establishment of new international agencies over monetary exchange rates, relief and rehabilitation, food and agriculture, and so on, since these would provide services ('functions') to citizens of national states and thus gradually build loyalties to international organization. He called the process 'federalism by installments'. The functional approach was also the one chosen for the European Community.

77 **The world as a total system.**
Kenneth Boulding. Beverly Hills, CA: Sage, 1985. 183p. bibliog.
In these lectures, originally presented at the United Nations University in Tokyo in 1984, the eminent economist and peace researcher pushes system theory to its limits. Boulding regards the world as a 'total system' and as a 'mosaic of partial systems: physical, biological, social, economic, political, communicative, and educational systems. His first chapter is an exposition of how we think of systems. The United Nations is regarded as a nascent political system, little able to restrain the Cold War in the Orwellian year of 1984. Boulding hopes his book will 'provoke a movement among the educational systems of the world for both research and teaching about the world as a total system.' Compare his earlier book, which inspired many, *The meaning of the twentieth century: the great transition* (1964).

78 **World military and social expenditures, 1986.**
Ruth Leger Sivard. Washington, DC: World Priorities, 1976- . annual. 52p.
Here is an annual account of the use of world resources for social and military purposes, providing an objective basis for evaluating public policy. It includes haunting statistics ('just people with the tears wiped off') and clear graphs. Topics include: scale and spread of militarization; technology and research and development devoted to military purposes; weapons in the 'last frontier' (space); risks to the public in economic burdens, social neglect, militarized political power, and wars (120 since 1945); reversing the tide by official and citizens' diplomacy; and tables of relevant statistics for most member states of the United Nations.

79 **World politics and international law.**
Francis A. Boyle. Foreword by Louis B. Sohn. Durham, NC: Duke University Press, 1985. 366p. bibliog.
This is a vigorous defence of the 'legalist-moralist' school of political science favouring international law and organization against the 'realist' school concentrating

on national power and self-interest. Boyle boldly discusses several difficult cases for a foreign policy based on international law and organization – ranging from the Israeli Entebbe raid of 1976 to the U.S.–Iranian hostage crisis of 1979-81. 'The theme is slowly developed that in the long run national interest is better served not by practicing power politics and relying on the use or threat of force, but by strengthening those international institutions that can provide a neutral environment for first slowing down a crisis and then finding an equitable solution acceptable to most of the parties in conflict.' Boyle is much impressed with the founder of the realist school Hans Morgenthau's abandonment of power politics in 1978 on the ground that it was leading inexorably toward a nuclear Third World War; in its place Morgenthau favoured the alternative of the deliberate 'formation of a world government'. Boyle concludes: 'They [international lawyers] must restore the U.N. Charter and fundamental principles of international law and organizations to their rightful position as the paramount basis for conducting American foreign policy. Otherwise, the future of mankind will be left in the brutal hands of geopolitical practitioners of Machiavellian power politics such as Kissinger, Brzezinski, Haig, and Kirkpatrick, and their students, associates and protégés.'

International law

80 The common law of mankind.
C. Wilfred Jenks.   London: London Institute for World Affairs, 1958.
456p.

This is a broad historical and judicious account of the 'revolutionary' changes in international law since World War II. The author's thesis is that: 'Contemporary international law can no longer be reasonably presented within the framework of the classical exposition of international law as the law governing the relationships between States but must be regarded as the common law of mankind in an early stage of its development.' Three general problems are addressed: the new law's scope, universality, and relation to international organization. The particular problems that Jenks treats, like European integration, colonial policy, employment policy, and control of atomic energy are now somewhat dated but are still handled in an admirable way by a 'good craftsman' of international law. The book is excellent for beginners. 'For the first time in history, we have the elements of a universal legal order.'

81 The concept of custom in international law.
Anthony A. D'Amato. Foreword by R. Falk.   Ithaca, NY: Cornell University Press, 1971. 286p. bibliog.

Custom is one of the major sources (in addition to treaties) of international law. The author's book is typical of the shift in jurisprudence away from the positivist conception of law as the command of the sovereign to a behavioural conception of law as process, whose basis of obligation is consensus. Since the international community lacks a 'governmental presence' (in Falk's terms), custom among its sovereign members is the first source of 'law' among them; treaties, the second. D'Amato treats customary international law as a way station between 'old power politics' and a 'world government having central legislative, executive and judicial functions'.

82 **The concept of law.**
H.L.A. Hart.   Oxford: Clarendon Press, 1961. 263p. bibliog.
This is a classic on law, analytical jurisprudence, moral and political philosophy, and descriptive sociology. It is broader in view than J.L. Austin's positivism ('law is the command of a sovereign'). Hart is commonly required of beginning law students. International law is regarded as a body of primary rules (customs, treaties, declarations defining obligations and duties) and secondary rules (constitutions defining rights to which states have given their consent or, as when new states come into existence, assume). The difficulties that the system of international law has no legislature, no independent courts, and no centrally organized system of sanctions are disposed of by contrasting the different social contexts of law within states and between them. International authorities that would be more like municipal are described as a unitary world state, federal state, or regime.

83 **Contemporary issues in international law: essays in honour of Louis B. Sohn.**
Edited by Thomas Buergenthal.   Kehl, Strasbourg, Arlington:
N.P. Engel, 1984. 571p. bibliog.
Human rights, the law of the sea and the environment, and international organizations are here treated with rigour, soundness, and imagination – the qualities his admiring students find in Professor Sohn. These three general topics, says the editor, 'comprise the international law of peaceful cooperation, a cooperation that has as its goal a world in which peace, the rule of law, and justice are shared by mankind as a whole'. Students who are in search of recent light on these topics may find it here. The book concludes with a complete list of Sohn's publications to 1984, which themselves are of great importance, especially in the area of 'the United Nations and problems of world order and peace'.

84 **Contemporary views on the sources of international law: the effect of U.N. resolutions on emerging legal norms.**
Stephen M. Schwebel, Christopher Osakwe, and Oscar M. Garibaldi.
American Society of International Law Proceedings, vol. 73 (1979),
p.300-33.
This volume explores legal attitudes found in the U.S., Soviet Union, and Third World on whether U.N. General Assembly resolutions give rise to new legal norms. The situation is transitional, but on a continuum of legal opinion the Soviet Union is most opposed to recognizing General Assembly resolutions as declaratory of international law, and the Third World least. This article is valuable for surveying exactly the middle ground between a recommendation and a binding agreement. All these observers recognize the theoretical necessity for a popularly representative world legislature and discuss consensus as an interim form of real majority rule. Garibaldi, for instance, remarks that accepting General Assembly resolutions as law would be analogous on the national plane to agreeing to a 'claim in Great Britain [that] the law is laid down not only by the Queen in Parliament but also by pronouncements of the Trade Union Congress'.

85 Custom as a source of international law.

Michael Akehurst. *British Yearbook of International Law*, vol. 47 (1974-75), p.1-53.

Custom is the oldest and most reliable of the sources of international law. This article explores how international law can be inferred from the practice of states and then how custom is related to treaties. This is a learned article, probably of interest only to international legal publicists.

86 Essays on international law and organization.

Leo Gross. Dobbs Ferry, NY: Transnational Publications, 1984. 2 vols. bibliog.

This is a collection of a lifetime's papers, especially on the development of international law by the U.N., problems of organization in the U.N., and adjudication of disputes by the International Court of Justice. The essays 'reflect [Professor Gross's] singular combination of idealism and realism, his taste for a more effective international law heavily salted with a sense of the limitations imposed by the hard facts of international life'. An index helps the general reader into the specialized essays. The essay, 'On the degradation of the constitutional environment of the United Nations', is especially relevant for U.N. reform. To counter unconstitutional proceedings to evict South Africa from the General Assembly, and Israel from UNESCO, ILO, and IAEA, the author proposes to count abstentions as negative votes, and, if this fails to discipline the majority, to refuse to pay assessments or to withdraw from the U.N.

87 In fairness to future generations: international law, common patrimony, and intergenerational equity.

Edith Brown Weiss. Preface by Richard Falk. Tokyo: U.N. University; Dobbs Ferry, NY: Transnational Publishers, 1988. 385p. bibliog.

This is the lead volume in a series on 'Innovation in international law'. New world conditions – technological change, the inability of state governments to meet global challenges, the danger that present national policies (nuclear deterrence, non-calculation of environmental costs) threaten future life prospects – require an 'anticipatory' approach to international law. This book deals with the nascent international obligation to conserve natural resources and the environment for future generations, rather as the right of property in domestic legal systems requires its preservation for future use by others. Topics include: planetary obligations, planetary rights, implementation, nuclear wastes, biological resources, forests, water, soils, cultural resources, climate. There are valuable appendixes on equity, environmental law, and protecting the cultural heritage. 'Traditionally only areas not subject to national jurisdiction have been considered as global commons. But from the intergenerational perspective, the planet is a "global commons" shared by all generations.'

88 **Global law-making and legal thought.**
Nicholas G. Onuf.   In: *Lawmaking in the global community*. Edited by
Nicholas G. Onuf.   Durham, NC: Carolina Academic Press, for Center
of International Studies, Princeton, 1982, p.1-81.
This learned volume is a sequel to *The future of the international legal order* (1969-
72). Onuf traces the history of positivism, culminating with the authoritative list of
the sources of international law given in Article 38 of the Statute of the International
Court of Justice. He then proceeds through recent challenges to positivism, beginning
with sociological jurisprudence, continuing through the debate over the law-making
'powers' of the General Assembly, and ending with such new departures as
neocolonialism and regimes. 'In an age of science, law, and legislation, it appears that
we have no vocation for the making of a global legislature. Without one, we cannot
make Austinian law, or so it would seem, and without Austinian law, we cannot even
hope to control the legal processes indispensable to a well-managed world.' The
foreword by Richard A. Falk on the 'whole enterprise of law without government or
governance' will perhaps be clearer to beginning students of international law.

89 **The growth of world law.**
Percy E. Corbett.   Princeton, NJ: Princeton University Press, 1971.
216p. bibliog.
Written during a dark ebb in the Cold War, this book nevertheless is one of the
clearest and most intelligible studies of the transition of international law from a law
of states to a supranational law of the world community. It is not so optimistic as
many books written about the time of the founding of the U.N., nor so pessimistic as
those written after forty years of Cold War, when the idea of 'world law' had almost
been forgotten. Hence, it should be useful to students seeking a hopeful yet realistic
perspective for the future. Corbett surveys the progress of international law
(especially across the divide of 1945), the progress marked by the establishment of
the League of Nations and the United Nations, the challenge of modern war to human
survival, and finally the new realities of world economic life and demand for
international protection of human rights. 'We may never reach a stage of world
government where the central authority will be armed with such powers as are normal
in federal systems. But, insofar as universal interests are recognized and brought
under collective implementation, the state will necessarily be subordinated to
supranational agencies exercising, where persuasion fails, some measure of coercion.
This truth must be faced even at the risk of temporarily increasing resistance.'

90 **International law: a contemporary perspective.**
Edited by Richard A. Falk, Friedrich Kratochwil, and Saul H.
Mendlovitz.   Boulder, CO: Westview, 1985. 702p. bibliog.
Written at another low ebb in the progress of international law, when the end of the
Cold War and the return to the United Nations could scarely be imagined, this volume
remains instructive for 'legalists' or 'moralists' in confrontation with 'realists',
especially if international war resumes again or the United Nations is not
strengthened while the opportunity lasts. The book 'is based on a conviction that the
structures of human activity on a global scale necessarily has a normative element
that is best studied in relation to the place of law'. Three doctrines of the conviction
are emphasized: (1) There is much unobtrusive observance of international law
occurring daily, as in travel, commerce, and community. (2) The current organization

of international society into states claiming sovereign independence and acting on the basis of particular interests, rather than shared interests or the common good, limits what can be achieved by a law based on voluntary compliance. (3) But the habit of thinking legally could contribute to the rise of a 'Grotius for our time' – who might devise a law comprehending 'global interests as well as national interests, planetary loyalities as well as national loyalties, non-state actors as well as state actors'.

91   International law and the future.
Myers S. McDougal. *Mississippi Law Journal*, vol. 50 (1979), p.259-334.

The author is one of the founders, with Harold Lasswell, of the school of thought that international law is not the command of the sovereign, but the 'process of authoritative decision through which the members of a community seek to clarify and secure their common interests'. McDougall here reflects on the future of international law in the spirit of the World Order Models Project, Club of Rome, Trilateral Commission, and Richard A. Falk's specific suggestions to improve legal processes for the achievement of public order values. McDougall agrees with Falk that humanity is moving out of the Westphalian state system into a pluralistic system of states, peoples, and individuals, 'with central guidance coming from an as yet unidentified source'. Like a good international lawyer, who is familiar with the lack of a source of central guidance, McDougall devotes the rest of his long article to a 'policy-oriented framework of inquiry' in order to guide statesmen and citizens during the transition. Topics include: the transnational character of current problems, goals of world community, authoritative decision-making to secure the common interest, the contemporary global constitutive process, conditions affecting world public order, possible futures, optimum future. The latter he does not describe as 'world government', since most of its proponents have not shown the policies and reforms necessary to establish it, nor as 'lesser modifications of the existing anarchy', since their proponents ignore the larger processes of authoritative decision and effective power. His own solution is somewhere between these extremes – a kind of continual, élite and democratic pursuit of human rights and peace.

92   International law: a treatise.
L. Oppenheim. Edited by H. Lauterpacht.   London: Longmans, Green, 7th ed., 1948-52. 2 vols. bibliog.

This is a classic of international law (first published in 1906). Vol. I: Peace; Vol. II: Disputes, war and neutrality. Here is the place to go for a brief, authoritative account of the law of nations, sovereignty, international personality, rights of states, state responsibility, national territory, freedom of the seas, the position of individuals in international law (changing by 1948), heads of state and government, diplomats, envoys, international transactions, treaties, the laws of war, peaceful and compulsory settlement of disputes, and especially the legal organization of the international community (League of Nations and United Nations). 'The historic idea of a "general international organization" . . . connotes an association of States of potentially universal characteristics for the ultimate fulfilment of purposes which, in relation to individuals organized in political society, are realized by the State. The achievement of these purposes is as essential to the Law of Nations as it is to the international law of the State.' By 1948, Oppenheim's *International law* recognized the necessity for the 'obligatory jurisdiction of international tribunals', 'international legislation', some form of popular 'representation', and the 'ultimate goal of a supra-national legal ordering of mankind'.

93 International law in 'her infinite variety'.
R.R. Baxter. *International and Comparative Law Quarterly*, vol. 29 (October 1980), p.549-66.

The author writes on 'hard' vs. 'soft' law – treaties vs. U.N. resolutions. *Rules* of international law are now generally accepted as obligations for states and individuals, even though they are not enforceable by sanctions. *Norms*, the author argues, also do so. Norms include international agreements, alliances, declarations of policy, joint communiqués, and resolutions of the U.N. General Assembly. The Helsinki Accords of 1975 and the Stockholm Declaration on the Human Environment of 1972 are typical; though not 'enforceable', they have created many new rights and duties. Four degrees of 'intensity of agreement' are set out for norms. 'The lawyer is indeed a social engineer and in that role, he must be able to invent or to produce machinery that will assist in the resolution of disputes and differences between the States.'

94 International law in theory and practice.
Oscar Schacter. Dordrecht, The Netherlands: M. Nijhoff, 1991. 431p. bibliog.

Here is a recent theoretical and practical account of international law by a former American member of the U.N. Legal Affairs Department and now an eminent scholar and international legal publicist. International law is understood sophistically as a relatively autonomous body of binding rules and obligations for states – even though they lack a superior authority – *and* as the decentralized pursuit of common social ends through the exercise of legitimated state power. It cannot be reduced to politics, yet it is more than the rules maintaining the status quo. This view tends to unite international lawyers, who are often divided between the instrumentalists, who stress the primacy of purposes and values, and the positivists, who stress the constraints of agreed rules and obligations. Schachter treats such objections as that international law is subject to state power or is based only on their continuing consent. Readers interested in the debate between the normative theorists and the realists will find Schachter's earlier chapters on the nature and sources of international law most helpful; those with more practical concerns will turn to his later chapters on the prohibition of the threat and use of force, self-defence, peaceful means for the settlement of international disputes, enforcement of international law, limits on state applications of its domestic law on persons or in situations outside its territory, the new law of the sea, international business, human rights, protection of the environment, and collective security after the Cold War.

95 The international society as a legal community.
Hermann Mosler. Alphen aan den Rijn, The Netherlands: Sijthoff & Noordhoff, 1980. 327p. bibliog.

This is an up-to-date text by a judge of the ICJ on both international legal relationships and international organizations. 'The purpose underlying the choice of the topics treated in these pages is to show how the international society, consisting of States and organizations set up by States, constitutes a community governed by law.' Topics include: international society and legal community, subjects of international law, the position of the individual, sources of law, treaties, custom, principles and rules, evidence, responsibility, international organizations (large section), regimes, economic cooperation, and contemporary settlement of disputes. The author is strict yet not devoid of vision: 'Recent history's answer to the political disorder of sovereign States prevailing before the two [world] wars has not been the *civitas maxima*, a centralized or federal State or a confederation of States, but a multitude of specialized international organizations with a political forum in the United Nations.'

96 Law and force in the new international order.
Edited by Lori F. Damrosch and David J. Scheffer.   Boulder, CO: Westview, 1991. 325p.

Papers originally presented at a joint U.S.–Soviet conference on International Law and the Non-use of Force, Washington, 1990, are here collected. Topics include: legitimate use of force for self-defence and collective security (as in Iraq); interventions by invitation, against 'illegitimate' regimes, for humanitarian purposes (as to protect human rights), and against international crimes (such as drug trafficking and terrorism); restraints on force by new arms control agreements; and improved judicial tribunals for the settlement of disputes without force. The end of the Cold War provides a new opportunity to establish the 'primacy of law over politics', as Mikhail Gorbachev expressed it. The book 'constitutes the first published result of a collaborative effort [between] U.S. and Soviet experts to rethink international law in the light of new political conditions'.

97 The law-making function of the specialized agencies of the United Nations.
Charles H. Alexandrowicz.   Sydney: Angus and Robertson, 1973. 181p.

A typical example of international legislation is the making of regulations governing civil aviation by the International Civil Aviation Organization (ICAO) Council. The Council, representative of states, acts unilaterally, not multilaterally, and its regulations do not require the specific consent of states. Its actions are not contracts, dependent on mutual performance, nor are they treaties, requiring ratification by states. In the fields of science and technology, the world is already legally one. The author, a British barrister, conducts a comparative study of all such cases of international making of internal procedural rules, rules of external practice, and amendment of agencies' constitutions. This is already done when linking national postal systems, allocating the radio spectrum, regulating civil aviation, collecting weather data, and repaying international loans of money. Because such acts are passed by majority rule and yet are binding on all, as in municipal legislation, international technical legislation creates a precedent for 'political' legislation, occupied now by 'power politics'. 'While the obsession with the paramount nature of sovereignty still reigns supreme in power politics, the law of the Specialized Agencies, in so far as it follows in the wake of scientific and technical progress, has tended to intensify methods of functional cooperation and promote a measure of world integration.'

98 Law, morality, and the relations of states.
Terry Nardin.   Princeton, NJ: Princeton University Press, 1983. 350p. bibliog.

Here is a philosophical exposition of international law as the set of customary *practices* guiding or limiting sovereign states in their pursuit of divergent purposes – as opposed to deliberately chosen *purposes* governing states in their pursuit of shared purposes. 'Like the hedges to which Hobbes likened the laws, practices keep travelers on the roads but do not prescribe their destinations.' To Nardin, the state system is at most a society, not a community. He does not regard it as a decentralized version of the civil state, nor as an anarchy lacking either government or rules. A 'legal order without a state' is quite possible. He acknowledges visions, particularly by Kant, of a confederation of independent states in order to move toward a more centralized civil state, but regards this as remotely in the future. Even the United Nations, which aimed to establish common principles and purposes (Articles 1 and 2) for promoting cooperation among existing states, he treats as having 'abandoned international law' and marking 'one of the low points in the fortunes of the practical conception of international society'. Its failures to maintain international peace and security, to secure human rights, or to achieve greater economic and social justice reflect the lack of international consensus on values and ends. The practical conception of international law – based on custom, treaties, and legal scholarship – he concludes, is 'possibly the only understanding upon which a pluralist world order can be constructed'. Although this view contributes very little to the historic project of international organization, the reader will find much that is informed and balanced on international morality and law. The chapter on international justice is particularly clear.

99   The law of nations: an introduction to the international law of peace.

James Leslie Brierly. Edited by Humphrey Waldock.   New York: Oxford University Press, 6th ed., 1964. 442p.

This brief masterpiece of international law is intended as an introduction for students and laypersons. It is excellent on the origins of the modern international system and on such notions as the state, sovereignty, the basis of state obligation, the sources of international law, and the legal organization of international society. The sixth edition carries the account of the expansion of international law only about as far as the U.N. shortly after its founding, but Brierly's discussion of its foundations is still relevant at a time when the idea of U.N. reform is in the air.

100   Legislative powers in the United Nations and specialized agencies.

Edward Yemin.   Leiden, The Netherlands: A. W. Sijthoff, 1969. 230p. bibliog.

International law lags behind changes in international society. Custom and treaty cannot keep up. What is needed, the author argues (against the tradition of the sovereignty of states), is *international legislation*. By this Yemin means a unilateral act of a higher authority, binding on the members of the community, and consisting of a general rule or norm. In the case of the world community, which lacks a legislature, this evolving legal function is performed by the U.N. General Assembly and Security Council and by the governing bodies of the specialized agencies during the amendment process. Yemin does not consider whether these bodies engage in international legislation when passing ordinary resolutions. To him, the fundamental step toward such legislation was taken when states adhered to an international organization in which amendments binding on all could be reached without unanimity, that is, by, say, a two-thirds majority.

101 **A manual of international law.**
Georg Schwarzenberger and E.D. Brown.   Milton, England:
Professional Books, 6th ed., 1976. 612p. bibliog.

This is a clear, authoritative account of international law 'as a system of fairly stable
and interlocking rules of international customary law on which, from time to time,
more ambitious superstructures, varying in permanence and significance, have been
grafted by way of treaty'. The manual is historical and realistic in presentatation, as
well as brief. It is especially clear on the fundamental 'principles' of international law
(sovereignty, recognition, consent, good faith, freedom of the seas, international
responsibility, and self-defence), on its 'subjects' (states, and increasingly
intergovernmental organizations, international non-governmental organizations, and
individuals), the law of treaties, the law of the U.N. and its system of functional
agencies and institutions, and U.N. reform in the nuclear age. 'The difficulties
obstructing progress towards territorial or functional world federalism are not
primarily of a technical character. . . . The obstacles are of a more fundamental and
less rational character. Prejudices of a national and racial character, differences in
economic and social structure or in political ideologies and religious belief are
elevated into barriers which prevent any further integration of existing international
society.' Schwarzenberger calls his approach to international law 'inductive,
interdisciplinary and relativist'.

102 **A modern law of nations: an introduction.**
Philip C. Jessup.   New York: Macmillan, 1948. 236p. bibliog.

This is an eloquent plea, written shortly after the end of World War II and the first use
of nuclear weapons, to 'begin the systematic re-evaluation of the traditional body of
international law'. It is typical of creative international legal opinion at another
historic opportunity. Jessup calls for an international law applicable not only to states,
but also to individuals, for an international criminal law in order to maintain world
peace, and for a modification of absolute national sovereignty. 'Until the world
achieves some form of international government in which a collective will takes
precedence over the individual will of the sovereign state, the ultimate function of
law, which is the elimination of force for the solution of human conflicts, will not be
fulfilled.'

103 **The nature and process of legal development in international
society.**
Oscar Schachter.   In: *The structure and process of international law:
essays in legal philosophy, doctrine, and theory.* Edited by R. St. J.
Macdonald and Douglas M. Johnston.   The Hague: M. Nijhoff, 1983,
p.745-808.

'International law develops through treaties and custom.' The author goes beyond this
short and familiar answer to discuss philosophically, historically, and politically 'how
the international legal system is continuously being forged to meet the problems
brought about by the conflicts and passions endemic to the human species'. Schachter
constantly contrasts the received doctrines of international law with the new realities
of life on the planet (the law develops out of changing conditions, problem-solving,
historical progression, and power politics). This article is a clear and relatively short
survey of international law and its continuing controversies by a masterful
international lawyer. He concludes with valuable reflections on 'general principles of

law, equity, and justice'. The reason why states and peoples pursue equity, he writes, is not merely 'moral idealism; it has its origin and basis principally in the necessities of contemporary international relations'.

104 **Principles of public international law.**
Ian Brownlie. Oxford: Clarendon Press, 3rd ed., 1979. 743p.

The author provides a standard, authoritative text of the international law of peace, based on the modern practice of states, the practice of international organizations, and the decisions of international and municipal courts. Brownlie is rather more positivist (empirical) than, say, Schwartzenberger or Falk. The treatment of international organization, for instance, is entirely in terms of what the law is, not what it might be. This is the place to go for the busy government official, corporate lawyer, law professor, and law student.

105 **The relevance of international law.**
Edited by Karl Deutsch and Stanley Hoffmann. Cambridge, MA: Schenkman, 1968. 280p.

This volume of essays in honour of Professor Leo Gross is an attack on international law and organization as irrelevant to international politics and to political science. Hoffmann claimed that contemporary international affairs exhibited a 'revolutionary' and 'heterogeneous' nature, as opposed to a 'moderate' and 'homogeneous' one. The causes were dissolution of the classical balance of power, worldwide revolutionary insurgence, suicidal nuclear weapons systems, nationalistic fervour, ideological division of the world, uncurbed exponential population growth, and headlong technical and industrial innovation. This was an environment for the expedient and wise conduct of diplomacy, aided by military power, not international law. Books like this mark the triumph of 'realism'.

106 **The role of the United Nations General Assembly resolution in determining principles of international law in United States courts.**
Gregory J. Kerwin. *Duke Law Journal* (September 1983), p.876-99.

This article treats the tendency of General Assembly resolutions (technically non-binding) to be cited by U.S. courts as sources of international law. Two cases are considered: the arbitration of Texaco Overseas Petroleum Co. *v.* Libyan Arab Republic (1977) and the appeal of Filartiga *v.* Peña-Irala (1980). The author is doubtful that the General Assembly can yet serve as a world legislature, but he ably reviews the arguments on both sides.

107 **The role of the United Nations in the development of international law.**
Nico Shrijver. In: *The U.N. under attack.* Edited by Jeffrey Harrod and Nico Schrijver. Aldershot, England: Gower, 1988, p.33-56.

The author reviews the U.N. role in codification of international law, the special role of General Assembly resolutions, and the role of the International Court of Justice. Shrijver documents impressive 'progress' (350 multilateral treaties negotiated under U.N. auspices, several binding resolutions like the arms embargo against South Africa (1977), establishment of subsidiary organs like the International Law Commission and UNCTAD, 49 ICJ judgments and 18 advisory opinions). He acknowledges reluctantly the 'stagnation and even decline' of international law (maintaining the status quo, political preemption by the Security Council, ICJ judgments binding only for the parties concerned and for each particular case). 'One has to enter the "grey zones" of politics, "soft" law, and "hard" law in order to understand the role that international law could and should play in the fields of development, the maintenance of peace and security, and the promotion of respect for human rights.'

108 **Scope and meaning of article 2(4) of the United Nations Charter.**
Toslim O. Elias. In: *Contemporary problems in international law: essays in honor of Georg Schwarzenburger on his eightieth birthday.* Edited by Bin Cheng and E.D. Brown. London: Stevens & Sons, 1988, p.70-85.

Article 2(4) provides: 'All members shall refrain in their international relations from the threat or use of force against the territorial integrity of political independence of any state, or in any other manner inconsistent with the purposes of the United Nations.' The author surveys legal opinion on the scope and meaning of this fundamental principle, especially with respect to challenges by Thomas Franck (1970) and Michael Reisman (1984). Elias concludes that reprisals or armed intervention, even for humanitarian purposes (as to protect human rights) is illegal. The exemption for self-defence is exploded by reviewing the International Court of Justice's judgment in the case of Nicaragua *v.* United States of America (1986). The deeper problem is that the prohibition against the threat or use of force seems to undermine nuclear deterrence in the Cold War, so the author supports various initiatives in NATO and the former Warsaw Pact to conclude a treaty on the non-use of military force. (By the 1990s, such non-use was becoming a customary reality.)

109 **Transnational law.**
Philip C. Jessup. New Haven: Yale University Press, 1956. 113p. (Storrs Lecture on Jurisprudence).

Here is an eloquent case for expanding international law during the transition from the 'society of states' to the 'world state'. 'Transnational law' was defined as 'a law which regulates actions or events that transcend national frontiers'. The author was a distinguished teacher of law at Columbia University, a diplomatist who helped end the Berlin blockade in 1949, and a judge of the International Court of Justice.

110 **Transnational law in a changing society: essays in honor of Philip C. Jessup.**
Edited by Wolfgang Friedman, Louis Henkin, and Oliver Lissitzyn. New York: Columbia University Press, 1972. 324p. bibliog.

Here are valuable essays reflecting the widening of international law from a law strictly of states to one of states, organizations, and individuals on the U.N.'s twenty-fifth anniversary.

111 Treaty series.
United Nations. New York: United Nations, 1946- . 1,503 vols by 1988.

In accordance with Article 102 of the U.N. Charter, every treaty and international agreement entered into by a member-state is registered or filed with the Secretariat and then is published in the U.N. continuing series. By 1988, almost 26,000 such treaties and agreements had been so published. The U.N. Treaty Series continues the League of Nations Treaty Series beginning in 1921. (In effect, this series ends the general practice of secret convenants, secretly arrived at.) It includes multilaterial, bilateral, inter-state and state-organization instruments. Text is in English and French.

112 The United Nations – A general evaluation.
Bert V.A. Roling. In: *U.N. law/fundamental rights: Two topics in international law*. Edited by Antonio Cassese. Alphen aan den Rijn, The Netherlands: Sijthoff & Noordhoff, 1979, p.23-28.

The author is a professor of international law at the University of Groningen and a co-founder of the International Peace Research Association. Roling evaluates the U.N. by the standard of peace since 1945 – not *justice*, which was not given to either General Assembly or Security Council as a primary responsibility. (There was too much difference of opinion about justice, as determined by national interests, values, and power.) Roling concludes that the U.N. has failed to keep the peace (thirty international wars to 1970), but by entering the field of human rights, it has made surprising progress in promoting justice. That is, the U.N. could do little more than the League to prolong 'negative peace' (interval between wars), but was operating in so changed an international environment, which required a general international organization to solve global problems beyond the powers of sovereign states, that it made its first great gains in 'positive peace' (reign of justice). Roling traces this progress in the areas of anti-colonialism, ending racial discrimination, and the struggle against economic exploitation. He foresees a long struggle for 'world unity'. 'Students and scholars should be prepared for this coming controversy, where the demands of narrrow nationalism should be opposed and answered by the demands of humanity as a whole.'

113 The United Nations and the control of international violence: a legal and political analysis.
John F. Murphy. Totowa, NJ: Allanheld, Osmun, 1982. 212p. bibliog.

This is a study of the U.N. record in coping with international violence in its several forms: state-to-state armed conflict, revolutionary wars, and 'unconventional' violence (assassination, surrogate warfare, state-sponsored terrorism, and private terrorism.) The focus is on the principles of the U.N. Charter and of international law in order to determine their adequacy in today's world. Secondary focus is on U.N. practice by the Security Council, General Assembly, Secretary-General, and International Court of Justice. The general approach is historical and interdisciplinary through case-studies, avoiding the usual split between international lawyer, social scientist, and policy analyst. Murphy concludes (before the end of the Cold War) that 'reform' should not take the form of Charter amendment, but of creative use of the existing organization. 'International law is a dynamic process constantly undergoing change.'

114 **The United Nations and the development of international law.**
Nagendra Singh. In: *United Nations, divided world*. Edited by Adam
Roberts and Benedict Kingsbury. Oxford: Oxford University Press,
1988, p.159-91.

Here is a conventional view of international law by a judge of the International Court
of Justice. Judge Singh reviews methodically all the sources of international law:
U.N. Charter, General Assembly, International Law Commission, International Court
of Justice, and the specialized agencies. The Charter, by comparison with the League
Covenant, provided at least nine new principles of law, such as the prohibition against
the use of force in the settlement of disputes. Certain General Assembly resolutions
have acquired the force of law, such as that granting independence to colonial
countries and peoples (Resolution 1514 of 1960). Binding conventions have also
emerged from conferences such as that on the Law of the Sea. The International Law
Commission and International Court of Justice have made small but appreciable
contributions to bringing order to the anarchy of sovereign states. The judge
concludes with discussion of four kinds of problems with contemporary international
law – particularly closing its gaps and enforcement.

115 **The United Nations and the politics of law.**
Robert E. Riggs. In: *Politics in the United Nations system*. Edited by
Lawrence S. Finkelstein. Durham, NC: Duke University Press, 1988,
p.41-74.

Riggs accepts the traditional view of international law as a body of rules and
principles binding upon states. He disputes the new view of law as the process of
General Assembly enactment of non-binding resolutions and subsequent citation by
courts and diplomats. This, argues Riggs, fits all rules along a continuum, erasing the
distinction between law and non-law. It will not heighten respect for Assembly
resolutions, but weaken the obligatory power of real law. Nevertheless, Riggs is
constrained to discuss new sources of international law beyond treaty and custom:
internal procedural rule-making, repetition of declarations until their principles
become customary (Universal Declaration of Human Rights), legal obligations set by
specialized agencies (World Bank), amendment of founding conventions, and
difficulties like falling into arrears on financial contributions and non-enforcement.

116 **The United Nations, lawmaking, and world order.**
Samuel S. Kim. In: *The United Nations and a just world order*.
Edited by Richard Falk, Samuel Kim, and Saul Mendlovitz.
Boulder, CO: Westview, 1991, p.109-24.

Kim takes a bold new view of international law, whose sources now include the
General Assembly, for it is the 'only available global forum with universal
membership and the competence to discuss any matters of international concern
where member states can seek a fit between national and common interests as a way
of expressing the general will and of translating this will into law'. Kim discounts
custom (a heritage of colonialism), the International Court of Justice (only 48
judgments to 1982), and the International Law Commission ('progressive
development' of the law has been handed back to the General Assembly). His notion
of international law is sociological, hard to distinguish from politics in the U.N. There
can still be law even without a government at the world level. 'The international

lawmaking process has shifted from the "sources of law" to the consensual mode of global bargaining and decision making.'

117   **United Nations law making: cultural and ideological relativism and international law making for an era of transition.**
Edward McWhinney.   New York: Holmes & Meier for UNESCO, 1984. 274p. bibliog.

The author, a distinguished Canadian legal scholar, anticipates the end of the Cold War which he treats as virtually accomplished by the coming of détente in the early 1970s. The book, then, is a judicious and well-informed account of the full range of international law-making in an 'era of transition', especially with respect to the Western liberal, socialist, and developing worlds, which he regards as rather permanent divisions of international relations. (If the socialist tradition is not extinguished by events of 1989-91, McWhinney's views will seem particularly fair.) Topics of law-making include: dialectical developments of law under conditions of peaceful coexistence, recognition of the temporal nature of the 'new' international law (adaptable to new conditions), sources (customs, conventions, principles, publicists), General Assembly resolutions, International Law Commission codification, International Court of Justice judgments, Charter amendment, the Secretary-General's roles, values to govern legislation later, such as self-determination, economic sovereignty, and peace. The author does not attempt to prophesy the content of the new international law *after* the transition, except to say that it will be a 'living law' synthesizing the liberal democratic, social democratic, and developing traditions, as in general acceptance of political, economic and social human rights.

118   **The world community: a planetary social process.**
Myres S. McDougal, W. Michael Reisman, and Andrew R. Willard.
University of California Davis Law Review, vol. 21 (1988), p.807-972.

This is a long, closely reasoned and annotated article on the future of international law, embedded in a larger world social process already producing what can be descriptively termed a 'world community'. International law is not understood as an Austinian 'closed system' but as a Lasswellian 'world community process'. The process is described with great analytical care in terms of the participation of individuals in world politics as they make demands on situations based on their values and strategies. The outcomes are then compared with future perspectives. The article is designed to bring clarity and synthesis to the work of international relations specialists, historians (diplomatic, economic, and popular), international lawyers, and official decision-makers. Particularly helpful is the authors' treatment of the relationships among states, individuals, transnational parties, and civilizations. This is one of the boldest, most serious recent expositions of the idea that all humanity now constitutes a single world community.

119   **World treaty index.**
Peter H. Rohn, director.   Santa Barbara, CA: ABC-Clio, 2nd ed., 1984. 5 vols.

A quick reference to some 44,000 treaties and agreements from 1900 to 1980 can be found here. Information given in the main entry section (vols 2-3) consist of: date of signature, cross-reference to source (e.g., U.N. Treaty Series), type of agreement (e.g., protocol, treaty), title, date of entry into force, topic or field of application (e.g., dispute settlement), and parties (multilaterial, bilateral, unilateral). Readers can search for treaties by date, topic, party, or keyword. Originally intended as a catalogue of cases for theory-building in political science, the *Treaty index* has become a convenient entrée into the vast realm of international treaties and agreements. For actual texts of treaties, readers will have to turn to given sources. The first volume contains valuable statistical profiles of 'party' (regional) groups by treaty topics over time.

A survey of treaty provisions for the pacific settlement of international disputes, 1949-1962.
See item no. 423.

The international regulation of armaments: the law of disarmament.
See item no. 672.

See also General Assembly (p.96ff.), International Court of Justice (p.120ff.), International Law Commission (p.125ff.), Arbitration (p.170ff.), and Judicial settlement (p.180ff.).

U.N. reform

120 **After consensus, what? Performance criteria for the U.N. in the post-Cold War era.**
Kendall W. Stiles and Maryellen MacDonald.   *Journal of Peace Research* (Oslo), vol. 29 (1992), p.299-311.

The new consensus is that, at least in the North, the U.N. has 'utility'. (That has long been the consensus in the South.) But how will this utility be measured? Mere support for the ideology of freedom or of socialism will no longer do, since Northern values have converged around 'social democratic principles'. The authors suggest four criteria: (1) consistency with the Charter and other founding documents; (2) operational goals set by agency executives and published so that others can test them; (3) past trends, apart from charters and policy goals; and (4) imagining the situation without the U.N. (By analogy, one might evaluate a church in accordance with scripture, creed, tradition, and absence, leaving its functions to the state.) Stiles and MacDonald discuss their criteria for use in social science.

121 **An agenda for peace: preventative diplomacy, peacemaking, and peacekeeping. Report [of the Secretary-General pursuant to the statement adopted by the Summit Meeting of the Security Council on 31 January 1992].**
Boutros Boutros-Ghali.   New York: United Nations, 1992. 53p. (DPI/1247).

Here are the Secretary-General's proposals for U.N. reform, following the historic first meeting of the Security Council at the level of heads of state and government. The end of the Cold War has given nation-states and their peoples a 'second chance to create the world of our Charter'. He proposes improved fact-finding and early-warning capabilities within the U.N., preventive deployment of aid workers and, in certain cases, peacekeeping forces before a crisis erupts, general acceptance of the compulsory jurisdiction of the International Court of Justice, development of peace enforcement units under Article 43, financing of peacekeeping by contributions from members' defence (not foreign affairs) budgets, and a new concept of 'post-conflict peace-building'. Peace-building, as in Namibia and Cambodia, is the wider use of peacekeeping forces, police, and civilian personnel to establish order, the rule of law, and even new representative sovereign governments. 'Reform is a continuing process, and improvement can have no limit. Yet there is an expectation, which I wish to see fulfilled, that the present phase in the renewal of this organization should be complete by 1995, its fiftieth birthday.'

122 **Alternative pasts: a study of weighted voting at the U.N.**
Hanna Newcombe, Christopher Young, and Elia Sinaiko.
International Organization, vol. 31 (1977), p.579-86.

This is a statistically rigorous report on the political effects of U.N. General Assembly votes caused by introduction of any of twenty-two weighted voting formulae (one-nation-one vote, proportional to population, proportional to U.N. assessment, the Clark–Sohn steps, square root of population, etc.). Most of the weighted voting formulae would tend to arrest or reverse the General Assembly's trend to vote pro-South, pro-Arab, and pro-supranational resolutions (peacekeeping, disarmament, human rights). The authors prefer a weighted voting system to counter the effects of mini-states in the system, to satisfy democratic justice (one-person-one-vote), to reflect the realities of power, and to stop the anti-West, anti-Israel trend in the General Assembly. But they argue that, to be just, a weighted voting reform would have to be linked with a package of measures for greater economic equalization. 'Although for the present this aspiration is utopian, the ultimate objective would be a democratic General Assembly in a world of equality.'

123 **A bargain for humanity: global security by 2000.**
Douglas Roche. Foreword by V. Petrovsky.   Edmonton: University of Alberta Press, 1993. 189p. bibliog.

The author is a seasoned Canadian statesman. Roche looks forward to the U.N.'s fiftieth anniversary in 1995 as an opportunity for a new 'global compact' in order to protect the future of civilization. He looks at the confusing spectacle of world politics after the Cold War (North–South collision, Persian Gulf War, difficult peacekeeping missions) from the perspective of a revitalized United Nations. Russian, Canadian, and U.S. policies are especially examined for their potential contributions to new global policies of common security, sustainable development, preservation of the earth's environment, and 'transforming' world leadership. He closes with a practical yet visionary 'bargain for humanity'.

124 **Beyond Cold War thinking: security threats and opportunities. Report [of the Twenty-fifth United Nations of the Next Decade Conference, 1990].**
40p. (Stanley Foundation, 216 Sycamore St., Suite 500, Muscatine, IA, 52761.)

After the Cold War, the Stanley Foundation hosted a high-level conference of officials and foreign policy experts from the United Nations, United States, (former) Soviet Union, (former) East and West Germany, Canada, Mexico, Poland, Algeria, India, and China. It included, for example, Yashushi Akashi, Alexei Arbatov, Maurice Bertrand, James Jonah, Krzystan Ostrowski, Olara Otunnu, Thomas Pickering, and Gary Sick. The end of the Cold War, they agreed, would lead to a shift from military to economic power in the ranking of national states, a shift from a bipolar to multipolar world, an increased focus on Europe over the Third World in the short term, and increased importance of global issues like the environment, the transnational economy, communications, trade, overpopulation, and drugs. Security issues would become much more complex than the old standoff between NATO and the Warsaw Pact. A 'new international security regime' would grow out of the Conference on Security and Cooperation in Europe, continued arms control, and transfer of military funds. It would attack the causes of war by supporting the establishment of democracies, limiting population growth, and promoting economic development 'tempered by social justice'. The United Nations, which 'atrophied' during the Cold War, could now play an important role in peacekeeping, peacemaking, settling regional disputes, and addressing the causes of war. Reform would take the form of creating a small, representative policy council or ministerial board to manage United Nations economic functions.

125 **Building a more democratic United Nations.**
Edited by Frank Barnaby. Portland, OR: Frank Cass, 1991. 313p.

This volume contains the proceedings of the first international Conference on a More Democratic U.N., New York, October 1990. It contains substantial contributions from the non-governmental organization (NGO) community on how to 'democratize and revitalize the United Nations'. Ideas include a second house of the General Assembly representative of peoples, increased interim NGO access, improved global communications, and U.N. restructuring (weighted voting, binding triad, limits on Security Council veto, following up on Gorbachev's initiatives). The book is a compendium of rather radical proposals to allow 'We the Peoples' to have more direct representation in the United Nations and hence to increase its collective authority for the maintenance of peace and security.

126 **Building peace: reports, 1939-1972.**
Commission to Study the Organization of Peace. Metuchen, NJ: Scarecrow, 1973. 2 vols.

The Commission to Study the Organization of Peace was founded in 1939 by two leaders of the League of Nations Association, James T. Shotwell and Clark M. Eichelberger. They aimed to create an enduring research group, independent of other associations and of any government, 'to engage in a thorough and comprehensive study of all aspects of the problem of international peace, with special emphasis on plans for a future world organization to maintain peace and to promote the progress of mankind'. Forty-seven of its select members attended the San Francisco conference on the establishment of the United Nations Organization in 1945 as consultants to the U.S. delegation. In years following, the commission continued to make timely and far-seeing recommendations for strengthening the U.N. that had some influence on U.S. policy, as John Foster Dulles, once a member and later Secretary of State, admitted in 1949. These two volumes contain all the commission's reports from 1940 to 1972. They are a record of practical, yet idealistic steps toward a 'world community based on law and justice' that will be of interest to anyone seriously contemplating U.N. reform after the Cold War. Topics include: Charter review in 1955 (9th report), strengthening the U.N. (10th), responding to the influx of new states (17th), and the U.N. of the future (20th).

127 **Can the United Nations be reformed?**
Maurice Bertrand. In: *United Nations, divided world: the U.N.'s role in international relations.* Edited by Adam Roberts and Benedict Kingsbury. Oxford: Clarendon Press, 1988, p.193-208.

This is an excellent account of the history and issues of U.N. reform, culminating in the anti-U.N. mood in the American Congress, which produced the Kassebaum Amendment (1985) to cut U.S. contributions to 20 per cent unless weighted voting on budget decisions in the General Assembly were introduced. The minor reforms of the Committee of Eighteen – providing for consensual (not weighted) decisions on the budget by the Committee on Programme Coordination – are set out. Bertrand then turns to a fundamental political analysis of the problems of the U.N. system in the modern interdependent world. The United Nations cannot reform itself, he argues. The 'need for reliable policy institutions at the international and global level' is being satisfied *outside* the United Nations, as in the Group of 7. Bertrand argues that interdependence or consensus has still progressed so little that the U.N. Charter is almost as utopian as a constitution for a world federal state. Reform, then, should take the form of creating institutions for the *negotiation of consensus,* especially in economic and security fields. Only in technical fields like the mails or communication is there enough consensus for real global management. Hence, he proposes establishment of an 'Economic Security Council' and other changes in the model of the European Community and more North–South summits like that at Cancún in 1981. Compare *A successor vision* (item no. 163).

128 **The case for a United Nations parliamentary assembly.**
Dieter Heinrich. New York: World Federalist Movement, 1992. 26p. (Available from World Federalist Movement U.N. Office, 777 United Nations Plaza, New York, NY 10017.)

Here is a well-thought-out political proposal to create a 'parliamentary assembly' (sometimes also called a 'second chamber') as a subsidiary organ of the General Assembly, on the model of the European Community's European Parliament. The purpose would be to strengthen the authority of the U.N. by extending the principle of representation from that of states, as in the present General Assembly, to that of peoples – in effect establishing a second, popular or democratic house, beside the house of states, in the nascent world legislature. The safe and practical course, Heinrich argues, is to provide, at first, that national parliaments elect the world representatives and that their powers remain advisory. In time the U.N. Charter could be amended to provide for direct popular elections to the second chamber and for law-making powers in conjunction with the first chamber or house of states, as in bicameral federal legislatures. Meanwhile, even an indirectly elected and advisory parliamentary assembly would bring the voice of individual citizens into the U.N.'s deliberations, fostering international cooperation, assisting in the drafting of treaties, reinforcing the trend toward democracy in state members, building support in turn for the U.N. because of the popular link, gathering the practical expertise and political will for U.N. reform, and 'fostering a new planetary ethos by symbolizing the idea of the world as one community'.

129   **The case for global economic management and U.N. system reform.**
David B. Steele.   *International Organization*, vol. 39 (1985), p.561-78.

The International Trade Organization was defeated in 1948, and the New International Economic Order in 1977. Now there is 'a perceived need not only to increase the roles of some of the existing agencies [IMF, World Bank] and either to coordinate or to combine their secretariats, but also to form some higher-level guiding body with an element of discretionary power, which would establish the major lines of short- and medium-term global economic management'. This need is reflected in recent calls for a new 'Bretton Woods' conference. Steele surveys the extent of the world economic problem (Third World debt, U.S. deficit, reduced trade, extreme economic cycles, volatile exchange rates, uncooperative interest rate policies). He then outlines the standards and limits of 'global economic management' (Special Drawing Rights as a unit of account, global open market operations, world forecasting, negotiating fora, countercyclic policy). Precise suggestions are made for 'restructuring' the IMF, IBRD, GATT, UNCTAD, and UNIDO.

130   **The case for the binding triad.**
Richard Hudson.   New York: Center for War/Peace Studies, 1983. 30p. (Special Study No. 7. Available from Center for War/Peace Studies, 218 E. 18th St., NY 10003.)

The binding triad is a realistic yet progressive proposal to reform the General Assembly's voting rules and powers so that decisions could be reached by three concurrent two-thirds majorities: of states (as at present), of world population, and of economic power (as measured by financial contributions to the U.N.). Amendments to Articles 13 and 18 would be required. Hence, the General Assembly would acquire the legitimacy (consent by meaningful majorities) to enact law binding on states and individuals. Practical demonstrations on real issues, like the Arab–Israeli conflict, have been made in a continuing series of international conferences at Mohonk, New York.

131   **The challenge of peace: God's promise and our response.**
National Conference of Catholic Bishops.   Washington, DC: U.S. Catholic Conference, 1983. 87p.

This is a pastoral letter on war and peace. It is a major statement from a Christian and moral point of view on the threat of nuclear war, on 'conventional' or 'just' wars, on deterrence policies, on arms control and disarmament, on personal conscience, and on promoting peace – particularly through strengthening the United Nations or establishing a 'global authority adequate to the needs of the international common good'. It recommends verifiable agreements to halt testing, production and deployment of new nuclear weapon systems; deep cuts in nuclear arsenals; a comprehensive test ban; strengthened nuclear non-proliferation regime; controls on the conventional arms trade; protection and promotion of human rights; and U.N. reform. Many of these proposals have become or are becoming fact with the end of the Cold War; so attention could now be focused on the positive moral and political analysis of the 'interdependent world' and of the needs for 'global systems of governance'. (See 'Shaping a peaceful world', p.73-84.) 'Major global problems such as worldwide inflation, trade and payment deficits, competition over scarce resources, hunger, widespread unemployment, global environmental dangers, the growing power of transnational corporations, and the threat of international financial collapse, as well as the danger of world war resulting from those growing tensions, cannot be remedied by a single nation-state approach. They shall require the concerted effort of the whole world community.'

132 Collective management: the reform of global economic organizations.

Miriam Camps and Catherine Gwin.   New York: McGraw-Hill for Council on Foreign Relations, 1981. 371p. bibliog.

The authors provide here a study of the need in the next ten to twenty years for improved economic institutions at the global level. Areas of concern include: relief of world poverty, increased production and trade, international management of money, and fairer international economic development. For the student, the book is an excellent introduction to global economic organizations, such as the World Bank (IBRD), GATT, IMF, and UNDP, since it is written not from the point of view of U.S. policy and interests alone, but from that of the 'perceived interests of most states'. For the government official or serious citizen contemplating reform, it is full of exact and practical guidance. U.N. reform, Camps recognizes, must some day confront the one-nation-one-vote basis of representation in the General Assembly, but for the future foreseeable at time of writing she did not expect that Charter amendment was likely. Hence, she concentrated on ways to strengthen the Economic and Social Council (Ecosoc) and to bring the specialized agencies into real cooperation.

133 Common crisis, North–South: cooperation for world recovery.

Independent Commission on International Development Issues.

Willy Brandt, Chairman.   Cambridge, MA: MIT Press, 1983. 174p.

Three years after the commission's report, North–South (item no. 152), Brandt and the others wrote this memorandum on implementation (or rather lack of implementation) of its recommendations. An emergency programme to find a way out from the economic crises of the early 1980s toward a New International Economic Order is again outlined very specifically in the fields of finance, trade, food, energy, and the negotiating process. 'We believe that the world's economic and monetary system must now be reconsidered and restructured under circumstances nearly as serious as those of 1944, when the lingering horrors of 1930's economic disasters inspired the new Bretton Woods institutions – GATT, IMF, and World Bank.' Typical recommentations are establishment of the Special Drawing Right as the principal international reserve asset, creation of a world development fund and renegotiation of an international trade organization.

134 **Common responsibility in the 1990s. Stockholm Initiative on**
     Global Security and Governance. [22 April 1991.]
     Swedish Prime Ministers Office, 22 April 1991. 48p. (Distributed by
     World Federalist Assn., 418 Seventh St., SE, Washington, DC 20003.)

This is a little-known recent work in the tradition of *Common crisis* (item no. 133),
Common security (item no. 135), and *Our common future* (item no. 153). Signatories
include: Willy Brandt, Gro Harlem Brundtland, Ingmar Carlsson, Shridath Ramphal,
Jimmy Carter, Robert McNamara, and Julius Nyerere. It contains fundamental
proposals, at the end of the Cold War, on peace and security, development,
environment, population, human rights, and 'global governance', and it includes a
call for a 'World Summit on Global Governance' in 1995, similar to the Bretton
Woods conference in 1944 or the San Francisco conference in 1945. 'We are at a
moment in history, perhaps not experienced since the end of the Second World War,
when questions of how to assure peace and security can be addressed in a
constructive and fundamental way by the nations of the world. It is a unique moment
of opportunity, but also of great risk.'

135 **Common security: a blueprint for survival.**
     Independent Commission on Disarmament and Security Issues. Olof
     Palme, Chairman. Prologue by Cyrus Vance.   New York: Simon &
     Schuster, 1982. 202p.

This report, prepared during another period of collapse of détente and escalation of
the arms race, found roots of the problem of war in ideas of national security and
nuclear deterrence. 'The principle of common security which underlies this Report
asserts that countries can find security in cooperation and not at each other's expense.
This principle applies to economic as well as military security.' The proposed
programme includes graduated steps to large-scale mutual reductions of military
forces in Europe and eventual withdrawal of nuclear weapons. In their place would be
substituted improved U.N. institutions of collective security and peaceful resolution
of disputes. Many of its ideas were implemented by Gorbachev and Bush by 1990.
Many more are still to be achieved.

136 **The conquest of war: alternative strategies for global security.**
     Harry B. Hollins, Averill L. Powers, and Mark Sommer.
     Boulder, CO: Westview, 1989, 224p. bibliog.

Written as the end of the Cold War loomed on the horizon, this slim and thoughtful
book argues that the historical opportunity has arrived to make the *abolition of war*
(nuclear and conventional war, with attendant proliferation and military spending) a
realistic goal, like the abolition of slavery in the last century. The authors are
advocates of bold, courageous political initiatives: 'Taking a bold step with
unmistakable boldness strikes an emotional chord that fatally compromised and
technically obscure half measures like traditional arms control can never inspire.'
What is needed is 'fundamental system change'. Transitional strategies include: U.N.
reform, minimum deterrence, qualitative disarmament, non-provocative defence,
civilian-based defence, verification, use of international law, and economic
conversion of military industry to civilian. The goal is a *common security* system.

137 **The constitutional foundations of world peace.**
Edited by Richard A. Falk, Robert C. Johansen, and Samuel S. Kim.
New York: SUNY Press, for the World Order Models Project, 1993.
388p.

The world has become interdependent, yet the citizens, or their representatives, are rarely consulted about the formation of national 'foreign' policy and virtually never about 'global governance'. 'It is time', argues Betty A. Reardon, the series editor, 'for serious consideration of how to restructure the international system toward both greater democracy and more effective and humane planetary management.' The end of the Cold War permits a return to thinking about the *constitutional* foundations of a peaceful world, but the approach now is broader and more sophisticated than world government thinking after World War II. It is much concerned with the whole of world problems (the global problematique), with values in addition to peace (social justice, economic plenty, environmental preservation, political participation), and with the *transition* to a better-ordered world. This book is an up-to-date exposition of 'world order thinking', as led by Saul Mendlovitz. World law is never separated from world politics. U.N. reform is ably surveyed, with nothing more drastic proposed than Marc Nerfin's reformed General Assembly representative of states, major economic powers, and world citizens. The authors' goal is a 'world of greater security, prosperity, and justice'.

138 **A dangerous place: the United Nations as a weapon in world politics.**
Abraham Yeselson and Anthony Gaglione.   New York: Grossman,
1974. 240p.

All states use the Security Council and the General Assembly as arenas for the pursuit of national self-interest rather than as fora for the pacific settlement of their differences. Four conflict strategies within world politics are set out: embarrassment, status, legitimization, and socialization. 'U.N. reform', unless fundamental, will only make the U.N. a more dangerous place, the authors argue. The non-governmental organization (NGO) community generally has not been able to summon the concern, energy, and intelligence to restore the dream of a United Nations.

139 **Enhancing the capacity of the United Nations in maintaining peace and international security: a common interest of Japan and the United States.**
James S. Sutterlin.   New York: United Nations Association–United
States of America, 1992. 44p. bibliog. (Occasional Paper No. 5).

This is a clear and plain-spoken discussion of the enhanced role of the U.N., rather in the spirit of the Secretary-General's *Agenda for peace* (q.v.). Conflict prevention, conflict resolution, peace building, peacekeeping, and regional crisis management are discussed with a view toward realistic improvements. Reform of the Security Council by the admission of Japan as a permanent member, with or without veto, is regarded as distant since revision of the Charter was specifically excluded by the Council in its historic January 1992 summit. Sutterlin argues that the U.S. and Japan, as the first and second world economic powers, should take the lead in the U.N., but he remembers that the *authority* of the Security Council depends on its reputation for impartiality.

140   **Fateful visions: avoiding nuclear catastrophe.**
       Edited by Joseph S. Nye, Jr., Graham T. Allison, and Albert
       Carnesale.   Cambridge, MA: Ballinger, 1988. 299p. bibliog.
Written after the Reykjavik summit (1986) but before the officially declared end of
the Cold War (1990), this able work edited by three leading Harvard professors
surveys a wide range of alternative visions of desirable worlds: abolition of nuclear
weapons, strategic defence (SDI), no first use policy, non-provocative defence,
civilian defence, U.S.–Soviet cooperation, Soviet transformation, U.S. world
hegemony, internationalism, and world government. The authors are realistic and
doubtful: every alternative to policies of massive nuclear deterrence and NATO
strategy is seen as possibly increasing the likelihood of nuclear or conventional war.
Compare Hollins, *Conquest of war* (item no. 136).

141   **The future of international governance: post-war planning without
       having the war first.**
       Harlan Cleveland and Lincoln Bloomfield.   *Journal of Development
       Planning*, vol. 17 (1987), p.5-17.
This is an earlier and in some ways clearer statement of the 'rethinking international
governance' project at the Hubert H. Humphrey Institute of the University of
Minnesota. As the end of the Cold War approached, the authors judged that 'local
sovereignty' was still stronger than 'world community' in its hold on people's
loyalties. Yet the global *problematique* – peaceful settlement of disputes, regulation
of the world economy, management of the planetary environment, control of matters
that formerly were thought to be within the domestic jurisdiction of states like
population growth or the status of women – calls for new international institutions.
Six 'misguided' assumptions of the U.N. are set out – first, for example, that World
War II convinced nascent 'world society' that war was intolerable, or, sixth, that
international organization was a way-station to 'supranational government'.
Alternative assumptions are drawn from the precedents of post-World War
international cooperation, in which sovereignty is pooled, not ceded – e.g., guarantees
for territorial integrity, protection of diplomats, non-proliferation of weapons,
immunity of civilian aircraft and ships, humanitarian aid to refugees, and
decolonization. 'The beginning of wisdom in fashioning a third try at world order (the
League of Nations and the United Nations counting as the first two) may be precisely
the pragmatic notion that no one is supposed to be in charge.'

142   **The future of the U.N.system: some questions on the occasion of an
       anniversary.**
       Marc Nerfin.   *Development Dialogue* (Uppsala), vol. 1 (1985),
       p.5-29.
The author surveys what has changed in world politics since the U.N. was founded in
1945 – decolonization, Third World grouping, population explosion – and what has
not – hegemony of North over South. A 'general crisis' or world problematique has
emerged: economic crisis, social crisis, institutional crisis. Nerfin finds that most
criticism of the U.N. misses the external factors of its decline – such as the decline of
U.S. hegemony itself – and the internal ones – such as the proliferation of agencies
and programmes. U.N. reform requires, he argues, that governments and peoples re-
examine their faith in collective action and decide what functions they want the U.N.
to serve, how it shall make decisions, how to pay for itself, and whom to represent.

He supports a *tricameral* General Assembly, representative of 'Princes' (states), 'Merchants' (large economic powers), and 'Citizens' (individuals).

143 The future role of the U.N. in an interdependent world.
Edited by John P. Renninger.   Dordrecht, The Netherlands: M. Nijhoff for UNITAR, 1989. 283p.

The proceedings of the Moscow roundtable on the future of the U.N. are published here. The principal paper is by Maurice Bertrand, 'The process of change in an interdependent world and possible institutional consequences'. This is a major continuation of Bertrand's fundamental analysis. Also included is Sidney Dell, 'The future of the international monetary system'. Soviet responses follow Gorbachev's lead but show flexibility. Renninger is fair toward the Clark and Sohn plan, *World peace through world law* (item no. 177).

144 Goals for mankind: a report to the Club of Rome on the new horizons of global community.
Ervin Laszlo and the International Project Team.   New York: Dutton, 1977. 434p. bibliog.

Written at the height of controversy over the New International Economic Order, this book, prepared for the general reader, draws back from the fray and attempts to identify and compare the goals (professed, covert and unconscious) of national communities and such nascent international communities as the United Nations, International Labour Organization, multinational corporations, the World Council of Churches, and the Roman Catholic Church. The study is more respectful of differences than the World Order Models Project on 'values' or even the U.N. on human rights. Ingenious tables show the 'gap' in goals and hence the difficulties in bringing about great cooperation and eventually unity among communities. The final part shows creatively how world religions, secular political philosophies, and popular revolutionary movements can overcome the 'inner limits' to build 'world solidarity'. 'A new world order will come about when the people of all nations demand of their leaders that they be given a constructive role in building the shared human future; when a new global ethos emerges based on trust and solidarity; when a new standard of humanism crystalizes as the norm of conduct in all major areas of public policy.'

145 Gulf crisis lessons for the United Nations.
Erskine B. Childers.   *Bulletin of Peace Proposals* (Oslo), vol. 23 (1992), p.129-38.

The Persian Gulf War was a watershed event, but not because it restored the United Nations to a functioning organization to maintain international peace and security, argues this seasoned former U.N. official. To people of the South, the war was 'a high technology massacre in a continuum of centuries of white Northern assault', while the U.N. was 'the nearly ruined captive of the Northern powers'. The watershed was that the war revealed such deep problems for the future as 'non-endogenous borders' of about half the U.N. members, inaction on oil and other resource inequities, inadequate early warning, abuse of Chapter VII, the 'undemocratic' character of the veto, defence of human rights only when it serves great power *Realpolitik*, financial withholdings as a lever on U.N. decisions, and double standards.

146   **Interdependence and the reform of international institutions.**
      C. Fred Bergsten. *International Organization*, vol. 30 (1976),
      p.361-72.

The world is entering the third wave of institution building. The first established the
U.N. system (1945); the second, regional bodies like the European Community and
the Organization for Economic Cooperation and Development (1957); the third, the
international organizations addressing the global problematique, like the U.N.
Environmental Programme and the World Food Council (1972). The functional
purpose of such institutions is 'to provide an *international* framework within which to
manage issues where *national* management has become inadequate, or to handle
better those issues where earlier international arrangements had failed'. The political
purpose is to legitimize the existing status of Great Power relations and to integrate
newcomers. For future institution building, cooperative policies provide longer-term
benefits than unilateral ones; narrowly specialized functional agencies succeed better
than multipurpose ones; membership must be universal; and competent secretariats
invite trust. Hence, the author argues against 'dusting off' the International Trade
Organization (abandoned in 1948), which would be too general and probably limited
to industrialized countries. Future difficulties include accommodating demands for
national sovereignty, restoring participation in the international system by the
(former) communist countries, moving from U.S. leadership to collective leadership,
and avoiding paralysis due to interdependence (or linkage), economic interests, and
security. Bergsten proposes a new ocean regime, regimes for the global 'commons'
such as the air and outer space, an institution to control terrorism, and especially a
new international financial institution to govern foreign direct investment and
multinational enterprises. The goal is international 'governance'.

147   **Keeping faith in the United Nations.**
      B.G. Ramcharan. Foreword by B. Urquhart.   Dordrecht,
      The Netherlands: M. Nijhoff, 1987, 354p. bibliog.

A view of the future of the U.N. is here based on official statements of governments
during the fortieth anniversary and on the Secretary-General's reports, particularly
since 1982. Comparisons with the twenty-fifth anniversary (1970) are explicitly
made; those with the fiftieth (1995) are implied. In part, the book is a response to the
criticism of M. Bertrand and is written in a spirit of exactness and fairness that is rare.
Ramcharan, a U.N. staff officer based in Geneva, discusses the U.N.'s image
problem, controversy with the U.S., other governmental attitudes, the conception of
the organization as it grew despite the Cold War, the problem of international
authority, non-implementation of decisions, performance or effectiveness, sectoral
problems in the system, and efficiency. His suggestions for improvement are
conservatively within the concept of an organization with powers only of *persuasion*,
not of coercion or *enforcement*, but he is most radical in the area of human rights. He
supports the new international humanitarian order (1981) and envisages that
peacekeeping forces could be transformed into 'humanitarian forces' protecting
human rights. Stronger international courts and equity tribunals to settle disputes
about human rights, however, are hardly imagined.

148   **Learning from the Gulf.**
      Brian Urquhart. *New York Review of Books*, 7 March 1991, p.34-37.

The Persian Gulf War was, like the Korean War, an international response to an act of
aggression. At the time, those whose hopes were most pinned on the United Nations

as the guarantor of a new world order saw the response as a sign that, after the Cold War, the U.N. Charter would finally begin to work as it was designed. This important article by the former Under-Secretary-General responsible for peacekeeping warned that the 'United Nations has so far not provided a *system* for peace and security so much as a last resort, or safety net'. A true system – as opposed to occasional collective warfare – he argued would have to be based on 'vigilance, consensus, common interest, collective action, and international law'. It would maintain a global watch on international peace and security, anticipate conflict, mediate disputes, act before the level of war was reached, protect the weak, and deal authoritatively with aggressors. Urquhart surveys the types of conflict short of armed invasion likely to occur in the future – notably ethnic and religious conflict – and he sets out the principles of a new collective security system.

149   **The limits of international organization: systematic failure in the management of international relations.**
Giulio M. Gallarotti. *International Organization*, vol. 45 (Spring 1991), p.183-220.

This is a critique of traditional arguments about the need for 'extensive supranational government' from federalists, functionalists, neofunctionalists, modernization and interdependence theorists, and managerialists. International organization can fail (1) when it attempts to manage tightly coupled systems, as of international monetary exchange rates; (2) when it offers a substitute for more substantive and long-range resolutions of international problems or of responsible domestic or foreign policy, as in passing vague U.N. resolutions or continuing the peacekeeping operation in Cyprus; (3) when it intensifies international disputes, as when the U.N. was used by the West to condemn the Soviets for invading Hungary in 1956 or by the Soviets to embarrass the U.S. over the Dominican Republic in 1965; (4) when it generates moral hazard, as in the escape clauses of GATT providing insurance to domestic industries caught in balance of payments difficulties. The author concludes that, where the above results are possible, *limited* international organization is preferable.

150   **The management of peace.**
Harlan Cleveland. *G.A.O. Journal*, vol. 11 (Winter 1990-91), p.4-23.

This is a report on the project on 'rethinking international governance' by a former Assistant Secretary of State. With the end of the Cold War, the management of international relations by 'mutual terror' technological leadership, economic 'growth', and self-interested foreign aid for 'development' is challenged by the domestic troubles of the two superpowers, the decline of big-power satellite systems, the 'backlash from Nature', and 'from publics moved by the emerging ecological ethic'. Since national governments are failing to cope, Cleveland rejects a design for 'global governance' on the model of a world state. The alternative is enhanced international cooperation on the 'extranational' model of the European Community. A world community would propose world policies and actions, consult with NGOs and the popularly elected world parliament, encourage public debate in the media, and submit the proposals to the world council of minorities, who could not amend but only accept or reject them *in toto*. Taxation on international activities that most benefit from world regulations – travel, transport, communications, financial transactions, use of the seabed or space – is recommended. Compare Bertrand, *A third generation world organization* (item no. 164).

151   **New genesis: shaping a global spirituality.**
Robert Muller.   New York: Doubleday, 1982. 192p.

The Assistant Secretary General (unofficially the philosopher of the United Nations) looks forward to world law supplanting national law. Love is the key to overcoming violence.

152   **North–South: a program for survival.**
Independent Commission on International Development Issues.
Willy Brandt, Chairman.   Cambridge, MA: MIT Press, 1980, 304p.

This impressive report, at the climax of the 'North–South dialogue' (1974-81), argues that mutual interests as well as human solidarity could combine in a new global politics to end hunger and poverty in the South, which threatened (and still threatens) to bring down the North. 'Equal in importance to contracting the dangers of the arms race, we believed [reshaping North–South relations] to be the greatest challenge to mankind for the remainder of this century.' Their most controversial proposal is the transfer of resources – grants, low-interest loans, goods and technologies – from the North to the South (up to 0.7 per cent of developed nations' GNP). This is a classic text on the world economic problematique.

153   **Our common future.**
World Commission on Environment and Development. Gro Harlem Brundtland, Chairman.   New York: Oxford University Press, 1987. 400p.

This is a recent and most influential report on the environment. It brought the term, 'sustainable development', into parlance. Humanity is not faced with a choice between a healthy environment *or* economic development to supply basic needs, but can achieve both through development that is sustainable. This implies common international policies on population, food, ecosystems, energy, industry, urban life, the seas, space, security and peace. 'In the broadest sense, the strategy for sustainable development aims to promote harmony among human beings and between humanity and nature.'

154   **Reform and restructuring of the U.N. system. President's report and Secretary's report.**
Jimmy Carter and Cyrus Vance.   Washington, DC: Department of State, June 1978. 43p. (International Organization and Conference Series 135, Pub. No. 8940).

This 'Carter Report' contained the most substantive U.S. proposals on U.N. reform before the end of the Cold War. It approved more meetings of the Security Council at the foreign minister's level and fact-finding missions not subject to veto. Carter and Vance saw no prospect of weighted voting in the General Assembly but approved more use of consensus decision-making in all organs. They approved greater recourse to the International Court of Justice for preliminary opinions, supported establishment of a U.N. peacekeeping reserve and many improvements in its training, supply and financing, and approved strengthening the U.N. human rights regime, instead of a high commissioner for human rights. They made many suggestions on improving economic programmes, especially technical assistance, and suggested new revenue sources to eliminate the U.N. deficit (in 1977, $129,000,000 total).

155 **The reform of the United Nations.** [A volume in the series,] **Annual review of United Nations affairs.**
   Joachim W. Müller.   New York: Oceana, 1992. 2 vols.
The author presents a comprehensive report (vol. 1) and documentation (vol. 2) on the U.N. reform effort from 1985 to 1990. Achievements include: new planning and budgeting procedures, reductions in personnel, restructuring of the Secretariat, some streamlining of intergovernmental machinery, improved public information activities, reorganization of conference services, and changes in monitoring, evaluation, and inspection. The reform effort began and ended in a financial crisis. It revealed the major interest groups in contemporary world politics: the U.S.A. (very critical), the U.S.S.R. (newly supportive), Japan (now second-largest financial backer), Western Europe (the broker in negotiations), and the Third World (rhetorically very supportive). A thorough analysis of the results was made by the Secretariat in 1990. Muller reports that the 'general view' was that the reforms had 'largely failed in the economic and social fields'. His superior in the Secretariat, Margaret Anstee, explains that this is understandable, for 'the enterprise in this case has the equivalent of a Board of 166 Directors [states-members in the U.N. system]'. Hence, the process of reform continues. Maurice Bertrand's reform proposals are noted, but the more substantial work of creating an 'Economic United Nations' remains for the future.

156 **The reform of the United Nations.**
   David B. Steele.   London: Croom Helm, 1987. 191p. bibliog.
Written by a long-time international civil servant with experience in WHO, UNICEF, and U.N. social development research institutions, this is a broadly informative and radical book on U.N. reform, on a par with Maurice Bertrand's *A third generation world organization* (item no. 164). Steele aims to answer recent criticism of the U.N. He reviews past reform efforts, notably that of 1974-79 which saw establishment of the post of Director General for Development. The problem is to escape from the 'dilemma of attainable and irrelevant or radical but unattainable reforms'. He recommends (as does Bertrand) a long-term process of debate culminating in a general review conference in accord with Articles 108 and 109 or independently. Three areas offer potential for increased collective control: global economic management, environmentally sustainable development, and international security, peace, and disarmament. The book was written before the end of the Cold War, but its political judgement that the North must re-acquire proportionate weight over the South still offers clarity. The non-aligned are the 'middle ground to the superpowers', Steele argues, in any fundamental U.N. reform. The objective is a 'United Nations which avoids both undue heterogeneity as well as monolithism'. 'The U.N. Charter needs to be a fixed point as governments come and go, but it has to reflect the major power realities within a long time trend. . . . The world is at the mercy of unbalanced competitive powers checked by only the limited moral force of the U.N. system.'

157 **Renewing the United Nations system.**
   Erskine Childers and Brian Urquhart.   *Development Dialogue*, no. 1 (1994). 213p. (Available from the Ford Foundation, 320 East 43rd Street, New York, NY 10017.)
This will probably remain the most widely read and discussed proposal of U.N. reform at least up to the fiftieth anniversary in 1995. The two seasoned former U.N officials boldly confront the confusion and uncoordination of the U.N. *system*. Their recommendations touch every organ and organization, yet almost all can be

implemented without amendment of the Charter or the founding documents of the specialized agencies. They would create only one additional unit, but many others would be consolidated or streamlined. They are aware of history and often go back to the founding for principles. 'Our objective in this study is to examine the system as it now is, and to suggest adjustments and modifications which might gradually transform it into the effective mechanism of a future world community.' The specialized agencies would be brought back to their original close relationship to the United Nations; a new intergovernmental consultative board somewhat on the model of the European Commission would oversee the functioning of the whole system; the Bretton Woods system would be reformed, particularly by changing the weighted voting procedure in the IMF and by establishing the original ITO; the Trusteeship Council, whose work is now virtually done, would be reconstituted as a council on diversity, representation, and governance; the new High Commissioner for Human Rights would be assisted by an 'ombuds-panel' to improve implementation; a parliamentary assembly, representative of peoples, would be added as a deliberative body to the General Assembly.

158 **Report of the Special Committee on the Charter of the United Nations and on the Strengthening of the Role of the Organization.**
United Nations, General Assembly. Official Records, 32nd session, 33rd supp., 1977. 248p. (A/32/33).
After the Charter review conference provided for in Article 109 was never held – because after 1955 there was no 'appropriate time' – this committee has reported annually on issues of U.N. Charter interpretation (virtually never on amendment). Typical contents: The role of the U.N., maintaining international peace and security, peaceful settlement of disputes, economic and social quesitons, decolonization, rationalization of procedures, administration, finance. Later reports stressed development of an international conciliation service.

159 **Reshaping the international order: a report to the Club of Rome.**
Jan Tinbergen, coordinator. New York: Dutton, 1976. 325p.
Here is an answer to the question: 'What new international order should be recommended to the world's statesmen and social groups so as to meet, to the extent practically and realistically possible, the urgent needs of today's population and the probable needs of future generations?' A group of twenty-one collaborators and hundreds of correspondents produced the report in response to the 1974 spring session of the U.N. General Assembly, which produced the resolution and programme of action to establish the New International Economic Order (NIEO). Its aim was to remove the 'manifest injustices' in the present international system. Since the authors did not believe reforms could be limited to economic rules, they addressed the full range of political, social and cultural changes to bring about a *new international order*. Readers today may overlook Parts I and II, in which the West was held largely to blame for global inequalities and the underdeveloped world accepted little responsibility for its own uplift. But they should study Part III, on the needed reforms, which remain pending after the end of the Cold War. Important reforms are proposed for the international monetary order, development institutions, food products, industrial development, trade relations, energy, scientific research, transnational corporations, the environment, arms control and disarmament, ocean management, and negotiation packages. The fundamental goal is 'a life of dignity and well-being for all world citizens'. To achieve this, national sovereignty will have to be reinterpreted as 'functional sovereignty' or 'decentralized planetary sovereignty'.

160 **Restructuring the U.N. system: institutional reform efforts in the
context of North–South relations.**
Ronald I. Meltzer. *International Organization*, vol. 32 (1978),
p.993-1018.

'U.N. focus in this area has evolved from piecemeal efforts to supplement national
economic programs within developing societies', the author argues, 'to concerted
demands for systemic changes within North–South relationships involving major
concessions from industrialized countries on current international economic practices,
principles, and outcomes.' Western governments, Meltzer has found, look on U.N.
reform less in terms of establishing the New International Economic Order (NIEO),
and 'more in terms of creating increased institutional rationalization and more
efficient resource management'. This article concentrates on the report of the Group
of Experts, 'A new United Nations structure for global economic cooperation' (May
1975), and on the deliberations of the Ad Hoc Committee on Restructuring the
Economic and Social Sectors of the U.N. System (1975). The principal political
players in that round of U.N. reform were the United States, the European Economic
Community, and the Group of 77. Out of these efforts came the establishment of the
post of Director General for Development and International Economic Cooperation
and 'the most ambitious internal reorganization plans since the U.N.'s inception'. The
context of North–South relationships is well surveyed. Typical was the G-77's
opposition to the U.S. proposal to create small consultative groups organized around
specific policy matters in order to facilitate intergroup agreements, rather than vest
the General Assembly with powers to discuss and negotiate such general reforms as
NIEO.

161 **Reviewing the United Nations Charter.**
Lawrence S. Finkelstein. *International Organization*, vol. 9 (May
1955), p.213-31.

This is typical of U.S. opinion as the review conference provided for in Article 109
came due at the height of the Cold War. (At the time, West Germany was being
admitted into NATO, and the Warsaw Pact was being organized.) The author assumes
that far-reaching amendment was impossible, but still there was much room for
'change and growth without resort to amendment'. The Uniting for Peace Resolution
(General Assembly Resolution 377 (V), 3 November 1950), the Security Council
convention in which an abstention is not a veto, the use of Article 39 to authorize the
enforcement action in Korea (1950-53) were all 'extensions of the language, if not the
purpose, of the Charter'. Amendment in 1955 or 1956 would only increase tensions
by the West and the Soviet bloc and hence destroy the U.N.'s 'usefulness as a bridge
between the two camps'. Finkelstein concludes by quoting Osten Unden of Sweden
who, in an address before the General Assembly on 24 September 1954, concluded
from the experience of the U.N. and of the League before it: 'It is the policies which
nations pursue, particularly the great ones, and not the machinery of international
instruments, which determine the large issues of peace and war.'

162 **The role of the United Nations in the new world order.**
Michel Doo Kingué.   New York: UNITAR, 1991. 21p.
(E.91.III.K.CR/33).

This is a report of a high-level panel of national ambassadors to the U.N., the
president of UNA–USA, and several UNITAR scholars on the meaning of U.S.

President George Bush's 'new world order' at the 'end of the Cold War' (1990). The consensus of the participants was that the new world order should be an 'order based on justice and peace, democracy and development, human rights and international law'. Practically, this meant that the U.N. Charter should begin to function as it was designed to do; without amendment, it could be interpreted to deal with such new concerns as nuclear disarmament, relief of poverty, and protection of the environment. The U.N.'s role was to develop a working system of collective security, expand the Security Council's and Secretariat's capacity to anticipate and prevent conflicts, develop peacekeeping and enforcement under Article 42, improve regional arrangements under Chapter VIII, promote the rule of law, accept some limitations of sovereignty in order to defend human rights (that is, limit the scope of Article 2(7)), promote economic and social development to reverse the worsening of world poverty, admit economic security into the concept of 'international security'. Yet, practically, it was still wise to await bureaucratic reforms in the U.N. before undertaking reforms of its social and economic functions. Modest proposals were made to strengthen the Security Council by the permanent admission of Germany, Japan, Brazil, India, and Nigeria. The Stockholm Initiative, *Common responsibility*, was noted as 'likely to inspire the international community in its efforts to reform the United Nations'.

163 A successor vision: the United Nations of tomorrow.

U.N. Management and Decision-Making Project. Edited by Peter Fromuth. New York: UNA–USA, September 1987. 116p.

This is a report of an international panel, including Elliot Richardson, Robert McNamara, Cyrus Vance, and Nancy Kassebaum of the U.S., Helmut Schmidt of the Federal Republic of Germany, Thomas Koh of Singapore, and Brian Urquhart of the U.N. They propose extensive reforms of U.N. economic functions in order to build consensus for later political reforms. The work supersedes the Bertrand report below. Proposals include: elimination of the General Assembly's Second (social) and Third (economic) Committees, enlargement of Ecosoc to plenary size, merger of the Special Political Committee with the Fourth (decolonization) Committee, creation of a new commission to coordinate the work of the development agencies and Bretton Woods financial organizations, and creation of a new ministerial board to conduct global watch, consensus building, and common action. Ten supporting studies are also available.

164 A third generation world organization.

Maurice Bertrand. Dordrecht, The Netherlands: M. Nijhoff, 1989. 217p.

This book by a retired U.N. official who served in the Joint Inspection Unit has had perhaps the greatest influence of all recent works on U.N. reform. Reflections on the U.N. after forty years, argues Bertrand, lead to the conclusion that the time has arrived to establish a third-generation world organization. This should be not a world government but an 'economic U.N'. Reform of the political organs of the U.N. – the Security Council and the General Assembly – is now impossible, he thinks, but much could be done to rationalize and integrate its complex and decentralized economic functions, beginning in the Economic and Social Council and proceeding through the specialized agencies and programmes of the system. The goal is to build international consensus by improved negotiation processes; only then can serious proposals be considered for undertaking common 'management' of global problems. The book includes long extracts of his parting report, *Some reflections on the reform of the U.N.* (1985), A/40/988 (q.v.).

165 **Towards a more effective United Nations.**
Brian Urquhart and Erskine Childers. *Development Dialogue*
(Uppsala, Sweden), (1991). whole issue. (Includes two proposals:
'Reorganization of the United Nations Secretariat: a suggested outline
of needed reforms', p.9-40; and 'Strengthening international response
to humanitarian emergencies', p.41-85.)

Here are serious proposals by two seasoned former U.N. officials, under the auspices
of the Dag Hammarskjöld Foundation and the Ford Foundation, to reorganize the
Secretariat under four new Deputy Secretaries-General, with consequential
elimination of ten Under Secretaries-General. The four new departments are: (1)
Political, Security and Peace Affairs; (2) Economic, Social, Development and
Environmental Affairs; (3) Humanitarian and Human Rights Affairs; (4)
Administration, Management and Conference Services. The next step is reform of the
remainder of the U.N. system. (A modified version of this proposal was actually
instituted by Secretary-General Boutros-Ghali in 1991.) The second proposal makes
many practical suggestions to meet the 'continuous humanitarian emergency' after
the end of the Cold War. The new Deputy Secretary-General for Humanitarian Affairs
would consolidate related functions primarily in UNDRO and UNDP but also in
UNHCR, UNICEF, FAO, and WHO. Compare their sequel, *Renewing the United
Nations system* (1994) (item no. 157).

166 **The United Nations and illegitimate regimes: when to intervene to
protest human rights.**
Igor I. Lukashuk. In: *Law and force in the new international order.*
Edited by Lori F. Damrosch and David Scheffer. Boulder, CO:
Westview, 1991, p.143-58.

A 'legitimate' regime has come to mean a freely elected government responsive to the
will of the people. The Russian author surveys the history and principles of
intervention, especially to preserve 'democracy' – socialized or liberal (Brezhnev or
Reagan doctrines). After the Cold War, legitimacy will have to be determined not by
state hegemons, but by 'collective recognition', as by the O.A.S., O.A.U., or U.N.
Lukashuk supports strengthening the U.N. by creating a parliamentary assembly to
widen its representativeness from states to peoples. 'The world community is
becoming an increasingly important and unified social and political system.'

167 **United Nations based prospects for a new global order.**
Thomas M. Franck. *New York University Journal of International
Law and Politics*, vol. 22 (Summer 1990), p.601-40.

The end of Cold War is not a time for 'smug satisfaction' but an 'opportunity . . . to
rethink the basic structures and processes of the international system'. Franck gives
credit to Soviet 'new thinking' for opening the opportunity, and he reviews the
uneven American response. He suggests improvements to the U.N.'s political process,
administration, judicial settlement, and coordination of the system. He approves the
idea of a popularly elected lower chamber in the General Assembly, and argues for
elimination of duplicate or independent economic functions under Ecosoc and the
specialized agencies. Franck urges statesmen to uphold *democracy* as the norm of
what Gorbachev called a 'new global system'. How? Use self-determination to
undermine totalitarian regimes, increase human rights monitoring, widen U.N.
supervision of elections, and enhance popular participation in government.

168   **The United Nations: its problems and what to do about them.**
Charles M. Lichenstein, Thomas E.L. Dewey, Juliana G. Pilon, and
Melanie L. Merkle.   Washington, DC: Heritage Foundation, 1986.
36p. bibliog.

Convinced that the administrative and budgetary reforms contemplated by the
General Assembly's Group of Eighteen in response to U.S. charges of 'inefficiency'
and 'mismanagement' in 1985 did not go to the heart of the 'present U.N. institutional
structure and . . . political and organizational dynamics which are the primary cause
of the organization's present condition', the authors offered 'fundamental rethinking
of the structure and role of a world organization'. They found that the U.N. has failed
to keep the peace, legitimized national liberation movements, maintained a double
standard in human rights investigations (El Salvador but not Cuba) and in
condemnations of terrorism (Israel but not Libya, Iran, U.S.S.R.), favoured socialist
rather than free market development aid, blamed the West for world poverty (though
it provides 92 per cent of official aid), provided a 'haven for Soviet bloc espionage
against the U.S.', and charged the U.S. 'unfairly' for one-fourth of the budget. They
offered such reforms as adopting weighted voting in the General Assembly on
budgetary matters, reducing the number of top-level posts in the Secretariat,
admitting the FBI into the U.N. to combat espionage, rotating General Assembly
meetings between New York and Moscow, terminating programmes after two years
unless explicitly reauthorized, opening *all* U.N. meetings to the public (including
Security Council executive sessions and the Secretary-General's good offices),
restricting distribution of documents, shortening General Assembly sessions from
three months to six weeks, convening the Conference on Disarmament every two
years instead of every six months, and the like. If reforms were not forthcoming, they
urged Congress to 'defund the U.N.' and even withdraw the U.S. from membership.

169   **United Nations: reforms might help it to work.**
Sadruddin Aga Khan and Maurice Strong.   *International Herald
Tribune*, 9 October 1985.

The authors propose that contributions by member states to the U.N. budget should be
redistributed so that no nation pays more than ten percent. This would eliminate the
'problem' of U.S. contributions of twenty-five percent, which tends to become a lever
of U.S. policy to dominate the organization.

170   **The United Nations: structure and leadership for a new era.
Report [of the Twenty-Second United Nations Issues Conference,
1991].**
Muscatine, IA: Stanley Foundation, 1991. 24p.

Here is discussion of practical U.N. reform in the short term. The context was the
Persian Gulf War and the election of a new Secretary-General. The aim of reform is
to improve the effectiveness of the U.N., not to cut its budget; member governments
must take the lead, because U.N. officials cannot independently reform the system;
major powers have special responsibility, but small countries and NGOs have
contributions to make; reform should serve the interests of all states, for the U.N.
remains a universal organization. Richard Stanley concludes: 'We must work toward
a system in which justice and the rule of law supplant the rule of force, a system in
which the rights of the weak are respected and the nations accept a shared
responsibility for peaceful resolution of conflict.'

171 **The United Nations system: coordinating its economic and social
work.**
Martin Hill.   Cambridge: Cambridge University Press for UNITAR,
1978. 252p.

This is a careful study of U.N. 'restructuring' in response to the General Assembly's
Declaration on the Establishment of a New International Economic Order and its
Charter of the Economic Rights and Duties of States (1974). The author was an
experienced international civil servant in both the League and the United Nations.
Hill deals first with the problems of coordination, especially the U.N. system's
deliberate decentralization (so that the agencies would survive if the U.N., like the
League, failed). He then surveys challenges to the system (interdependence,
decolonization, world poverty), and follows with a cogent analysis of coordination to
date, especially by the Administrative Committee on Coordination (ACC) and the
Advisory Committee on Administrative and Budgetary Questions (ACABQ). His
solutions, which may seem rather technical, are placed in perspective for the general
reader (in chapter 8) and proceed very clearly to the attitudes, practices, and policies
of governments (chapter 10). The responsibilities of the General Assembly, ACC,
Secretary-General, U.N. Development Programme, and other departments are boldly
yet judiciously described so that the reader gets a sense of the world constitutional
process in progress. In many ways, this book anticipates the proposals for reform of
Maurice Bertrand.

172 **The United Nations: the next twenty-five years.**
Commission to Study the Organization of Peace. Louis B. Sohn,
editor.   Dobbs Ferry, NY: Oceana, 1970. 263p.

Here are older but carefully considered proposals for modification of the Security
Council veto, acquisition of legislative capacity by General Assembly, compulsory
jurisdiction of International Court of Justice, improved peaceful settlement of
disputes, disarmament, economic development, protection of human rights,
managerial reforms, finance. The book contains very plain and persuasive arguments
for the development of world law, applicable not only to states but also to individuals.
In 1995 the twenty-five years will be up: the book is still of great relevance.

173 **A U.N. revitalized: a compilation of UNA–USA recommendations
on strengthening the role of the United Nations in peacemaking,
peacekeeping, and conflict prevention.**
Compiled by Russell M. Dallen, Jr.   New York: United Nations
Association of the United States of America, 1992. 10p.

This is a volume of succinct, substantial suggestions for the Secretary-General's
report, *An agenda for peace* (item no. 121), covering the Security Council, Military
Staff Committee, peacekeeping, peace enforcement, the Seccretary-General, the
International Court of Justice, weapons proliferation, international terrorism, an
international criminal court, and the role of non-governmental organizations. Many of
these proposals will remain immediately implementable for years.

174 **The U.N. under attack.**
Edited by Jeffrey Harrod and Nico Schrijver. Preface by Sir Shridath
Ramphal. Aldershot, England: Gower, 1988. 156p.
This is a collection of lectures at the Institute of Social Studies in The Hague on the
occasion of the U.N.'s fortieth anniversary. It is a response to the 'erosion of
multilateralism' by 1985, but not an anticipation of the end of the Cold War. It
contains thoughtful reflections on U.N. reform in the areas of world authority,
decision making, international law, international finance, trade, food, labour, and
education. The final essay concludes cautiously that humanity may be ready to move
beyond functionalism and hegemony to real international cooperation, marked by the
declarations of 'new orders' since the 1970s: the New International Economic Order
of the U.N. General Assembly and UNCTAD, the New World Information and
Communication Order of UNESCO, the Health for All Programme of WHO, and the
World Employment Programme of ILO.

175 **World federation: a critical analysis of federal world government.**
Ronald J. Glossop. Jefferson, NC: McFarland, 1993. 262p. bibliog.
The author engages the 'realists', the internationalists, the 'world order' theorists, and
the religious conservatives in an extended debate about how humanity at the end of
the Cold War will 'run the world in general'. The book is written in a rational spirit
by a professor of philosophy and is recommended to students and to all public-
spirited citizens who would like an up-to-date account of the alternative of
constitutionally limited, democratic, federal world government. (World government is
usually misunderstood as a unitary world state involving the abolition of nation-states
– a concept not intended in the term 'world federation'.) The case for world
federation is primarily that it would abolish war on earth just as national governments
abolish war within their territories. The transition is the great difficulty, since national
citizens would have to develop a sense of responsibility as world citizens, would have
to elect world representatives to a world legislature for the enactment of the world
laws, and then would have to obey the laws out of respect for their justice (rather than
out of fear of their punishments). Glossop explores the slow but possible transitions
of U.N. reform (by Articles 108 and 109), the Clark–Sohn plan for systematic Charter
amendment, the Binding Triad proposal (amendments to Articles 13 and 18), the
establishment of a U.N. parliamentary assembly (as a subsidiary organ under Article
22), regional federation (E.C., etc.), and the Stockholm Initiative on Global Security
and Governance (1991).

176 **A world federation of cultures: an African perspective.**
Ali A. Mazrui. New York: Free Press, 1976. 508p.
This is one of the forward-looking volumes of the World Order Models Project. The
author regards projects of world government as premature until the values of a world
culture are more widely shared. 'It is a postulate of our perspective, therefore', the
author writes, 'that the transmission of ideas and their internalization are more
relevant for world reform than the establishment of formal institutions for external
control.' Mazrui thinks that humanity is no nearer world government than it was after
World War I, but it is much nearer to a world culture. Hence, he provides here a long
sociological analysis of kin-based, political, economic, and intellectual cultures and
cultural convergence. He concludes with a proposal (in the appendix) for a 'cultural
federation', as a model for U.N. reform during a transition to a more effective world
political organization.

177 World peace through world law.
Grenville Clark and Louis B. Sohn. Cambridge, MA: Harvard
University Press, 1958; 2nd ed., 1960; 3rd ed., 1966. 540p.

This is a classic model for systemic U.N. reform. Six principles are put forward: (1)
Genuine peace cannot be expected until an effective system of enforceable world law
reaching to individuals is established in the limited field of war prevention; (2) the
world law against organized violence must be explicitly stated in constitutional and
statutory form; (3) world judicial and equity tribunals and enlarged mediation and
conciliation organs must be established to provide alternative means for peaceful
resolution of disputes; (4) permanent international armed ('police') forces are
necessary for enforcement should the tribunals fail; (5) such a legal system requires
general and complete disarmament; (6) international economic development organs
must be expanded to redress economic injustice. The book is laid out in parallel
columns showing the existing U.N. Charter and a fundamentally reformed one,
followed by explanatory comments, so that the reader can see exactly *how* the
fundamental law of a limited and participatory world governing authority could be
written.

178 A world without the United Nations: what would happen if the United Nations shut down.
Edited by Burton Pines.   Washington, DC: Heritage Foundation,
1984. 176p.

This influential 'conservative' work advocates U.S. withdrawal from the U.N., though
the U.S. might still remain in several specialized agencies. The book defies
conventional wisdom on interdependence and multilateralism. 'How would a world
without a U.N. look? For one thing, it would remain a world filled with multinational
bodies. . . . Once independent, they [the specialized agencies] could deal solely with
the technical matters in which they are expert and need not be hampered by the
resolutions of a "mother" organization that declares Zionism to be racism and that a
New International Economic Order is needed to redistribute the world's resources
from the successful industrial nations to the developing countries. . . . This could all
function as well as it now does without the U.N.'s costly Secretariat, its cronyism,
legions of bureaucrats, its high salaries and lavish perquisites, and its anti-Western
ideology.' Though often inaccurate and unfair, this volume is the major source for
criticism of the U.N. system and hence for American policies of withdrawal of
funding. For a similar view on the left, see Charles Krauthammer, 'Let it sink: Why
the U.S. should bail out of the U.N', *New Republic*, 24 August 1987.

Empowering the United Nations.
See item no. 304.

The restructuring of the United Nations economic and social system.
See item no. 324.

The Declaration on the Peaceful Settlement of International Disputes (Manila).
See item no. 392.

The United Nations and the problem of economic development.
See item no. 1032.

United States policy

179 **American values and multilaterial institutions.**
Inis L. Claude, Jr.   In: *States and the global system: politics, law, and organization*, Inis J. Claude, Jr.   New York: St. Martin's, 1988, p.102-11.

Americans believe – more than other people about their country – that the United States embodies political and social values that are wanted abroad and ought to be extended. Claude refers to them under the general head of 'constitutional democracy'. This motivation, he argues, is behind their approach to both foreign policy and international organization. The World Court, League of Nations, and United Nations were all American in inspiration. Americans reject the export of their values by imperialism, but they genuinely hope to do so by international organization without 'multilateral concealment of a unilateral quest for hegemony'. Claude warns that regarding international organizations as 'moral' institutions superior to states is to court disillusionment and then to retreat from necessary participation in an imperfect world political system. In the preceding chapter, 'America and international organization', he concludes: 'There is now less consensus and more confusion and uncertainty about international organization among Americans than at any other time since World War II, and probably since World War I.'

180 **Around the cragged hill: a personal and political philosophy.**
George F. Kennan.   New York: Norton, 1993. 272p. bibliog.

This is a book of ripe wisdom by an influential American diplomat and scholar, the architect of the containment policy of 1947. Increasingly through the years of the Cold War, Kennan became a dissenter from the more military and imperious qualities of this fundamental American foreign policy. Here, near the end of his career, Kennan tries to state his own 'coherent personal and political philosophy'. He warns that, like all his works, it remains a 'collection of critical observations'. In his discussion of the United Nations – in a chapter, appropriately, on the nation – Kennan confronts the problem of the increasing unreality of the doctrine of sovereign equality; he supports the 'creation of a spectrum of potential political statuses larger than that of the national state but smaller than that of a relatively meaningless universality'. In the chapter on non-military foreign policy, he returns to his idea of regional cooperation on the lines of the then proposed North American Free Trade Agreement between the United States, Canada, and Mexico. But as for the U.N. and global organization generally, he favours at most 'moral support' and workmanlike 'international collaboration' without the 'political and verbal posturing to which many of us seem to be inclined'. Kennan, like most of his compatriots, is still far from an idealist of the United Nations (human rights figure very slightly in his thought), but his book can be read as a sign of shifting conservative opinion in the United States.

181 **Beyond globalism: remaking American foreign economic policy.**
Raymond Vernon and Debora L. Spar.   New York: Free Press, 1989. 246p.

Despite its title, this book by two leading Harvard professors (with the collaboration of their students) is not about a renunciation of international economic policy or a reversion to American economic nationalism. 'If the U.S. government', they write, 'is to retain its objective of promoting open competitive markets, if its actions are to be more than the outcome of a series of pitched battles by special interest groups, it will need the support of international institutions reasonably capable of maintaining the rules of the road.' They set out, with sure knowledge of executive policy and democratic politics, the changing international context (Europe, Japan, developing countries); the obsolescence of the Bretton Woods system; the refusal of all countries to delegate real decision-making powers to international institutions, especially the ill-fated International Trade Organization; the escape of transnational corporations from international regulation; the loss of a domestic interest in foreign aid; and in general, incoherence and decline in principled U.S. leadership of global economic cooperation, symbolized by the frustrating negotiations in GATT. The authors' policy recommendations steer between 'ineffectual' global institutions and unilateral use of 'threats and promises'. Their solution is 'thinking in parts' – that is, concentrating on limited membership international institutions like OECD and its IEA, created as a foil to OPEC, or the U.S.–Canadian Free Trade Agreement (1987). America, to these thinkers, is becoming a regional power.

182 **Changing our ways.**
Commission on America and the New World, Carnegie Endowment for International Peace. Washington, D.C.: Brookings Institution, 1992. 90p.

This is an attempt to provide a 'coherent vision' for U.S. foreign policy at a moment like that at the end of World Wars I and II. The U.N. is given a prominent place, especially in peacekeeping, as U.S. forces are withdrawn from abroad. It is an excellent source for seeing the United Nations in the context of the 'sole surviving superpower'. The authors urge the United States to restore U.S. domestic economy without sacrificing international free trade, temper U.S. world leadership in collective security, merge NATO gradually into the CSCE, admit Germany and Japan to the Security Council (they are silent on the veto), raise taxes on energy for economic, environmental, and security reasons, and shift the attack on the drug trade to reducing demand at home rather than interdicting production and sale abroad. The report calls for 'a new Dumbarton Oaks'. 'The enormity of the task of organizing for more effective multilateral action leads us to propose that the United States initiate an international assessment of the family of U.N. agencies and other major mulilateral organizations. This assessment should include a re-examination of the rationale for each organization, the assignment of responsibilities among them, and the possible revision of their charters.'

183 **Creating the entangling alliance: the origins of the North Atlantic treaty organization.**
Timothy P. Ireland. Westport, CT: Greenwood, 1981. 245p. bibliog.

The Atlantic Alliance had two goals, the first short-term and the second long-term: (1) to counter the threat of Soviet-sponsored subversion and enable Western Europe to recover from World War II; (2) to recreate a balance of power in Europe, especially by integrating Western Germany into Europe and securing France against future German aggression. This history concentrates on the second, more politically creative side of the story. The United Nations is little mentioned, except for the lip service paid to Article 51, but the story is pertinent since it shows how far the United States would go to create a *working* collective security system that could be a model for an eventual universal system under the U.N.

184 **The creation of the North Atlantic alliance.**
Alan K. Henrikson. In: *American defense policy*. Edited by John
Reichart and Steven Strum. Baltimore, MD: Johns Hopkins
University Press, 1982, p.296-320.
This is an historically rich essay on the origins of NATO in a *working* collective
security system. It is suggestive about widening the membership (even to include the
Soviet Union) and undertaking greater social and economic integration in accordance
with the alliance's Article 2. (By the formation of the North Atlantic Cooperative
Council, including Russia and other members of the former Warsaw Pact, in 1991,
some of these predictions were coming to pass. Such NATO reform is a precedent for
U.N. reform in the field of collective security.)

185 **A dangerous place.**
Daniel P. Moynihan with Suzanne Weaver. Boston: Atlantic, Little
Brown, 1978. 297p.
This is a readable, witty book, critical of the United Nations, by the U.S. ambassador
at the time of the 'Zionism is a form of racism' resolution (1975). Moynihan
subsequently became a leading Senator and was sometimes affectionately referred to
by the press as an 'American national treasure'. His book probably has done more
than any other to express American disenchantment with the U.N., preparatory to the
less cultivated and more inaccurate attacks of the Heritage Foundation. No one has
written better of the U.N. as a 'theatre of the absurd', as a politicized arena for the
'tyranny of the majority'. The book tugs at nationalist heartstrings and does little to
harmonize international discords.

186 **Defining purpose: the United Nations and the health of nations.**
Final report [to the President and Congress].
United States Commission on Improving the Effectiveness of the
United Nations. Rep. James A. Leach, co-chairman. Privately
printed; 10 September 1993. 116p. (Copies available from
Rep. Leach's office.)
Here is the report of a bipartisan commission established by Congress 'to examine the
United Nations system as a whole' and to prepare 'recommendations on ways to
improve the effectiveness of the United Nations'. Hearings were held in six cities to
sound out articulate American public opinion. 'The end of the Cold War', said Rep.
Leach on issuing the report, 'has created the most propitious moment since 1945 for a
U.S.-led United Nations to fashion common responses to the common problems of
mankind.' The committee, however, could not reach consensus. The majority
recommended establishing a 5,000 to 10,000 troop volunteer standing U.N. rapid
reaction military force, increasing peacekeeping appropriations, creating a high
commissioner for human rights, establishing an international criminal court,
promoting free trade and global markets, admitting Germany and Japan to the
Security Council as permanent members without veto power, reforming U.N.
management and administration to restore the independence of the international civil
service, and securing U.N. financing by paying U.S. arrearages but reducing future
U.S. assessments to 15-20 per cent. The minority opposed granting any larger
responsibilities to the U.N. 'It is far from clear', wrote co-chairman Charles
Lichenstein, 'that the United Nations is ready for the post-Cold War world. . . . U.S.
leadership in the world begins at home.' The split reflects U.S. Congressional and

public disenchantment with the U.N. and lack of will to lead a reform process. Executive leadership, like Franklin D. Roosevelt's, is lacking.

187   **The future of international law and American foreign policy.**
Francis A. Boyle. Introduction by Ramsey Clark.   Ardsley-on-Hudson, NY: Transnational Publications, 1989. 487p. bibliog.

Boyle begins this book with a quotation from George Kennan on Grenville Clark and Louis B. Sohn's monumental work, *World peace through world law* (q.v.). 'Today, two decades later . . . the logic of [Clark and Sohn's proposals] is more compelling. It is still too early for their realization on a universal basis; but efforts to achieve the limitations of sovereignty in favor of a system of international law on a regional basis are another thing' (*New York Review of Books*, 21 January 1982). Boyle puts this admission together with Hans Morgenthau's acceptance of Louis Sohn's position (1978) and concludes that the 'mortal intellectual enemies' of the moral and legal conduct of foreign policy had, in the twilight of their careers, abandoned 'Machiavellian power politics' for the more traditional theory of American diplomacy in which respect for international law and international organization was accorded a place alongside economic and military power. The Clark–Sohn plan is rooted in that broader foreign policy tradition. Boyle devotes special attention to the *teaching* of international law, since the realists 'have left in their wake an entire generation of American foreign policy decision makers who really believe that international law and organizations are totally irrelevant to the conduct of international relations'. He applies the legal policy approach to such cases as Israel and the Middle East, Libya, nuclear, biological, and chemical weapons, and Star Wars.

188   **Handbook of foreign policy analysis: methods for practical application in foreign policy planning, strategic planning, and business risk assessment.**
Daniel Frei and Dieter Ruloff.   Dordrecht, The Netherlands: M. Nijhoff for UNITAR, 1989. 392p. bibliog. (E.89.III.K.ST/25).

The world today is not like a set of territorially sealed and legally independent sovereign states – it is more like Marshall McLuhan's 'global village'. It is interdependent, complex, changing very rapidly, and of the highest importance to states and individuals. The threat of nuclear war and the uncertainties of world capitalism are typical of the new international environment. This unusual book is a 'scientific' guide to the perplexed international civil servant, national policy-maker, business person, scholar, and student in order to help them cope with the new flow of information. The book shows how to plan a study, gather and analyse data (especially by computer), consider analogies, and use decision trees. Motto: *Gouverner c'est prévoir*.

189   **On the law of nations.**
Daniel P. Moynihan.   Cambridge, MA: Harvard University Press, 1990. 211p.

This is a powerful essay, by the respected U.S. senator, ambassador, and professor of government, on recovering respect for international law in the conduct of American foreign policy. At the end of the Cold War (written at the beginning of the Persian Gulf War), Moynihan asks, 'By what rules can we expect to conduct ourselves in the next century?' He traces American respect for international law among the Founding

Fathers, Woodrow Wilson, F.D. Roosevelt, and even Truman in response to North Korean aggression in 1950. But with the Cold War, 'the "superpower" conflict simply took precedence'; 'the "legalistic approach to international affairs" was [felt, especially in the Reagan administration] inadequate to cope with the realities of communist aggression.' Thesis: 'A political culture from which the idea of international law has largely disappeared places its initiatives [Grenada, Nicaragua, Panama] in jeopardy.' International law is part of the Supreme Law of the Land, and as such is the ground of freedom at home and 'an essential cement for the international community'. In the future, international law and a strengthened U.N. system will be vital for 'new world-order questions': arms control, human rights, environmental protection, and the abolition of the threat and use of force to settle international disputes.

190 **The making of a security community: the United Nations after the Cold War.**
Peter J. Fromuth. *Journal of International Affairs*, vol. 46 (1993), p.341-66.

The Cold War has left a political heritage of unfamiliarity with negotiating a 'universal security consensus', which now is vital for building a security 'community'. We are still thinking, argues the author (now in the U.S. State Department), in terms of absolute independence (national sovereignty), when our security depends on cooperation with many states in an interdependent world. Common security, then, *requires* U.S. participation in peacekeeping missions even when they are not narrowly within traditional American interests. Fromuth explores what such a cooperative U.S. security policy would mean in practice within a revitalized U.N. Security Council. Its approaches to Iraq, Somalia, former Yugoslavia, and Libya, while hardly unanimous, yet showed the way forward. Proliferation, ethnic conflict, and threats to human rights are among the global problems of the future that the Security Council is in the best position to address.

191 **New world disorder: a critique of the United Nations.**
Kim R. Holmes. *Journal of International Affairs*, vol. 46 (1993), p.323-40.

The 'general collapse of Soviet support for client states and groups' explains far more of recent improvements in international relations than does the 'triumph of the multinational ideal' or the 'ideals of global democracy', argues the author. As long as the U.N. remains a 'mere instrument of nation states', their sovereign interests – and not simply their interests in international cooperation – will determine events. Holmes (much influenced by the Heritage Foundation) finds new threats to world order in the collapse of remaining empires (U.S.S.R. and potentially China and India), nationalism, and religious fundamentalism. Another new one is what Brian Urquhart calls the 'unraveling of national sovereignty', which used to protect small states like Mexico or Cuba from great power intervention. A standing U.N. army could intervene, too. Peacekeeping is already gliding into 'U.N. warmaking', as in the Persian Gulf. Limited peacekeeping operations rarely contributed to the *making* of peace; in the future, they will need powers to wage war in order to overcome local fighters. If the U.S. gets involved in expanded peacekeeping, it will have to risk the lives of American soldiers in places far removed from U.S. interests. Holmes would have the U.S. support U.N. peacekeeping only when a 'valid U.S. security interest is at stake' (though this would convert the U.N. into an agency of every state-member's foreign policy). Small powers, he hopes, will revert to defence of national sovereignty (even though to do so would destroy what little they have won with the U.N.). Compare Fromuth (item no. 190).

192   **Out of the cold: new thinking for American foreign and defense policy in the 21st century.**
Robert S. McNamara.   New York: Simon & Schuster, 1989. 223p.
This essay, written before 1989 by one of the United States' most vigorous Secretaries of Defence and one of the world's most respected international civil servants, argues in favour of a positive Western response to the 'new thinking' of Soviet leader Mikhail Gorbachev. Some of McNamara's argument has been outdated by events, including Gorbachev's fall, but the reader will find here an apt example of the best 'liberal' American thinking in the same spirit. McNamara proposes an East–West code of conduct emphasizing preventive diplomacy, conversion of military industrial plants, non-involvement in regional conflicts, and increased recourse to the U.N. He claims that such a code would have precluded Soviet invasion of Afghanistan and U.S. intervention in Vietnam.

193   **The political role of the United Nations: advancing the world community.**
John W. Halderman.   New York: Praeger, 1981. 219p.
This is a study by a retired U.S. Foreign Service Officer of the peaceful settlement functions of the U.N. Halderman contrasts these with national defence policies, which are not his focus. He argues that the objective of debate in the General Assembly and of decision in the Security Council must be to build *consensus*, that is 'world community', as a precondition to an effective world organization able to settle 'all significant' disputes'. He is opposed to Charter reform on the grounds that the 'problem is always to transform written provisions into reality' and that the Charter is already a reasonably 'adequate constitutional instrument'. What is necessary is the will to apply it. The book may be taken as reflective of shifting or dissenting opinion in the State Department.

194   **The politics of international law: U.S. foreign policy reconsidered.**
David P. Forsythe. Foreword by Richard Falk.   Boulder, CO: Lynne Rienner, 1990. 181p. bibliog.
This short book puts the politics back into international law, and the law back into foreign policy-making. The author traces the actual influence of international law on statecraft in five case-studies: reinterpreting the ABM Treaty, covert intervention in Nicaragua, overt intervention in Grenada, refugees in the Western hemisphere, and withholding assessed financial contributions to the U.N. The work is deliberately framed to restore the study of law to that of military and economic power in the political science of international relations, which till 1990 was dominated by the 'realist' paradigm. 'The central value judgment permeating this work is that the United States cannot make a lasting contribution to world order by seeking short-term national advantage, but rather will promote its most fundamental national interests by adjusting its foreign policy to the transnational and cosmopolitan values found in contemporary international law.'

195   **Practical internationalism: the United States and collective security.**
Richard N. Gardner.   *SAIS Review*, vol. 12, no. 2 (Summer-Fall 1992), p.35-49.

Now that the Cold War is over, the author tries to steer between the Scylla of a 'New Isolationism' and the Charybdis of a 'New Nationalism'. The first would ignore the necessity of defence in an interdependent world, and the second would play for imperial power, which the American people reject. 'Practical Internationalism' will rely on NATO, CSCE, O.A.S., and especially, as stated at the G-7 summit in July 1992, on a 'revitalized United Nations'. Gardner reviews recent U.N. successes in reversing Iraq's aggression, peacekeeping, peacemaking, and preventive diplomacy. He supports establishment of a U.N. rapid deployment force under Article 43 as a practical approach to enforcement of Security Council decisions. He also discusses ways to use the U.N. to strengthen the non-proliferation regime. The time has arrived, Gardner concludes, to enlarge the Security Council by the admission of Germany and Japan as permanent members without veto, provided they are prepared to send their armed forces abroad on international peacekeeping and enforcement missions.

196   **The promise of world order: essays in normative international relations.**
Richard A. Falk.   Philadelphia: Temple University Press for Center of International Studies (Princeton), 1987. 332p. bibliog.

This volume includes recent dissenting essays on American foreign policy by an author whose breadth of mind and political consciousness enable him to effectively challenge the reigning 'realist' paradigm of the theory and practice of U.S. foreign relations. The essay, 'Beyond deterrence: The essential political challenge', may be taken as typical. The 'great challenge' is to overcome the disparity between 'realist' assessments and 'more cosmopolitan imperatives of a more cooperative framework of demilitarized relationships' that might save the United States from disasters like the Vietnam War and the threat of general nuclear war. To 'demilitarize politics' will require social demands for normative conduct, substitution of U.N. institutions for diplomatic resolution of disputes, and an awakening of the political imagination.

197   **The prudent peace: law as foreign policy.**
John A. Perkins.   Chicago: University of Chicago Press, 1981. 246p. bibliog.

Here is an argument that adherence to international law is a *realistic* approach to U.S. foreign policy. 'The issue we should be considering is not the feasibility of law as a system of enforceable restraints but the necessity of law as a strategy for the resolution of conflict.' Perkins, a distinguished Boston attorney, considers the difficulties that international law is not addressed to the central concerns of foreign policy (the Cold War), is insufficiently defined to guide policy, and is not universally observed. He argues that a wise foreign policy cannot be seen as merely self-interested, but must be 'right' and 'something a people believe in'.

198 **Relations in a multipolar world.** [Part 1.] **Hearings, [26, 28, 30 November 1990].**
U.S. Senate. Committee on Foreign Relations. 101st Cong., 2nd sess. (CIS No.: 91-S381-26. SuDoc No.: Y4.F76/2:S.hrg.101-1200/pt.1).

This is the record of hearings to examine U.S. foreign policy and international relations in view of recent world political developments, especially the easing of Cold War tensions. Daniel P. Moynihan speaks on ending the Cold War, and C. William Maynes, on international organization.

199 **Revitalizing international law.**
Richard A. Falk.   Ames, IA: Iowa State University Press, 1989. 241p. bibliog.

Here is a sustained argument, in essays published since 1975, for restoring respect for international law in U.S. foreign policy as it existed before the 'realist' theory of international relations drove what little of it is possible in a world of competing sovereign states out of the minds of American policy-makers. Falk accepts the logic of *raison d'état* from Hobbes to Kissinger, but he warns that deterrence, unrestrained by moral or legal limits, will almost certainly lead to 'nuclear catastrophe', and that use of force, without international authority, leads to 'barbarism' and 'imperial geopolitics', which in turn lead to the 'end of life on earth'. These shrewd, engaged essays discuss international law from the perspective of declining state sovereignty before the emergence of an effective central world authority during the 'quest for world order'. The present (illegal) practice of use of force is confronted with the (revolutionary) challenge of nuclear weapons and even of environmental warfare. Falk closes with reflections on the new status of individuals in international law, as in the law of human rights and the Nuremberg principles. He argues that 'constitutional government' now depends on the impartial 'third party' rule of law.

200 **Right vs. might: international law and the use of force.**
Louis Henkin, Stanley Hoffmann, Jeane Kirkpatrick, Allan Gerson, William D. Rogers, and David J. Scheffer.   New York: Council on Foreign Relations, 1989; 2nd ed., 1991. 200p. bibliog.

This is an authoritative discussion of the 'proper role of international law in the formulation of American foreign policy'. The first edition dealt with the U.S. invasion of Grenada (1983) in order to restore order and keep communism at bay; the second brings the intervention in Panama (1989), the war against Iraq (1990-91), and the prospects for the post-Cold War world into the picture. The included essays are representative of the wide range of American governmental, defence, scholarly, historical, and journalistic opinion as brought together in three years of debate at the Council. Traditionalists argue that U.N. Charter Articles 2(4) and 51 still contribute to building the world rule of law in the face of international violence of lesser degree than armed invasion. Neorealists argue that the time has come to recognize that the U.N. Charter is based on assumptions that are even more untrue in 1991 than in 1945. Consensus on international peace and security is minimal; a concert of great powers is unavailable for enforcing by their authority and, when necessary, by their military force the nascent rule of law. Hence, the U.S. must be free to intervene to respond to others' abuses or to protect human rights and democracy. International legal empiricists occupy a somewhat middle position. With the end of the Cold War, a 'new world order' must be creatively based on a 'modern compact on legitimate uses of armed force under the U.N. Charter'. Policy-makers will have to attend to the 'global interest'. Collective humanitarian intervention must take hold in international law; 'otherwise the new world order will simply perpetuate the illegalities of the status quo'.

201   **In search of American foreign policy: the humane use of power.**
Lincoln P. Bloomfield.   New York: Oxford University Press, 1974.
182p.

'The truly hard-nosed advice may well be that which recommends interpreting the national interest far more broadly – that is, by taking bold moves to pool authority and giving a new lead to cooperation rather than unilateral direction.' The author admits that the U.N. is 'ineffective', and he recognizes that Charter reform to make the General Assembly more representative, say, of states in proportion to their power and wealth, is unacceptable to the 'majority'. Hence, he favours a wise U.S. diplomacy that would build coalitions of like-minded states in the U.N. and would *unilaterally* accept General Assembly resolutions as binding only when they represent a 'meaningful majority' of states, population, and wealth (effectively the binding triad). Written after the disaster of the Vietnam War, the book is a refreshing critique of the policies of 'toughness' and 'strength', which students will still find iconoclastic. 'The major forces affecting human life on the planet are increasingly trans-national and require purposeful steps toward world order.'

202   **Status of U.S. participation in the United Nations system.**
Hearings, [23 September 1988].
U.S. House of Representatives. Committee on Foreign Affairs. 100th
Cong., 2nd sess. (CIS No.: 89-H381-42. SuDoc No.:
Y4.F76/1:Un35/95).

These hearings on the Presidential decision to release the remaining instalment of Fiscal Year 1988 contributions to the U.N. budget, based on certification of U.N. reform measures, reflect recent Congressional opinion.

203   **Time of fear and hope: the making of the North Atlantic Treaty,**
1947-1949.
Escott Reid.   Toronto: McClelland & Stewart, 1977. 315p. bibliog.

This book explains why the weakness of the U.N. collective security system led to a strong Atlantic security system under Article 51. The North Atlantic Treaty then became the real collective security arrangement on which the U.S. relied in Europe for its defence – not the U.N. Charter. The author, an assistant to Lester Pearson, one of the principal architects of the treaty, remarks that in the original conception the North Atlantic alliance was but a 'temporary expedient', pending the time when the U.N. Security Council would be sufficiently unanimous to provide for a *general* collective security system. Then the Atlantic alliance would evolve into a community, 'a community which would increasingly acquire the characteristics of a federation'. This book could be formative for all students who look towards the expansion of NATO towards the east and eventually into a working general security system.

204 The United Nations and United States security policy.
Ruth B. Russell. Washington, DC: Brookings Institution, 1968. 510p.

This is a standard account of the founding of the U.N. in 1945 through a low point in U.S. (and other nations') reliance on the U.N. for its security and economic cooperation in 1967. The containment policy had then entered its 'coexistence' phase, but relapses into 'confrontation' (the Vietnam War, the Reagan military buildup) were to come. The author surveys 'myth and reality' in the U.N. Charter's approach to international peace and security, and discusses hesitant developments in arms control, collective enforcement (Korean War), peacekeeping (new in 1956), decolonization, efforts to limit the use of force by extension of international law, and the financial crisis growing out of the U.N. peacekeeping operation in the Congo. The book is a relic of sympathetic views toward the U.N. during the Cold War.

205 The United Nations and U.S. foreign policy: a new look at the national interest.
Lincoln P. Bloomfield. Boston: Little, Brown, 1960; revised ed., 1967. 268p.

The author, who served eleven years in the State Department, admits that the Cold War has dispelled many of the 'extravagant' hopes that were once placed in the U.N. for 'ending the scourge of war'. But, in the depths of the Vietnam War, he tried to fill the 'void' in U.S. policy toward the U.N. by systematically stating America's 'general political goals and objectives', its 'over-all strategic doctrine in the political realm', the 'larger national interest'. This was a voice howling in the wilderness in 1967, but at the end of the Cold War it could be just the book to help strategic thinkers to adjust to new realities. Bloomfield discusses the value of the U.N. to national security, to international cooperation, and to peaceful settlement of international disputes. He closes with reflections on the ultimate goal of a 'world order' – including world community and world government – under the 'rule of law'.

206 The United Nations: constitutional developments, growth, possibilities.
Benjamin V. Cohen. Cambridge, MA: Harvard University Press, 1961. 106p.

A former U.S. ambassador to the U.N., Cohen interprets the Charter in the spirit of *McCulloch v. Maryland* (1819) for its 'implied' powers. 'While the American Constitution established a government with organs endowed with power to act, the United Nations Charter established an instrument for international cooperation. But both created an organism capable of life and growth; the life and growth in each case depending not simply on the written injunctions of the founding fathers but on the vision and wisdom of succeeding generations.' Cohen applies loose construction to the Charter to justify such early developments as the rule in the Security Council that an abstention by a permanent member does not constitute a veto, but he also applies it to issues still alive thirty years later, such as whether the U.N. has authority to intervene in 'domestic' affairs despite Article 2(7). Written at a time when practical faith in the U.N. was not completely extinguished in the upper ranks of U.S. leadership, this short and clear book can still inspire youth and concerned citizens after the Cold War when formal Charter amendment seems impossible.

207 **The United States and multilateral institutions: patterns of changing instrumentality and influence.**
Edited by Margaret P. Karns and Karen A. Mingst.   Boston: Unwin, Hyman for Meshon Center Series on International Security and Foreign Policy, vol. 5, 1990. 366p.

This text is designed to guide students and graduate students in international relations courses into the new post-Cold War world, which is increasingly institutionalized. Primary focus is on U.S.–IGO relationships. By the 1990s, the editors find, even critics of the U.N. in the former Reagan administration had 'discovered the value of many international institutions and the potential for institutional reform'. Chapters are provided on the U.N. (as it relates to national security), IAEA, IMF, World Bank, GATT, FAO, WHO, UNESCO, and the International Bill of Rights. Karns and Mingst conclude that, for the future of multilateralism in U.S. foreign policy, the benefits of IOs outweigh their constraints. 'Although others can share the costs, there is as yet no rival for the role of leadership for multilateralism.'

208 **The United States in the new global economy: a rallier of nations.**
Research and Policy Committee.   New York: Committee for Economic Development, 1992. 90p.

Here is a confident call by American business people and educators for U.S. leadership in creatively responding to the challenges of the new global economy. 'Now that communism has collapsed and the Cold War is at an end, the spotlight is turned on market systems and democracy. America must articulate a sense of direction and purpose that inspired the American people and the citizens of other nations to move boldly into the twenty-first century.' Principles: collective security, free trade, sustainable development, reduction of U.S. federal budget deficits, shift from military to economic strength, investment in people. The book articulates U.S. interests in an integrated global economy, advocates 'reconstruction' of Eastern Europe and C.I.S. republics, accepts use of international institutions and 'sharing decision making power' in the U.N. Security Council, and acclaims American world leadership in the future. The work contains valuable graphs and economic indicators.

209 **United States participation in the United Nations.**
United States Department of State. *Report* by the President to the Congress for the Year 1991.   Washington, DC: U.S. Department of State, Bureau of International Organizational Affairs, 1992. 311p. (Pub. No. 9974).

This official report is organized along lines of traditional U.N. emphases and then of U.S. interest: political affairs, disarmament and arms control, economic development, social and humanitarian issues, human rights, science and technology, trusteeship, legal developments, administration and budget, specialized agencies. The material is presented factually, without political analysis. The treatment of 'U.N. reform', or 'Nicaragua *v.* United States of America', or 'Rights of the child' glosses over deep U.S. distress with the world organization. Yet in many areas the U.S. finds the system useful. Policy-makers, international officials, non-Americans, scholars, students, and citizens will find this volume essential to begin to understand the actual U.N. system and its problems.

210 **U.S. policy in international institutions: defining reasonable options in an unreasonable world.**
Edited by Seymour M. Finger and Joseph Harbert. Foreword by Cyrus Vance. Boulder, CO: Westview, 1978, revised ed., 1982. 217p. bibliog.

This book was written at a time of American 'disenchantment' with the U.N., yet also a time, in one contributor's view, when Americans could take a more 'realistic view of the world and of the limits of U.S. power' in an 'evolving international system'. Here are expert articles, rarely longer than ten pages each, on U.S. cooperation with the U.N. and other international organizations in the common areas of disarmament, peacekeeping, human rights, trade and development, currency exchange, regulation of multinational corporations, the law of the sea, oil supplies, and the future United Nations.

211 **U.S. policy toward international institutions.**
Seymour M. Finger. *International Organization*, vol. 30 (1976), p.347-60.

At a time of détente with the Soviet Union, when the Cold War had given way to at most a cold peace, the author recommended that the United States 'should' satisfy its security interests in Europe through NATO, and in Asia, Africa, and Latin America through the United Nations (peacekeeping, peacemaking, disarmament). Its economic interests could be met through the World Bank group, regional development banks, IMF, GATT, OECD, and even UNCTAD. Finger did not advocate establishing new institutions (like the Security Council's Military Staff Committee or an international trade organization) because the necessary prior step is 'to change governmental attitudes and policies'. He called for policies less 'narrowly nationalistic, short-sighted, or callous toward the developing countries'.

212 **The U.S., the U.N., and the management of global change.**
Edited by Toby Trister Gati. New York: New York University Press for UNA–USA, 1983. 380p.

Written before the Heritage Foundation's attacks on the U.N, the Reagan administration's demotion of the U.N. ambassador from cabinet rank, withdrawal from UNESCO, and Mikhail Gorbachev's initiatives ending the Cold War and supporting a process of U.N. reform, this collection of expert essays reflects a positive view of the U.N. system at the height of its evolution before the opportunities opened by the end of the Cold War. Hence, it remains an excellent book to explain the history, organization, and deeper issues – like human rights and the north–south conflict – that are still with us. Use in conjunction with Finkelstein's *Politics in the U.N. system* (1988) (item no. 55).

213 **Vision for the 1990s: U.S. strategy and the global economy.**
Edited by Daniel F. Burton, Jr., Victor Gotbaum, and Felix G. Rohatyn. Cambridge, MA: Ballinger for the UNA–USA Economic Policy Council, 1989. 164p.

This is a prospectus for a U.S. long-term economic strategy in the international market place. The expert authors concentrate on the U.S. policy problems in the areas of technology, finance, and labour. More specific problems include commercializing new innovations, international debt, needs for long-term planning in manufacturing, volatility of financial markets, job flight to manufacturing plants abroad, growth of service sector jobs, worker protection, and workplace innovation. The authors anticipate the emergence of a 'global market' and the need for radical adjustment of the American domestic economy.

214 **Washington Weekly Report.**
    Edited by Steven Dimoff. UNA–USA Washington Office (1010 Vermont Ave., NW, Suite 904, Washington, DC 20005). 40 issues per year.

Here is the best source for thorough and up-to-date information on law and policy affecting the U.N. in Congress and the Presidential administration.

215 **Whose collective security?**
    Edward C. Luck and Toby Trister Gati. *Washington Quarterly*, vol. 15 (Spring 1992), p.43-56.

This is a compact, politically clear account of the U.N. contribution to international security, addressed to the élite policy-making community in Washington. The answers to the question in the title is that collective security belongs to all nations. The U.N. cannot, as some small nations fear, become a cover for U.S. domination, yet the U.S. still exercises preponderant leadership. The Security Council could be made more representative by the permanent admission of Japan and Germany, even by Charter amendment, yet the whole Council is collectively responsible for international peace and security. With the end of the Cold War, standby U.N. armed forces and activation of the Military Staff Committee under Article 43 could share the burden of enforcement of international decisions. Occasions for interventions are apt to increase in the future as the international community refuses to allow non-interference in domestic affairs to shield gross abuses of human rights. Financing reforms, such as a tax on international commerce or arms sales, could reduce the inequitable burden on the U.S. 'Multilaterial crisis management, peacekeeping, and collective security should be as fundamental to the defense of U.S. national security interests in the 1990s as participation in the North Atlantic Treaty Organization (NATO) has been during the past 45 years.'

The International Court of Justice.
See item no. 339.

Disarmament and the U.N.: strategy for the United States.
See item no. 657.

See also National missions (p.128ff.).

Soviet policy

216 Address to the General Assembly of the United Nations.
Mikhail S. Gorbachev. *General Assembly official records*, Plenary.
43rd sess., 7 December 1988. (A/43/PV.72).

This is a powerful, historic address on the new realities of a 'mutually interrelated and integral world' and on the necessity for a reformed and strengthened United Nations to build 'unity in diversity'. Initial press and official attention focused on his announced *unilateral* initiative to cut Soviet armed forces by 500,000 men, but the bulk of the speech was about a far deeper transformation of international relations from armed rivalry to the rule of law. 'Today, we have entered an era when progress will be shaped by universal human interests. Awareness of that dictates that world politics, too, should be guided by the primacy of universal human values.' 'Being in favor of demilitarizing international relations, we want political and legal methods to prevail in solving whatever problems may arise. Our ideal is a world community of States which are based on the rule of law and which subordinate their foreign policy activities to law.' Gorbachev made many concrete suggestions, some still in the future, for negotiations on nuclear and conventional arms reductions, ending regional conflicts, expanding the Helsinki process (CSCE), economic cooperation, reducing international debts, protecting the environment, cooperation in space, economic conversion of military industries, deliberate winding down of the Cold War, and strengthening the U.N.

217 Domestic reform and international change: the Gorbachev reforms in historical perspective.
Valerie Bunce. *International Organization*, vol. 47 (1993), p.107-38.

Gorbachev's reforms (1985-91) were similar to those of Alexander II (1855-81). Bunce finds similar historical patterns in periods of Russian stagnation: international security, Russian conservatism, expanding Russian power. In periods of reform the pattern is: instability in Europe, liberalization of Russian politics, and Russian downward mobility in the international system. (The implication is that Gorbachev's reforms will be undone by an authoritarian successor. Bunce completely passes over any permanent innovations that Gorbachev may have made within the U.N. system.)

218 Governability of the world.
Georgi Shakhnazarov. *International Affairs* (Moscow), vol. 34, no. 3 (March 1988), p.16-24.

The world is increasingly 'interrelated, interdependent, and integral', Shaknazarov argues. Neither great-power theory nor the theory of competing social systems explains the facts of convergence. Lenin's theory of social development above class and national conflict of interests implies interdependence, economic internationalization, and 'a more governable world'. H.G. Wells, Albert Einstein, and other advocates in the West saw world government as the completion of the growth of sovereign and hence peaceful political units after city-states (Greek, *polis*) and nation-states. After World War II, the attack on the narrowness of *national sovereignty*, in the historical circumstances of the time, could not be disentangled from neocolonialism and U.S. hegemony over a war-ravaged world. But now colonialism is dead, U.S. hegemony is declining, and even the 'global socialist experiment' has suffered 'general failure'. Hence the project of *governing* the world, by law and by a government in which sovereign states could participate more equally, has at last become possible. In functional fields like air transport, shipping, and international communications, it is already far advanced. The great problem now is to extend 'governability' to economic development and to war and peace. Transitional steps could be taken in nuclear arms reductions, conventional force reductions in Europe, and protection of human rights. 'Sovereignty, the people's will, is not infringed in any way by the voluntary delegation of part of one's powers to an international or supranational agency.'

219   **Nobel lecture.** [Oslo, 5 June 1991.]
      Mikhail S. Gorbachev.   *Les prix Nobel* (Stockholm): *The Nobel prizes*, 1990, p.259-71 (Russian), p.272-83 (English).

Delivered after the victory of the international coalition in the Persian Gulf War – at the height of interest in a 'new world order' – and six months before the unanticipated breakup of the U.S.S.R., this dramatic address outlined the principles of *perestroika* (reform): 'from confrontation to interaction and, in some cases, partnership'. New thinking, said Gorbachev, was 'based on the conviction that at the end of the 20th century force and arms must move aside as the main lever in world politics'. In their place would have to be solidarity – 'a policy in both internal and in international affairs which combines the interests of its own people in the interests of the world community'. The new principles, then, include solidarity, the universality of civilization, unity in diversity, the indivisibility of peace, lawfulness, constitutional means in place of force, democracy, human rights, mixed economy, a common European home, 'de-ideologizing relations among states', protection of the environment, and a new system of international security. To his audience in Oslo, Gorbachev did not specifically mention the United Nations, but the implication was either that the U.N. could be reformed into such a new system of 'cooperation and joint creativity' or that a new global institution would be established. 'The world needs *perestroika* no less than the Soviet Union.'

220   **The reality and guarantees of a secure world.**
      Mikhail Sergeyevich Gorbachev.   *Pravda* and *Isvestia*, 17 September 1987. Translated in: Foreign Broadcast Information Service, *Daily Report: Soviet Union*, 17 September 1987, p.27.

This stunning article signalled the new Soviet leadership's intention to end the Cold War and turn to the United Nations. 'Objective processes are making our complex and diverse world increasingly interrelated and interdependent. And it increasingly needs a mechanism that is capable of discussing its common problems. . . . The United Nations organization is called upon to be such a mechanism by its underlying idea and its origin.' Gorbachev reaffirmed the agreement in principle reached with President Reagan at the Reykjavik summit to institute a program for the 'stage-by-stage elimination of nuclear weapons', then he turned to an international alternative to the national strategy of nuclear deterrence. He introduced the concept of 'military sufficiency', proposed an accord on defence strategy, demilitarized zones, dissolution of military blocs, return home of troops stationed abroad, and verification agreements. Echoing Maxim Litvinov in the League of Nations before World War II, he declared that 'security is indivisible'. Suggestions for strengthening the U.N. included utilizing the Security Council as a 'multilateral center for lessening the danger of war', widening the use of peacekeeping observers and forces, improving means for the peaceful settlement of disputes, building a new world economic order, admitting the relation between disarmament and development, aiming at 'ecological security', protecting human rights, expanding humanitarian assistance, and cooperation in health. But his comments on international law were what was most revolutionary about this article. 'We are convinced that a comprehensive system of security is, at the same time, a system of universal law and order ensuring the primacy of international law in politics.'

221 **The river of time and the imperative of action.**
Mikhail S. Gorbachev. Westminster College, Fulton, Missouri, 6 May 1992. (Available from Office of Press Relations, Fulton, MO, 65251-1299.)

This historic address recalls Winston Churchill's 'Iron Curtain' address in 1946. Gorbachev, by now ousted from power in the breakup of the Soviet Union, reflected on the 'missed chance' at the start of the Cold War 'to initiate a world order different from that which existed before the war'. The implication, he held, was that by 1992 a similar opportunity could be lost. 'In pushing forward to a new civilization', he stated, 'we should under no circumstances again make the intellectual, and consequently political, error of interpreting victory in the "Cold War" narrowly as a victory for oneself, one's own way of life, for one's own values and merits. . . . This was altogether a victory for common sense, reason, democracy, and common human values.' He surveyed emerging challenges of ethnic conflict, narrow nationalism, North–South splits, rebirth of economic protectionism, ecological catastrophe, and the need to restructure the United Nations. 'An awareness of the need for some kind of global government is gaining ground, one in which all members of the world community would take part.' Specific reforms mentioned include admitting Germany and Japan to the Security Council, deleting the 'hostile states' language from the Charter, expanding peacekeeping, establishing a global emergency watch facility in the Secretariat, and better links to the world economy. The necessary goal is a 'democratically organized world community'.

222 **U.N. mirrors the whole world.**
Andrei Igorevich Kolosovsky. *International Affairs* (Moscow), vol. 36, no. 2 (February 1991), p.21-29.

A new statue outside the U.N. depicts St. George breaking up Pershing-2 and SS-20 missiles. The Cold War is over. The author credits 'new political thinking, coupled with democratisation processes inside the country [U.S.S.R.]', as a major factor for improved Soviet–American relations and the reunification of Germany. Kolosovsky analyses the 'most significant transformation since the end of World War II'. The end of ideology may have come, and universal values may be proclaimed, but unless regional and global mechanisms capable of maintaining peace and stability are devised, the new world order will break down again. New threats can be seen in social and economic problems of both the Soviet Union and the Third World. He calls for continued Big Five cooperation in the Security Council – as during the repulsion of Iraqi aggression against Kuwait – and for advance consultations with non-permanent members in a spirit of impartiality. That will solve the 'problem of unity'.

223 The world community is amenable to government [*upravlyayemo*].
Georgi Shakhnazarov. *Pravda*, 15 January 1988, p.3.

Shakhnazarov, a past president of the Soviet Political Science Association, was
widely recognized as a key adviser to Gorbachev and a source of 'new thinking', of
which this daring article is an example. Shakhnazarov admits that world government
is theoretically necessary to 'save mankind from perishing', but historically, when the
idea was most popular (after use of atomic bombs), it became entangled in U.S.
foreign policy. Now the success of anticolonialism and the attainment of military
strategic parity by the Soviet Union have created conditions where management and
even government of global problems could be approached, not on the basis of denial
of sovereign independence, but on that of the 'balance of interests of the various
states'. Governability (what in the West is now called governance) is explored in the
fields of crime control, environmental protection, disease (AIDS) control,
international trade, 'regulation' of human rights, and U.N. reform. Such world
centralization of functions, the author argues, is consistent with 'Soviet socialist
patriotism', which 'has nothing in common with blind nationalism'. At this early date
in the progress of *perestroika*, Shakhnazarov still imagined that 'by rectifying its
shortcomings, broadening the zone of social justice, and enriching the rights of the
individual, socialism will prove its total superiority over capitalism'.

British policy

224 British foreign policy: tradition, change, and transformation.
Edited by Michael Smith, Steve Smith, and Brian White. London:
Unwin, Hyman, 1988. 287p. bibliog.

This is a recent, very able study of British foreign policy, written before the end of
the Cold War but at a time when 'tradition and transformation' were marked by loss
of the British Empire and 'adjustment to life as a secondary or regional actor in world
affairs'. The United Nations hardly fits into the authors' analyses, except in
North–South relations and with respect to one or two of the specialized agencies. The
paradigm operative here is 'realist' power politics.

**225 The expanding role of the United Nations and the implications for
U.K. policy. Report and proceedings.**
Great Britain. House of Commons. Foreign Affairs Committee. David
Howell, chairman. London: HMSO, 1992-93. 11 reports and 2 vols.
(HC 235-i-xi, I, II).

'After nearly 45 years hobbled by the Cold War, the world now looks to the United
Nations to do what the founding fathers set it up to do.' The implications for U.K.
policy imply a 'central interest' in the U.N. As the Foreign Secretary said in his
address to the U.N. in 1992: 'International order is threatened in the short-term by the
unleashing of extreme nationalism and challenges to the rule of law. In the medium-
term, the inescapable challenge is to reinforce the system of collective security based
on the U.N. Respect for good government and human rights must move to the centre
of the stage.' These reports contain up-to-date extensive coverage of peacekeeping,

finances, diplomacy, disarmament, humanitarian aid, human rights, sanctions, and international cooperation. The final two volumes authoritatively review key issues, Boutros-Ghali's *An agenda for peace* (see item no. 121), experiences and problems (1945-87), preventive diplomacy, peacekeeping, peacebuilding, humanitarian intervention, enforcement, regional arrangements, human rights work, finance, institutional change, and implications for U.K. policy.

226 **International relations: British and American perspectives.**
Edited by Steve Smith.   Oxford: Blackwell for British International Studies Association, 1985. 242p. bibliog.

Here is a valuable survey of British thinking on international relations – including international political economy, transnationalism, international organization, trilateralism, utopianism, and history – with special attention to the parallel approaches (realism, idealism, empiricism, legalism) but differing emphases of British and American scholars. 'American political writing sometimes seems to reflect a deep-seated constitutionalism: a belief that form or structure will determine content or practice. . . . Britain, on the other hand, has a long tradition of suspecting any but the most limited attempts to effect European integration . . . [and her scholars and statesmen] doubt the prospects of international organizations ever playing a more substantial role in world affairs.' The introductory chapter contains a particularly far-seeing and balanced list of landmark volumes in the literature on international relations, which the student, trying to winnow the wheat from the chaff, will find very helpful.

227 **Keeping the peace: the United Nations and the maintenance of international peace and security.**
Nigel D. White.   Manchester: Manchester University Press, 1993. 267p.

This is a major revision of the author's 1989 study, *The United Nations and the maintenance of international peace and security*. Here, partly in response to Secretary-General Boutros-Ghali's *An agenda for peace* (1992), which recognized 'that an opportunity has been regained to achieve the great objectives of the Charter', White casts particular attention on the U.N.'s involvement in the Persian Gulf War, on its new peacekeeping operations in former Yugoslavia, Western Sahara, Cambodia, Somalia, and Central America, and on its embargoes against Libya and South Africa. His earlier historical, geopolitical, legal, and practical analyses of the Security Council and General Assembly – always in 'tension' – are retained. Readers will find this volume succinct, fair, unadorned, and critical. Of peacekeeping, White writes, 'It is clear from the [non-U.N.] operations in Lebanon and Sri Lanka, that the term "peacekeeping", like so many legal concepts, is abused by States. The surest way of maintaining the integrity of the peacekeeping function is to retain it within the United Nations.'

228 **National security in a new world order.**
Laurence Martin.   *The World Today* (London), vol. 48 (1992), p.21-26.

The director of the Royal Institute for International Affairs here doubts that the end of the Cold War will lead to any more 'order' or 'security' than the end of any of the other great wars in the last two centuries. Any 'change in the very nature of the system', Martin holds, is due to the 'success of patient containment . . . precipitated . . . by the robust strategy of the Reagan Administration and the staunchness of its allies'. The Second World has been vanquished. As for the Third World, 'the Western victors have less need either to meddle or to help'. He foresees a future of 'local' international conflict, which could be contained by a working collective security system. The Persian Gulf War – 'primarily [an] American act licensed by the United Nations' – will not be typical of such a system. U.N. peacekeeping in former Yugoslavia might. So may prevention of open war between Pakistan and India. 'Abstention', he argues, may then be the realistic U.N. course in case of domestic conflicts that border on threats to international peace and security (as later in Rwanda). In Europe, NATO forms a 'security community' that dares not let down its guard against a resurgent Russian threat. The U.N. could have a role in Europe, though only as a legitimator or auxiliary, not an enforcer. A European Defence Community could yet evolve.

229   **The new international actors: the United Nations and the European Economic Community.**
Edited by Carol A. Cosgrove and Kenneth J. Twitchett.   London: Macmillan, 1970. 272p. bibliog.

This anthology of British writers on transnationalism is presented 'without the jargon'. The authors concentrate on the U.N. and E.C., which 'can and do exert influence on a similar scale to that of many medium-sized powers'. Influence is measured in terms of the organization's autonomous decison making, encouragement of functional cooperation affecting inter-state relations, and modification of its member states' foreign policies. The U.N. is studied by comparison with the 'failed' League and with respect to the 'management of power', which is its fundamental responsibility. The essays were mostly written in the 1960s (one as early as 1942), but they still provide a clear view of what was a new phenonenon in international relations.

230   **The new United Nations: appearance and reality.**
Rosalyn Higgins.   Hull: University of Hull Press, 1993. 27p.

A leading British scholar on the U.N. here re-examines it in the light of new historic opportunities.

231   **Peacekeeping as a growth industry.**
Laurence Martin.   *The National Interest*, vol. 32 (Summer 1993), p.3-11.

This article sounds 'cautionary notes' about enthusiasms for a new world order (1990), peacekeeping, and 'an almost lighthearted readiness to trample across borders and the idea of sovereignty'. To intervene in civil conflicts like those in Kurdistan (Iraq), Somalia, and (former) Yugoslavia – that is, to cross the line protecting domestic jurisdiction – is to face ethnic conflict in perhaps half the organized states of the world. To support secession or to cross borders ostensibly to protect human rights, as in Yugoslavia, is to expose minorities to the greater danger of breakdown of all law and order. Martin prefers a slower, more cautious approach, starting with transforming NATO into a peacekeeper, especially with respect to future crises in the Russian 'near abroad'. *Pas trop de zèle* is the right motto.

232   **Problems and prospects of the United Nations.**
       Brian Urquhart.   *International Journal* (Toronto), vol. 44 (1989),
       p.803-22.

The author admits that the U.N. Charter, despite its advances on the League of
Nations Covenant, was based on such false assumptions as the indefinite continuation
of World War II allied unity, pre-atomic weaponry, and sovereign self-sufficiency.
The result was 'twenty-five years of improvisation' (to 1970), as peacekeeping and
the role of the Secretary-General advanced. Urquhart sets out the main U.N.
achievements in decolonization, human rights instruments, and economic
development through further 'storm and stress' until about 1985. Mikhail
Gorbachev's new thinking finally put an end to the Cold War, Sir Brian argues, but
the 'renaissance' at the U.N., he warns, is not being sustained by the other great
powers. The technological revolution, over-population, and industrial pollution are
not being addressed as common global problems. He sees great obstacles to
meaningful U.N. reform.

233   **Reform of the United Nations?**
       Keith Hindell.   *The World Today*, vol. 48 (1992), p.30-33.

The author, a BBC journalist, finds the prospects for U.N. reform improved. '. . . the
initiative has passed to the developed market economies'; 'radical changes' are
foreseeable. Sovereignty (Article 2(7)) is yielding to a right of intervention to protect
human rights; the IAEA could be given real powers to guard against nuclear
proliferation; some 'supranational authority' is needed to cope with the global
problematique of climate change, environmental pollution, AIDS, migration, drugs,
and international crime. The Security Council, set in the mould of the victorious allies
in World War II, is due for reform; Japan proposes new permanent members, *without*
veto. The United States opposes a U.N. review conference, Hindell argues, 'lest [the
Council] should become a more effective peace broker and security enforcer than
itself'. He closes with approving references to the Stockholm initiative, *Common
responsibility*.

234   **The United Nations after the Gulf War.**
       Anthony Parsons.   *The Round Table*, vol. 319 (1991), p.265-73.

The former British ambassador and representative to the U.N. takes up the question
whether, in the recent Persian Gulf War, the Security 'Council was hijacked by the
United States with British collusion' or 'functioned as it was designed to do by the
Founding Fathers'. Sir Anthony finds that U.N. enforcement is much improved over
that of the League of Nations, but in practice Chapter VII had little restraint on the
150 wars that have occurred since 1945. What were needed were powers of *coercion*.
A 'change for the better' began in 1987 with Gorbachev's new policies, which
immediately put an end to the Iran–Iraq War (U.N. Res. 598). The Iraqi attack on
Kuwait was the 'first major post-Cold War test' of the Council, which comported
itself well, considering that it had no U.N. forces under Article 43 or dared to act
under Article 42. He concludes: 'The most important lesson of all, in the new and
favourable international conjuncture, is the need for pre-emptive diplomacy before
crises explode into warfare.'

235   **The United Nations and the national interests of states.**
Anthony Parsons. In: *United Nations, divided world.* Edited by Adam
Roberts and Benedict Kingsbury.   Oxford: Oxford University Press,
1988, p.47-60.

The Cold War has prevented the U.N. from guaranteeing collective security
on a world-wide basis. Meanwhile, the author, a retired British diplomat, contends,
'what the U.N. can do is to ameliorate disputes, to defuse crises, and to act as a
catalytic agent to persuade the parties to come together and negotiate.' The U.N.
offers public multilateral diplomacy in the Security Council and General Assembly,
private diplomacy in the good offices of the Secretary-General, and an escape route or
ladder for states on the verge of hostilities to climb down. Parsons reviews the
historical record of successful U.N. security functioning from the Suez crisis of 1956
to the Falklands in 1982. Failures like inability to prevent the Iran–Iraq War in 1980
or the Israeli invasion of Lebanon in 1982, however, call for the Secretary-General's
earlier intervention, which could be encouraged, says the author, by limiting him to a
single term.

236   **The United Nations in 1992: problems and opportunities.**
Brian Urquhart.   *International Affairs* (London), vol. 68 (1992),
p.311-19.

Sir Brian here prefers 'pragmatic idealism' to 'realism' when considering policies
toward the U.N. '"Realism" is often a euphemism for short-sightedness, and policies
lacking in the necessary courage or vision. . . . We are in a situation which is so
revolutionary and so different from that of preceding generations that it may well be
that idealism, with an element of Utopian thinking, is a far more realistic approach
than self-styled realism.' The problems that now confront the world, at a 'defining
moment' include the erosion of national sovereignty, the population explosion, and
systemic changes to earth's environment. His solutions are to 'strengthen the U.N.'
(1) in its maintenance of international peace and security, to permit transfers of funds
from national defence to social and international programmes; (2) in its management
of global problems, on the model of the specialized technical agencies; and (3) in its
'development of a world society based on law'. The latter he describes – in the face
of lingering realist ridicule – only so far as calling for a legal *system*, with a strong
International   Court of Justice and effective monitoring and enforcement of
international treaties and customary law.

237   **The United Nations in the new world order.**
Nicholas Hopkinson.   London: HMSO, 1993. 41p.

The author, the associate director of Wilton Park and a far-seeing commentator on
European and British foreign policy, here looks to the U.N. as a forum for
cooperation in troubled times ahead. As he said in a recent conference on refugees
and migration, if European investment and aid does not increase in developing
countries, eliminating poverty at the source, then the West will have to spend even
more money to police borders, protect the innocent in the streets, screen asylum-
seekers, and feed millions of immigrants.

United Nations, divided world.
See item no. 22.

The anarchical society.
See item no. 31.

Armed peace: the search for world security.
See item no. 643.

The international nuclear non-proliferation system.
See item no. 716.

History

238 **Charter of the United Nations: commentary and documents.**
Leland M. Goodrich, Edvard Hambro, and Anne P. Simons.   New
York: Columbia University Press, 1946; 3rd ed., 1969. 732p. bibliog.

This is a magisterial study of the drafting of the U.N. Charter, its form and content,
and its early work (to about 1948). Probably the most valuable of the book's features
is its article-by-article commentary. Here readers can find out the sources and variants
for such important articles as those on purposes (Article 1), principles (2), functions
and powers of the General Assembly (11), veto power in the Security Council (27),
provision of armed forces to the Security Council (43), right of self-defence (51), the
International Court of Justice (92), and Secretary-General (97). The authors write
coolly, so readers will have to be attentive to the hidden meanings behind many of the
judicious expressions. The book was written at a time when, as the authors conclude,
'there is as yet no reasonable assurance that [the U.N.] will succeed where the League
failed'.

239 **The defeat of an ideal: a study of the self-destruction of the United
Nations.**
Shirley Hazzard.   Boston: Little, Brown, 1973. 286p.

Here is an iconoclastic study of the 'failure' of the U.N. through the depths of the
Cold War. 'It is not my purpose here, in dwelling on the interior nature and
experience of the United Nations, to minimize or overlook the vast political forces at
work or in abeyance there; but rather to trace a more intricate relation between the
two than has yet been suggested, and to depict a set of reciprocal, and mutually
destructive, repercussions.' In effect, this is a study of the inadequacies of
international bureaucracy, as it has evolved since the mid-19th century, to meet the
needs of the interdependent world as it approaches the 21st. Hazzard's goal is U.N.
'reform'. She knows that reform must come about 'through the insistence of the
peoples of the world' but minces no words against an organization that 'has made
itself inaccessible to reform'. Readers must not mistake the primary cause for the
weakness of the U.N. in the unwillingness of state governments – and ultimately of
their peoples – to establish a representative world authority with real powers.

240   **Dumbarton Oaks: the origins of the United Nations and the search for postwar security.**
Robert C. Hilderbrand.   Chapel Hill: University of North Carolina Press, 1990.
'The Great Powers, by the time they came to Dumbarton Oaks [the estate in Washington, DC, where the Charter was first drafted], were all working toward the creation of an organization that would be enough like the Four Policemen to keep the peace and enough like the League of Nations to keep the small nations happy. It would, in addition, have to be an organization that they could control, at least where their own vital interests were concerned.' Hilderbrand sees 'Federation of the World' as the ideal standard for measuring how little was achieved in the United Nations.

241   **The evolution of the United Nations system.**
Amos Yoder. New York: Crane Russak, 1989. 270p. bibliog.
Written by an experienced U.S. diplomat, this history aims 'to bridge the intellectual gap between internationalists and the power brokers who believe that only material power counts in international relations'. The book is written in a quiet, reasonable tone that may be best for the student or the confused beginner. The book was written during the Gorbachev era, but just before the end of the Cold War seemed possible.

242   **Federalism, world.**
Joseph Preston Baratta.   In: *World encyclopedia of peace*. Edited by Ervin Laszlo and Jong Youl Yoo.   Oxford: Pergamon, 1986. vol. 1, p.311-21.
Earlier plans of a union of states to establish peace were not strictly federalist. Even Immanuel Kant spoke only of a *confederation* of free and independent states. But with the failure of the League of Nations and the coming of the Second World War, a number of experienced people in America and Europe began planning for a world federal system – with powers to enact law reaching to individuals, delegated to it by the national states – in order to preserve the peace. Clarence Streit, Robert M. Hutchins, G.A. Borgese, and Grenville Clark drafted model world constitutions. A world federalist movement sprang up opposed to the new U.S. policy of containment and committed to continued progress of the U.N. At its height in 1950, it consisted of some seventy-three national and associated organizations in twenty-two nation-states, uniting about 151,000 people. The Korean War ended the fledgling mass movement. Nevertheless, the movement left behind substantial plans, of which Grenville Clark and Louis B. Sohn's *World peace through world law* (q.v.) is probably the most practicable, and it produced a body of fundamental political thinking about how to establish the rule of law at the world level. 'What world federalists are really calling for is a new kind of world political wisdom.'

243   **A history of the United Nations.**
Evan Luard.   New York: St. Martin's, 1982; 2nd ed., 1989. 2 vols.
This critical narrative history extends from the 'lessons of the League' to the establishment of the United Nations Organization in 1945, and through the Korean War, Suez crisis, and other world events involving the U.N. until 1965. The author, who has written many books on the U.N., concentrates on the central responsibility of the organization – the maintenance of international peace and security. The earlier

chapters on the origins of the U.N. may be of most interest to readers contemplating reform. There are very few notes, and this is a book for the general public.

244   **A history of the United Nations Charter: the role of the United**
       States, 1940-1945. Ruth B. Russell and Jeannette B. Muther.
       Washington, DC: Brookings, 1958. 1,140p. bibliog.
This is the standard political history of the founding of the United Nations from the Atlantic Charter (1941) to the San Francisco conference and immediate Senate approval of the U.N. Charter for ratification (1945). It records the shift in the fundamental U.S. foreign policy from isolationism to international cooperation (in 1947 it would change again to containment of communism). It gives an account of U.S. leadership, after a great war, to put international relations on another basis than spheres of influence and balance of power. It recounts the courageous statesmanship, innovative diplomacy, responsible legislative oversight, and generous will of the American people that brought about the creation of a universal organization of states dedicated to ending 'the scourge of war'. The story here is detailed and exact. Here will be found an historical explanation for the Security Council veto, for the enforcement provisions of Chapter VII, for the novel inclusion of an Economic and Social Council with its competence in human rights, for the lack of legislative powers in the General Assembly, for the amendments at the San Francisco conference (suggestive for a future review conference), and for Senate consent *without reservations*. The authors in their final reflections discuss the weaknesses in the U.N. but argue that no stronger form of general international organization was acceptable in 1945.

245   **The influence of history on the literature of international law.**
       R.P. Anand.   In: *The structure and process of international law:*
       essays in legal philosophy, doctrine, and theory. Edited by R. St. J.
       Macdonald and Douglas M. Johnston.   The Hague: M. Nijhoff, 1983,
       p.341-80.
On a broad historical view, international law is far older and widespread than the European form that emerged at the end of the Wars of Religion (1648). Nevertheless, the author, a leading Indian scholar, traces the history of European international law through the colonial period and the founding of the United Nations in the aftermath of World War II. Two consequences were immediately apparent: the absolute sovereignty of the state was limited by majority rule in the U.N. (except for the five permanent members of the Security Council), and the colonized peoples could no longer be denied sovereign independence as states on the European model. Anand traces subsequent developments of the law under the noisy rivalries of sovereign power politics. 'Despite the vast horizontal extension of the international society and multipolar division of the world, the new world was one world.' Hence the growth of regional collective security systems like NATO, rapid growth of customs and treaties 'in the absence of a world legislature', and expansion of the law of the sea, air, and space. He concludes: 'international law has passed from the phase when it was primarily a law of coexistence to a new law of cooperation'.

246   **Multilateralism: the anatomy of an institution.**
       John Gerard Ruggie.   *International Organization*, vol. 46 (Summer
       1992), p.561-98.

Multilateralism is a core feature of the international institutional order. This article recovers the meaning of multilateralism from historical practice and suggests why it may continue to play a significant role as it has since the end of World War II. Historically, multilateralism began in institutional arrangements to define and stabilize the international property rights of states, was developed to manage coordination problems, and still promises to resolve collaboration problems. Examples include: extraterritoriality, the International Telecommunications Union, and the universal, multipurpose League of Nations and United Nations.

247   **Nation against nation: what happened to the U.N. dream and what
       the U.S. can do about it.**
       Thomas M. Franck.   New York: Oxford University Press, 1985.
       334p.

This is a sharp critique of politics in the U.N., generally from the U.S. perspective. Franck concludes with discussion of withdrawal. One possible alternative, he suggests, is a 'broader-based NATO for the defense not of boundaries but of democratic principles'. He recognizes that the proper alternative is world government, but the time for 'noble visions' was in 1945. 'Instead, there were grand illusions.'

248   **Postwar foreign policy preparation, 1939-1945.**
       Harley Notter.   Washington, DC: Department of State, 1949. 726p.
       (Pub. No. 3580, General Foreign Policy Series 15).

This is the official history of the U.S. part in founding the United Nations. Starting with rather open ideas of a 'federalized international organization – or government' (fall 1942), the Subcommittee on International Organization of the Advisory Committee on Post-War Foreign Policy, led by Sumner Welles and later by Leo Pasvolsky, went beyond Roosevelt's idea of the Four Policemen and Churchill's of Regional Councils to propose a general international organization at Dumbarton Oaks (1944) and San Francisco (1945).

249   **Power and the pursuit of peace: theory and practice in the history
       of relations between states.**
       Francis H. Hinsley.   Cambridge: Cambridge University Press, 1963.
       418p. bibliog.

This often-cited and influential book takes a broad historical approach to finding a solution to the problem of war. Hinsley surveys our stock of ideas on international peace, beginning in the Wars of Religion and continuing through the establishment of the League of Nations. Finding the international organization achieved to date wanting, he then turns to another analytical, historical study of the modern state system, whose tendency to war is still the great unsolved problem of the 20th century. This leads him to some final reflections – plainly designed to be 'scientific' and 'sane' – on improvements in the physical deterrents and public restraints on state action of the United Nations or any successor international organization.

250 **Second chance: the triumph of internationalism in America during World War II.**
Robert A. Divine. New York: Atheneum, 1967. 371p. bibliog.
This is a standard narrative history of the U.S. part in the creation of the United Nations. Emphasis is on the progress of public opinion and national politics – not diplomacy. 'In 1919 the Senate had refused to sanction American participation in the League of Nations; in 1945 few feared a repetition of that tragedy. After Pearl Harbor a small group of articulate internationalists had set out to convince the American people that their refusal to join the League had led to the Second World War. Only a new organization of nations, they preached, could guarantee an end to wars. By June of 1945, the internationalists had created such overwhelming public support that Senate approval of the U.N. Charter was a certainty. The American people were determined not to waste their second chance.'

251 **A short history of international organization.**
Gerard J. Mangone. New York: McGraw-Hill, 1954; Westport, CT: Greenwood, reprint ed., 1975. 326p.
Here is a history of the 'development of international organization along constitutional lines with attention to procedure and law, hoping to indicate a potential, though by no means inevitable, growth toward world order'. The author takes a long view, going back to the first proposals of international organization at the end of the Wars of Religion, and continuing through the Congress of Vienna, the Concert of Europe, and the League of Nations. The United Nations is covered only through its first relatively confident phase to 1954. Mangone discusses the association of the specialized agencies within the system and the rise of regional, even more 'collaborative' organizations, notably the Council of Europe (1949) and European Coal and Steel Community (1951). This is a history by a judicious and broad-spirited writer who expresses certain basic truths about sovereign states, international organization, world government, and the rule of law with a clarity not often found forty years later.

252 **Swords into plowshares: the problems and progress of international organization.**
Inis L. Claude, Jr. New York: Random House, 1956; 4th ed., 1984. 458p. bibliog.
This clear and still instructive study of the history, constitutional problems, contributions to peace, and future of international organization was written as the United Nations slipped into its marginal but persistent role for the maintenance of international peace and security during the Cold War. Claude provides plain-spoken accounts of peaceful settlement of disputes, collective security, disarmament, preventive diplomacy, debates in the General Assembly, trusteeship over former colonies, and functionalism in the specialized agencies. He concludes with discussion of the ideal of world government and then of practical next steps in international organization to achieve a working world order.

253   **United Nations conference on international organization, San Francisco, California, April 25 - June 26, 1945: Documents.**
London, New York: U.N. Information Organizations, 1945-55.
22 vols. New York: Readex Microprint, 1981.

Here is the complete verbatim record of the founding conference of the United Nations, including speeches, plenary sessions, commission debates (which produced the General Assembly, Security Council, and other organs), committee work, the journal, amendments to the Dumbarton Oaks draft charter, and final Charter. A major historical source, this work appears in English, French, some Spanish and Russian.

254   **United Nations conference on international organization, San Francisco, California, April 25 - June 26, 1945: Selected Documents.**
U.S. Department of State.   Washington, DC: Department of State, 1946. 991p. (Publication 2490, Conference Series 83).

This is the one-volume collection of proceedings during the final drafting of the U.N. Charter at San Francisco in 1945. It records controversy over the Security Council veto, enlargement of the functions of the Economic and Social Council, and Latin American demands for regional security arrangements (Art. 51 – later to become the foundation of NATO). China and fourteen small nations at the time expressed willingness to limit their national sovereignty.

255   **United Nations Documents, 1941-1945.**
Royal Institute of International Affairs.   London and New York: RIIA, 1946. 271p.

This short collection of valuable documents on the founding of the U.N. includes the Atlantic Charter (1941), United Nations declaration (1942), Lend-Lease agreement (1942) Moscow declaration (1943), UNRRA constitution (1943), Teheran Conference declaration (1943), International Labour Organization declaration at Philadelphia (1944), Bretton Woods agreements establishing the World Bank and International Monetary Fund (1944), Dumbarton Oaks draft of the U.N. Charter (1944), ICAO conference (1944), Yalta agreements (1945), San Francisco conference on the U.N. Charter and International Court of Justice Statute (1945), Potsdam agreements (1945), FAO constitution (1945), UNESCO constitution (1945), proposals for an international trade and employment organization (ITO, 1945).

256   **The United Nations in a changing world.**
Leland Goodrich.   New York: Columbia University Press, 1974.
280p. bibliog.

This work is by a leading American scholar of the United Nations who provides a cool and reasoned perspective in the depths of the Cold War. Goodrich believed that it was neither possible nor tolerable for the U.N. to evolve as the modern state did, in large part, by 'physical force'. 'Consequently, we have the problem of achieving comparable results by consent.' When he wrote, two years after the Stockholm conference on the environment (1972), he saw little prospect of 'global community' (and hence of 'world government'). But he looked forward to what twenty years later would be called global governance: 'some form of institutionalized cooperation between pluralistic communities, with a great variety of institutions, and structural, functional, and procedural arrangements'. He surveys the history of the U.N. as an 'evolving political system' with special attention to representation, power, the Secretary-General and his staff, maintaining peace and security, peacekeeping, protection of human rights, decolonization, and economic development. The book may be read as a traditional internationalist account, respectful of the realists, with an expectation of progress only as the result of leadership by the great powers.

257 **The United Nations in historical perspective: what have we learned about peacebuilding?**
Chadwick F. Alger. In: *The United Nations and a just world order.* Edited by Samuel Kim, Richard Falk, and Saul Mendlovitz. Boulder, CO: Westview, 1991, p.87-108.

This is a normative and structural overview of the U.N. system. Alger briefly reviews its history and reflects politically on the meaning of its work. He offers valuable reflections on universality, self-determination, human rights, economic development (six stages from national development alone to ecological balance or sustainable development), growth of the U.N. system, voting and consensus, and the role of the peoples in a system of states. He sees a transnational politics emerging, guided by citizen diplomats and visionary world scholars. 'The conflict produced by contending approaches to reorganize the U.N. system is helpful. . . . Actually, what is needed are institutions that are most responsive to the diverse and conflicting interests of the people of the world. . . . Fortunately the U.N. system offers a vast laboratory for experimentation.'

258 **The United States and 'collective security': notes on the history of an idea.**
Richard N. Current. In: *Isolation and security.* Edited by Alexander DeConde. Durham, NC: Duke University Press, 1957, p.33-55.

The author traces the American roots of the idea of a 'league to enforce peace' or 'collective security'. Woodrow Wilson and Franklin D. Roosevelt are the heroes of this tale, but there has always been an opposition, represented historically by William Borah and Herbert Hoover, that peace cannot be based on repeated bouts of international force. Current passes rapidly over the deceptive achievement of collective security in the United Nations of 1945 and the lip-service paid to the U.N. to cover reversion to a system of alliances. 'True, the systems of collective security were designed for "police action" against an "aggressor", not for "war" against an "enemy" . . . In fundamentals it was hard to distinguish from the timeworn statecraft of alliances designed to achieve for their adherents some kind of "balance", which usually meant pre-dominance.'

259 **The United States and the United Nations, 1945-1990.**
Gary B. Ostrower. New York: Twayne, forthcoming (1995). (Twentieth Century International History Series).

This will be an interpretive and narrative diplomatic history of the U.N. system, with special attention to its political and economic features.

260 The United States and the United Nations: the search for international peace and security.
Lawrence D. Weiler and Anne P. Simons.   New York: Manhattan Press for the Carnegie Endowment for International Peace, 1967. 589p.

This is a basic study of the history of the founding of the United Nations and the coming of the Cold War. The authors were convinced 'that international organizations – and especially the United Nations – are essential for the mangement of today's world and the search for tomorrow's peace', yet they had to recount how the hopes for 'ending the scourge of war' were soon disappointed. The book is still valuable for providing historical perspective on the opportunity lost after the Second World War by analogy with that after the Cold War.

261 The world beyond the Charter: a tentative synthesis of four stages of world organization.
C. Wilfred Jenks.   London: Allen & Unwin, 1969. 199p.

Written by a 37-year veteran of the League and the United Nations and one of the most prominent legal champions of international organization. Even in the depths of the Cold War, Jenks could look forward to a better world after its end. 'I believe that we are living through the birth-pangs of a world community and that the task of endowing that community with effective political institutions capable of maintaining the peace, entrenching human freedom, and promoting the general welfare, is the supreme political task of our time and perhaps of any time.'

Decolonization: The British, French, Dutch, and Belgian empires.
See item no. 329.

Remnants of empire: the United Nations and the end of colonialism.
See item no. 332.

International peacekeeping: history and strengthening.
See item no. 569.

Peacekeeping in international politics.
See item no. 581.

Uncertain mandate: politics of the U.N. Congo operation.
See item no. 593.

Collective security.
See item no. 608.

Diplomats, scientists, and politicians.
See item no. 656.

Pugwash – the first ten years.
See item no. 685.

The struggle against the bomb: One world or none.
See item no. 693.

The United Nations and disarmament.
See item no. 705.

Financing the U.N.

262 **Financing an effective United Nations.**
Independent Advisory Group on U.N. Financing. Shijuro Ogata and
Paul Volker, co-chairmen. New York: Ford Foundation, 1993. 34p.
(Available from Office of Communications, Ford Foundation, 320 E.
43rd St., New York, NY 10017.)

Here is a high-level study of financing for U.N. peacekeeping and its expansion at the
end of the Cold War. Future needs for peacekeeping can be foreseen in Sudan, former
Yugoslavia, Liberia, Afghanistan, Asian republics of the former Soviet Union,
Myanmar (Burma), Kashmir, Assam, Sri Lanka, Kurdistan. The U.N. peacekeeping
budget was $3,600 million in 1992-93 – up from $364 million in 1986-87. The cost is
still a bargain: the increment of $1,460 million in 1992-93 was about equal to the
budget of New York City fire and police departments. Recommendations to
governments include charging peacekeeping dues to national military defence
budgets.

263 **Financing the United Nations system.**
John G. Stoessinger with Gabriella Rosner Lande. Washington, DC:
Brookings Institution, 1964. 348p. bibliog.

This older work is basic on the history and problems of financing the Congo
peacekeeping operation. From the perspective of the 1990s, this was the 'first' U.N.
financial crisis, so this earlier work may offer historical perspective. The study covers
the U.N. political framework, the lessons of the same financial crisis for the League
of Nations (penury, irrelevance, death), costs of membership, budgeting, and new
sources of revenue (private contributions, U.N. services, levies on international
activities, taxation, exploitation of the global commons in Antarctica, the deep sea,
and outer space). But then as now, financing depends on 'what the member states
want the United Nations to be'.

264 **An international redistribution of wealth and power.**
Robert F. Meagher. New York: Pergamon, 1979. 303p.

This is a study of the earlier U.N. financial crisis, which culminated in the Helms
amendment in 1978 halting U.S. contributions to U.N. technical assistance
programmes. That was a rehearsal for the Kassebaum amendment of 1985. Meagher
deals fairly with the larger question of the demand of the great majority of humanity
and states for a more equitable sharing of wealth and power.

265   **United States financing of the United Nations.**
Robert F. Meagher.   In: *The U.S., the U.N., and the management of
global change*. Edited by Toby Trister Gati.   New York: New York
University Press for UNA–USA, 1983, p.101-28.

This is an excellent account of U.N. financing issues through the Helms amendment
of 1978 – similar to the Kassebaum amendment coming later in 1985. Causes of
Congressional dissatisfaction were: loss of U.S. and West European influence;
disagreement with such General Assembly actions as seating the People's Republic of
China in place of Nationalist China, or passing the 'Zionism is racism' resolution;
resentment at Third World demands for a larger share of wealth and power in their
New International Economic Order (NIEO); objections to financing U.N. technical
assistance programmes out of obligatory assessments; complaints about the general
rule of assessments; demands for limiting the growth of U.N. budgets.

**Image and reality; questions and answers about the United Nations;
how it works and who pays for it.**
See item no. 6.

Report of the Secretary-General on the work of the organization, 1993.
See item no. 11.

An agenda for peace.
See item no. 121.

The financing of United Nations peacekeeping operations.
See item no. 565.

Organs of the United Nations Organization

General Assembly

266 **Conscience, law, force, and the General Assembly.**
Julius Stone. In: *Jus et societas: essays in tribute to Wolfgang Friedman.* Edited by Gabriel M. Wilner. The Hague: M. Nijhoff, 1979, p.297-337.

This is an examination of the 'legal and moral bases of the pretensions of the General Assembly as an arbiter of global issues'. The author treats this matter in relation to the history of sovereign relations, the international law of 'unequal' treaties, Security Council Resolution 242 of 1967 aiming to settle the Arab–Israeli conflict, and General Assembly resolutions of 1974 to settle the whole Palestinian situation. He concludes with a severely negative view of the quasi-legal or fully legal status of resolutions of the General Assembly. He argues that the 'degree of deliberation' originally permitted in the Assembly by the founders of the United Nations has been transformed into a 'tyranny of manipulated majorities' of the Communist, Asian, and African blocs who use the forum for rhetorical attacks upon the West rather than for responsibly allocating resources (such as new OPEC wealth) to solving common problems. The Assembly has become an 'ever more dangerous weapon against the vital interests of Western States'. Stone counsels Western withdrawal or non-payment of assessments as a 'positive step toward relaxation' of tensions. The article is a virtual ideological manifesto for Western policies of damage-limitation at the United Nations during the 1980s. Read appreciatively, it is a politically perceptive call for U.N. reform to create organizational structures for the practical negotiation of consensus – 'for adjustment mechanisms which work'.

267 **Conference diplomacy: an introductory analysis.**
Johan Kaufmann. Dordrecht, The Netherlands: M. Nijhoff, 1968; rev. 2nd ed., 1988. 208p. bibliog. (E.88.III.K.PS/11).

Despite warnings of a 'crisis of multilateralism', the practice of multilateral diplomacy has grown greatly in the last forty years. This book, written by an experienced ambassador from the Netherlands to the United Nations, defines conference diplomacy and provides practical guidance to the diplomat. It outlines the characteristics of a 'delegation', reviews such qualities of a successful negotiator as truthfulness and courage, examines the role of 'groups' (nascent political parties), and provides guidance on tactics, instructions from home governments, and speeches. This is a book for the practitioner, then the scholar.

268   **Dimensions of conflict in the General Assembly.**
Hayward R. Alker, Jr.   *American Political Science Review*, vol. 58 (Sept. 1964), p.642-57.

This is an older, qualitative study of voting behaviour in the General Assembly (1961-62) with respect to various conflicts influencing the votes, such as the East–West conflict, the emerging North–South (self-determination) conflict, membership issues in the Cold War, the 'Moslem factor', supranationalism, and others. The article will be of interest mostly to political scientists familiar with factor analysis, but the determined general reader will be impressed with the possibilities of objective analysis of free human behaviour. The author concludes that the challenge of modern international conflict is 'to persuade others and ourselves of the United Nations' universal supernationalist possibilities'.

269   **The effect of resolutions of the General Assembly of the United Nations.**
D.H.N. Johnson.   *British Yearbook of International Law*, vol. 32 (1955-56), p.97-122.

The author approaches the question of the moral, political, quasi-legal, or full legal 'effect' of General Assembly resolutions by review of a narrow International Court of Justice advisory opinion of 1955 on the Assembly's competence in the South West Africa mandated territory. The World Court ruled that a two-thirds vote in the U.N. General Assembly was just as binding as a unanimous vote in the old League Assembly – in effect countenancing consensus rather than consent as a legal basis for obligation. That is, the ruling marked the passing of absolute national sovereignty. Judge Lauterpacht is quoted exactly on this point. Johnson concludes that General Assembly resolutions have more than a moral effect; they have a political and a *legal* effect, certainly on states that vote for them, and potentially on states opposed, since the resolution constitutes a 'subsidiary means for the determination of rules of law' capable of being used by an international court.

270   **The effect of the resolutions of the United Nations General Assembly.**
Gabriella R. Lande.   *World Politics*, vol. 19 (October 1966), p.83-105.

The Security Council was established as the United Nations' primary political organ, empowered to take action to maintain international peace and security. The General Assembly was secondary, empowered only to make recommendations on a broader range of issues. The thinking was that great power unanimity would permit common action to end the scourge of war, while the weakness of world community would require a deliberative body to slowly build consensus, that is, the 'principles on which world peace and the ideal of solidarity must rest'. But with the frustration of the Council through the Cold War, attention turned to the Assembly, which offered unsuspected potential for both political creativity and action. This article examines the authority, influence, and legitimacy of the General Assembly up to 1965 and measures the effectiveness of its resolutions in terms of state compliance and secondary outcomes. Typical examples include its approach to disarmament, nuclear arms control, termination of colonialism, advancement of human rights, and regulation of the uses of outer space.

271 **The effect of resolutions of the United Nations General Assembly on customary international law.**
Stephen M. Schwebel. *American Society of International Law Proceedings,* vol. 73 (1979), p.301-09.

The General Assembly is not a world legislature; hence its powers are merely recommendatory. The author, then a legal adviser to the U.S. State Department and later a judge of the World Court, considers whether recommendations are acquiring a legal (binding) character. State representatives in the Assembly, when voting, do not think of themselves as creating or changing international law, yet a series of consistent resolutions exhibits an emerging custom or general practice, which is one of the sources of international law. He explores a case in the law of the sea negotiations, where a *declaration* that the ocean floor beyond national jurisdiction was the 'common heritage of mankind' was treated (by the chairman of the Group of 77) as *international law* prohibiting unilateral exploitation – a point contradicted (by the U.S. representative) on the grounds that it was only a resolution without binding force. Schwebel then contrasts such 'confrontation' with 'consensus'. If it is genuine consensus, it is adopted with the support of all states present. If it is 'fake consensus', as in the adoption of the New International Economic Order (NIEO) in 1974 despite the declared objections of almost forty states, it is another name for confrontation. The article, then, is a warning about consensus.

272 **The General Assembly in world politics.**
M.J. Peterson. Boston: Allen & Unwin, 1986. 320p. bibliog.

Here is a fresh study of the functioning of the General Assembly 'without falling into the exaggerations being offered by neoconservatives or liberal internationalists'. The author investigates why, how, and to what degree states ignore the United Nations, particularly its general deliberative organ, the General Assembly. Some, mainly in the United States, see the U.N. 'as the weapon of a radical Third World–Soviet bloc alliance out to discredit the West, destroy free enterprise, and abolish democracy'; others, mainly in the Third World, see it 'as a place where the weak and the developing can protect their interests, restrain the strong, and promote a more equitable world order'. In the absence of a world government to bring order to anarchical world society, argues Peterson, the General Assembly still affects world politics by 'filtering' and 'channeling' the interactions of sovereign states by its rules and institutions. Some political outcomes – like the voluntary South African withdrawal from Namibia – cannot be understood without reference to the General Assembly. He traces the political process in the Assembly from desires to agenda to decisions and to implementation. He admits that the U.S.-led coalition (1945-64) has given way to a Third World coalition (1964-), but the latter at time of writing was splitting into pro-Moscow, pro-Washington, and truly non-aligned. (The collapse of Soviet power since 1991 has surely left but two poles.) The book is written with a focus on current trends similar in spirit to the most disinterested British scholarship.

273 **The General Assembly of the United Nations: A study of procedure and practice.**
Sydney D. Bailey. London: Stevens & Sons, 1960; New York: Praeger for the Carnegie Endowment for International Peace, rev. ed., 1964. 377p. bibliog.

The author sees the U.N. General Assembly on a course of historic evolution like that of the Parliament of Great Britain. This study focuses primarily on procedure, rather than politics, on the grounds, as Eleanor Roosevelt said in 1958, that at the United Nations tensions are so high that often 'good procedure' means 'the difference between success and failure'. Bailey sets out magisterially the practice of 'parliamentary diplomacy', the groups of contentious states ('an embryonic party system'), the agenda, the general debate, decisions and recommendations, committees and subsidiary organs. On the eve of Algerian independence and the great influx of former colonies into the U.N. as sovereign states, Bailey predicted that the General Assembly would acquire an 'importance' greater than any of the other organs.

274 **Parliamentary diplomacy: an examination of the legal quality of the rules of procedure of organs of the United Nations.**
Philip C. Jessup. *Recueil des Cours*, vol. 89 (1954), p.185-320.

The negotiation of consensus resolutions in the General Assembly is distinguished from traditional diplomacy and from national parliamentary procedure. This influential article remains an excellent introduction to the work of the U.N., which is transitional between the exchange of ambassadors and the enactment of law in a world legislature. Jessup explores the analogy between the development of law in early national societies and that of international law in the world today. One difference is that the world has not passed through a 'period of absolutism which in turn needed to be checked by the development of democratic institutions'! But the rules of procedure are certainly law in both institutions, and majority rule for resolutions provides the beginning for binding enactments of law by the General Assembly. The article is also a circumstantial and practical guide to the state representative in the U.N. One point of advice is not to ridicule the principles of the U.N. 'Pure opportunism and the absence of an underlying theory or principle is not persuasive. The sophisticated outsider mocks at the high-sounding principles enunciated in the United Nations Charter, but no competent delegate does so within the United Nations.'

275 **On the quasi-legislative competence of the General Assembly.**
Richard A. Falk. *American Journal of International Law*, vol. 60 (1966), p.782-91.

The author takes issue with the positivist conception of international law, enshrined in Article 38 of the ICJ Statute – that such law must be based on evidence of consent by sovereign states. Falk accepts General Assembly resolutions as law when adopted by *consensus* (without a vote). Hence the Assembly's 'quasi-legislative competence'. To justify this view, he cites decisions by a Japanese court based on *draft* rules of air warfare, by the U.S. State Department on Soviet violation of an *informal* testing moratorium, and by the U.N. members who rejected the ICJ judgment in the *Expenses* case. Other evidence indicates a 'trend from consent to consensus as the basis of international legal obligations'. Falk emphasizes that such consensus, as for Res. 1653 (XVI) of 1961 condemning use of nuclear weapons, to be effective must cross the 'fissures of the Cold War'. (After 1990, this condition was increasingly met.) He recognizes that the new Afro-Asian states are upsetting the old (imperialist) doctrines of international law and are seeking 'revision in the structure of international order'. When they form consensus with the big powers, as in resolutions condemning South African apartheid, the legislative effect is strong enough to lead to serious economic sanctions. Falk plainly argues the case for a world legislature: 'If international society is to function effectively, it requires a limited legislative authority, at minimum, to translate an overriding consensus among states into rules of order and norms of obligation despite the opposition of one or more sovereign states.'

276   **Unanimity, the veto, weighted voting, special and simple majorities, and consensus as modes of decision in international organizations.**
C. Wilfred Jenks.   In: *Cambridge essays in international law: essays in honour of Lord McNair.*   Cambridge University Faculty of Law. London: Stevens, 1965, p.48-63.

This is an authoritative account of consensus, which, since unanimity was unavailable and majority rule openly challenged the sovereign equality of states, had become, twenty years after the founding of the U.N., the most generally respected and hence effective mode of taking important decisions. The author traces the origins of the practice and its use in the programmes and specialized agencies of the U.N. system. Jenks predicts that consensus offers a way out from the unacceptability of weighted voting and the irremovability of the veto.

277   **U.N. General Assembly resolutions and international law: rethinking the contemporary dynamics of norm creation.**
Christopher C. Joyner.   *California Western International Law Journal,* vol. 11 (1981), p.445-78.

This is another legal argument on the legislative competence of the General Assembly. Its competence is transitional, and there is much legal dispute. Joyner carefully surveys this dispute, which on balance is negative; then he turns to the 'contemporary dynamics of international norm creation', which is more positive. In human rights, restraints on use of force, and outer space, the Assembly has manifestly advanced international law (both custom and treaties). At time of writing, he also expected progress in the law of the sea. He concludes that while the General Assembly is not a new source of law, like a world legislature, it contributes to the growth of customary and treaty law.

278   **For a U.N. second assembly: summary of a proposal.**
International Foundation for Development Alternatives Dossier (Nyon, Switzerland), vol. 64 (March-April 1988).

This article surveys some eighty-eight non-governmental organizations now supporting the proposal to establish a popularly representative but advisory second chamber of the General Assembly, created as another subsidiary body under Article 22. First to support it was the Medical Association for the Prevention of War (1983).

279   **The United Nations and law-making: the political organs.**
Rosalyn Higgins.   *American Society of International Law
Proceedings*, vol. 64 (1970), p.37-48.

The argument here is that the political organs of the U.N. do develop international
law (treaties and customs), for the organs exhibit state practice and also engage in
acts and pronouncements. In this article, Higgins particularly discusses decisions of
the U.N. organs about their own jurisdiction, declarations of existing law, resolutions
clarifying the law, those settling competing claims as to the law, and those adopting
new rules of law. She finds U.N. legal obligation rooted in consent, when the vote is
unanimous, or consensus, when majority rule has applied or in new areas like atomic
testing or cooperation in outer space where the votes of the superpowers 'weigh'
more than those of states not yet ready to enter the area. The General Assembly,
strictly, has no legislative competence, yet its contributions to customary international
law is immense, she argues. The law also grows by the Assembly's interpretation of
the Charter, which restrains the tendency of states to interpret it in their own
sovereign interests. Moreover, the Security Council has constitutionally binding
authority, which it exercises in the regulation of sanctions like those against
Rhodesia. And the International Court of Justice, in the controversial *South West
Africa* case (1966), provided a clear indicator of the law when it left the General
Assembly to condemn apartheid. She concludes that the U.N. does not enact *positive*
law, since it has not a 'superior authority to enforce it'; nor does it reveal *natural* law,
since it plainly pronounces and revises its resolutions. It enacts *customary* law. This
view is close to the American 'law as process' school.

280   **The United Nations Declaration on Friendly Relations and the
system of the sources of international law.**
Gaetano Arangio-Ruiz.   Alphen aan den Rijn, The Netherlands:
Sijthoff & Noordhoff, 1979. 341p. bibliog.

This is an extended legal essay on the General Assembly's declarations as law-making
acts, taking as a typical case its Res. 2625 (XXV) of 1970 on the Friendly Relations and
Cooperation among States, which reaffirmed the principles in the U.N. Charter's Article
2. The author, a professor of law at the University of Rome, concludes that the
declaration *cannot* serve as a possible material source of international law. But he adds a
long appendix on the theory of international organization which is much more interesting
from the point of view of future U.N. reform. He clarifies the notions of international
community, organization, state sovereignty, the place of the individual, and federal
government. The U.N., he argues, is not yet legally or sociologically the organization of
the universal community of people or of states. The *peoples* of the world, if they had
been really involved, could have created a juridical entity over and above the states in
1945, and in principle they could still do so. Meanwhile, the General Assembly is a
diplomatic forum for governments, not a world legislature.

281   **United Nations procedures and power realities: the international
apportionment problem.**
Richard N. Gardner.   *Department of State Bulletin*, vol. 52 (10 May
1965), p.701-11.

A State Department study of 1962 concluded that weighted voting in the Security
Council and the General Assembly would *not* be in the U.S. interest, since the
population factor would favour (slightly) the communist bloc. Other reforms

considered: dual voting (concurrent majorities), bicameralism, selective representation in key committees, informal relations with the secretariats of the U.N. and specialized agencies, and new conciliation procedures (especially in UNCTAD). The author, then Deputy Assistant Secretary of State for International Organization Affairs, inclined toward the last, since consensus was lacking for the more binding reforms. Readers after the end of the Cold War, however, may find Gardner's candour about such reforms refreshing.

282 **The Uniting for Peace Resolution on the thirtieth anniversary of its passage.**
Harry Reicher. *Columbia Journal of Transnational Law*, vol. 20 (1981), p.1-49.
The Uniting for Peace Resolution (Res. 377A (V)) was passed by the U.N. General Assembly in November 1950 during the Korean War in order to allow the Assembly to recommend action to counter acts of aggression when the Security Council was paralysed by the veto. The Soviets, then strict constructionists of the Charter, called it the 'Disuniting for War Resolution'. The author exactly surveys the history of the resolution, the legal preconditions for its exercise, the power of its recommendations, and the timetable for action. He reviews the cases when it has been applied: Korea (1950), Suez (1956), Hungary (1956), Congo (1960), Bangladesh (1971), Middle East (1980), and Afghanistan (1980). He concludes that the resolution did not (stealthily) create new powers for the General Assembly, but 're-legitimized what was already there'.

Alternative pasts: a study of weighted voting at the U.N.
See item no. 122.

The case for a United Nations parliamentary assembly.
See item no. 128.

See also International Law Commission (p.125ff.).

Security Council

283 **Consultation and consensus in the Security Council.**
Feng Yang Chai. New York: UNITAR, 1971. 55p. (PS No. 4).
This is a study on consensus in the Security Council, where, as in the General Assembly, it became by the 1960s a contender to voting for the making of respected and hence effective decisions. The author, an experienced member of the Secretariat, surveys the precedents and rules justifying the practice, analyses its concept and types, surveys the political factors favouring it (particularly the demise of 'speeches and votes' public diplomacy), compares it to conciliation, and assesses its merits and demerits. The conclusion seems to be that, like majority rule in democratic governments, consensus in international organizations is not the ideal rule but the 'only possible one'.

284   **The genesis of the veto.**
       Dwight E. Lee.   *International Organization*, vol. 1 (1947), p.33-42.

Here is an early, traditional account of why the Security Council was constituted of five permanent members possessed of a veto and six (now ten) non-permanent members not so possessed. Giving them all a veto (a rule of unanimity), as in the League Council, would have prevented establishment of a 'body capable of quick and effective action against a disturber of the peace', while giving a veto to the surviving great powers recognized their responsibility 'to guarantee it the necessary military weight'. The veto, then, was a compromise between 'democracy' and the 'realities of the concentration of power'. Lee passes over the limitations of sovereignty accepted by the states not given a veto in even a modified majority rule system. But he traces the struggle at the San Francisco conference over whether the Security Council or the General Assembly would be dominant in the new organization.

285   **The problem of the veto in the Security Council.**
       Emanuel C. Udechuku.   *International Relations* (London), vol. 4
       (1972), p.187-217.

Here is a critical article of the *arcana* of the veto – including the rule of 1946 that an abstention by a permanent member does not constitute a veto, or that a double veto may be cast, first to determine whether a matter is procedural or substantive, then, if substantive, to prevent a decision on the matter itself. The author explains why the veto power was established (to protect the nations primarily responsible for implementing decisions) and its effects (never an enforcement action against a permanent member or its ally or interest). He reviews the General Assembly Uniting for Peace resolution (1950) as one escape.

286   **The procedure of the U.N. Security Council.**
       Sydney D. Bailey.   Oxford: Clarendon Press, 1975; 2nd ed., 1988.
       424p. bibliog.

This is a standard, up-to-date study of the Security Council. Much changed between the first and second editions: the membership remains at fifteen, though Germany and Japan are knocking at the door; there is much more participation by non-members; the veto, once much used by the Soviet Union, has become mainly a Western device; informal consultation has increased. Bailey, a leading British scholar, ably surveys the institutional role of the Security Council within the U.N. system, its meetings in practice, its representatives, diplomacy and debate, voting, relations with other organs, subsidiary organs, and the future. It contains the best published list of vetoes (1946-86). The U.S. cast its first veto in a dispute over Southern Rhodesia in 1970. Statistically, the veto has not produced quite the paralysis reputed in the U.N. Of 186 issues 'seized' by the Council since 1946, there have been no vetoes on 127; on another 32 issues, there were 88 vetoes but still 459 resolutions; on the remaining 27 issues – all affecting great power vital interests (Czechoslovakia, Israel) – vetoes prevented any decision. The author admits that the threat of a veto may have prevented other issues at stake in the Cold War from being introduced at all. He concludes that amendment of the Charter – possible only at revolutionary moments in world history – does not have as much potential as flexible interpretation of the Rules of Procedure. What are needed, above all, are new national policies toward the U.N. Security Council, of which he lists ten.

287   **The Security Council as an instrument for peace.**
Hugh Caradon. In: *Multilateral negotiation and mediation:*
instruments and methods. Edited by Arthur S. Lall.   New York:
Pergamon, 1985, p.3-13.

The U.N. Security Council has the assets of small size and speed of response within
hours of a call to meet. Its procedure has evolved away from the veto toward private
negotiation and informal consultation. Open debate has become 'little more than a
ritual'. The search now is for *consensus*. The author discusses proposals for change
such as increasing Council membership (to twenty-one) and abolishing the veto (at
least for new permanent members). China favours such changes; the U.S. and U.K.
accept only a limited list of issues exempt from the veto; France and the (former)
U.S.S.R. are opposed. Caradon recounts the story of the Council's dramatic
cooperation over Res. 242 on peace in the Middle East in 1967 to show how effective
it can be when member-states are unable to settle a crisis by themselves.

288   **The Security Council in a universal United Nations.**
Arthur S. Lall.   New York: Carnegie Endowment for International
Peace, 1971. 42p. (Occasional Paper No. 11).

This short study contains fundamental criticism of the Security Council, going
beyond the usual complaints against the undemocratic veto or the unrealistic absence
of Germany and Japan as permanent members. The great power unanimity or
hegemony relied upon in 1945, Lall argues, has been superseded by new centres of
power as in China, is corruptible like all power, and cannot be maintained as a closed
and privileged system in the face of modern communications. Lall traces failure of
the Council to act – particularly on the eve of the Israeli–Arab Six Day War of 1967 –
to its unrepresentative character and to the corruptions of power. The Cold War, he
thinks, was less a cause for the Council's inaction than the fact that its permanent
members will not act when their interests are unaffected, even though they have
pledged responsibility for international peace and security. Hence, the fundamental
flaw in the Council is *representation by great powers*, which are the states most often
in conflict over their interests. To solve this, Lall inclines to a 'wider diffusion of the
decision-making power in the Security Council' – as by representation by regions
(E.C., O.A.S., etc.) or by 'small' states (some larger than France or Britain) that are
more aware of non-hegemonic issues like equitable economic development or
protection of the environment. He surveys proposals – still being discussed twenty-
five years later – to limit the veto or enlarge the Council by the permanent admission
of Brazil, India, and Japan. (Germany was not admitted to the U.N. until 1973.)
Regional representation by such states would have several advantages: it breaks away
from 'a provocative hegemony based on the possession of nuclear weapons'; it
recognizes the reality of regional associations of states; it reduces the 'potentially
dangerous confrontation' of the 'northern hegemony'; and by rationalizing and
enlarging the 'vital center' of the Council, it should increase its effectiveness.

289   **The Security Council's role in the settlement of international**
disputes.
Louis B. Sohn.   *American Journal of International Law*, vol. 78
(1984), p.402-04.

Here is a short, clear, forceful argument that the Council can act *sua sponte*, on its
own initiative, to investigate a dispute, to recommend a procedure for adjustment, or

even to suggest appropriate terms of settlement – without awaiting a state or the Secretary-General to place the matter on its agenda. Professor Sohn, like Professor Bailey, makes many suggestions for small changes in the Rules of Procedure to improve effectiveness, thus avoiding politically explosive Charter amendment. He also suggests giving the president the power to refer a matter to the Council and, too, establishing regional monitoring groups to watch and report. Compare Davidson Nicol, *The United Nations Security Council* (item no. 293).

290 Security regimes.
Robert Jervis. *International Organization*, vol. 36 (1982), p.357-78.

This article contains a standard definition of a 'regime' in current international relations theory, to which the U.N. Charter and Security Council practice make small contributions: 'Those principles, rules and norms which permit nations to be restrained in their behavior in the belief that others will reciprocate. . . . The concept implies not only norms and expectations which facilitate cooperation, but a form of cooperation which is more than the following of short-run interest.' Jervis doubts that any such international security regime yet exists. The fitful peace (150 wars) since 1945 has been produced rather by nuclear stalemate and balance of military power. One conceivable example of a real regime, he notes ironically, is Grenville Clark and Louis B. Sohn's *World peace through world law* (q.v.).

291 The United Nations, collective security, and international peacekeeping.
Brian Urquhart. In: *Negotiating world order: the artisanship and architecture of global diplomacy.* Edited by Alan K. Henrikson. Wilmington, DE: Scholarly Resources, 1986, p.59-67.

Urquhart here calls for a 'change of attitude' on the part of the leaders of the superpowers. This is now somewhat dated, since Gorbachev led the way to ending the Cold War. Nevertheless, this essay, by the former U.N. official most responsible for the development of peacekeeping from Dag Hammarskjöld's original conception, reveals the deeper, persistent issues of an effective collective security system. It needs to identify the 'common interest'; superpowers must recognize their stewardship over the 'fate of everybody else'; they must deal with security questions 'on their merits'. Urquhart's suggestions for U.N. reform are similar to Boutros-Ghali's later *An agenda for peace* (q.v.).

292 The United Nations in the Gulf crisis and options for U.S. policy.
David J. Scheffer.   New York: United Nations Association–U.S.A., 1991. 34p. (Occasional Paper No. 1).

This is the best exact record of what the Security Council did to mobilize the U.N. in response to Iraqi aggression against Kuwait. The meaning of each relevant article of the Charter is dramatically revealed. Article 42, which expressly provides for collective military action, has never been invoked and was not invoked in the case of the Persian Gulf War. Crucial resolutions were phrased, 'pursuant to Chapter VII'. Concepts revealed include: collective self-defence, collective security, enforcement, sanctions, humanitarian assistance, financing. Long-term implications: peacekeeping, peace building, Middle East settlement, international criminal court, General Assembly role, Big Five cooperation, revival of Military Staff Committee.

293 **The United Nations Security Council: towards greater effectiveness.**
Davidson Nicol with Margaret Croke and Babatunde Adeniran.   New York: UNITAR, 1982. 334p. bibliog. (E.82.XV.CR/15).

In response to growing state demands for 'improving the effectiveness of the Security Council in the discharge of its responsibilities', UNITAR in 1981 convened a seminar, reported here, of the Secretary-General, eighteen past presidents of the Council, international officials, and scholars. The book, then, is a practical, informed overview of the Security Council by practitioners who anticipated the 'ending of the cold war' and looked upon the Council as an 'institution in which the vital currents of world power were constantly faced'. Topics covered: basic facts, role of the president, informal consultations, formal meetings, and world attention. The authors conclude with suggestions for the Council to prevent conflict rather than merely react to events. Certain Charter articles would permit the Council to meet periodically not just to respond to crises but to review the general international situation, to regulate armaments, to develop international armed forces, to establish a subsidiary organ to monitor dangerous situations, to receive reports from regional organizations, to allow the president or the Council as a whole to bring matters to its attention, to set up a committee of the whole to oversee implementation of its decisions, to appoint an ombudsman or 'wise men' to improve implementation, to increase public accountability, and to regard economic and social development as the foundation of international peace and security. These ideas led to the historic Security Council summit ten years later and to *An agenda for peace* (q.v.).

294 **Voting in the Security Council.**
Sydney D. Bailey.   Bloomington: Indiana University Press, 1969. 275p. bibliog.

This is a full-scale study of the veto power to 1967, superseded by the author's *The procedure of the U.N. Security Council* (1988).

See also Enforcement (p.213ff.).

Secretary-General

295 **Anarchy or order: annual reports, 1982-1991.**
Javier Pérez de Cuéllar.   New York: United Nations, 1991. 362p. (E.91.I.52).

This is a collection of the Secretary-General's clear and often courageous reports on the work of the organization through his tenure (1982-91). No index or commentary is provided. Here the diligent reader will find out how the principal international civil servant talks sense to the political leaders of national states. At the time of the Reagan military buildup and loose talk about 'winning a nuclear war', the Secretary-General warned of a 'crisis in the multilateral approach in international affairs' and explained patiently that 'Governments in fact need more than ever a workable system of collective security in which they can have real confidence'. Pérez de Cuéllar provides a fair-spoken account of the U.N.'s part in the momentous events that led to the ending of the Cold War. He includes a 'vision of what can be accomplished through the United Nations in bringing about a safer, more equitable, and more prosperous world' (1987), and he offers hope for the 'banishment of war from international relations' (1989).

296 **Bending with the winds: Kurt Waldheim and the United Nations.**
Seymour M. Finger and Arnold A. Saltzman.   New York: Praeger,
1990. 129p. bibliog.

How could a man who had hidden his war-time service with the German *Wehrmacht* in the Balkans (and possible complicity in war crimes there) have risen to the office of Secretary-General of the United Nations? This book is not just an exposé but a serious exploration of what the office of Secretary-General meant through the Cold War and of how, as that war ended in about 1988, a new Secretary-General, Javier Pérez de Cuéllar, was able to assume a more active role and give 'new life to the United Nations'. The authors close with suggestions for a revitalized U.N. and a more effective Secretary-General at a 'crossroads' like that in 1945.

297 **Betrayal: the untold story of the Kurt Waldheim investigation and
cover-up.**
Eli Rosenbaum with William Hoffer.   New York: St. Martin's, 1993.
538p.

This is a well-documented narrative of the investigation of 'Kurt Waldheim's life lie'. It contains an appendix of Waldheim's military service, most of which, through 1945, was in Montenegro, Bosnia, Albania, and Greece, where he took part in campaigns against the Yugoslav partisans and in deportations of prisoners to slave labour camps in Norway and Germany. He also assisted in Waffen-SS operations that deported Greek Jews to Auschwitz. The principal author of this book was general counsel for the World Jewish Congress and now serves in the U.S. Justice Department. The U.N. connection is treated on occasion throughout the story, but the implication is plainly that the election of such an apparent war criminal to the post of Secretary-General was an international scandal.

298 **Building the future order: the search for peace in an
interdependent world.**
Kurt Waldheim. Edited by Robert L. Schiffer. Foreword by Brian
Urquhart.   New York: Free Press, 1980. 262p.

Here is a synthesis of the Secretary-General's key reports and statements over his two terms (1971-81), edited when primary attention, as Brian Urquhart says, was focused on Waldheim's 'civilized and constructive approach to the great problems' of the world. The aim, says the editor, is 'to suggest the extent to which the United Nations . . . is now involved in some way in practically every major global problem and in practically every area of human activity, and how the Secretary-General, in overseeing and directing the work of the Organization, daily encounters "the height of human aspiration and the depth of human frailty"'. The book is divided into sections parallel to the U.N.'s main concerns (maintenance of international peace and security, creation of conditions of well-being, etc.) and hence provides a picture of the U.N. as it took up new global responsibilities, notably in economic development and human rights.

299 **In the cause of peace: seven years with the United Nations.**
Trygve Lie. New York: Macmillan, 1954. 473p.

These are memoirs of the tumultuous first years of the U.N. (1945-53). The organization, in Lie's view, was developing international law toward enforceable world law within a universal world society. Meanwhile, however, the U.N. remained a voluntary association of nations, not a world government. The Secretary-General recounts, from his elevated vantage point, the beginnings of the Cold War, starting up the U.N. Organization, the Baruch plan for the international control of atomic energy (which failed), the civil war in Greece and the Truman doctrine, the Palestinian crisis and the founding of Israel, the Soviet blockade of Berlin, Chinese Communist representation (delayed until 1971), and the Korean War.

300 **The challenge of peace.**
Kurt Waldheim. Preface by Brian Urquhart. New York: Rawson Wade, 1980. 158p.

This is a book of reflections by Secretary-General Waldheim through the bulk of his years in office (1971-81), during a slow ebb in the fortunes of the U.N. Urquhart emphasizes the constitutional weakness of the office: 'It is unique in its range, its moral acceptance, and its almost complete lack of conventional power.' Waldheim very politically, without offensiveness, surveys the work of the U.N. during these years when U.S.–U.S.S.R. détente failed and the Cold War resumed. Chapters on 'A mirror of the world' and 'Powers and limitations of the United Nations' are still instructive. In the last chapter, 'Into the future', he dared to hope for only slow progress. 'Rome was not built in a day. . . . If national sovereignty and national interests are still primary motivations of governments, there is an increasing willingness to discuss international responsibility and control as the indispensable framework of an interdependent world.'

301 **The challenging role of the U.N. Secretary-General: making 'the most impossible job in the world' possible.**
Edited by Benjamin Rivlin and Leon Gordenker. Foreword by Brian Urquhart. New York: Praeger, 1993. 301p. bibliog.

This book is a major re-evaluation of the Secretary-General's role in world politics after the end of the Cold War. Originally, as Brian Urquhart explains in his foreword, the Secretary-General was conceived in the tradition of the Secretary-General of the League of Nations, as a chief administrative officer – a 'moderator', as Franklin D. Roosevelt once called him. But the world has changed greatly after another world war. The U.N. is no longer a bureaucratic and diplomatic organ, but one that necessarily has responded to needs that no state can meet alone, particularly in peacekeeping, economic development, and all the 'global problems'. Moreover, the U.N. is now responding to problems within states, especially human rights violations and needs for humanitarian assistance, which can no longer be ignored as not affecting international peace and security. The Secretary-General is increasingly drawn into this new global problematique. Leon Gordenker concludes with summary reflections on the transition of the Secretary-General from administrator to leader within an institution still aiming at international cooperation.

302   **Countenance of truth: the United Nations and the Waldheim case.**
Shirley Hazzard.   New York: Viking, 1990. 179p.

Beginning as an exposé of former U.N. Secretary-General Kurt Waldheim (who, after
his U.N. service, was revealed to have fought in Hitler's *Wehrmacht* and possibly to
have supported expulsions of Greek Jews), this readable and absorbing book turns to
a general indictment of the moral and political pretensions of the United Nations. It
became one of those books, like the Heritage Foundation tracts, that captured the
American public's disenchantment with the U.N. Hazzard chronicles the subversion
of the international civil service, particularly by the United States after 1949 (the FBI
installed an office to conduct loyalty tests right inside the new Secretariat building in
1953), and carries the story through comparable abuses by the Soviets (who seconded
their nationals on very temporary rotations), and by the Third World (who took every
advantage of 'equitable geographic distribution'). Brian Urquhart defended the U.N.
at the crossroads of power politics in the pages of the *New York Review of Books*.
Hazzard closes her book with a reference to Maurice Bertrand's *Some reflections on
the reform of the United Nations* (1985). 'Any new organization', she writes, 'that is to
contribute to the conduct of world affairs a meaning far beyond governmental
maneuvering will be brought forth by public pressure stimulated by the rightful and
insistent hopes of a fresh generation.'

303   **Dag Hammarskjöld revisited: the U.N. Secretary-General as a
force in world politics.**
Edited by Robert S. Jordan.   Durham, NC: Carolina Academic Press
for the Institute of International Studies, University of South Carolina,
1983. 197p. bibliog.

Here are retrospective and critical essays by leading scholars and international civil
servants on the office of Secretary-General. The emphasis is on Hammarskjöld and
the U.N. as he tried to guide it out of the Cold War. 'Secretary-General
Hammarskjöld and all who have followed him have made great gains for the process
of multilateral diplomacy, a first step in the direction of an ultimate goal to create a
world community.' Mark Zacher's essay on 'Hammarskjöld's conception of the
United Nations' role in world politics' is probably the most future-oriented, for it
looks at both his innovations in conflict management (peacekeeping) and his views on
institutional development of the U.N. ('organic growth' toward 'world federation').
Such growth involved the progress of peaceful coexistence, international cooperation,
evolution of the national missions to the U.N. in close contact with the Secretariat,
gradual acceptance of Security Council decisions as binding and then of General
Assembly resolutions as 'common law', and finally continued expansion of the
Secretary-General's executive action, as in fielding peacekeeping missions.
Hammarskjöld sometimes dared to play the role of a *vox populorum*, the voice of the
general will of humanity, but he always remembered that he could not get too far
ahead of states and their peoples.

304   **Empowering the United Nations.**
Boutros Boutros-Ghali.   *Foreign Affairs*, vol. 71 (Winter 1991-92),
p.89-102.

The Secretary-General sees a historic opportunity 'to expand, adapt, and reinvigorate
the work of the United Nations so that the lofty goals as originally envisioned by the
Charter can begin to be realized'. He reviews recent peacekeeping operations

(fourteen new ones since 1988; five completed) and calls for speeded-up deployments (now delayed for three to four months), a start-up capital fund, equipment stocks held in reserve, and designated national units of soldiers and police, trained in peacekeeping techniques and ready to be detached for U.N. service. A U.N. *standing* force is rejected as 'impractical and inappropriate' for the time being. He also repeats his call for stronger 'peace enforcement units' to compel parties to a ceasefire to respect it, even though such enforcement 'goes beyond peacekeeping'. He reflects on the U.N. role in collective security and economic and social development, on declining absolute national sovereignty in favour of 'universal sovereignty that resides in all humanity', and on the necessity for international cooperation. U.N. reform will take many years, he argues, for the 'world is still in some ways in its "Middle Ages" when it comes to international organizations and cooperation'. As the feuding barons were only slowly disciplined by the monarchical states, after which those states were transformed into modern republics, so the international system will only slowly learn to cooperate. 'Governments increasingly prove ineffective in efforts to guide or even keep track of these [political and economic] flows of ideas, influences, and transactions.' For the spirit of the U.N. to thrive, the *culture* of states and peoples in their international relations must undergo a transformation. 'Peace-building' to restore inter- and intra-national order after conflict will be part of this transformation. So will 'empowerment of people in civil society and . . . at all levels of international society'.

305 **In the eye of the storm: a memoir.**
Kurt Waldheim. Bethesda, MD: Allen & Adler, 1986. 278p.
Written just before the storm broke (1986) over his World War II German army service, this book is a personal account of Waldheim's 'background, actions, and aspirations' in forty years of diplomatic service, including his years as U.N. Secretary-General (1971-81). Events covered include his wartime service (to 1941), entry into the diplomatic corps, the Austrian treaty of 1955 ending the post-war occupation, U.N. service, the Yom Kippur War of 1973, peacekeeping, the new majority of Third World states, human rights, refugees, the Iranian hostage crisis of 1979-81, the war in Afghanistan, and the 'tarnished image' of the U.N. – 'the creature of its sovereign member states'. He closes with some thoughtful reflections on power politics and the eclipse of the U.N. by the Cold War. 'It was the tragic involvement of Europe in two world wars that engendered in me, as in so many of its citizens, the hope that national power politics could be overcome, and gave birth to my dream of a supranational world government.'

306 **The first fifty years; the Secretary-General in world politics, 1920-1970.**
Arthur W. Rovine. Leiden, The Netherlands: Sijthoff, 1970. 498p. bibliog.
The office of Secretary-General has slowly expanded toward greater power and responsibility for the maintenance of world peace. This history concentrates on the 'political' development of the office as a neutral third party in the resolution of conflict. It has less to say about the Secretariat's role in economic development, promotion of human rights, or advancement of international law. It exhibits the 'great sweep of history' as the world develops a 'chief executive'. Secretaries-General covered: Sir Eric Drummond (1920-33), Joseph Avenol (1933-40), Sean Lester (1940-46), Trygve Lie (1946-53), Dag Hammarskjöld (1953-61), U Thant (1961-71).

Rovine closes with an analysis of the Secretary-General's resources and functions in the evolving U.N.

307 Hammarksjöld.
Brian Urquhart. New York: Harper, 1972. 655p.
This is a vivid biography of the most creative and resourceful Secretary-General, written by a close associate. Hammarskjöld devised the practice of preventive diplomacy and peacekeeping in order to reconfirm the value of a general international security organization at a time of headlong decline into the Cold War. Urquhart tells the story with a view to the long-term significance of the U.N. Hammarskjöld 'showed that one man, if sufficiently spirited and courageous, could stand up for principle against even the greatest powers. . . . In speaking up for the common interest in peace and decency, he also showed the potential of the office of the Secretary-General, as a political organ of the United Nations, to act when intergovernmental organs, and especially the Security Council, were frustrated by the conflicting interests of the great powers.'

308 International administration: its evolution and contemporary applications.
Edited by Robert S. Jordan. New York and London: Oxford University Press, 1971. 299p. bibliog.
This is a very broad study of international administration or international civil service, with special attention to the British secretariat tradition, E.C. regional experience, and U.N. administration of early peacekeeping operations. It concludes with Dag Hammarskjöld's classic essay, 'The international civil servant in law and in fact' (1961), written in response to Nikita Khrushchev's charge, 'While there are neutral countries, there are no neutral men.'

309 International bureaucracy: an analysis of the operation of functional and global international secretariats.
Thomas G. Weiss. Lexington, MA: Lexington Books, 1975. 187p. bibliog.
By the mid-1970s, as 'realist' indifference to international organizations began to wear thin, studies like this from a 'world order' perspective began to appear. 'The working hypothesis for this book is that the unwieldy administrative structures of functional secretariats are counterproductive to the idealistic goals that they have been created to pursue.' The author judges the system of bureaucratic secretariats by the standard of a 'more equal distribution of the world's resources', and he makes 'modest' recommendations for reform, such as further decentralizing the specialized agencies and increasing the turnover of staff (to increase the 'commitment to planetary interests'). Very closely studied are UNICEF and ILO.

310 The international civil service: changing role and concepts.
Edited by Norman A. Graham and Robert S. Jordan. New York: Pergamon for UNITAR, 1980. 245p. bibliog.
The traditional ideal of an international civil service was a 'cadre of permanent career officials recruited on the basis of merit who would place their loyalty to the organization above all other loyalties'. The authors discuss challenges to this ideal by

the Third World demand for equitable geographical distribution, the Soviet bloc practice of temporary assignments, and Western charges of politicization. Administrative reforms are proposed for recruitment, career development, and admission of women.

311 **International peace and security: thoughts on the twentieth anniversary of Dag Hammarskjöld's death.**
Brian Urquhart. *Foreign Affairs*, vol. 60 (Fall 1981), p.1-16.
Here is a rare article in the lead journal of American foreign policy, which, the editor notes, tends to 'neglect' the U.N. Urquhart bravely draws on Hammarskjöld's leadership in order to call for 'renewed study' of the U.N. as it enters a 'period of public doubt and skepticism'. He supports the concept of a 'strong and independent United Nations' as founded by national governments in 1945 in their common interests. In the depths of the Cold War, Hammarskjöld had a vision of an 'international conscience' forming within the U.N., which he as Secretary-General could guide using the small nations as innovators, great powers as reluctant allies, and international law as the lasting achievement of their cooperation. Urquhart focuses on why states, especially the permanent members, are reluctant to have recourse to the Security Council, even though in times of supreme crisis, as in the Cuban missile crisis of 1962, or the Middle East war of 1973, the Council has substantially helped to avoid a larger war. He calls the cause 'expediency' – another name for sovereign power, while international organization has been made too weak and hence is unreliable to keep the peace. The article is a patient appeal to reason leading to the world statesmanship of Secretary-General Javier Pérez de Cuéllar in 1982.

312 **The nature of United Nations bureaucracies.**
Edited by David Pitt and Thomas G. Weiss.   Boulder, CO: Westview, 1986. 199p. bibliog.
This is a recent work of collaborative social science on the 'dynamics of the people and structures charged with international cooperation' – not on the politics or economics of the U.N. Scholars are beginning to shift their sights from national organizations to international ones. The authors come from the 'humanistic, liberal middle' and 'write from sorrow rather than anger about the declining fortunes of the U.N. They do not want its dissolution, even if they want its reform.' Although this book will be of interest primarily to peace researchers, attentive readers will be able to glean useful information on the U.N. bureaucracy, UNCTAD, UNESCO, regional organizations, and other specialized agencies. The last chapter by Paul Streeten, 'The United Nations: unhappy family', is full of clever observations and prescriptions on UNESCO, WHO, FAO, ILO, UNIDO, UNCTAD, and UNDP. Streeten would like them all to become ministries within a limited world government, or, failing that, to be linked by a better career civil service.

313 **Public papers of the Secretaries-General of the United Nations.**
Edited by Andrew W. Cordier and Wilder Foote.   New York: Columbia University Press, 1969-77. 8 vols.
This is the full record of the collected political speeches and writings most likely to be of use for history of Secretaries-General Trygve Lie, Dag Hammarskjöld, and U Thant. For Kurt Waldheim, see: *Building the future order* (item no. 298); for Javier

Pérez de Cuéllar, see: *Anarchy or order* (item no. 295); and for Boutros Boutros-Ghali, see: *Report on the work of the organization* (item no. 11).

314   **The role of the U.N. Secretary-General.**
Javier Pérez de Cuéllar.   In: *United Nations, divided world*. Edited by
Adam Roberts and Benedict Kingsbury.   Oxford: Oxford University
Press, 1988, p.61-77.

Here are wise and authoritative reflections about the political and administrative functions of the Secretary-General. Pérez de Cuéllar does not mince words about the fundamental weakness in the U.N.: 'No authority delegated to the Secretary-General, and no exercise by him of this authority, can fill the existing vacuum in collective security. The vacuum is due to dissension among the Permanent Members of the Security Council, to the failure of member states to resort to the Charter's mechanisms for the settlement of disputes, and to their lack of respect for the decisions of the Security Council.' He reviews the Secretary-General's role in preventive diplomacy, mediation, and good offices, including his proper action when parties to a conflict seem 'immune to rational persuasion'. He supports a greater information gathering function in the Secretariat, defends independence in the international civil service, calls for resolution of the financial crisis, a concludes with his personal faith.

315   **The secretariat of the United Nations.**
Sydney D. Bailey.   New York: Praeger for the Carnegie Endowment
for International Peace, 1962; rev. ed., 1964. 128p. bibliog.

This is a somewhat dated but still useful historical and political study of the U.N. Secretariat by a perceptive British scholar, who draws many clarifying comparisons to national politics. 'The General Assembly and the [Security, Economic and Social, and Trusteeship] Councils are like legislatures; the International Court is a judiciary; the Secretariat is analogous to a civil service. . . . The differences, however, are significant. . . . In the United Nations system there are several "legislatures", not one, and there is no "government". . . .' The author has a vivid sense of the U.N. on a course of historic change. The book will offer much light when read with another written in its spirit after the Cold War.

316   **The Secretary-General of the United Nations: his political powers
and practice.**
Stephen M. Schwebel.   Cambridge, MA: Harvard University Press,
1952. 299p. bibliog.

This is an early, rather confident and glowing account of the establishment of the office of the U.N. Secretary-General and of its history through most of Trygve Lie's term (1946-53). Very little is said about the coming of the Cold War. The U.N. Secretary-General was given more of a 'political role' (mostly in Article 99) than the League's comparable official, but Schwebel emphasizes that this potential will have to be cautiously realized. He includes a haunting note on the resignation of the League's Joseph Avenol at a time of general failure of the organization (1940). The book may be regarded as an historical document of the early U.N. Secretariat. Compare Rovine, *The first fifty years* (item no. 306).

317 **Sheathing the sword: the U.N. Secretary-General and the prevention of international conflict.**
Thomas E. Boudreau. Foreword by James S. Sutterlin. New York: Greenwood, 1991. 188p. bibliog.

The 'global political role' of the Secretary-General is based on Articles 98 and 99 of the U.N. Charter. The end of the Cold War provides the author with an occasion for this re-examination of the at times independent political role of the Secretary-General. Boudreau briefly lays down the constitutional foundations of the Secretary's power, recounts the history of the office from Trygve Lie to Javier Pérez de Cuéllar, then devotes the last half of the book to 'reform and renewal'. Preventive diplomacy, global watch, early warning, an independent international intelligence service, ambassadors in troubled states, enhanced quiet diplomacy, conciliation and intervention, satellite communication, and a multilateral war risk reduction centre are discussed in depth. He concludes with a call for states-members to work with the Secretary-General in a 'preventive partnership'.

318 **Trygve Lie and the Cold War: the U.N. Secretary-General pursues peace, 1946-1953.**
James Barros. DeKalb, IL: Northern Illinois University Press, 1989. 445p.

This is a critical history of the first Secretary-General (1946-53). The author finds that neither Lie nor the new U.N. was a match for the 'power struggle' between the surviving great sovereign powers that emerged from World War II – the United States and the Soviet Union. He credits Lie with attempting more than Secretaries-General under the League, but his weakness was fundamentally constitutional. 'The problem that Lie faced and failed to surmount can be traced not only to its insoluble nature but to false assumptions by Lie as to the influence that a secretary-general can wield in world politics, keeping in mind the lack of real physical power in military terms.'

319 **U.N. élites: perspectives on peace.**
Christine Sylvester. *Journal of Peace Research*, vol. 17 (1980), p.305-23.

This survey of 126 high-ranking officials in the U.N. Secretariat and members of permanent delegations sought their views about 'peace'. The author finds that they value economic welfare and social justice more than maintenance of peace and security. This finding is consistent with trends of the U.N. agenda and known predilections of 'nationalistic élites to attain preferred ends'. Sylvester infers that 'peace is valued largely by global minded élites' and concludes that 'cognitive and socialization impediments to peace . . . may require reconciliation before policy progress can be made'. Stripped of jargon and the illusions of quantification, this amounts to saying, The U.N. is an organization of sovereign states that have barely begun to perceive their common interests in cooperation.

320 **The U.N. Secretary-General and the maintenance of peace.**
Leon Gordenker. Foreword by Leland Goodrich. New York: Columbia University Press, 1967. 380p.

This is a study of the Secretary-General's influence on the U.N. Organization and on states in cases when the use of armed force has recently occurred or threatens to occur immediately. The book was written in the afterglow of Dag Hammarskjöld's brilliant leadership in setting up the U.N. Emergency Force (UNEF I, 1956-67), the first 'peacekeeping' force. It is significant that no scholar in the 1930s would have undertaken a similar study of the Secretary-General of the League. By 1967, the Secretary-General of the United Nations necessarily had acquired (if he had not been expressly granted) far greater authority to intervene in breaches of the peace, though his powers were decidedly limited (Article 99).

321 U Thant: the search for peace.
June Bingham.   New York: Knopf, 1966. 300p. bibliog.

This laudatory biography was completed while U Thant was still Secretary-General. Only the epilogue, 'The view from the 38th floor', deals with his U.N. experience. At that point, he was noted for his broad views on food distribution, equitable economic development, education, good offices in ending the war in Vietnam, and peacekeeping missions to Cyprus and Kashmir; his (legally required) decision to withdraw the peacekeeping force from the Sinai, which touched off the Six Day War in 1967, was still ahead. The author includes several appendixes on Burmese history and the Buddhist Eightfold Path, which help to explain this humble international public servant.

322 View from the U.N.
U Thant.   Garden City, NY: Doubleday, 1978. 508p.

Here are memoirs of the Secretary-General's difficult two terms (1961-71). Events covered include: the Soviet Union's *troika* proposal for a plural chief administrative officer, U Thant's frustrated mediation to end the Vietnam War, his more successful effort to resolve the Cuban missile crisis, his legally required but politically disastrous decision to withdraw UNEF I, which precipitated the Arab–Israeli Six Day War of 1967, his frustration over U.S. intervention in the Dominican Republic in 1965 and Soviet intervention in Czechoslovakia in 1968, and his tragic inability to settle the war between India and Pakistan that resulted in the separation of Bangladesh in 1971. He closes with eloquent reflections on the 'global challenges' now facing humanity – particularly the division of the world into rich and poor, North and South. He surveys the slow progress of the first U.N. Development Decade (1961-71) and the achievements of WHO and other specialized agencies. 'A new quality of planetary imagination is demanded from all of us as the price of human survival. . . . I am making a plea . . . for a dual allegiance . . . to the human race as well as to our local community or nation. . . . Perhaps my own Buddhist upbringing has helped me more than anything else to realize and express in my speeches and writings this concept of world citizenship.'

Economic and Social Council

323 ECOSOC: options for reform.
John P. Renninger.   New York: UNITAR, 1981. 33p. (Policy and Efficacy Studies No. 4. C.81.XV.PE/4).

By 1977, there was widespread consensus that the Economic and Social Council (Ecosoc) 'is not working well at a time when the world is beset by very grave problems both in terms of the state of the world economy and the issue of global economic relations'. The author reviews the official responsibilities and the practical problems of Ecosoc (duplication of effort, lack of focus, dispersal of authority, legacy of distrust). He recounts past reform efforts, particularly that in 1979 establishing a Director-General for Development and International Economic Cooperation directly below the U.N. Secretary-General. Bolder measures include abolition of Ecosoc, expanding it to plenary size, and limiting its role. Compare proposals by Maurice Bertrand for an 'Economic Security Council' in *A third generation world organization* (1989) (item no. 164) or those of the United Nations Association–U.S.A. in *A successor vision* (1988) (item no. 163).

324 **The restructuring of the United Nations economic and social system: background and analysis.**
Davidson Nicol and John P. Renninger. *Third World Quarterly*, vol. 4 (1982), p.74-92.

'Eighty percent of the budgets of the organizations in the U.N. system are today devoted to the promotion of economic and social development.' The authors survey the 'growth and fragmentation' of the system and review past attempts at reform, particularly in response to the New International Economic Order (NIEO, 1974-79). Proposals were made to create a post of Director-General for Development directly under the Secretary-General, to consolidate most funds for pre-investment, to revitalize Ecosoc, replace UNCTAD by an international trade organization (ITO), and coordinate the specialized agencies. Only the first was achieved. Nicol and Renninger describe the reform process from the points of view of the developing countries (they wanted a link to NIEO), the developed ones (a more cost-effective U.N.), and the bureaucracy (careers advanced). NIEO was defeated, efficiency was set back, and only a few careers were advanced. They conclude, however, that the effort 'brought increased attention to the issue of reform and rationalization and helped establish the parameters within which future reform efforts will be initiated'. (By 1985, Maurice Bertrand would launch another attempt to create an 'Economic U.N.', building on this earlier attempt.)

325 **The United Nations Economic and Social Council.**
Walter R. Sharp. New York: Columbia University Press, 1969. 322p.

This is a study of Ecosoc as it began to 'slide into obsolescence'. The author, a pre-quantitative political scientist, discusses the organ's origins, operations, representative character (its size had recently been increased from 18 to 27, and it would be enlarged again to 54 in 1973), decision-making, economic policy forum, administration and budget, coordination of the specialized agencies and other U.N. programmes (failing), and its future. He foresees that Ecosoc could continue to decline, or be radically reformed into a 'functionally centralized model', or, between these two extremes, be salvaged by a 'pragmatic course'. The book may still be of interest to those who cannot find another introduction to Ecosoc.

326 **World economic survey, 1993: current trends in the world economy.**
Department of International Economic and Social Affairs.
New York: United Nations, 1947- . annual. 258p. (E.93.II.C.1).

This is an annual analysis of major current trends, emerging issues, and national and international policies in the world economy. The 1991 edition covers the state of the world economy, a net zero growth in output due to the transition in the Soviet Union from a command economy to the market system, uncertainty about the multilateral approach to trade (GATT), continued net transfer of financial resources *from the developing countries* to the developed, implications of the Persian Gulf War for the oil market, complex problems of Eastern Europe and the Soviet Union as they undergo economic reform, the continuing debt crisis, military spending after the Cold War, and the poverty of women. It includes a statistical annex of standardized macroeconomic and international financial data.

A successor vision.
See item no. 163.

A third generation world organization.
See item no. 164.

See also Economic development (p.338ff.).

Trusteeship Council

327   **Colonialism, neo-colonialism, and decolonization.**
      Mohammad Hakim Aryubi. *UNESCO Courier*, vol. 26 (November 1973), p.28-31.
This brief article summarizes the achievements of decolonization since 1945, and especially since the General Assembly's Declaration on the Granting of Independence to Colonial Countries and Peoples (1960). The author points out the remaining colonies to be freed (in 1973): Angola, Mozambique, Southern Rhodesia, Namibia. Other articles in this issue of the *Courier* convey the atmosphere of decolonization: 'freedom fighters', 'liberation movements'.

328   **Decolonization and world peace.**
      Brian Urquhart. Austin: University of Texas Press, 1989. 121p.
Here is a short book on decolonization from the U.N. point of view, written by the official who largely presided over peacekeeping. Urquhart takes a broad political view in which the 'old order' of a 'hegemony of a few great empires' was put on a course of replacement, in 1945, by a 'world of sovereign, independent states working together in a system of collective security'. By the mid-1980s, the excesses of self-determination, the demands for a new international economic order by the emerging majority of the human race, the superimposition of East–West rivalry on Third World national conflicts, he argues, had produced a situation ripe for a third approach to 'reliable and effective international systems'. We are in the midst of the 'revolution' of managing the transition to 'one world'.

329 **Decolonization: the British, French, Dutch, and Belgian empires, 1919-1963.**
Henri Grimal. Translated by Stephan DeVos.   Paris: A. Colin, 1965;
Boulder, CO: Westview, 1978. 443p. bibliog.

The French author here presents a broad and judicious history of the whole process of decolonization, which in general was the converse of European expansion since the 15th century. The independence of colonies of Europeans like the U.S.A. was achieved, as Turgot said, just as ripe fruit drops from the tree, but that of native people, regarded by Western powers as 'backward', was very much harder. The First World War broke the mystique of European superiority, and the Second brought actual victories of 'coloured' peoples. It spread ideas like self-determination until the demand for independence and self-government became a flood. Grimal traces the long preparation for decolonization, then recounts the achievement first in Asia (1945-54), second in Africa (1956-63). The U.N.'s part – along with other outside forces such as the Christian churches, Marxist ideology, and the anticolonial policies of the U.S.A. – is fully treated, as is the somewhat limited role of the Trusteeship Council over former mandated territories. Grimal in his conclusion credits 'colonial nationalism' with decolonization, even though many peoples, especially in Africa, did not have an historical past in a national state. They accepted colonial boundaries for their new states, no matter how absurd. Nationalism on European models was the last heritage of colonial masters. Grimal is aware of alternatives like commonwealth and political federation, especially to build the economic foundations of independence, and he closes the history with the thought that colonial empires will cease to exist only when the dependent peoples have achieved full equality.

330 **International trusteeship system.**
Liu Chieh.   *International Conciliation*, vol. 448 (February 1949),
p.97-106.

This is a short introduction to the trusteeship system, written soon after the founding of the United Nations. The author explains the principles and purposes of trusteeship (Charter, Chapter XI), its operations (Chapter XII), and the Trusteeship Council (Chapter XIII). The colonial system, which antedated even the League of Nations, technically remained outside the trusteeship system, but the Charter contemplated that the former would be displaced by the latter (Article 77.1(c)). Chieh distinguished between the Administering Authorities, which exercised sovereign administrative, legislative, and judicial powers over the trust territories, and the Trusteeship Council, which 'supervised' the Administering Authorities – an early instance (as in the U.N. Temporary Executive Authority peacekeeping operation in West Irian, 1962-63) in which the U.N. exercised sovereign powers, despite formal denials.

331 **Problems of the trusteeship system: a study of political behavior in the United Nations.**
George Thullen.   Geneva: Droz, 1964. 217p. bibliog.

The author recounts the history and politics of trusteeship, especially through the decade before 1964, when 'anticolonialism nearly eclipsed security issues at the center of United Nations attention'. Thullen's work is more analytical than earlier descriptive studies, like those of Murray and Toussaint. All the imperial colonies were not in the trusteeship system, but the Trusteeship Council brought the trust territories into the modern world, and the General Assembly hurried and guided the rest. Thullen includes a close study of French and British Togoland.

332 Remnants of empire: the United Nations and the end of colonialism.
David W. Wainhouse.   New York: Harper & Row for the Council on Foreign Relations, 1964. 153p.

This is a history of decolonization during its final years. The author gives due credit to the U.N. Trusteeship Council and to subsidiary organs of the General Assembly. In retrospect thirty years later, the relatively peaceful dismantling of the European empires and the achievement of self-government by the former dependent peoples must seem like a quiet triumph for the United Nations – a model for the cooperative solution of other great political and social problems in the nascent world community. Wainhouse tells the story with comprehension and exactness in the cases of Portuguese, South African, British, Australian, New Zealand, and U.S. colonialism (the French case is left out). Anticipating the coming Third World challenge to the U.N., he warned in 1964: 'Until a new relationship of mutual cooperation between newly independent nations and the more advanced Western states can develop, much will still be heard of colonialism and neocolonialism.'

333 The trusteeship system of the United Nations.
Charmian E. Toussaint.   New York: Praeger for London Institute of World Affairs, 1956; Westport, CT: Greenwood, 1976. 288p. bibliog.

This is a standard account of the U.N. trusteeship system by a British scholar sympathetic to the better colonial systems of 'some Powers'. 'The importance of the Trusteeship System is that it complements, rather than replaces, national colonial administration. It tackles the problem of colonial rivalry between States and thus contributes to the maintenance of international peace and security.' Toussaint covers the system's history, its scope and aims, its law and institutions, the Trust Agreements, supervision by the Trusteeship Council, administration, and relation to dependent (colonial) territories outside the system, but does not take up the larger issue – still hard to anticipate in 1956 – of decolonization.

334 The United Nations and decolonization.
David A. Kay.   In: *The United Nations: past, present, and future*. Edited by James Barros.   New York: Free Press, 1972. p.143-70.

By the end of the 19th century, J.A. Hobson and others argued convincingly that the imperial struggle for colonies was a principal cause of war. By 1972, the work of decolonization by the League of Nations and then the United Nations was so far advanced that it was possible for the author to make this brief retrospective assessment. Kay sets out the provisions in the U.N. Charter designed to bring former colonies into the trusteeship system *or* to leave them as non-self-governing territories but to enjoin special responsibilities on their colonial governments. (The latter were eight times more numerous.) He then describes the work of the General Assembly particularly after the Declaration on Colonialism of 1960, partly influenced by the Soviet Union in its struggle with the West. He carries the story as far forward as the then (1972) very difficult cases of Rhodesia, South Africa, Angola, and Mozambique. There were in all then forty-four territories still under colonial rule. (By 1994, there were ten non-self-governing ones left.)

335 **The United Nations and decolonization: the role of Afro-Asia.**
Yassin El-Ayouty. The Hague: M. Nijhoff, 1971. 286p. bibliog.
Africa has been the scene of the most dramatic progress of decolonization. At the
founding of the U.N., there were 4 African member-states; by 1960, there were 22; by
1971, 41 (by 1985, 50). The author explains how this happened in a large work of
'constitutional interpretation', particularly of the U.N. Charter's Chapter XI. His
purpose, he writes, is 'to explain how the growing influence of a particular U.N. bloc
[the 31 Afro-Asian states before 1960] has resulted in the adoption of successive
General Assembly resolutions which modified the meaning of certain Charter
provisions. This process of political interpretation of the Charter is indicative of the
evolution of political organizations such as the U.N.'

336 **The United Nations trusteeship system.**
James N. Murray, Jr. Urbana, IL: University of Illinois Press, 1957.
283p. bibliog.
This is a standard early account of the trusteeship system on the eve (1955) of its
triumphs of decolonization. Murray traces the history of international responsibility
for non-self-governing peoples under first the League of Nations and second the
United Nations, and then he examines the functioning of the Trusteeship Council. The
first trust territory, Italian Somaliland, is treated in a case-study. He recognizes that
the struggle for independence of the peoples in the administered territories could be
regarded as the primary cause of their liberation, but he remains convinced that the
Trusteeship Council performed the intercessions with sovereign states that did the
actual political work. Trusteeship, he argues imaginatively, 'provides a microcosm of
the general process of international politics'.

International Court of Justice

337 **The future of the International Court of Justice.**
Edited by Leo Gross. Preface by Philip C. Jessup and Edvard Hambro.
Dobbs Ferry, NY: Oceana, 1976. 2 vols.
At a time when the World Court and the hope of a world built on law seemed to be in
atrophy, the American Society of International Law assembled a panel of leading
international lawyers and practitioners 'to study the Court, to diagnose its ills, and if
possible to suggest remedies'. These two learned volumes discuss the ICJ's role in the
peaceful settlement of disputes, its place in the U.N. system, its relation to national
state policies and its use and potential for the future. Enlargement of the contentious
jurisdiction of the Court to international organizations, business corporations, and
individuals (by Sir Gerald Fitzmaurice) is one suggestion for the future. The editor
cites the disappointing outcome of the General Assembly's review of the ICJ (1970)
and concludes with Judge Lachs that a 'real breakthrough' may come from increased
use of (legally non-binding) advisory opinions. He adds many more technical
recommendations, most requiring no amendment of the Court's Statute. To explain
why the Court is so little resorted to, he admits that its judgment in the *South West
Africa* case (1966) brought its fortunes to a 'nadir', but the remedy seems to have
been to 'throw the case back into the political arena'. The Court 'rehabilitated' itself

in the *Namibia* opinion (1971) only by reverting to 'teleological interpretation' somewhat outside the bounds of legal reasoning. Gross ends with gloomy reflections on the 'parochial attitude' of states, the 'opposition to the law itself' of communist bloc states, and the frustration of 'rule-of-law oriented states'.

338 **The International Court of Justice.**
Department of Public Information. New York: United Nations, 9th ed., 1983. 45p. (E.83.I.20).
This is a short, official introduction to the World Court. It includes history, organization of the Court, access (by states), jurisdiction in contentious cases, the law applied, procedure, advisory opinions, and main cases.

339 **The International Court of Justice.**
Monroe Leigh and Office of the Legal Advisor. In: *Digest of United States practice in international law, 1976*. Edited by Eleanor C. McDowell. Washington, DC: Department of State, 1977, p.650-80. (Pub. 8908).
In 1976, Julia Willis prepared a study, 'Widening access to the International Court of Justice', to which the State Department here replies. Because of the world's increasing 'transnational' activity (business, commerce, economics, politics, science, environment, education, U.N. System International Court of Justice 163 culture, and humanitarian relief), the United States should, the Department advised, 'announce in an appropriate forum that it favors, in principle, amendment of the Statute of the International Court of Justice and the U.N. Charter to incorporate an advisory "preliminary opinion" in recourse from national appellate courts to the ICJ on issues of international law'. This would promote 'uniformity' in the law and 'flexibility' in procedure. It would give individuals, corporations, and non-governmental organizations *indirect* access to the Court. (The Department opposed *direct* access.) The Department also supported amending the Statute to permit the United Nations to appear before the Court in contentious proceedings against a state or another international organization. But, in view of opposition to Charter amendment by the U.S.S.R., China, and the U.S., both reforms should be supported only 'in principle', leaving actual amendment to a 'more propitious time'. This article, which prints Willis's study of current practice historical precedents, and proposed reforms, is a window on U.S. policy toward the Court.

340 **The International Court of Justice: an analysis of a failure.**
John K. Gamble, Jr., and Dana D. Fischer. Lexington, MA: Lexington Books, 1976. 156p.
The authors' criteria for evaluating the Court are (1) the effect of its (few) judgments on the resolution of (many) international disputes, and (2) its contribution to the development of international law, even the effect of its potential use in world politics. They survey the literature on the Court, its work (using some quantitative techniques), states' relation to it, and a statistical model for predicting future use of the Court. In thirty years, the ICJ rendered judgments on only twenty-six disputes and gave only fourteen advisory opinions. Virtually all East–West conflicts of the Cold War failed to reach the Court, as did most important international problems. Hence, its development of international law has been constrained, and all that seems left is

unsupported 'hope for the future'. Decentralized arbitral tribunals as in the proposed law of the sea or environmental treaties may be more acceptable.

341   **The International Court of Justice and some contemporary problems: essays on international law.**
Taslim O. Elias.   The Hague: M. Nijhoff, 1983. 374p. bibliog.

The author, a judge and president of the World Court, gathers together his writings on the '*living* law of the United Nations' into five parts: judicial process (notably as related to cases on nuclear testing), development of international law (especially in economic and social fields), the legal aspects of the proposed New International Economic Order, human rights, and the end of colonization in Africa. Readers who focus on the small number of judgments of the Court, and hence doubt its usefulness for the resolution of disputes within a world dominated by power politics, may be impressed in this book by how much the Court contributes to those few issues which are brought before it by states.

342   **The International Court of Justice and the Western tradition of international law.**
Edward McWhinney.   Dordrecht, The Netherlands: M. Nijhoff, 1987. 158p. bibliog.

Here are clear, timely lectures on the challenge to international law caused by U.S. withdrawal from the World Court over the Nicaragua suit. The author, an eminent Canadian legal scholar, surveys international law as it has been criticized by the decolonized and Soviet worlds, reviews the transition from positivist to process jurisprudence, discusses the 'emerging constitutionalism of world order', and then launches into the crisis at the World Court. He answers such charges as an anti-Western majority on the Court, or a drift from legal into political decisions, and concludes – before the Cold War ended – that the Court is still trying to reconcile liberal, socialist, and decolonialist values in an 'era of transition'. This is a remarkably readable and humane account of the World Court.

343   **The International Court of Justice at a crossroads.**
Edited by Lori Fisler Damrosch.   Dobbs Ferry, NY: Transnational Publishers, 1987. 511p.

In response to U.S. withdrawal from the compulsory jurisdiction of the World Court after Nicaragua's suit over the mining of its harbours (1986), the American Society of International Law assembled a panel of forty distinguished experts on the Court to discuss the grave issues of this 'watershed'. For instance, what now is the meaning of compulsory jurisdiction (Article 36(2) of the Statute)? What happens to ICJ dispute settlement clauses in countless treaties? What can still be done to strengthen the potential usefulness of the Court? Here readers will find an up-to-date learned account of the history and principle of compulsory jurisdiction, of the distinction between 'legal' disputes suitable for resolutio by the Court and 'political' disputes that remain outside international adjudication, and of U.S. policy toward the Court. In the general conclusion, three misunderstandings are found: The U.S. did not leave the Court – it left only Article 36(2). Those who disagreed with the decision to withdraw from Nicaragua's case did not all support compulsory jurisdiction. The Court is not 'simply another U.N. political body' in which a Soviet judge could (although he did not) rule against the U.S. in the case of Nicaragua, nor did only the U.S. judge rule that the

Court had no jurisdiction (four did). This book is a must for serious study of the World Court.

344 The International Court of Justice: its role in the maintenance of International peace and security.
Oliver J. Lissitzyn. New York: Carnegie Endowment for International Peace, 1951. 118p. bibliog.

This is an early, traditional account of the World Court, when hopes were still high for its contribution to ending the scourge of war. The Court could not prevent outbreaks of violence, but it offered by its very existence an alternative for peaceful settlement; it created an atmosphere of respect for law; and it promised to expand the present, limited acceptance of compulsory jurisdiction into a mutually beneficial world rule of law. The author views the ICJ in a slow historic progression (even the U.S. Supreme Court had a very light case-load for fifty years). His chapters on 'The function of law in the world community' and 'The need for the development of international law' will remind the reader of certain hard-won truths. The book still serves as an introduction to the Court.

345 Judging the World Court.
Thomas M. Franck. New York: Priority Press for the Twentieth Century Fund, 1986. 112p. bibliog.

Here is a sharp response to U.S. withdrawal from the jurisdiction of the ICJ as a result of Nicaragua's suit against the United States in 1984. At a time of wavering American adherence to the idea and practice of an international court ruling by law, Franck very ably surveys the work of the World Court, its history, the case against the Court (bias, judicial overreach, poor fact-finding, vanishing clientele), and the usefulness of the Court (ability to rely on neutral principles over the long term, rule of law as a superior ideology to communist revolution or democratic use of force). He concludes his short book with recommendations to use the Court and hence to strengthen the system of international law: increase the use of chambers of three or more judges; increase the requests for advisory opinions to elucidate, not implement, the law; revise the Vandenberg reservation. Franck recognizes that a 'peaceful world order' depends in part on a growing legal and judicial tradition and that a revived World Court or any conceivable new court or equity tribunal implies a 'diminution of sovereignty'. But in the modern, interdependent world no nation enjoys 'total sovereignty'. Hence he urges the U.S. to return to the Court, while cautiously retaining for the immediate future its 'military option'. He rejects 'extremes of both unilateralism and multilateralism'.

346 Reviving the World Court.
Richard A. Falk. Charlottesville: University Press of Virginia, 1986. 197p.

The author, who served as counsel to Ethiopia and Liberia in the controversial *South West Africa* case (1966), argues that, although the Court was established to 'represent the main forms of civilization and of the principal legal systems of the world' (Statute, Article 9), it remains predominantly Western, without strong developing country or Marxist jurisprudence. Hence, 'the World Court cannot be revived without the awakening of non-Western governments to its potential importance and the commitment of their representatives on the Court to the development of a non-

Western jurisprudence, including authoritative sources.' He sees the case of *Nicaragua v. the United States* (1984-86) as another 'big case' affecting the future of international adjudication, but does not dare to develop his proposed Marxist or Third World approaches (which in the circumstances would have tactically failed). The book will not offend those readers who wish, as Falk does, 'to bring law and judicial methods back into the mainstream of planetary activity committed to the urgent possibility of bringing about a just and peaceful world'.

347   **The role and record of the International Court of Justice.**
Nagendra Singh.   Dordrecht, The Netherlands: M. Nijhoff, 1989.
443p.

This is an authoritative treatise on the World Court by a distinguished Indian judge (since 1973) and president (1985-88). Originally given as the Tagore Law Lectures at the University of Calcutta, the book reflects Judge Nagendra Singh's conviction that the U.N.'s primary purpose to maintain international peace and security can be in part fulfilled by the ICJ's settlement of disputes in accordance with international law and principles of justice. 'The last forty years of valuable experience', he writes, 'should teach the sovereign states that their ultimate salvation lies in greater use of the Court rather than more frequent use of force.' For the future, he recommends greater use of advisory opinions, increased contentious proceedings (seventy per cent of which are successfully resolved), and more recourse to chambers.

348   **Strengthening the International Court of Justice. Hearings.**
United States Senate, Committee on Foreign Relations. 93rd Cong., 1st sess. 10-11 May 1973. 293p. (CIS No. S381-22. SuDocs No. Y4.F76/2:In8/42).

These hearings include proposals by Professor Louis B. Sohn on allowing regional organizations to request advisory opinions from the World Court, allowing the U.N. General Assembly to request such opinions, and granting individuals limited access. Other suggestions are made by Judge Philip C. Jessup, Leo Gross, Stephen Schwebel, Charles Yost, Ambassador Arthur Goldberg, Senator Robert Taft, Senator Alan Cranston, and Walter Hoffman.

349   **The World Court: what it is and how it works.**
Shabtai Rosenne with Terry D. Gill.   Dordrecht, The Netherlands: M. Nijhoff, 1962; 4th rev. ed., 1989. 320p. bibliog.

This is a standard descriptive text (not a contentious treatise) on the Internat Court of Justice, written for 'the politician, the diplomat, the member of parliament, the student of international law and international relations, and the enquiring members of the public at large'. Although at the time of this revision the number of states accepting the optional clause for the compulsory jurisdiction of the Court (Article 36(2) of its Statute) had not grown but had even declined by the withdrawal of the United States and Israel, 'the developing countries are beginning to realize that the Court does not merely express the judicial values of a certain part or parts of the world, but that it applies rules of international law, whose main purpose is precisely to protect the interests of the weak and to balance, in law, the power of States in order to attain an equity that does not exist in fact.' The author authoritatively discusses the history of the founding of the Court, its judges, jurisdiction, trial procedure, and case-by-case accounts. General readers will probably most be drawn to the landmark cases of *South West Africa* (1966) and *Nicaragua v. the United States* (1986). Rosenne's concluding assessment, warning of an increased unwillingness of states to have recourse unilaterally to the Court after *Nicaragua*, still finds that 'it is the International Court, together with the International Law Commission, which has infused new dynamism into the international law of today'.

See also International Law Commission (p.125ff.) and Judicial settlement (p.180ff.).

International Law Commission

350   **The International Law Commission.**
      Ian M. Sinclair.   Cambridge: Grotius for University of Cambridge, Research Centre for International Law, 1987. 177p.

These are the Hersch Lauterpacht memorial lectures. The author, who served on the ILC from 1981 to 1986, is knowledgeable, sympathetic, and yet critical of the commission as a 'fen of stagnant waters'. As the most recent study of the ILC's contribution to international law, this work will repay close examination. Sinclair covers its constitution, working methods, achievements in codification, and contributions to law. After the Vienna Convention on the Law of Treaties of 1969, however, the commission's work slowly failed to win state ratification and its agenda became crowded with items 'peripheral to the main thrust of the codification process'. He finds a division not between members from developing countries and industrialized ones, as charged in the UNITAR study of 1981, but between those 'who adhere to a somewhat old-fashioned view of State sovereignty and those who genuinely wish to engage in creative but realistic law making'. He makes practical suggestions for speeding up the commission's work, such as not debating all topics on the agenda at each session.

351   **The International Law Commission: its approach to the codification and progressive development of international law.**
      B.G. Ramcharan.   The Hague: M. Nijhoff, 1977. 227p. bibliog.

This official and rather traditional account of the ILC, a subsidiary organ of the General Assembly, was prompted by the ILC's own review of its approach and programme (1967-73). Its approach to 'the progressive development of international law and its codification' remains empirical and pragmatic, yet its future programme, the author argues, must become more 'dynamic', for international law is silent in areas of new concern like space, the environment, and a new economic order. (By the 1980s, this creative work had passed from the ILC to the more political General Assembly.) This book covers the ILC's history, working methods, juristic methodology, political approach, and relation to regional legal bodies.

352 **The International Law Commission: the need for a new direction.**
Mohamed El Baradei, Thomas M. Franck, and Robert Trachtenberg.
New York: UNITAR, 1981. 31p.

The International Law Commission is a group of fifteen experts in international law
serving in their individual capacity and dedicated, in accordance with Article 13 of
the U.N. Charter, to the 'progressive development of international law and its
codification'. The commission has compared itself to the General Assembly, at the
'legislative' level, and to the International Court of Justice, at the 'judicial'; they are
'complementary' and are the 'principal judicial and legal organs of the United
Nations system'. Since about the time of the Vienna Convention on the Law of
Treaties (1969), however, the commission has ceased to play its major role in the 'law
making process'. The new Third World states do not want further codification of
'international law', which seems to them to be a relic of European colonialism; hence,
new departures in space and environmental law have been given to ad hoc bodies of
the General Assembly, and this precedent has been followed in the fields of law of the
sea, hostage-taking, and human rights. The Sixth Committee does not give 'political
guidance' to the commission to enter new areas of law where there is little state
practice, and the commission itself has been reluctant to shift from codification to
progressive development. To speed up the commission's work, the authors
recommend making it full-time, or, if the cost is too high, at least creating full-time
rapporteurs. To enter new fields of law, they suggest reducing its agenda (last set in
1949) and moving from draft treaties to reports and model rules (like those on
arbitration). The authors are wedded to the virtues of independent experts, however,
and do not favour making the commission more representative of states and people –
thus converting it into something more like a world legislature. Their last
recommendation is to establish an international legal research centre to assist both the
International Law Commission and the General Assembly.

353 **The work of the International Law Commission.**
United Nations. New York: United Nations, 4th ed., 1988. 325p.
bibliog. (E.88.V.1).

This is an official account of the International Law Commission's work, primarily in
the codification of customary and conventional international law. The book covers the
commission's history, organization, programmes, methods of work, relationship to
governments, and relation to other inter-governmental organizations. (Article 26 of
the Charter permits it to consult with national organizations and NGOs concerned
with progressive development of international law and its codificiation, but so far the
commission has been reluctant to move so far from state practice.) The book provides
a complete list of its reports, draft conventions and model rules, topics currently
under consideration, and multilaterial conventions actually concluded following ILC
consideration (e.g., earlier Law of the Sea conventions and Vienna Convention on the
Law of Treaties).

354   **Yearbook of the International Law Commission, 1989.**
      United Nations.   New York: United Nations, 1949- . 50+ vols.
      (E.91.V.4).

These are summary records of the meetings of the International Law Commission (analogous to the Official Records of the General Assembly). For the forty-first session in 1989, the agenda included the Draft Code of Crimes against the Peace and Security of Mankind and other topics. Multilateral conventions cited during the commission's deliberations included those relating to human resources, diplomatic relations, the law of treaties, law of the sea, nuclear and space activities. Government officials and scholars will be primarily interested in these volumes, but the ordinary citizen might leaf through them to gain a sense of 'international legislation'.

Closely Associated Entities

National missions

355 **American ambassadors at the United Nations: People, politics, and bureaucracy in the making of foreign policy.**
Seymour M. Finger. Foreword by Henry Cabot Lodge.   New York: UNITAR, 1992. 363p. (E.92.III.K.RR.36).
This is a study of both American foreign policy toward the U.N. (the subject of first chapter) and of the formation and execution of Presidential policy by the U.S. representatives to the U.N. The book is a deliberate study of the role of bureaucracy – especially those officials who are willing to take responsibility and make difficult decisions – in the making of American foreign policy. The author is a former ambassador who served five years in the U.S. mission. Finger carefully recounts the story of every U.S. representative from Edward Stettinius to Vernon Walters. In some cases, the representative has had a demonstrable influence on policy, as in the proposal to establish the United Nations Development Programme in 1957 or the World Food Programme in 1960. In his last chapter, the author reaffirms the value of the U.N. to the U.S. and advocates increased recourse to the specialized agencies where weighted voting offers the United States 'a degree of influence comparable to its economic importance'. In the Security Council, the veto protects the U.S., and in the General Assembly, the talk can be listened to, but safety ignored. He quotes President Carter's pleas for U.N. reform without elaboration.

356 **Diplomats' views on the United Nations system: An attitude survey.**
Thomas M. Franck, John P. Renninger, and Vladislav B. Tikhomirov.
New York: UNITAR, 1982. 38p. (Policy and Efficacy Study No. 7).
High-level members of national delegations to the U.N. find economic and social cooperation more important than maintenance of peace and security. This partly reflects the fact that 63 per cent of the diplomats in the study were members of the Group of 77. Satisfaction with the Trusteeship Council was similarly high; with the Security Council, low. The most common reasons given for ineffectiveness were 'lack of power' by the organ to enforce its decisions and recommendations and 'lack

of commitment' by certain member states. On the stalled North–South dialogue, 77 per cent thought they had 'promoted better mutual understanding', yet the 'economic and political climate' still prevented new agreements. The statistics confirm general impressions.

357 The 'other' State Department: The United States mission to the United Nations – Its role in the making of foreign policy.

Arnold Beichman. Foreword by Leland Goodrich.   New York: Basic Books, 1968. 221p. bibliog.

This is a basic book about that vital but somewhat anomalous element in the U.N. system – the national 'mission', headed by an ambassador or permanent representative. The mission is very much an embassy of the state member, yet, as William Jordan used to say, it is 'partly in the Secretariat'. Beichman studies the U.S. mission to the U.N. during the period 1946-68, when admittedly the American ambassador could not commit the United States to any international action without consulting his government, but at least he was a member of the President's cabinet. (This last status was lost during the Reagan administration, but by Clinton's a woman was appointed and she was brought back into the cabinet. This could be a mark of the future.)

358 Permanent missions to the United Nations.

United Nations, Protocol and Liaison Service.   New York: United Nations, April 1993. 347p. (No. 272).

Updated frequently, this handy volume lists the ambassadors (permanent representatives), counsellors, secretaries, and other diplomats of all the embassies (missions) of the states-members of the U.N. in New York. It also includes international civil servants of the specialized agencies that maintain liaison offices in New York (ILO, FAO, WHO, UNESCO, etc.), diplomats of non-member states (Holy See, Switzerland), and officials of IGOs (Commonwealth, E.C., O.A.U.). Member-states of the principal U.N. organs (Security Council, etc.) and standing organs (Military Staff Committee) are listed too. Hence, when looking for the right name and address, this is the reference work to go to.

359 Ralph Bunche: The man and his times.

Edited by Benjamin Rivlin. Foreword by Donald McHenry.
New York: Holmes & Meier, 1990. 279p. bibliog.

Ralph Bunche was a black American State Department official who helped draft the chapters of the U.N. Charter on trusteeship in 1944, which were effective by the 1960s in ending colonialism for nearly half of the world's population. He was also the U.N. mediator in Palestine in 1948, after Count Folke Bernadotte's assassination, and Bunche largely settled the first Arab–Israeli War. In 1950 he was awarded the Nobel Peace Prize. This volume of admiring essays covers Bunche's youthful race consciousness, his work as an Africanist and decolonizer, and finally his world statesmanship at the United Nations. Brian Urquhart writes the account of Bunche's contributions to peacekeeping. His memory deserves recalling at a time when talented Americans tend to avoid the U.N.

360   **Representing America: Experiences of U.S. diplomats at the U.N.**
Linda M. Fasulo. Foreword by Elliot Richardson.   New York:
Praeger, 1984. 343p. bibliog.

This is a book of interviews with surviving American representatives to the United
Nations from W. Averell Harriman (1944) to Jeane Kirkpatrick (1981-85). The
author, a young woman who had served in U.N. internship programmes in New York
and Geneva, connects the interviews with lively introductions. In effect, the work is a
history of the U.N. as told by American participants whose first duty was 'to carry out
U.S. policy decisions'. Fasulo, in her afterword, answers the main U.S. criticisms of
the U.N. (politicization, financial irresponsibility, unenforceability of resolutions) and
she recommends that the American people, 89 per cent of whom still favour U.S.
membership (1983), reassess the role they want the U.N. to play in the world and in
U.S. foreign policy. She particularly urges that future Presidents and the State
Department involve the U.S. representative at the U.N. to a greater degree in the
making of policy.

361   **Your man at the U.N.: People, politics, and bureaucracy in the
making of foreign policy.**
Seymour M. Finger.   New York: New York University Press, 1980.

This is a study of U.S. representatives to the U.N., with particular attention to Henry
Cabot Lodge (1952-61), Adlai Stevenson (1961-65), and Arthur Goldberg (1965-68).
The author, who himself served in the U.S. Mission, draws out the contributions to
policy of the strong personalities who have served there. Finger is at pains to contrast
the 'master players' with the 'inert bureaucracy' and the 'slow and cumbersome
legislature'. The President remains the principal U.S. foreign policy-maker, but,
Finger argues, the permanent representative to the U.N. has and should have an
important influence. The U.N. ambassador, unlike all other ambassadors, negotiates in
a standing diplomatic conference and reports not through an area Assistant Secretary
of State but often directly to the President. Compare Finger's *American ambassadors
at the United Nations* (item no. 355).

See also United States policy (p.65ff.).

Groups

362   **Developments in decision making in the United Nations.**
Johan Kaufmann.   In: *The U.N. under attack*. Edited by Jeffrey
Harrod and Nico Schrijver.   Aldershot, England: Gower, 1988,
p.17-32.

The author discusses the emergence of bloc voting (as early as 1949), the
Secretariat's role, influence of chairmen, non-governmental organizations, private
sector businesses (as in cocoa negotiations in UNCTAD), weighted voting in the IMF
and World Bank, and the tripartite system in the ILO. New political conditions
include the admission of many new non-aligned states, the rise of nationalism in place
of the liberal internationalism at the founding of the U.N., the aversion of the

superpowers to bringing conflicts involving themselves into the Security Council, loss of confidence in the impartiality and effectiveness of the organs and agencies in the system, and fear of 'politicization' (use of specialized fora for general purposes). Kaufmann suggests improvements in *management* (more opportunity for negotiations) and *structure* (economic security council, merger of specialized agencies).

363 Global bargaining: the legal and diplomatic framework.
Gidon Gottleib. In: *Law-making in the global community*. Edited by Nicholas G. Onuf. Durham, NC: Carolina Academic Press, 1982, p.109-30.

As big-power bloc politics declines, and smaller states combine in 'global political parties' or groups, the author argues, a 'new world order' is emerging 'shaped more by bargains, compromises, and necessity than by grand architectural designs', such as proposals for U.N. Charter reform or for a world constitution. Gottleib surveys seven kinds of diplomatic decision making in international organizations, notably *parliamentary diplomacy*, based on the legal fiction of state equality, and *parity diplomacy*, based on the more realistic equality of groups of states like the G-77 and NAM. This equality, or parity, 'is anchored neither in ideological claims of equality nor in the theory of representation. It emanates from the realities of power relationships and from the need to manage the problems of interdependence and of world order.' He further analyses such rules for decision-making (by states, groups, or other combinations) as unanimity, majority rule, and consensus. Gottleib concludes with a warning that informal, non-voting procedures, though they have achieved such progressive results to date as the Helsinki accords (1975) and the Law of the Sea (1982), are harder for Congress, the legal and economic communities, and the public to monitor and ultimately to control.

364 The Group of 77: evolution, structure, organization.
Karl P. Sauvant. New York: Oceana, 1981. 232p.

This is a not unfriendly study of the Group of 77 (actually 122 in 1980) the – developing countries that collaborated to establish UNCTAD (1964) and launch the New International Economic Order (NIEO, 1974). All agree that 'little progress has been made', yet the group 'has become an important moral and political force in international economic relations'. Hence, this short study can be read as an exposition of the group system, which some observers liken to the beginnings of transnational political parties. The G-77, since it is composed of states-members of the U.N., has made the most concerted effort at U.N. reform and hence bears examination as a model for future reform.

365 The Non-Aligned Movement and the 'Group of 77': towards joint cooperation.
Karl P. Sauvant. *Non-Aligned World*, vol. 1 (January-March 1983), p.23-73.

Disappointment with North–South trade as an engine of economic growth leads this official of the U.N. Centre on Transnational Corporations to South–South economic and technical cooperation under the head of 'self-reliance'. 'In contradiction to the prevailing associative development strategy with its orientation towards the world market and heavy reliance on linkages with the developed countries', Sauvant writes, 'self-reliance seeks greater selectivity in North–South linkages, accompanied by a greater mobilization of domestic and Third World resources (to satisfy primarily indigenous needs) and a greater reliance on domestic and Third World markets.' So fundamental a new strategy requires that the Non-Aligned Movement and the Group of 77 shift their approach to a New International Economic Order (NIEO). Sauvant provides an elaborate analysis of the two groups for the purpose of improving their economic cooperation and self-reliance in both direct action unilaterally amongst themselves and in bargaining multilaterally with the North. The article, even for those not directly concerned with economic development, is a revealing window on these two important groups of actors on the international stage. If groups are incipient transnational political parties, Sauvant reveals their history, organization, and programmes. Their goal is not yet U.N. reform, but in pursuit of economic cooperation they have brought about several special sessions of the General Assembly on development and many meetings of foreign ministers on the same subject. This contributes to the institutionalization of U.N. summits like the European Council in the E.C.

366   **The Non-Aligned Movement: the origins of a Third World alliance.**
Peter Willetts.   London: Frances Pinter, 1978. 310p. bibliog.
This is a quantitative study of the diplomacy and foreign policy behaviour of th Non-Aligned Movement (NAM). In his final chapter, Willetts draws a portrait of the NAM and finds that anti-neocolonialism is a 'strong hypothesis' to explain the group. 'Despite the origin of the word, the Non-Aligned could not be described either as a group of states that had refused to join alliances or as a group that was distinguished by non-involvement in Cold War disputes.' Sometimes members supported the East, sometimes the West. Hence he concludes that the end of the Cold War will not lead to disappearance of the group. It remains 'an established part of the international system. What could destroy it is 'a dispute that cuts right across the Third World, such as a failure by the cartels of primary producers of oil and other raw materials to provide economic support for the poorest developing states'.

367   **The Non-Aligned, the U.N., and the superpowers.**
Richard L. Jackson.   New York: Praeger, 1983. 315p. bibliog.
Written by a U.S. Foreign Service Officer while the Cold War remained a constant reality of international relations, this book is a history of the Non-Aligned Movement (NAM, about 101 Third World nations), an analysis of the NAM's relation to the U.N., and a critique of its 'alignment' with the Soviet Union. The author admits that the NAM majority in the U.N. is the result of a 'power vacuum created by U.S.–Soviet division and lack, over the years, of consistent Western leadership', but he is not inclined to grant that their 'rhetoric' and 'taxation without adequate representation' might be desperate devices of the poor to achieve justice in an international organization designed by the rich to have almost no powers. He concludes that a new U.S. approach to the NAM must be based on 'real convergence of interests'. With the end of Soviet confrontation by the 1990s, this probably still remains the conservative U.S. diplomatic strategy.

368   **Structural conflict: the Third World against global liberalism.**
Stephen D. Krasner.   Berkeley, CA: University of California Press,
1985. 363p. bibliog.

Here is a challenge, from a 'modified realist' orientation, to the conventional wisdom
concerning Third World economic development, especially after the proposed New
International Economic Order (NIEO, 1974) and call for Global Negotiations (1979).
Krasner regards states as the principal actors in the international system, while
multinational corporations and international organizations are dependent upon them;
but states operate within established international 'regimes' (customary principles,
norms, rules, and decision-making procedures around which the actors' expectations
converge). His great complaint against the NIEO is that it aimed to replace the liberal
market-oriented international regime with an authoritative one under a powerful
United Nations. This book could hardly be more hostile to the cause of world
economic justice ('Third World policies are responsible for Third World poverty'),
but it is aware of many uncomfortable facts ('Latin American countries led the fight
for extended economic zones in the ocean', quite inconsistently with the view that
Third World states care more for justice than for power). As a study of the Third
World as a 'group', it is clea and challenging. Krasner specifically examines the Third
World attacks on the Bretton Woods financial institutions, multinational corporations
operating in the liberal economic order, air and sea transport, and the 'global
commons' of the deep sea, Antarctica, space, and the radio spectrum. In his
conclusion, Krasner proscribes further conference diplomacy or policies that interfere
in states' domestic affairs. He prescribes policies taking advantage of the still-existing
liberal economic regime – policies in areas like security, nuclear non-proliferation,
and migration, where 'authoritarian state allocation' is the accepted norm. He also
prescribes collective policies in raw materials trade like oil where the market leaves
industrialized countries at the mercy of a few developing ones.

369   **The Third World coalition in international politics.**
Robert A. Mortimer.   Boulder, CO: Westview, 1980; 2nd ed., 1984.
194p. bibliog.

This is a history of the Group of 77, particularly through the period of its col
diplomacy to establish a New International Economic Order (NIEO, 1974-77), and
then, after Fidel Castro became chairman of the Non-Aligned Movement, through the
diplomatic struggle over the Global Negotiations (1979-). The author, a political
scientist, is vividly aware of growing poverty in the Third World and of South–South
conflicts, yet he writes not as a moralist but as a realist trying to demonstrate how the
poor countries, in today's system of world politics, might defend themselves against
the rich. 'Distributive issues will not be settled on moral grounds', Mortimer writes.
'The Third World has every right to appeal to moral sensibilities, but rich states are
likely to be influenced only by power. The conceptual focus of this work is upon
power, not policy, but it is hoped that the study will stimulate reflection as well upon
the values that the United States should be pursuing in its relations with the Third
World.'

370 **The weak in the world of the strong: the developing countries in the international system.**
Robert L. Rothstein. New York: Columbia University Press, 1977. 384p.

This is a study of the developing countries (Third World, Group of 77, Non-Aligned Movement) at the peak of their concerted agitation for the New International Economic Order. The American author rejected the then-current argument that the West was to blame for Third World poverty and hence had a moral obligation to redistribute income or at least to improve the terms of trade. Rather, he holds (and it was a perspective that prevailed) that Third World nations shared the responsibility, had choices available to them, and were overdue for reforms of their own exploitative élites. Hence, the focus in this book is on domestic policy-making as it affects the external policy of most of these states. Rothstein closes with a chapter on 'justice in the international system' but the matter was moot while East and West were locked in a life-and-death struggle.

Transnational parties: organizing the world's precincts.
See item no. 69.

World treaty index.
See item no. 119.

Small states and the peaceful settlement of disputes.
See item no. 443.

See also Regional agencies (p.190ff.), U.N. Conference on Trade and Development (p.393ff.), and the New International Economic Order (p.397ff.).

Non-governmental Organizations

371 **The growth of international nongovernmental organization in the 20th century.**
Kjell Skjelsbaek. *International Organization*, vol. 25 (1971), p.420-42.

The author, a peace researcher in Oslo, finds about 3,000 transnational, non-profit organizations in the world, not counting multinational business enterprises (which are treated in other articles in this issue). Such organizations (NGOs) represent at least two countries, and at least one of their members is not a government. He surveys statistically their historical growth, distribution over the continents, field of activity, and the influence o the Northwest (Europe and North America). The causes of their growth are the need to manage transnational inteıactions, economic and technological development in the host country, and a pluralistic ideology. The consequences are a substitution of positive interactions for violence and threats of violence, a reduction of exploitation, and hence a more peaceful and just world. Skjelsbaek admits that the

Third World, because of its poverty, has not yet produced enough NGOs to balance the Northwest.

372 How could nongovernmental organizations use U.N. bodies more effectively?
Antonio Cassese. *Universal Human Rights*, vol. 1, no. 4 (1979), p.73-80.

The author briefly surveys the three types of NGOs accredited to Ecosoc under the U.N. Charter's Article 71: category I, category II, and roster. The Inter-Parliamentary Union is typical of the first, the International Committee of the Red Cross of the second, and the Trilateral Commission of the third. Generally, NGOs have made an 'outstanding contribution' to the work of the U.N., particularly in the field of the implementation of human rights. But Cassese suggests that they could have more influence if they entered the field of standard setting, conducted more 'imaginative' research, and pursued the global (not individual) approach of A/Res/32/130 (1977). Implementation can still be aided by providing reliable information to the Human Rights Committee, informing the public of the committee's work, and exposing states for violations.

373 International nongovernmental organizations and transnational integration.
Louis Kriesberg. *International Associations* (Brussels), vol. 18 (1972), p.521-25.

By *integration* is meant 'positive interactions' and 'collective identification' of peoples across national borders. The author, a social scientist, investigates how and to what degree international non-governmental organizations (INGOs) contribute to 'transnational 180 Non-governmental Organizations Bibliography on integration'. Kriesberg finds that, within an INGO, the active leaders usually learn to cooperate and 'converge'; but, with respect to national member organizations, the integration may be unfelt or slow to form; and with respect to non-members, including rival INGOs, the public whom INGOs aim to serve, and the governments whom they try to influence, it may be very tentative. Three factors do improve integration: homogeneity of members' interests and tastes (not nationality), goals of service to their own members (even if they are drawn from antagonistic societies, like Arab and Israeli states), and more democratic structures, which encourage active participation of individuals (especially in committee work, as opposed to general meetings). Most of his examples are taken from the *Yearbook of international organizations* (see item no. 750).

374 Methods of multilateral management: interrelationship of international organizations and NGOs.
Angus Archer. In: *The U.S., the U.N., and the management of global change*. Edited by Toby Trister Gati. New York: United Nations Association – U.S.A., 1983, p.303-26.

This is a basic account of the contribution of NGOs to the work of the U.N. syst especially since the first FAO food conference in 1963, when NGOs began to take up the cause of international economic and social justice. By the 1970s, they were involved in issues of human rights, environment, trade, habitat, women, New

Closely Associated Entities. Non-governmental Organizations

International Economic Order (NIEO), disarmament, and peace. In effect, NGOs represent the beginnings of popular representation at the U.N. Archer concludes that they have a positive contribution to make to deliberations at the U.N., as well as to inform and educate the public at large. Compare the essay by Nigel Rodley in the same volume.

375 **Monitoring human rights violations in the 1980s.**
Nigel S. Rodley. In: *Enhancing global human rights*, by Jorge I. Dominguez, Nigel S. Rodley, Bryce Wood, and Richard A. Falk. New York: McGraw-Hill, 1979, p.117-51.

'The principal role of monitoring human rights violations will remain with non-governmental organizations.' The author surveys the rise of human rights standards and the current concern to improve implementation. He passes over the rudimentary U.N. system for monitoring to focus on the elements of a reliable system composed of vigilant NGOs, such as Amnesty International, the International Commission of Jurists, and the Red Cross. He concludes with a speculation on a *worldwide NGO*, a kind of federation of all human rights NGOs.

376 **A new role for non-governmental organizations in human rights.**
Virginia Leary. In: *U.N. law/fundamental rights*. Edited by Antonio Cassese. Alphen aan den Rijn, The Netherlands: Sijthoff & Noordhoff, 1979, p.197-210.

Individuals and non-governmental organizations (NGOs) are increasingly recognized as 'subjects' of international law, in addition to states. They have *rights*. This article explores the role of NGOs like Amnesty International in creating those rights – that is, in 'international law-making'. The right of people to be exempt from torture is now well established as an international civil right. The author surveys the history and work of NGOs in advancing human rights. Generally the strategy has been to influence the General Assembly to issue declarations against torture, then to support negotiations to reach a binding convention declaring torture an international crime, like aggression, apartheid, and genocide. The first was achieved in 1975 (the second, in 1984).

377 **Non-governmental organizations at the United Nations: identity, role, and function.**
Pei-heng Chiang. New York: Praeger, 1981. 355p. bibliog.

This is a standard study of non-governmental organizations (NGOs), as contrasted with intergovernmental organizations (IGOs). The International Committee of the Red Cross is typical of the former; the Food and Agricultural Organization of the latter. They are formally related in the U.N. Charter's Article 71. Much interest now is drawn to NGOs, since they are rooted in Western traditions of free association and offer some competition to IGOs and even to states, because of the functions they perform and the loyalties they inspire. On a broad, historical perspective, NGOs seem transitional to a supranational organization of individuals, a 'functional common-wealth'. This study examines their more recent political role. Human rights NGOs have performed critical exposure of abuses that no state would dare; policy NGOs bring imagination and dissent to staid U.N. bureaucracies; and most NGOs since 1972 have been drifting to the environmental, economic, and social issues that sometimes the developing countries, sometimes the developed, think are more important (food,

136

women). Chiang's study is rooted in the theory of interdependence, recognizing the role of non-state actors in addition to states, and in the theory of functionalism. But the bulk of it is historical and practical. He concludes that NGOs are guardians of freedom in the system and are links to the peoples of the world on whom the U.N. ultimately depends. Yet he warns that, while the Cold War dragged on, NGOs were in danger of 'losing their democratic character' by being dominated by the more powerful U.N. or states.

378 **Pressure groups in the global system: the transnational relations of issue-oriented non-governmental organizations.**
Edited by Peter Willetts. London: Frances Pinter, 1982. 225p.

In the post-realist approach to international relations, which looks beyond states to transnational organizations and actors, this scholarly study goes beyond multi-national corporations to 'issue oriented pressure groups' – that is, to international non-governmental organizations (NGOs) that have had a demonstrated influence on 'global politics'. Included are the anti-apartheid movement, the Palestine Liberation Organization, Amnesty International, Oxfam, Friends of the Earth, the Decade for Women (1975-85), and NGOs assisting refugees in cooperation with the U.N. High Commissioner for Refugees. The editor draws some surprising conclusions about these successful NGOs by comparison with national associations. NGOs pursue strategies of both challenging governmental authority and challenging society's allocation of goods in customary patterns of legitimacy. NGOs aim to influence the public first, then parties, legislatures, and, lastly, executives. The international NGOs (INGOs), like the intergovernmental organizations (e.g., the U.N.), are weaker than their (sovereign) members; often they are financially able to do little more than exchange information, but they cooperate under U.N. auspices. Their strengths are rooted in personal commitment, the specialized knowledge their leaders acquire, and their lack of cumbersome bureaucracy. NGOs protect themselves by claiming to be 'non-political'. They have few economic or military resources, as states do, but NGOs 'can communicate political ideas', which, in a world linked by aeroplanes, telephones, and television, are what count in global politics.

379 **The role of international nongovernmental organizations in the implementation of human rights.**
David Weissbrodt. *Texas International Law Journal*, vol. 12 (1977), p.293-320.

The popular demand to 'do something' about human rights abuses abroad is challenging the realists' notion that international law is useless. International non-governmental organizations (INGOs) are a link between the peoples of the various states and international organizations, including the U.N. They also link people to still-visionary schemes of an international criminal court or a world government. The author, with elaborate documentation, explores the powers of these INGOs. States are sensitive to criticism of their treatment of the people, and they hesitate to criticize one another. INGOs, because of their legitimacy based on the support of the people, can point the 'finger of shame'. He traces the quasi-legal processes of INGO exposure of human rights violations.

380   **Sisyphus endures: the international human rights NGO.**
       Jerome J. Shestack.   *New York Law School Law Review*, vol. 24
       (1978), p.89-123.

This article is basic on the NGO contribution to human rights, with special attention
to the problem of slowing the tide of abuse. The author, president of the International
League for Human Rights, one of the principal NGOs in the field, surveys the NGOs
and their functions: consultation, education, mediation, participation in government
action, catalyst for government action, and restraint on government action. For the
foreseeable future, he argues, since the U.N. will not have world governmental
powers to protect and promote human rights, NGOs will have to try to influence
governments 'outside of the U.N. structure'. World opinion can already be appealed
to, in the field of human rights, as a nascent general will. Shestack measures the
effectiveness of NGOs and answers criticisms that, by naming states in violation of
human rights, they 'threaten their existence at the U.N.'. He closes with ten
suggestions for improved performance.

381   **Transnational forums for peace.**
       William M. Evan.   In: *Preventing World War III: Some proposals.*
       Edited by Quincy Wright, William M. Evan, and Morton Deutsch.
       New York: Simon & Schuster, 1962, p.393-409.

This is an early study of 'transnational' non-state actors. 'The addition of new organs
of a transnational character would add other voices to those now heard in U.N.
deliberations. A multiplicity of voices, especially in a crisis, may generate ideas for
new alternatives and bring pressure to bear on governments to entertain new
alternatives, thus facilitating the resolution of conflicts.' Four forums are proposed:
Forum for regional supranational communities; Forum for international science and
professional associations; Forum of multinational business enterprises; and Forum of
universities.

The International Committee of the Red Cross.
See item no. 757.

Functions of the United Nations Organization

Preventive diplomacy

382 **The international law and practice of early warning and preventive diplomacy: the emerging global watch.**
B.G. Ramcharan. Dordrecht, The Netherlands: M. Nijhoff, 1991. 185p. bibliog.

'Preventive diplomacy', as used by Dag Hammarskjöld, was prior to all the *corrective* means of peaceful settlement, and broader in concept from what is now called 'global watch'. Ramcharan uses 'global watch' to mean, since domestic conflict is now a prime source of international conflict, the competence of the Secretary-General and hence the Security Council to investigate domestic affairs, not to intervene in them. Such investigation is allowed, the author argues, for the purposes of protecting human rights and democracy (sources of the legitimacy of governments) or protecting social minorities and indigenous peoples, whose abuse can cause international concern. The author surveys innovations (since 1985) in the office of the Secretary-General for fact-finding, early warning, and preventive diplomacy, especially observation of elections and resolution of internal conflicts. He reviews new principles and policies and discusses new institutions, notably Pérez de Cuéllar's Office for Research and Collection of Information. He then examines the practice of early warning about political crises, humanitarian emergencies, environmental disasters, and demands for basic needs. Ramcharan concludes that early warning is already established as a feature of international cooperation, meets a common need, and will likely grow in the future. He sets out ten legal principles to guide the U.N. and member-states when dividing the labour of taking urgent action to meet emergencies and disasters.

383 **Lebanon, 1958: Preventive diplomacy. [And] More preventive diplomacy.**
Brian Urquhart. In: *Hammarskjöld.* New York: Harper Colophon, 1972, p.261-314.

This is a convenient and instructive source for entering into the concept of preventive diplomacy, as Dag Hammarskjöld, who invented the practice, used the term. The former Secretary-General realized that preventive action was far more effective than corrective action, and he sought to enlist the middle powers, like Canada, in efforts to keep the Cold War from spreading. The U.N. Observer Group in Lebanon (UNOGIL, 1958) was a 'classical case of preventive diplomacy'.

384 **Preventive diplomacy.**
Boutros Boutros-Ghali. In: *An agenda for peace,* by Boutros Boutros-Ghali. New York: United Nations, 1992, p.13-19. (DPI/1247).

The Secretary-General discusses an array of currently acceptable measures to prevent conflict before it breaks out. These include confidence building measures (exchange of military missions, regional risk reduction centres, etc.), fact-finding (information provided by member-states, missions sent out by Security Council), early warning (reports by regional organizations), preventive deployment of peacekeeping troops or humanitarian agencies on the request of one country, and demilitarized zones.

Peaceful Settlement of Disputes (Chapter VI) and conflict resolution

385 **Alternative to war: conflict resolution and the peaceful settlement of international disputes.**
Keith Suter. Sydney: Women's International League for Peace and Freedom, 1981; 2nd ed., 1986. 151p.

'Opposition to nuclear weapons is not enough', writes this Australian scholar. 'There has to be simultaneous development of alternative ways of settling disputes.' This compact book pays special attention to the role of non-governmental organizations (NGOs), such as his publisher, in 'talking to governments and seeking their support for more effective machinery for the peaceful settlement of disputes'. Suter describes the history of peaceful settlement (the only other means is settlement by force), with particular reference to such cases as the Falklands/Malvinas crisis (1982) and the Iranian hostage seizure (1979-81). He concludes the book with practical suggestions for building public opinion behind peaceful settlement, launching a public campaign for mediation and conciliation like that for disarmament, and establishing such NGO initiatives as a centre for conflict resolution, a centre for human rights and responsibilities, and even a 'supranational independent thinking organization' (like that of Edward de Bono).

386 **An alternative to war or surrender.**
Charles E. Osgood. Urbana, IL: University of Illinois Press, 1962. 183p.

Graduated reciprocation in tension reduction (GRIT) was a concept of conflict reduction proposed by the author in the depths of the Cold War. As long as nuclear weapons exist and the possibility of Great Power tension continues, GRIT offers a practical way to avoid war. Osgood argues that Russians and Americans are equally motivated by a search for security, and that tensions can be reduced without sacrificing ideology. GRIT was similar to recent ideas of build-down and common security.

387   **Conflict and defense: a general theory.**
Kenneth Boulding.   New York: Harper & Row, 1962. 349p.

The author, an economist who had great influence on the peace movement (he co-founded the *Journal of Conflict Resolution* in 1957), here expands the 'theory of oligopoly, that is, of competition among a few firms', into a general theory of international conflict that could undergird the 'broad movement for the abolition of war'. Boulding concludes with a chapter on conflict resolution and control, which covers avoidance, conquest, reconciliation, compromise, and award of a third party. The latter is further analysed as mediation, conciliation, arbitration, adjudication, and political settlement. 'It is easy to see that the institutions that might have prevented the two world wars were simply not present; it is more difficult to specify the institutions that will prevent a third, a possibly last, world war.'

388   **Conflict and peace in the modern international system: a study of the principles of international order.**
Evan Luard.   Basingstoke, England: Macmillan, 1968; Boston: Little, Brown, 2nd rev. ed., 1988. 318p.

The author clearly understands that, before the rule of law can maintain order in international society, there will have to be a long period when 'understanding and conventions' (customary international law) must be improved. Luard surveys empirically the history of international conflict – particularly external wars, civil wars, and wars over frontiers and colonies; he then discusses realistically but not cynically such devices to reduce conflict as arms control, disarmament, world authority (U.N.), developing international law, and growing world public opinion as a check on governments. The book is often used in the teaching of international relations.

389   **Conflict in world society: a new perspective on international relations.**
Edited by Michael Banks. Foreword by Herbert Kelman.   Brighton, England: Wheatsheaf, 1984. 234p. bibliog.

The British, under the influence of 'generalist' John Burton, have developed a school of thought on 'world society' rather like American 'interdependence' theory. Old problems of international politics are being reinterpreted in the light of a 'pluralistic world view which most scholars in the discipline now accept'. This edition of new thinking includes a study of the origin, development, and resolution of conflict (by Anthony de Reuck); another on the usefulness of social psychology in the resolution of conflict (by A.N. Oppenheim); and a third on the problem-solving workshop (by Margot Light). Burton's proposed International Facilitating Service (a professional NGO offering conflict resolution to governments and other parties) remains suggestive.

390 Conflict: resolution and provention.

John W. Burton. Foreword by Samuel W. Lewis. New York:
St. Martin's, 1990. 295p. bibliog.

Conflict resolution has emerged as a new discipline in the study and conduct of international relations – distinct from coercive settlement and management by nuclear deterrence and military preparedness. This lead volume in a series of four supported by the U.S. Institute of Peace aims to clarify the concepts and settle the terminology of the field. Burton himself, a major innovator, prefers the term *provention* in the title to avoid the connotation of containment in *prevention*. Provention emphasizes provision of devices to eliminate sources of conflict and promotion of conditions favoring collaboration for their resolution. In this book, Burton methodically sets out the approach, political context, technique of conflict resolution, and 'provention'. In his conclusion, he looks on conflict resolution as a 'political system' in place of communism and Western liberalism, exhausted by their mutual struggle in the Cold War.

391 Conflict resolution in 1988: the role of the United Nations.

Brian Urquhart. In: *SIPRI Yearbook, 1989: world armaments and disarmament.* Oxford: Oxford University Press, 1989, p.445-60.

By 1988, the warming trend in the Cold War was creating, in the view of this seasoned U.N. official, 'a global context in which peaceful settlement of disputes can take hold'. Urquhart describes this context in terms of an effective Security Council and continued bilateral agreements on arms control and European policy. He gives credit to Soviet General Secretary Mikhail Gorbachev's 'new rules for coexistence' (1987), which called for an expanded U.N. role in international affairs. U.S. President Ronald Reagan could only find 'cause for shaking the head in wonder' (1988), but he also reciprocated, if slowly, with constructive counter-proposals on medium-range missiles and regional conflicts. Urquhart reviews the contribution of U.N. peace-keeping operations and emphasizes the continuing need for superpower cooperation in the international authority behind them. Conflicts in Afghanistan, Iran–Iraq, Namibia, Western Sahara, Cyprus, and Kampuchea (Cambodia) were ripe for U.N. settlement. He concludes that the causes of the 'reversion to negotiation and the techniques of peaceful settlement' are: the improvement of East–West relations, Gorbachev's 'reshaping of Soviet international policy', American responsiveness, the readiness of the Security Council, the Secretary-General's 'creative and patient diplomacy', and the latent capacity of the whole U.N. system. He predicts more 'uphill and nerve-racking work' to achieve the world 'rule of law'.

392 The Declaration on the Peaceful Settlement of International Disputes (Manila).

Bengt Broms. In: *Essays in international law in honour of Judge Manfred Lachs.* Edited by Jerzy Makarczyk. The Hague: M. Nijhoff, 1984, p.339-53.

The Manila Declaration of 1982 was the outgrowth of over a decade's efforts to revise the U.N. Charter or, failing that, to reform or strengthen its existing structures for maintaining international peace and security. This scholarly article concludes that while 'the Declaration does not create new and original methods for the settlement of international disputes, it is important that these principles have been collected and included in one single legal document'. For text, see Osmańczyk, *Encyclopedia of the*

United Nations (item no. 4). The Manila Declaration is the next step to a treaty on peaceful settlement and possibly to a revised U.N. Charter.

393 **The dispute settlement clause of the 1986 Vienna Convention on the Law of Treaties.**
Moritaka Hayashi. *New York University Journal of International Law and Politics*, vol. 19 (1987), p.327-56.

The Vienna Convention on the Law of Treaties codified the international law for treaties between states and international organizations (like the U.N.) and the law for *treaties* between *international organizations*. One of its most controversial parts, which required a formal vote, was Article 66, on dispute settlement. The author, a Japanese minister for legal affairs, traces the history of this article and of the convention as a whole. Article 66 provides for a *binding advisory* opinion of the ICJ to settle a dispute between a state and an international organization, or between two international organizations, in cases involving the most well-established (*jus cogens*) norms of international law. An alternative article provided only for voluntary conciliation in such cases, but it was voted down. Objections that the compulsory procedure 'infringed upon state sovereignty', 'stretched the limits of international law and practice in consultative procedures', and compelled the General Assembly and the Security Council to discuss such a case in the future 'on its merits' were answered by pointing to existing consistent international legal practice. The author fully approves of the result. 'The 1986 Convention is the first occasion that the international community has adopted such a comprehensive system of ICJ procedures in a multilateral treaty. Thus, the 1986 Convention can be characterized as landmark international legislation as far as dispute settlement is concerned.' (Hayashi does not comment on the ICJ's 1986 *Nicaragua* decision!)

394 **Dispute settlement through the United Nations.**
Edited by K. Venkata Raman.   New York: Oceana for UNITAR, 1977. 489p. bibliog.

This is a compilation of major studies by UNITAR scholars on the procedures and mechanisms for the peaceful settlement of disputes within the United Nations system. Emphasis is on the practical needs of diplomats, experts, and others directly involved in dispute settlement. Some 86 disputes and 15 ICJ cases are discussed. Thorough attention is given to disputes between India and Pakistan, in Cyprus, the Middle East, Bangaladesh, and Vietnam. The study is virtually exhaustive up to 1977. Topics include: peaceful settlement, third-party roles, mediation, international law, intervention in internal conflict, procedure, consultation and consensus in the Security Council, and good offices of the Secretary-General.

395 **Draft general treaty on the peaceful settlement of international disputes: a proposal and report.**
American Bar Association, Standing Committee on World Order under Law. Louis B. Sohn, principal author.   *International Lawyer*, vol. 20 (1986), p.261-91.

The General Act for the Pacific Settlement of International Disputes was adopted by the U.N. General Assembly in 1949 and entered into force the next year. An act by the same name was adopted by the League of Nations in 1928 but was ratified by only seven states and never entered into force. This private draft by the ABA in 1986 provides for clearer general obligations, negotiation, good offices, mediation, inquiry, conciliation, arbitration, and judicial settlement. The roles of the Security Council, General Assembly, and International Court of Justice are explicitly set out. Novel guidelines for a statute of a permanent conciliation commission, another statute of a permanent arbitral tribunal, and a resolution on advisory opinions of the ICJ are also provided.

396 The future of dispute settlement.

Louis B. Sohn. In: *The structure and process of international law: essays in legal philosophy, doctrine, and theory.* Edited by R. St.J. Macdonald and Douglas M. Johnston. The Hague: M. Nijhoff, 1983, p.1121-46.

The author ably surveys the present state of international dispute settlement, especially as found in Chapter VI of the U.N. Charter, but also elsewhere as in European conventions and the law of the sea. The basic techniques are negotiation, good offices, mediation, inquiry and fact-finding, conciliation, arbitration, and adjudication by international courts. Sohn's suggestions for the future include accepting greater diversification (decentralization) of dispute settlement; broadening the jurisdiction of the ICJ, especially by widening the scope of advisory opinions as in the E.C.; and establishing a U.N. mediation and conciliation service.

397 Global conflict: the domestic sources of international crisis.

John W. Burton. Foreword by Edward E. Azar. Brighton, England: Wheatsheaf, 1984. 194p. bibliog.

Said to be 'Burton's General Theory' of conflict resolution – analogous to Keynes' *General theory of employment, interest, and money* – this book succinctly provides the 'analytical framework' for a successor to the theory of power politics. Burton argues that the contemporary emerging politics of common security, or protection of human rights (even if 'domestic'), or preservation of the environment are rooted in 'human needs concerned with development as well as survival'. That is, the structures and institutions of international life – especially those now being defended by military force in the interests of shallow elites – are being revealed as not based on the 'individual', and hence they are being revolutionized. The securit one people is not based on the insecurity of another, but on the security of all. The United Nations, in his analysis, is a 'failure', for it cannot address domestic conflicts that spill over into the international system. The U.N. then attempts to resolve the conflicts when they have enlarged to national dimensions by an adversarial process utilizing the threat of international force. (In the *Federalist Papers*, this fault was called the attempt to legislate for communities, as contradistinguished from the individuals whom they contain.) Burton's prescription is to introduce conflict resolution into government negotiations, especially by second-track diplomacy and by scholarly collaborations. When he wrote this book, the global conflict between Russia and America seemed to be a fact of international relations; ten U.N. System Peaceful Settlement of Disputes 193 years later the cry of 'human developmental needs' had yet to be fully heard in the West.

398 **Handbook on the peaceful settlement of disputes between states.**
U.N. Office of Legal Affairs, Codification Division. New York:
United Nations, 1992. 229p. (OLA/COD/2394. E.92.V.7).
This is the long-awaited authoritative and comprehensive guide to 'peacemaking' –
that is, to peaceful settlement of disputes (Chapter VI). Its subject is not to be
confused with enforcement (Chapter VII). Peacemaking includes: negotiation,
inquiry, good offices, mediation, conciliation, arbitration, adjudication or judicial
settlement, resort to region agencies or arrangements, adaptations of familiar means,
or novel means specified in treaties. Roles of the principal international organs are
also set out: Security Council, General Assembly, Secretariat, International Court of
Justice, specialized agencies (including GATT), and non-permanent institutions
provided for in multilateral treaties. The bibliography includes works in languages
other than English. The handbook can be envisaged as a basis for drafting a universal
convention on the peaceful settlement of disputes, perhaps during the Decade of
International Law (1990-99). Compare Sohn's *Draft general treaty on the peaceful
settlement of international disputes* (item no. 395).

399 **How wars end: the United Nations and the termination of armed
conflict, 1946-1964.**
Sydney D. Bailey. Oxford: Clarendon Press, 1982. 2 vols. bibliog.
The author closely studies seven cases of conflicts that were brought to the U.N.
Security Council and resolved, or at least were brought to ceasefires: Indonesia
(1947-48), Kashmir (1947-49), Palestine (1947-49), Indonesia (1948-49), Korea
(1950-53), Sinai and Suez (1956-57), and Cyprus (1964). The Vietnam War is not
treated since it never came before the Security Council. The cases may seem
somewhat remote from concerns after the end of the Cold War, but Bailey provides a
wise historical perspective that the serious reader will easily apply to current
conflicts, especially those in which peacekeeping is frustrated. His goal is to explain
'How to stop wars'. He defines terms, sets out the diplomatic processes in the
Security Council, discusses problems in the field, and concludes with humanitarian
questions.

400 **The intermediaries: third parties in international crisis.**
Oran R. Young. Princeton, NJ: Princeton University Press, 1967.
427p. bibliog.
This is a standard theoretical and empirical analysis of third-party intervention –
particularly that of the Secretary-General in the Sinai and Congo crises, which saw
the creation of peacekeeping forces. Young also considers the potential intervention
of non-aligned states, regional organizations, and NGOs. In a dark time, he foresaw
that the U.N. could play an intermediary role in Soviet–American crises, as had
happened already in the Cuban missile crisis of 1962, and would happen again in the
Middle East crisis of 1973 and in response to Gorbachev's initiatives in 1988. The
book is still a staple of international relations theorists.

401 **International conflict resolution.**
Edited by Ramesh Thakur. Foreword by David Lange. Boulder, CO:
Westview, 1988. 309p. bibliog.
This book is a report of an important scholarly conference on conflict resolution held
in New Zealand in 1987, but it is broader and more politically reflective than many

such works. Prime Minister David Lange, who had astonished the world by closing his country's seaports to vessels carrying nuclear weapons, writes that the conference came to three conclusions: (1) There are ways to avoid or end conflict without war or 'systematic appeasement'. (2) Conflict today is rooted less in disputed national boundaries than in 'issues of equity and justice' within and between nations. (3) The nuclear threat symbolizes the 'inadequacy of war as a means of resolving differences between nations'. Ramesh Thakur, who in his thinking about the causes and cures of modern conflict is not above quoting the Buddha and American Indian visionaries, briefly skirts the idea of a unitary world government only to fall back on something more like a world federation. 'Continued survival of the species may come through the cohesive integrity of traditional civic society fulfilling basic needs, rather than through the homogenization of an integrated nation-state or world-state. . . . One suggestion that came up in discussions was the idea of geographically dispersed, functionally compartmentalized supranational governments for dealing with such subjects as ocean management and human rights, subjects that transcend national frontiers.' Topics include: comprehensive security, Soviet 'new thinking', the history of wars, new approaches to conflict resolution, disarmament, mediation, peacekeeping, the Third World critique of the superpowers, the role of the churches, environmentalism, and a working global security system in place of nuclear deterrence.

402 **International conflict resolution: theory and practice.**
Edited by Edward E. Azar and John Burton. Brighton, England: Wheatsheaf, 1986; Boulder, CO: L. Rienner, 1986. 159p. bibliog.

International conflict resolution has become a sophisticated scholarly discipline, of which this book of essays is an example. But theory has not quite caught up with practice, nor do the practitioners read much of the new literature of the theorists – as both Michael Banks in the first essay and Ambassador John W. McDonald in the last acknowledge. This book attempts to bridge the gap. It contains excellent chapters on traditional international relations theory (which 'leads logically to threat and deterrence systems'), on the new theory of conflict resolution in a 'world society . . . with no institutionalized means of resolving conflicts peacefully', and on practical procedures and problem solving processes, as applied to Soviet–U.S. relations and the frustrating case of Lebanon. An essay by Anthony D. Smith on class, ethnicity, and nationalism looks forward to 'inter-communal' politics – which some saw as 'unrealistic' in U.N. System Peaceful Settlement of Disputes 195 1985. Readers today might find it increasingly suggestive in the era of ethnic conflict. But Ambassador McDonald cautions: '"The international community", absent a world government, is not in a position to manage or negotiate these suggested changes.' The book is a study of 'Track II diplomacy' – private or citizen diplomacy in support of official or governmental (Track I) diplomacy.

403 **International dispute settlement.**
John G. Merrills. London: Sweet & Maxwell, 1984; 2nd ed., Cambridge: Grotius, 1991. 288p.

This second edition of a magisterial text brings its account of peaceful settlement up to the post-Cold War period. Merrills places the instrumentalities of the United Nations (Chapter VI) into the broad and general context of diplomatic negotiation (still the basic means of peaceful settlement), inquiry, mediation, conciliation, arbitration, adjudication through the World Court (a U.N. organ), the law of the sea, and regional organizations. He is aware of the failings of the U.N., but he finds, with U Thant, that 'the failure of the United Nations is the failure of the international community'. As Merrills explains, 'The United Nations, then, is in no sense a world government, but a diplomatic forum in which persuasion, argument, negotiation, and a search for consensus are the means available for handling international disputes.' His suggestions for improving the capacity of the U.N. include earlier recourse to Chapter VI by the Security Council, greater cooperation between the United States and the Soviet Union (now Russia), better financing and intelligence-gathering for the Secretary-General's good offices, better linkages between peacekeeping and actual dispute settlement (peacemaking), and general U.N. reform. Weaknesses in the whole U.N. system, he concludes, 'will therefore not be rectified until a sufficient number of influential states decide that they are prepared to accept an organization which can act effectively, rather than one whose activities are to be judged solely by the criterion of immediate national advantage'.

404 **International disputes: case histories, 1945-1970.**
Michael D. Donelan and M.J. Grieve.   New York: St. Martin's for
David Davies Memorial Institute of International Studies, 1973. 286p.

This volume of fifty case-histories complements the earlier two volumes (below) on international disputes in their political and legal aspects. Here will be found brief and exact accounts of many famous disputes, such as that in Poland (1941-47), which could be said to mark the beginning of the Cold War, or the Cuban missile crisis (1962), which marked its height. The United Nations and other international organizations are mentioned in context so that the objective reader will gain a sense of proportion about their contribution to dispute settlement. The authors are inclined to see the system of states as a 'world society', yet they are compelled by the facts in 1970 to regard it as an 'inter-state society' of 140 sovereign states. But this makes true 'world politics', in which individuals would feel a common consciousness as world citizens and would take common action to meet world problems, impossible, though there is already, they argue, *world economics*. 'To speak of world politics, still more to attempt to theorize about it, is an absurdity. It will remain so until all human beings are members of one state, a world community with a world authority.' Nevertheless, in an excellent introduction, Donelan and Grieve explain associations of states, their conflicts (over property, honour, power), bargaining, the reality of both competition and cooperation, statesmanship, and teaching international relations in a democratic society where the citizen wants and needs to know 'how his country should act'. They conclude that 'it is in the area of reason and justice that the great questions of international politics lie'.

405 **International disputes: the legal aspects.**
Edited by Humphrey Waldock. Foreword by Francis Vallat.   London:
Europa Publications for the David Davies Memorial Institute, 1972.
325p.

The threat and use of force for the settlement of international disputes has been prohibited in customary law and treaties (U.N. Charter, Article 2(4)). States furthermore have accepted the obligation to settle their disputes by peaceful means (Article 2(3)). Yet wars continue. As Sir Francis explains in his foreword to this fundamental study, 'an obligation of this kind requires content and machinery to be effective'. The whole book is an informed and critical study of how the rule of law can be made a reality within the U.N. system. Each of the means of peaceful settlement – negotiation, mediation, etc. – is treated in a separate chapter. The authors do not think the machinery of peaceful settlement in Chapter VI is inadequate. 'The real core of the problem is, and always has been, the attitudes of Governments towards the use of the various institutions and procedures of settlement.' The authors respond to legal objections that international law is uncertain and that compulsory jurisdiction cannot so easily be lifted out of the law of individual relations and applied to the much more complicated relations between states. They argue politically for the 'real benefits' of third-party settlement, and they make specific suggestions for the improvement of U.N. procedures, including completion of the long-awaited 'Handbook of peaceful settlement procedures [states]' (published in 1992).

406 **International disputes: the political aspects.**
F.S. Northedge and M.D. Donelan.   London: Europa Publications for the David Davies Memorial Institute of International Studies, 1971. 349p.

There are many studies of the *legal* aspects of international disputes. This clear and vigorous work is a study of their *political* aspects. The authors note that states are reluctant to employ third-party dispute settlement techniques (inquiry, mediation, conciliation, arbitration, adjudication, resort to regional agencies); states prefer two-party negotiation or other means (U.N. Charter, Article 33(1)). Northedge and Donelan then ask, 'What are the conditions, political, economic, military, or other, which facilitate or, as the case may be, militate against, the peaceful settlement of international disputes?' They approach this question not from an omniscient historical or sociological point of view, but from that of the statesman. They professedly aim at finding the 'unconscious general wisdom' of the current practitioners of statecraft in a world without strong central authority. With respect to the external forces at work and to the conditions to be favoured, they look for 'wisdom concerning human performance in politics'. The topics covered are: origins of disputes, their development, solutions. They conclude that, even under an ultimate world government, disputes will still need to be resolved by international institutions that are already in existence, and 'good statecraft' will have to use this machinery in order to arrive at a more lawful and orderly world. They are doubtful that, if the Cold War should wind down, a 'dyarchy of the super-powers' or even the whole U.N. Security Council could long provide the justice and legitimacy needed for the peaceful resolution of disputes. They urge all people to work for a more universal system. 'No social order can remain secure unless it accords with the sense of justice of most people most of the time.'

407 **Is there a role for the United Nations in conflict resolution?**
Raimo Väyrynen.   *Journal of Peace Research,* vol. 22 (1985), p.189-96.

The U.N. has a role, but not in cases of planned and determined aggression, as in the the Soviet invasion of Afghanistan (1979), the Iran–Iraq War (1980), the Israeli invasion of Lebanon (1982), the Argentine–British war over the Falklands/Malvinas (1982), or the genocide in Kampuchea (1975-79). The author was writing before the end of the Cold War, when it seemed that even Namibia would remain under the control of South Africa. His suggestions for strengthening the United Nations include meetings of the Security Council at the level of foreign ministers, increased fact-finding capability, an anticipatory intelligence network, and a limited right of intrusion into states' internal affairs.

408　Justice without law?

Jerold Auerbach.　New York: Oxford University Press, 1983. 182p.

The author of *Unequal justice*, who there warned of a 'plague of lawyers' in American life, here presents a philosophical and historical account of non-legal means of dispute settlement (mediation, conciliation, arbitration) within U.S. society. The book has virtually nothing to say about international conflict resolution, but it shows that the new techniques are rooted in the American 'communitarian' experience, and hence it points to a world community that resolves its conflicts without adversarial and contentious litigation. In fundamental ways, Auerbach argues, international relations are a search for 'justice without law', international law is far weaker (some say non-existent) than national law. It is not impossible that conflict resolution techniques introduced into the less organized field of world politics may have successes that will hasten their development within *national* societies, particularly in America.

409　The Kennedy experiment.

Amitai Etzioni.　*Western Political Quarterly*, vol. 20 (1967), p.361-80.

The author treats President Kennedy's statesmanship from his 'Strategy of peace' speech at American University (10 June 1963) to his assassination (22 November 1963) as a test of a psychological theory of international relations, which holds that unilateral initiatives to reduce tensions between states will, like similar gestures between persons, be reciprocated by the other side. The article is an early defence of the psychological analysis of international behaviour, which eventually received a respectable place in deterrence doctrine and theories of non-centralized conflict resolution. Since the causes of war are psychological, Etzioni argues, eliminating fears in the attitudes of people will have more effect on ending war than mere disarmament. He traces the effects of Kennedy's gestures: a partial nuclear test ban, cooperation in the U.N., a reduction of trade barriers, a spirit of détente in the Cold War. In terms of peaceful settlement, where the 'dispute' was the entire Cold War, Kennedy's initiative would probably have to be classified as a grand act of conciliation.

410　Legal institutions: the development of dispute settlement.

Peter Stein.　London: Butterworths, 1984. 236p.

This is an elementary account of the main institutions found in most developed legal systems, such as the Roman, English, French, and German ones. It has little to say about international law or the United Nations, but the attentive reader will find here a discussion of the fundamental issues of 'dispute settlement in order to preserve the peace of the community' that are very relevant to the peaceful settlement of disputes at the world level. Stein aims to help the student to identify 'institutions' ('established ways of doing things'), find the law, and recognize the institutions in which the law copes with recurring and new problems. Developed legal systems, he concludes, include dispute settlement; they are now are moving beyond settlement to prevention of conflict, imposition of duties, protection of rights and achievement of larger social goals such as equitable economic development and protection of labour. Where the law originally was concerned only with 'horizontal' relations between individual and individual, now it encompasses 'vertical' relations between the individual and his or her community.

411 **Managing international crises.**
Edited by Daniel Frei. Beverly Hills, CA: Sage for the International
Political Science Association, 1982. bibliog.

At the time this collection of political science papers from around the world was
assembled, the superpower conflict seemed to be at a permanent impasse marked by
working nuclear deterrence. Hence, the authors here devoted themselves to managing
confrontation between 'secondary powers'. The frequency of international crises,
straining the capacity of modern diplomacy to cope with them, had increased fourfold
since 1960, and each crisis threatened to escalate into 'uncontrollable war'. Hence,
crisis management had become, in the view of the editor, a replacement for *strategy*.
Most of the contributors emphasized better training of diplomats in crisis
management. Only one, Kinhide Mushakoji, pointed to the potential of the United
Nations. The U.N. itself, he showed, was 'in crisis'.

412 **Nonmilitary aspects of security: a systems approach.**
Dietrich Fischer. Aldershot, England: Dartmouth Publishing for
U.N. Institute for Disarmament Research, 1993. 222p. bibliog.
(Available from Ashgate Publishing, Old Post Road, Brookfield,
VT 05036.)

This study is a theoretical discussion of non-military threats to security: threats to
survival, health, economic well-being, environment, and political rights. Threats are
classified by source (domestic, foreign, global) and by intention (deliberate threats,
dangers from ignorance or negligence, natural dangers). There is little discussion of
specific countries, historical trends, policy problems. But it contains an excellent
overview of concepts of security (realist, neo-realist, idealist), definitions (military
and political), the emerging international reality of interdependence. It concludes with
a synthesis of elements of a comprehensive system of global security, with specific
correlations to U.N. programmes or agencies that could more adequately address the
non-military threats. A humane and diligent study.

413 **An overview of international dispute settlement.**
Richard B. Bilder. *Emory Journal of International Dispute
Settlement*, vol. 1 (1986), p.1-32.

American lawyers are trained in an adversarial system. Conflict resolution or the
peaceful resolution of disputes requires a more cooperative approach, to which this
substantial article is an excellent introduction. Bilder offers international lawyers a
'framework for thinking' about the subject. He defines a 'dispute', explains the
continuing need to settle disputes, reviews obligations on states in the U.N. Charter to
settle, and discusses politically the techniques of settlement (coercion, voluntary
relinquishment, chance, voting, negotiation, good offices, mediation, fact-finding,
inquiry, conciliation, arbitration, judicial settlement, resort to U.N. or other global or
regional organizations). He defends the relevance of international law to dispute
settlement: the law establishes obligation based on shared interests in an orderly
world, and it 'provides salient rules and principles which generally shape the parties'
perceptions of legitimacy and guide their efforts to reach agreement'.

414 **Peace and disputed sovereignty: reflections on conflict over territory.**
Friedrich Kratochwil, Paul Rohrlich, and Harpreet Mahajan.
Lanham, MD: University Press of America for Columbia University
Institute of War and Peace Studies, 1985. 159p.

The Falklands/Malvinas dispute is a classic case of an old conflict over boundaries
and sovereignty that finally erupted into war (1982). The authors consider seven other
similar cases (e.g., Japan's Kurile Islands, the Ethiopia–Somalia border, the Gulf of
Maine) and provide an appendix of scores of similar disputes. Their study searches
for a pattern of border disputes that escalate into violent conflict, seeks the conditions
for peaceful settlement without intervention by third parties, and explores the role of
impartial third parties in settlement. They conclude with practical suggestions for the
strengthening of conciliation.

415 **Peaceful settlement of disputes and international security.**
Louis B. Sohn. *Negotiation Journal*, vol. 3 (1987), p.155-66.

Sohn briefly reviews the main means of peaceful settlement. He then comes to grips
with problems of implementation, which are generally rooted in nations' sense of
injustice, as in the recurrent ceasefires and renewed outbreaks of violence in the
Middle East. 'The crucial question is really not just devising better methods for
settling disputes', he writes, 'but finding a way of improving the general acceptability
of the settlements arrived at by whatever method has been used.' He points out that
modern theories of law emphasize consensus in order to achieve just solutions rather
than coercion by exercise of the Security Council's enforcement powers. The framers
of the U.N. Charter did give the Council power to *decide* on measures to remove
threats to the peace or to stop aggression, but they wisely gave the Security Council
and the General Assembly powers only to *recommend* terms for the actual settlement
of disputes (Articles 11(2) and 37(2)). To explain why states still do not utilize the
existing legal means of settlement (arbitration and adjudication), Sohn reviews the
whole issue of *consent* in treaties providing for such means. He suggests obtaining
special consent after a dispute has arisen (Article 36(2)), limiting the scope of a
binding judgment, arranging for more non-binding advisory opinions, or removing the
dispute from the interstate plane by granting individuals and corporations standing
before international courts and tribunals, as in the E.C. He also suggests
improvements to negotiation and conciliation, and urges gathering U.N. provisions on
peaceful settlement into a code, which seems to have become the *Handbook on the
peaceful settlement of disputes between states* (1992) (item no. 398).

416 **Peaceful settlement of international disputes: an alternative to the
use of force.**
Galina Georgievna Shinkaretskaia. In: *The non-use of force in
international law.* Edited by W.E. Butler. Dordrecht, The
Netherlands: M. Nijhoff, 1989, p.39-52.

Writing in the Gorbachev era of 'restructuring', this Soviet international legal scholar
argues against the view, widely held, she remarks, in the West, 'that modern
international relations are based to a significant extent on power, and that violence as
a means of conducting policy is wholly lawful'. She shows this is false because of the
consistency of Articles 2(3) and 2(4), and because of the 'duty' to resolve their
disputes peacefully that states have accepted by adherence to the Charter. The whole

book will be of interest to practitioners and theorists of the non-use of force since it contains a full exchange by Soviet and British scholars. Topics include: history, principle, role of U.N. and Commonwealth, self-defence, economic power.

417 **Prototypes of peacemaking: the first forty years of the United Nations.**
Mary Allsebrook. Foreword by Lord Caradon. Harlow, England: Longman, 1986. 160p. bibliog.

Often it is claimed that the United Nations is effective in humanitarian assistance or even in economic aid, but is very ineffective in the resolution of political disputes. The author surveys over 200 disputes that came before the Security Council, General Assembly, Secretary-General, Economic and Social Council, Trusteeship Council, International Court of Justice, or other U.N. bodies (20 current in 1985) in order to draw the lessons of history for the future. She concludes that peacemaking is most successful if initiated before open hostilities have broken out; that peacekeeping or policing is complementary to peacemaking; that Security Council missions, General Assembly support for human rights (even if they infringe on a country's domestic jurisdiction), and Secretary-General's good offices will increase; that rhetorical politicization of the U.N. could be reduced by Security Council conciliation using subcommittees and even by a permanent settlement service within the Secretariat; that the U.N. needs an early warning or crisis anticipation system, perhaps by 'ambassadors' of the Secretary-General in troubled regions; and that the permanent members of the Security Council – especially if the Cold War winds down and all members accept coexistence – could assist peaceful resolution by voluntarily limiting the veto power, abstaining from voting in disputes to which they are parties or are directly interested, and devising means for monitoring and otherwise increasing the implementation of its policy decisions.

418 **Resolving deep-rooted conflict: a handbook.**
John W. Burton. Lanham, MD: University Press of America, 1987. 74p. bibliog.

This is a reprint of 'Procedures for facilitated international conflict resoluti a paper prepared for the U.S. Foreign Service Institute (Occasional Paper No. 4, 1985). 'Deep-rooted' conflicts between persons or nations involve not only interests, but also deep motivations, values, and needs that cannot be compromised. Traditional settlement of disputes by peaceful or coercive means were conceived as win–lose, and hence judicial, legal, or ultimately military means were practiced. This slim book sets out the new theory of win–win non-violent conflict resolution suitable for relations between states. It is called *facilitated* conflict resolution since the theory and practice depends on the role of a facilitator or panel of facilitators. In face-to-face situations, they aim at sustainable understanding and accommodation of parties in deep conflict, rather than at compromise, as in traditional mediation. Fifty-three rules of procedure for sponsorship, entry, preparation, analysis, search for options, policies, and follow-up are provided.

419 **The role of international institutions as conflict adjusting agencies.**
Louis B. Sohn. *University of Chicago Law Review*, vol. 28 (1961), p.205-57.

This long and learned article, written before the Cold War completely dimmed hopes in the United Nations, remains a luminous introduction to the peaceful settlement of international disputes, that is, to peacemaking (Chapter VI). Sohn defines and discusses diplomatic negotiation, good offices, inquiry, mediation, conciliation, arbitration, adjudication or judicial settlement, and resort to regional arrangements. He admits that states have been slow (since 1920) to accept legal resolution of even justiciable disputes – symbolized by the Connally reservation to U.S. acceptance of the compulsory jurisdiction of the ICJ, exempting domestic matters as determined by the United States (1946). To widen acceptance, he discusses how to expand the Court's jurisdiction, how to elect the most respected judges, and how to improve the international law applied by the Court. He also clarifies such fundamental and often misunderstood concepts as 'obligation', 'disputes', 'situations', 'questions', 'competent organs', 'recommendations', 'decisions', the distinction between 'legal' and 'political' disputes, and 'domestic jurisdiction'. Sohn concluded bravely before the Vietnam War, the war in Afghanistan, and scores of other wars: 'With a little courage and a lot of persistence, it may be hoped that almost all important disputes between nations will become amenable to a satisfactory process of settlement.'

420   **Settlement of disputes relating to the interpretation and application of treaties.**
Louis B. Sohn.   *Recueil des Cours*, vol. 150 (1976), p.195-294.
bibliog.

This long and expert article takes up the problem of the interpretation of treaties, especially as provided in their 'special compromissory clauses'. Settlement of such interpretation is mainly by arbitration or by adjudication before the World Court. Not included are 'general compromissory clauses', for the settlement of *all* disputes , or ordinary 'compromis', for the ad hoc settlement of existing ones. Sohn examines the methods of legal dispute settlement and the main preconditions for resorting to arbitration or adjudication. He closes with an examination of the 'veritable code on dispute settlement' in the emerging Law of the Sea convention. He is aware that large, powerful states may employ 'extra-legal, political and economic pressures' to bring about a settlement, but legal settlement, he maintains, is based on equality before the law – applicable to large and small states alike.

421   **Social conflicts and third parties: strategies of conflict resolution.**
Jacob Bercovitch.   Boulder, CO: Westview, 1984. 163p. bibliog.

This is a short social science text on conflict management and resolution, with special attention to third-party intervention. The approach is broad and inclusive, dealing with conflict resolution in the family, factory, nation, and world. The section on international conflict takes up but one chapter. The author correctly understands U.N. peacemaking in the terms of Chapter VI of the Charter. The work has some quantitative data, but methodologically it is primarily based on 'verbal data' from interviews with practitioners. It studies 'third-party intervention from the perspective of the interveners themselves'.

422   **The structure of impartiality: examining the riddle of one law in a fragmented world.**
Thomas M. Franck.   New York: Macmillan, 1968. 344p.

This older but brilliant book will still be useful to students who are trying to understand the philosophical foundations of third-party dispute settlement in an anarchic world – in Franck's terms, how 'even a much less organized society [than the national state] may nevertheless govern much of its conduct by laws'. He argues that law is progressively rooted in power (one party), compromise (two parties), and impartial settlement as by a court (third party). He suggests that, since politicians cannot be expected to lead, lawyers and citizens must 'denationalize international disputes' in order to build up the 'morality of impartiality'.

423 **A survey of treaty provisions for the pacific settlement of international disputes, 1949-1962.**
United Nations.   New York: United Nations, 1966. 901p.

This survey, which reprints 301 treaties, complements the earlier *Systematic survey of treaties for the pacific settlement of international disputes, 1928-1948*, which reprinted 234. But after World War II, the number of treaties concerned solely with pacific settlement declined from 207 to 8 – reflecting humanity's loss of faith in the efficacy of such treaties in a supreme crisis. Hence, the new survey includes treaties on international cooperation that contain *provisions* for pacific settlement, which is the current more modest yet politically more sophisticated approach. Here the reader will find the text of modern treaties with such provisions: treaties of alliance (e.g., North Atlantic Treaty, Warsaw Pact), treaties of regional cooperation (E.C.), agreements on communications and transportation, agreements on economic matters (GATT) and on commodities (sugar, olive oil), conventions of social and humanitarian interest (human rights), bilateral agreements on trade, exchange, and economic cooperation, treaties of friendship (U.S.S.R. and Hungary, U.S. and Japan), agreements on treatment of nationals, on frontiers and boundary waters.

424 **Toward a strategy of peace.**
John F. Kennedy.   *Department of State Bulletin*, vol. 44 (1963), p.2-6.

This is Kennedy's historic speech at American University on 10 June 1963. The former President, soon after resolution of the Cuban missile crisis, urged an end to the Cold War. He pointed out the 'common interests' of the United States and the Soviet Union – above all, mutual abhorrence of war – and he warned that weapons originally designed for deterrence had caught up both countries in a 'vicious and dangerous cycle in which suspicion on one side breeds suspicion on the other, and new weapons beget counterweapons'. To break out of this cycle, Kennedy called for a comprehensive test ban and announced a unilateral U.S. moratorium on nuclear testing in the atmosphere. The long-range American interest, he explained, was 'general and complete disarmament'. And since disarmament alone would not enhance national security, he further called for effective international control – 'strengthening the United Nations . . . into a genuine world security system – a system capable of resolving disputes on the basis of law, of insuring the security of the large and the small. . . .' Finally, Kennedy ca for a peace based on human rights, especially freedom from fear and freedom of speech.

425 **The United Nations and collective management of international conflict.**
Ernst B. Haas.   New York: UNITAR, 1986. 73p. (E.86.XV.ST.19).

In an effort to measure the effectiveness of international conflict management, the author found 319 disputes from July 1945 to September 1984. Of these, 137 reached the U.N. agenda, 30 the O.A.S., 27 the O.A.U., 24 the Arab League, and 5 the

Council of Europe. (Such a quantitative study could not account for *potential* conflicts that the Security Council or the Secretary-General diffused through quiet diplomacy, which may, judging by Boutros-Ghali's report of 1993, be as high as 100 per year.) Haas's conclusion: 'There is a decline in the effectiveness of the United Nations and the regional organizations.' Yet he also finds that the U.N. has a better record of abating (half were abated), if not settling, disputes; peacekeeping, which gains only time for the negotiation of a settlement, is a good example. Moreover, he points out, there is no lack of disputes *referred* to the U.N. Haas sternly explains that *success* in *settling* a dispute is most often correlated, not with U.N. impartiality, but with a preference of one of the permanent members of the Security Council, or with a two-thirds majority in the General Assembly led by a superpower, or with a temporary coalition put together by a daring Secretary-General and supported by a superpower. 'The most persistent weakness of the United Nations is that it is unable, except in rare circumstances [like decolonization] to settle any dispute with finality.' To make things better, Haas does not suggest any palliatives like strengthening peacekeeping. Governments, rather, must learn to accept 'constraints' on their war powers in circumstances that have led to war in the past. He argues that, after forty years of the Cold War, governments *have learned* to accept such constraint, 'though it has not been cumulative, nor equally internalized by all states, and is subject to reversals'. After constraint, he sees little sign that the national states have learned 'reciprocity', on which the rule of world law could be based. But these are developing in the social and economic fora of the U.N.

426   **The United Nations and the control of international violence:
      a legal and political analysis.**
      John F. Murphy.   Totowa, NJ: Allanheld, Osmun, 1982. 212p.

The author, who has been both a legal adviser in the U.S. Department of State and a professor of international law interested in the U.N.'s practical contributions to dispute settlement, here treats first 'traditional violence' of the sort the U.N. was designed to prevent and stop – aggression and armed invasion across borders. He then treats 'non-traditional violence', which has plagued the U.N. and exceeded current international law and practice to cope with it – revolutionary warfare and violence, wars of assassination, surrogate warfare, and terrorism. He recommends giving the Secretary-General an early warning system, widening acceptance of the ICJ's compulsory jurisdiction (that was before the *Nicaragua* case), improving the General Assembly's powers of negotiation, conciliation, and mediation, and 'creatively and energetically' using the U.N. to resolve conflicts in southern Africa and the Middle East.

427   **The United Nations and the resolution of international conflicts.**
      Raimo Väyrynen.   *Cooperation and Conflict*, vol. 20 (1985),
      p.141-71.

The U.N. has little – but not no – power to resolve conflicts between the superpowers or between their allies. After a long decline of the U.N. from the period of U.S. hegemony, through decolonization, to the more recent fragmentation and disagreement, the author argues, the kind of conflicts referred to it were 'peripheral' to the centres of power, and the U.N. experienced difficulties in settling them. Vayrynen, a Finnish scholar, argues that strengthening U.N. peacekeeping missions will require both political and technical reforms. The political consensus and diplomatic activity in the Security Council, on which peacekeeping depends, could be enhanced by granting the Secretary-General greater fact-finding powers and by convening the Council more often at the level of foreign ministers. Council and Secretary, in turn, would be assisted by better communications and intelligence facilities, including international technical means on satellites, and by standing international military forces on the Nordic model. The U.N., Väyrynen concludes, has always been a creature of its environment, so such enhancements will be a reflection of shared needs in a multipolar world.

428   **Why we still need the United Nations: The collective management of international conflict, 1945-1984.**
Ernst B. Haas.   Berkeley, CA: Institute of International Studies, University of California, 1986. 104p.
'To attribute failure to the United Nations and to regional organizations is to endow these entities with a degree of autonomy they do not possess.' The author shows, historically and statistically, that collective conflict management has had a respectable rate of success, though the trend is downward. But as long as collective management is an aspect of foreign policy of sovereign states, rather than of an autonomous world organization, Haas argues, the search for the causes of decline must enter the field of national culture and policy, which remains reluctant to utilize collective means of peaceful settlement. Things could be better, he wryly remarks, if 'nation-states cease being themselves'. Haas carefully measures the 'marginal but not absent' impact of the U.N. on moderating international conflict, and he takes up the hard question, whether the U.N. can deal with the underlying, rather than the proximate, causes of such conflict. Can the U.N. settle any dispute with finality, or will it merely contain it until it reappears in the next crisis? His conclusion is negative, historically; the reason is that 'the U.N. is and always has been viewed by its members as an instrument of foreign policy'. Haas closes with his own prescriptions for U.N. reform, which fall between the extremes of world federalism and muddling through.

Negotiation

429   **The art and science of negotiation.**
Howard Raiffa.   Cambridge, MA: Belknap, Harvard University Press, 1982. 373p. bibliog.
The author of this practical and theoretical book began his career as a decision analyst and game theorist, and he ended as a teacher of a course on competitive decision-making at the Harvard Business School. Hence, Raiffa approaches negotiation very inclusively as dispute settlement between individuals, labour and management, business firms, nations, and (he expects whimsically) planets. International negotiation is treated within this larger context. Particular attention is focused on negotiations over the Panama Canal, Middle East, and Law of the Sea. He concludes that, like theories of the firm, theories of negotiation tend to be adequate only to a first approximation; thereafter, what is needed is a 'bag of analytical tools along with a sprinking of specialists . . . who can interact on an ad hoc, consultative basis with decision makers'.

430 **Bargaining and negotiation in international relations.**
Jack Sawyer and Harold Guetzkow. In: *International behaviour: a social-psychological analysis*. Edited by Herbert C. Kelman. New York: Holt, Reinhart & Winston, 1965, p.466-520.

International negotiation, in which the participants are bound by instructions from their governments, is contrasted elsewhere in this book with domestic negotiation, where individuals are freer to act in accordance with their sense of the merits. Sawyer and Guetzkow provide here a rather traditional theory of international negotiation, emphasizing its conditions, goals, processes (decision to enter, matrix of choices between compromise and intransigence, communication, persuasion, threats and promises, *fait accompli*, new alternatives), and its outcomes.

431 **Bargaining in international conflicts.**
Charles Lockhart. New York: Columbia University Press, 1979. 205p. bibliog.

The author approaches negotiation (a term he does not use) from the perspective of economic, administrative, or psychological bargaining theory. He applies his theories to severe international conflicts like the Cuban missile crisis, which he interprets uniformly as consisting of an intolerable violation, an act of resistance, a confrontation, and an accommodation. The practical implications for settlement are unclear, however, and even the author in his conclusion admits the predictive power of his theories are 'vague'. This is a book for international relations theorists.

432 **Further explorations of track two diplomacy.**
John W. McDonald. In: *Timing the de-escalation of conflicts*. Edited by Louis Kriesberg and Stuart J. Thorson. Syracuse, NY: Syracuse University Press, 1991, p.201-20.

International war is decreasing in frequency, but domestic conflict threatening international peace and security is increasing. In 1987, there were in the world thirty-six conflicts in which more than 1,000 people were killed, but only four were cross-border wars (Iran–Iraq, Libya–Chad, Thailand–Laos, Vietnam–China). The author sets out the advantages of 'track two' or citizen diplomacy for resolving conflicts short of war. The work of the National Resources Defense Council (a U.S. citizens organization) to build confidence in the verification of a comprehensive test ban is typical. McDonald includes guidelines to newcomers to track two diplomacy, so that they will not work at cross-purposes to negotiators in track one. Compare McDonald's *Multi-track diplomacy: A systems approach to peace* (1993), available from the Institute for Multi-track Diplomacy, 1133 Twentieth Street, NW, Suite 321, Washington, DC 20036.

433 **Getting to the table: the processes of international prenegotiation.**
Edited by Janet G. Stein. Baltimore, MD: Johns Hopkins University Press, 1989. 273p.

Negotiation is the most frequently used peaceful means of international settlement, but many disputes (of which the Arab–Israeli dispute is typical) never or rarely reach the negotiation stage. How does one bring angry parties to the negotiation table? This book addresses the vital problem of *prenegotiation*. The authors treat it as a process, particularly for the formation of agendas and initial bargaining positions. The process is illustrated in the cases of the North American Free Trade Agreement, the Uruguay Round of GATT, arms control (Soviet and U.S. sides), and the Arab–Israeli conflict. The editor concludes, 'A valid theory of prenegotiation can make an important contribution to the larger theory of negotiation.'

434   **Getting to yes: negotiating agreement without giving in.**
Roger Fisher and William Ury.   Boston: Houghton Mifflin, 1981; 2nd ed., 1991. 163p.

This popular book on negotiation has had great influence on establishing negotiation as a field of professional study in universities and business consulting firms. Louis B. Sohn advised the authors on international negotiation. Its features are treated throughout along with domestic negotiation. The approach is thoroughly practical and down to earth. Fisher and Ury call it neither soft (making too many concessions) nor hard (aiming only to win), but *principled negotiation*, 'hard on the merits, soft on the people'. The second edition contains an added section of ten questions people ask about *Getting to yes*. An analytical table of contents serves in lieu of an index.

435   **How nations negotiate.**
Fred C. Iklé.   New York: Harper & Row for the Center for International Affairs of Harvard University, 1964; reprinted ed., 1982. 274p. bibliog.

This is a standard work on negotiation, deliberately conceived at the Harvard Center for International Affairs to match the rigorous studies on the problems of war and of preventing it through deterrence and arms control that had been developed by U.S. strategic thinkers during the previous fifteen years. Iklé treats negotiation rather as certain colleagues treated nuclear weapons – as neither good nor bad in themselves, since the character of the men who controlled them was the important factor. 'But negotiation is only an instrument: it can be used on the side of the angels as well as by the forces of darkness.' This is a realistic, bright book from the Kennedy era that has had wide influence and cannot be ignored even now by serious theorists and practitioners.

436   **International negotiation: a multidisciplinary perspective.**
Janice G. Stein.   *Negotiation Journal*, vol. 4 (1988), p.221-31.

The author, an expert on prenegotiation, introduces a dedicated issue of the journal on 'the process of dispute settlement'. She expressly leaves out the two dominant disciplinary perspectives – history and political science (notably game theory) – and seeks 'new perspectives' from a political linguist, a sociologist and ethnographer, an anthropologist, a psychologist, a political psychologist, and a management specialist. They look upon negotiation as a rather common, purposeful form of social communication. They address the specific phenomenon of international negotiation, emphasizing the 'importance of context', but are rather frustrated by the methodological problems for social science of inadequate evidence in the record of the complex political, diplomatic, social, and intellectual proceedings.

437 **International negotiation: art and science.**
Edited by Diane B. Bendahmane and John W. McDonald, Jr.
Washington, DC: Foreign Service Institute, Department of State, 1984.
85p. bibliog. (SuDocs No. S1.114/3:N31/984).

This short work aims 'to synthesize the best of the practitioner's experience and skill and the best of the theoretical and conceptual work of the academic'. Topics include: negotiation in theory and reality, negotiation in Congress, mediation, relevance of domestic conflict resolution to international dispute settlement, teaching negotiation, prenegotiation, and cross-cultural communication. David Newsom's chapter, 'Domestic models of conflict resolution: Are they relevant in the international context?' is typical. He doubts that domestic experience will reveal new techniques for the resolution of difficult international conflicts. Domestic conflict resolution, in the United States, takes place under the rule of law, where there are 'broad understandings about how conflicts are resolved'. This is hardly true for the international context. Moreover, domestic disputes are between individuals or organizations, while international ones are between separate political systems; international negotiations involve complex bureaucratic supervision and constitutional constraints. His view comes down hard on the 'art' of negotiation.

438 **Negotiation: the alternative to hostility.**
Jimmy Carter. Macon, GA: Mercer University Press, 1984. 57p.

The former President here presents, with simplicity and grace, his reflections on negotiation after several historic successes, particularly the Israeli–Egyptian Peace Treaty of 1979. 'We need', he says, 'the same kind of bright thinking, unanticipated approaches, and unorthodox ideas to achieve the ancient goals of better justice and peace in the world.' Carter discusses negotiations over the Panama Canal Treaty, SALT II, majority rule in Zimbabwe, release of the American hostages from Iran, and the Israeli–Egyptian Treaty, drawing out the 'procedures and principles' of each that may be applied in the future. The process in many ways is the opposite of litigation, for negotiation aims to help all sides to win. He discusses the 'general framework', differences in national attitudes, the problem of premature public statements to the press, the use of threats and promises, and the value of a deadline. He applies seven rules to future talks on Middle East peace and nuclear arms reduction.

439 **Modern international negotiation: principles and practice.**
Arthur S. Lall. New York: Columbia University Press, 1966. 404p.

This book, written by a former Indian diplomat and professor at the School of International Affairs at Columbia University, remains an extended account of bilateral and particularly multilateral diplomacy within the ambit of the United Nations. All of the examples are drawn from before 1966, when of course the Cold War had dimmed the first light from the U.N., but Lall was especially fitted by his non-aligned national background and natural intelligence to perceive the beginnings of great things. In his chapter on conference diplomacy, for example, he points out that the resolution of the General Assembly in 1954 establishing the Disarmament Commission in place of the Security Council's twin and fractious Atomic Energy Commission and Commission on Conventional Armaments was 'tantamount to a legislative alteration of the Charter'. Readers interested in the history of peaceful settlement at the U.N. will find this book a rich secondary source.

440 **Perspectives on negotiation: four case studies and interpretations: Panama Canal treaties, Falkland/Malvinas islands, Cyprus dispute, Zimbabwe's independence.**
Edited by Diane B. Bendahmane and John W. McDonald, Jr.
Washington, DC: Foreign Service Institute, Department of State, 1986.
315p. bibliog.

This is a collaborative study from the U.S. State Department's perspective of long-term practical negotiation of four diverse and very difficult international disputes. In the final chapter, seventeen 'lessons' are drawn, e.g., (1) 'A continuous negotiation process increases the likelihood of settlement'; (2) 'A continuous negotiation process, within a power framework, decreases the likelihood of long-term resolutions'. The approaches include both 'track one' (official) and 'track two' (citizens') diplomacy. The conclusion emphasizes procedural flexibility, equitable conditions, and shrewd tactics.

441 **Processes of international negotiations.**
Edited by Frances Mautner-Markhof.   Boulder, CO: Westview, 1989.
541p. bibliog.

The pace, magnitude, and complexity of international negotiations have been rapidly increasing, and yet the acceptability, effectiveness, and implementation of the settlements have been decreasing. 'The processes of negotiations are in general taking more and more time and lagging behind the evolution of the international environment.' This book is a compendium of papers on modern negotiation given at an Australian institute of applied systems analysis. Participants came from most East and West developed countries and the U.N. Topics include: the role of international organizations; trade negotiations; cultural, psychological, and political factors; theoretical foundations and methods of analysis; training for negotiation; and negotiation on development and environmental issues. Both theorists and practitioners are represented.

442 **The SALT experience.**
Thomas W. Wolfe.   Cambridge, MA: Ballinger for the Rand Corp.,
1979. 405p. bibliog.

The Strategic Arms Limitation Talks I and II (1969-79) are here treated from four points of view: history, the institutional setting, the evolution of strategic policies, and the final pursuit over six years of a SALT II treaty. (During the Cold War some sixteen arms control treaties were negotiated between the United States and the Soviet Union.) The U.N. was hardly involved, but these negotiations between superpowers illustrate the worst of the problems between sovereign state antagonists, which will surely be met with again in the future by states or international organizations. In the last chapter, Wolfe allows his 'biases' to show. He wrote the book as if SALT were an 'institutional process' for the readjustment of power between the U.S. and the U.S.S.R., but it could be treated in three other ways: as the 'onl realistic alternative' to eventual nuclear war, as a distraction from 'unilatera strategic planning' on which effective deterrence is based, or (his own view) as a political symbol of 'superpower ability to both compete and cooperate'. By 1992, when the SALT II treaty had been supplemented by the INF, CFE, START, and other treaties and agreements (some with breakaway republics of the old Soviet Union), which cut even deeper into nuclear and conventional arms, the third alternative would seem to be the true one.

443 Small states and the peaceful settlement of disputes.
Mircea Malitza. In: *Multilateral negotiation and mediation: instruments and methods.* Edited by Arthur S. Lall. New York: Pergamon, 1985, p.77-88.

The author, a Romanian diplomat, suggests that small and medium-sized states can contribute to practical negotiations the 'principle of the comprehensive formula'. This is a diplomatic balance of the conflicting interests and cooperative values in any dispute designed to induce the parties to conduct themselves 'in harmony with the fundamental tendencies of the international community'. Some degree of international institutionalization is required, the author argues, to guarantee the parties against risks, discontinuity, and erosion of cooperation. Small and medium-sized states can maintain such a principle because they are more remote from great power responsibility and are more sympathetic to the local situation. If they set the example by renouncing force, their 'political' contribution to dispute settlement is then invaluable.

Inquiry and fact-finding

444 Factfinding and commissions of inquiry.
H.G. Darwin. In: *International disputes: the legal aspects.* Edited by Humphrey Waldock. London: Europa, 1972, p.159-77.

The author treats inquiry broadly, first outside international organizations (with discussion of cases), then, as fact-finding, within the U.N. He emphasizes that fact-finding is incidental alone, but vital in combination with the other peaceful means.

445 Fact-finding by the Secretary-General of the United Nations.
M. Christiane Bourloyannis. *New York University Journal of International Law and Politics*, vol. 22 (Summer 1990), p.641-69.

Fact-finding, a form of inquiry (investigation) used by the Secretary-General in order to fulfill his early warning responsibility to the Security Council under Article 99, significantly expanded under Javier Pérez de Cuéllar. He requested heads of U.N. agencies and field offices abroad to inform him of developing humanitarian crises. He also established the Office for Research and Collection of Information (ORCI) to discover potential threats to the peace. But his calls for satellite monitoring and independent intelligence-gathering have gone unanswered. The author surveys fact-finding missions since 1985 and proposals by states for expanding the function.

446 Fact-finding: the revitalization of a Dutch initiative in the U.N.
Dick A. Leurdijk. *Bulletin of Peace Proposals*, vol. 21 (1990), p.59-69.

A permanent U.N. organ for fact-finding has been proposed since 1962. The end of the Cold War has created a new opportunity for establishing such a body, analogous to a permanent conciliation and mediation service. Impartial fact-finding, the author argues, could support peaceful settlement, monitor its implementation, and provide verification for arms control agreements. Leurdijk recounts the history of the original Dutch initiative. Fact-finding, like peacekeeping, remains a flexible and pragmatic device; 'institutionalization', he admits, 'is still out of the question'.

The international law and practice of early warning and preventive diplomacy.
See item no. 382.

The implications of establishing an international satellite monitoring agency.
See item no. 671.

Good offices

447 **Humanitarian good offices in international law: the good offices of the United Nations Secretary-General in the field of human rights.**
Bertrand G. Ramcharan.   The Hague: M. Nijhoff, 1983. 220p.
bibliog.

In a world of sovereign states, each insistent on non-interference in its internal affairs, the protection and promotion of human rights and all humanitarian action to save lives by the United Nations, using existing legal procedures and the various human rights commissions and committees, is often frustrated. Could less formal or legal processes, such as the good offices of the Secretary-General, help to relieve human suffering while international law is so underdeveloped? The author provides here a comprehensive study of the Secretary-General's good offices in the field of human rights, in addition to those for the resolution of disputes. Ramcharan sets out the basis, in the Charter and in interpretations of the Charter, of the Secretary-General's power to exercise good offices. He exhibits models of humanitarian action; discusses cases in Bangladesh (1971), Southeast Asia (1979), Cyprus (1964-82), and Iran (1979-80); and explains the role of the proposed High Commissioner for Human Rights. He or she would not be a world attorney for the people, but an inquirer, conciliator, mediator, and assistant.

448 **The good offices function of the U.N. Secretary-General.**
Thomas M. Franck.   In: *United Nations, divided world.* Edited by
Adams Roberts and Benedict Kingsbury.   Oxford: Oxford University
Press, 1988, p.79-94.

The author reviews the history of the Secretary-General's 'good offices', from Trygve Lie's inquiry into the Greek civil war in 1946 to Pérez de Cuéllar's mediation into the Cyprus dispute in 1986. Franck argues that the role is so vital that the General Assembly should establish a $40 million trust fund to support good offices. This would enable the Secretary-General to post U.N. ambassadors in the capitals of key countries to gather facts and maintain a U.N. presence. He also thinks that a single term of seven to eight years would strengthen the Secretary-General, since his decisiveness and impartiality would not appear to be reduced by a desire for a second term.

449 **'Good offices' in the light of Swiss international practice and experience.**
Raymond R. Probst.   Dordrecht, The Netherlands: M. Nijhoff, 1989.
182p. bibliog.

The author, an accomplished Swiss diplomat and secretary of state, here treats good offices historically and practically from the point of view of first Switzerland, then the United Nations, as the conciliatory third party. Switzerland's neutrality (she is still not a member of the U.N.) is vital to the performance of good offices. Switzerland is the Protecting Power for both the Vienna Conventions on diplomatic and consular relations (1961, 1965) and the Geneva Conventions on the treatment of wounded soldiers and sailors, prisoners, and civilians in time of war (1949, 1977). She has been the host of the International Committee of the Red Cross and the League of Nations. Switzerland has taken part in numerous arbitrations and missions of a political nature – most recently in assisting at the resolution of the U.S.–Iran crisis (1980-81). In the future, the state may provide reliable verification of comprehensive arms control agreements as part of the end of the Cold War. Probst provides a full chapter on 'new forms' of good offices – those conducted, sometimes on Swiss models, by NGOs like the Red Cross and by international organizations in the U.N. system and Europe (most notably the CSCE). Students will find his first chapter on the notion of good offices helpful for its contrast with other peaceful means; scholars and diplomats will find the later chapters on the Swiss analogy instructive.

450 **The good offices of the United Nations Secretary-General in the field of human rights.**
Bertrand G. Ramcharan.   *American Journal of International Law*,
vol. 76 (January 1982), p.130-41.

Good offices, a form of inquiry, conciliation, and mediation, originated in the field of the settlement of international disputes. But since U Thant's time, it has been extended into the humanitarian field. The author focuses on the nature, law, and practice of good offices in the field of human rights primarily by the U.N. Secretary-General, but also, by analogy, by officials of the U.N. High Commissioner for Refugees, International Labour Organization, UNESCO, Red Cross, Council of Europe, and O.A.S. He concludes that such good offices have become part of the 'common law of organized international cooperation'.

Mediation

451 **Alternative dispute resolution: a lawyer's guide to mediation and other forms of dispute resolution.**
Alexander H. Bevan.   London: Sweet & Maxwell, 1992. 128p.

Litigation, which is premised on an adversarial system, is proving so slow, costly, and still unjust, observes the author, that many people are turning to mediation and other techniques of peaceful settlement, based on cooperation. This book is a British version of the American pioneering technique of conflict resolution within the domestic field of states. International mediation is not formally treated, but the technique has been applied in the European Community and between the states of the United States.

452 **Bernadotte in Palestine, 1948: a study in contemporary humanitarian knight-errantry.**
Amitzur Ilan. Basingstoke, England: Macmillan for St. Antony's College, Oxford, 1989. 308p. bibliog.

Count Folke Bernadotte was a U.N. mediator sent to Palestine after the establishment of the state of Israel and the Arab invasion in 1948. His purpose was to end the war and to assist the parties to find a just and equitable peace. Four months later he was gunned down by a Jewish assassin. The American, Ralph Bunche, then continued the mediation. The author of this scholarly narrative biography examines this tragic but ultimately constructive (if not permanently successful) case of U.N. mediation at length. Ilan concludes that 'while [Bernadotte] worked to bring about a partition solution based on a temporary strategic equilibrium which looked equitable to him and to the major western powers, he actually helped to bring about a new and lasting equilibrium, which suited Israel better but hurt the Arabs'. Compare Rubin, below, on Henry Kissinger after three more wars.

453 **Dynamics of third party intervention: Kissinger in the Middle East.**
Edited by Jeffrey Z. Rubin. New York: Praeger for the Society for the Psychological Study of Social Issues, 1981. 303p. bibliog.

From the beginning of the October 1973 war in the Middle East to the end of the Arab–Israeli negotiations in August 1975, Henry Kissinger, then U.S. Secretary of State, conducted an historic case of third-party mediation. He succeeded in bringing Egypt, Jordan, and Syria to sign disengagement agreements with Israel, two new U.N. peacekeeping operations were set in place (UNEF II and UNDOF), two non-U.N. multinational observer missions were also established in the Sinai (Multilateral Force and Observers and Sinai Field Mission), and a process was set in motion that resulted in the Egyptian–Israeli peace treaty of 1979. The authors here provide an intense examination of his work. Dean Pruitt argues that, although people have regarded Kissinger as a miracle man, his work came out of the book of industrial mediation, with two differences – he wielded power over the parties, particularly Israel, and he represented the United States, which had strong interests in the area. Apparently because U.N. mediators have neither power nor interests, they are left out of the analysis, but the reader interested in international mediation will find here an impressive example of effective mediation of the sort that someday must be internationalized.

454 **International law, mediation, and negotiation.**
Manfred Lachs. In: *Multilateral negotiation and mediation: instruments and methods*. Edited by Arthur S. Lall. New York: Pergamon, 1985, p.183-95.

The author, a judge of the ICJ, discusses international negotiation and mediation. International law grows by negotiation, as in the General Assembly's Declaration of Permanent Sovereignty over Natural Resources (1962) or in the declarations, covenants, and conventions on human rights. Mediation is treated here as an adjunct to negotiation, in tense situations when an impartial and trusted third party can help to bring the parties to the negotiating table. The ultimate third party, vital in disarmament negotiations, Judge Lachs points out, is the 'pressure of world opinion'. He closes with a brief review of summit conferences in order to advance negotiations.

455 **International mediation: a study of the incidence, strategies, and conditions of successful outcomes.**
Jacob Bercovitch. *Cooperation and Conflict*, vol. 21 (1986), p.155-68.

Of 72 international disputes since 1945, 44 were mediated, some more than once. The total, then, is 210 mediation cases. The author identifies three conditions for success: (1) clear identity of the parties, (2) low salience or low intensity of the dispute, and (3) fairness, knowledge, authority, and resources of the mediator. This article brings together, tests, and resolves the claims of most of the previous literature on mediation.

456 **International mediation in theory and practice.**
Edited by Saadia Touval and I. William Zartman. Boulder, CO: Westview for the School of Advanced International Studies, Johns Hopkins University, 1985. 274p. (SAIS Paper No. 6).

The editors present a theory of mediation, then, to improve practice, get down to cases: Algerian mediation in the U.S.–Iranian hostage dispute (1980-81), Algerian mediation again in the Iran–Iraq conflict (1975), British mediation in the Zimbabwe struggle (1976-79), U.S. involvement in the Namibia negotiations (to 1985), Soviet mediation in the Indo-Pakistan conflict at Tashkent (1966), O.A.U. efforts, O.A.S. experience, and Red Cross mediation. Hence, both state and NGO mediation is treated. The editors conclude with a discussion of mediators' motives (defensive and expansionist), disputants' motives (face-saving, cost-saving), impartiality (not negated by considerations of power politics), timing and synchronization (most important at beginning), and leverage (delicate). They define 'success' as 'a contribution toward a formal agreement promising the reduction of conflict'. Full *resolution* of the conflict can never be promised.

457 **International mediation: the view from the Vatican – lessons from mediating the Beagle Channel dispute.**
Thomas Princen. *Negotiation Journal*, vol. 3 (1987), p.347-66.

Arbitration of this dispute by Queen Elizabeth II (1977) did not prove acceptable, so the Pope then mediated. After further delays, including the Falklands/Malvinas War, Chile and Argentina negotiated an acceptable treaty (1984). The author analyses the Pope's success as rooted in his moral authority and in the disinterested and non-military role of the Holy See in international relations. The Vatican's mediators were all clergy, who are trained to listen, to be patient, to try to reconcile differences. They set a standard of impartiality for all international mediators.

458 **The mediators.**
Deborah M. Kolb. Cambridge, MA: MIT Press, 1983. 230p. bibliog.

The author looks on mediation as both an art and a science. Her focus is domestic labour mediation, especially as practised in the U.S. Federal Mediation and Conciliation Service and the Board of Conciliation and Arbitration. There is virtually no discussion of international mediation, but as an introduction to the subject, where the practice is effective and guided by law, this little book could be very instructive. Labour mediators, Kolb writes, contribute to industrial peace less by solving every conflict than by 'preserving the existing social order'. The analogy with international mediation is suggestive.

459 **Mediation: a comprehensive guide to resolving conflicts without litigation.**
Jay Folberg and Alison Taylor.   San Francisco: Jossey-Bass, 1984.
392p. bibliog.

This is a large-scale study of mediation within the emerging practice of conflict resolution. Its field is limited to domestic situations, not international, except by implication. A large store of experience and effective techniques is being accumulated for eventual application in the larger field. This book is intended to help professionals, trainers, and ordinary people interested in promoting cooperation. Topics include: history, definitions, stages of mediation, concepts, skills, applications, professional dimensions. Mediation promotes 'cooperation' and 'self-determination', unlike litigation. The authors conclude: 'The principles applicable to consensual resolution of disputes in these small-scale situations are similar to those used to nonviolently resolve conflicts between nations.'

460 **Multilateral negotiation and mediation: instruments and methods.**
Edited by Arthur S. Lall.   New York: Pergamon, 1985. 206p. bibliog.

The 'multilateral instruments' treated in this collection of specialized article are the U.N. Security Council, O.A.S., Arab League, Commonwealth, small and medium-sized states as mediators, the Committee on Disarmament, the North–South 'dialogue', and other forms of diplomatic cooperation. Their contributions to dispute settlement can be understood as, first, mediation, then if effective, negotiation, which is how the editor presents them. At date of publication (1985), there was an air of futility about such international initiatives (no peace in the Middle East, rearmament rampant, North and South at an impasse), but more hopeful times will still require serious negotiators and mediators to confront problems like those analysed in this book.

461 **Multilateral mediation: practical experiences and lessons.**
Victor H. Umbricht.   Dordrecht, The Netherlands: M. Nijhoff for
UNITAR, 1989. 429p.

Dr. Victor Umbricht was a distinguished Swiss businessman and international civil servant who here presents an exact and useful record of his international mediations in terminating the affairs and debts of the East African Community (Kenya, Tanzania, and Uganda, 1967-77). He also includes a shorter account of his mediations in the aftermath of the separation of Bangladesh from Pakistan (1972) and of the Vietnam War (1976-78). He concludes with practical lessons gleaned from his experience and likely to be useful to other individual mediators in the future. Reflecting on the political impossibilities that confront a mediator, he ends, 'judgment is the essence'.

462 **New approaches to international mediation.**
Edited by C.R. Mitchel and K. Webb.   New York: Greenwood, 1988.
255p. bibliog.

Scholarly interest in international mediation increased as the Cold War wound down. The editors begin this collection of analytical papers with an essay on the history of such mediation, and they later explore individually issues of bias and neutrality. Cases include mediation in the Falklands/Malvinas conflict, in Namibia, in South Tyrol, in South Africa, and in the Sudan civil war (mediated by the World Council of Churches). The last essay, by Dennis Sandole, speculates on the paradigm shift from

Functions of the U.N.O. Peaceful Settlement of Disputes. Mediation

political realism (power politics) to conflict resolution (cooperation). Compare works by John Burton (q.v.).

463 Non-official mediation in disputes: reflections on Quaker experience.
Sydney D. Bailey. *International Affairs* (London), vol. 61 (1985), p.205-22.

The role of consultative non-governmental organizations (NGOs) in the settlement of international disputes – in addition to inter-governmental organizations like the U.N. – is here described and defended. The Society of Friends (Quakers) is a particularly good example. Quakers have assisted in peaceful settlement in Palestine (1948), Kashmir (1952-53), the Middle East (1955), East and West Germany (1962-73), India–Pakistan (1965), Biafra (1968-69), Middle East (1967-), and Rhodesia–Zimbabwe (1972-80). Bailey explains that the Quakers' reputation for impartiality was more significant in their success than management expertise. Their problems are comparable to those of diplomats. Other NGOs with similar experience include the Holy See, International Committee of the Red Cross, and the International Peace Academy.

464 Ralph Bunche: an American life.
Brian Urquhart. New York: W.W. Norton, 1993. 496p. maps.

This new illustrated biography of the black American U.N. mediator in Palestine and the international civil servant, Ralph Bunche, will surely, like Urquhart's biography of Dag Hammarskjöld and his own autobiography, help a broad public to appreciate the work of the United Nations, especially for the peaceful settlement of disputes. Bunche was the 'pragmatist', while Hammarskjöld was the 'metaphysician', as Urquhart writes in a photo caption of the two. 'Ralph was both an idealist and a realist', said U Thant in a eulogy after his death. 'He believed resolutely in the necessity of making the United Nations work, but he never underestimated the difficulties and frustrations of the peacemaker.'

465 Strengthening international mediation.
William L. Ury. *Negotiation Journal*, vol. 3 (1987), p.225-29.

The author is concerned that techniques of peaceful settlement, like mediation, must be enlarged until they are adequate to the challenge of nuclear confrontation, which 'could imperil the world'. The ultimate dispute for resolution is the Cold War or any military contest that threatens the existence of large states. Uri develops the precedents of mediation in the Israeli–Egyptian conflict (1973-75), the transfer of power to the black majority in Zimbabwe (1979), and the settlement of the Beagle Channel dispute between Argentina and Chile (1977-84). He suggests six steps for improvement: anticipation of conflict, settlement before the verge of hostilities, pre-negotiation, using new conflict resolution techniques, empowering the third party, and follow-up. He reviews the proposal to establish a permanent international mediation and conciliation service, but, since political leaders and diplomats prefer their freedom of action, he discusses at some length an *informal* approach.

466   **United Nations mediation of regional crises.**
Frederic L. Kirgis, Jr., Thomas M. Franck, Richard W. Nelson,
Francese Vendrell, and Gay J. McDougall.   *American Society of*
International Law Proceedings, vol. 80 (1986), p.135-51.

The authors explore the implied powers of the Secretary-General for mediation. (The
word occurs once in the Charter, in Article 33.) He may mediate at the request of the
Security Council (Articles 24, 36, 37), General Assembly (14), a state (35), or on his
own authority (97-99). A case of the latter was Hammarskjöld's personal fact-finding
mission to Laos during its civil war (1959). Another was U Thant's effort to mediate
in the Vietnam War, though it was never brought before a U.N. organ (1964-65). The
Secretary-General, Franck writes, has been the 'important winner in the intra-
institutional power struggle'. But he is on a 'short leash' of information, time, and
money. Other authors review the record of the Secretary-General's mediation in the
Middle East, Central America, and southern Africa. They agree that mediation has
necessarily expanded despite the U.N. Charter's relative silence, and that perhaps
thirty U.N. ambassadors, as Trygve Lie proposed in 1949, at a cost of $50 million per
year, would help resolve conflicts before they escalate into war.

467   **U.N. mediation: More effective options.**
Paul E. Mason and Thomas F. Marsteller, Jr.   *SAIS Review*, vol. 5,
no. 2 (Summer-Fall 1985), p.271-84.

A permanent U.N. mediation service or, alternatively, a U.N. commission on good
offices, mediation, and conciliation are here discussed at length. Both proposals meet
three major problems: lack of a systematic approach to dispute settlement in the U.N.,
critical delays in beginning the process, and refusal of some parties to meet for
negotiation of a settlement. The authors argue that a permanent mediation service
would be a valuable addition to the U.N.'s ad hoc mediations, and, if placed within
the Secretariat, would retain its flexibility while reaffirming its impartiality. The
commission on good offices, mediation, and conciliation, on the other hand, since it
would be composed of all member-states and would function under the General
Assembly or the Security Council, could not work in confidentiality and almost
certainly would become politicized. Neither proposal would change the voluntary
character of mediation, but the service, the authors conclude, because it would be
composed of experts, would be more 'fair'; the commission, composed of states,
would in the present international system, preserve more 'control by member
governments'.

468   **The ways of the peacemaker.**
K. Venkata Raman.   New York: UNITAR, 1975. 142p.
(E.75.XV.PS/8).

Mediation and good offices are relatively unstructured and informal methods used by
the U.N. and other third parties to assist parties to a dispute to find solutions through
negotiation. The functions of mediators include: establishing contacts between the
disputants, infusing moderation in their negotiations, and sometimes suggesting fresh
approaches and new ideas to clear deadlocks. The author sets out the advantages of
such informal methods to the more formal ones of arbitration, adjudication, or
placement on the agenda of the Security Council. His specific emphasis is on the
proper *procedures* of mediation and good offices in the U.N. context. Such
procedures will avoid problems that may, on past experience, defeat the process.

These procedures deal with initial consent, expectations of the parties, public debate, international authority, contact between the parties, a working basis of intermediary assistance to the parties, and consideration of the substantive issues.

Conciliation

469 **Conciliation and arbitration procedures in labour disputes: a comparative study.**
International Labour Organization.   Geneva: International Labour Office, 1980. 183p.

'The problem of settling labour disputes cannot be viewed in isolation.' This slim book is a comparative study of different *national* systems of dispute settlement in labour–capital–state relations. The principal means of settlement are litigation, conciliation (or mediation), and arbitration. The book concentrates on conciliation (a non-legal means) and arbitration (a legal means), though all means are related. The ILO does not itself intervene, but limits itself to guiding responsible parties in the variou national systems. Here the reader will find comparable practice in European countries, the United States and Canada, and several Third World countries. The mature practice in industrialized countries has gone beyond early emphasis on preventing strikes and lockouts to prevention of the disputes that lead to strikes and lockouts. Hence conciliation and mediation are favoured over arbitration and litigation. Moreover, emphasis on the law and executive enforcement has given way to conciliation and administrative policy in the dynamic business and labour environment. The conclusion looks forward, not to uniform world systems of labour, but to the sharing of diverse national experiences and to the adaptation of workable ideas to the unique cultural and national setting.

470 **Peaceful settlement of international trade disputes: analysis of the scope of application of the UNCITRAL conciliation rules.**
Isaak I. Dore.   *Columbia Journal of Transnational Law*, vol. 21 (1983), p.339-52.

Conciliation is contrasted with arbitration. The former is amicable, cannot proceed without the participation of the parties, and produces a recommended settlement; the latter is adversarial (though all must agree on the choice of arbitrators), can continue even if a party fails to appear or produce requested documents, and leads to a binding award. The peaceful settlement of international trade disputes by conciliation and arbitration is highly advanced and hence is suggestive for the settlement of issues affecting international peace and security. The author traces the history and scope of application of the U.N. Commission on International Trade Law (UNCITRAL) rules as applied to both conciliation and arbitration.

471 **Resolving disputes between nations: coercion or conciliation?**
Martin Patchen.   Durham, NC: Duke University Press, 1988. 365p. bibliog.

The author, a social psychologist, asks the question, 'How can we avoid war while at the same time maintaining the things we hold dear?' He draws on the new discipline of conflict resolution in order to analyse the conduct of foreign policy, especially deterrence (threat) and alliance (promise). It is a 'realist' analysis in which the United Nations hardly figures. When Patchen speaks of 'conciliation' – in contrast with 'coercion' – he means not the technique of peaceful settlement but what Hans Morgenthau correctly meant by 'appeasement' – that is, compromising with another state that is apparently maintaining a policy of the status quo. The threat and use of force, or coercion, by contrast, is suited for a state pursuing a policy of expansion. The book should be of interest to theorists.

472 **The role of the Advisory, Conciliation, and Arbitration Service (ACAS) in British Labor Relations.**
Peter Parker.   Washington, DC: Society of Professionals in Dispute Resolution (SPIRD), 1983. 7p. (Occasional Paper No. 83-3).
The ACAS is in Britain what the Federal Mediation and Conciliation Service is in the United States. Hence, this paper is merely representative of the growing literature on domestic conflict resolution. Parker discusses conciliation, mediation, and arbitration in British labour relations. He does not comment on international conciliation, but the reader can imagine future applications.

473 **The use of conciliation for dispute settlement.**
K.D. Kerameus.   *Revue hellénique de droit international*, vol. 32 (1979), p.41-53.
The author examines the use of conciliation in Greek civil procedural law. In principle, 'conciliation, especially under the supervision of a court, is, as a rule, the best way to settle a dispute; [for] it avoids judicial contest and promotes peace as a principal ideal of justice'. Historically, however, conciliation settles far fewer cases than adjudication; for advocates know that the Greek people prefer a 'pugnatious contest' in the courts, judges do not have time because of crowded work schedules to utilize conciliation, and adjudication costs are low. The author does not apply the Greek example to international conciliation, but he concludes that conciliation serves where the law is weak, which is the case with international law.

Arbitration

474 **Arbitrage dans le commerce international. Arbitration in international trade.**
René David.   Deventer, The Netherlands: Kluwer, 1985. 482p. bibliog.
The French author writes from a businessman's – not a lawyer's – perspective. International commercial arbitration is flourishing (285 cases per year settled by the International Chamber of Commerce in Paris, not counting those settled by other arbitration associations). The cause, David argues, is that international business is more concerned with the swift and inexpensive administration of justice than with the contribution of each case to the corpus of international law as found in a court. Moreover, business people in the new global economy are in search of a new international commercial law, a *lex mercatoria*, without the accidental and irrational limitations of many national civil laws. They prefer conciliation to litigation, which leaves behind hard feelings, and they find arbitration particularly suited to the

revision of long-term contracts in rapidly changing national and international circumstances.

475 Arbitration and mediation: synthesis or antithesis?

Vincent Fischer-Zernin and Abbo Junker. *Journal of International Arbitration*, vol. 5, no. 1 (March 1988), p.21-40.

All the means for the peaceful resolution of disputes listed in the U.N. Charter glide into one another. Arbitration, for instance, is usually called a 'legal' means, yet an arbitrator may propose a forum for negotiation, help the parties find a compromise, and even propose terms of settlement. Is that not mediation? The German authors here compare and contrast mediation and arbitration, with a view to reducing the costs of litigation as proposed by their American counterparts. The article is grounded in the new concepts of conflict resolution or 'alternative dispute resolution'. Mediation, the authors argue, is institutionalized in civil law countries, whereas arbitration (and adjudication), in which the judge is regarded as an umpire between contentious parties, is rooted in the common law. The international trend, as in the UNCITRAL Conciliation Rules and the Zurich Mini-Trial Procedure, favours mediation. Arbitration, then, should be developed in the direction of mediation (and conciliation).

476 Arbitration of international disputes *ex aequo et bono.*

Louis B. Sohn. In: *International arbitration:* liber amicorum *for Martin Domke.* Edited by Pieter Sanders. The Hague: M. Nijhoff, 1967, p.330-37.

Sohn here explores the legally provided but as yet seldom used basis for arbitration *ex aequo et bono,* according to what is equitable and good. Since international law is relatively underdeveloped, and since arbitrators frequently must decide particular cases in accordance with what seems right, 'equity' – understood, the U.S. Senate Foreign Relations Committee once said, as not the old English concept but as what is 'equally right or just to all concerned' – offers a way to close a gap in international law or even to depart from or to change the law. Sohn proposes that, in place of the many unused arbitral clauses accepting jurisdiction *ex aequo et bono,* a special equity tribunal could be set up authorized to render an *advisory* opinion on such basis *when requested* by the U.N. General Assembly or Security Council after a request by a party to a dispute for settlement *ex aequo et bono.* He argues: 'If States were more certain that a recommendation of the General Assembly or the Security Council would be based not on political manoeuvring in these bodies but on a well-considered opinion of a special group of experts, deciding *ex aequo et bono,* they might be less reluctant to accept United Nations decisions as binding. Arbitration treaties having shown the way, the United Nations can breathe new life into this important method of settling international disputes. To paraphrase an ancient maxim, *ex aequo et bono pax oritur.*'

477 Case for a tribunal to assist in settling trade disputes.

Guy Ladreit de Lacharrière. *World Economy,* vol. 8 (1985), p.339-52.

The author, the French judge in the ICJ, reviews the dispute settlement procedures of the GATT and proposes a new tribunal to settle trade disputes on the model of the new provisions in the Law of the Sea convention. The judge regards as 'Utopian' any proposal to grant GATT 'a direct effect in municipal law, so that it could be invoked by individuals', for that would amount to converting states to 'full compliance with the law in international trade relations'. Such 'changes would amount to making the GATT the guarantor, no longer of a commercial order with legal components, but of a legal order in the commercial sphere'. Hence, his tribunal is, like Sohn's proposal above, a panel of professional experts whose opinions would slowly contribute to customary international law.

478 **A dictionary of arbitration and its terms: labor, commercial, international; a concise encyclopedia of peaceful dispute settlement.**
Compiled by Katharine Seide. Dobbs Ferry, NY: American Arbitration Association Library, 1970. 334p. bibliog.

This is a handbook of arbitration useful to the arbitrator, practitioner, party, scholar, or advanced student interested in the actual conduct of arbitration. The focus is primarily on international commercial (private) arbitration, as befits its prevalence, but terms found in international (public) arbitration between states are also included, as are terms related to U.N. specialized agencies.

479 **Economic and political implications of international commercial arbitration.**
Richard N. Gardner. In: *International trade arbitration: a road to world-wide cooperation.* Edited by Martin Domke. New York: American Arbitration Association, 1958, p.15-26.

Although old, this article explores implications being fully revealed only after the end of the Cold War. International commercial arbitration, Gardner argues, brings security, prosperity, freedom, and justice. The volume contains other suggestive articles, notably, Quincy Wright, 'Arbitration as a symbol of internationalism'.

480 **The function of international arbitration today.**
Louis B. Sohn. *Recueil des Cours*, vol. 108 (1963), p.1-113. bibliog.

This long article remains a succinct and judicious introduction to international arbitration for the settlement of disputes between states. (Commercial arbitration is omitted.) Sohn addresses the questions of the role allocated to arbitration in the U.N. Charter; the sorts of disputes that could be arbitrated, if not adjudicated; the basis of arbitrators' decisions in law or equity; improved structures of arbitral tribunals; and nations' experience with arbitration and its consequences for the future. Sohn argues that many international political disputes could go to arbitration, just as legal ones go to adjudication. He closes with a proposal for a *permanent* arbitral court, rather like the world equity tribunal proposed in the 1930s and revived in Grenville Clark and Sohn's *World peace through world law* in 1958 (q.v.). Such an equity tribunal could perform 'quasi-legislative functions' until world society developed enough of a sense of common justice to permit establishment of 'the Parliament of Man'.

481 **Guide to international arbitration and arbitrators.**
Parker School of Foreign and Comparative Law, Columbia University. Ardsley-on-Hudson, NY: Transnational Juris Publications, 1989; 2nd ed., 1992. 2 vols. bibliog.

The first volume of this authoritative guide is a reference to international rules and institutions, national institutions and rules, codes of ethics for international arbitrators, and the New York Convention on the Recognition and Enforcement of Foreign Arbitral Awards (1958). It then begins a list, continued into the second volume, of qualified international arbitrators ready to serve on arbitral panels. The work is not a text explaining the nature of arbitration, but a reference and guide to its practical conduct. The field is expanding rapidly beyond commercial transactions to investment, joint ventures, transfers of technology, and industrial and economic cooperation.

482 The international arbitral process: public and private.

J. Gillis Wetter.   New York: Oceana, 1979. 5 vols. bibliog.

This is a large-scale work on both international arbitration affecting peace and security ('public international arbitration') and international commercial arbitration ('private'). The author has set himself two goals: 'to provide the international lawyer with most of the basic texts and information which are required for practicing in the field as arbitrator, advocate, and counsel', and to exhibit 'all the contradictions and difficulties of law and the process manifested in actual practice'. The work is a standard introduction to the field, its length actually an asset. The first chapter is on 'war or peace' – the ultimate concern even of commercial arbitration. Wetter in an epilogue sums up his philosophy of a dynamic, living law, crafted by the hands of professional lawyers. In commercial cases, there exists a national legal framework; but in cases of war and peace, the international law must be supplemented by equity. In both areas, arbitral tribunals are autonomous compared to courts, which is another source of their flexibility. Moreover, arbitration is a system of procedure, not an application of law, which gives the technique its usefulness in the immensely complicated international setting of the future.

483 International arbitration – back in favour?

D.H.N. Johnson.   *Yearbook of World Affairs, 1980*, vol. 34 (1980), p.305-28.

The Cold War between East and West and the economic conflict between North and South have been, argues this British legal scholar, 'too deep and too pervasive to render recourse to arbitration a realistic solution in most cases'. Yet Johnson shows at length why arbitration may be preferable to judicial settlement by the ICJ. Arbitration permits states to retain more control over the proceedings, it is more flexible than adjudication, and it provides a tribunal in which states have more confidence in complex international circumstances. Johnson reviews in some detail the eight principal international arbitrations since 1945 – most notably the Beagle Channel arbitration, which was still frustrated by 1980 (the Pope finally settled it in 1984).

484 International arbitration: improving its role in dispute settlement.

Joseph Preston Baratta.   Washington, DC: Center for U.N. Reform Education, 1989. 56p. bibliog. (Monograph No. 7).

International arbitration as a pacific means for the resolution of disputes affecting international peace and security is defended and evaluated. It is compared to international *commercial* arbitration. Improvements, modelled on the arbitral provisions of the law of the sea, include increased provisions for arbitration in a new convention on the peaceful settlement of disputes, in new treaties on the environment, the seas, outer space, trade, human rights, arms control and disarmament, and in a new permanent mediation and conciliation service. Equity provides a practical ideal for moving the society of nations toward the world rule of law.

485 **International arbitration law.**
Mauro Rubino-Sammartino. Deventer, The Netherlands: Kluwer, 1989. 537p. bibliog.

This is a text, written from a professedly 'ideal' perspective, of the law of international arbitration, both commercial (private) and inter-state (public). The author foresees that both will become a 'unity'. The book will be of interest to international lawyers and arbitrators, scholars, and advanced students. It concludes with a chapter on the continual search for improvements. Rubino-Sammartino is concerned to reduce the number of national attacks on arbitral awards, so he proposes a one-arbitrator system (with a time limit to complete the process in one year), an appellate arbitral panel, a self-executing mechanism after appeal, an addendum to the New York Convention, and a supranational court of appeal.

486 **International arbitration: three salient problems.**
Stephen M. Schwebel. Cambridge: Grotius Publications, 1987. 303p.

The three problems are: (1) the 'severability' of the arbitral clause of a contract that is later found invalid, as by fraud, and hence requires exercise of the arbitral clause; (2) the 'denial of justice' by a state that refuses to arbitrate in accordance with an arbitral clause in a contract with an alien; (3) the 'authority of a truncated arbitral tribunal' (one in which a member refuses to participate) to still render a valid award under international law or the law selected for the arbitration. These questions come up mainly in private international commercial arbitration, but in principle they also arise in public international arbitration between states affecting their peace and security. The author, the distinguished American judge in the ICJ, concludes: (1) The arbitral clause is severable – that is, the clause continues to apply even if the contract is invalid. (2) There is a denial of justice, for a state may not claim sovereign immunity before a tribunal that is not an instrument of state sovereignty, and the alien has a right to justice even if he may not plead international law in a municipal court. Arbitration exists 'to insulate the litigants from parochial municipal rules of standing, pleading, and evidence.' (3) Withdrawal of an arbitrator from the tribunal is a wrong under customary international law and hence cannot bar the truncated tribunal from rendering a valid award.

487 **International commercial arbitration: a peaceful method of dispute settlement.**
Michael F. Hoellering. *Arbitration Journal*, vol. 40, no. 4 (1985), p.19-26.

International arbitration affecting peace and security has not grown as has international commercial arbitration. The author, general counsel of the American Arbitration Association (AAA), here recounts the progress of international commercial arbitration as commerce has spread across the globe in the 20th century. He defines the practice and the law, the sources of information, the role of NGOs like the AAA, the International Chamber of Commerce, the New York bar associations, and others. Particular emphasis is given to U.S. practice. Hoellering concludes that arbitration's great contribution to world peace is its preservation of friendly relations even in a contentious suit.

488 **International commercial arbitration: International Chamber of Commerce arbitration.**
W. Laurence Craig, William W. Park, and Jan Paulsson.   Dobbs Ferry, NY: Oceana for the ICC Court of Arbitration, 1984. 2 loose-leaf folders, updates from 1990. bibliog.

This is a standard guide and reference to the Court of Arbitration of the International Chamber of Commerce. The focus is on the rules of the ICC Court, rather than the national and international law that might or might not apply to the substantive or procedural issues. Topics covered include: the Court of Arbitration as an institution, the agreement to arbitrate, ICC arbitration in practice, hearings and proof, the role of state courts, and current trends in international commercial arbitration. There is relatively little attention to the United Nations, except for the UNCITRAL Model Law on International Commercial Arbitration.

489 **Iran–United States Claims Tribunal in action.**
Aida B. Avanessian.   Dordrecht, The Netherlands: Graham & Trotman, 1993. 325p. bibliog.

This work, originally a Ph.D. dissertation at the University of London, is a technically exact and yet legally liberal account of the recent arbitral tribunal. The author is convinced that 'the Tribunal will leave its mark on the international commercial community, its law, and the process of international arbitration'. Further, she predicts that the tribunal will vindicate 'a means of dispute settlement in circumstances where political considerations are of no less importance than legal issues'. These conclusions are drawn by close examination of the tribunal's jurisdiction, the claimants, the respondents, the awards, and enforcement. Avanessian, herself Iranian, finds that the tribunal has been successful in settling the crisis, advancing the process of arbitration in inter-state commercial disputes, and providing a 'wealth of precedent that will serve the field of international law well for years to come'.

490 **The Iran–United States Claims Tribunal: controversies, cases, and contribution.**
Rahmatullah Khan.   Dordrecht, The Netherlands: M. Nijhoff, 1990. 343p. bibliog.

The author, an Indian professor of law who assisted Iran in its presentation of cases to the tribunal, tries here, after nine years of its arbitration, to draw a balanced assessment. He surveys conflicting opinions, yet argues, 'Never before have two powers so hostile to each other resorted to such a peaceful procedure for settlement of their disputes.' Khan first examines at length the charges of non-validity in setting up the tribunal and of its 'bad bargain'. Second, he discusses the personal problems of the arbitrators (one was forced to resign, another refused to sign the awards), which affected the composition and status of the tribunal. Third, he weighs the jurisdictional issues, especially over residual Iranian jurisdiction and dual nationality. Lastly, he is quite critical of the legal consequences of this arbitration as they affect the impact of revolution on foreign property, the right and degree of control of alien property in the host state, and the standard of compensation applied by the tribunal. The most controversial product of the tribunal was its expropriation awards. Khan concludes that the 'precedential value' and 'doctrinal contribution' of the tribunal are suspect, and he warns Third World countries that international arbitration with a great power is 'inherently hazardous'.

491 **The Iran–United States Claims Tribunal: a review of developments, 1983-84.**
David P. Stewart. *Law and Policy in International Business*, vol. 16 (1984), p.677-753.

Following the Iranian Revolution and the taking of U.S. hostages, the Iran–United States Claims Tribunal was set up in 1981. Its purpose was to resolve thousands of economic claims arising from the rupture of relations between the two countries. The tribunal is an arbitral panel which, because of its broad jurisdiction in both public and private international law and its powers to settle disputes aggregating over $1,000 million, vividly illustrates the usefulness today of international arbitration. The entire issue of the above journal is devoted to the tribunal. David Stewart's article recounts its history and progress through 1984. He focuses on categories of claims, jurisdictional issues (e.g., dual nationality), choice of law, property rights, and relation of tribunal proceedings to municipal law in Iran, the U.S., and Holland. Stewart concludes that 'the Tribunal . . . has demonstrated that international arbitration of claims on the basis of respect for law can be pursued even in the most difficult circumstances.'

492 **Law and practice of international commercial arbitration.**
Alan Redfern and Martin Hunter. Foreword by Sir Robert Jennings. London: Sweet & Maxwell, 1986. 462p.

This is an authoritative text on the practice and the law of international commercial arbitration, written by two English lawyers with twenty years' experience. They are at pains to preserve the flexibility of arbitration, in contrast to litigation before national courts and adjudication before the World Court. They admit that writing about arbitration is rather 'like peering into the dark', for there is no universal 'law' to be applied in arbitration, and arbitration remains a private *form of proceeding* whose awards and procedures are rarely published. Yet they are encouraged by the United Nations UNCITRAL Model Law on International Commercial Arbitration (adopted 1985) and by the convergence of national law in anticipation of the global market place. This book will remain a standard for both the beginner and the professional because, as Judge Jennings remarks, 'it has so much to teach of practical wisdom'.

493 **Multi-party arbitration: identifying the issues.**
Sigvard Jarvin. *New York Law School Journal of International and Comparative Law*, vol. 8 (1987), p.317-25.

The author surveys the work of the Court of Arbitration of the International Chamber of Commerce in cases of dispute over large-scale international construction projects. Multi-party arbitration saves money and produces more consistent results. But there are problems: loss of confidentiality over inventions, marketing, other contracts; loss of consensus (consent) on the arbitration; difficulties in anticipating conflicts among subcontractors. Jarvin proposes solutions and concludes that international commercial arbitration still has advantages over national or local courts.

494 **Negotiating the Iranian settlement.**
Lloyd N. Cutler. *American Bar Association Journal*, vol. 67 (1981), p.996-1000.

This article, by an American attorney and adviser to President Carter who helped bring about the Algiers Declarations (1981) leading to return of the U.S. hostages and establishment of the Iran–U.S. Claims Tribunal, reviews the political costs and benefits of resorting to arbitration in a case affecting national honour. The Algiers Declarations, Cutler writes, 'show that, in circumstances in which a military response to a particular aggressive use of force may not be practicable, it can be practicable to repel the aggression by economic, political, and legal measures.' (Ten years later the forces in the Middle East that Carter and his team sought to contain burst out in the Persian Gulf War.) Algeria proved to be a vital mediator in establishing the arbitral tribunal. Warren Christopher, the U.S. negotiator in Algiers, led the lawyers who tied together the elaborate package.

495 **Present-day relevance of the Hague peace system, 1899-1979.**
Georg Schwartzenberger.   In: *Yearbook of World Affairs, 1980.*
Boulder, CO: Westview for London Institute of World Affairs, 1980, p.329-50.

The Hague peace system, which antedates and is distinct from the U.N. system (including the International Court of Justice), is based on the Hague Conventions of 1899 and 1907, which emphasize arbitration, inquiry, mediation, and conciliation. The author reviews its existence, record of settlement, and promise for the future, especially if adjudication under the ICJ continues to decline. Schwartzenberger analyses, with biting legal irony, a wrong decision of the ICJ about an arbitral commission on human rights abuses that was never set up under the Eastern European peace treaties of 1947, and then an error of the International Law Commission in its section on arbitration in the Draft Convention on the Peaceful Settlement of Disputes of 1949. Both provided loopholes to states to avoid their obligations even in agreed *compromis* clauses. The voluntary Hague system was thus gravely weakened, while the compulsory system of the ICJ never attracted fifty adherents, most of them with 'derisory' reservations.

496 **Private law sources and analogies on international law: with special reference to international arbitration.**
Hersch Lauterpacht.   Hamden, CT: Archon Books, 1970. 326p.
bibliog.

One of the sources of international law is 'the general principles of law recognized by civilized nations'. Lauterpacht provides here a treatise, written in the first glow of the League of Nations (originally published in 1923), on the applicability of such principles, drawn from 'private' (national) law, to the development of 'public' international law. It is done in such a way that citations from private law in suits before the PCIJ would not be thrown out as 'misleading analogies'. Lauterpacht also provides a virtual digest of international arbitration to 1923. The book is old, but its issues are perennial.

497 **The questionable validity of arbitration and awards under the rules of the International Chamber of Commerce.**
Antoine Kassis.   *Journal of International Arbitration*, vol. 6, no. 2 (June 1989), p.79-100.

The author provocatively challenges the practice of 'administered arbitration', as under the ICC, by comparison with the older and wider process of *ad hoc* arbitration. Kassis finds the former inconsistent with basic rules of law since its awards are unenforceable in state courts. He also replies to defenders of the ICC system. The article seems to reflect the ambiguity of the present international legal system – where world economic conditions require a higher law than state law for the resolution of disputes, but equity in arbitral processes remains overrulable by state courts. Arbitration will be strengthened if it can meet Kassis's objections.

498   **Reports of international arbitral awards.**
U.N. Office of Legal Affairs, Codification Division.   New York: United Nations, 1948-90. 20 vols.

Here the reader will find a complete record of (public) international arbitration between states affecting their peace and security.

499   **Resolving transnational disputes through international arbitration.**
Edited by Thomas E. Carbonneau.   Charlottesville, VA: University Press of Virginia, 1984. 301p.

This collection of expert papers covers arbitration in public international law (arbitration between states affecting their peace and security), arbitration in private international law (commercial arbitration), and arbitration in transnational commerical settings. The approach is comparative, with special attention to English, French, and Soviet (socialist) practice. Dean Rusk contributes an essay on international arbitration of political disputes. He thinks it can supplement negotiation – still the fastest and least expensive means of peaceful settlement – when governments are willing to settle, domestic opinion is opposed to the concessions likely in negotiation, parties recognize the need for a third party, and there is law available or rules agreeable in a *compromis*. Louis Sohn in his essay sets out the potential for future arbitration – some sixty arbitral clauses in multilateral treaties since 1970 and very flexible provisions in the law of the sea. Arbitration, he concludes, 'may become the wave of the future.'

500   **The role of arbitration in recent international multilateral treaties.**
Louis B. Sohn.   *Virginia Journal of International Law*, vol. 23 (1982-83), p.171-89.

Legal procedures for the settlement of disputes are advantageous for small and economically weak states since the principle of equality before the law will prevail. They are also advantageous for large states, the author argues, since such states are in a minority in alternative international institutions like the U.N. General Assembly. Sohn observes that arbitral clauses in recent multilateral treaties seem to be favoured over those providing for adjudication before the ICJ because the former gives states more psychological assurance of a just and acceptable outcome. In this article, he surveys arbitration procedures found in multilateral treaties, discusses use of arbitration as a settlement technique, reviews efforts at codification, and examines the model Law of the Sea arbitral provisions. Arbitration, he dares to hope, 'may become the wave of the future'.

501   **Settling U.S. claims against Iran through arbitration.**
Erik Suy.   *American Journal of Comparative Law*, vol. 29 (1981), p.523-29.

This short article written shortly after establishment of the Iran–United States Claims Tribunal, sets out the types of claims that may be made – basically those of one government against another, or those of national citizens against a government. Since Iran violated treaties on diplomatic relations, most of the claims of the first type were expected to be made by the U.S. against Iran; since Iranian courts were 'not available', claims of the second type were *not* expected to be those of Iranians against Americans. Suy discusses the implications of this arbitral tribunal for national municipal and constitutional law (it seems to be another step toward recognizing the individual as a subject of international law). He concludes on an economic note: 'The agreement set in my view an historical example, not of how to solve a hostage situation, but rather how to deal with the international financial and commercial consequences of the collapse of a regime, of a revolution, or of a change in the socio-economic system of a State. . . . In a period when the legal principles concerning nationalization and compensation have become very controversial, the case law of the Arbitral Tribunal will, no doubt, give new impetus to the development of international economic law in the relations between North and South.'

502 Survey of international arbitrations, 1794-1970.

Alexander M. Stuyt. Leiden, The Netherlands: Sijthoff, 1972. 572p.

There have been over 464 international arbitrations affecting peace and security since the Jay treaty between the United States and Great Britain of 1794 provided for arbitration to settle the northern boundary of Maine. This reference volume lists these historic cases and hence is a valuable secondary source for historians, theorists, and practitioners.

503 The Taba award of 29 September 1988.

Derek W. Bowett. *Israel Law Review*, vol. 23 (1989), p.429-42.

The *compromis* that set up the arbitral panel provided for conciliation and fact-finding in addition to an award. The author traces the course of this recent arbitration which settled a dispute over sovereign territory left over from the 1979 peace treaty between Egypt and Israel. Bowett's account presents arbitration in the microcosm of this technical yet highly emotive case. He concludes that important results were obtained in the Taba case: both parties had every opportunity to present their arguments, the award was according to law, and the parties respected the arbitrators' verdict.

504 The world arbitration reporter.

Edited by Hans Smit and Vratislav Pechota. Stoneham, MA: Butterworth for the Parker School of Foreign and Comparative Law, Columbia University, 1986-88. 6 loose-leaf binders (updatable)

This updatable reference will be invaluable to the arbitrator, international lawyer, scholar, and student. Contents: Vol. 1: International legal framework; Vol. 2 and 2A: National legislation; Vol. 3 International arbitral institutions and rules; and Vol. 4 and 4A: National arbitral institutions and rules.

Judicial settlement/Adjudication

505   **Acceptance, and withdrawal or denial, of World Court jurisdiction: some recent trends as to jurisdiction.**
Edward McWhinney.   *Israel Law Review*, vol. 20 (1985), p.148-66.
The author, a leading Canadian scholar, reviews (since 1970) the Western and Soviet decline in support for the principle of international adjudication of disputes. The generally favoured method now is bilateral diplomatic negotiations – which is, indeed, one of the peaceful means recognized in Article 33 of the U.N. Charter. McWhinney cites several decisive ICJ cases marking the shift, most recently *Nicaragua v. U.S.A.*, which provoked the United States to withdraw from the case (and soon from the compulsory jurisdiction of the World Court) on the ground that the dispute was 'political' (January 1985). He examines the Special Chambers of the Court as a device to return the great powers to adjudication, even though such chambers are 'Eurocentric'. They are acceptable in an 'era of transition such as we live in today'.

506   **Adjudication in the International Court of Justice: progress through realism.**
Abraham D. Sofaer.   *Record of the Association of the Bar of the City of New York*, vol. 44 (1989), p.462-92.
'A special opportunity seems to be at hand [with the end of the Cold War] to promote the use of the International Court of Justice (ICJ) in resolving international disputes.' The author, a former legal adviser to the U.S. State Department, briefly reviews the decline of adherence to the mandatory (compulsory) jurisdiction of the ICJ (by 1985 only the U.K. among the permanent members of the Security Council still accepted the optional clause, Article 36(2) of the Statute). He then reviews the great growth of international law through multilateral treaties (such as the Montreal Protocol of 1987 for the protection of the ozone layer), which require the adjudication of the Court for the resolution of disputes. To explain why the ICJ is not meeting the need, he reviews the history of its founding – largely due to 'messianic' U.S. leadership in the 'quest for a rule to replace violence in the world'. Woodrow Wilson even had a vision of 'international government' to augment the limited role of a judicial branch. But in 1946, when the Court was refounded, the U.S. did not accept unqualified compulsory jurisdiction (the Connally reservation absolutely rejected interference in domestic jurisdiction), and subsequent history demonstrates that all states shrink from third-party international adjudication. Sofaer then reviews realistic arguments against the existence of international law that could settle disputes leading to war – or of judges or lawyers able to create such law to adjudicate fairly between the 'two worlds' of liberalism and communism. (By implication, a world legislature would be no more competent to enact world law reaching to individuals.) His solution is to limit the jurisdiction of the World Court, insist on state consent, and permit recourse to chambers only partially representative of all the principal legal systems in the world.

507 **An argument to expand the traditional sources of international
law – with special reference to the facts of the South West Africa
cases, [and] The South West Africa cases: an appraisal.**
Richard A. Falk.   In: *The status of law in international society*, by
Richard A. Falk.   Princeton, NJ: Princeton University Press, 1970.
p.126-73, p.378-402.

The second of these chapters from Falk's innovative book on the autonomy and
relevance of international law presents a rather descriptive account of the 'triumph of
judicial conservatism' in the ICJ's dismissal of the case brought by Liberia and
Ethiopia against South Africa over its administration of South West Africa (Namibia)
in 1966. The first chapter presents a more prescriptive argument in response to the
judgment – proposing a legal (not political) response in the form of interpreting (not
amending) Article 38(1) of the Court's Statute to admit norms of conduct reflected in
consistent resolutions of the General Assembly, particularly those condemning
apartheid, as new sources of international law. That is, international law, Falk holds,
is evolving rapidly in response to the increasing interdependence of the world, and the
Court must catch up. Both chapters provide a stimulating account of the Court's
historic judgment of 1966.

508 **Case concerning military and paramilitary activities in and
against Nicaragua (*Nicaragua v. United States of America*): merits.**
Judgment of 27 June 1986.
International Court of Justice.   *Reports of judgments, advisory
opinions, and orders, 1986*, p.14-546.

Here will be found the full text of the historic judgment, covering failure of the
respondent to appear, jurisdiction of the Court, justiciability of the dispute,
establishment of facts, acts imputable to respondent, applicable law, the votes and
opinions of the judges. Judge Lachs (of Poland) quotes Oliver Wendell Holmes: 'The
remoter and more general aspects of the law are those which give it universal
interest.'

509 **Compulsory jurisdiction and defiance in the World Court: a
comparison of the PCIJ and the ICJ.**
Gary Scott and Karen D. Csajko.   *Denver Journal of International
Law and Policy*, vol. 16 (1988), p.377-92.

Two years after the Court's *Nicaragua* decision, the authors find that state defiance of
the Court (in preliminary objections) is increasing. To gain historical perspective,
they look back on the interwar Permanent Court of International Justice, which was
not so defied, but they conclude this was illusory. Both PCIJ (1921-39) and ICJ
(1945-70) were products of 'postwar legal idealism'. Now, with the return of 'normal
international politics', even the pretence of adjudication, they imply, is being abandoned.
(They seem not to be worried by the analogy with what ended the PCIJ's effective life in
1939.)

510   **Evidence, the Court, and the Nicaragua case.**
Keith Highet.
The ICJ and compulsory jurisdiction: the case for closing the clause.
Gary L. Scott and Craig L. Carr. *American Journal of International Law*, vol. 81 (1987), p.1-56, 57-76, followed by colloquium.

Soon after the ICJ rendered its judgment in the case of *Nicaragua v. United States of America* (1986), dismayed and delighted international lawyers debated its causes and probable effects in the pages of this leading American journal. The former tended to feel that the non-appearance of the United States as a strategy will 'backfire', since the very necessity for adjudication of legal disputes will draw the U.S. back to the ICJ. The latter felt that compulsory jurisdiction was fully revealed as premature at the present historical stage of development of the 'law–politics distinction' in international life.

511   **The future of the International Court of Justice.**
Lyndel V. Prott.   In: *Yearbook of World Affairs, 1979*.   Boulder, CO: Westview for London Institute of World Affairs, 1979, p.284-303.

Since the *South West Africa* decision in 1966, there has been a slow decline in state recourse to the ICJ and in scholarly enchantment. 'The current mood of all discussions is reflected in certain truisms about the Court: that it is under-used and that its business should be increased.' The author examines several state and expert proposals to reform the Court. All have the purpose of increasing states' confidence in the Court. But reforms of the Court's procedure and working methods, widening access by international organizations, NGOs, and individuals, widening jurisdiction by allowing states to choose from a list of topics for judicial settlement, and changing the election procedure to increase 'impartiality' – these seem to Prott inadequate, even if they were acceptable. He then broadens his inquiry into the fundamental issues of state confidence: the unpredictability of the Court, the uncertainty of the applicable law, the shallowness of the Court's support amongst the general public and hence legal élites. These reflections lead Prott into more fundamental inquiries into the (Western) meaning of 'court', 'law', and 'judge'. He closes with rather radical suggestions that, in the future, adjudication might more acceptably be pursued, not through a universal law, but through regional legal systems, especially where mediation, conciliation, and alternative forms of dispute settlement might be allowed greater scope.

512   **The function of law in the international community.**
Hersch Lauterpacht.   Oxford: Clarendon Press, 1933; Hamden, CT: Archon, reprinted ed., 1966. 469p.

This is an old but still illuminating account of the difference between 'legal' and 'political' disputes – that is, between 'justiciable' and 'non-justiciable' disputes over 'rights' and conflicts of 'interest'. The book is a classic defence of the compulsory jurisdiction of international legal tribunals, made at a time (1933) similar to ours, when no great power threatened to destroy all international legal obligations. Lauterpacht considers all the evasions, still being heard, to judicial settlement: the importance of political disputes (all disputes, he argues, are political), the absence of an international legislature (a difficulty, but a legislature is not the only instrument of change in the law of a society), and doubts as to the impartiality of judges (the real reason is the refusal to submit interests to justice).

513 **The International Court of Justice and domestic jurisdiction.**
Henri Rolin. *International Organization*, vol. 8 (1954), p.36-44.

Here is early analysis of the scope of U.N. Charter's Article 2(7), which was interpreted at the time as barring the ICJ from settling a dispute between Iran and Great Britain over British exploitation of Iranian oil. The author points out that Article 2(7), unlike the analogous article in the League Covenant, omits reference to international law as the standard for determining domestic jurisdiction, and also omits reference to any U.N. organ to decide about jurisdiction if contested. He concludes that Article 2(7) does *not* widen the scope of traditional domestic jurisdiction nor exempt governments from gross misuse of such jurisdiction.

514 **International dispute settlement and the role of international adjudication.**
Richard B. Bilder. *Emory Journal of International Dispute Resolution*, vol. 1 (1987), p.131-73.

The author begins with the *Nicaragua* case at the ICJ (1984-86), which provoked the United States to withdraw from its acceptance, with reservations, of the compulsory jurisdiction of the Court (7 October 1985). This was a major setback for the project of judicial settlement. Bilder here gives an overview of the general characteristics of international adjudication, its necessity for effective world legal order, its political advantages and disadvantages, its contrast with ad hoc arbitration, and its long-term prospects. He lists the advantages as: adjudication is dispositive (ends the dispute), important, principled, authoritative, impersonal, serious, orderly, reduces tension, gains time, sets precedents, helps develop international law, and re-enforces the system of legal international relations. And the disadvantages as: adjudication involves the risk of losing, is unpredictable, may not be impartial, imposes a binding judgment, may produce an illusory settlement, may escalate, may freeze the dispute, is inflexible, conservative, costly, and may be used for propaganda or harassment. Bilder concludes that, on balance, 'the benefits to the U.S. national interest of acceptance of the compulsory jurisdiction of the Court far outweigh the risks'. He suggests correctives to the disadvantages and urges the U.S. to return to the World Court. 'From the foundations of the Republic, the principle of respect for law has been a firm tenet of U.S. foreign policy. . . . Perhaps a few nations can hope to 'free-ride' on an international legal system supported by most others – invoking the benefits of international law when it is to their advantage but ignoring the law when respect for law seems at the moment inconvenient or disadvantageous. But this course is not open to our country. For, if *we* choose not to play by the rules of the game, there may not be any game left worth playing.'

515 **Judicial procedures relating to the use of force.**
Richard B. Bilder. In: *Law and force in the new international order.*
Edited by Lori F. Damrosch and David J. Scheffer. Boulder, CO: Westview, 1991, p.269-97.

International law does not require states to submit disputes involving the use of force to settlement by judicial procedures, as by arbitration or adjudication under the ICJ. But there are advantages to voluntary recourse to judicial settlement, according to the author. Adjudication may peacefully resolve the problem or make compromise politically possible, especially when a state is likely to lose a test of force. The whole issue of adjudication after the Cold War is here authoritatively discussed.

Functions of the U.N.O. Peaceful Settlement of Disputes. Judicial settlement/Adjudication

516 **Judicial remedies in international law.**
Christine D. Gray. Oxford: Clarendon Press, 1987. 250p. bibliog.

'Judicial remedies', in a world where the legal system is not based on compulsory jurisdiction as in national states, where arbitral and judicial settlement of disputes is rare compared to negotiation and even coercion, where a world legislature and consequently a centralized judicial system is lacking, have a relatively modest role in international dispute settlement but still an important one. This informed and resourceful book examines such remedies with special attention to their practicality for states, and hence with a view to increasing their use in the future. Covered are international arbitral practice, adjudication in the World Court, comparison with practice in the European Community, special tribunals as for human rights, the Iran–U.S. Claims Tribunal, and commercial arbitration generally. Gray concludes with guarded favour for popular actions in international courts, for an international criminal court, and for state liability for environmental pollution, but she warns that the international regime cannot develop without proper attention to implementation and reduction of 'state responsibility'.

517 **Judicial settlement of international disputes: International Court of Justice, other courts and tribunals, arbitration, conciliation.**
Edited by Hermann Mosler and Rudolf Bernhardt. Berlin: Springer Verlag for Max Planck Institute for Comparative Public Law and International Law, 1974. 572p.

The international symposium of some sixty-one legal experts, of which this book is a record, were asked three questions: (1) Does the ICJ, as it is presently shaped, correspond to the requirements which follow from its functions as the central judicial body of the international community? (2) To what extent and to which subject matters is it advisable to create and develop special judicial bodies with a jurisdiction limited to certain regions or to certain subject matters? (3) To what extent and for which questions is it advisable to provide for the settlement of international legal disputes by other organs than permanent courts? The answers generally are: (1) No. (2) Special Chambers offer one alternative when states will accept them and the international law to be applied. (3) Arbitration and even political means for the determination of law remain further alternatives. Bernhardt concludes darkly: 'For the foreseeable future, the judicial solution represents only one of several possible means for the settlement of international conflicts, even over matters of law, and is generally applied only to conflicts of lesser political importance. The hope, repeatedly expressed and manifested in numerous treaties at the turn of the century and between the two world wars, that international adjudication and arbitration might make a more substantial contribution to overcoming fundamental disputes and differences between States, or even make court judgments a substitute for war, proved an illusion and will remain so for the foreseeable future.'

518 **Judicial settlement of international disputes: jurisdiction, justiciability, and judicial law-making on the contemporary International Court.**
Edward McWhinney. Dordrecht, The Netherlands: M. Nijhoff, 1991. 189p.

This is a spirited response to recent debate on the World Court, prompted by U.S. Reagan administration attacks in the wake of the *Nicaragua* rulings (1984-86).

Functions of the U.N.O. Peaceful Settlement of Disputes. Judicial
settlement/Adjudication

McWhinney, a Canadian legal scholar, briefly reviews the past benefits of the ICJ to
the U.S. – including so recent a case as *United States v. Iran* (1980) – then undertakes
a broadly historical, jurisprudential argument in favor of the Court's 'constitutional-
legal legitimacy in the exercise of such a new, community policy-making role',
analogous to that of the great national constitutional courts like the U.S. Supreme
Court. The key to his thinking is a studied critique of the 'law/politics' distinction in
international law, which, unlike municipal law, grants the World Court jurisdiction
over few 'legal' questions, while leaving 'political' ones for other organs of the U.N.
or outside it in the anarchical world society altogether. McWhinney agrees with
Richard Falk that more non-Western influence in the Court is healthy for the
development of a truly universal international law. The 'new' Court – since the
disastrous *South West Africa* decision (1966) – has moved into the 'policy-making
role' consistent with the transformation of the 'world community' by decolonization
and the attainment of independent self-government by all peoples throughout the
world.

519 **The law and practice of the International Court.**
Shabtai Rossene.   Leiden, The Netherlands: Sijthoff, 1965;
Dordrecht, The Netherlands: M. Nijhoff, 2nd rev. ed., 1985. 811p.

The first edition of this authoritative book on the role of the World Court in the
settlement of international disputes, when that role seemed flourishing, appeared the year
before the Court's controversial *South West Africa* judgment; the second, twenty years
later, appeared when the author had to admit that, quantitatively, the work of the Court
had 'fallen off', and qualitatively, the law and practice of the Court had suffered a
'revolution', marked by the resistance of governments and the criticism of political
scientists and international lawyers. The fundamental explanation, Rosenne agrees with
many, is that 'the old and established international order is clashing with the aspirations
of those who are dissatisfied with inherited international law and do not accept its
Eurocentred manifestations'. In the second edition, Rossene has not attempted to
incorporate the 'new jurisprudence' from the General Assembly and elsewhere into his
book on the Court, now become rather antiquated. Apart from a few updated references,
the reader will find here the same classic account, which always emphasized the political
and legal interrelations in the work of the Court. Topics include: history and constitution,
organization, jurisdiction, contentious practice and procedure, and advisory opinions.

520 **The law and procedure of the International Court of Justice.**
Gerald Fitzmaurice.   Cambridge: Grotius Publications, 1986. 2 vols.

Despite the recent date of publication, this authoritative study of the World Court
principally covers its work only to 1959. (Sir Gerald was a judge of the ICJ from
1960 to 1973.) The author concentrates here on 'statements of principle . . . from the
standpoint of international law and procedure'. He has not produced a study of the
cases heard by the Court, but of the principles (rules) found in those cases and
applicable to new ones. Hence, there is no admission in this work of a 'decline' in the
burden of the Court, nor of a 'revolution' in its role of settling international legal
disputes or determining international law, as Shabtai Rossene admits. The topics
covered are: general principles, sources of law, treaty interpretation, international
organizations and tribunals, the United Nations, jurisdiction, competence, procedure.
Many articles on Hersch Lauterpacht as scholar and judge conclude the second
volume.

521 **The prospects of international adjudication.**
C. Wilfred Jenks.   London: Stevens, 1964. 805p.

This volume, written in expectation of an *advance* of international adjudication as an adjunct to international organization and wise diplomacy, is worth recalling after the Cold War in order to recover the promise of the rule of law to world peace and world order. Jenks concludes at one point: 'Fundamentally the problem of compulsory jurisdiction is political and psychological; legal and technical ingenuity can find a solution . . . for all the technical and procedural elements of the problem, but the heart of the matter lies elsewhere. The essence of the question is confidence; confidence in the stability and adequacy of the law, and confidence in the integrity and predictability of the courts and tribunals administering the law.' Jenks argues that confidence can be increased by accepting the *risks* of international organization, as has been the way forward for every major step in the progress of humanity from the elimination of private vengence, to federalism, to the formal renunciation of war as an instrument of national policy. The book explains proposals for further development of adjudication, advisory proceedings, standing of international organizations, general principles of law, equity, international public policy, application of municipal law, consent, inductive and deductive reasoning, compliance, and execution of international judgments. Jenks concludes with a long chapter on 'the rule of law in world affairs'.

522 **Reflections on the South West Africa cases.**
Julius Stone.   In: *Of law and nations: between power politics and human hopes*, by Julius Stone.   Buffalo, NY: W.S. Hein, 1974, p.331-47.

This chapter, written by a master of the 'realist' school of criticism of international law ('the plight of nations is too grave and retractable for rescue by facile legalism'), is still a revealing analysis of the case that did more than any other to undermine respect for the Court, especially by the new nations in Africa and Asia. Disposing of first the legal then the political controversies about the case, Stone comes to the fundamental difficulty of state refusal to accept third-party settlement of disputes affected with a national interest – as in South Africa's regard for apartheid, or Western nations' refusal to delegate powers to a common judge. 'If decisive power to cut through [conflicts threatening the peace] is not available and direct paths are blocked by power, movement towards adjustment is unlikely to come from speciously tidy and definitive designs for decision by impartial judges under "the rule of law".' Hence, Stone called for political alternatives like General Assembly resolutions condemning apartheid and 'establishing' the independence of Namibia, which by 1974 were still about a decade from bearing fruit.

523 **The relevance of international adjudication.**
Milton Katz.   Cambridge, MA: Harvard University Press, 1968. 165p.

This is a book of lectures addressed to lawyers and the educated public about the slow growth of international law and its limited ability to curb violence and resolve disputes. The analogy with municipal law, which does perform these functions, is imperfect, for there is no government of the world, though Katz regards international organizations as 'international governmental organizations' and hence a step in that direction. The bulk of the book is a discussion of the ICJ's perplexing ruling in the *South West Africa* case (1966), implying that the issue of apartheid had to be

removed from legal processes and transferred to political ones, as in the U.N. General
Assembly. But his chapter on the Cold War, which rendered all such adjudication so
moot, may be most interesting to readers after it, for Katz compares the conflict
between communism and capitalism, between economic democracy and political
democracy, to the 'cold war over slavery between North and South' in the mid-19th
century. The U.S. government at the time, like the U.N. after World War II, was
relatively weak compared to the states, and the Supreme Court, though appealed to, was
inadequate, as Abraham Lincoln said in his First Inaugural, to settle 'vital questions
affecting the whole people'. The implication is that, at the end of the Cold War, the
challenge of a 'socialist law' or a 'proletarian law' has been abandoned, freeing the
World Court for the application of one common law of all humanity. Katz concluded that
the ICJ had necessarily deferred to the General Assembly and the Security Council,
which were assisting in the making of that common law, that is, were taking 'political
action infused with . . . a sense of law'.

524 **The role of controversy in international legal development.**
Shabtai Rosenne. In: *The structure and process of international law.*
Edited by R. St.J. Macdonald and Douglas M. Johnston. The Hague:
M. Nijhoff, 1983, p.1147-85.

The author takes up the serious problem for the future of adjudication that most new
states admitted to the U.N. do not regard themselves as bound by customary
international law bequeathed by Europe on the grounds that it is the 'law of European
imperialism, colonialism, and aggression'. Combined with 'rampant nationalism' and
'revolutionary dogma', this turn of national sovereignty could undo the restraints of
international law achieved over centuries. Rosenne sees three profound effects: (1)
The individual is demanding standing before international law, in addition to states,
since the community to which he or she belongs is increasingly felt to be the world.
(2) National security has proved to be an illusion under modern conditions, and even
collective security seems unachievable unless political and military security is
supported by social and economic security of all peoples. (3) An international law
protective of developing states and redressing the inequalities of the old Eurocentric
law is required by justice. Hence has arisen the movement to replace customary law
with treaty law and to avoid the ICJ. Rosenne worries that erosion of the principle of
the equality of states, first to favour developing countries, then to recognize national
liberation movements and finally individuals as 'subjects' of international law, will
not be compensated by increased legislative capacity of the U.N. General Assembly,
which remains a diplomatic conclave. Yet he does not conclude, even in our
'revolutionary times', that the solution might be to turn politically to the creation of
one popularly representative chamber of the present house of states in order to
establish a world legislature.

525 **Some limitations of adjudication as an international dispute
settlement technique.**
Richard B. Bilder. *Virginia Journal of International Law*, vol. 23
(1982), p.1-12.

As the compulsory settlement of disputes by courts is the hallmark of an effective
legal system at the national level, so it has been taken as the standard at the
international level. Bilder confronts the fact that nations are very reluctant to submit
significant disputes to impartial tribunals. He argues that, at the present stage of
international community development, adjudication is chancy, uncompromising,

unrealistic, adversarial, and non-precedental. On the other hand, he counter-argues that adjudication *can* settle cases in which prestige but not interests are at stake, technical cases, and cases in which judicial delay is politically desirable. As an international lawyer, he reluctantly concludes that the non-legal means of settlement (negotiation, conciliation, etc.) hold more promise.

526 States and the World Court: the politics of neglect.
Inis L. Claude, Jr. In: *States and the global system: politics, law, and organization*, by Inis L. Claude, Jr. New York: St. Martin's, 1988, p.160-73.

The World Court is little used for the adjudication of disputes, but, Claude argues, that is not a realistic measure of state compliance with international law. Just as, within states, out-of-court settlements reflect the rule of law, so, at the international level, the diplomatic means for the settlement of disputes (negotiation, etc.) are part of working international law. Claude also includes in his broad concept of law increased recourse to the *political* organs of the U.N., especially the General Assembly, after the Court's disappointing judgment in the *South West Africa* case of 1966.

527 Step-by-step acceptance of the jurisdiction of the International Court of Justice.
Louis B. Sohn. *American Society of International Law Proceedings*, vol. 58 (1964), p.131-36.

Since by 1964 the ICJ was manifestly not proving to be effective in resolving international disputes, Sohn proposed a 'step-by-step approach which will gradually increase the Court's permanent jurisdiction'. Such steps would include, first, granting the Court jurisdiction only over the interpretation of treaties; then, jurisdiction over specified areas of international law like state recognition or the high seas; then, jurisdiction through regional arrangements, like the nascent Atlantic community; and finally, jurisdiction over disputes referred by the U.N. Security Council or General Assembly. Sohn argues that, as states gained confidence in adjudication in small cases, they would be more willing to accept it in large ones.

528 Suggestions for the limited acceptance of compulsory jurisdiction of the International Court of Justice by the United States.
Louis B. Sohn. *Georgia Journal of International and Comparative Law*, vol. 18 (1988), p.1-18.

In anticipation that the U.S. will reconsider its withdrawal from the compulsory jurisdiction of the ICJ (1985), Sohn here considers at length 'limited' acceptance of such jurisdiction. He proposes a draft reservation (less drastic than the old Connally reservation), carefully stating which matters the Court would have jurisdiction over (e.g., interpretation of treaties), and which not (those affecting national security or a collective security alliance). He concludes that such limited acceptance would enable the United States 'to reclaim its image as the main defender of world order under law'.

529   **The United States and the compulsory jurisdiction of the
International Court of Justice.**
Edited by Anthony C. Arend.   Lanham, MD: University Press of
America, 1986. 250p.

In response to a U.S. statement of intention to withdraw from the World Court (April
1984) over the *Nicaragua* case, the Center for Law and National Security at the
University of Virginia held a panel discussion on the issues by leading international
lawyers Louis B. Sohn, Fred L. Morrison, and W. Michael Reisman. Professors Sohn
and Morrison argued for modified participation in the Court (revision of the Connally
and Vandenberg reservations); Reisman argued for complete withdrawal. After the
meeting, the U.S. did formally withdraw (October 1985). The editor concludes that
the international system is in a 'state of disequilibrum', marked by Third World
claims of a right to use force to achieve self-determination, Second (socialist) World
challenges to the philosophical foundations of a liberal capitalist legal order, and First
World willingness to use force to promote democracy. He warned that returning to
modified participation by accepting only chambers of the Court would limit the law-
finding role of the Court, since representatives of all principal legal systems would
not be in the chamber.

530   **Who tolled the death bell for compulsory jurisdication? Some
comments on the judgments of the ICJ.**
Peter H. Kooijmans.   In: *Realism in law-making: essays on
international law in honour of Willem Riphagen.* Edited by Adriaan
Bos and Hugo Siblesz.   Dordrecht, The Netherlands: M. Nijhoff,
1986, p.71-87.

In the *Nicaragua* judgment (1986), the World Court held that it had jurisdiction
because the United States had accepted compulsory jurisdiction in legal disputes
under Article 36(2) of the Court's Statute (the optional clause) in 1946, and further
had agreed to the compromissory clause in its Treaty of Friendship, Commerce, and
Navigation with Nicaragua in 1956. Both (U.S.) Judge Steven Schwebel and
Professor Frederick L. Kirgis, Jr., argue that to apply a compromissory clause in a
commercial treaty to a highly political dispute was a desperate expedient to save the
Court's compulsory jurisdiction after forty years of frustration. 'Did not the Court,
out of sheer love for the system of compulsory jurisdiction', asks the Dutch author,
'give it the kiss of death?' Kooijmans reviews, with Sir Humphrey Waldock, the slow
decline of the *optional* system of compulsory jurisdiction ('the States themselves . . .
have been tolling the death-bell'), and he concludes that the Court has 'hastened the
process' of destruction of *conventional* compulsory jurisdiction, too. But he still sees
a future for judicial settlement, particularly in the increasing recourse of non-
European states to the Court on the basis of bilateral special agreements.

531   **The work of the jurisprudence of the International Court of
Justice, 1947-1986.**
Eduardo Jiménez de Aréchaga.   *British Yearbook of International
Law*, vol. 58 (1987), p.1-38.

The author, a former judge and president of the ICJ, sums up its accomplishments
under the heads of its contributions to the development of the law of the U.N. Charter,
to the codification and progressive development of general international law, to the

solution of territorial disputes, and to the rapid growth of customary international law. Under the first head, for instance, are discussed the Court's judgments on the legal personality of international organizations, the legitimacy of peacekeeping operations, protection of human rights, decolonization, admission of states to the U.N., and protection of the right of U.N. staff members. The whole article will serve students, beginning scholars, and concerned citizens as an elementary summary of matters that may be assumed in more technical accounts of the ICJ.

532 **The World Court's compulsory jurisdiction under the optional clause: past, present, and future.**
Niklas Kebbon. *Nordic Journal of International Law*, vol. 58 (1989), p.257-86.

The project of creating, by use of the optional clause (Article 36(2) of the Statute), a universal system of compulsory jurisdiction for the legal settlement of disputes between states has to be adjudged a failure. The author describes and analyses impediments to the creation of an international system of compulsory jurisdiction and elaborates on the possible future role of the World Court. He makes several non-technical suggestions for enhancing its role. Reasons for the decline in the prospects for a strong and respected international court include: lack of confidence in the predictability and impartiality of the ICJ, communist and former colonized worlds' dissent from classical (European) international law, and recourse to the General Assembly as a quasi-legislative organ. Kebbon sees some hope in U.S. lawyers' demands for a return to compulsory jurisdiction under a more specific reservation, and in the Non-Aligned Movement's call for a Decade of International Law and a third Hague or second San Francisco conference by 1999.

Regional agencies

533 **The Arab League and peacekeeping in the Lebanon.**
Istvan Pogany. Aldershot, England: Avebury, 1987. 214p.

In 1976, in response to the Lebanese civil war, the Arab League established a non-U.N. peacekeeping force, the Symbolic Arab Security Force. Within a few months, it was transformed into the Arab Deterrent Force (ADF), dominated by the Syrians. Pogany closely compares these Arab League peacekeeping forces with the U.N. Interim Force in Lebanon (UNIFIL, 1979) and the non-U.N. four-power Multinational Force (MNF, 1982). The reasons for the failure of the Arab peacekeeping forces are not much different from those for the failures of UNIFIL and MNF: civil anarchy, Israeli obduracy, ambiguity of mandates, lack of international authority. The author concludes that peacekeeping has inherent limits: such forces 'cannot *impose* peace on unwilling states or on entire peoples'. Moreover, the bounds of international legality were surely crossed by the ADF's resort to massive firepower and to taking instructions from Damascus.

534 **Arab unity: hope and fulfillment.**
Fayez A. Sayegh. New York: Devin-Adair, 1958. 272p.

This is a sympathetic treatment of the history and ideal of Arab unity, carried as far as the establishment of the United Arab Republic (Egypt, Syria, and Yemen, 1958) and the proposal for a federation of the Arab Maghrib, before their collapse. Little is said of the Arab League's ability to resolve conflict, but here will be found the idealism of Arab unity and brotherhood.

535 **The Inter-American dilemma: the search for Inter-American cooperation at the centennial of the Inter-American system.**
L. Ronald Scheman. New York: Praeger, 1988. 210p. bibliog.

The author recognizes that the U.N. system of international organizations is disunited and in trouble because it is not effectively dealing with global problems and has lost the hold of the imagination of people everywhere. He also knows that the O.A.S. as the 'flagship' of regional organizations has reached a stage of 'paralysis' after a century of Pan-Americanism. Scheman's thesis is that the sectoral, functional approach to international problems should be replaced by a 'federal', integrated approach based on strengthened regional organizations. He does not agree with critics that federalism detracts from a global design, nor that it is misplaced idealism in a world of big-power politics. 'A federal approach to global problems is a real issue in our international life. A wide range of matters are best handled on a smaller scale. There is no rational argument why nations should wait for global accords before they enter into partial agreements any more than a city should wait to clean up toxic wastes until a national or international agreement is reached.' A chapter on the O.A.S. and the United Nations vividly sets out the advantages of a federal structure for regional organizations. Dispute settlement would continue the O.A.S.'s tradition of emphasis on mediation and conciliation, backed by collective defensive power (as in NATO) and presumably by strengthened regional judicial institutions. That states and their peoples might agree to such a reform, he argues, is proved by the facts that about three-fourths of the international organizations established by states since 1945 are regional, and that 'they obviously serve a need and provide a type of service which [states] are not getting from the U.N.'

536 **International conflicts and collective security, 1946-77: the United Nations, Organization of American States, Organization of African Unity, and Arab League.**
Mark W. Zacher. New York: Praeger, 1979. 297p.

Disappointment with universal collective security organizations like the U.N. leads this political scientist to study regional security organizations. He tries to identify the factors of success in those cases when regional organizations have terminated conflicts (the most important is 'coalition configuration'). He also seeks the conditions that must be met if collective security organizations (regional or universal) are to attain a more permanent role in international conflict management (multipolarity and more transnational actors are two). Zacher quotes Henry Kissinger, who said, 'The United Nations is not a world government', and presumably, the regional organizations are not governments either, able to settle conflicts by apprehending the individuals accused of violating the laws. But he does not speculate on such a remote prospect. An appendix provides a list of 116 wars from 1946 to 1977.

537 **International law, dispute settlement, and regional organizations in the African setting.**
H.A. Amankwah. In: *Third World attitudes toward international law.* Edited by Frederick E. Snyder and Surakiart Sathirathai.
Dordrecht, The Netherlands: M. Nijhoff, 1987, p.197-217.
The author carefully relates the O.A.U. to the U.N., especially by Articles 52(2) and 24(1). He reviews the O.A.U.'s record in dispute settlement, as in the Algeria–Morocco border case (1962-64) and the Nigerian–Biafran civil conflict (1966-70). He compares the O.A.U. to the O.A.S., which has powers to use collective force but has not had appreciably more success in keeping the peace. Amankwah has no explanation for why the O.A.U.'s Commission of Mediation, Conciliation, and Arbitration has never been used.

538 **International regional organizations: constitutional foundations.**
Edited by Ruth C. Lawson. New York: Praeger, 1962. 387p. bibliog.
This is a convenient collection of the founding documents of the principal regional intergovernmental organizations established after 1945: the North Atlantic Treaty (1949), the Warsaw Pact (1955), the Treaty of Rome establishing the European Economic Community (1957), the Charter of the Council for Mutual Economic Assistance (1959), and charters for the Arab League (1945), O.A.S. (1948), and many others, twenty-five in all. Each document is introduced by a historical and analytical note and followed by a specific bibliography. This is a most valuable reference.

539 **The international role of the Association of Southeast Asian Nations.**
Leonard Unger. In: *Negotiating world order: the art and architecture of global diplomacy.* Edited by Alan K. Henrikson.
Wilmington, DE: Scholarly Resources, 1986, p.149-63.
This is an historical and diplomatic analysis of ASEAN (Thailand, Malaysia, Singapore, Indonesia, Philippines, Brunei – but not Vietnam, Laos, and Cambodia). ASEAN was originally designed (1967) to meet the needs of newly independent nation-states just emerging from colonial dependency. Its purposes were social and economic, not defensive, for defence was potentially divisive. Even today the goal is a 'zone of peace, freedom, and neutrality'. For defence, ASEAN has appealed to the U.N., which prevented Vietnam from receiving recognition until 1977.

540 **The League of Arab States and regional disputes: a study of Middle East conflicts.**
Hussein A. Hassouna. Dobbs Ferry, NY: Oceana, 1975. 512p. bibliog.
The author surveys ten disputes, from the Yemen situation in 1948 to the whole Arab–Israeli conflict, 1948-75. He carefully evaluates the Arab League's capacity for resolving regional disputes, especially by conciliation, mediation, good offices, fact-finding, arbitration, and the influence of the League's Secretary-General. The relationship between the Arab League and the United Nations is clearly spelled out. Hassouna admits that the League machinery of peaceful settlement is 'limited', so he proposes both political reforms under the existing charter (e.g., substituting for the Council a judicial body for arbitration) and constitutional reforms (e.g., providing for

a two-thirds vote in place of present unanimity in the Council). He ends on a hopeful note, looking forward to a 'Arab Confederation of States'.

541 **The League of Arab States: a study in the dynamics of regional organization.**
Robert W. MacDonald.   Princeton, NJ: Princeton University Press, 1965. 407p. bibliog.

The Arab League was twenty years old when the author of this model study completed his 'judgment of the degree of efficiency with which the organization is approaching its self-described goals of regional, functional, and political integration'. MacDonald traces the historical roots of the regionalist versus universalist approaches to peace, especially with respect to the U.N. Charter's Chapter VIII. He is careful not to abstract the League from its political context in the Arab region. The League's constitution, organization, policy formation, functional programmes, collective security, and dispute settlement procedures are fully discussed. He concludes that Arab League success has been mixed at best – Sudan, Libya, Morocco, Tunisia, Kuwait, and Algeria were brought into existence with the help of the League, and many states were helped 'to shed the remaining vestiges of a former European hegemony'; but there has been continual internal crisis (Iraq–Egypt) and external wars (Israel). Functional cooperation has been a reality, as has cooperation with the U.N. MacDonald ends with critical judgments on the theory and practice of regionalism: nationalism and doctrines of national sovereignty still militate against regionalism; even if regions could be effectively united (as Europe seems to be doing), there would still be potential for 'warfare *between* regions'; and functional cooperation with the U.N. is an uncertain solution since 'functionalism has been taken over by the Great Powers as a basis for national policy'.

542 **Memoirs.**
Jean Monnet. Translation by Richard Mayne. Introduction by George Ball.   Garden City, NY: Doubleday, 1978. 544p.

For the learner, this autobiography by the architect of the European Community is still the best introduction to the field of regional organization in Europe. The 'international dispute' that Monnet aimed to settle was the centuries-old hatred and warfare between Germany and France. His method was to unite, first, their coal and steel industries, then their entire economies and the economies of their neighbours, so that war became economically impossible and slowly, psychologically, unthinkable. He was seeking 'new political methods, and . . . [the] right moment for changing the way people *thought*'. He was convinced that 'international cooperation' is incapable of making necessary decisions; hence, he aimed at 'joint sovereignty' over the basic industries of Europe. 'Over and above coal and steel', he declared, the Schuman Plan 'is laying foundations of a European federation.' He concluded: 'Have I said clearly enough that the Community we have created is not an end in itself? It is a process of change, continuing that same process which in an earlier period of history produced our national forms of life. Like our provinces in the past, our nations today must learn to live together under common rules and institutions freely arrived at. The sovereign nations of the past can no longer solve the problems of the present: they cannot ensure their own progress or control their future. And the Community is only a stage on the way to the organized world of tomorrow.'

543 **New departures in the exercise of inherent powers by the U.N. and O.A.S. Secretaries-General: the Central American situation.**
Hugo Caminos. *American Journal of International Law*, vol. 83 (1989), p.395-402.

The O.A.S. Charter lacks a provision allowing its Secretary-General to exercise any initiative along the lines of the U.N. Charter's Article 99. Nevertheless, under pressure of the Contadora and Lima Support Groups, both Secretaries-General by the end of 1987 were authorized to assist the governments of Central America to bring about an end to years of hostilities. The author traces these developments through the establishment of the International Verification and Follow-up Commission (August 1987). (Subsequently, there have been two U.N. observer missions sent to the region: the U.N. Observer Group in Central America, 1989-92, and the U.N. Observer Mission in El Salvador, 1991- .)

544 **The North Atlantic Alliance as a form of world order.**
Alan K. Henrikson. In: *Negotiating world order: the art and architecture of global diplomacy*. Edited by Alan K. Henrikson. Wilmington, DE: Scholarly Resources, 1986, p.111-35.

NATO is not a mere alliance or regional military bloc arrayed against an enemy state or bloc of states; it is an incipient Atlantic or even global collective security *order*. It is consistent with the U.N. Charter (Article 51) and was established 'to strengthen the U.N. Organization *in the only way possible* in the international circumstances of the deepening Cold War'. Henrikson traces NATO's potential universality, managerial complexity, and suitablitiy for future negotiations with the Soviet Union and its Warsaw Pact allies. Gorbachev's unilateral initiatives, ending the Cold War, are not anticipated, but Henrikson rightly analyses the continuing need for security. He points out such devices for a new order as the concept of common security (in place of national security), a more cooperative regional order (in place of the previous hegemonic one), and the contemporary reality of interdependence.

545 **The O.A.S. and U.S. foreign policy.**
Jerome Slater. Columbus, OH: Ohio State University Press, 1967. 315p. bibliog.

From a U.N. perspective, the manipulation of the O.A.S. by the United States does not augur well for the independence of regional organizations in resolving disputes. During the CIA-masterminded coup in Guatemala in 1954, Henry Cabot Lodge in the Security Council adeptly prevented any international inquiry. He warned that interference with U.S. policy would doom the U.N. Charter in 1954 as surely as not acceding to the veto would have in 1945. The book exhibits 'conflict' as much within the organization – over U.S. attempts to transform it into an anti-communist, anti-dictatorial alliance – as without – over externally fomented communist subversion.

546 **The Organization of American States.**
Ann Van Wynen and A.J. Thomas, Jr. Dallas, TX: Southern Methodist University Press, 1963. 530p.

This standard work is an historical, constitutional, and political account of the O.A.S. Its treatment of peaceful settlement of disputes within the Americas is presented in terms of principle and of fact (to 1962 and the Cuban missile crisis). One of the authors' tests for an effective regional organization is its ability to settle disputes peacefully; in 1962, on the eve of a long struggle with international communism, the O.A.S. could hardly have a very high score. But the authors remember the historic reasons for founding the organization, and they conclude with hope that 'genuine regional legal order' will yet flourish.

547   **The Organization of American States and international order in the Western hemisphere.**
Alejandro Orfila.   In: *Negotiating world order: the art and architecture of global diplomacy*. Edited by Alan K. Henrikson. Wilmington, DE: Scholarly Resources, 1986, p.137-47.

The O.A.S. was founded in 1948 to advance the aspirations shared in Latin America for democracy, human rights, non-intervention, and economic development. The author traces the difficulties in achieving these ideals, as in the Falklands/Malvinas war or the U.S. invasion of Grenada (Panama and Nicaragua came later). He makes various suggestions for curing the 'existing malaise of the O.A.S.' in the face of new challenges by 'global issues'.

548   **Pan-Africanism and East African integration.**
Joseph S. Nye, Jr.   Cambridge, MA: Harvard University Press, 1965. 307p. bibliog.

This study is offered as a complement to studies of attempts to integrate the sovereign states of Europe into a federal union. The failure of Tanzania, Uganda, and Kenya to federate in 1963 Nye looks upon as casting doubt on the dream of integration. Even pan-Africanism has degenerated into 'pan-African nationalism'. What is left is functional cooperation between sovereign states. One of the casualties, though Nye does not make much of it, was the legal settlement of disputes within the putative regional federation.

549   **Peaceful settlement among African states: roles of the United Nations and the Organization of African Unity.**
Berhanykun Andemicael.   New York: UNITAR, 1972. 63p. bibliog. (PS No. 5).

The U.N. Charter permits both initial resort to regional agencies (Article 52(2)) or involvement at any time of the General Assembly or Security Council (Articles 11(2) and 34) in order to settle a dispute. This study generally finds that the U.N. has followed, in the 1963-68 period, the 'Try O.A.U. First' principle. The author, himself an Ethiopian, examines four kinds of African conflicts: border disputes, differences over the future of neighbouring non-self-governing territories, internal conflicts, and inter-state friction. His study covers the Algeria–Morocco boundary dispute, Somalia's early disputes with Ethiopia and Kenya, the Congo crisis after 1964, the Nigerian civil war, and Ghana's friction with Guinea and Ivory Coast. He concludes that the O.A.U., though tried first, could 'normalize' a conflict, but not finally *settle* it without the assistance of various ad hoc bodies of senior civil servants or national heads of state, or without the good offices of the U.N. Secretary-General and the still more remote international authority of the Security Council. The O.A.U.'s own Commission of Mediation, Conciliation, and Arbitration has never been used, apparently because parties in dispute prefer not to submit to its mechanical processes.

550   **The peaceful settlement of disputes among African states, 1963-1983: some conceptual issues and practical trends.**
Tiyanjana Miluwa.   *International and Comparative Law Quarterly*, vol. 38 (1989), p.299-320.

The O.A.U. Charter provides for peaceful settlement, yet the record of African adherence to this principle is disappointing. Why? The author explains that Africans (and Asians) 'lack confidence' in the international judicial system because of its European origins and bias, which was revealed markedly in the ICJ's disastrous *South West Africa* judgment in 1966. But why then do they also seem to lack confidence in *political* means, particularly in the O.A.U.'s own Commission of Conciliation, Mediation, and Arbitration, which has never been used? Miluwa reviews the founding of the commission and the resort in some fifty disputes from 1963 to 1983 to alternative ad hoc devices usually linked to a head of state. He concludes that the 'try O.A.U. first' principle is unhistorical and that upgrading the commission to a court would be unrealistic.

551   **Peace in parts: integration and conflict in regional organizations.**
Joseph S. Nye, Jr.   Boston: Little, Brown, 1971. 210p.

Chapter 5 of this tough-minded, influential book tests the hypothesis that the control of intra-regional conflicts by regional political organizations contributes to peace. Nye examines the record of the O.A.S., O.A.U., and the Arab League in resolving some nineteen historic cases of conflict that involved them. He finds that the three organizations have helped abate conflicts and end fighting in about half the cases, and provide a permanent settlement in a third, which compares roughly to the U.N. success rate of one in three, though the U.N. receives far harder cases. Hence, the hypothesis of regional political conflict resolution is roughly confirmed, like a similar hypothesis that regional economic organization helps to create functional links between states and also contributes to peace. Nye is cautious about extrapolating results based on so few instances into the future.

552   **Regional cooperation for development and the peaceful settlement of disputes in Latin America.**
Edited by Jack Child.   Dordrecht, The Netherlands: M. Nijhoff for the International Peace Academy, 1987. 158p. (Report No. 26).

This work, produced in cooperation with three Peruvian research organizations, aimed to recommend long-term improvements in peaceful settlement in Latin America at a time of massive Cold War conflict in Central America. General conclusions included: (1) Development, democracy, peace, and security are mutually reinforcing. . . . (6) Terrorism, which is condemned, may be distinguished from revolutionary struggle, which cannot be. (7) East–West tensions should be decoupled from regional solutions. . . . (10) The Contadora and Lima Support Groups are a new development in diplomacy that help the region grope toward its own solutions. Supportive papers provide a rich fund of case-studies, conflict resolution methods, confidence-building measures, peacekeeping, and third-party roles in the future, including those of the O.A.S. and the U.N.

553 **Regional international organizations: structures and functions.**
Edited by Paul A. Tharp, Jr. New York: St. Martin's, 1971. 276p.
bibliog.

The editor interprets the proliferation of major regional intergovernmental
organizations (twenty by 1971) as a 'process of political evolution as profound as the
change from feudalism to the nation-state that occurred in Europe several centuries
ago'. The book presents regional organizations in functional terms first chosen for the
political institutions of nation-states: articulation and aggregation of interests,
socialization, rule-(law-)making, and rule adjudication. These concepts are illustrated
in the cases primarily of the European Community, Scandinavia, O.A.S., O.A.U.,
COMECON (now defunct), and economic organizations in Africa and Latin America.
Joseph Nye contributes a concluding essay on U.S. policy toward regional
organizations. Pan-Americanism, the Atlantic alliance, support for economic
integration in Europe and Latin America, and support of regional and U.N. conflict
management and peacekeeping have been long-standing U.S. foreign policy concerns.
For the future, if the bipolar system should decay, Nye argues that U.S. policy will
still have other options than 'to promote autonomous regional organizations as a part
of a long-run vision of world order'.

554 **Regionalism and world order.**
Ronald J. Yalem. Washington, DC: Public Affairs Press, 1965. 160p.

By 1919, it was evident that national states, acting alone, could no longer preserve
themselves, but the problems of establishing an effective universal international
organization have suggested to some statesmen and internationalists that more
progress might be made with regional organizations. This thoughtful study examines
the assumptions and history of regionalism since 1920, with particular attention to its
support or undermining of the universal approach to peace and security. Yalem's
standard is 'world order' – 'conceived as an ideal condition of the international
system of sovereign states in which relations between states are governed on the basis
of law and noncoercive procedures rather than power politics and force'. He finds
promise in the E.E.C., if it becomes a federation, and danger in NATO, if similar
regional security agencies become opposed to each other around the globe. Yalem
speculates in his conclusion about the consequences of a 'normalization of relations
between the major ideological systems', that is, an end of the Cold War. He is
doubtful that either the U.N. or regional organizations will be able to appreciably
contribute to disarmament or to the rule of law without the long-term 'elimination of
mutual suspicion and distrust'. Regionalism, he concludes, is 'only a partial solution' to
universal problems in an interdependent world.

555 **Regional politics and world order.**
Edited by Richard A. Falk and Saul Mendlovitz. San Francisco:
W.H. Freeman, 1973. 475p.

This collection of thoughtful essays focuses on the processes of regional cooperation
and integration as they may contribute to *world order* – understood as a preferred
world where the values of peace, economic abundance, social justice, ecological
balance, and political participation are realized. Since by the 1990s the expression
'new world order' would capture the vision of a world after the Cold War, this book
may yet give timely instruction. The authors give special attention to regions as
addressed by the United Nations, especially by its regional economic commissions,
which have led Johan Galtung to propose regional security commissions under the

U.N. Attention is also given to fledgling regional human rights and environmental organizations and to the somewhat more independent regional intergovernmental organizations like the O.A.S. In an appendix, documenting the world order school's link with the earlier world government movement, the editors reprint 'The preliminary draft of a world constitution' (1948, 1965).

556 The role and impact of the O.A.U. in the management of African conflicts.

Bukar Bukarambe. *Survival*, vol. 25 (1983), p.50-58.

The Organization of African Unity was founded in 1963 to defend the sovereignty of the new states emerging from colonialism and to promote their cooperation under the U.N. Charter. Ultimately, the goal was a 'supra-national' pan-Africanism. The author reports on progress in maintaining regional security. The O.A.U. confronts five problems: its own size (fifty members) and diversity (Arab and Black), the fragility of members' political and economic systems, superpower rivalry (notably in Somalia after 1977), ideological differences ('responsible for the demise of the East African Community'), and élite personality and power conflicts. Bukarambe (a Nigerian) argues that pan-Africanism as an ideal has not been able to produce the consensus necessary for the O.A.U. to solve its diverse political, economic, and military problems. He closely examines the O.A.U.'s record of conflict management in Chad and Western Sahara, and finds four operational problems rather like those of the larger United Nations. The O.A.U.'s resolutions are only advisory, its members foment nationalism, each state fears its neighbours, and the organization is not given the resources to pursue common interests. He closes with suggestions for reform such as making O.A.U. resolutions binding and dues compulsory. All depends on a 'sudden re-awakening to necessity'.

557 The role of the Commonwealth in the peaceful settlement of disputes.

Peter Slinn. In: *The non-use of force in international law*. Edited by W.E. Butler. Dordrecht, The Netherlands: M. Nijhoff, 1989, p.119-35.

The Commonwealth is a voluntary association of forty-eight states bound together by historic ties and by regular meetings of heads of government. It is not a 'regional' organization nor strictly speaking an international organization with a legal 'personality'. Nevertheless, the Commonwealth has had a role in dispute settlement, particularly in Zimbabwe and southern Africa. Its forms of cooperation and consultation, without legal coercion, have long seemed suggestive for the wider world from the times of Lionel Curtis to those of Peter Slinn.

558 Territorial conflicts in Latin America and procedures for settlement.

Association for Research and Specialization in Ibero-American Themes (Madrid). In: *UNESCO yearbook on peace and conflict studies, 1984*. Paris: UNESCO, 1986, p.147-79.

A research team here surveys border and territorial disputes and their peaceful settlement (conciliation, arbitration, etc.) over the long term, as far back as the independence of Latin America (1810). There exist a number of still-unresolved border conflicts, an unregulated conventional arms trade, and a potentially catastrophic refusal to adhere to the Tlateloco Treaty for the Prohibition of Nuclear

Weapons in Latin America. The authors conclude that there is a 'sufficiently wide choice' of means for peaceful settlement of *all* such conflicts. What is wanting is an insistent public opinion and the 'political will, courage, and good faith' of national leadership.

559 **Towards a Pax Africana: a study of ideology and ambition.**
Ali Mazrui. Chicago: University of Chicago Press, 1967. 287p.

This is a brilliant, impassioned defence of the federal ideas of Kwame Nkrumah. It is out of such 'ideology and ambition', argues the author, that regional integration – and the rule of law for the resolution of disputes – may be effected. The United Nations comes into Mazrui's account in the context of decolonization and non-alignment, but he does not overlook so seemingly small but vastly consequential a point that the U.N.'s very voting system encourages some small powers to *remain* small. Regional federation would require apportioning votes on the basis of population or economic power, not 'sovereign equality'.

560 **World order and local disorder: the United Nations and international conflicts.**
Linda B. Miller. Princeton, NJ: Princeton University Press for Center of International Studies, 1967. 235p. bibliog.

This book is an early study of a problem that has loomed large after the decline of superpower conflict – whether the United Nations should intervene in essentially domestic conflicts in order to preserve life or protect human rights. But the problem has existed for the U.N. at least as far back as the Spanish question (what to do about Franco) in 1946. The author takes up cases of 'internal conflict' that threatened international peace and security, and hence became seized by the U.N., in three broad areas: colonial wars, breakdown of law and order, and proxy wars. Miller concludes that, although U.N. involvement in such conflicts has often been disappointing (to 1967), its improvement will depend on self-restraint by powerful third-party states and possibly on new norms of state conduct developed by the General Assembly. Her hope is that international society will develop into a 'transnational political community'.

Peacekeeping ('Chapter VI 1/2')

561 **The blue berets.**
Michael Harbottle. London: Cooper, 1971. 157p. bibliog.

This is an illustrated history of the major U.N. peacekeeping operations to 1971 (UNEF, ONUC, UNFICYP, UNTEA, with comment on the Korean enforcement action), by a former (British) chief of staff of the Cyprus operation. The story of peacekeeping, Harbottle argues with a certain irony, 'should have pride of place in history books'.

562 **The blue helmets: a review of United Nations peacekeeping.**
United Nations. New York: United Nations, 1990. 449p. maps.
(E.90.I.18).

This is the U.N.'s official account of peacekeeping, which serves as an even-handed introduction for the student and a reference for the scholar. Peacekeeping is a 'holding action', an adjunct to the means of peaceful settlement of disputes set out in Chapter VI of the Charter. Peacekeeping operations are generally classified as observer missions or peacekeeping forces. They are normally established by the Security Council and directed by the Secretary-General with the consent of the states-parties involved. The military personnel are contributed voluntarily by member-states. U.N. observers are unarmed, while peacekeeping soldiers are lightly armed but not allowed to use their weapons except in personal self-defence. Peacekeepers do not intervene in the parties' domestic affairs, and they maintain strict impartiality. The book describes past and present U.N. operations up to the one in Namibia in 1989-90. Valuable appendixes summarize data on each operation.

563 **The evolution of United Nations peacekeeping.**
Marrack Goulding. *International Affairs* (London), vol. 69 (1993), p.451-64. (Cyril Foster Lecture. University of Oxford, 4 March 1993).

The former Under Secretary-General for peacekeeping operations explains peacekeeping after the Cold War. Classical peacekeeping was based on the principles of U.N. authority, consent of the parties, impartiality, national contributions of troops, and non-use of force. Peacekeeping operations since 1988 fall into six types: preventive deployment (Macedonia), traditional operations, implementation of a comprehensive settlement (Namibia, El Salvador, Angola, Cambodia, Mozambique), operations to protect humanitarian relief (Somalia, Bosnia), deployment where institutions of state have largely collapsed (Somalia, Congo), ceasefire enforcement (Bosnia). Somalia was a failure, Goulding argues, not because of inadequate rules of engagement, but 'because of the absence of recognized political authorities with whom the United Nations could reliably conclude agreements for the deployment and activities of the peacekeepers'. He welcomes the trend toward enforcement ('a decisive moment in the development of the organization'). But since it means 'going to war', he asks: By what criteria does the Security Council decide to use force? How can it ensure that force will succeed? Will the international community pay the cost in money and lives? How should command and control for war operations be improved, particularly at U.N. headquarters? In the future, he cautions, the Secretary-General and the Security Council will bear the responsibility of finding a middle way between rushing into every crisis and exercising such restraint that states doubt the 'real usefulness of the United Nations' and return to the 'bad old ways of unilateral military action'.

564 **The evolution of U.N. peacekeeping: case studies and comparative analysis.**
Edited by William J. Durch. New York: St. Martin's for Henry L. Stimson Center, 1993. 509p. bibliog.

This book sets a standard for the study of peacekeeping after the Cold War. It does not confuse peacekeeping with peace enforcement ('the U.N. needs to walk before it can run'), and it surveys the whole gamut of U.N. operations in a consistent comparative style. (Non-U.N. operations, like the Multinational Force in Beirut, are left out, presumably because their lack of international authority, loss of impartiality, and abandonment of the principle of non-use of force discourage repetition. Certain regional operations, like the Commonwealth Monitoring Force in Zimbabwe, however, have followed U.N. guidelines and worked well.) The book is written for those already familiar with international relations, the history of the Cold War, and the basic structure and functions of the United Nations, so it will be instantly intelligible to all those who speak the language of defence and foreign policy. The introduction and first three chapters by the editor are particularly clear. Each historic operation (to 1988) in the Mediterranean and Middle East, South Asia, Southeast Asia, Africa, and the American continents is fully described. An epilogue sketches operations since 1988 in El Salvador, Cambodia, former Yugoslavia, and Somalia. Cases are described in terms of their origins, political support, U.N. mandate, funding, planning and implementation, and assessment. There is relatively little discussion of the need for strengthening peacekeeping or for U.N. reform in general.

565   **The financing of United Nations peacekeeping operations: the need for a sound financial base.**
Susan R. Mills.   New York: International Peace Academy, 1989. 33p. (Occasional Paper No. 3).

A sound financial base is obviously needed for peacekeeping, but the author, a U.N. deputy controller, cannot enter into the larger political issues of member-state neglect of one of the more successful international activities. Mills limits herself to an exact accounting of past and present financing methods. These are: the regular budget (six operations), voluntary contributions by parties concerned (two), and special assessments (eight through 1989). She discusses the first U.N. financial crisis caused by the refusal of France and the Soviet Union to pay for ONUC in the Congo, the small bond issue of 1961, the futility of disciplining states by Article 19, and the Working Capital Fund and Special Account to enable the Secretary-General to cope with persistent shortfalls. She reviews the General Assembly debate through 1989 and concludes that states are not facing up to their financial responsibilities.

566   **The future of peacekeeping.**
Indar Jit Rikhye.   New York: International Peace Academy, 1989. 36p. (Occasional Paper No. 2).

In 1988, as the Cold War wound down, U.N. peacekeeping began a rapid expansion, with new missions in Afghanistan, Iran–Iraq, Angola, Namibia, and soon Cambodia. (In three years, as many new missions were operating as had been established in the previous forty-five.) In this short work, General Rikhye, who first served in UNEF I and is now president of the International Peace Academy, reflects on the accomplishments of peacekeeping and on its practical future. Peacekeeping gains time for negotiation, but it cannot by itself achieve lasting peace: 'only parties to the conflict can achieve this'. Peacekeeping has been a device to end wars. Rikhye wishes that member-states would go to the U.N. to end their conflicts before war. In the future, he argues, peacekeeping could be given new roles to quell incipient conflict, secure borders, provide confidence-building measures, verify arms control agreements, assist weak governments in maintaining internal law and order, combat terrorism, provide humanitarian aid, interdict drug trafficking, and begin naval peacekeeping.

567 **An Inter-American peace force within the framework of the O.A.S.: advantages, impediments, implications.**
James R. Jose.   Metuchen, NJ: Scarecrow, 1970. 334p.

The Inter-American Peace Force was an O.A.S. peacekeeping force established in the aftermath of the U.S. intervention into the Dominican Republic in 1965. It was withdrawn a year later after the threat of a communist electoral victory had been dispelled. The author closely examines this case in order to discuss the prospects of establishing a *permanent* 'Inter-American Force'. Jose concludes that such a force, though theoretically it would contribute to national and regional political stability, probably cannot be created because of the absence of political consensus (especially over a 'supranational' system) and because of the 'predominance of the United States'.

568 **International peacekeeping at the crossroads.**
David W. Wainhouse.   Baltimore, MD: Johns Hopkins University Press, 1973. 634p.

This is an authoritative study of peacekeeping through 1973, before UNEF II was established in another round of expansion. (Regional peacekeeping under the Arab League and O.A.S. is also included.) The author presents elaborate case-studies and concludes with a study of U.S. support of peacekeeping compared with the support of other countries.

569 **International peacekeeping: history and strengthening.**
Joseph Preston Baratta.   Washington, DC: Center for U.N. Reform Education, 1989. 120p. bibliog. (Monograph No. 6).

'Peacekeeping', says Sir Brian Urquhart, 'is the projection of non-violence onto the military plane.' The history of peacekeeping is recounted in thirty related narratives and is summarized in a comparative table. Both U.N. and non-U.N. observer missions and peacekeeping forces are included. Peacekeeping forces introduced into anarchic situations – as in West Irian (1962-63) and Namibia (1988-89), in which the U.N. temporarily exercised sovereign powers in supervising elections and maintaining law and order until the new government was established – provides a precedent for subsequent operations as in Cambodia (1992-93). Many of the recommendations in this study, largely based on U.S. proposals during the Carter administration, are being implemented: creation of a U.N. peacekeeping reserve, national training in the techniques, joint contingency planning, cooperative airlift and supply, shared finance, and enhanced negotiations of settlements in the time gained. The author is resolute, with Dag Hammarskjöld, not to strengthen peacekeeping along the lines of international armed forces as contemplated in Chapter VII. 'Peacekeepers', Baratta concludes, 'should come to look more like marshals and less like soldiers.'

570 **International peacekeeping in Lebanon: United Nations authority and multinational force.**
Ramesh Thakur.   Boulder, CO: Westview, 1987. 356p. bibliog.

This book is a studied challenge to attempts by Great Powers to mount peacekeeping forces outside the framework of the United Nations. Thakur compares the U.N. Interim Force in Lebanon (UNIFIL, 1978), established by the Security Council, with the Multinational Force in Beirut (MNF, 1982), established by the United States, Great Britain, France, and Italy. The latter broke up and withdrew in disgrace after its international authority (diplomatic notes) and legitimacy (power, not consent) were questioned, and after its troops abandoned U.N. standards not to use force and always to maintain impartiality. UNIFIL, on the other hand, had international authority and legitimacy, and so was accepted by the local population, but the inadequacy of its mandate and the irresolution of the Security Council to improve it detracted from the operation's small but symbolic powers. MNF had power without authority and legitimacy; UNIFIL had legitimacy and authority without power. Both are needed for effective peacekeeping forces. To underline his arguments about the mistake of avoiding the U.N., Thakur includes a haunting chapter on the non-U.N. observer mission in Vietnam after the Geneva accords of 1954.

571 **International peace observation: a history and forecast.**
David W. Wainhouse.   Baltimore, MD: Johns Hopkins University Press, 1966. 662p.

This is a scholarly study of some seventy cases of third-party peace observation missions since 1920. Since observation glides into peacekeeping forces in interpositional roles, Wainhouse includes ONUC, UNTEA, UNFICYP, and suggestive missions to Korea and Hungary in the depths of the Cold War. The book includes a section on strengthening peace observation.

572 **Keeping the peace between Egypt and Israel, 1973-1980.**
Nissim Bar-Yaacov.   *Israel Law Review*, vol. 15 (1980), p.197-268.

This article deals with the 'foreseen and unforeseeable problems', which brought about 'changes in the traditional pattern of peacekeeping' in the Middle East after 1973. Covered are: the introduction of UNEF II, two disengagement agreements, the introduction of the U.S. Sinai Field Mission on the Giddi and Mitla Passes (because UNTSO was unacceptable), the peace treaty between Egypt and Israel in 1979, and the introduction (not complete as the article went to press) of the non-U.N. Multilateral Force and Observers deployed between Egypt and Israel (1981). Bar-Yaacov takes the view, respecting the basic principles at work in these novel arrangements, 'that the security arrangements provided for in each of the two disengagement agreements and in the peace treaty represent the continuous application of one and the same security system, based on the principle of separation of forces, limitation of forces and of armaments, and the employment of third-party personnel charged with supervising the implementation of the relevant obligations of the parties'. This is a valuable Israeli account to balance similar accounts by Pelcovits (U.S.) and Mackinlay (U.K.).

573 **The Multinational Force in Beirut, 1982-1984.**
Edited by Anthony McDermott and Kjell Skjelsbaek.   Miami: Florida International University Press, 1991. 293p.

This is a full-scale study, by the widest range of Western, Lebanese, and Israeli authors, of the ill-fated, four-power Multinational Force (MNF). The general verdict, say the editors, is that the MNF was 'ill-conceived, ill-briefed, and uncoordinated' as a peacekeeping operation. The pros and cons of its organization outside the U.N. framework are debated, with the balance of argument, judging by the operation's failure, tipping toward the folly of ignoring U.N. practice. The charge, particularly of Lebanese critics, that it was 'intervention in the guise of peacekeeping' seems to be, if unintentional, confirmed. The editors admit that planners of the intervention can be faulted for 'lack of understanding of the social and religious complexities on the ground and, above all, how they were changing throughout the period from 1975'. From a U.N. point of view, the implication is that future U.N. peacekeeping operations must not make similar mistakes.

574 **Negotiations before peacekeeping.**
Cameron R. Hume. New York: International Peace Academy, 1991. 40p. (Occasional Paper No. 5).

Peacekeeping operations are introduced with the consent of the parties, but how is that consent obtained? Answer: By prior negotiation. The author here closely examines the different negotiations leading up to five U.N. operations: UNTSO (Palestine, 1948), in which a mediator figured prominently; UNDOF (Golan Heights, 1974), with the help of a mediator backed by the United States; UNIFIL (Lebanon, 1978), in which the Security Council could not find the unanimity necessary for a strong mandate; UNIIMOG (Iran–Iraq, 1988), in which the permanent members cooperated effectively; and UNTAG (Namibia, 1989), where the United States and the Soviet Union cooperated to end their Cold War proxy war in Angola, linked to Namibia. Hume recounts these cases with special attention to the factors of successful negotiation.

575 **The peacekeepers: an assessment of peacekeeping operations at the Arab–Israeli interface.**
John Mackinlay. Preface by Gen. F. Bull Hansen. London: Unwin & Hyman, 1989. 239p.

The problems of peace in the Middle East are so intractible that the author focuses on the development of new peacekeeping operations in the wake of the 1967 and 1973 Arab–Israeli wars. UNEF I, whose withdrawal on Egyptian demand permitted the outbreak of the 1967 Six Day War, has to be accounted a failure, except for its innovations as the first peacekeeping force in international relations. UNEF II was established in 1974 on new principles, but Israel had little confidence in it. Four other peacekeeping forces, two outside the U.N. framework, were subsequently established, and these are the subject of Mackinlay's careful account: UNDOF on the Golan Heights (1974), UNIFIL in Lebanon (1978), MFO in the Sinai (1981), and MFN in Beirut (1982). Mackinlay recognizes that peacekeeping is primarily a *political* activity, but he argues that its military component is vital in the beginning. He concludes with reflections on the characteristics of success or failure. Compare Bar-Yaacov, *Keeping the peace* (item no. 572).

576 **The peacekeeper's handbook.**
International Peace Academy. Foreword by Indar Jit Rikhye. New York: Pergamon, 3rd ed., 1984. 439p.

This training manual on the relatively non-violent techniques of peacekeeping has been compiled by comparison with the instructions or guidelines of several of the leading troop-contributing nations. It is here offered as a general handbook of 'knowledge which national armed forces can use in the preparation of their contingents for international peacekeeping'. The emphasis is clearly on peacekeeping in the context of peacemaking (negotiation and mediation) and peacebuilding (rehabilitation and reconstruction). The book is designed for the classroom or the field. Topics include: U.N. organs, principles and procedures of U.N. peacekeeping, standard operating procedures, logistics, communications, economic operations and humanitarian relief, training, civilian police, and international law. The chapter on peacekeepers' attitudes is typical. Traditional military attitudes, especially of elite troops, such as 'You're in there to win', 'Shoot first or get shot', or disparagement of other peoples' military abilities, must be countered by the U.N. attitude, 'We don't use force', 'We have no enemies'.

577 **Peacekeeping and peacemaking.**
Richard N. Swift. In: *The United Nations: The next twenty-five years.* Commission to Study the Organization of Peace. Louis B. Sohn, chairman. Dobbs Ferry, NY: Oceana, 1970, p.149-65.

The author does not assume that Great Power conflict (in 1970 that between the United States and the Soviet Union) will easily go away. Hence, his recommendations for improvements to U.N. peacekeeping are designed to be acceptable in a hostile environment, which is realistic. One idea is to urge the President to formulate a policy on recourse to U.N. peacekeeping in appropriate circumstances as a substitute for U.S. action. Others are to use American funds to help other nations train units for U.N. service, earmark certain U.S. units for rapid U.N. service, establish a U.N. start-up contingency fund, develop a U.N. military staff and armed forces under Article 43, revive the dormant Panel for Inquiry and Conciliation, and create an observer corps for early warning. Twenty-five years later, most of these ideas are still being discussed.

578 **Peacekeeping and peacemaking after the Cold War.**
Lynn E. Davis. Santa Monica, CA: Rand Summer Institute, 1993. 36p.

The author, now U.S. Under Secretary of State for International Security Affairs, reviews, in this succinct paper completed before her appointment, the contributions of the U.N., CSCE, WEU, NATO, other regional organizations, Germany, and Japan to keeping the peace. For conflicts that meet the conditions for success of traditional U.N. peacekeeping operations, she finds, U.N. or regional peacekeeping can help. But for conflicts that do not meet those conditions, an array of responses from affirmation of principle to confidence-building measures to conflict resolution to peacemaking and peace enforcement may be required. Alternative responses include preventive diplomacy, peace building, and upholding international norms (like human rights), though none promises complete success. 'Keeping the peace in the post-Cold War era will be difficult, and the prospects for success are low for conflicts involving ethnic and religious groups. But this is no reason to despair. What is needed is a multifaceted approach to peacekeeping and peacemaking that is integrated with political, economic, and diplomatic measures.'

579 **Peacekeeping and the Inter-American system.**
John Child. *Military Review,* vol. 60, no. 10 (October 1980), p.40-54.

This article, by a U.S. Army Latin America specialist, introduces the concepts of peacekeeping to the military community, surveys Latin American participation in U.N. peacekeeping operations (1948-80), then turns to observer missions and the one peacekeeping force (Dominican Republic, 1965-66) within the Western hemisphere (fourteen cases, 1932-76). Peacekeeping missions within the Inter-American system have been based on the League of Nations (one case), the Rio Treaty of Reciprocal Assistance (1947), and the Charter of the Organization of American States (1948). (The

Bogotà Treaty of Pacific Settlement [1948] was too rigid and has never been sufficiently ratified to enter into force.) Col. Child finds that peacekeeping within Latin America remains constrained by 'resistance to unilateral U.S. actions which might violate the deeply rooted principles of nonintervention and state sovereignty'. He suggests enhancements of both U.N. and O.A.S. operations that do not give rise to 'historic fears of intervention by the United States'. For instance, U.S. contributions should be limited to logistics. Child also looks forward to Canadian participation and that of the Inter-American Defense Board.

580   **Peacekeeping: appraisals and proposals.**
Edited by Henry Wiseman.   New York: Pergamon for the
International Peace Academy, 1983. 461p.

In 1983, after UNEF II had proven its worth in contributing to Israeli–Egyptian peace but UNIFIL had just been overrun by an Israeli invasion into Lebanon, there was beginning to be widespread critical attention to peacekeeping. This book is a *tour d'horizon* of historical experience, national perspectives (Egypt, Israel, Canada), operations (U.N. headquarters, field problems, International Peace Academy training, technology), regional peacekeeping (O.A.S., O.A.U., International Commission for Control and Supervision in Vietnam), and future peacekeeping. Both Henry Wiseman and K. Venkata Raman contribute essays on future peacekeeping that are firmly grounded in U.N. practice yet extend the art of the possible.

581   **Peacekeeping in international politics.**
Alan James.   London: Macmillan for International Institute for
Strategic Studies, 1990. 378p. maps.

This is a broadly conceived, analytical history of peacekeeping, beginning with some frontier delimitation commissions under the League of Nations and continuing through the observer missions and peacekeeping forces of the United Nations and non-U.N. coalitions. The author, a British professor of international relations, has been at pains to avoid technical jargon ('peacekeeping can be seen as little more than a modern application of an ancient arrangement – that of the use of impartial and non-threatening go-betweens'). He divides his subject into cases of 'back yard operations' (those in a major power's sphere of influence), those in a 'club house' (group of kindred states), in a 'neighbourhood' (region), on 'high street' (strategic standoffs of the Cold War), and at 'dangerous crossroads' (flash points of nuclear war). The functions of such peacekeeping operations are the diffusion, stabilization, and, in the best of circumstances, resolution of disputes. 'The quite considerable use which has been made of military people in a non-threatening and impartial way', James concludes, '. . . suggests that states have found the device of value when they wish to wind down the intensity of international conflicts and problems, or even to wind them up.'

582   **Peacekeeping in Vietnam: Canada, India, Poland, and the**
International Commission.
Ramesh Thakur.   Edmonton: University of Alberta Press, 1984. 375p.
bibliog.

This is a valuable critical history of the International Commission of Supervision and Control (1954-73) and International Commission of Control and Supervision (1973-75), which are little remembered because of their failure to avert a second war in

Vietnam. The history provides a pensive sidelight on both the Vietnam War and the promise of international peacekeeping. 'The argument', writes Thakur, 'is that because of the above interrelationships [between Canada, India, and Poland], peacekeeping is successful when it is limited to narrow, precisely defined tasks of overseeing a military disengagement upon the cessation of hostilities, but fails when extended to embrace political tasks of conflict resolution, and is not viable against the self-defined vital interests of a superpower.'

583 **Peacekeeping, Lebanon: the facts, the documents.**
Ghassan Tueni. New York: Wm. Belcher Group, 1979. 477p.
The ambassador of Lebanon to the U.N. here provides an account of the dispatch of UNIFIL, the peacekeeping force sent to Lebanon in response to an Israeli invasion in 1978. It is not about the prior Arab Deterrent Force (1975). The documents include speeches, minutes, resolutions of the Security Council, reports, letters, even TV transcripts, from March 1978 to June 1979.

584 **Peacekeeping on Arab–Israeli fronts: lessons from the Sinai and Lebanon.**
Nathan A. Pelcovits. Boulder, CO: Westview for the Foreign Policy Institute, School of Advanced International Studies, Johns Hopkins University, 1984. 181p.
This is a close, comparative study of the four new peacekeeping operations (two set up outside the U.N. framework) that were established after the 1973 Yom Kippur War: UNDOF on the Golan Heights (1974), UNIFIL in Lebanon (1978), MFO in Sinai (1981), and MNF in Beirut (1982). (UNEF II [1974-79] is treated as not problematical.) UNIFIL has not kept the peace, and MNF ended in disaster. The author seeks to find out why. He concludes with novel recommendations for three peacekeeping missions designed to meet the difficult political, social, and military conditions in Lebanon: UNIFIL extended to the Israeli border and authorized to evict the PLO, a joint MNF–Arab League operation in the centre, and UNDOF extended from the Golan into the Beca'a Valley. Because the Lebanese civil war (or foreign intervention) has ended since the book was written, Pelcovits's recommendations may be dated, but they still are instructive for improving the design of future peacekeeping operations in the volatile Middle East. Compare Mackinlay, *The peacekeepers* (item no. 575).

585 **Peacekeeping operations and the quest for peace.**
Paul F. Diehl. *Political Science Quarterly*, vol. 103 (1988), p.485-507.
Peacekeeping was invented in 1956 when it was clear that collective security, the threat or use of force by the former allies as contemplated in Chapter VII of the U.N. Charter, was unrealistic and unacceptable to states and their peoples. As U Thant plainly summed up the matter in 1963: 'The idea that conventional military methods – or to put it bluntly, war – can be used by or on the behalf of the United Nations to counter aggression and secure the peace, seems now to be rather impractical.' Diehl describes the origins of classical peacekeeping, reviews cases (to 1988), and discusses factors of success (sure financing, fortunate geography, clarity of mandate, unified command and control, and neutrality).

586 The power to keep peace: today and in a world without war.

Lincoln P. Bloomfield. Berkeley, CA: World without War Council, 1971. 249p.

'This book asks: "If some form of police force is required [for the United Nations to provide international security], how can it be organized, maintained, controlled, and deployed?"' The work contains a fair and thoughtful critique of world government as an alternative ideal, which seemed implied in the U.S. disarmament proposals of 1960-62. 'No abstract conception of community or brotherhood', Bloomfield warned in the depths of the Cold War, 'whether expressed in political or moral terms, by itself carries anywhere enough authority to restrain contemporary belligerents.' Similar critical analyses are contributed by Hans Morgenthau, Stanley Hoffmann, Thomas C. Schelling, and Henry V. Dicks.

587 From Rhodesia to Zimbabwe: the politics of transition.

Henry Wiseman and Alastair M. Taylor. New York: Pergamon for International Peace Academy, 1981. 170p.

The Commonwealth mounted a non-U.N. peacekeeping force in Rhodesia (1979-80), which undertook the relatively novel function of monitoring elections. It was completely successful. 'The purpose of this case study', write the authors, 'is not to provide a capsulated history of the genesis of a new nation state in central Africa, but to focus on the interaction of the modalities of a ceasefire and an electorial process under the authority of a British governor so as to achieve, with all deliberate speed, a democratic black majority government in Zimbabwe.'

588 In the service of peace in the Middle East, 1967-1979.

Ensio Siilasvuo. London: Hurst, 1992. 388p. maps.

Readers in search of a more personal story of U.N. peacekeeping may find it here. Ensio Siilasvuo was the (Finnish) force commander of UNEF II, the peacekeeping operation set up after the 1973 Yom Kippur War. UNEF II functioned ideally as classic peacekeeping operations should, gaining time necessary for the parties to negotiate a settlement, which Egypt and Israel did in 1979. Siilasvuo tells the dramatic story of U.N. peacekeeping, starting with UNTSO and UNEF I, continuing through the 1967 and 1973 wars, and ending with UNEF II, UNDOF, and UNIFIL. As he returned to Finland in 1980, proud of the U.N.'s success yet disappointed by the continuing conflicts of the United States, Soviet Union, PLO, and Israel, he was struck by the heartfelt thanks of Jewish shopkeepers. 'Where do you think you are going?' they protested. 'You belong here. Otherwise we will never have peace here.'

589 Soldiers without enemies: preparing the United Nations for peacekeeping.

Larry L. Fabian. Washington, DC: Brookings, 1971. 315p. bibliog.

This sophisticated U.S. study, written at a low ebb of U.N. peacekeeping (UNEF I had been withdrawn and the Six Day War of 1967 had ensued), is still useful for its discussion of the rationale and practical arrangements of a 'stand-by' (not standing) system for the readiness of national contingents for rapid U.N. deployment on peacekeeping missions. Implementation of Article 43 – the Military Staff Committee – is discussed from a U.S. point of view.

590   **The Suez crisis,** [and] **The October war.**
Brian Urquhart.   In: *A life in peace and war*, by Brian Urquhart.
New York: Harper & Row, 1987, p.131-39, 234-53.

These two chapters in Urquhart's own autobiography recount the origins of the first peacekeeping force (UNEF I, 1956) and its successor (UNEF II, 1973). Together – despite the disastrously weak mandate of the first, which forced U Thant, on Egypt's demand, to withdraw it, precipitating the Six Day War – exemplify 'classic' peacekeeping, for they assisted negotiation of the Egyptian–Israeli peace treaty of 1979. Peacekeeping, writes Urquhart, who, after Dag Hammarskjöld and Lester Pearson, did most to develop the practice, is a 'symbol of international consensus'. 'It is the projection of non-violence onto the military plane.' Because this book reveals the political context of the U.N., it is still the best introduction to peacekeeping.

591   **The theory and practice of peacekeeping.**
Indar Jit Rikhye.   New York: St. Martin's, for International Peace
Academy, 1984. 255p. maps.

This work is an historical analysis of peacekeeping operations and a discussion of its future in the U.N. system. It includes regional peacekeeping and non-U.N. multilateral forces in its view. General Rikhye was chief of staff of UNEF I and later military adviser to the Secretary General (to 1969). At time of writing, the 'over-riding factor' for the success of peacekeeping, he held, was the attitude of the superpowers. Ten years later, this is still true of one superpower, but all powers must cooperate if the full potential of peacekeeping is to be released.

592   **The thin blue line: International peacekeeping and its future.**
Indar Jit Rikhye, Michael Harbottle, and Bjørn Egge.   New Haven,
CT: Yale University Press, 1974. 353p. maps. bibliog.

The International Peace Academy was founded in 1971 for 'the advancement of practical education in peacekeeping and in mediation, negotiation, and peaceful action for human rights and social development'. It 'directs its attention to the practical needs of peacekeeping, peacemaking, and peacebuilding for solving problems on the ground'. This book is a first report of the Academy, so is rather dated. Rikhye's *Theory and practice of peacekeeping* (1984) is one update (see above), but in the 1974 work the historian will find an account of classic peacekeeping and a record of courageous thought about the 'future of peacekeeping' should the 'dynamic concept' of the U.N. ever come to prevail.

593   **Uncertain mandate: politics of the U.N. Congo operation.**
Ernest Lefever.   Baltimore, MD: Johns Hopkins University Press,
1967. 254p. bibliog.

The United Nations did not first become involved in domestic conflicts with the application of *military* force in the 1990s. It did so first in the Congo peacekeeping operation in 1960-64. The Cold War revisionist historian, Ernest Lefever, here presents an informed and critical account of the operation, *Opération des Nations Unis au Congo* (ONUC), which may be of interest for comparative purposes. 'The U.N. operation did not prevent a political confrontation between the West and the Communist states in the Congo', Lefever writes, 'but it did impose legal and political constraints working for a unified state and a moderate government. . . . The effect of the United Nations Force [ONUC] was a net gain for the United States and a net loss for the Soviet Union. . . . But measured against its primary political goal – international stability – it made a modest but constructive contribution.'

594 **UNIFIL: international peacekeeping in Lebanon, 1978-1988.**
Bjørn Skogmo. Foreword by Brian Urquhart.   Boulder, CO: Lynne Rienner, 1989. 279p. bibliog.

The U.N. Interim Force in Lebanon (UNIFIL) was not given a mandate to deploy in a continuous band along the southern Lebanese border, to disarm or evict the PLO militia, or to obviate Israel's need to establish a clandestine security zone along the border patrolled by a rebel Lebanese militia. The operation could be viewed as a case-study of the failure of the Security Council to properly exercise its political responsibility for peacekeeping when it was nearly paralysed by the Cold War, which is how this experienced Norwegian diplomat views UNIFIL. His study remains instructive, for the Council will never be completely free of the conflicts of national interest, and peacekeeping of the future must not be frustrated by the political and constitutional constraints of the Council. Skogmo concludes that UNIFIL should not be withdrawn, for it is a 'custodian for a concept of international law' and a reminder of the 'lack of authority that the members of the Security Council have been able or willing to invest in their own decisions'.

595 **The United Nations and internal conflict.**
Oscar Schachter.   In: *Law and civil war in the modern world.* Edited by John N. Moore.   Baltimore, MD: Johns Hopkins University Press, 1974, p.401-22.

This chapter is a systematic and authoritative discussion of the U.N.'s role in settling internal conflicts (civil wars), despite Article 2(7). The discussion is somewhat dated (peacekeeping operations are barely mentioned among the U.N.'s peaceful means of dispute settlement), but its account of U.N. purposes, occasions calling for intervention, political factors influencing the U.N., and array of means available to the U.N. are still instructive when considering the threats to world order from ethnic conflict or break-up of states, as in Bosnia-Herzegovina, in the post-Cold War world.

596 **The United Nations and peacekeeping: results, limitations, and prospects; the lessons of 40 years of experience.**
Edited by Indar Jit Rikhye and Kjell Skjelsbaek.   Basingstoke, England: Macmillan for International Peace Academy and Norwegian Institute of International Affairs, 1990. 200p.

The papers collected here from a conference in 1988 were the most advanced on peacekeeping prior to its great expansion with the end of the Cold War. The authors include a Minister of Foreign Affairs, a Minister of Defence, officials from such ministries, uniformed officers on the Military Staff Committee, U.N. officials (Brian Urquhart, Marrack Goulding, James Jonah), former peacekeeping commanders, and leading scholars. The papers expound 'traditional' peacekeeping already encountering problems of command and control and of financing that would soon loom much larger.

597 **United Nations peace-keeping.**
United Nations. Foreword by Kofi Annan. New York: United
Nations, 1993. 57p. (DPI/1399).

This is an invaluable little booklet containing a succinct overview of U.N.
peacekeeping ('a way to control conflicts and promote peace'), a list of current
operations, another list of past operations, and a simple map. Each operation is
uniformly described, usually on one page, in terms of name, dates, place,
headquarters, mandate, strength, fatalities, expenditures, financing, Secretary-
General's representative, force commander, and countries contributing soldiers,
administrators, and police. An excellent short reference.

598 **United Nations peacekeeping and the non-use of force.**
F.T. Liu. Foreword by Brian Urquhart. Boulder, CO: Lynne Rienner
for International Peace Academy, 1992. 46p.

The author, who spent thirty-seven years in the U.N. Secretariat dealing with
peacekeeping and retired as Assistant Secretary-General for Special Political Affairs,
argues cogently that *use of force* by the U.N. contradicts the basic 'principle of the non-
use of force except in self defense . . . based on practical as well as idealistic
considerations'. His paper is an answer to all those who argue that peacekeeping should
be strengthened in the direction of national or even international military forces. Liu
fully defends the principles of consent, voluntary contributions, impartiality, and
international authority, which are the keys to success in peacekeeping. Peacekeepers do
not make war; they assist peacemakers in negotiating an end to the conflict. Non-use of
force is not easy, however, and Liu devotes much of his paper to its practical
improvement.

599 **United Nations peacekeeping: management and operations.**
F.T. Liu. New York: International Peace Academy, 1990. 43p.
(Occasional Paper No. 4).

Peacekeepers enter areas of conflict not to wage war but to maintain peace. The
author, who spent nearly forty years serving the U.N., ending as Assistant Secretary-
General with responsibility for peacekeeping, here discusses the practical
management of operations: direction and control, the force commander, national
military contingents, logistical support, and finance. Liu's ideas on finance include
limiting the duration of certain peacekeeping operations (like UNFICYP) or requiring
concerned parties to pay a larger share (UNIFIL). He concludes that continued
progress will require 'the sustained and unequivocal support of the Member States,
especially the five permanent members of the Security Council'.

600 **U.N. peacekeeping, 1946-1967: documents and commentary.**
Rosalyn Higgins. London: Oxford University Press, for Royal
Institute for International Affairs, 1969, 1970, 1980, 1981. 4 vols.
bibliog.

By 1969, interest in U.N. peacekeeping, especially in the Middle East, justified this
four-volume compilation, with explanatory commentary, of 'all the documentation' of
'all U.N. peacekeeping operations' to date. The material will be of great value to
historians, international lawyers, and policy-makers. The volumes cover the Middle
East (UNTSO, UNEF I, UNOGIL, UNYOM), Asia (UNSF, UNMOGIP, UNIPOM,

and the Korean enforcement action), Africa (ONUC), and Europe (UNSCOB, UNFICYP).

601   **U.N. peacekeeping: the changing utility of military force.**
Robert C. Johansen.   *Third World Quarterly*, vol. 12, no. 2 (April 1990), p.53-70.

The author argues that, for the purposes of maintaining peace, national military force is proving less useful than multilateral peacekeeping. He contrasts the defeat of U.S. forces in Vietnam and the stalemate of Soviet forces in Afghanistan with the progress of U.N. peacekeeping in Namibia and Angola since 1988. Johansen suggests that 'an imaginative approach to U.N. peacekeeping can become the linchpin in developing an overall strategy for reducing the role of military power in international relations'. Peacekeepers, because they have no enemies and do not seek to defeat armies or overcome whole societies, he argues, are transitional to true international police who seek to enforce law on individuals and punish only the leaders who violate world norms. He reviews the politics of strengthening peacekeeping and concludes that, by analogy with the history of rearmament, 'citizen and congressional pressure will be needed to re-orient U.S. priorities'.

602   **The uses of law in international peacekeeping.**
Oscar Schachter.   *Virginia Law Review*, vol. 50 (1964), p.1096-114.

Peacekeeping was new in 1964. The author, then with the Legal Division of the U.N. Secretariat, sought to trace the legal precepts and principles that would maintain the legitimacy and impartiality of the operations. Law provides a *locus standi* for impartial third-party intervention, Schachter argues. It provides standards and rules to facilitate discussion and settlement among the disputants. It relieves suspicions of competitive ideological blocs by guiding U.N. officials and peacekeepers in conformity to agreements negotiated in the General Assembly or Security Council. Schachter shows the law at work in these ways in U.N. observer missions along demarcation lines and in frontier areas (UNSCOB, UNMOGIP, UNTSO) and in the new peacekeeping forces (UNEF I, ONUC, UNFICYP, UNYOM). He particularly emphasizes the authority of the Security Council (Chapter VII), the prohibitions against the use of force (Article 2(4)), respect for non-intervention in domestic jurisdiction (Article 2(7)), economic and social aid (Chapters IX and X), and impartiality of officials (XV).

603   **Whither U.N. peacekeeping? An analysis of the changing military requirements of U.N. peacekeeping with proposals for its enhancement.**
Mats R. Berdal.   London: Brassey's for International Institute for Strategic Studies, 1993. 83p. (Adelphi Paper 281).

This strategic study of peacekeeping as it has entered its 'second generation' (electoral assistance, human rights monitoring, humanitarian relief, disarmament), is based on two assumptions: (1) While world politics may no longer be polarized by the struggle between communism and democracy/capitalism, it is still divided by 'profound differences of interest and value'. (2) Since political will of member-states is tied to their perceptions of national interests, greater effectiveness of the U.N. in protecting those interests by enhanced peacekeeping is likely to increase the 'willingness of member states to commit resources and political capital' to peacekeeping, other means of peaceful settlement, and U.N. reform. The study examines the changing nature of U.N. peacekeeping since 1988, the challenges facing peacekeeping in the 1990s (especially challenges to its classic principles of non-use of force and consent of the parties, with consequential need for improved planning and military intelligence), and lastly, how to enhance the practice if it becomes more frequently used on the international stage. Improved financing is treated as a direct consequence of military enhancements that will produce greater political effectiveness. The author is careful not to confuse peacekeeping with enforcement.

A life in peace and war.
See item no. 9.

The Arab League and peacekeeping in the Lebanon.
See item no. 533.

A draft concept of second generation multinational operations.
See item no. 610.

Enforcement (Chapter VII)

604 **Allocating competences to use coercion in the post-Cold War world: practices, conditions, and prospects.**
W. Michael Reisman. In: *Law and force in the new international order*. Edited by Lori F. Damrosch and David J. Scheffer. Boulder, CO: Westview, 1991, p.26-61.

The author presents a critical view of the 'intellectual pathology' of regarding the U.N. system of collective security under the five permanent members of the Security Council as either legal or reliable. He accepts the principle that law does not abolish force, but limits and regulates it for only authorized uses. He searches for the 'operational code' of actual practice in the use of force since 1945 and considers both 'proactive' coercion (state use of military force to change international custom, as in wars of national liberation and the Brezhnev and Reagan doctrines) and 'reactive' coercion (tolerable defence against low-intensity conflict). Reisman concludes that international law under the U.N. Charter is evolving, without express amendment and without the 'centralization of authoritative force and an effective monopoly over who can use it' necessary to a full constitutional order. Meanwhile there has to remain some latitude for the threat and use of force by responsible and enlightened independent sovereign governments.

605 **Authorized uses of force by the United Nations and regional organizations.**
Oscar Schachter. In: *Law and force in the new international order*. Edited by Lori F. Damrosch and David J. Scheffer. Boulder, CO: Westview, 1991, p.65-93.

This study was prepared during the U.N.'s second major enforcement action involving armed force – the Persian Gulf War (1990-91). The first was the Korean

War (1950-53). Schachter surveys the international legal categories for the use of force and discusses what will be required to give the U.N. more regular enforcement powers, especially under Articles 42, 43, and 47. He also discusses the rather evasive claim of 'collective self-defence' under Article 51, whose abuses the ICJ rejected in the case of *Nicaragua v. United States of America* (1986). He warns against enlarging the force available to peacekeeping operations.

606 **Civil wars: guidelines for states and the United Nations.**
Louis B. Sohn. In: *Law and civil war in the modern world.* Edited by
John N. Moore. Baltimore, MD: Johns Hopkins University Press,
1974, p.582-87.

Professor Sohn clarifies and synthesizes the debate among international legal publicists throughout this substantial volume by formulating some precise guidelines for states and the United Nations with respect to permissible and prohibited activities in case of civil wars. The basic principle is: 'No military intervention by one state in an internal armed conflict in another state is permissible, except in an extreme emergency requiring instant response and subject to immediate termination of such emergency action on request of the United Nations or an appropriate regional organization.'

607 **Collective responses to illegal acts in international law: United Nations action in the question of Southern Rhodesia.**
Vera Gowlland-Debbas. Foreword by Georges Abi-Saad. Dordrecht,
The Netherlands: M. Nijhoff, 1990. 753p. bibliog.

This exhaustive legal study of the U.N.'s political acts toward Southern Rhodesia, after Ian Smith threatened to bring it into the U.N. as a white racist state, will no doubt set a standard for years to come. The case set a precedent for the rule of law, the author argues, for the General Assembly found illegal and invalid Rhodesia's declaration of independence and refused to recognize the new regime; moreover, the Security Council for the first time imposed mandatory economic, financial, and diplomatic sanctions on the grounds that the situation in Rhodesia constituted a threat to international peace and security under Chapter VII (Article 41) of the Charter. The author interprets these events as upholding the new norm of self-determination (racial justice) above state power, enforced by the 'collective response' of the 'international community'. In effect, international law is shedding its subordinate role of maintaining the status quo for states, and is taking up a more dynamic and interventionist role, obliging states to adhere to norms essential for the protection of the world community.

608 **Collective security.**
Roland N. Stromberg. In: *The encyclopedia of American foreign policy: studies of the principal movements and ideas.* Edited by
Alexander DeConde. New York: Scribners, 1978. vol. 1, p.124-33.

This short article is a masterpiece of historical compression and analytical clarity – a good place to begin in order to understand collective security. The idea arose in 1914, though the term was coined only in the 1930s. 'Collective security may be defined as a plan for maintaining peace through an organization of sovereign states, whose members pledge themselves to defend each other against attack.' It failed utterly under the League of Nations by 1939, and was only revived in 1945 under the United Nations because of the argument that the League had failed, not for the reason that its members retained their absolute freedom of action, but because the United States had never been a member. Stromberg traces the subsequent failure of collective security through the Korean War, though there have been some partial realizations of the principle in U.N. peacekeeping and NATO, while war regularly returned to disrupt international relations. He criticizes collective security for assuming that states are normally 'peace-loving' and that war is caused by 'the occasional transgressions of a bad nation'. He also finds it wanting for freezing the status quo, not accommodating the demands of once colonized peoples for justice, and waging war to prevent war. Stromberg's own solution is to 'face the formidable task of creating a world community able to support a world government'.

609 **Consultation and consensus in the Security Council.**
F.Y. Chai. In: *Dispute settlement through the United Nations.* Edited by K. Venkata Raman. Dobbs Ferry, NY: Oceana for UNITAR, 1977, p.517-75.

Consensus, which in the General Assembly means the adoption of a resolution without a vote, in the Security Council means the adoption of a resolution or decision by unanimous agreement, with or without a vote. Consensus has been growing since the 1960s and seems to represent a form of diplomatic decision-making based more on consultation and less on public debate. The author traces the origins of the practice (especially dissatisfaction with 'speeches and votes' as a substitute for serious negotiation), compares it to conciliation, and assesses its value. Unanimous decisions, like Res. 242 of 1967, which was adopted by consensus, reflect broader support and hence tend to be more effective.

610 **A draft concept of second generation multinational operations, 1993.**
John Mackinlay and Jarat Chopra. Providence, RI: Thomas J. Watson Institute for International Studies, Brown University, 1993. 39p.

Funded by the Ford Foundation, and with the cooperation of the United Nations and the Academic Council on the United Nations, this 'manual' aims 'to develop a doctrine for a common approach to second generation U.N. operations'. (The first generation was the creation of peacekeeping operations from 1956 to the enforcement operation in the Persian Gulf War of 1990-91.) The manual has been distributed to sixty-three foreign or defence ministries involved in U.N. forces, and it is also under review by the CSCE, Group of 7, ASEAN, O.A.U., and O.A.S. A second edition, incorporating these state and regional organization assessments, and including sections on the *civil* elements of U.N. forces, should be ready in 1994. The manual reviews probable needs for U.N. peacekeeping or enforcement forces after the Cold War, specific missions, and legal authorization and limits, especially at 'level two' (preventive deployment, internal conflict resolution, assistance to interim civil authorities, humanitarian relief, and guarantees of movement). Truly effective economic and diplomatic sanctions and 'high intensity operations' (international war) are reserved for 'level three'. The principles of second-generation forces conclude the short work. This is a realistic work, not ranging far beyond the current international practice of states, but aiming to make force the servant of legality.

611   **Economic sanctions.**
Robin Renwick.   Cambridge, MA: Center for International Affairs,
Harvard University, 1981. 118p. bibliog. (Harvard Studies in
International Affairs No. 45).

This is a study, parallel to the early work of Margaret Doxey, of the effects of the two
major cases of application of economic sanctions under international auspices to change
the political behaviour of a single state – namely, the League of Nations sanctions
against Italy in 1935-36, and those of the United Nations against Southern Rhodesia in
1965-79. The author was a British diplomat, actually the head of the Rhodesia
Department of the Foreign Office. He sought to test the widespread belief that sanctions
have no effect. Renwick concludes that sanctions, despite problems of application like
long lead times and lack of international solidarity, do have effects and do impose
penalties, though they cannot stop determined aggression (Italy) or quickly change
government policy (Rhodesia). They are symbolic of the 'penalty', available within well-
organized states but not yet in the international community, 'imposed to secure
obedience to a law'.

612   **Economic sanctions and international enforcement.**
Margaret P. Doxey.   New York: Oxford University Press for Royal
Institute of International Affairs, 1971; 2nd ed., 1980. 161p. bibliog.

This short, sophisticated study examines the 'collective exercise of coercion by
economic means', as in economic warfare and blockades, regional boycotts, League
of Nations sanctions (as of Italy in 1935-36), and U.N. sanctions (North Korea,
China, Portugal, South Africa, and Rhodesia). In international law, use of economic
sanctions by international organizations is, like war, a collective punishment upon a
whole society in order to 'uphold standards of behaviour expected by custom or
required by law' of *élites*. Doxey discusses such problems of international sanctions
as finding consensus, defining goals, selecting means, and accepting costs. She has no
measures of effects of sanctions, which are inseparable from those of other factors. In
the case of Rhodesia, the effects were less economic than political, for after fifteen
years the 'U.N. norms of non-discrimination and majority rule progressively
delegitimized the Rhodesian and South African concepts of white minority rule and
apartheid'.

613   **Economic sanctions: ideals and experience.**
M.S. Daoudi and M.S. Dajani.   London: Routledge & Kegan Paul,
1983. 263p. bibliog.

As the world becomes more economically interdependent, the role of economic
sanctions will probably become more effective. The authors confirm this view, but
readers will have to be patient, since Daoudi and Dajani first show that the 'paradigm
shift' from a general belief that sanctions are an effective coercive weapon in
international politics, to the current one that they are ineffective or at best symbolic,
is an illusion. They date the shift to the weakness of the U.N. sanctions against
Rhodesia in 1965-79 or the failure of the OPEC oil embargo to defeat Israel in 1973-
74. A chapter on League of Nations and United Nations sanctions may be informative
to reflective readers. The authors conclude that 'sanctions do forestall the use of
force' by more symbolic than material effects, like exposing the moral injustice of
apartheid.

614   **Economic sanctions reconsidered: history and current policy.**
       Gary C. Hufbauer, Jeffrey J. Schott, and Kimberly Ann Elliott.
       Washington, DC: Institute for International Economics, 1985; 2nd ed.,
       1990. 2 vols.

This book presents a 'comprehensive analysis of the use of economic sanctions for
foreign policy purposes'. Most of the 116 cases examined are of sanctions imposed
unilaterally by the United States and other nations, but cases of U.N. sanctions, as
against South Africa, or of those undertaken by the Arab League, European
Community, and other regional organizations are also included. Hence, the reader
interested in international sanctions will find them here comprehensively treated
within the whole. Even national economic sanctions are an alternative to war, so their
use must be adjudged a reduction of the severity of conflict, if not of its incidence.
Generally, the authors find a 36 per cent 'success' rate for all their cases, and a lower
rate for international cases. International sanctions through the U.N. or coalitions,
they conclude, 'seldom yield desirable results'. They are useful only to 'increase the
moral suasion of the sanction', 'isolate the target country from the global
community', and 'preempt foreign backlash, thus minimizing corrosive friction
within the alliance'.

615   **Effective sanctions on South Africa: the cutting edge of economic
       intervention.**
       Edited by George W. Shepherd, Jr.   New York: Praeger for
       Consortium on Human Rights Development, 1991. 148p. bibliog.

By 1991, Nelson Mandela had been released from prison and it was time for a scholarly
analysis of the effect of international sanctions on moving the conflict over apartheid
into negotiations. This study includes appendixes listing all U.N. arms and economic
embargoes against South Africa (from 1962), national embargoes, and national
violations of the sanctions. The authors conclude that sanctions do work, that the
movement for racial equality in the world is not spent, that NGOs have been able to
implement economic sanctions when major powers declined, that 'domestic disputes'
can no longer evade international law – which has great implications for correcting
other major human rights violations – that certain economic models permit objective
assessment of the effect of sanctions, and that 'international economic measures are
replacing military intervention as a means for settling major world conflicts'.

616   **Enforcement of human rights in peace and war and the future of
       humanity.**
       Nagendra Singh.   Dordrecht, The Netherlands: M. Nijhoff, 1986.
       252p.

The author, the (Indian) president of the World Court, recognizes that the
enforcement of human rights has to take place on the national level (by law), on the
international level (by declaration and treaty), in peace time (by national courts,
European Court of Human Rights, and U.N. commissions and committees, ICJ
chambers, and a new world tribunal of human rights), and in war time (by national and
international armed forces). The book is little concerned with the expansion of
peacekeeping into domestic affairs for humanitarian purposes or for the protection of
human rights; it is concerned with the larger question of the world's legal enforcement of
rights on the model of national states, where armed forces are always provided as a last
resort. Judge Singh writes refreshingly from the perspective of the Indian legal system.

617 **Enforcing international law, a way to world peace: a documentary history and analysis.**
Benjamin B. Ferencz. Introduction by Louis B. Sohn. New York: Oceana, 1983. 2 vols. bibliog.

'Enforcement' is not understood narrowly in these splendid volumes as international coercion by economic sanctions or armed force (war), as in the conceptions of the U.N. Charter's Chapter VII. In addition to coercion, Ferencz includes appealing to regional organizations and to ad hoc coalitions, peacekeeping, clarifying the norms of international behaviour, widening the acceptance of judicial authority, making the U.N. more effective, demilitarizing states, establishing a small, safe, but effective international force, and above all, pursuing peace with justice. All these are devices for improving the enforcement of international law. Readers should not be deterred by the bulk of the two volumes: the analysis is pointed, and the documents entrancing. Ferencz concludes: 'There are no reasonable alternatives to the peaceful enforcement of international law. . . . International cooperation must replace the prevailing international anarchy. What is required is the determination by all countries – their statesmen and their peoples – to further every program and procedure that leads to more effective law enforcement. In the interests of all, the sovereignty of the state must be replaced by the sovereignty of the law.'

618 **Enforcing restraint: collective intervention in internal conflicts.**
Edited by Lori Fisler Damrosch. Foreword by Max Kampelman.
New York: Council on Foreign Relations Press, Project on International Organizations and Law, 1993. 403p.

The interdependence of the world has progressed so far that, only a few years after the euphoria of opening the Berlin Wall and ending the Cold War, the burning question for the maintenance of peace is whether the international community should intervene in internal, or domestic, disputes, as in Yugoslavia. The U.N. Charter's Article 2(7) is becoming a dead letter. The editor surveys the shifting international legal situation – in which 'state system values' are increasingly challenged by 'human rights values', and in which the world community of states and peoples is newly willing to endorse strong collective action (usually by the U.N.) in cases of genocide, interference with the delivery of humanitarian aid, violations of ceasefire agreements, collapse of civil order, and irregular interruption of democratic governance. The authors of the specialized articles then examine, case by case, the complex new situations in (former) Yugoslavia, Iraq, Haiti, Liberia, Somalia, and Cambodia. Damrosch contributes an instructive chapter on the 'civilian impact of economic sanctions', and Tom Farer, a modest one on a 'paradigm of legitimate intervention'. This is an informed and prudent book that all readers in search of new thinking on enforcement would be wise to consult. It does not depart, as Farer says, from 'a thinly institutionalized, if not altogether anarchic, political system'.

619 **Financial sanctions against South Africa. Report [on implementation of sanctions and other action against apartheid].**
Group of independent experts appointed by the Governing Body of the International Labour Organization. Geneva: International Labour Office, 1991. 61p. bibliog.

This resourceful, official study by the ILO attempts to assess the impact of financial sanctions on South Africa as imposed by the International Monetary Fund, World

Bank, Commonwealth, European Community, Bank for International Settlements, United States, Canada, U.K., France, Germany, and other nations. In 1990, Nelson Mandela had just been released from prison, yet it was impossible to predict the pace and constitutional results of the anti-apartheid struggle. The authors concluded that financial sanctions had curbed only the buoyancy and growth of the South African economy, but they urged that foreign and international banks should not reschedule South African debt in order to maintain pressure on the authorities.

620 **Freezing assets: the U.S.A. and the most effective economic sanctions.**
Mahvash Alerassool. New York: St. Martin's, 1993. 238p. map. bibliog.

In 1979, the United States froze the financial assets of Iran in response to the Iranian revolution and the hostage crisis. Since then the U.S. has implemented similar policies against Nicaragua, Libya, Panama, Kuwait, and Iraq. The author, a lecturer at the London School of Economics and Political Science, here presents a 'study of the international financial, political, and legal implications of freezing sovereign assets and an assessment of its effectiveness as an economic sanction'. The U.N. Security Council did pass one freeze resolution (Res. 661 of 6 August 1990), but this came long afterwards and was more related to the Persian Gulf War. The reader will find here a comprehensive account of the freezing of assets, with the U.N. given its minor part. Alerassool argues 'that domestic and international economics and politics cannot be separated'.

621 **International sanctions in contemporary perspective.**
Margaret P. Doxey. New York: St. Martin's, 1987. 175p.

The author, a leading scholar in the field, here brings her analysis of international sanctions up to 1986. By this date, sanctions had had some appreciable influence on bringing black majority rule to Zimbabwe, but their effect on the independence of Namibia would not be fully felt until 1989, and those on the end of apartheid in South Africa, for several more years. Doxey presents an excellent, succinct summary of the whole record of U.N. enforcement within the scope of Chapter VII, including the Article 39 action against Korea in 1950-53. (The Gulf War, similarly authorized, of course comes later, in 1990.) Also studied are the authoritative basis for economic or military sanctions, League of Nations practice, sanctions by regional organizations, by coalitions of states when the veto prevents U.N. action (as in the Iran hostages case), and by individual states as an instrument of foreign policy. She concludes generally, before the end of the Cold War, 'that resort to sanctions by governments over the past decade has not accompanied or reinforced any trend towards increased authority for international institutions in dealing with international misconduct'. She also finds 'that collective economic measures have not generally proved a reliable means of bringing compliance'. Sanctions are too indiscriminate, damaging not only the target society but also the neighbouring ones, and even the imposing power. Ethical and prudential reasons limit use of sanctions, as when they would only increase suffering in a developing country or lead to debt defaults. But as symbolic measures, economic sanctions are non-lethal and hence preferable to use of force. She closes with a worry 'that "sanctions" will lose their status as measures which genuinely support universally accepted standards of behaviour'. 'Given the real progress which has been made since the Second World War in developing rules which limit both the use of force and the abuse of human rights, this would be a retrograde development.'

622 **Multilateral sanctions in international law: a comparative analysis.**
C. Lloyd Brown-John. New York: Praeger, 1975. 426p. bibliog.
The author defines 'sanctions' – moral, political, economic, financial, and physical – then surveys international sanctions, particularly in the difficult and revealing cases of League sanctions against Italy (1935-36), O.A.S. sanctions against the Dominican Republic (1960-61), and U.N. sanctions against Rhodesia (1966). He finds his view confirmed: 'Sanctions, and especially economic sanctions, can be used to enforce decisions of multilateral international agencies taken in pursuit of international law and its violators.'

623 **A proposal for United Nations security forces.**
Én Verden. World Association for World Federation. Oslo: Én Verden, 1989. 20p. (Available from World Federalist Movement Office, 777 United Nations Plaza, New York, NY 10017.)
This is a proposal by a Norwegian group of experts, including Gen. Frederik Bull-Hansen and Lt.Gen. Odd Bull, both of whom have commanded peacekeeping operations, to go beyond peacekeeping based on consent, to the international armed forces able to deter or halt large-scale conflict by defeat of the parties, as contemplated in Chapter VII. The authors recommend that *all* nations earmark forces for a 'dual national/U.N. general war prevention and peacekeeping role', with the designation of such contingents as 'U.N. Security Forces'. Provision is made for U.N. observers (under authority of the Secretary-General); U.N. land, sea, and air force reserve contingents; U.N. special alert forces (provided in rotation by the smaller countries); U.N. strategic reserves (provided by the permanent members of the Security Council); and an elaborate military command under a developed Military Staff Committee as in Article 47. The authors argue: 'Since preventing war and conflicts is the main *raison d'être* for the U.N., this organization needs and deserves good professional military service at all levels and also proper military command responsibility in executing the various missions and tasks undertaken.' Compare Stanley, *To unite our strength* (item no. 629).

624 **Sanctions against South Africa: exploding the myths.**
Barbara Rogers and Brian Bolton. Manchester: Manchester Free Press and Holland Committee on Southern Africa, 1981. 104p.
This is a close study of sanctions against South Africa by the European Community. The European imports from, and exports to, South Africa are exactly quantified in order to address the question of the effect of the sanctions. The authors conclude with recommendations for multilateral action by the U.N. Security Council or E.C. Commission to further reduce the extent of existing trade with South Africa. Hence, the book is an argument *for* international sanctions, not an analysis of the *effect* of them.

625 **Sanctions: the threat to South Africa.**
Tony Koenderman. Johannesburg: J. Ball, 1982. 278p. bibliog.
The United Nations Security Council, regarding South Africa's apartheid and armament policies as threats to international peace and security, imposed a mandatory arms embargo against the state in 1977. This was added to a wide array of other sanctions – financial, economic, trading, diplomatic, transport, communications,

sport, and educational. Hence, sanctions against South Africa provide a dramatic test case of this instrument of enforcement under Chapter VII. The author, himself a South African, is critical of outside efforts to 'accelerate the revolution', preferring 'orderly change' through economic growth of all the states south of the equator. The book may offer a corrective to accounts of sanctions written from a superior internationalist perspective.

626   **The sanctions weapon: a summary of the debate over sanctions against South Africa.**
       Africa Research Centre for the Black Caucus.   Cape Town: Buchu
       Books, 1989. 112p.

At a time when no public airing of the issue of sanctions had taken place within South Africa, the authors of this booklet, reporting to a caucus of black American workers in companies operating in the Western Cape region, aimed to present an objective summary of the debate. 'Such a summary, it was hoped, would enable those who read it as well as those with whom they had contact to make informed decisions and thus to become less liable to being pressurised in one direction or another by belief in a magic formula.' Hence, the work is a valuable source for a reader who wants to quickly discover the whole context of the question of sanctions. The U.N. by no means imposed them all, but it led the debate.

627   **The U.N. in a new world order.**
       Bruce Russett and James S. Sutterlin.   *Foreign Affairs*, vol. 70, no. 2
       (Spring 1991), p.69-83.

This article in the leading U.S. journal of foreign policy comes straight to the point of 'military enforcement measures by the United Nations' on the model of the Persian Gulf War (1990-91) and Korean War (1950-53). 'More occasions are likely to follow', the authors assert. They review the history and principles of peacekeeping after 1956 and argue that after 1990 consent and non-use of force may have to be modified to meet the challenges in places like the Persian Gulf. The necessity for deterrence and eventually coercion will require implementation of Chapter VII, they affirm. The Korean and Gulf precedents, however, left behind many problems, particularly undue reliance on one state and risk of loss of international consensus. Russett and Sutterlin discuss the issue of U.N. command as if Senate and Presidential jealousy of their war powers can be overcome by reasoning about the necessities of international cooperation for the provision of troops, unified command, integrated training, secure lines of supply and communication, sure financing, and the *esprit* of the whole force. An effective U.N. enforcement capacity, they conclude, can defeat aggression, deter breaches of the peace, and reduce even the need for peacekeeping.

628   **The United Nations and the maintenance of international peace and security.**
       N.D. White.   Manchester: Manchester University Press, 1990. 240p.

At time of writing, the East–West status quo was undergoing 'seismic strains'. The author takes a fresh look at the security functions of the U.N., providing, first, a geopolitical analysis of the Security Council, then, constitutional and practical accounts of its functioning. Similar accounts of the General Assembly and of peacekeeping follow. White regards his work as a synthesis of older article-by-article analyses and newer case-studies. At every point the language of the Charter is illuminated by the experience of nearly fifty years. Here the American reader will find the virtues of cumulative, British scholarship. The account of the Security Council's competence under Chapters VI and VII is particularly clear.

629   **To unite our strength: enhancing the United Nations peace and security system.**
John M. Lee, Robert von Pagenhardt, and Timothy W. Stanley.
Lanham, MD: University Press of America for International Economic Studies Institute, Washington, 1992. 166p.

The authors – each an American with extensive military, defence, and academic experience – move from international economics to peacekeeping 'because of a particular conviction that the only path to sustainable economic progress on a global basis is for countries to redirect resources away from wasteful military competition toward economic goals'. The end of the Cold War, in their view, provides an opportunity for such redirection. The United States cannot play the role of world policeman. The United Nations remains as the collective organization to end the 'scourge of war'. Hence follow their policy-oriented proposals for strengthening U.N. peacekeeping, enforcement, and collective security. These include establishing a 'peace management committee' as a subsidiary organ of the Security Council, giving the Secretary-General an 'executive agent' for the management of peacekeeping and enforcement, creating a standing U.N. military force (the 'legion'), earmarking national units for U.N. duty (especially quick-reaction forces), and financing the forces by raising a 'peace endowment' of $3,000 million, which is modest compared to national defence costs. The authors regard the 'imminent threat or use of force by the U.N. as a last resort', after preventive diplomacy and negotiation have begun the process of settlement, but they view its availability as vital to the larger U.N. diplomatic processes. This is a practical, knowledgeable book on how U.N. military forces could be safely and effectively organized. It was funded by the U.S. Insitute of Peace.

International peacekeeping: history and strengthening.
See item no. 569.

Peacekeeping and peacemaking after the Cold War.
See item no. 578.

The Suez crisis [and] **The October war.**
See item no. 590.

United Nations peacekeeping and the non-use of force.
See item no. 598.

Peace building

630 **Post-conflict peace-building.**
Boutros Boutros-Ghali.   In: *Report on the work of the organization*,
by Boutros Boutros-Ghali.   New York: United Nations, 1993, p.156-
61. (A/48/1, DPI/1420).
Secretary-General Boutros-Ghali introduced the term 'peacebuilding' in his *Agenda
for peace* (1992). Here he expands his meaning. 'Peace-building encompasses more
than the reconstruction of the peace after the cessation of hostilities. . . . The objective
of peace-building is to involve hostile parties in mutually beneficial undertakings
which not only contribute to economic and social development but also reinforce the
confidence necessary for the creation of lasting peace. . . . Peace-building begins with
practical measures to restore the civil society, reinvigorate its economy, repair the
land and restore its productivity, repatriate and resettle displaced people and refugees;
it also entails reducing the levels of arms in society, as a component of the volatility
that induces violence.' His examples include mine clearance and electoral assistance.
But peace building could be understood in more radical terms as the U.N.'s temporary
exercise of sovereign powers in order to restore government, law, and order to a
member or potential member state that has suffered civil strife, as in West Irian
(1962-63), Namibia (1989-90), or Cambodia (1992-93).

631 **Obstacles to peacebuilding.**
Alvaro de Soto and Graciana del Castillo.   *Foreign Policy*, vol. 94
(Spring 1994), p.69-83.
The authors go beyond peacekeeping to peacebuilding in the complex military and
civil situations that are typical of new threats to the peace – as in Namibia, Cambodia,
and El Salvador. In El Salvador, the whole process began with negotiations in 1990,
which culminated in the peace agreement of 1992 (peacemaking). It was followed by
U.N. supervision of the military accords (peacekeeping). Then came U.N. support for
carrying out political, social, and institutional reforms without recurrence to violence;
the World Bank and IMF also offered economic stabilization and structural
adjustment programmes (post-conflict peace building). But now the peace accords
(especially land redistribution) are in conflict with the economic stabilization
programme. The authors use El Salvador's dilemma to critique the Bretton Woods
financial organizations as they reach their 50th anniversary. Much closer coordination
is needed than the present twice-yearly meetings with the Administrative Committee
on Coordination. Cold War reasons for resistance by the World Bank to coordination
with the United Nations have disappeared.

632 **What is proper soldiering? a study on new perspectives for the
future uses of the armed forces in the 1990s.**
Michael Harbottle.   Chipping Norton, England: Centre for
International Peacebuilding, 1991. 30p.
'Security', writes this former commander of the U.N. peacekeeping force in Cyprus,
'is no longer purely a politico-military consideration, but must embrace those non-
military aspects of economic, humanitarian, and environmental security.' Hence,
Harbottle discusses at length in this innovative paper the 'non-violent role of the
armed forces'. Topics include: peace building, disaster relief, and environmental

security. He calls it 'a new philosophy of service'. Peace building is understood, not as something that comes after peacekeeping, but as *including* both peacekeeping and peacemaking. UNFICYP (the U.N. force in Cyprus) provides his first example, for it not only kept the Greek and Turkish armies apart, but delivered the mail, shipped school books, evacuated civilians to hospitals, and ended blood feuds. The qualities required of peacekeepers include, he finds, a readiness to mediate, conciliate, negotiate, and arbitrate. An annex sets out the activities to conserve the environment already being undertaken by national armed forces, including those of Britain and the United States.

International Criminal Court

633 The case against the Nazi war criminals: opening statement for the United States of America and other documents.
Robert H. Jackson.   New York: Knopf, 1946. 217p.

This short work, now a historical document, is still worth studying as an introduction to the question of establishing an international criminal court. The Nuremberg Tribunal is a classic example of what such a court should be. Justice Jackson effectively argues that no *ex post facto* law was being applied, that a fair trial based on evidence was possible, that victors' justice belonged to all the world, and that no individual could escape responsibility on the grounds of acts of state. 'International law', he roundly affirmed, 'is more than a scholarly collection of abstract and immutable principles. It is an outgrowth of treaties and agreements between nations and of accepted customs. . . . It grows, as did the Common Law, through decisions reached from time to time in adapting settled principles to new situations.' He admitted that judicial action could not prevent future wars, for it comes only after the event and then only if the war-makers are caught. Courts like the Nuremberg Tribunal could contribute to all the political, economic, social, and religious efforts to establish peace by strengthening the common law of nations. 'But the ultimate step in avoiding periodic wars, which are inevitable in a system of international lawlessness, is to make statesmen responsible to law.' Jackson consistently carried this principle so far as to apply it to the United States: 'And let me make it clear that while this law is first applied against German aggressors, . . . if it is to serve a useful purpose it must condemn aggression by any other nations, including those which sit here now in judgment.'

634 An international criminal court: a step toward world peace; a documentary history and analysis.
Benjamin B. Ferencz. Introduction by Louis B. Sohn.   Dobbs Ferry, NY: Oceana, 1980. 2 vols. bibliog.

The U.N. is currently deliberating on a Draft Code of Offenses against the Peace and Security of Mankind. Ferencz's volumes document the history of international criminal law in an effort to include in the new code: aggression, genocide, apartheid, terrorism, and other universally recognized crimes against humanity. Thesis: The law of force must be replaced with the force of law.

635 **The jury is still out on the need for an international criminal court.**
Michael P. Scharf. *Duke Journal of Comparative and International Law,* vol. 1 (1991), p.135-68.

This is a pessimistic review of the history of efforts to establish an international criminal court, starting with unexercised provisions in the Treaty of Versailles (1919) to the International Law Commission's recommendations at the beginning of the U.N. Decade of International Law (1990). The court's practical prosecution of international criminals is discussed, along with the problems it would pose for existing international law enforcement. In conclusion, the author finds that the risks and costs outweigh the purported benefits. (Scharf has since modified his views and now concludes that such a court 'could work'. 'I was but a wordsmith for the State Department', he says of his 1991 article.)

636 **Nuremberg in retrospect: legal answer to international lawlessness.**
Robert H. Jackson. *American Bar Association Journal,* vol. 35 (1949), p.813-16, 881-87.

The American chief prosecutor at the Nuremberg trials here presents an authoritative account of their legal basis. International law at the start of the 20th century, Justice Jackson reminds us, recognized absolute state sovereignty, the legality of war, acts of state, and individual irresponsibility under superior orders. At mid-century, he argues, the Nuremberg prosecutions brought international customary law into conformity with treaty law and even with the 'standards of the future'. The very establishment of the tribunal, apart from its verdicts, was in conformity with a new sense of public rejection of 'international lawlessness'. Its conduct was in accordance with the highest standards of the Anglo-American, Continental, and Soviet legal systems. Its judgments were based on international treaties and agreements to which Germany was a party, on the criminal law of Germany itself (as it had been enforced before the Nazis came to power), and on the international 'common law', which, like natural law, should have informed those who conducted slave labour and racial extermination that such policies were criminal. Jackson claims that the prosecutors at Nuremberg, like the English common law judges, *applied law* – they did not create it. But he openly avows that they set a 'civilized legal precedent' for an international law of limited state sovereignty and of individual responsibility.

637 **The Nuremberg trials in international law.**
Robert K. Woetzel. New York: Praeger, 1960; 2nd ed., 1962. 287p. bibliog.

This book is an analysis of the legal aspects of the Nuremberg trials – their basis in international law, individual responsibility in the law of the time, and the nature of 'crimes' against peace, war crimes, and crimes against humanity. The author also addresses political questions – that the verdicts were 'victors' justice' since only Allied judges served in the tribunal; that the law was retroactive law not binding on the defendants at the time they acted; that the Allies, under conditions of total war, committed many of the same crimes; and that subsequent violations of the law of Nuremberg, since they have gone unpunished, weaken the law of nations. These matters are all discussed fairly and cogently by Woetzel. He is convinced that something new has appeared in international law: 'No government any longer possesses an undisputed right to treat its subjects as it pleases.' He concludes in favour of a permanent international criminal court – a proposal that has been before the United Nations since 1951.

638   The Nuremberg trial: landmark in law.
Henry L. Stimson.   *Foreign Affairs*, vol. 25 (January 1947), p.179-89.
Stimson regarded the Nuremberg trials as an enforcement action of the Kellogg–Briand pact for the renunciation of war (1928). The adherents, including Germany, renounced war as an instrument of national policy – that is, renounced aggressive war – and they pledged to resort only to peaceful means for the resolution of their disputes. (The pact's two operative clauses became in 1945 the U.N. Charter's Articles 2(3) and 2(4).) Like Jackson, Stimson denied that *ex post facto* law was applied. The article is a stirring defence, in the circumstances of the first international criminal court, of the long-term advantages to states of enforcing the principle that aggressive war is a personal and punishable crime. 'It is this principle upon which we must henceforth rely for our legal protection against the horrors of war.'

639   Principles of international law recognized in the charter of the Nuremberg Tribunal and in the judgment of the Tribunal.
United Nations. International Law Commission.   *American Journal of International Law*, vol. 44 (1950), p.125-34.
There are seven principles, of which I quote four:
  1. Any person who commits an act which constitutes a crime under international law is responsible therefor and liable to punishment. . . .
  3. The fact that a person who committed an act which constitutes a crime under international law acted as Head of State or responsible Government official does not relieve him from responsibility under international law. . . .
  5. Any person charged with a crime under international law has the right to a fair trial on the facts and law.
  6. The crimes hereinafter set out are punishable as crimes under international law: a. Crimes against peace. . . . b. War crimes. . . . c. Crimes against humanity. . . .

640   Report of the International Law Commission on the work of its forty-second session, 1 May – 20 July 1990.
United Nations. International Law Commission.   U.N. General Assembly Official Records, 45th session, A/45/10, 10th supplement, 1990, p.36-54.
The International Law Commission here presents its plan for an international criminal court within the context of its Draft Code of Crimes against the Peace and Security of Mankind. The court is seen as the principal means for the enforcement of the code. The difficult question of implementation of judgments led to two basic approaches: an 'international detention facility' or 'implementation under national systems'. The commission finally proposed three alternatives: (1) an international criminal court with exclusive jurisdiction, which would require states to cede their jurisdiction over international crimes; (2) concurrent jurisdiction between the international court and national courts, in which states would decide on a case-by-case basis whether to submit a case to the international court; (3) an appellate international court, with review competence only. All those interested in an effective international criminal

court in the tradition of the Nuremberg Tribunal will want to study this document closely.

641 Report of the World Federalist Association on an international criminal court.

Bryan F. MacPherson. Washington, DC: World Federalist Association, 1991. 21p.

This is a legal and political analysis of the existing system of international law enforcement, the potential contribution of an international criminal court, its establishment and funding, its composition, jurisdiction over individuals, crimes to be punished, and procedures. 'The current system of prosecuting and punishing international and transnational crime', writes the author, 'has been insufficient to deal with many serious crimes, particularly war crimes and genocide, but also including drug trafficking and political terrorism. Too often major international criminals are able to avoid responsibility for their actions because of inadequacies in the current extradition system. Furthermore, trials of war criminals conducted by tribunals of the opposing side often give the appearance of unfairness. . . . An international criminal court would represent a powerful symbol of the community of nations' commitment to a world order that is based on the rule of law and of the determination of the community of nations that international crimes not go unpunished.'

642 Toward a feasible international criminal court.

Edited by Julius Stone and Robert K. Woetzel. Foreword by Charles S. Rhyne. Geneva: World Peace through Law Centre, 1970. 325p.

The Genocide Convention (1948) and the Nuremberg Principles (1950) have boldly declared that the individual can be prosecuted under international law for crimes against the peace and crimes against humanity. But the effort to establish a permanent international criminal court to prosecute individuals for such crimes has raised a deep and systematic challenge to international law, which hitherto has been a law only of states. All the essays in this scholarly book deal with individual responsibility. The reasons why states are reluctant to permit establishment of an international criminal court, as Julius Stone explains in his introduction, is that they fear 'that action in future contingencies affecting their security might be hampered by risks of criminal liability'. Moreover, states fear that, since individuals and groups of individuals are the aggrieved parties in such crimes, granting individuals standing before an international court will expose them to harassment and trivial complaints. Hence, at the time this collection of the best thinking on an international criminal court from the 1950s and 1960s was assembled, the authors proposed a 'minimal' court for even a few states, with jurisdiction over the most strictly defined international crimes, like genocide. Human rights offences, they recommended, could for the time being be heard and redressed by the U.N. Commission on Human Rights. The aim was to develop a record of safe practice in order to win the adherence of reluctant states. The rule of law is in all states' interests. As Charles Rhyne writes, 'That an international legal order must be the answer to international peace is proven by the success of order under law within nations.'

Disarmament

643 **Armed peace: the search for world security.**
Edited by Josephine Howe.   New York: St. Martin's 1984. 191p.
bibliog.

The British authors in this volume on arms control and disarmament take as their starting point the recommendations in the Palme commission report, *Common security* (1982). Since they were writing during the Reagan military buildup, their views may seem rather dated, yet many of the most advanced proposals for the post-Cold War world are rooted in their thinking. Topics include: disarmament and security in Europe, strategic arms control, chemical arms control, non-proliferation, a comprehensive test ban, common security (later taken up by Mikhail Gorbachev), the arms trade, and peacekeeping. The U.N.'s role in disarmament comes into the picture, but it is tangential to that of national states.

644 **Arms control agreements: a handbook.**
Jozef Goldblat.   New York: Praeger for Stockholm International
Peace Research Institute, 1983. 328p. bibliog.

This book is a standard introduction, analysis, and reference to all bilateral and multilateral arms control (and disarmament) agreements between states from 1945 to 1982. Hence, it is more inclusive than similar U.N. references, and so it will instruct the reader about the larger international legal and political context. Goldblat covers the history of disarmament efforts from the Hague conferences and League of Nations to the United Nations until about 1961, when the goal of 'general and complete disarmament under effective international control', though still ritually repeated, was in practice replaced by the more limited goal of 'arms control'. He then discusses the legal obligations of the arms control agreements, their effects on reducing the likelihood of war, verification of agreements, and the actual texts. He concludes: 'Arms control measures clearly cannot remove the motives for acquiring arms, but they may help to minimize the risk of war started by accident or miscalculation, or even by design.'

645 **Arms control and disarmament agreements: texts and histories of negotiations.**
U.S. Arms Control and Disarmament Agency.   Washington, DC: U.S.
ACDA, 1972; 6th ed., 1990. 459p.

This official reference contains brief histories and the texts of all major arms control treaties and agreements concluded from 1925 to 1988 (twenty-eight, of which eleven are multilateral). Included are the recent Intermediate-range Nuclear Forces (INF) Treaty of 1987, but not the Conventional Forces in Europe (CFE) Treaty of 1990, the Strategic Arms Reduction (START) Treaty of 1991, or subsequent U.S. agreements with the Russian Federation and other C.I.S. republics to reduce the stockpile of nuclear weapons.

646   **Arms control and the arms race.**
Readings from *Scientific American*. Introductions by Bruce Russett
and Fred Chernoff.   New York: W.H. Freeman, 1985. 229p. bibliog.

These illustrated and informative articles appeared in the popular journal *Scientific
American* from 1972 to 1985. They provide a graphically clear account of the slow
progress of arms control through the Cold War as it turned alternately colder and
hotter. The U.N. is given relatively little coverage, except for verification and non-
proliferation. The emphasis, in a rather unscientific spirit, is on national arms policies
of defence, coupled with some bilateral efforts at limitations in the common interest.
The topics covered are: the debate over Truman's decision to build the H-bomb in
1950 rather than try again at the international control of atomic energy; the Non-
proliferation (NPT) Treaty, Anti-ballistic Missile (ABM) Treaty, Strategic Arms
Limitation (SALT II) Treaty (1979 – never ratified); the negotiating process for
strategic arms; doctrines of 'limited nuclear war', 'pre-emptive attack', 'launch on
warning', and 'ballistic missile defense'; European theatre weapons; neutron bombs,
medium-range and tactical nuclear weapons, precision-guided munitions (later much
used in the Persian Gulf War), and chemical weapons.

647   **Arms control and national security: an introduction.**
Arms Control Association. Preface by Spurgeon M. Keeny, Jr.
Washington, DC: Arms Control Association, 1989. 176p. bibliog.

'This book offers the student and concerned citizen an overview of the current arms
control scene and the more knowledgeable practitioner a convenient reference for
specific arms control topics.' The book is amply illustrated and current to 1989.
Topics include: the history of arms control, its goals, its relation to national security,
the SALT I (1969-72), SALT II (1972-79), and START (1982-89) negotiations, the
ABM treaty (1972) and the issue of ballistic missile defence, anti-satellite weapons,
command and control of nuclear forces (especially in crises and after accidents),
European nuclear and conventional forces, testing, proliferation, chemical weapons,
verification and compliance. The INF treaty (1987) is covered, but the CFE treaty
(1990) and START treaty (1991) and subsequent further agreements came after
appearance of this informative book.

648   **Arms control: the multilateral alternative.**
Edited by Edward C. Luck. Foreword by Elliot L. Richardson.   New
York: New York University Press, UNA–USA Policy Studies Book,
1983. 258p. bibliog.

Of sixteen historic arms control agreements from 1959 to 1992, eleven were
multilateral. The tendency in recent years, after this book went to press, was
downward, hence the titles of several included essays: 'The rise and fall of
multilateral arms control', and 'Is there life after the second U.N. special session of
disarmament?' Yet there are more than two states concerned about limitation of
armaments, and general treaties are necessary if the superpowers disarm down to
levels where they would be threatened by former 'middle' powers. A year before this
book appeared, one million people marched in the streets of New York in support of
U.N. efforts. The book aims to explain why the very extensive discussions at the U.N.
– at the special sessions and the Committee (now Conference) on Disarmament in
Geneva – come to so little action. An association of sovereign states needs much
convincing before its members, realistically and cooperatively, reduce the arms on

which they believe their defence is based. This volume is particularly concerned with U.S. policy toward the U.N. disarmament process. After the Cold War, potential, recognized here, was beginning to be realized in renewal of the Non-proliferation (NPT) Treaty (1990), agreement on the Chemical Weapons Treaty (1993), and conventional arms control.

649 **The arms race and arms control.**
Stockholm International Peace Research Institute (SIPRI).
Introduction by Frank Blackaby.   Cambridge, MA: Oelgeschlager, Ginn & Hain, 1982. 242p.

'This book is for those who want well-researched information on what is going on in the world of armaments and disarmament.' The facts about the balance of power (that is, of weapons), the neutron bomb, preparations for a first strike, testing, and European alternative defence approaches are covered in this compact volume. Because SIPRI is unaffiliated with either of the superpowers, its information has become a standard for policy-makers, legislators and parliamentarians, negotiators, scholars, students, and the concerned public. This book, prepared for the second U.N. special session of disarmament (1982), is somewhat dated – the trends continued upwards ($600,000 million total world military expenditure in 1981, $1,000,000 million in 1990), and the turnaround is by no means automatic – yet it still offers clarity and exactness about the whole problem.

650 **Challenges for the 1990s for arms control and international security.**
Committee on International Security and Arms Control, National Academy of Sciences. Foreword by Frank Press.   Washington, DC: National Academy Press, 1989. 78p.

This report of a high-level American and Soviet seminar follows one published two years earlier on very deep cuts in strategic nuclear arsenals. In effect, the short work is a picture of responsible American thinking changing in response to Mikhail Gorbachev's initiatives. The goal which arms control could help to attain, argued former U.S. Under-Secretary of the Navy R. James Woolsey, was 'strategic and conventional force stability'. Retired Soviet Academician Roald Sagdeev argued that the goal was 'common, or mutual, security – a system that would provide a chance for the coherent development of future military configurations based on a drastic reduction of overarming'. The discussants looked forward to conventional arms control, a chemical weapons treaty, and renewal of the NPT regime.

651 **Challenges to multilateral disarmament in the post-Cold War and post-Gulf War period.**
U.N. Department for Disarmament Affairs.   New York: United Nations, 1991. 335p. bibliog. (Disarmament Topical Papers No. 8. E.91.IX.18).

By 1991, with the disintegration of the Soviet threat and the firm international response to aggression against Kuwait, great progress began to be made in arms control and disarmament. This book is a report of a conference held in Kyoto of nearly a hundred participants from diplomatic corps, parliaments, the scholarly community, and non-governmental organizations on the 'new challenges facing the world today' and on 'a possible common course of action'. Important papers on security were given by representatives of Australia, Japan, the Philippines, the U.S., and the U.S.S.R. Others were given on regional approaches, non-proliferation, conversion of military industries, monitoring, and verification. Yasushi Akashi, then Under-Secretary-General for Disarmament Affairs, concludes with hope for 'real disarmament' and concern for 'ethnic, religious and cultural antagonisms' that may become the new threat to national and international security.

652 **Comprehensive study on nuclear weapons.**
U.N. Department of Political and Security Council Affairs. New York: United Nations, 1981. 172p. (Study Series No. 1. E.81.I.11. A/35/392).

'Nuclear weapons', it was said in the *Final document* of the first U.N. General Assembly special session on disarmament (1978) (see item no. 666), 'pose the greatest danger to mankind and to the survival of civilization. It is essential to halt and reverse the nuclear arms race in all its aspects in order to avert the danger of war involving nuclear weapons.' This U.N. study, next after a similar one of 1968, presents factual information on the nuclear arsenals by 1981 (40,000 nuclear warheads), trends in the technological development of nuclear weapons systems (multiple warheads, increased accuracy), and effects of their use (destruction of cities, fallout zones, disruptions of the global economy). The study also examines doctrines of deterrence and credible threats, quantitative and qualitative 'improvements', and the effects of treaties and negotiations on control of such weapons.

653 **Concepts of security.**
U.N. Department for Disarmament Affairs. New York: United Nations, 1986. 53p. (Study Series No. 14. E.86.IX.1. A/40/553).

'One nation's security is often another's insecurity', write the authors of this official U.N. report to the General Assembly. By the 1980s, international interdependence had grown to the point that national security could not be understood as a sufficient standard for the conduct of a national state. A new concept – recognizing the viability of a state's economy within the world economy, the preservation of the environment, the protection of all states from armed attack – emerged in the Palme commission's phrase, 'common security'. This concept was taken up by Mikhail Gorbachev and has led to revivals of 'collective security' and to still newer coinages of 'cooperative security'. This study aimed to demonstrate to national policy-makers 'that the security of nations can no longer be divorced from the security of the entire international community of which they are an ever more integral part'. Topics include: overview of security concepts, current problems and threats to international security, and measures to promote international peace and security. One of the latter is disarmament and arms limitation.

654 **Confidence- and security-building measures: from Europe to other regions.**
U.N. Department for Disarmament Affairs. New York: United Nations, 1991. 178p. (Disarmament Topical Papers No. 7. E.91.IX.17).

Since 1975, when the Conference on Security and Cooperation in Europe (CSCE) became a permanent institution of East–West relations, confidence-building measures, like prior notification of military manoeuvres exceeding 25,000 troops or exchange of military observers of such manoeuvres, have contributed to the reduction of tensions and hence to the array of causes that brought about the Conventional Forces in Europe (CFE) Treaty in 1990. This collection of expert papers analyses the European experience with what are now called, more ambitiously, confidence- and *security*-building measures; discusses their sequence from transparency to verification to constraint; and proposes their extension to Asia, Southeast Asia, the Middle East, Africa, and Latin America. Ultimately, the goal, as Yasushi Akashi concludes, is to create the 'regional and global structures that can contain and defeat the impulses behind aggressive behaviour'.

655 **Confidence-building measures in the Asia–Pacific region.**
U.N. Department for Disarmament Affairs. New York: United Nations, 1991. 175p. (Disarmament Topical Papers No. 6. E.91.IX.16).

American, Japanese, Chinese, and Russian experts participated in a conference, following the Persian Gulf War and signing of the START treaty, on confidence-building measures in the highly armed and dangerous Northeast Asia and Southeast Asia regions. This report contains their informed views. Suggestions are made, for instance, for North and South Korea, the Sino-Soviet border, the Sea of Japan near Sakhalin Island, and the countries within the Asia–Pacific Economic Co-operation Conference.

656 **Diplomats, scientists, and politicians: the United States and the nuclear test ban negotiations.**
Harold K. Jacobson and Eric Stein. Ann Arbor, MI: University of Michigan Press, 1966. 538p. bibliog.

This is a history of events leading to the Partial Test Ban Treaty of 1963. It was written shortly after conclusion of the negotiations, when it was hoped that the treaty, though limited, would mark a 'turning point'. Judging by the history of arms control agreements, all of which, with the exception of the Antarctica Treaty of 1959, post-date the Partial Test Ban, this hope seems to have been, very slowly, fulfilled. War, of course, has not been abolished, nor has the international security system been strengthened to the point where nations will no longer feel a need for *national* defence establishments. But this history of the leading case of the turning may be instructive to those who imagine the completion of the process in a comprehensive test ban and general disarmament.

657 **Disarmament and the U.N.: strategy for the United States.**
Lincoln P. Bloomfield and Harlan Cleveland. Princeton, NJ: Aspen Institute for Humanistics Studies, 1978. 78p.

This policy paper was prepared for official and public discussion prior to the U.N. General Assembly's first special session on disarmament in 1978. In retrospect, there was a sense of opportunity in the air then, not unlike that in the early 1990s. President Carter had called for nuclear disarmament at the U.N. in 1977, the Third World countries had called for the special session, and the U.N. had issued another troubling study on the harmful effects of the arms race on international peace and security. States, NGOs, and scholars had contributed a plethora of proposals that, then as now, offered practical next steps: a comprehensive test ban, strengthening the NPT regime, qualitative halts, controlling arms trafficking, zones of peace, reduction of military

budgets, etc. The authors warn that the U.N. forum may pit the Third World, anxious
to reduce superpower arms but not its own, against the industrialized West, intent on
damage limitation and determined to maintain its 'defence'. Because most states at
the session will be interested not in disarmament but in economic and social
development, Bloomfield and Cleveland counsel the U.S. to pursue a realistic but
flexible strategy aimed at sharing non-military technologies, focusing on human needs
and rights, and cooperating in the peaceful settlement of disputes. The U.N. cannot be
expected to function as a 'global government' – which is implied in the goal of
general and complete disarmament under effective international control.

658 **Disarmament and world development.**
Edited by Mac Graham, Richard Jolly, and Chris Smith.   Oxford:
Pergamon, 1978; 2nd ed., 1986. 306p. bibliog.

Expenditure on arms leaves less to address the problems of poverty, but will
disarmament produce a 'disarmament dividend'? The editors admit that, in the midst
of the Cold War, those who study the relationship between disarmament and
development cannot promise so much. In the second edition of this leading study,
they concentrate on the barriers to disarmament and on the link between armament
and underdevelopment in the South (war, arms dependency, military regimes,
poverty). They then show some possible ways toward alternatives to armament, for
instance, by producing trade goods that meet basic needs or converting military
industry to civilian, since the latter provides more employment. The Inga Thorsson
report to the U.N. on the relation between disarmament and development is printed in
full. Abundant quantitative data support the arguments.

659 **Disarmament: a periodic review by the United Nations.**
Edited by the U.N. Department for Disarmament Affairs.   New York:
United Nations, 1978- .

This quarterly journal includes discussion papers circulated at U.N.-sponsored
seminars held around the world. For example: Yasushi Akashi, 'Is there still life after
SSOD III?' *Disarmament*, vol. 11 (Autumn 1988), p.17-22. The journal is a scholarly
enterprise of the World Disarmament Campaign and serves as a forum for statesmen,
scholars, and NGO leaders to share their views on arms limitation and disarmament.

660 **Disarmament fact sheets, 17- .**
U.N. Centre for Disarmament; later, Department for Disarmament
Affairs.   New York: United Nations, Department of Public
Information, 1981- .

These are short (10-20p.) summaries of topics of current interest, negotiations,
studies, documents, and treaties. They are intended for wide distribution to non-
governmental organizations (NGOs) and the general public. For example: 17. Comprehensive study on nuclear weapons; 21. Relationship between disarmament and
development; 22. Relationship between disarmament and international security;
27. Economic and social consequences of the arms race; 30. U.N. fellowships on
disarmament; 33. Non-proliferation of nuclear weapons; 37. Comprehensive test ban;
38. Conventional disarmament; 42. U.N. and disarmament, 1945-1985; and 49. U.N.
information materials on disarmament.

661 Disarmament: its politics and economics.

Edited by Seymour Melman. Boston: American Academy of Arts and Sciences, 1962. 398p. bibliog.

This volume of expert papers was assembled in September 1962, shortly after negotiation of the McCloy–Zorin agreement on the principles for the negotiation of 'general and complete disarmament under effective international control', and just before the Cuban missile crisis, which all but terminated the hopeful movement toward general and complete disarmament. Both the United States and the Soviet Union contributed draft treaties on the subject, which are conveniently printed here in the appendixes. After the Cold War, readers who may barely be able to imagine that great things could be done in the field of disarmament would be well advised to consult the record of what was once actually proposed.

662 On disarmament: the role of conventional arms control in national security strategy.

Edited by Ralph A. Hallenbeck and David E. Shaver. New York: Praeger, 1991. 229p. bibliog.

Conventional arms control is by no means beyond the wit of man. The major effort has been made in Europe, as this strategic study, completed just before the signing of the Conventional Forces in Europe (CFE) Treaty (1990), ably shows. Readers must be prepared to enter the field with appreciation for technical detail within NATO planning, but the early chapters on background, objectives, procedures, and issues will probably be instructive for all. Two final chapters on the 'post-CFE environment' look farthest into the future – assuming that the U.S. policy of containment has been made obsolete by the collapse of Soviet authoritarianism. This could mean a 'renaissance of the United Nations'. It also could mean that 'alternative defense' – here subjected to a rare mainstream defence analysis – could be suitable to the reduced risks of military attack.

663 Draft treaty for a comprehensive program for common security and general disarmament.

Marcus G. Raskin. Washington, DC: Institute for Policy Studies, 1982; rev. ed., 1986. 73p.

The author takes the U.S. Draft Treaty on Disarmament of 1962, which he helped write in the Kennedy administration, and updates it. Raskin has envisaged a three-stage process of disarmament to be completed over fifteen years (1990-2005). His major innovations concern the structure and powers of an international disarmament organization and the practical process of verification. The organization would consist of a secretary-general and staff, trained in quasi-judicial functions of dispute settlement and drawn from all nations, and a smaller executive board of inquirers, composed of the five permanent members of the U.N. Security Council and thirteen rotating members elected by the General Assembly. There is no 'conference' of all states. The board of inquirers would be responsible for the implementation of the disarmament programme, which would include further agreements with states, relations with the U.N., technical questions, adjudication, reporting, finance, public communication, and enforcement. A vigorous programme of TV and other media coverage of the progress of disarmament would maintain public pressure when states might be inclined to renege. Processes in case of proved violations include fines and (subject to the Security Council) use of international force. To control the force, provision is made for enactment of a parallel 'World Security Agreement', which would activate the Military Staff Committee of Chapter VII of the Charter but limit U.N. forces. Enforcement is entirely by nascent processes of world law, and verification includes citizen watchfulness. The idea is to 'humanize and socialize' the disarmament process.

664 **Economic and social consequences of the arms race and of military expenditures.**
Department for Disarmament Affairs. New York: United Nations, 1983. 70p. (Study Series No. 11. E.83.IX.2. A/37/386).

This report, the third since 1977 and 1971, analyses the 'extremely harmful effects on world peace and security' of the arms race. Driven by mutual fear, ignorance of others' motives, competition, and by a kind of 'vicious circularity between its technological and strategic momentum', the arms race is not only outpacing the U.N.'s efforts to return to a spirit of cooperation, but also is consuming the best of the world's material and intellectual resources. The chapter on declining socio-economic development everywhere is alarming. By the end of the 1970s, high military spending and high rates of economic growth were proving to be negatively related, as inflation and unemployment combined in 'stagflation'. Military manufacturing was less productive than civilian, and the 'goods' did not circulate in the economy. The authors' analysis of the social and economic damage of the arms race and its possible consequences in a third world war is so severe that in retrospect a reader may wonder if their argument did not help statesmen – apparently first in Mikhail Gorbachev's circle – to turn back from the brink.

665 **Encyclopedia of arms control and disarmament.**
Edited by Richard Dean Burns. New York: Scribners, 1993. 3 vols. bibliog.

This is a major new systematic reference work in the field of arms control and disarmament under U.N. auspices and outside the U.N. Individual scholarly essays are broadly inclusive and written with historical perspective. Techniques covered: limitation and reduction of weapons; demilitarization, denuclearization, and neutralization; regulating or outlawing specific weapons; controlling arms manufacture and trafficking; law of war; and stabilizing the international environment. Methods of achieving arms control and disarmament include: retribution, unilateral measures, bilateral and multilateral negotiations, and verification. Prospects for the post-Cold War world are emphasized. Essays are included on: national and regional practice, themes, and institutions; history to 1945; and arms control achievements since 1945. Treaties are reprinted in vol. 3. The U.N. contribution is covered in a long essay by Tobi Trister Gati and Edmund T. Piasecki.

666 **Final document of the first special session on disarmament, 1978.**
U.N. General Assembly. New York: United Nations, 1978. 27p. (A/S-10/10. DPI/679).

Variously called 'the bible of disarmament' and 'the greatest State paper of all time', the *Final document* of the first U.N. General Assembly special session on disarmament firmly sets out the final objective of 'general and complete disarmament under effective international control', within the context of more immediate goals to eliminate the danger of nuclear war and to halt and reverse the arms race. The document includes an analysis of the problem ('Mankind today is confronted with an unprecedented threat of self-extinction . . .'), a declaration of the common interest ('All the peoples of the world have a vital interest in the success of disarmament negotiations'), a programme of action, a review of U.N. machinery to assist, and a reference list of specific state proposals for reform.

667   **The future of American defense.**
Philip Morrison, Kosta Tsipis, and Jerome Wiesner.
Scientific American, vol. 270 (February 1994), p.38-45.
This is a bold proposal to sharply lower U.S. defence spending on the grounds that the Soviet threat against Central Europe has evaporated, and that the threats of Iran, Iraq, North Korea, and Libya can be contained by far smaller, rapidly deployable U.S. forces. The U.N. has a small place in the thinking of these eminent American liberal strategists, except when they say that, in a relatively disarmed world, 'wider international sharing of economic progress and political decision making could help ease tensions between nations', or that, to improve the collective early warning system, 'the U.S. should seriously consider sharing substantial chunks of the costs and results of its intelligence activities with American allies and with the U.N.'

668   **The game of disarmament.**
Alva Myrdal.   New York: Pantheon, 1976; 2nd ed., 1982. 397p.
With the announced end of the Cold War and the signing of the START treaty and other agreements by 1992 to substantially *disarm* in the fields of strategic nuclear weapons, tactical nuclear weapons, and even conventional forces in Europe, readers may not be as critical as this courageous woman from a 'lesser power' – Sweden's Alva Myrdal. Yet arms races continue, and, without the 'effective international control' that the U.N. always ties to its goal of 'general and complete disarmament', threats of war will increase again. Myrdal's goal is a more 'rational' level of defensive armament within the existing international system of organizations and states. 'My striving has been to widen the view to global proportions. And I firmly believe that trying to serve not your own country above others but mankind as a whole will in the long run serve the true interests of all nations. This is my main value premise by which I seek to present the reasons for disarmament, for holding military capacities to a sensible low by mutual agreement, formalized or not.' Students will find this a plain-spoken, revealing book, not written in the code of most accounts by scholars from one or the other of the nuclear powers. All the basic concerns and approaches are here – except U.N. reform to increase the effectiveness of collective or common security.

669   **The great illusion: 'Star Wars' and world order.**
Gerard C. Smith.   In: *Negotiating world order: the artisanship and architecture of global diplomacy.* Edited by Alan K. Henrikson.
Wilmington, DE: Scholarly Resources, 1986, p.69-78.
The American negotiator provides an introduction to arms control when it seemed that the Reagan administration was aiming to *deregulate* strategic nuclear arms. Still in the future were the INF treaty (1987), the CFE treaty (1990), START (1991), and the cancellation of Star Wars (1993). Nevertheless, Smith's essay is an instructive example of the tortuous logic of arms control by a practitioner who exposes the illusions (which may return) of 'nuclear defense'. Smith closes with an appeal for a

comprehensive test ban – 'the world's best hope to get the nuclear proliferation problem under some control'.

670   **A handbook of verification procedures.**
Edited by Frank Barnaby. Foreword by Michael Harbottle.   New York: St. Martin's, 1990. 357p.

This volume, edited by the former SIPRI director, brings together half a dozen thoughtful British essays on the wider scope for verification since the Soviets accepted on-site inspection under the INF treaty (1987). Barnaby reviews the role of the International Atomic Energy Agency (IAEA) in verifying the Non-proliferation Treaty, and he sets out again the virtues of an International Satellite Monitoring Agency, though it is still opposed by the powers that have developed the technology. Other authors discuss satellite monitoring, verification of a comprehensive test ban, of a cut-off of fissile material, of the START and INF treaties, and of future agreements to end the nuclear arms race and reduce conventional forces.

671   **The implications of establishing an international satellite monitoring agency.**
U.N. Department for Disarmament Affairs.   New York: United Nations, 1983. 110p. (Study Series No. 9. E.83.IX.3. A/AC.206/14).

In 1978, France proposed that, in order to enhance the U.N.'s monitoring capability in conjunction with a comprehensive disarmament plan, the U.N. should be given an agency to monitor military activities by satellite – in effect, to be granted international technical means for verification. This study reports on this highly technical but vital proposal to enhance fact-finding, early warning, and international security. The total cost for a three-satellite system in a third phase of implementation was as much as $1,288 million, plus annual operating costs of $250 million – which was prohibitive in 1983, but, considering the acceptable costs of peacekeeping by 1993 ($3,600 million), not permanently out of the question.

672   **The international regulation of armaments: the law of disarmament.**
Göran Lysén.   Uppsala: Iustus Förlag, 1990. 246p. bibliog.

Just before the end of the Cold War, the author summarized and expounded the 'Law of Disarmament' as a new branch of international law, analogous to nuclear law, space law, and environmental law. He begins with the reflection that humanity has tried to base peace on good faith, force, and law (as in the League of Nations and United Nations). Since the advent of nuclear weapons, peace has been practically based on fear or mutual deterrence, and Lysen sees the law of disarmament as fitting into this fact of contemporary world politics. He concludes, 'As a matter of fact, public international law includes a regulation of armaments as a part of *ius pacis.*'

673 **Interrelationship of bilateral and multilateral disarmament negotiations.**
U.N. Institute for Disarmament Research. Preface by Jayantha Dhanapala. New York: United Nations for UNIDIR, 1988. 258p. (GV.E/F.88.0.1. UNIDIR/88/1).

Since the Non-proliferation Treaty of 1968, most of the arms control treaties have been bilateral, between the U.S.A. and the U.S.S.R. The exceptions are not very substantial: the Sea Bed Treaty (1971), the Biological Weapons Treaty (1972), the Environmental Modification Convention (1977). (In 1993, the Chemical Weapons Treaty broke out of this pattern.) Why has there been so little progress in multilateral negotiations, involving all states, and why has arms control not led to disarmament? As Soviet 'new thinking' began to be respected in the West, UNIDIR hosted a conference of government officials, diplomats, and scholars at Baku on the Caspian Sea in 1987 to explore the neglected relationship between bilateral and multilateral disarmament negotiations. 'Security in our interdependent, indivisible world', argued Alexander Kislov of the Institute for World Economics and International Relations (IMEMO) in Moscow, 'can only be universal. . . . This formula [of "disarmament and development"] reflects the new political thinking which rejects militarism and the cult of force in the international arena and is oriented towards co-operation.' In his spirit, the participants critically discussed both bilateral and multilateral negotiations for nuclear arms limitation and reduction, prevention of an arms race in space, conventional and chemical weapons control, and confidence-building measures and verification.

674 **Joint statement of agreed principles for disarmament negotiations. [And] Letters exchanged between U.S. and U.S.S.R., 20 September 1961.**
John J. McCloy and Valerin A. Zorin. In: *Yearbook of the United Nations, 1961.* New York: United Nations, 1962. p.10-11.

The McCloy–Zorin principles mark the closest approach to a general East–West agreement on disarmament. Even the treaties and agreements since the INF treaty (1987), while for the first time *lowering* arms levels, are not comprehensive. The McCloy–Zorin agreement established the principle of 'general and complete disarmament under effective international control', which has been the ultimate goal of U.N. disarmament negotiations at least through the *Final document* of the first special session on disarmament (1978). Text is also in Jozef Goldblat, *Arms control agreements* (SIPRI, 1978), p.75-76. Compare U.S. and Soviet draft treaties on disarmament of 1962 (see item no. 702).

675 **Kennedy, Khrushchev, and the test ban.**
Glenn T. Seaborg with Benjamin S. Loeb. Foreword by W. Averill Harriman. Berkeley: University of California Press, 1981. 320p.

John F. Kennedy in 1963 seized one of those rare historic opportunities to achieve a mutually advantageous arms control agreement. But the president and his Soviet counterpart were unable – generally because of mutual distrust – to agree to a *comprehensive* test ban, which might have broken the spiral of the arms race. This book by a seasoned policy-maker, the chairman of the U.S. Atomic Energy Commission from 1961 to 1971, examines in detail how mutual suspicions operated 'to thwart the hopes of the largest part of the world community'. The book remains a practical guide to the wise and timely future negotiation of a comprehensive test ban.

676   **Limitations and safeguards in arms control agreements.**
John B. Rhinelander.   In: *Law and force in the new international order*. Edited by Lori F. Damrosch and David J. Scheffer.   Boulder, CO: Westview, 1991, p.247-57.

The author provides an overview of arms control agreements to the Intermediate-range Nuclear Forces (INF) Treaty (1987), Conventional Forces in Europe (CFE) Treaty (1990), and Strategic Arms Reduction (START) Treaty (1991). He includes optimistic proposals for a CFE II and START II as well as a permanent nuclear Non-proliferation Treaty (NPT) and a comprehensive test ban treaty (CTBT). A following comment by John H. McNeill covers dispute resolution mechanisms in the treaties, such as the U.S.–U.S.S.R. Standing Consultative Commissions in SALT I (1972). Progress depends, he argues, on winding down the Cold War.

677   **The master of the game: Paul Nitze and the nuclear peace.**
Strobe Talbott.   New York: Knopf, 1988. 416p.

The author, a prominent journalist and later Deputy Secretary of State in the Clinton administration, here presents an intriguing biography of one of the leading American arms control negotiators. Paul Nitze was an architect of the Anti-Ballistic Missile (ABM) Treaty within SALT I, a sharp critic of SALT II, and an early negotiator of the INF treaty. Talbott has written books on the last two – *Endgame* (1979) and *Deadly gambits* (1984). This third book on Nitze continues the series. Their very titles convey Talbott's wry sense of the nature of arms control negotiations on which the very fate of the earth may depend – an elaborate game, with cities for counters! The United Nations barely figures in this story – 'a first draft of history' – but readers who are looking for a realistic account of how international negotiations are actually conducted by flesh and blood Americans could well find it here.

678   **The naval arms race.**
U.N. Department for Disarmament Affairs.   New York: United Nations, 1986. 100p. maps. (Study Series No. 16. E.86.IX.3. A/40/535).

The sea forms 71 per cent of the earth's surface; about the same percentage of humanity live within 300 kilometres of a sea coast. This expert study reviews the history of efforts to reduce or eliminate the deployment of strategic and tactical weapons on and under the sea (most recently nuclear weapons and sea-launched cruise missiles), in order to realize the sea's full potential for food, trade, exploration, and development for the benefit of all humanity. Suggestions are made for naval disarmament, within the context of general disarmament under effective international control, including: quantitative, qualitative, and geographical restraints, confidence-building measures, verification, and modernization of the laws of sea warfare (restricted zones, limits on indiscriminate weapons, protection of the marine environment). Particular attention is given to the new law of the sea and to peaceful uses of the sea under conditions of 'security and stability at significantly lower levels of conventional naval arms and armed force'. Security, the authors conclude, must include economic and social development. 'Without development, there will be no peace.'

679 **Naval confidence-building measures.**
U.N. Department for Disarmament Affairs. New York: United
Nations, 1990. 320p. (Disarmament Topical Papers No. 4.
E.90.IX.10).

Confidence-building measures have been applied first on land in Europe, but with the
end of the Cold War they began also to be applied at sea. This large volume is a
report on two conferences, one in Denmark, the other in Bulgaria, of foreign
ministers, officials, naval officers, and experts, who discussed possible reductions of
tension and eventual disarmament among the principal navies of the world. The
principle at work, said Yasushi Akashi in his introduction, is 'seeking undiminished
security at constantly lower levels of armament and armed forces'. He particularly
warned of such new challenges to peace at sea as the vulnerability of all maritime
traffic to precision-guided munitions, the danger of accident and provocation during
close naval manoeuvres, and the strategic problem of naval nuclear arms. The
participants explored the practical potential of confidence-building measures at sea,
conventional force stability, naval nuclear control and disarmament, the law of the
sea, and the role of the U.N.

680 **Nuclear issues on the agenda of the Conference on Disarmament.**
Thomas Bernauer. New York: United Nations for UNIDIR, 1991.
107p. bibliog. (GV.E.91.0.16. UNIDIR/91/68).

While the nuclear-weapons states engage in bilateral negotiations, non-nuclear-
weapon states attempt to protect themselves by multilateral negotiations in the
Conference on Disarmament (CD) in Geneva. No treaty has emerged from the CD
since a declaration of 1968. (In 1993, the Chemical Weapons Treaty, after over
twenty years in the CD, was finally signed.) Nevertheless, four nuclear issues as they
affect all states have been discussed in the CD: security assurances to non-nuclear-
weapon states, prevention of nuclear war, cessation of the nuclear arms race, and a
comprehensive test ban. This report examines the first three; a separate study
discusses the ban. A large volume of protest has been registered, but until the
superpowers settled their Cold War, progress was minimal. Compare Schmalberger,
In pursuit of a nuclear test ban treaty (1991) (item no. 686).

681 **Nuclear weapons: a comprehensive study.**
U.N. Department for Disarmament Affairs. New York: United
Nations, 1991. 148p. (Study Series No. 21. E.91.IX.12. A/45/373).

This is the most up-to-date, impartial study of nuclear weapons at a time when
Russian and American statesmen seem determined to reduce or even eliminate the
threat of nuclear attack from their relations. The appendix contains a compilation of
the official doctrinal positions of the five nuclear-weapons states and of their
inventories of nuclear weapons. The study proper covers the existing weapons (1990),
trends in their future development, doctrines and strategies, testing, effects of use in
nuclear war, the special problem of nuclear weapons for international security, the
bilateral and multilateral limitation of nuclear arms, and secure disarmament. The
authors conclude with calls for continued Russo-American negotiations to reduce
their stockpiles, for involvement of the other nuclear powers, and for cooperation of
all states through the Conference on Disarmament.

682   **Outline of basic provisions of a treaty on general and complete disarmament in a peaceful world, 18 April 1962.**
United States Department of State.   In: *Disarmament: its politics and economics*. Edited by Seymour Melman.   Boston: American Academy of Arts and Sciences, 1962, p.279-308.

This is a rare draft of a U.S. treaty on disarmament in accordance with the McCloy–Zorin principles. It provides for a staged process of disarmament, to be completed in seven years, under supervision of an international disarmament *organization*. Compare the Soviet *Treaty on General and Complete Disarmament* (item no. 702).

683   **Prevention of an arms race in outer space: a guide to the discussions in the Conference on Disarmament.**
Péricles Gasparini Alves.   New York: United Nations for UNIDIR, 1991. 203p. bibliog. (GV.E.91.0.17. UNIDIR/91/79).

Bombers have been succeeded by intercontinental ballistic missiles, which may yet be succeeded by orbiting offensive and defensive satellites of 'Star Wars' technology. To prevent an arms race in space, a number of international treaties have been negotiated: the Treaty on . . . the Moon and Other Celestial Bodies (Outer Space Treaty, 1967), the ABM Treaty (1972), and the En Mod Convention (1977). By 1985, it was evident that ambiguities in the treaties and the need for new treaties to cope with innovations in aerospace technology required comprehensive and sustained negotiations in a multilateral framework (outer space is often listed as part of the 'common heritage of mankind'). Hence, the Conference on Disarmament's Prevention of an Arms Race in Outer Space (PAROS) Committee was formed. This book covers the discussion in the PAROS Committee. The topics covered are: history, issues, present international legal situation, and proposals of participating states for improvement. The latter include amendments to the Outer Space and ABM treaties and to the Registration Convention of 1961; new treaties prohibiting satellite weapons, use of force in space, and anti-satellite weapons; confidence-building measures; an international satellite monitoring agency; and a verification agency.

684   **The prevention of nuclear war: a United Nations perspective.**
William Epstein.   Cambridge, MA: Oelgeschlager, Ginn & Hain for UNITAR, 1984. 114p.

After the second U.N. special session on disarmament (1982), and at a time of sharply increased fear of nuclear war, the author brought his years of experience in the U.N. Secretariat to explain to the public and to statesmen the history and the prospects of nuclear disarmament by multilateral treaty and agreement. Epstein admits at the start that 'it is probably not possible, indeed it is highly unlikely, that far-reaching measures of disarmament can be achieved without parallel progress in improving on strengthening international security'. The book deals only briefly with this prior question, which to some extent in the next ten years was answered by the dismemberment of the Soviet Union and by increased attention to U.N. reform. Epstein sets out briefly and clearly the history of bilateral and multilateral negotiations (twenty-two treaties and agreements, of which nine are multilateral). He explores such issues as: reducing the risk of nuclear war; banning the use, especially first use, of nuclear weapons; ending the arms race, as by a comprehensive test ban and an extended Non-proliferation Treaty; and future U.N. capabilities such as an international space monitoring agency.

685 **Pugwash – the first ten years: history of the conferences of science and world affairs.**
Joseph Rotblat. New York: Humanities Press, 1968. 244p.
Scientists, who made the atomic and hydrogen bombs, have also been in the lead to control them internationally. Inspired by a manifesto by Bertrand Russell and Albert Einstein warning that 'a war with H-bombs might quite possibly put an end to the human race, which now requires the abolition of war', the first conference of scientists from East and West devoted to saving the planet from disaster was held in Pugwash, a peaceful fishing village in Nova Scotia, in 1957. Its significance, writes the author, a leading British physicist and co-signatory of the Russell–Einstein manifesto, was that for the first time an international conference of scientists was held 'not to discuss specific technical matters, but the social implications of scientific discovery'. Pugwash conferences have since been held annually all over the world, and the scientists attending them have had a notable influence on governments, other scientists, and public opinion in favour of disarmament, arms control, and effective international control. The Pugwash movement is one of the NGOs whose authority, scientific and technical competence, and public prestige enabled it to have a moderating influence on the Cold War and to point the way toward eventual peace. Rotblat continued the story to 1971 in his *Scientists in the quest for peace*.

686 **In pursuit of a nuclear test ban treaty: a guide to the debate in the Conference on Disarmament.**
Thomas Schmalberger. New York: United Nations for UNIDIR, 1991. 132p. bibliog. (GV.E.91.0.4. UNIDIR/91/16).
A comprehensive test ban (CTB) as a key to substantial nuclear disarmament was proposed in 1958 and was partially achieved in the Partial Test Ban Treaty of 1963. A CTB, if verified, would have military, environmental, and political effects that would increase states' confidence in international security. A CTB would make development of new military weapons impossible and would degrade reliability of existing weapons. It would end any further danger of underground leakage of radioactivity, now that France (1974) and China (1980) have ceased their atmospheric tests. It would prevent proliferation and prove to all nations that the nuclear-weapon states were willing to end their competition in nuclear arms. This work surveys the issues and progress toward a CTB, especially since the end of tripartite negotiations between the U.S., U.K., and U.S.S.R. in 1980. Much attention is devoted to monitoring and verification.

687 **Reduction of military budgets: international reporting of military expenditures.**
U.N. Department of Political and Security Council Affairs. New York: United Nations, 1981. 197p. (Study Series No. 4. E.81.I.9. A/35/479).
An international panel of experienced practitioners in the field of military budgeting prepared this expert study, with the cooperation of fourteen states, including Australia, Indonesia, France, Germany (FRG), Italy, Sweden, Mexico, Canada, and the U.S.A. Hence, this report provides a rather rare comparative and statistical snapshot of the levels of military spending in 1981. It can be viewed as a step toward greater transparency, and hence alleviation of fear, about military expenditures. The panel concludes with recommendations for widening the use of their reporting

instrument (questionnaire sent to national states). The aim of the General Assembly in establishing the panel was to expose the 'detrimental effects [of global military expenditures] on international security and on economic and social developments'.

688 **Reduction of military budgets: refinement of international reporting and comparison of military expenditures.**
U.N. Department for Disarmament Affairs. New York: United Nations, 1983. 99p. (Study Series No. 10. E.83.IX.4. A/S-12/7).

This is a continuation of the above report, with the participation of sixteen states members, including the U.S.A. (The series extends back to 1974 and continues to through to 1986 and beyond.) This study brings into the analysis of security such factors as a nation's gross domestic product, the quality of its defences, the preparedness and determination of its population to defend themselves, and the military and economic power of its allies and adversaries. New attention to verification of arms control and disarmament agreements is evident, as if, by 1983, questions of implementation had succeeded those of the very necessity of agreements.

689 **The relationship between disarmament and development.**
U.N. Department of Political and Security Council Affairs. New York: United Nations, 1982. 189p. (Study Series No. 5. E.82.IX.1. A/36/356).

Disarmament and economic development are widely viewed within national governments as separate problems. Defence, in the absence of reliable international institutions of collective security, is regarded as an absolute necessity, regardless of the cost; expenditure on economic and social problems is rooted in more volatile domestic politics. Many officials doubt the wisdom or practicality of drawing attention to the relation between the two. This study examines the basis for such perceptions and attitudes. It goes on 'to investigate, systematically and in depth, the range of the relationship between the prospects for balanced and sustainable global economic and social development on the one hand, and disarmament on the other, through the reallocation of real resources'. The authors find that 50 million people are engaged in military activities world-wide, that about 30 per cent of industrial production is given over to military products, that about 6 per cent of petroleum and 10 per cent of critical minerals are so consumed, that military research and development (R&D) amounts to one quarter of all R&D, that the arms trade amounts to $26,000 million per year, and total military expenditures (in 1980) to $500,000 million or 6 per cent of world output. This was thought then to be 'astonishing', but in ten years it would double. The conclusion is obvious. For the parallel study, see the next item.

690 **Relationship between disarmament and international security.**
U.N. Department of Political and Security Council Affairs. New York: United Nations, 1982. 55p. (Study Series No. 8. E.82.IX.4. A/36/597).

Nations cannot be expected to disarm until their security can be assured by an international system of security. This study describes the United Nations system for the maintenance of international peace and security. It analyses the effectiveness of the U.N., which must deserve some credit for humanity's avoiding a third world war, yet has not proved sufficient to obviate the need of national armaments. The reason, it is argued in this U.N. study, is not because of 'provisions of the Charter' but because of lack of 'political will' by the member-states. 'The effectiveness of the Organization depends first and foremost upon the readiness of Member States to fulfil their obligations under the Charter. . . .' Hence, all the suggestions here are to improve the cooperative political will, or, technically, to improve the implementation of Security Council decisions, on which the U.N. security system is designed to rely. Suggestions include: International Atomic Energy Agency assistance in verifying the nuclear non-proliferation (NPT) regime, progressing toward a chemical weapons disarmament treaty (achieved in 1993), maintaining the disarmament of outer space, progressing toward conventional force reductions in Europe (CFE treaty in 1987) and in other regions, introducing confidence-building measures, expanding peacekeeping, establishing Article 43 reserve forces, and enhancing the U.N.'s Chapter VI means for the peaceful settlement of disputes. The authors cite such precedents as the cooperation of the United States and the Soviet Union to stop the Middle East War of 1973 and cooperation in their Standing Consultative Commission within the framework of the SALT I treaty of 1972. By the 1990s, thanks to Soviet and American leadership, many of these interim policies had been tried, so it was possible to look at Charter reform – particularly in the constitution of the Security Council – in order to strengthen the international security system.

691   **Status of multilateral arms regulations and disarmament agreements.**
U.N. Department of Political Affairs.   New York: United Nations, 4th ed., 1993. 2 vols. (E.93.IX.11).

The texts of all multilateral arms control and disarmament treaties and lists of all signatories and parties to the treaties will be found in this basic reference. (Bilateral treaties, including some of the most important ones between the United States and the Soviet Union, are omitted.) Here can be found, for example, the Antarctica Treaty of 1959, the Partial Test Ban Treaty of 1963, the Non-proliferation Treaty of 1968, the Biological Weapons Convention of 1972, and the Treaty of Rarotonga, establishing a South Pacific nuclear free zone, of 1985. Compare Goldblat, *Arms control agreements* (item no. 644).

692   **Stemming the tide: arms control in the Johnson years.**
Glenn T. Seaborg with Benjamin S. Loeb.   Lexington, MA: Lexington Books, 1987. 495p. bibliog.

This is a readable history by a leading participant in the early nuclear arms race, who discusses the threat of proliferation (foreseen as early as the Franck report of June 1945), the disappointment over a comprehensive test ban in 1963, the abandonment of the nuclear Multilateral Force as a pan-Atlantic unified defence force, the drafting of the Non-proliferation Treaty during the Johnson administration, and the beginnings of the SALT I negotiations. Seaborg concludes with some wise reflections on the necessity for arms control, the tendency to exploit it as propaganda, and the prison of animosity that may again, if some other threat than nuclear weapons arises, mislead humanity.

693   **The struggle against the bomb.** [3 vols. Vol. 1:] **One world or none: a history of the world nuclear disarmament movement through 1953.**
Lawrence S. Wittner. Foreword by Martin J. Sherwin.   Stanford, CA: Stanford University Press, 1993. 456p. bibliog. (Nuclear Age Series).

'A new type of thinking is essential if mankind is to survive', wrote Albert Einstein in 1946. Readers in search of an inclusive and humane account of the disarmament movement – not written from a narrow national perspective, but with appreciation for the historic task of humanity to abolish war – may find it here. The author provides an international history of popular demands to bring nuclear weapons under control as well as of the diplomacy of the arms control and disarmament treaties. He particularly addresses the 'question of why, despite the clear necessity of freeing humanity from the threat of nuclear destruction, that movement has not been more effective'. Wittner recounts the history of the popular response to Hiroshima and Nagasaki in Japan, the United States, Europe, Eastern Europe, the Soviet Union, and internationally; he then treats the Communist-led peace movement; and he ends with a review of U.S.-led efforts in the U.N. to establish the international control of atomic energy (the Baruch plan) and the decisions of Britain and the Soviet Union to develop their own bombs.

694   **Study on all the aspects of regional disarmament.**
U.N. Department of Political and Security Council Affairs.   New York: United Nations, 1981. 59p. (Study Series No. 3. E.81.IX.2. A/35/416).

This study, pursuant to the first U.N. General Assembly special session on disarmament (1978), examines the prospects of regional disarmament in conjunction with, or even prior to, universal disarmament. The Antarctica treaty (1959), which provides for an absolute prohibition of all military activities and for instant verification by any party, is a model for what may be possible elsewhere. The study examines the harder cases of Latin America (Treaty of Tlateloco, 1967), Europe (Conference on Security and Cooperation in Europe, 1975), 'zones of peace' in the Indian Ocean, Southeast Asia, and the Mediterranean, and 'nuclear-weapon-free zones' in half a dozen places. It concludes with a survey of conceivable measures for reduction of threats without loss of security. 'Given the political will', the authors argue, 'there is a vast and, to a large extent, unexplored potential for progress in disarmament if the global approach is supplemented with determined and systematic efforts at the level of the different regions.'

695   **Study on the climatic and other global effects of nuclear war.**
U.N. Department for Disarmament Affairs.   New York: United Nations, 1989. 61p. bibliog. (Study Series No. 18. E.89.IX.1. A/43/351).

Nuclear explosions cause three large effects – blast, heat, and radiation. Nuclear war, the authors of this expert study agree, would very probably produce 'global environmental disruption'. A nuclear winter will complete the war of death and destruction. Readers during lulls of anxiety over weapons of mass destruction may feel this prospect remote, but the effects of acid rain and deforestation are already visible to all, and, in an anarchic world, wars with the weapons at hand are already a constant occurrence.

696 **Study on conventional disarmament.**
U.N. Department for Disarmament Affairs. New York: United
Nations, 1985. 67p. (Study Series No. 12. E.85.IX.1).
Although nuclear disarmament has had highest priority in the U.N., conventional
disarmament has been a concern since the founding of the organization, and in the
1990s it will surely become more important. When this study was prepared, some 150
armed conflicts since 1945 had taken the lives of twenty million people. The authors
survey the nature and causes of the conventional arms race, of which one is the very
weakness of the U.N. collective security system, and they discuss at length many
approaches to conventional disarmament.

697 **Study on defensive security concepts and policies.**
U.N. Department for Disarmament Affairs. New York: United
Nations, 1993. 64p. (Study Series No. 21. E.93.IX.12. A/47/394).
'Defensive security' is a new term that has acquired scholarly acceptance in place of
other new terms like 'non-offensive defense' and 'reasonable sufficiency'. Since
defence is universally accepted as a legitimate right of states, and since *security* is
their primary interest (self-preservation), the combined term is considered acceptable.
Its meaning is not far removed from 'common security' (1982) or 'collective security'
(1930). This study sets out the more technical meanings of the term. The emphasis is
on cooperation, transparency, and restructuring.

698 **Study on deterrence: its implications for disarmament and the
arms race, negotiated arms reductions, and international security.**
U.N. Department for Disarmament Affairs. New York: United
Nations, 1987. 142p. (Study Series No. 17. E.87.IX.2. A/41/432).
Deterrence, in international relations, is the establishment of fear in an enemy or
adversary sufficient to 'dissuade' him from military attack on a national state, because
of that state's effective defences and credible threat of counter-attack even after
absorbing a first blow. The doctrine of deterrence emerged after the United Nations
soon proved incapable of providing international security (1946). Deterrence is a
substitute for international cooperation in an association of sovereign states – and
even for the rule of law under a participatory world federal government. So
fundamental is deterrence to the national security of states at the present time of
inadequate world organization, that the authors of this U.N. study could not agree on
its definition and features. Each author's paper is printed here individually; in the last
part, views are summarized under the heads of NATO countries, Warsaw Pact
countries, and non-aligned countries. Here the reader will find plain statements why
major nations refuse to disarm under the protection of the United Nations. For the
future, the West argued in 1987 that 'while one can continue to rely on deterrence
with confidence . . . one should not be satisfied forever with a system of deterrence
that is too heavily dependent on the residual possibility of catastrophic destruction.'
The East argued that 'there is no alternative to cooperation. . . . The only way of
dealing with deterrence is to replace it with . . . common security, peaceful
coexistence, and disarmament.'

699 **Study on the economic and social consequences of the arms race and military expenditures.**
U.N. Department for Disarmament Affairs. New York: United Nations, 1989. 82p. (Study Series No. 19. E.89.IX.2. A/43/368).

Six years after the last similar study, the authors find that the debate about whether military spending encourages or prevents economic growth has been resolved. 'For most countries, there is a trade-off between military spending and socio-economic development', they conclude. The negative effects of military spending in recent years are carefully examined in the fields of economic development, human resources, technology, inflation, debt, society, and conversion. In 1989, there was no appreciable reversal of the nuclear or conventional arms race – but the argument in this U.N. study that arms brought neither security nor prosperity seemed decisive. Common security had become a necessity – as had general disarmament under effective international control.

700 **Study on the role of the United Nations in the field of verification.**
U.N. Department for Disarmament Affairs. New York: United Nations, 1991. 90p. (Study Series No. 20. E.91.IX.11. A/45/372).

As disarmament has come to seem necessary by the 1990s, the question of verification (literally 'to make true') in order to insure compliance with agreements has loomed larger. This study reviews the concept and process of verification, compares national and international processes, and sets out particularly the U.N. contributions in the field. These include standard setting and specific responsibilities under several of the arms control and disarmament treaties. Suggestions are made for expanding the U.N.'s role in data collection, exchange of experts, fact-finding by the Secretary-General, aerial surveillance, satellite monitoring, and even an international verification *system.* A U.N. role should be acceptable to states, the authors conclude, since successful implementation of disarmament agreements is in the common interest.

701 **Transparency in international arms transfer.**
U.N. Department for Disarmament Affairs. New York: United Nations, 1990. 193p. (Disarmament Topical Papers No. 3. E.90.IX.9).

Since the limitation or reduction of conventional arms is even more difficult than that of nuclear arms (all states trade conventional arms, and they are widely used), one approach is to increase 'transparency' – that is, the exact, quantitative knowledge of the trade – in order to reveal the magnitude and implications of the problem prior to disarmament. This work is a report of a conference of experts pursuant to a General Assembly resolution of 1988 calling for a study of transparency. (The U.N. Arms Control Register, established in January 1992, is the fruit in part of their work.) The working group on possible multilateral action discussed the full range of issues and a virtual agenda of future action. Transparency might begin with confidence-building measures, then move to a register of imports and exports, then of stockpiles, then of production. But the register would have to be global to prevent abuses. The U.N. could move from fact-finding to verification to a 'watchdog' group of experts to monitor arms supplies. But always it would be necessary 'to show goodwill and cooperation in the process of sharing information'.

702 **Treaty on general and complete disarmament under strict
international control, draft, 22 September 1962.**
U.S.S.R. Ministry of Foreign Affairs. In: *Disarmament: its politics
and economics*. Edited by Seymour Melman. Boston: American
Academy of Arts and Sciences, 1962, p.309-31.
This is a Soviet draft treaty on disarmament in accordance with the McCloy–Zorin
principles. It is comparable to a U.S. draft (printed in the same volume). Both
foundered on fear of impartiality in the international disarmament organization to
which sovereign powers would have to be delegated.

703 **Unconventional approaches to conventional arms control
verification.**
Edited by John Grin and Henny Van der Graaf. New York:
St. Martin's for Inter-university Network for Studies on Technology
Assessment in Defence, Centre for Verification Technology,
Amsterdam, 1990. 276p.
The 'unconventional approaches' are: an all-European verification system; verifying
the defensive or offensive structure of national armed forces; and verification of
production and R&D facilities. The book is intended for both professionals and
concerned citizens. Essays cover the history of verification in Europe, organizational
options, especially under the Conference on Security and Cooperation in Europe
(CSCE), data exchanges, a satellite system, aerial monitoring, seismic sensors, and
other technical aids. The authors conclude that many new departures are now possible
in the 'revolutionary situation in Europe'.

704 **Unilateral nuclear disarmament measures.**
U.N. Department for Disarmament Affairs. New York: United
Nations, 1985. 18p. (Study Series No. 13. E.85.IX.2. A/39/516).
Unilateral measures include those announced and taken, without demand for a
reciprocal response, in order to reduce tension without abandoning all armaments on
which national security is still assumed to be based. Charles Osgood's 'graduated and
reciprocated initiatives in tension reduction' (GRIT, 1962) is one example. The
purpose is 'to create gradually an atmosphere of confidence and mutual trust within
which negotiations on critical issues will have a better chance of succeeding'. This
short study explores so desperate an escape from the nuclear arms race. Soon after the
study appeared, Mikhail Gorbachev boldly offered such unilateral initiatives.

705 **The United Nations and disarmament, 1945-1985.**
U.N. Department for Disarmament Affairs. New York: United
Nations, 1985. 166p. (E.85.IX.6).
This official U.N. publication presents a 'broad historical overview' of the U.N.'s part
in arms control and disarmament negotiations to 1985. It is a product of the U.N.'s
World Disarmament Campaign, launched in 1982 and dedicated to informing the
organizations of the U.N. system, member-states, non-governmental organizations,
and hence all segments of the world's population, especially elected representatives,
the media, scholars, teachers, and students. The style is non-contentious, as befits an
organization of states. Topics include: history of U.N. efforts, 1945-85; the

disarmament bodies (notably the Conference on Disarmament in Geneva); the goal of general and complete disarmament under effective international control; nuclear disarmament; a comprehensive test ban; non-proliferation; nuclear-weapon-free zones; biological and chemical weapons elimination; disarmament of outer space; prohibition of environmental modification; control of conventional weapons; and economic consequences of the arms race.

706 United Nations disarmament yearbook, 1991.

U.N. Department for Disarmament Affairs. New York: United Nations, 1992. 513p. (E.92.IX.1).

This annual reference (begun in 1976) 'focuses to a large extent on specific, active issues and is oriented towards professionals and serious students in the field of arms control and disarmament . . . [and] in the study of peace and security'. In 1991, the effects of the end of the Cold War were beginning to be felt on the reduction of military budgets, the termination of the Warsaw Pact, the shift of NATO toward a pan-European security system, the dissolution of the U.S.S.R., the signing of the START treaty (1991), an agreement on transparency in the conventional arms trade (the U.N. register, 1992), and imminent completion of the Chemical Weapons Treaty (1993).

707 United Nations General Assembly and disarmament, 1989.

U.N. Department for Disarmament Affairs. New York: United Nations, 1990. 198p. (E.90.IX.5).

This annual reference volume contains the texts of General Assembly resolutions on disarmament, with votes. There are brief introductions and occasional summaries.

708 Verification and disarmament: an international verification agency or international disarmament organization.

Joseph Preston Baratta. Washington, DC: Center for U.N. Reform Education, 1988. 60p. bibliog. (Monograph No. 4).

This is a relatively non-technical examination of the nature and practice of national and international verification and a survey of proposals for an international *agency* by the United States, Soviet Union, France, and the Six-Nation Group. The author then examines proposals for a larger-scale international *disarmament organization*, including the McCloy–Zorin agreement (1961), the American and Soviet draft treaties on general and complete disarmament under effective international control (1962), and the Clark–Sohn plan for systemic U.N. reform (1958). Baratta argues that verification can never be absolutely certain, but, with the 'politics of common security' emerging after the Cold War, it can be sufficient to support trust and, eventually, the rule of law.

709 Verification: How much is enough?

Allan S. Krass. London: Taylor & Francis for SIPRI, 1985. 271p.

This is a standard and authoritative study of the verification of national compliance with international arms control agreements. Verification has always been required of arms control and disarmament treaties since the Antarctica treaty of 1959, but by 1985 the availability of 'national technical means', especially spy satellites, suggested ways to make progress without the intrusive devices of ground inspections, though these, too, may be required for the greatest assurance. Politically, in a world of divided sovereignties, there can never be absolute assurance. Krass shows, in his criticism of the 'Wiesner curve' (which assumed a context of acute distrust and hence very high levels of inspection to give assurance that an enemy was not secretly rearming), that disarmament steps would tend to increase trust and even lead to what was being called 'common security', so that the necessary level of verification in such an international milieu could safely be *low*. He concludes that, technically, existing and developing means of verification can support the next round of U.S.A.–U.S.S.R. bilateral agreements (SALT II, START, etc.), and by implication multilateral agreements under negotiationn (INF, CFE, chemical weapons). But Krass expects the disarmament regime to be maintained by the national parties, not the U.N. In a subsequent round, if détente and bilateral arms control progresses (in 1985 he could not imagine the collapse of the Soviet Union and the negotiation of genuine *disarmament* agreements), then 'the ultimate goal of genuine international disarmament verified by international means would be within reach'.

710 **The verification issue in United Nations disarmament negotiations.**
Ellis Morris.   New York: United Nations for UNIDIR, 1987. 103p.
(GV.E.87.0.4. UNIDIR/87/14).

This is an historical and comprehensive account of the political, rather than the technical, aspects of verification within the U.N. It 'traces the development of national positions on verification in the multilateral arms control negotiations conducted in the various United Nations committees on disarmament from 1962 to 1986.' These negotiations dealt with general and complete disarmament, a comprehensive test ban, a freeze on vehicles, a cut-off of production of fissionable materials, nuclear-free zones (as in Latin America), the Non-proliferation Treaty, the Sea Bed Treaty, and the Chemical Weapons Treaty. The differing approaches of the five permanent members of the Security Council, the non-aligned nations, the socialist countries, and the Western countries are all detailed in this reference work.

711 **Verification of disarmament or limitation of armaments:**
instruments, negotiations, proposals.
Edited by Serge Sur.   New York: United Nations for UNIDIR, 1992.
267p. bibliog. (GV.E.92.0.10. UNIDIR/92/28).

This large-scale U.N. study was completed during another momentous year of changes in international relations, as the Persian Gulf War led to a triumph of the international coalition opposed to aggression, and as the Soviet Union broke into its constituent republics. All of the expert articles here, while they provide an adequate account of *national* technical means, make every effort to bring *international* means of verification into the picture. Topics include: verification of nuclear testing, cut-off of production of fissionable material for weapons, START verification, ballistic missile defences (SDI, 'Star Wars'), *short*-range nuclear forces control, verification of a chemical weapons ban, of biological weapons, of conventional weapons, transparency, naval arms control, space weapons, the role of international organizations, and U.N. monitoring of Iraqi compliance with the Security Council resolution designed to protect the Kurds (1991).

712 **The verification revolution.**
Alan Krass.   Cambridge, MA: Union of Concerned Scientists, 1989.
63p.

The 'revolution' is technological and political: new U.S. satellites and generally available seismic sensors can securely verify Soviet compliance with arms control agreements under negotiation; and the Soviets are, since Gorbachev came to power, willing to accept on-site inspection, as under the Intermediate-range Nuclear Forces (INF) treaty of 1987. 'For the first time', Krass writes, 'the U.S. confronts the dilemma of being able to get just about as much verification as it is willing to give in return.' The author briefly surveys the techniques, confronts the political question of how much verification is enough, and precisely discusses the requirements for the START treaty, a modified ABM treaty (permitting space-based defences), and a comprehensive test ban. He concludes with difficulties of verifying limits on submarine launched cruise missiles, mobile ICBMs, space weapons, and the like.

713 **World disarmament: an idea whose time has come.**
Edited by Ron Huzzard and Christopher Meredith.   Nottingham:
Spokesman, Bertrand Russell House, 1985. 238p.

Edited at a dark time for disarmament – President Reagan and Secretary Andropov seemed to be presiding over another worsening of the Cold War – this book collects some of the most far-visioned articles from the British and American peace movement. The articles taken together are a studied commentary on the *Final document* of the first U.N. special session on disarmament (1978), which is here reprinted in full. 'The greatest State paper of all time', British politician and statesman Philip Noel-Baker called it. A succinct paper of Lord Noel-Baker, 'From warfare to welfare', arguing that the arms race is the *cause* of world poverty, is included. Other articles discuss the role of public opinion, NGOs, the U.N. Disarmament Campaign, the Freeze movement, and ending interventionary roles for national defence forces.

Common security.
See item no. 135.

See also Non-proliferation (p.251ff.).

Non-proliferation

714 **The diplomacy of nuclear proliferation.**
Joseph S. Nye, Jr.   In: *Negotiating world order: the artisanship and architecture of global diplomacy.* Edited by Alan K. Henrikson.
Wilmington, DE: Scholarly Resources, 1986, p.79-94.

This is a clear account of the nuclear 'non-proliferation regime', which has since changed somewhat. France and China have declared their intention to adhere to the Non-proliferation Treaty (NPT) (1992), but North Korea has threatened to withdraw

(1993). Several suspected nuclear states (Israel, India, Pakistan, Iraq) are outside the treaty or in violation, but others (South Africa, Brazil, Argentina) have terminated their programmes. Nevertheless, Nye well describes the diplomacy of maintaining a regime in which the bulk of states are induced to voluntarily renounce a weapon that five others hold as an ultimate threat, endangering the whole world. The review conference in 1995 will test the regime.

715   **Doomsday weapons in the hands of many: the arms control challenge of the '90s.**
       Kathleen C. Bailey.   Urbana, IL: University of Illinois Press, 1991. 158p.

There are four proliferations: nuclear weapons, chemical weapons, biological and toxin agents, and ballistic and cruise missiles. (The proliferation of conventional weapons is not brought into the study, apparently because it is so familiar and intractible.) The author sets out 'the scope and nature of the proliferation problem'. She mentions international control efforts and places the Geneva Protocol, Non-proliferation Treaty, and Biological Weapons Treaty in the appendix, but virtually all her discussion of remedies is about U.S. policy. The U.N. is hardly mentioned. Readers will find this an intelligible book within the presumptions of U.S. power.

716   **The international nuclear non-proliferation system: challenges and changes.**
       Edited by John Simpson and Anthony G. McGrew.   New York: St. Martin's, 1984. 209p. bibliog.

This volume of mostly British expert essays was prepared in time for the third NPT review conference (1985), but already the authors were looking forward to the general conference to decide whether to allow the treaty to lapse or to extend it indefinitely in 1995. The editors acknowledge such challenges as the 'reawakening of "cold war" antagonisms between the superpowers' (in 1984), the qualitative nuclear arms race, the lifting of bans on nuclear exports to India and military aid to Pakistan in response to the Soviet invasion of Afghanistan, the oil crisis of 1973 that inclined states toward nuclear power, competition from other nuclear suppliers, and even Britain's purchase of the Trident missile. The essays cover non-proliferation policies in the nuclear-weapon states, the IAEA safeguards system, the pressures on the international nuclear industry, U.S. and British policies (especially the 'implicit folly' of a narrow approach, argued trenchantly by D. Keohane), technical reforms, and wider, vigilant national policies. 'What appears to be needed', the editors conclude, 'are policies that offer the opportunity to create new trade management structures and that will resolve existing contradictions between long and short run policies, assist in reinforcing an international social fabric of shared norms and expectations concerning non-proliferation, and generally improve the atmosphere of international non-proliferation discussions.'

717   **International nuclear proliferation: multilateral diplomacy and regional aspects.**
       Ashok Kapur.   New York: Praeger, 1979. 387p. bibliog.

This is an analytical study by a Canadian political scientist who made special efforts by widespread travel and interviews to discover the views of 'potential proliferators': India, Pakistan, South Africa, Japan, Brazil, and Argentina. 'The task of this study',

Kapur writes, 'is to see how national perceptions of the environment shape the national decisions about nuclear power; to see if there are attitudes and policies in the thinking of states that differ from the conventional wisdom of North American arms control literature; to see if the central scholarly and policy assumptions that permeate American thinking are shared by a bulk of humanity; to see if there are theoretical and practical alternatives to the sterility of some parts of the U.S. literature on arms control and disarmament.' Hence, the book, while quite informative about the NPT 'regime', and five alternatives, presents the account from a critical perspective of the states 'discriminated against'.

718   **International politics of nuclear energy.**
      Charles K. Ebinger.   Beverly Hills, CA: Sage for Center for Strategic and International Studies, Georgetown University, 1978. 87p. bibliog. (Washington Papers No. 57).

Following the OPEC oil crisis of 1973-74, Western reliance on nuclear power seemed the only short-term solution to dependency on foreign energy supplies. But nuclear power ran straight into the problem of proliferation of nuclear weapons. In the middle of the Carter presidency (1977), the author conducted interviews with foreign officials in Washington and abroad in order to discover why there was such acute suspicion of U.S. policies toward both nuclear power and non-proliferation. He finds that, as the Soviet Union and Britain found U.S. policy discriminatory and hence decided that they would have to develop nuclear weapons for their national security, so other nations by the 1970s were similarly motivated. Yet U.S. (and Soviet) policy was designed only to limit other states' 'technical capacity to go nuclear', not 'to promote new institutional mechanisms to limit nuclear weapons proliferation'. Ebinger writes, with great pertinence: 'Although the issues reased by a study of the international politics of nuclear energy (strategic deterrence, proliferation) form a cornerstone of most contemporary geostrategic doctrines, most nations of the world reject the theoretical assumptions that underlie this dogma. Thus, most of the nuclear "have-not" nations reject the notion of superpower strategic nuclear parity as a stabilizing geopolitical force; they reject the hierarchical ordering of "responsible states"; they reject the argument that horizontal nuclear proliferation is more of a threat to world stability than the vertical proliferation of nuclear weapons held by the superpowers; and they assert the right of all sovereign nations to foster their economic independence and strategic security.'

719   **The last chance: nuclear proliferation and arms control.**
      William Epstein.   New York: Free Press, 1976. 341p.

In 1976 – following India's successful test of a nuclear device, the decision of the U.S. and U.S.S.R. to deploy multiple independently targetable re-entry vehicles (MIRVs), and the frustrations at the first NPT review conference – the author regarded control of the military weapons that threatened to destroy all civilization as 'the most important problem facing the world'. The book is more than a narrow study of the prospects of the Non-proliferation Treaty (NPT). It is a history and analysis of the nuclear arms race, with special attention to the rather late (1968-) strategy of controlling the horizontal proliferation of nuclear weapons. (Control of their vertical proliferation was relegated to the SALT and START negotiations.) Epstein gives equal attention to the security needs of nuclear and non-nuclear states, he reviews the safeguards of the International Atomic Energy Agency (IAEA), and he discusses such 'radical suggestions' as phasing out civilian nuclear power, reviving the Baruch plan for a supranational authority to manage all nuclear materials and facilities, strengthening the universal collective security system of the U.N. (Chapter VII), and abandoning the focus on arms control to turn to more fundamental problems of world order like alleviating world poverty.

720 **Maintaining a non-proliferation regime.**
Joseph S. Nye, Jr. In: *Nuclear proliferation: breaking the chain.* Edited by George H. Quester. *International Organization*, vol. 35 (1981), p.15-38.

This whole special issue on non-proliferation is based on such 'optimistic' assumptions that nuclear proliferation is not desirable for the world, is not inevitable, can be stopped by means short of a brutal exercise of American power, can be avoided without surrender of American power to other nuclear powers (like the Soviet Union or a loose group of new, small nuclear powers), and does not require surrender of that power to the United Nations by progressing toward general and complete disarmament under strict and effective international control in accordance with Article VI of the NPT. Joseph Nye's article is squarely within this framework. He argues that the non-proliferation 'regime' (NPT, IAEA safeguards, suppliers under Article IV, norms, and sanctions) can be maintained by flexible and vigilant U.S. policies, not unlike those he pursued as Deputy Under-Secretary of State from 1977 to 1979. One of these was the International Nuclear Fuel Cycle Evaluation (INFCE) programme. Disarmament? 'The best is sometimes the enemy of the good', he argues. 'But given the difficulty of constructing international institutions in a world of sovereign states, and the risks attendant upon their collapse, political wisdom begins with efforts to maintain the existing regime with its presumption against proliferation.'

721 **The Non-proliferation Treaty: on the road to 1995.**
Lawrence Scheinman. *IAEA Bulletin* (Vienna), vol. 34, no. 1 (1992), p.33-40.

With the end of the Cold War, the author sees two scenarios of regional and ethnic conflict that could have serious implications for the permanent extension of the NPT in 1995. Threshold states in Korea, South Asia, and the Middle East may conclude that their security interests require nuclear weapons like present nuclear-weapon states; or they may decide their security would be better served by maintaining the non-proliferation regime. Scheinman reviews the impending debate from the perspective of a *general security* regime, anchored in a treaty. The treaty would build on recent strategic arms agreements and require very deep cuts in existing nuclear-weapon states' stockpiles; it would uphold the norm of the non-legitimacy of the spread of nuclear weapons; and it would provide confidence-building measures, verification, and safeguards to ensure compliance.

722 **Non-proliferation: the why and the wherefore.**
Edited by Jozef Goldblat. London: Taylor & Francis for SIPRI, 1985. 343p. bibliog.

The Non-proliferation Treaty (NPT, 1968) has been very widely ratified, but two nuclear powers – France and China – and a number of 'threshold' states continue to refuse to sign: Argentina, Brazil, India, Pakistan, Israel, South Africa, and Spain. 'The purpose of this book', Goldblat writes, 'is to examine the reasons why the ruling élites in these countries, with varing degrees of popular support, have been in favour of acquiring nuclear weapons or at least of keeping open the option to do so.' He provides a clear and informative introduction to the whole subject of non-proliferation. Each one of the threshold states is treated in a separate essay. For comparative purposes, selected states-parties to the NPT, who decided *not* to go nuclear, are also discussed: Canada, Egypt, South Korea, Sweden, Switzerland, and Taiwan. (After the Cold War, only India, Pakistan, and Israel seemed to be holding out.) Goldblat finds that the main reasons for not adhering to the NPT are claims for the deterrent value or political value of nuclear weapons. These reasons are the very converse of those that persuaded Switzerland, Sweden, and South Korea to adhere to it. Open acquisition of nuclear weapons, they reasoned, could be understood as a provocation by neighbouring states, and eventually in a crisis they would invite a conventional or even nuclear attack. Moreover, acquisition would reduce the credibility of conventional defence, while modern conventional arms can achieve most of the same effects as tactical nuclear weapons without the radioactive and political fallout. Goldblat emphasizes the 'transitional' nature of the NPT regime – it depends on superpower progress in bringing *their* nuclear arms race under control, in a general movement toward nuclear disarmament. Article VI of the treaty must be implemented before there is mass withdrawal under Article X. Why non-proliferation?: 'to prevent a bad situation from getting worse'. Wherefore?: 'to facilitate nuclear disarmament'.

723 **NPT: the logic of inequality.**
Joseph S. Nye, Jr. *Foreign Policy*, vol. 59 (Summer 1985), p.123-31.
In anticipation ultimately of the 1995 NPT review conference, the author confronts the 'basic, long-run security problem that the superpowers have tended to neglect' – not that the treaty is discriminatory or hypocritical or racist, but that nuclear 'deterrence' between the superpowers, which has provided a credible umbrella against proliferation, 'will fail'. This danger will grow more acute, Nye warns, with civil wars and revolutions in 'today's anarchic world'. To stabilize deterrence, he recommends U.S. policies of good faith on Article VI – reversing the then current round of nuclear modernization (vertical proliferation), abandoning doctrines of the usefulness of nuclear weapons, and respecting the arms control process. 'But maintaining the NPT regime will remain at the heart of an effective policy', he concludes. Yet he adds, revealingly, that the Great Powers, not the U.N., will maintain the 'police function . . . in international politics'.

724 **Nuclear non-proliferation: an agenda for the 1990s.**
Edited by John Simpson. Cambridge: Cambridge University Press, 1987. 237p.
This British volume is particularly focused on the 1995 NPT review conference. One set of essays is devoted to 'the world in 1995' (international system, Third World perspectives, nuclear trade relations, new technologies); another is on 'strengthening the non-proliferation regime'; and a third, on extending the regime (amending the NPT or even abandoning it and allowing 'internal restraints' to preserve order). The editor closes with an agenda of issues and policy choices. He predicts that a comprehensive test ban will be the symbolic issue in 1995, that renewal of the NPT will be vital to a secure *regime* because it has become a virtual 'security treaty rather than a disarmament one', and that verification and remote monitoring will be vital.

725 **Nuclear non-proliferation and global security.**
Edited by David B. Dewitt. New York: St. Martin's, 1987. 283p.
This Canadian study looks at non-proliferation particularly from the standpoint of the United Nations. The 'proliferation of actors [159 member-states in 1987] has brought with it the need to regulate the complex network of state interactions, confirming the importance of international organizations and institutions', Dewitt writes. 'Yet the dilemma of state security in the face of competition and conflict continues to undermine the visibility of a working system of co-operative global management.' The book is based on the assumption that, even if more states voluntarily decide not to develop nuclear weapons, nuclear technology will continue to spread; so the relevant question is, How can temporary instabilities or their effects be contained? The authors emphasize strengthening and renewing the NPT by 1995 for both 'global security' and regional security.

726 **Nuclear non-proliferation and the Non-proliferation Treaty.**
Edited by Michael P. Fry, Patrick Keatinge, and Joseph Rotblat.
Foreword by Prime Minister Charles Haughey. Berlin: Springer-Verlag, 1990. 198p. maps.
This volume is a report of a Pugwash (scientific) symposium held in Ireland in 1989. At that date, 'an extraordinary change in the climate of East–West relations' was evident, but the nuclear force levels were still high, and the danger of other states acquiring nuclear weapons had not dissipated. Nevertheless, here is some genuine 'new thinking' on the NPT regime, with emphases on strengthening the IAEA's safeguards, improving regional security (as by nuclear-weapons-free zones and credible guarantees by nuclear powers not to use their weapons against smaller states), continuing the progress of the Soviet–American talks to reverse the nuclear arms race, and, lastly, fulfilling Article VI obligations toward general disarmament (as by a comprehensive test ban). Looking forward to the 1995 NPT review conference, the editors call attention to an Indian proposal to replace the treaty with a new one on a comprehensive system of international peace and security, abolishing discrimination between nuclear-weapon and non-nuclear-weapon states, and aiming at total elimination of nuclear weapons by 2010.

727 **Nuclear proliferation: preventing a threat to world peace.**
Marvin S. Soroos. In: *Beyond sovereignty: the challenge of global policy*, by Marvin S. Soroos. Columbia, SC: University of South Carolina Press, 1986. p.163-94.
The danger of nuclear war will be increased if additional states to the present five openly acquire nuclear weapons and the means to deliver them. India's test of an atomic device in 1974 is a warning that nuclear 'have-not' nations will not endure forever the threats of the 'haves'. This informative chapter reviews the facts of nuclear proliferation, the Non-proliferation Treaty (NPT) of 1968, the safeguards provided by the International Atomic Energy Agency (IAEA), and the 'regime' of treaty, inspections, technology sharing, and proposed 'internationalization' of handling weapons-grade by-products. Partial nuclear disarmament and a comprehensive test ban (in the offing by 1991) would not be safe, Soroos argues, without general disarmament and strengthening the U.N.

728 **Nuclear proliferation today.**
Leonard S. Spector. Cambridge, MA: Ballinger for Carnegie
Endowment for International Peace, 1984. 478p. bibliog.

This book on non-proliferation is written from a broad internationalist perspective but
not strictly that of the United Nations. It looks at the dangers in the 'emerging
nuclear-weapon states' of India, Pakistan, Israel, Libya, Iraq, Argentina, Brazil, and
South Africa. Unlike some scholars in the mid-1980s, Spector concludes that non-
legal 'constraints on the spread of nuclear arms are . . . growing. The renunciation of
nuclear weapons is slowly becoming a norm of international conduct. . . .' Students
will find this a particularly readable book.

729 **Nuclear war, nuclear proliferation, and their consequences.**
Edited by Sadruddin Aga Khan. Oxford: Clarendon Press, 1986.
483p.

In 1985, on the eve of the third NPT review conference, a prestigious preparatory
conference of world leaders (e.g., Sweden's Prime Minister Olof Palme, Senator
Edward Kennedy), U.N. officials (Aga Khan, High Commissioner for Refugees, Hans
Blix, IAEA Director-General), national officials, scholars, scientists (Carl Sagan,
Yevgeny Velikov), and a broad representative audience, was held in Geneva. The
group came to several conclusions: that the NPT must be maintained and
strengthened, that the superpowers must make greater progress toward disarmament
under Article VI, that regional security will take the impetus out of proliferation, and
that peaceful uses of nuclear energy were less and less attractive.

730 **Nuclear weapons proliferation and nuclear risk.**
Edited by James A. Schear. Aldershot, England: Gower for
International Institute for Strategic Studies, 1984. 185p. (Adelphi
Library No. 10).

The strategic papers here address three general problems in the mid-1980s: the
fragility of the East–West nuclear balance, the dispersal of nuclear weapons
technology (symbolized by India's test of 1974), and frustration with Soviet–
American arms control negotiations. Joseph Nye, who was responsible for non-
proliferation in the U.S. State Department (1977-79), argues for sustaining the NPT
regime, but Kenneth Waltz, reflecting the mental world of these strategists, thought
that 'more [proliferation] may be better'. Problems of controlling the qualitative arms
race (vertical proliferation) and mobile ICBMs are brought out in the last two
chapters. The solution of general disarmament under effective international control
does not strike these thinkers as realistic. Deterrence will prevent nuclear war.

731 **Postures for non-proliferation: arms limitation and security
policies to minimize nuclear proliferation.**
Enid C.B. Schoettle and Stockholm International Peace Research
Institute. Preface by Frank Barnaby. London: Taylor & Francis for
SIPRI, 1979. 168p. bibliog.

This book, written after the first NPT review conference (1975) and after the first
U.N. special session on disarmament (1978), when there was great restiveness among
the 'second class' non-nuclear-weapon states, reviews the security policies of the
nuclear-weapon states in order 'to design effective policies to minimize the

proliferation of nuclear weapons'. The author concludes that a 'modified Low Postures Doctrine' would suit the nuclear-weapon states best. In effect, she justifies the emerging NPT regime. There is little discussion of the promised 'cessation of the nuclear arms race at an early date' in Article VI or of the wider goals of general disarmament under effective international control.

732 **Silent spread.**
Leonard S. Spector. *Foreign Policy*, vol. 58 (Spring 1985), p.53-78.

The author warns that nuclear weapons can be developed without testing. In fact, the bomb dropped on Hiroshima (U235 type, with gun trigger) had never been tested. Spector infers that, even without testing, Israel acquired the capacity to produce nuclear weapons in 1968-73, India in 1974, and South Africa in 1977; Pakistan, he suggests, could do so in 1986, Argentina and Brazil in the early 1990s. Although these predictions have not come true so soon, Spector's article remains a warning of secret proliferation. Nuclear power, he warns, is often a cover for a nuclear weapons programme. New 'rules of engagement' for the 'non-proliferation battle' are emerging. One is: 'If a country does not openly display its nuclear capabilities or break IAEA rules, it may approach and actually cross the nuclear weapons threshold with virtual impunity.' He shows this situation vividly in the case of the Dimona reactor in Israel, Tarapur in India, Valindaba in South Africa, New Labs in Pakistan, Osiraq in Iraq. Spector closes with policy recommendations for the United States and other 'advanced countries'.

733 **Without the bomb: the politics of nuclear non-proliferation.**
Michael Reiss. Foreword by Lincoln P. Bloomfield. New York: Columbia University Press, 1988. 337p. bibliog.

Although President Kennedy predicted a world of fifteen to twenty-five nuclear powers by the 1970s, only six have openly emerged to date. Why did Canada, Sweden, or South Korea decide not to develop nuclear weapons? The author finds four sources of restraint: domestic pressures, bilateral disincentives, international non-proliferation arrangements, and the general consensus against nuclear weapons. Reiss examines a wide range of cases, including the hard ones: Sweden, South Korea, Japan, Israel, South Africa, and India. He concludes that the most general restraint is the gradual realization that 'nuclear arms are simply not very useful instruments for achieving policy objectives'. The Soviet–American competition in such arms has not left them any more secure, and their superpower is based on a weapon that cannot be used. This readable book should especially appeal to students.

Functions of the U.N. System

International organizations

734 **The anatomy of influence: decision making in international organization.**
Edited by Robert W. Cox and Harold K. Jacobson. New Haven, CT: Yale University Press, 1973. 497p. bibliog.

This is a still useful collaborative study of the political decision-making process in eight specialized agencies loosely asssociated in the U.N. system from 1945 to 1970: ITU, ILO, UNESCO, WHO, IAEA, IMF, GATT, and UNCTAD. (The U.N. itself is passed over.) The authors deliberately 'pull back the veil of formal procedures', in these organizations in order to discover their 'political process'. They study 'influence', the effect of power. The influence of élites in national states, commercial businesses, international bureaucracies, and the public is the primary focus – not the doctrinaire and personified influence of states. The authors conclude that Western élites predominate even in UNCTAD; that GATT is becoming preoccupied with problems of the less developed countries; that to avoid preoccupation with problems of the poor, the rich countries are having recourse to 'shadow organizations' of less universal scope like OECD rather than ILO; that decision-making everywhere has become bureaucratized; that the preferred ideology of international organizations is shifting from functionalism (erosion of sovereignty by cooperation) to 'developmentalism' (aid because of need); that contending ideologies of capitalism and socialism are most visible in the larger organizations; that the more technical organizations (ITU, IAEA) permit more cooperation than the more political (ILO, UNESCO); and that the more 'salient' (important) the issues discussed in any organization, the less states will concede decision-making to it. Readers interested in learning more about the agencies may wish to skip over the theory, which is 'behaviorist' and quantitative, and go directly to the chapters.

735 **Beyond functionalism: attitudes toward international organization in Norway and the United States.**
Robert E. Riggs and I. Jostein Mykletun. Minneapolis: University of Minnesota Press, 1979. 224p. bibliog.

This comparative work discusses and critiques David Mitrany's and Ernst B. Haas's theories of functionalism. Both held, generally, 'that national government officials who become personally involved with the activities of international organizations will develop attitudes more favorable to international cooperation'. The authors test this proposition by a social science research design known as 'static group comparison'. The measuring instrument was a questionnaire mailed to civil servants and parliamentarians in both Norway and the United States. They find that increasing experience with the U.N. *does* lead to more favourable attitudes toward international cooperation and the U.N. in general. But (apparently because of the U.S.'s greater power and responsibility in world affairs) it *does not* lead the *U.S.* toward greater reliance on U.N. action and even less toward transfer of sovereignty to the U.N. Strangely, civil servants (supposedly more 'expert') in both countries, were not more disposed to international cooperation than were legislators. The authors conclude with speculations on a theory of world politics 'beyond functionalism' – sometimes called 'interdependence' – which is slowly replacing 'realism'. The territorial state is clearly declining, and world community is slowly being built.

736 **The concept of international organization.**
Edited by Georges Abi-Saad. Paris: UNESCO, 1981. 245p.

'Under the circumstances', writes the editor at a time when the Cold War showed no signs of abating, 'international organization is indispensable for the proper co-ordination of the [world] system through the co-operation of its members.' On this principle, the authors in this authoritative UNESCO study of international organization (IO) discuss the history and types of IO, its political processes (decision-making, functionalism, integration, struggle for power), and the perspectives of the Western liberal capitalist, socialist, and developing worlds. Because of the authors' knowledge, candour, and fairness, this is an excellent choice, as Prof. Abi-Saad says, for the student of international affairs.

737 **Encyclopedia of associations: international organizations.**
Edited by Grant Eldridge. Detroit: Gale Research, 28th ed., 1993. 2 vols.

Here is a standard reference work covering more than 13,500 international organizations (IGOs and NGOs). Extensive coverage of the U.N. system includes specialized agencies, programmes (e.g., UNDP), offices, and national branch offices (over 100); also private associations (UNAs) supporting the work of the U.N. in fields of peace, justice, economic development, disarmament, human rights, women's equality, education, and environmental protection. Entries include the organization's name and address, name of executive director, size, budget, activities, headquarters, facilities (libraries), services (computer networks), further associations, publications, meetings. Indexes (geographical, executive, and name) complement the subject keywords as finding aids. Compare *Yearbook of international organizations* (item no. 750).

738 **International administration: law and management practices in international organizations.**
Edited by Chris de Cooker. Dordrecht, The Netherlands: M. Nijhoff, for UNITAR, 1990. 380p. bibliog.

This is a study by experienced practitioners of the internal functioning – the law and management – of international organizations. It covers programmes within the U.N. system, such as the Secretariat, international civil service, ILO, and World Bank. Also covered are European Community organizations. Topics include: recruitment and retention, staff administration, changing roles and functions of staff members, their independence (privileges and immunities), legal responsibilities, relationship to member-states, social security, and judicial protection. One chapter is devoted to administration and structural reform, which has a valuable survey of proposals and notes. The book should be useful to managers within the system and to scholars interested in the management of complex international organizations.

739 **International agencies: the emerging framework of interdependence.**
Evan Luard. London: Macmillan for Royal Institute of International Affairs, 1977. 338p. bibliog.

The world has grown increasingly interdependent since the middle of the 19th century, when the first international organizations were established to regulate delivery of the mail around the world (UPU) and to communicate by telegraph (ITU). Since 1945 the number of problems requiring coordinated global attention has grown rapidly to include energy, food, population, aircraft hijacking, drug trafficking, regulation of TNCs, and protection of the environment; by the mid-1970s new problems were emerging like satellite communications and climate control. This readable and informative book aims to explain to the layperson and the serious student what are the nature and functions of the many (independent) international agencies, councils, organizations, and programmes that attempt to solve these global problems. Luard surveys the framework of international cooperation in the functional fields of posts, telecommunications, sea and air transportation, space, the sea bed, Antarctica, weather forecasting, energy, labour, health, social policy, trade, money, and economic development. He sees what is happening as a 'new layer of government' being superimposed 'over and above that traditionally performed by national administrations'. The two final chapters are very sensible about the problems of coordination of the autonomous agencies and of compliance by sovereign states.

740 **The international energy agency: state influence and transgovernmental politics.**
Robert Keohane. *International Organization*, vol. 32 (Autumn 1978), p.929-51.

The author applies his 'sophisticated' theory – that international relations are the product of both state behaviour and 'transnational coalitions' – to the International Energy Agency (IEA), founded in 1974 within OECD in response to OPEC's control of oil. The article, then, is a stimulating exercise in post-'realist' theoretical analyses. But it is also full of practical detail about energy, which has never been accommodated within a universal international organization. Keohane finds that transnational politics is important in IEA for the implementation of policy, but that inter-state politics is dominant for policy formation, as for the establishment of IEA itself. By implication, transnationalism is not yet strong enough to elevate energy to the level of the global *problematique*. 'Clearly, the IEA is not destined to become a supranational organization with authority to give orders to governments.'

741 **International institutions at work.**
Edited by Paul Taylor and A.J.R. Groom. London, New York: St. Martin's, 1988. 245p. bibliog.

This is an introduction to the work of international institutions, primarily the United Nations and its associated organizations. Less attention is paid to theory than to practical cooperation in areas of greater public concern by 1987: peace and security, economic cooperation, international civil service, labour, human rights, the law of the sea. Large parts of Maurice Bertrand's 'Some reflections on the reform of the United Nations' (1985) are included. The authors have a broad historical perspective, going back at least to the Congress of Vienna in 1815 – which helps to put the present dangers and opportunities of the U.N. in proper focus.

742 **International organization: a state of the art on an art of the state.**
Friedrich Kratochwil and John G. Ruggie. *International Organization*, vol. 40 (Autumn 1986), p.753-75.

The authors review the literature on 'international governance', which has passed through four phases: formal charters and institutions; actual organizational practices, especially when discrepant with constitutional designs; organizational roles within the context of international politics, e.g. nuclear safeguards, decolonization, functionalist integration; and international 'regimes' (informal unions based on international norms, state practice, and cooperation with international organizations, e.g., trade regimes, ocean regimes, non-proliferation regime). The second half of the article is an epistemological critique of regime theory.

743 **International organizations: a comparative approach.**
Werner J. Feld and Robert S. Jordon with Leon Hurwitz. New York: Praeger, 1983; 2nd ed., 1988. 330p.

This is a leading text on international organizations, newly edited to respond to U.S. scepticism about multilateralism, declining power of the Western industrial democracies since the oil price shocks of 1973 and 1979, and de-Westernization of the U.N. It includes: historical overview, survey of political science approaches, analysis of the existing inter-governmental organizations (IGOs) (not limited to those in the U.N. system), their bureaucracies and decision-making processes, their relations to governments and international non-governmental organizations (INGOs), regimes, and evaluation of their task performance. The growth of these international organizations has been very dramatic. The first IGO was the Rhine River Commission (1815). By 1914, there were 49 IGOs; by 1939, 86; by 1980, 378. The first INGO was the World Evangelical Alliance (1846). By 1914, there were 176; by 1939, 730; by 1980, 2,700. The authors conclude that, while the technical IGOs are flourishing, the economic and political ones are declining in task performance. Reasons for the decline include: state apprehension of loss of sovereignty, state disappointment with the organization as an adjunct to its foreign policy, state and popular perception that the organization's costs outweigh its benefits, state reversion to bilateral diplomacy and novel forms of 'intergovernmentalism', and state and popular 'waning enthusiasm for political and economic world organization in general'. The authors are not doctrinaire 'realists', but this pessimistic conclusion seems rooted in a Cold War frame of mind.

744 **National entanglements in international governmental organizations.**
Harold K. Jacobson, William R. Reisinger and Todd Mathers.
American Political Science Review, vol. 80 (March 1986), p.141-59.
The authors review the phenomenal growth in the number of IGOs (now more than 1,000), which they interpret as upholding 'functionalist predictions'. States create and join such organizations because their citizens demand to participate in national and international life, and because IGOs offer the benefits of technical cooperation. Cooperation, like free trade, will make states less bellicose, functionalism predicts. The authors measure the benefits of IGO membership quantitatively. They warn that too many more such organizations could make them 'progressively irrelevant'.

745 **Networks of interdependency: international organizations and the global political system.**
Harold K. Jacobson.   New York: Knopf, 1979, 2nd ed., 1984. 483p. bibliog.
This is a standard work by a leading American political scientist on international organization, including the U.N. His thesis: 'Humankind is crafting new political institutions that have already contributed significantly to greater global security, to better material welfare through a larger gross world product, and to higher standards of social welfare.' By 1984, some 600 IGOs were in existence. The book is 'optimistic', yet 'not unrealistic'. It is written from an independent, critical point of view – not always favourable to the U.N. – focusing on global problems and humanity's political response. It covers history, philosophical perspectives (federalism, functionalism, Marxism, Leninism), decision-making, structure of international organizations, peace and security, steps to a world economy, promotion of human dignity and justice, human rights, world communications, and the 'erosion of sovereignty' in an 'era of interdependence'. Jacobson concludes that, if additional apocalyptic catastrophes occur, there will be no escaping the logic that international organizations are inadequate to humanity's problems and hence must be centralized under some form of world government; or, if international organizations continue to resolve conflict and promote cooperation, it may be possible for humanity to live indefinitely within a 'non-hierarchical system'. Readers who cannot imagine a middle position between international anarchy (war) and world government will find these final remarks illuminating.

746 **Peace by pieces: United Nations agencies and their roles.**
Edited by Robert N. Wells, Jr.   Metuchen, NJ: Scarecrow, 1991. 482p. bibliog.
Expert articles are here provided on each of the specialized agencies: FAO, GATT, IAEA, IBRD (World Bank), ICAO, IFAD, ILO, IMF, IMO, ITU, UNCTAD, UNIDO, UPU, WHO, WIPO, and WMO. Before each article, the editor provides a brief summary of the agency's organization and functions; the specialist author then examines the agency 'at work'. Special attention is shown to the issue of 'politicization' (the introduction of global issues, like a new international economic order, into fora designed for technical issues, like civil aviation), which was greatly

accelerated by the admission of Third World states into the U.N. system. Fundamentally, politicization, practised now by the Third World no less than the West, marks the end of the functionalist dream that politics could be separated from technical cooperation. It also means the end of the homogeneity of member-states and hence of the imminent possibility of a politics of justice and law. The United States has already withdrawn from the ILO (1977-80), IAEA (1982-83), and UNESCO (1984-) over the issue, and the prospects for world integration seem dim. U.N. reform, to save the situation, will have to extend to the system of agencies.

747   **The specialized agencies and the United Nations: the system in crisis.**
Douglas Williams.   New York: St. Martin's for David Davies
Memorial Institute of International Studies (London), 1987. 279p.
bibliog.

The author, who had the advice of a group of distinguished British diplomats and scholars, discusses the crisis in the United Nations from the perspective of the crisis in at least some (the least technical or most political) of the specialized agencies in the system. The book addresses all the causes that have provoked the United States and Britain to withdraw from UNESCO, withhold funds, and generally relegate the U.N. to the 'outer margin of events'. These causes include the growth in membership often of miniscule states without democratic values, lack of consensus, cultural differences, reduction of the West to a minority in political and economic matters like the Arab–Israeli dispute or the North–South dialogue over a new international economic order, the Soviet Union's 'cynical' propaganda (1985-86), and the mandatory 25 per cent financial contribution by the U.S. when it has no proportionate control over the use of its funds. Williams very ably surveys politically the system and its problems. He discusses past attempts at U.N. reform from the Jackson report (1969) to the Bertrand report (1985), which he supports but warns is not getting as serious a hearing as U.S. Senator Nancy Kassebaum's amendment reducing U.S. contributions to 20 per cent if weighted voting is not introduced into the General Assembly on budgetary questions. He sees hope in the fact that some of the specialized agencies are functioning well. 'Despite the many difficulties of the present and the shortcomings of the past, the U.N. System as a whole has made an important contribution to promoting international prosperity and the organization of peaceful change.'

748   **United Nations specialized agencies: from functionalist intervention to international cooperation?**
Jeffrey Harrod.   In: *The U.N. under attack*. Edited by Jeffrey Harrod and Nico Schrijver.   Aldershot, England: Gower, 1988, p.130-44.

The author reviews the history and future role of the specialized agencies in the U.N. system – particularly WHO, ILO, UNESCO, and FAO. These are still very small ($1,500 million expenditure per year, employing 18,000 people – a fraction of the size of many corporations or cities), yet they are potentially large and effective. They have been justified as the beginnings of a world state, a realistic device to control power, a liberal internationalist approach toward cooperation, and a functional step toward international peace. In practice, they have lent themselves to the hegemony of the United States or of the Geneva Group of Western industrialized countries. But by the 1970s, the Third World began to resist such hegemony with its 'new orders' – the New International Economic Order, New World Information and Communication

Order, Health for All, and World Employment Programme. New orders and the research and publicity demonstrating the need for them have provoked the current political counter-attack, accusing U.N. organizations as nothing more than 'paper mills', 'document factories', and 'talk shops' – inefficient and corrupt. This criticism misses the mark, Harrod argues, for few states have left the U.N. organizations. A more substantial phase of U.N. reform is still ahead.

749 **The United Nations system at Geneva: scope and practices of multilateral diplomacy.**
United Nations Institute for Training and Research. New York: UNITAR, 1991. (E.91.III.K.LS/6).
This is a practical working guide to the U.N. system of offices, centres, programmes, and agencies in Geneva. Special attention is given to multilateral diplomacy and negotiations. The guide includes institutional histories, psychological dimensions, U.N. assistance to governments for shaping global and regional policies and strategies. A supplement covers diplomatic privileges and immunities for state delegates and international officials.

750 **Yearbook of international organizations, 1993-1994.**
Edited by Union of International Associations (Brussels). Munich: K.G. Saur, 30th ed., 1993. 3 vols. + index to comparable guides.
Vol. 1: *Organization descriptions*; Vol. 2: *Country directory*; Vol. 3: *Subject directory.*
Here is a standard reference for international organizations (IGOs and NGOs). By 1993, counting only 'conventional' international organizations, there were 286 IGOs and 4,696 NGOs. Counting most inclusively (subsidiary bodies, religious orders, multilateral treaties, and currently inactive bodies), there were 4,870 IGOs and 27,190 NGOs! Statistical appendixes show the historical progression. Entries include name and address, director, brief history, aims, structure, programme, finance, publications, members (by country), type of organization (federal, universal intergovernmental, regional, internationally-oriented national, etc.), and editor's note (conference, commercial, research, dormant, etc.). Very extensive entries are provided on the United Nations, its regional commissions, information centres, organs, specialized agencies, committees, programmes, offices, other bodies and related organizations. This is the place to go for exact updated information. Compare *Encyclopedia of associations: International organizations* (item no. 737).

International organizations: principles and issues.
See item no. 7.

The United Nations: a handbook.
See item no. 14.

The law-making function of the specialized agencies of the United Nations.
See item no. 97.

Postal union
Universal Postal Union (UPU)

751   **Report on the work of the Union, 1992.**
Universal Postal Union, International Bureau.   Berne: UPU, 1993.
139p.

This annual report contains detailed information on the legal status of the UPU and its members, the next Congress (Seoul, 1994), important meetings, postal services, technical cooperation, relations with the U.N., administration, and finance. By the end of 1992, there were 177 states-members of the UPU, and 174 had ratified the Vienna Constitution of 1964. The UPU has a weighted voting system, ranging from 0.5 units (Uganda) to 50.0 (U.S.A.).

752   **The Universal Postal Union: coordinator of the international mails.**
George A. Codding, Jr.   New York: New York University Press, 1964. 296p. bibliog.

This book is the standard, comprehensive account of the structure and organization of the UPU. The author traces the history of this long-lived IO (founded in 1874), and he analyses its structure and authority for the elements that explain its longevity. The necessity for swift and secure delivery of the mail, even in wartime, was the first of these; its legal independence from such more ambitious IOs like the League of Nations and the United Nations is a second, though the UPU is now a specialized agency of the U.N. Compare Codding's book on the UPU's sister organization, the even older (1865) ITU, *The International Telecommunications Union in a changing world* (item no. 836).

World weather
World Meteorological Organization (WMO)

753   **The regulatory regime for meteorology.**
David M. Leive.   In: *International regulatory regimes.*   Lexington, MA: Lexington Books, 1976. vol. 1, p.153-329.

This is a survey of WMO history, structure, and functions. Particularly covered are the WMO's programmes: the World Weather Watch; environmental programmes, especially on pollution; research, education, and training; and technical cooperation. Leive focuses on the regulatory regime, as a transitional device to a more centralized world legal order. Compare his similar studies of WHO (item no. 855) and FAO (item no. 877) in the same volumes.

754 **World Meteorological Organization annual report, 1992.**
Geneva, WMO, 1950- .
This is the official report of the organization.

Humanitarian aid

U.N. High Commissioner for Refugees (UNHCR)
U.N. Relief and Works Agency (UNRWA)
U.N. Disaster Relief Office (UNDRO)

755 **Calculated kindness: refugees and America's half-opened door, 1945 to the present.**
Gilburt D. Loescher and John A. Scanlon.   New York: Free Press, 1986. 346p. bibliog.
Here is a full-scale history and analytical study of U.S. refugee policy. The United Nations, UNHCR, UNICEF, UNRRA, IRO, UNRWA, and the principal NGOs in the field are brought into the account, so the reader can get a sense of their part in the policies of a Great Power. Since 1945, the United States has revived its invitation to the 'huddled masses yearning to breathe free', and more than two million refugees – many from Asia and Latin America – have been settled in the country. Refugees, if they cannot be repatriated, must be settled somewhere. The authors, though aware of the 'calculated kindness' of American policy, nevertheless find that that policy has become more 'humane' and 'fair' over the years.

756 **The global refugee problem: U.S. and world response.**
Edited by Gilburt D. Loescher and John A. Scanlan.   *American Academy of Political and Social Science Annals*, vol. 467 (May 1983), whole issue. 201p.
By 1939, it was already evident to perceptive editors of the *Annals* that the refugee problem was 'permanent'. The Holocaust in the Second World War demonstrated that 'when exacerbated by prejudice, isolationism, and restrictionism, [it] could be incalculably worse than had ever been imagined'. This volume of political and social science essays focuses on the growth and changing nature of the refugee problem by the 1980s. Leon Gordenker, for instance, argues that the U.N. High Commissioner for Refugees and other intergovernmental organizations 'serve as natural nuclei for expansion [since] more integrated modes of organization currently are of doubtful utility'. Ronald Scheinman argues that the definition of a refugee ought not to be expanded to include the large new class of economic migrants. Other essays deal with political and legal issues.

757 The International Committee of the Red Cross.
Georges Willemin and Roger Heacock. Dordrecht, The Netherlands:
M. Nijhoff, for Graduate Institute of International Studies (Geneva)
and Società Italiana per la Organizzazione Internazionale (Roma),
1984. 209p. bibliog. (International Organization and the Evolution of
World Society No. 2).

The International Committee of the Red Cross may be compared, by virtue of the
magnitude and effectiveness of its humanitarian aid, to the ILO, FAO, and WHO. Yet
it is one of the first international organizations ever founded (1863), and it remains a
'uninational international organization', founded by the Swiss government. (It is
something between a non-governmental organization and an *inter*national
organization. The world political system is full of anomalous creatures.) In recent
decades, especially by the 1980s, world society has been undergoing profound
transformations that challenge all forms of IOs: the spread of independent sovereign
states over all the earth, the redistribution of the balance of power into a multipolar
system, rising tension and conflict that break down old distinctions between internal
and international jurisdictions, great progress of science and technology that yet is
often not directed to human benefit, new demands for international cooperation, the
population explosion, 'transnational' relations, and a general focus on the human
person – on human rights – in the face of continued reaffirmation of the principle of
state sovereignty. This book is an exacting study of the Red Cross as it responds to
these growing challenges. The authors conclude that, in the struggle between
universalism and nationalism, 'the authority and influence of the ICRC have not
ceased to grow'.

758 Organizational expansion and limits in international services for refugees.
Leon Gordenker. *International Migration Review*, vol. 15 (1981),
p.74-87.

The budget for UNHCR has grown six times from 1976 to 1980 (to $500 million);
those for private volunteer agencies like Oxfam have also been rising. Refugees and
their causes, said Sadruddin Aga Khan in 1977, are 'an infallible indicator of the
world's political fever'. As the Cold War heated up in 1981, Gordenker concluded
that the limits of the expansion of UNHCR had been reached, 'barring some quite
drastic policy changes'. UNHCR cannot, by its statute, address the causes of refugee
flows (the oppression of governments); and the scale of operations is already so large
that the organization cannot protect people on an individual basis nor avoid
inefficiency and waste. He looked forward to contraction of such aid agencies, if they
could achieve their original purposes by repatriation and resettlement of people
temporarily under their protection.

759 The Palestinian question: dealing with a long-term refugee situation.
David P. Forsythe. *American Academy of Political and Social
Science Annals*, vol. 467 (May 1983), p.89-101.

The 'Palestine question' has gone through three stages: (1) resistance by Arab states
to refugee resettlement (1947-67); (2) violence by independent Palestinian groups
(PLO, etc.) to assert their claims to self-determination (1967-79); and (3)
international negotiations by Egypt, Israel, and the United States under the Camp

David formula to settle the question. In this context, the author, a leading scholar on human rights, recounts the story of UNRWA. By 1981, its budget was about $160 million, and it cared for 1.8 million refugees, 650,000 of whom lived in camps. UNRWA could not resettle the refugees, but it preserved their lives until the Palestinians were strong enough to recover their autonomy (nearly complete by 1994).

760   **The quality of mercy: Cambodia, holocaust, and modern conscience.**
William Shawcross.   New York: Simon & Schuster, 1984. 464p. bibliog.

Here is a broad, sensitive, historically informed narrative of one poor country whose refugee flows were only the final, visible result of the sorts of internal and international causes at work in many countries. 'I think Cambodia has an importance beyond itself', writes the author, who alerted the whole world to the killing fields, 'because there in its fragile heart paraded, throughout the 1970s, many of the most frightful beasts that now stalk the world. Brutal civil war, superpower intervention carelessly conducted from afar, nationalism exaggerated into paranoid racism, fanatical and vengeful revolution, invasion, starvation, and back to unobserved civil war without end.' Shawcross provides a full account of the roles of the UNHCR, UNICEF, and such NGOs as the Red Cross and Oxfam.

761   **The refugee in international law.**
Guy S. Goodwin-Gill.   Oxford: Clarendon Press, 1983. 318p. bibliog.

This book is an authoritative statement of the current international law on refugees. The author looks forward to development of the law within the broad context of guaranteeing the human rights of all people. He rejects the view that refugees are an 'accepted' result of every conflict, international or domestic. He concentrates on three core issues: the definition of a refugee, the right of asylum, and protection by international institutions (UNHCR), treaty law, and national municipal law. He concludes with a number of special measures to avert and relieve refugee crises, particularly in the context of a proposed new international humanitarian order (1981-82).

762   **Refugee law and policy: international and U.S. responses.**
Edited by Ved P. Nanda.   New York: Greenwood, 1989. 228p. bibliog.

The UNHCR now assists not only persons fleeing persecution (as in its original statute of 1950), but also exiles, asylum-seekers, displaced persons, those fleeing natural disasters and civil strife, and returnees. By 1988 the number of such refugees was about 13 million and growing. The editor surveys the nature and extent of the refugee problem and the international law affecting refugees. The right of asylum is internationally unrecognized, and millions of people who seek the protection of the refugee laws are turned away as ineligible. The authors of the specific articles discuss the international responses, the response of the United States, and the novel responses of citizen diplomats and churches. Nanda concludes that the time has arrived for another round of expansion of international law, to define international *obligations* especially for violations of human rights. He also argues that, at the national level, policy-makers must come to realize that military measures (as in Central America) are often the cause of refugee flows, and that, at the NGO level, actual assistance can best be helped by awakening public opinion.

763 **Refugees in international politics.**
Leon Gordenker.   New York: Columbia University Press, 1987.
227p. bibliog.

At the time of writing, the number of refugees, worldwide, year after year, was about 8-15 million. The author surveys the problem sympathetically, provides an historical perspective, and then expertly describes the international network of organizations – principally the UNHCR, with an annual budget sometimes exceeding $500 million – that attempt to cope with the human disaster. Professor Gordenker was challenged to show 'where multilateral co-operation can be seen to work well'. In this fine book, he concludes with a discussion of what the relatively successful international cooperation for the humanitarian purpose of aiding refugees implies for other purposes of the emerging world community, like the maintenance of international peace and security. He sets out at length the benefits to governments and people of internationalization: for receivers, the international channel ensures prompt and well-directed aid; for donors, the burden is distributed fairly and the risk spread; and even for governments probably responsible for causing the refugee flight, international standards give them a plausible pretext to their people for modifying their conduct and allowing the aid to flow in. But Gordenker, writing when the Reagan administration was particularly hostile to the U.N., was cautious about arguing 'that the example of the international treatment of refugees can be used as a universal guide to constructing additional organized international relationships'.

764 **Refugees: issues and directions.**
Edited by Dennis Gallagher.   *International Migration Review*, vol. 20
(1986), whole issue, p.141-501.

Refugees continue to be generated as fast as they are settled or repatriated. The annual total remains steady at over 10 million. This has led to a 'crisis of durable solutions'. Hence, 'international aid for refugees has become increasingly bogged down with expensive and continuing care and maintenance programs.' The problem is endemic to the Third World, where 95 per cent of all refugees flee from or into developing countries. Five per cent reach industrialized countries, where there is much media attention. The expert articles in this dedicated issue cover recent refugee movements, asylum, protection, the special problems of developing countries, adjustment, and resettlement.

765 **Refugees and international relations.**
Edited by Gilburt Loescher and Laila Monahan.   Oxford: Oxford
University Press, 1989. 430p. bibliog.

The editors find that most of the literature on refugees is merely descriptive, or narrowly legalistic, or historically uncritical. Convinced that, 'since refugees are a global problem, the search for solutions must also be global', they undertake in this book 'to understand refugee issues within their national and international political contexts'. They predict even larger refugee flows over the next twenty-five years, despite continuing sovereign state controls on the entry of foreigners. Hence, they focus on political constraints on the considerable theoretical authority of the UNHCR, on donor governments' national interests which override humanitarian concerns, on use of refugees as instruments of foreign policy ('freedom fighters'), and on the barrier of national sovereignty to addressing the root causes of the problem. The latter exists particularly in new states carved out of colonial empires and unable to provide the respect for human rights and the rule of law that would keep people content in their homelands. The current UNHCR, Jean-Pierre Hocke, begins the book with an up-to-date account of the international refugee situation. Other authors discuss the larger problem of South–North migration, such causes as population pressure and ecological disasters, the growing use of 'humane deterrence' (as in Hong Kong to discourage further Vietnamese boat people), the role of the churches and other NGOs, special European problems, and new responses generally based on respect for the positive contribution of refugees and immigrants on host countries. The conclusion sets out a 'more general, flexible, and cosmopolitan response' within the context of 'collective management and strengthening of existing international refugee institutions'.

766   **Refugees: a problem of our time; the work of the United Nations High Commissioner for Refugees, 1951-1972.**
Louise W. Holborn with Philip and Rita Chartrand.   Metuchen, NJ: Scarecrow, 1975. 2 vols. bibliog.

From the point of view of building a world community on which a free and respected world governing authority could be built, the expression of *international solidarity* for suffering humanity and the slow growth of the authority of the UNHCR are hopeful signs. This book is a closely documented, full-length history of the international response to refugees, beginning in the League of Nations period and continuing through the growth of the U.N. office of the High Commissioner for Refugees by 1972. The author covers the statute of the UNHCR, his work originally in Europe after World War II, the great expansion of the office after the Hungarian uprising of 1956, and its worldwide programmes thereafter. Individual chapters treat the refugee problem in every relevant country in the Western hemisphere, Asia, the Middle East, and Africa. Holborn concludes, in the spirit of David Mitrany: 'In a world in which desperate human problems transcend, but cannot escape national and regional authorities, functional arrangements such as those exemplified in the work of the UNHCR are increasingly relevant to the solution of the global problems of the twentieth century.'

767   **Refugees: a Third World dilemma.**
Edited by John R. Rogge.   Totowa, NJ: Rowman & Littlefield, 1987. 370p. bibliog.

This is a volume of specialized, often quantitative, social science studies of refugee problems and responses in Africa, Southeast Asia, South Asia, Western Asia, and Central America. Readers in search of particular country reports (e.g., Sudan, Tanzania) may find them here. Two chapters are particularly devoted to UNCHR (since 1970, its activities have increased eighteen times, as measured by dollars in its budget). Its budget is still made of voluntary contributions, and state contributors do influence its work, yet on balance, 'humanitarian considerations are far and away the most significant and powerful determinants of aid'. In this field, the world already acts as one.

768 **UNDRO News.**
Geneva: Office of the U.N. Disaster Relief Coordinator, 1966- .
This is the general interest magazine of UNDRO, addressed to the public and officials concerned with disaster relief. It contains stories and information on current disasters, U.N. responses, coordination, discussion of issues, and book reviews.

769 **The United Nations and refugees.**
Leon Gordenker. In: *Politics in the United Nations system.* Edited by Lawrence S. Finkelstein. Durham, NC: Duke University Press, 1988, p.274-302.
Humanitarian assistance to refugees enjoys almost as much international consensus as a uniform postal system or reliable telecommunications. Yet the UNHCR remains a 'dependency of an intergovernmental organization'. The commissioner's powers are limited, the legal definition of a refugee is narrow, protection of refugees touches national immigration policy which is jealously guarded, and funding is voluntary. Gordenker traces the history, structure, and decision-making processes of the agency. Africa gets less attention than Asia for local reasons. Because Palestinians are cared for by another agency (UNRWA), UNHCR is not accused of 'politicization'.

Children and youth

United Nations Children's Fund (UNICEF)
International Year of Youth (1985)

770 **Adolescent reproductive behaviour.** [Vol. I:] **Evidence from developed countries.**
U.N. DIESA. New York: United Nations, 1988. 178p. bibliog. (E.88.XIII.8. ST/ESA/SER.A/109).
Growth in world population increases concerns about teenage pregnancy. This study and the one below attempt to identify and quantify the factors affecting birth rates among adolescents. These factors are: exposure to sexual intercourse, marriage, contraceptive use, and abortion. For each factor, estimates of prevalence are given per country, so that similarities and differences are shown between countries. In developed countries, the overall social fertility rate has fallen to levels near replacement, but adolescent pregnancy, abortion, and birth rates vary considerably among countries.

771 **Adolescent reproductive behaviour.** [Vol. II:] **Evidence from developing countries.**
U.N. DIESA. New York: United Nations, 1989. 139p. (E.89.XIII.10. ST/ESA/SER.A/109/Add.1).
In developing countries, additional factors affecting adolescent birth rates appear to be a lingering cultural attitude that teenage fertility is not a problem and much less

availability of abortion and contraception. Early marriage is still very common; elsewhere, postponement of marriage is the main means available to reduce fertility. (It is striking that this volume has no chapter on abortion, unlike the one above for developed countries.) Data are given per country in Africa, Latin America, the Caribbean, Asia, and Oceana.

772   **Assessment of the impact of measures and activities accomplished during the International Youth Year: Participation, Development, Peace (1985).**
New York: United Nations, 1987. 43p. (E.87.IV.5. ST/ESA/200).
The International Year of Youth was undertaken in the context of admitted 'fragmentation . . . of the entire United Nations system' and of 'lack of a definitive consensus on development strategy'. The U.N., it is plainly stated here, 'cannot fulfill functions similar to those of a national Government or administration'. The Youth Year, like 'Years' on the environment, population, food, refugees, children, women, and disabled persons, was designed as a step toward consensus on 'international policy' – toward 'integration' of the presently unavoidable sectoral organization of the U.N. system. (Maurice Bertrand is cited for a critique of sectoral organization.) The Youth Year was supported by 158 national coordinating committees and there were many aspiring activities, including a world festival of youth in Moscow. But the general conclusion was that the year revealed that youth, too, were suffering in the world economic decline. A 'new perspective on youth' nevertheless emerged – 'that young people are increasingly seen as real agents for development, rather than merely passive recipients of it'.

773   **Blue and beautiful: planet Earth, our home.**
New York: United Nations, 1990. 48p. (E.90.I.15).
This is an attractively illustrated children's book on preserving the environment.

774   **Children and development in the 1990s: a UNICEF sourcebook on the occasion of the World Summit for Children, 29-30 September 1990, United Nations.**
UNICEF. Coordinated by Robert Ledogar.   New York: UNICEF, 1990. 256p. (E.90.XX.USA.8).
This sourcebook should prove invaluable to readers searching for comparative information about the conditions of children worldwide and for collective guidance on improving their protection everywhere. It is organized around an ambitious set of goals for children, such as: reducing the infant mortality rate to 50/1000 live births; providing access by all couples to birth control, and by all pregnant women to pre-natal care; eliminating iodine deficiency disorders; maintaining full immunization for 90 per cent of children in their first year; providing universal access to safe drinking water and to sanitation; and expanding basic education, especially for girls. Global goals, the authors argue, are necessary for problems that cross national boundaries – like drug abuse, AIDS, global warming, and other environmental issues. But even for those that must first be addressed by national programmes, such goals are amenable to élite advocacy, promote inter-agency cooperation, and emerge from common country experiences. Particular attention is devoted here to the Convention on the Rights of the Child (1990). The bulk of the book consists of strategies to reach its goals. The last chapter, on 'Children and the peace dividend', concludes that 'the amounts

needed for meeting the basic needs of children over the coming decade are paltry compared to the sums heretofore devoted to military expenditure and now no longer required for them.'

775 Children and the transition to market economy: safety nets and social policies in Central and Eastern Europe.
Edited by Giovanni A. Corina and Sándor Sipos.   Aldershot, England: Avebury for UNICEF, 1991. 251p. (E.91.XX.ITY.1).

The long decline of communist, centrally planned economies since about 1970, their collapse and breakup in 1989-91, and the difficult transition since then to democratic pluralism and market economy have had serious effects on the health and welfare of children. Economic reforms have required greater social sacrifices than expected, and safety nets have proved inadequately funded and designed. 'This book is a contribution to the growing debate on how to minimize the social costs of the transition to the market economy and [on] what social policies could be developed in the years ahead.' To save the children, the editors make many recommendations to policy-makers, such as setting up an 'early warning' child monitoring system for the public to alert the government. A more socially sensitive economic transition, they argue, will produce a more efficient economic system as well as draw on the 'ethic of solidarity'. Three models of such social policy are presented – that of the United States, Germany, and Sweden. The study makes use of the vast experience of UNICEF.

776 Convention on the Rights of the Child: world campaign for human rights.
New York: United Nations, 1991. 54p. (DPI/1101).

The Convention on the Rights of the Child was signed by sixty-one states in 1990. After receipt of twenty ratifications, it entered into force later that year. (The Declaration on the Rights of the Child preceded it by thirty years.) This short work contains the text of the convention and a brief, positive introduction. Considering that the child, historically, has not been accorded legal rights (in the U.S. case *In re Gault* of 1967, the Supreme Court held that the child has *no* rights), this international convention must represent an advance, particularly in states with a weak rule of law. However, the convention permits drafting children into the armed forces at age fifteen, execution for crime at eighteen, and arrest, detention, and imprisonment at any age, though 'in conformity with the law'. The intention is to protect children; the law, however, cannot be too far in advance of the world community.

777 A dream for peace: human rights drawings by Cambodian children.
U.N. Transitional Authority in Cambodia, Human Rights Component. Edited by Jamie Metzl.   New York: United Nations, 1993. 51p.

A book for children of all ages, in English and Cambodian. Quotes by Venerable Maha Ghosananda are included.

778   **A global, regional, and country assessment of child malnutrition.**
Beverly A. Carlson and Tessa M. Wardlaw.   New York: UNICEF,
1990. 128p. (Staff Working Paper No. 7. E.90.XX.USA.1).
Freedom from hunger and malnutrition is a basic human right. This study by
UNICEF, in cooperation with WHO and FAO, finds that about 150 million children in
the developing world (76 countries, excluding China) are malnourished or
underweight for their age. If current targets for food distribution by the year 2000 are
met, the number of malnourished children should be reduced to 75 million, rather
than increase to 178 million. The study breaks new ground in gathering quantitative
data for measuring the problem.

779   **Let's learn about the United Nations: a coloring book for children.**
Emery Kelen.   New York: United Nations, 1963.
Derso and Kelen were the original humorists of the United Nations, after 1945. This
colouring book continues their delights.

780   **Pepita's speech at the United Nations.**
Margaret and John Moore. Illustrated by Denise and Fernando.   New
York: United Nations, 1989. (E.89.17).
This is a wiser speech than most.

781   **Perspectives on contemporary youth.**
Edited by Janusz Kuczyński.   Tokyo: U.N. University, 1988. 268p.
(E.88.III.A.2).
This is the first formal report on the research component of the UNU's Project on
Youth (1983-). There is also a video component, produced by young participants in
a worldwide village network, *Young voices*. The report above studies the 'critical
situation' of youth from a variety of disciplinary perspectives. 'Even a cursory
glance', writes the editor, 'indicates that youth, and particularly its hidden creative
potential, is continuously contained and exploited for the wrong reasons.' The aim of
the work is to provide a 'synthesis of contemporary knowledge about youth'. Youth is
studied from the perspectives of sociology, literature, psychology, philosophy,
economics, and politics. There are case-studies on youth in Africa, Latin America,
Europe, Japan, India, and worldwide youth movements. The general tenor is that, as
the world, while the population rapidly expands, becomes increasingly young, young
people will find themselves 'on the threshold of historical transformation', as
Kuczyński writes, or of 'revolutionary orientations' like that at the breakthrough to
modernity, whose 'materialism, restriction, exploitation, and lack of opportunity for
self-fulfilment and creativity' will be rejected by many for 'dreams of a new life, a
new society, freedom and spontaneity, a new humanity', as S.N. Eisenstadt writes.

782   **State of the world environment, 1990: children and the
environment.**
UNEP and UNICEF.   New York: United Nations, 1990. 74p.
(E.90.XX.USA.2).
This is a book for schoolteachers about the environment or for students of children's
responses to environmental change.

783 **Universal Declaration of Human Rights: an adaptation for children.**
Ruth Rocha and Otavio Roth.   New York: United Nations, 1989. 46p.
'Everyone has the right to go to school, and school must be free. . . . Education should emphasize understanding, comprehension, tolerance, and friendship.' All the human rights are recast into simpler language and illustrated in a way that will catch a child's fancy. For children 6-12 years of age.

784 **World Declaration on the Survival, Protection, and Development of Children.** [And] **Plan of action for implementing the World Declaration in the 1990s.**
U.N. Department of Public Information.   New York: United Nations, 1990. 23p. (E.90.XX.USA.11).
At the Children's Summit in 1990, seventy-three heads of state and ministers agreed to this declaration and plan of action. The former sets out standards for political leaders, and the latter provides recommended actions for saving, protecting, and developing children.

785 **Youth: identifying measures for strengthening channels of communication between the United Nations and youth and youth organizations.**
New York: United Nations, 1985. 46p.
Prepared for the International Year of Youth (1985), this short work contains suggestions for maintaining young people's contacts with the U.N.

World population

U.N. Population Division
U.N. Fund for Population Activities (UNFPA)

786 **Concise report on the world population situation in 1989; with a special report on population trends and policies in the least developed countries.**
U.N. Department of International Economic and Social Affairs (DIESA), Population Division.   New York: United Nations, 1991. 31p. (Population Studies No. 118. E.90.XIII.32. ST/ESA/SER.A/118).
This concise report (seventh since 1968) covers population trends and policies at the global, regional, and least developed country levels. Topics include: rate of growth, structure of population, mortality, fertility, internal distribution, and international migration. The world's population is expected to reach 6,200 million by the year 2000, and 8,200 million in 2025.

787 **Long-range world population projections: two centuries of
population growth, 1950-2150.**
U.N. DIESA. New York: United Nations, 1992. 35p. (E.92.XIII.3).
Since the rate of growth is declining, the total world population is expected to level
off at not much more than 11,000 million well before 2150. The work provides long-
range projections for nine major regions of the world.

788 **Population growth and policies in mega-cities: Mexico City.**
U.N. DIESA. New York: United Nations, 1991. 34p. bibliog.
(Population Policy Paper No. 32. E.91.XIII.3. ST/ESA/SER.R/105).
This slim volume is one of a series that focuses on cities of more than eight million
inhabitants in developing countries. The emphasis is on broad policies relating
population to development in the spirit of the World Population Plan of Action.
Covered for each city are demographic trends, economic base, decentralization
strategies, key issues (labour, land, housing, water, etc.), and public investment. Other
cities studied by 1991 are: Bangkok (ST/ESA/SER.R/72), Bombay (67), Cairo (103),
Calcutta (61), Delhi (68), Dhaka (69), Jakarta (86), Karachi (77), Madras (75), Manila
(65), and Seoul (64).

789 **Population in the United Nations system: developing the legal
capacity and programs of U.N. agencies.**
Daniel G. Partan. Leiden, The Netherlands: Sijthoff, 1973. 219p.
U.N. action in the field of population has passed through three phases: statistical
studies (1950s), technical assistance to governments (1960s), and operational
responsibilities with impacts on individuals and non-governmental organizations. The
legal basis for such action is the 1974 General Assembly resolution providing that
population policies and programmes are matters within the 'internal competence' of
states, combined with the developing international law of human rights, which grants
the U.N. a certain 'international competence'. The author explores this legal dialectic
with respect to family planning, national population policy, international development
aid, the human environment, population research, training, and the work of WHO,
UNICEF, FAO, ILO, UNESCO, the World Bank, and the Regional Economic
Commissions.

790 **The prospects of world urbanization.**
U.N. DIESA. New York: United Nations, 1990. 223p. bibliog.
(Population Studies No. 112. E.91.XIII.11. ST/ESA/SER.A/112).
Not only is the world's population growing at the rate (1989) of 1,000 million per 12
years, but most of the increase will be concentrated in urban areas. The United States
became 50 per cent urbanized by 1920; the world will be, in 2010. The total urban
population then will probably be on the order of 3,800 million. In 1989, there were
twelve cities of ten million or more inhabitants; in 2000, there will be twenty-three,
seventeen in the Third World. Nevertheless, the *rate* of growth is declining
everywhere, even in South Asia and Africa. This report provides data on 205
countries in 24 regions.

791 **Studies to enhance the evaluation of family planning programmes.**
U.N. DIESA. New York: United Nations, 1984. 246p. (Population
Studies No. 87. E.84.XIII.9. ST/ESA/SER.A/87).

This is an expert study on the effectiveness and improvement of family planning
programmes. Addressed mainly to other experts, the study includes a scientific
critique of methods of measurement, eveluation, application of methods, and the
prevalence model. John A. Ross provides a final overview.

792 **Trends in population policy.**
U.N. DIESA. New York: United Nations, 1989. 387p. (Population
Studies No. 114. E.89.XIII.13. ST/ESA/SER.A/114).

Since the first U.N. World Population Conference at Bucharest in 1974, the U.N. has
been monitoring national population policies and reporting them in this series of
Trends and in the parallel *Concise reports*. The above volume in the series tabulates
qualitative data on 156 countries for 1974-89. Variables include: population growth,
fertility, contraceptive use, mortality, immigration, emigration, and spatial
distribution. The trends are then summarized quantitatively and discussed at the
global level.

793 **World population, 1992.**
U.N. DIESA. New York: United Nations, 1992. (E.92.XIII.12.
ST/ESA/SER.A/132).

This fold-out wall chart presents the basic historical and future facts of world
population (1950-2025) in a format that can be taken in at a glance. Figures are given
for world, regions, and countries. For the world in 1992, the percentage of the
population under 15 was 32 per cent; the median age, 24; and the urban concentration
was 43 per cent.

794 **World population at the turn of the century.**
U.N. DIESA. New York: United Nations, 1989. 126p. (Population
Studies No. 111. E.89.XIII.2. ST/ESA/SER.A/111).

This is the sixth report on world population, now projected to rise to 8,206 million by
2025. Maximum world population is not as high as previously predicted because
more and more countries, even in the Third World, have entered the 'demographic
transition' (steady state). Malaysia, South Korea, and Thailand are nearly there.
China, too, has achieved a very rapid decline in the population growth rate,
apparently, as in Japan, by permitting legal abortions on a large scale. The work
contains abundant figures and observations on all regions and most countries.
Example: 'Seventh observation. The decline in fertility is a function of development
levels and family planning efforts.'

795 **World population monitoring, 1989. Special report on the
population situation in the least developed countries.**
U.N. DIESA. New York: United Nations, 1990. 260p. (Population
Studies No. 113. E.89.XIII.12. ST/ESA/SER.A/113).

The developing regions of the earth, with about three-quarters of its population, are
growing at 2.1 per cent annually; the developed regions, at 0.6 per cent. This volume

looks particularly at the population problem in 41 least developed countries (excluding China). Impacts on economic development, hunger, disease (AIDS), the environment, refugees, housing, and education are assessed.

796   **World population policies.**
       U.N. DIESA.   New York: United Nations, 1990. 3 vols. (Population Studies No. 102. E.90.XIII.2. ST/ESA/SER.A/102/Add.2).
This series (begun in 1987) continues the *Population policy compendia* (1979-86), briefer summaries for each state-member of the U.N. (170 in 1990). Variables measured include: population growth, mortality, fertility, migration, urbanization.

797   **World population prospects: the 1992 revision.**
       U.N. Department for Economic and Social Information and Policy Analysis.   New York: United Nations, 1993. 677p. (E.93.XIII.7. ST/ESA/SER.A/135).
This is the latest revision (the first was in 1951) of the U.N.'s estimates of the world's population and its projections into the future. The 1992 revision takes into account the unions of Germany and of Yemen, the breakup of the U.S.S.R. into fifteen countries, new migrations, refugee flows, and even the impact of the Persian Gulf War. A separate chapter measures the demographic impact of AIDS on fifteen African countries. The world's population is expected to rise to about 8,200 million by 2025. Graphs and tables are particularly clear and complete. Some 211 countries in 22 regions are covered. This is probably the volume that most readers will consult for both general trends and detailed quantitative estimates.

798   **World population trends and their impact on economic development.**
       Edited by Dominick Salvatore.   New York: Greenwood, 1988. 238p. bibliog.
This volume of expert articles re-examines the seemingly self-evident proposition that unchecked population growth leads to declining standards of living in developing countries. Part I takes up this task; Part II deals with internal and international migration; and Part III examines technological change, the role of women, and the economic and social performance of small countries. The final essay concludes that, under many circumstances, it is reasonable for developed countries to put conditions on their aid to underdeveloped ones.

Demographic yearbook, 1991.

See item no. 800.

Statistics

U.N. Statistical Division

799 **Commodity trade statistics, [1992].**
U.N. Department of International Economic and Social Affairs
(DIESA), Statistical Division.   New York: United Nations, 1962- .
annual. vol. 41, nos. 1-1 to 1-31. (ST/ESA/STAT/SER.D/109-01 to
109-31).

'This series of publications contains the detailed import and export trade statistics of
most of the countries or areas of the world, presented by commodity and trading
partner.' The classification of commodities is according to the Standard International
Trade Classification. All values are given in thousands of U.S. dollars. Data are
presented for aggregates of world and region as well as for principal trading nations.
The flows of several thousand commodities (e.g., steam turbines, fresh apples) can
here be traced. There are as many 'numbers' within each annual 'volume' as
necessary to reproduce the tables for each state-member of the U.N. from Afghanistan
to Zimbabwe.

800 **Demographic yearbook. Annuaire démographique, 1991.**
U.N. DIESA.   New York: United Nations, 1948- . annual. 2 vols.
1: general tables; 2: special topics. (E/F.92.XIII.1.
ST/ESA/STAT/SER.R/21).

Official demographic statistics from 216 countries and areas are presented here.
World and regional summaries are printed first, then country data. Statistics include:
population, natality, foetal mortality, legally induced abortions, infant and maternal
mortality, general mortality, and nuptuality. In 1979, an *Historical supplement* was
issued, which presents time-series on population size, age, sex and urban/rural
residence, etc. for the thirty-year period, 1948-78. Readers will find there a wealth of
historical data collected in one volume.

801 **Energy statistics yearbook, 1990. Annuaire des statistiques de
l'énergie.**
U.N. DIESA.   New York: United Nations, 1956- . annual. 482p.
(E.92.XVII.3. SR/ESA/STAT/SER.J/34).

This yearbook provides 'comparable data on long-term trends in the supply of mainly
commercial primary and secondary forms of energy' (solid, liquid, and gaseous fuels,
electricity, and nuclear power). Data are presented by country, region, and world.

802 **Global report on human settlements.**
U.N. Centre for Human Settlements (Habitat). Foreword by Arcot
Ramachandran.   Oxford: Oxford University Press, 1987. 229p.

Habitat was founded in 1979 to assist governments in improving their settlement
policies, plans, and programmes. The objective of international cooperation to
improve housing is 'a satisfying living and working environment for the present and
future members of the world's community'. This first large-scale report sets out the

concept of human settlement within a strategy for development; it then traces global conditions, trends, and prospects for both developed and developing countries; it discusses such key policy questions as management of settlements, institutions, financing, land, infrastructure, construction, and shelter; and it concludes by returning to strategies for improvement. A statistical annex complements the book. Since the report is unillustrated, readers might like to compare *Human settlement*, edited by John R. Short (Oxford University Press, 1992).

803 **Human development report, 1991.**
U.N. Development Programme. Mahbub ul Haq, project director.
New York: Oxford University Press, 1990- . annual. 202p.

'The lack of political commitment, not of financial resources, is often the real cause of social neglect', is the principal finding here. The focus in this report is on public spending for human development. It differs from other socio-economic reports in that it has created two new measures – the human development index and the human freedom index. They supplement such conventional measures as per capita income. Here readers will find comparative national and regional data – attractively laid out – on financing for greater participation and choice in development, on access to income producing employment, on education, health, a safe environment, and democratic political life. Special attention is given to the needs of women and children. The report concludes with a 'political strategy' to establish a 'global compact' to commit political will to the fulfillment of all people's potential.

804 **Industrial statistics yearbook, 1991.**
U.N. Department for Economic and Social Information and Policy Analysis, Statistical Division. New York: United Nations, 1968- . annual. appeared 1993 in 2 vols. (E.93.XVIII.7. ST/ESA/STAT/SER.P/31).

Published since 1968, this annual compilation on world industry aims to meet the demand for information by the public and UNIDO. It is now published in two volumes annually: (1) general production statistics, and (2) commodity production statistics. The above 1993 edition contains data from 1987 to 1991. Industrial activity and structure for individual countries is first presented, then comparative index numbers for production and employment finish the volume.

805 **International trade statistics yearbook, 1991. Annuaire statistique du commerce international.**
U.N. DIESA. New York: United Nations, 1953- . annual. 2 vols. (E/F.93.XVII.2. ST/ESA/STAT/SER.G/40).

Vol. 1 presents trade statistics by country; vol. 2, by commodity. Data include: volume of imports and exports, economic categories of imports (by end use) and exports (by industrial origin), dollar value of trade, and value of commodities. Regional and world summaries are also given.

806 **International trade, 1993: statistics.**
Geneva: GATT, 1952- . annual. 120p. (GATT/1993-10).

Available in English, French, and Spanish, this annual volume presents GATT's statistics on world trade and merchandise trade by region and by product. Business people, government policy-makers, and international civil servants will find this an up-to-date reference work.

807   **The least developed countries, 1991 report.**
      UNCTAD Secretariat. Overview by K.K.S.Dadzie.   New York:
      United Nations, 1984- . annual. 187p. (E.92.II.D.1. TD/B/1312).
In 1972, the U.N. identified 24 countries as 'least developed' (LDCs); in 1991, the list had grown to 47. The LDCs' combined population exceeds 500 million. 'The LDCs are the weakest partners in the international community', admits the report. Yet, even in the depressed times of the 1980s, eleven of these LDCs achieved *improved* living standards, and six increased their per capital GDP. This volume of interpretation and analysis, which includes an annex of statistical data, deals with the particular problems of the LDCs for their governments and the international community. The UNCTAD Secretary-General, Kenneth Dadzie, sees 'grounds for optimism'. A reform process has long been under way to re-establish conditions for long-term growth (stabilization) and to improve the efficiency of public enterprises (privatization). There has also been progress in trade diversification and popular participation. But increased official development assistance (ODA), more favourable GATT negotiations, and further debt relief will also be required.

808   **Report on the world social situation, 1989.**
      U.N. DIESA.   New York: United Nations, 1952- . quadrennial. 126p.
      (E.89.IV.1. ST/ESA/213. E/CN.5/1989/2).
Socially and economically, the 1980s have been a decade of profound change. In Western Europe, economic growth has resumed, but unemployment remains high. In Eastern Europe, the reform process is causing major political, economic, and social upsets. In most of Asia, food and industrial production is consolidating. In Africa and Latin America, socio-economic conditions have worsened. This report gives special attention to the problems of developing countries, especially 'structural adjustment' (linked to debt) and rural development. Topics include: the family, women, food, inequality and poverty, new technologies, the environment, security and disarmament, drug abuse, terrorism, AIDS, migrants, refugees, and the critical social situation in Africa.

809   **The state of food and agriculture, 1981. World review: Rural**
      poverty in developing countries and means of poverty alleviation.
      Rome: FAO, 1957- . annual. 177p. bibliog. (Agriculture Series
      No. 14).
In 1981, there had been a 'frustrating lack of progress' in international cooperation over food and agricultural and rural development. The North–South summit at Cancún proved, in retrospect, to mark the end of 'global negotiations' – not their resumption. The world economy was entering a period of 'inflation, unemployment, monetary and exchange rate instability, and rising trade protectionism'. Nevertheless, FAO ploughed on, as this interpretive and statistical report demonstrates. It contains a review of the food and agricultural situation, long-term trends and prospects, the situation in rural areas, and means of alleviating rural poverty.

810   **Statistical yearbook. Annuaire statistique.**
      U.S. DIESA.   New York: United Nations, 1948- . annual. 38th ed.,
      1993. 1,109p. (E/F.93.XVII.1. ST/ESA/STAT/SER.S/14).

The *Statistical yearbook* has been appearing since 1948; the above 1993 edition contains data from 1981 to 1991. The yearbook provides a 'comprehensive compilation of internationally available statistics on social and economic conditions and activities in the world'. Population and social data, national accounts, government finance, labour forces, international trade, balance of payments are typical of the contents. There are summaries at the regional and world levels, but the bulk of the data are presented by nation.

811   **Statistical yearbook. Annuaire statistique. Anuario estadístico, 1993.**
      Paris: UNESCO, 1993. *c*.600p.

This yearbook prints reference data on education (enrolment, expenditure), science and technology (manpower, types of R&D, development), and culture (book production, newspaper circulation, film production, broadcasting, museums). An appendix lists member-states: the U.S. and U.K. are conspicuous by their absence.

812   **Trade and development report, 1991.**
      UNCTAD Secretariat. Overview by Kenneth K.S. Dadzie.   New
      York: United Nations, 1981- . annual. 209p. (E.91.II.D.15.
      UNCTAD/TDR/11).

In 1991, the world economy was in recession. The West was absorbing the unification of Germany, the centrally planned socialist countries were trying to convert to the free market, and the developing countries (generally in Africa and Latin America) had been stagnating for a decade. In trade, 'the developed market economy countries have forfeited their position in the vanguard of trade liberalization: some developing countries and economies in transition (such as Chile, Mexico, and Poland) have assumed the pioneering role', argues Secretary-General Dadzie. This interpretive and quantitative report covers the world economy, the effects of international markets on developing countries, recent trade policies, the savings shortage, financial fragility and reform, and the GATT talks (agricultural reform, intellectual property, banking services).

813   **World development report, 1993: investing in health; world development indicators.**
      World Bank.   New York: Oxford University Press, 1977- . annual.
      329p. bibliog.

Published since 1977, this statistical volume prints the most complete available figures for GNP per capita, growth of production, and other indicators for all countries. Fiscal and monetary accounts, international trade, and external finance (including ODA and debt) are included. Each volume also covers a special topic: that for 1993 was 'investing in health'; for 1992, 'development and the environment'; 1991, 'the challenge of development'; 1990, 'poverty'.

814 **World economic survey, 1992: current trends and policies in the world economy.**
U.N. DIESA. New York: United Nations, 1947- . annual. 232p. (E.92.II.C.1. E/1992/40. ST/ESA/231).

Addressed to governments, policy-makers, the U.N. General Assembly and Ecosoc, academics, and the public, this annual survey provides an overview of the world economy. It includes: output trends, macroeconomic policies, trends in world trade, savings and investment, the shortages of global savings, net financial transfers among countries, the oil and gas markets, conversion of military industries to civilian production, and lastly, entrepreneurship as a major factor of economic development. An annex contains world economic and financial statistics. This is an interpretive report – not a mere reference volume of computer-generated data.

815 **World economic survey, 1992-93: student edition.**
U.N. DIESA. New York: United Nations, 1991- . annual. 203p. (E.92.II.C.3).

For students and the general public, this concise edition will provide both clear explanations and reliable information on trends and issues in the world economy. Chapters cover the state of the world economy; the First, Second, and Third 'Worlds'; military conversion (the 'peace dividend'); international trade, finance, and energy; debt and development; and the causes, nature, and incidence of poverty. This modest-sized book is a virtual primer on the world economy. Compare the companion *Reader*.

816 **World health statistics annual. Annuaire de statistiques sanitaires mondiales.**
Geneva: WHO, 1962- . annual. *c*.500p.

Since 1977, the World Health Organization has been aiming at the goal of 'health for all by the year 2000'. This large volume is a record of the monitoring and evolution necessary to achieve such a goal. Twelve global indicators have been chosen (e.g., percentage of GNP spent on health, mortality rates). Measures are presented for regions and the basic developed/developing groupings. The bulk of the volume consists of vital statistics by country and region, and then of specific causes of death by country.

817 **The 1983 world programme on industrial statistics: principal indicators and related data.**
U.N. DIESA. New York: United Nations, 1981- . decennial. 980p. (E.90.XVII.7. ST/ESA/STAT/SER.P/27).

This work presents the latest available comparative industrial data (principal indicators, values, capital, energy) on the structure of world industry. The work is complete enough here to show data from 65 countries – of 174 from whom information was sought; two-thirds of the developed and one-third of the developing are represented. (In 2001, the 1993 report should be even more complete.) Data collected here would otherwise have to be found in national publications all over the globe. Machine-readable files are available.

818 **World statistics in brief: United Nations statistical pocketbook.**
U.N. DIESA.   New York: United Nations, 1964- . biennial. 117p.
(E.92.XVII.5. ST/ESA/STAT/SER.V/14).
Small enough to fit into a shirt pocket, this compact little booklet presents 'important
and frequently consulted statistical indicators' for all the states-members of the U.N.
Comparative figures are presented on population, economic activity, agriculture and
industry, international trade and prices, tourism, transport, communications,
education, health, and nutrition. Fold-out end-papers provide an easy-to-read key.
Data are provided for countries, regions, and world.

Annual bulletin of steel statistics for Europe, 1991.
See item no. 1213.

Statistics of world trade in steel, 1992.
See item no. 1221.

Compendium of statistics and indicators on the situation of women.
See item no. 1288.

1989 World survey on the role of women in development.
See item no. 1298.

The world's women, 1970-1990.
See item no. 1299.

Civil aviation

International Civil Aviation Organization (ICAO)

819 **Annual report of the Council, 1992.**
International Civil Aviation Organization. Montreal: ICAO, 1947- .
annual.
Here is the official report on the work of the organization.

820 **The freedom of the air.**
Edited by Edward McWhinney and Martin A. Bradley.   Leiden,
The Netherlands: A.W. Sijthoff, 1968. 259p.
To be fully enjoyed by all nations, freedom of the air must be subject to some legal
limitations. Similarly, all national rights and freedoms are secured by the rule of law,
and progress in the legal regulation of civil aviation in the interests of all may some
day set a precedent for the whole United Nations. This older book on the ICAO
reflects this perspective for the future. One of the innovations by 1968, since states
were unwilling to delegate necessary powers to the intergovernmental organization,
was the virtual asumption of such powers by the International Air Transport
Association, a mixed private–governmental association of airlines licensed by

governments (not quite an NGO). The book covers this association, regionalism, bilateral air transport agreements, problems like the conflict between scheduled and non-scheduled air services, registration of aircraft, air piracy, multinational airlines, and the related law of outer space.

821 **Conflict issues and international civil aviation decisions: three case studies.**
Young W. Kihl.   Denver, CO: University of Denver Press, 1971. 96p.
(Social Science Foundation Monograph, Series in World Affairs,
vol. 8, no. 1).

The author briefly surveys the history of the ICAO to 1967. By this date, some ten percent of world industrial production was related to air transport. Three cases decided by the ICAO – lateral separation over the Atlantic Ocean, origin and destination statistics exchange, and passenger liability – are studied in depth. Kihl finds that the ICAO has an 'essentially limited role in conflict settlement' solving only the technical problems, while leaving the substantive ones to the leading governmental actors.

822 **ICAO Bulletin** (Montreal), 1947-89[, and] **ICAO Journal,** 1990- .
monthly.

This is the 'official magazine of international civil aviation'. It is published in English, French, and Spanish editions, plus a quarterly digest in Russian. Earlier versions of the *Bulletin* carry the record back to the founding of the ICAO in December 1944; the *Journal* continues it from January 1990. By the latter date, the ICAO had a membership of 162 nation states, and the *Journal* reached readers in 186 nations and territories. Covered are a concise account of the activities of the ICAO and mostly scientific and technical articles on civil aviation around the globe.

823 **An introduction to air law.**
I.H.Ph. Diederiks-Verschoor.   Deventer, The Netherlands: Kluwer,
1983. 185p. bibliog.

This is a concise survey of the law of the air, with special attention to new technological innovations. Covered are history, the Chicago Convention of 1944, liability under the Warsaw Convention of 1929, damages, insurance, rights, assistance in distress, salvage, and penal law under the Tokyo Convention of 1963.

824 **Law-making in the International Civil Aviation Organization.**
Thomas Buergenthal.   Syracuse, NY: Syracuse University Press,
1969. 247p. bibliog.

This is an international legal study, from the procedural school, of the law and practice of the ICAO. The author is impressed with the potential of such a technical organization to show the way toward greater international cooperation. 'The relative sucess of [ICAO's] law-making techniques', Buergenthal concludes, 'demonstrate that it is by no means impossible for an organization of some 116 states [in 1969] to make considerable progress in regulating the conduct of governments.' He traces the influence of law on the political decision-making process of the organization in the fields of membership, technical legislation, dispute settlement, and amendments to its Convention of 1947.

825 **The multilateral agency: the approach, the perspective, and the means.**
Assad Kotaite.   Cambridge, MA: Massachusetts Institute of
Technology, 1981. 21p. (Flight Transportation Laboratory Report,
R-81-4).

The president of the ICAO Council here presents a brief lecture on the international
agency to students at MIT. The dream that airspace, like the high seas, should be free
to navigation and commerce did not survive the First World War. 'Therefore', Kotaite
explains, 'state security and economic considerations ensured that national
sovereignty of the airspace was the predominant principle.' He traces the origins of
the ICAO in order to meet the common challenges of the 'air age' after World War II.
The organization's progress in technical and legal areas has generally exceeded that
in regulation and economic spheres. He devotes much space to economic problems
through the 1970s – particularly disunity on fares and rates and an increasing trend
back toward bilateralism. The Special Air Transportation Conference of 1977, which
addressed regulatory and economic aspects of international civil aviation, marked a
new approach. He concludes with a survey of the more technical work, especially
studies and monitoring.

826 **Procedures for the settlement of aerial incidents.**
E.R.C. Van Bogaert.   *Studia Diplomatica* (Brussels), vol. 33 (1980),
p.511-37.

Since the international law of the air recognizes the sovereignty of the state over its
air space, the problem arises of aircraft, without authorization of the state concerned,
straying above foreign territory. There are three sorts of such 'incidents': accident,
defiance of an international agreement, or attack or error that leads to military
retaliation. The author explains how such conflicts are resolved by current
international law, which necessarily requires modification of exclusive sovereignty.
Van Bogaert's approach is broadly historical and legal. He treats only aerial disputes
between states – not those between air transport companies, which are generally
settled by negotiation rather than judicial procedures. The former class of disputes are
generally settled by diplomacy, adjudication before the ICJ, or by appeal to the ICAO
Council. The full range of cases from 1915 to 1977 – including the U-2 incident of
1960 – is discussed. He concludes that for the settlement of aerial incidents, most of
which are as common, as in Britain, of two to three per week, governments do not
have recourse to international jurisdiction, conciliation, or even diplomacy. In all but
'important' cases, governments settle by direct bilateral negotiation.

**The law-making functions of the specialized agencies of the United
Nations.**
See item no. 97.

Telecommunications

International Telecommunications Union (ITU)

827 **The coming information age: an overview of technology, economics, and politics.**
Wilson P. Dizard, Jr.   New York: Longman, 1982; 3rd ed., 1989.
250p. bibliog.

This book, written by a retired U.S. Foreign Service Officer and now a senior fellow at the Center for Strategic and International Studies in Washington, treats international communications primarily from the perspective of U.S. policy, though the United Nations and the ITU are brought into the account. As the 'air age' gave way to the 'atomic age', Dizard observes, so has the latter been replaced by the 'information age'. The U.N. has set a goal of a telephone within an hour's walk of every village by the early 21st century, and the number of electronic communications and computing devices on and orbiting the earth must be approaching the number of neurons in the human brain. (The next age may be that of the artificial global intelligence.) Dizard realistically faces the new prospects in his chapter on 'The politics of change'. Control of new information resources and communications channels is displacing the military and police as the forces of state. To preserve participatory democracy and a strong economy, he calls for reorganization of the U.S. federal government's communications establishment, policies to develop a 'full-service national information grid', and foreign policies favouring *export* of the American-designed communications network and opposing 'political restrictions on the growth of the world system'.

828 **Communications satellites: power politics in space.**
Larry Martinez.   Dedham, MA: Artech, 1985. 160p. bibliog.

This book – equally at home when discussing the inspiration of a technology that is uniting the world, or when delving into the practical technical details – surveys the states and IOs involved, examines the reasons for the 'politicization' of the ITU, and suggests a 'collective good' solution to the problem of equitably allocating the new, scarce but common resources of the orbit and radio frequency band. Underdeveloped countries fear that developed ones are gaining an unfair advantage by early entry into space; hence, they advocate long-range planning. Developed countries fear that the underdeveloped are pursuing a strategy to convert the ITU from a technical and passive standards-setting body into an aggressive international development agency using its budget – paid for by the rich – to finance satellite and telecommunications projects in the Third World. Martinez argues that the debate over access masks a hidden agenda over the New World Information and Communications Order (NWICO), the U.S. policy of anti-ballistic missile defence in space (SDI), and hence emplacing weapons in space. His solution is to disguise the collective good of the geosynchronous orbit and radio spectrum as a private good, by breaking the ITU into regional organizations, and INTELSAT into regional, national, and specialized competitors.

829 **Global communications and international relations.**
Howard H. Frederick.   Belmont, CA: Wadsworth, 1983. 400p.

In this comprehensive textbook on global communications, the United Nations and its specialized agencies dealing with communications figure as a detail. The 'centerpiece' of the book, explains the author, is the chapter on communications in war and peace. He has a normative approach, favouring use of global communications for peace and international understanding, but in an anarchic world he is constrained by the facts to emphasize the dangers of war. Readers will probably find the book realistic without loss of all idealism. Frederick, in the chapter on 'New world orders', critiques the U.N., the proposed NIEO and NWICO, the activities of UNESCO, and U.S. policy at the world level. In the chapter on 'Information law', he shows that without law there would be 'chaos in the airwaves' and argues in favour of a human right to *communication*. But a working world law of communications he leaves as a 'vision for the future'.

830 **Global *glasnost*: toward a new world information and
communications order?**
Johan Galtung and Richard C. Vincent.   Cresskill, NJ: Hampton
Press, 1992. 272p. map.

The New World Information and Communications Order (NWICO), like the New International Economic Order (NIEO), seemed by the 1990s to have been firmly defeated. Yet – since the First World retains control over the production, distribution, and consumption of news, and since its biases continue to favour stories relevant to itself (the 'center' countries), élites everywhere, personal rather than systemic cases, and negative events – the need for some kind of 'new global and human journalism' goes unmet. As the authors argue, 'the more global the problems, the more we need a new global journalism.' Galtung and Vincent re-explore the whole issue of a NWICO, especially with respect to the NIEO, and even other international orders (technical, military, political). They analyse the existing world communications situation and discuss the needs for a new kind of coverage of issues of peace, development, ecology, and war. This is a serious book, written gracefully and informatively by two leading social scientists.

831 **The hidden war of information.**
Enrique Gonzalez-Manet. Translated by Laurien Alexandre.
Norwood, NJ: Ablex, 1988. 173p. bibliog.

The author, a prominent Cuban journalist, here thoroughly discusses 'the socio-economic changes brought about by new information technologies'. Some of these include: the decline of the welfare state by deregulation and privatization; widening gap between rich and poor countries, aggravated by the latter's debt; acute inequalities in media and information infrastructures; massive structural unemployment caused by automation and informatics; unpreparedness of Third World governments for the post-industrial information revolution; Northern control of new data networks and satellite communications; and the struggle over the NWICO under the guise of 'free flow of information'. 'In the midst of these trends and dangers', Gonzalez-Manet writes, 'we find more than 800 million undernourished people, one billion illiterate, and 600 million unemployed. In this "computerized age", solutions must include these millions, or even more explosive problems will erupt.' Readers will find this book an impressive Third World view of the challenges ahead for the ITU, UNESCO and the United Nations in the field of communications.

832   **To inform or to control? The new communications networks.**
Oswald H. Ganley and Gladys D. Ganley.   New York: McGraw-Hill,
1982; Norwood, NJ: Ablex, 2nd ed., 1989. 263p. bibliog.
Communications has entered a 'period of extreme dynamism', when neither nations
nor the international community is able fully to control the new technologies or to
realize their full potential to inform their citizens and world society. This book,
addressed to political and industrial leaders, statesmen, and concerned citizens, aims
to draw out the implications for future management of industrial economies that have
become 'global'. 'Most of our stakes are now global', the Ganleys write. 'But
governments have not gone global.' They examine the international media,
transborder data flows, ITU allocation of the radio spectrum, international satellites,
communications in defence and peacekeeping, U.S.–Canada communications policy,
U.S. relations with other Western countries and with the communist (1989) and
developed worlds, and the emerging global telecommunications networks. They
conclude with calls for reform – already voiced by the Federal Communications
Commission – of the multinational organizations that are no longer coping with the
new needs brought about by intensification of communications and information.

833   **International broadcasting by satellite: issues of regulation,
barriers to communications.**
Jon T. Powell.   Westport, CT: Quorum, 1985. 300p. bibliog.
The arrival of direct broadcasting satellites in geosynchronous orbits and of
individual satellite dish receivers by the 1970s created new potentials for the free flow
of ideas as well as for centralized propaganda. The author makes the 'United Nations
the centerpiece for this book' since that is where controversies about the new
technology must be resolved. As a 1961 General Assembly resolution declared, 'The
United Nations should provide a focal point for international cooperation in the
peaceful exploration and use of outer space.' Powell faces squarely the political,
cultural, technological, and economic dimensions of sovereignty. He argues in favour
of such new concepts as the common heritage of mankind in space, the need for an
international legal structure, and the proposal to establish a world space organization
(1981) as a new specialized agency supplementing the earth-bound ITU. 'The
concepts of basic human rights, national sovereignty, privacy, cultural integrity, the
free flow of information, and the role of the United Nations', he concludes, 'should be
brought together into a broad international agreement, a "Covenant", from which
could be derived legal principles and laws to guide nations in their relations to each
other in an age of instantaneous communications.'

834   **International communications and world order.**
Leonard H. Marks.   In: *Negotiating world order: the artisanry and
architecture of global diplomacy*. Edited by Alan K. Henrikson.
Wilmington, DE: Scholarly Resources, 1986, p.47-56.
Here is a clear introduction to the ITU – historically a model for international
cooperation by independent sovereigns. 'Everyone recognized that there had to be
universality if there was going to be a functioning system of international
communications', the author writes. But ten large users, from the United States to the
Vatican, now use three-fourths of the radio spectrum, and Third World users are
demanding a larger share of frequencies and technical assistance. A crisis is growing
over access to geostationary communications satellites. The cooperative management

of the International Telecommunications Satellite Consortium (INTELSAT) is a model for the future, Marks concludes.

835 **International telecommunications and international law: the regulation of the radio spectrum.**
David M. Leive.   Leiden, The Netherlands: Sijthoff, 1970. 386p. bibliog.

One of the 'global commons' (in addition to the deep seabed, Antarctica, and outer space) is the radio frequency spectrum. This legal study closely examines the role of the ITU in apportioning and regulating the use of the spectrum. Covered are history, powers and procedures for regulation, rights and obligations of member-states, structure of the organization, the new frontier in outer space, and needs for new powers, legal principles, and improved institutional arrangements.

836 **The International Telecommunications Union in a changing world.**
George A. Codding, Jr., and Anthony M. Rutkowski.   Dedham, MA: Artech House, 1982. 414p. bibliog.

This is a 'current, comprehensive, and readable treatise on the ITU and what it does'. Reflecting the necessity for coordination of the vital techniques of communications that readily cross national frontiers, the International Telecommunications Union, the oldest existing IO, was established in 1865. It currently has a membership of 156 and is already addressing the future of communications satellites, optical transmission, dynamic radio systems, mass data storage, and computer information networks. The book covers its history, decision-making apparatus (notably the World Administrative Radio Conference and the Consultative Committees), the product (standards, frequency management, development assistance, and information), and problems and prospects. The authors conclude that 'the emerging communications revolution will demand even more of the ITU in the future', particularly from the member governments to devise a common strategy. Both technical and political problems, they affirm, can be solved 'with even a modicum of goodwill and understanding'.

837 **The International Telecommunications Union: ITU's structure and functions.**
Harold K. Jacobson.   In: *Global communications in the space age: toward a new ITU*.   New York: The John and Markle Foundation and the Twentieth Century Fund, 1972, p.38-55.

This brief book, dating from the period of first flux of Third World states entering the U.N. and its specialized agencies, calls for modest reforms and preservation of the ITU. One of the contributors, Abram Chayes, at the time had 'come to bury it'. Jacobson's chapter is informative within a generally critical American perspective.

838 **New communication technologies: a challenge for press freedom.**
Edited by Colin Sparks.   Paris: UNESCO, 1991. 109p. (Reports and Papers on Mass Communication No. 106).

This report is typical of UNESCO's continuing but chastened efforts – after the withdrawal of the United States and Great Britain – to advance the freedom of the press while it is mainly owned and operated by private corporations in the First

World. 'Media independence' and 'information pluralism' are its international ideals. The present report examines whether new communications technologies, such as the VCR and cable network, 'increase freedom and choice or, on the contrary, facilitate control and conformity', particularly in North America, Western Europe, Sweden, Ghana, Latin America, and Chile. Leonard Sussman provides a warning in his chapter, 'Exit the censor, enter the regulator'.

839 **Report on the activities of the International Telecommunications Union in 1992.**
ITU, Geneva.
This is the official annual report on the work of the organization.

840 **Technologies without boundaries: on telecommunications in a global age.**
Ithiel de Sola Pool. Edited by Eli M. Noam.   Cambridge, MA: Harvard University Press, 1990. 283p.
This posthumous volume extends Pool's award-winning *Technologies of freedom* into the international realm. Readers who, like Pool, are suspicious of governmental control of the new communications technology in intergovernmental organizations, will find this a broadly informative book, devoted to preserving freedom and diversity for all the world's peoples. His 'vision of a new world' focuses on five future trends: shrinking distances, merging modes of communications, overlap of communications and computers, growing information industry, and individualization of the mass media. His treatment of the UNESCO controversy over the attempt 'to codify the sovereign right of nations to control communications of foreign origin' draws attention to the alternative, championed by the United States, 'to codify the human right to communicate'.

841 **Telecommunications and economic development.**
Robert J. Saunders, Jeremy J. Warford, and Bjørn Wallenius.
Baltimore, MD: Johns Hopkins University Press for the World Bank, 1983. 395p. bibliog.
'What are the economic problems of the telecommunications sector in less developed countries. . . ? The principal problems center on the high capital cost of expanding telecommunications infrastructure, on the variety and diversity of the benefits of such investment, and on the organization and management of the sector.' This expert study takes up the large question of the relation between communications and economic development, and it is primarily addressed to policy makers. It surveys the principal organizational and management problems of expanding telecommunications, the macro- and micro-economic analysis of benefits of investment in the sector, measures of distribution of expanded services, and appropriate pricing policies. As a World Bank publication, it presumes that most effective action will be taken by national governments.

842 **Telecommunications: managing a technological revolution.**
Marvin S. Soroos.   In: *Beyond sovereignty: the challenge of global policy*, by Marvin S. Soroos.   Columbia: University of South Carolina Press, 1986, p.323-49.

The author surveys new developments in global communications – notably the geosynchronous orbit – which have expanded the scope of international cooperation in the old ITU. The field is one where the sovereign nations readily find a common interest; hence the ITU is a model of effective cooperation, with implications for weather forecasting, environmental protection, food production, and international education.

843 **The Third World and press freedom.**
Edited by Philip C. Horton. Foreword by John Chancellor.   New York: Praeger, 1978. 253p. bibliog.

This is a somewhat older record of a conference on the NWICO, when the issues were fresh, and before the United States and Great Britain ended debate by withdrawing from UNESCO. Do not news services from the developed world, the authors ask, have a responsibility to the developing world when presenting the news? How can journalists from the Third World organize themselves in groups to cross national boundaries? What is 'news' anyway – violence, human interest, social and economic development? Is freedom so great a value that in young countries with fragile polities endless scrutiny by the news media of shortcomings in the government or in its economic programmes should be allowed to destroy public trust? The thoughtful articles in this volume address these questions from the perspectives of all three 'worlds'.

844 **Transnational communications: wiring the Third World.**
Edited by Gerald Sussman and John A. Lent.   Newbury Park, CA: Sage, 1991. 327p.

Dedicated to 'the humble folk not invited to the "communications revolution"', this volume aims to discuss its potential for countries often overlooked in studies fixated on the leading industrial powers – the United States, Japan, and European Community. The contributors here return to serious consideration of the New World Information and Communications Order (NWICO, 1980), which was so critical of the First World's media and data monopolies in the Third World. Apart from Singapore, no other Third World nations – and no other First or Second World ones – have followed the United States and Great Britain out of UNESCO over the issues. But efforts at 'self-reliance' to establish a new communications order in the Third World alone have not been able to break the power of the 'transnational media and telecommunications monopolies'. Mexico's Televisa continues to circulate North American advertising and soap operas, and India's TV businessmen model their series *Khandan* after *Dynasty*. Here, information and communications issues are not viewed in isolation from such development issues as debt, export dependency, TNC penetration, technology and expertise deficiencies, links to military security, and often desperate shortages of food, housing, education, and health.

845 **World communications: a handbook.**
Edited by George Gerbner and Marsha Siefert.   New York: Longman,
1984. 527p.

This handbook is intended to be a 'guide for governments, corporations, scholars, students, and policy makers'. Emphasis simply on the West has been avoided; there are fifty-four brief contributions from twenty-five countries, North, South, East, and West. Topics include: global perspectives on information (U.S. policy, new world information order), transnational flows of news and images, satellites and computers, development issues, and international policies (INTELSAT, World Administrative Radio Conferences, the MacBride report, UNESCO). Readers in search of basic information on a wide variety of current communications issues may find it here.

Many voices, one world.
See item no. 909.

World health

World Health Organization (WHO)
U.N. Division of Narcotic Drugs

846 **The AIDS epidemic and its demographic consequences.**
United Nations and World Health Organization.   New York: U.N.
Department of International Economic and Social Affairs; Geneva:
WHO, 1991. 140p. (Global Programme on AIDS. E.91.XIII.5.
ST/ESA/SER.A/119).

This is a volume of proceedings of a U.N.–WHO workshop on modelling the demographic impact of the AIDS epidemic in pattern II countries (13-15 December 1989). It discusses progress to date and recommends policies for the future.

847 **Bulletin of the World Health Organization. Bulletin de
l'Organisation de la Santé.**
WHO, Geneva. 71 vols to 1993.

This is the scientific journal of WHO. Primary focus is on the progress of medical knowledge through international cooperation.

848 **Combatting drug abuse and related crime: comparative research on the effectiveness of socio-legal prevention and control measures in different countries on the interaction between criminal behaviour and drug abuse.**
Francesco Bruno.   Rome: U.N. Social Defence Research Institute, 1984. 251p. (Pub. No. 21).

This is a social-scientific study of the effectiveness of the laws in several countries to control drug abuse. Participants in the study were Brazil, Italy, Jordan, Malaysia, Sweden, U.K., and U.S.A. (None from the communist bloc would participate in 1984.) The author concludes: 'The efficiency of the [national penal] system, evaluated at an individual and subjective level, correlates significantly to the foreseen theoretic harshness, and even more significantly to the "knowledge" of the law and to the *perception* of harshness of the system . . .'.

849 **Consolidated list of products whose consumption and/or sale have been banned, withdrawn, severely restricted or not approved by governments.**
U.N. Department of International Economic and Social Affairs.   New York: United Nations, 1991. 4th ed., 807p. (E.91.IV.4. ST/ESA/224).

In an effort to protect health and the environment, the U.N., in cooperation with WHO and UNEP, maintains this large volume of harmful pharmaceuticals, chemicals, and consumer products. They have all been banned by one government or another; hence, the list serves to alert governments and to assist them in taking regulatory action. Chlorofluorocarbons, for instance, have been banned by Canada, Norway, and five other states.

850 **Drugs and punishment: an up-to-date interregional survey on drug-related offenses.**
Dušan Cotič.   Rome: U.N. Social Defence Research Institute, 1988. 146p. bibliog. (Pub. No. 30. E.88.III.N.1).

This study provides current quantitative and qualitative information on penal provisions in representative countries for drug-related offences. Europe, Asia, Africa, and Latin America are surveyed (thirty-one countries). The laws on drug abuse are changing throughout the world, which increases instability in drug-related criminal policy. This finding is most pronounced with respect to illicit possession and consumption; illicit production and trafficking is prohibited by law similarly everywhere.

851 **The first ten years of the World Health Organization.**
WHO. Foreword by M.G. Candau.   Geneva: WHO, 1958. 538p.

This official illustrated history covers the establishment of the WHO (1948), its methods of work, attacks on internationally transmitted communicable diseases (notably malaria), epidemiological work on sanitation and nutrition, recommendations on health care, nursing, maternal and child health, education, and public information. The illustrations recall to mind the triumphs of international cooperation to promote human health. Compare WHO's *Second ten years* (item no. 862).

852 **The global eradication of smallpox. Final report . . . December 1979.**
Global Commission for the Certification of Smallpox Eradication. Geneva: WHO, 1980. 122p. (History of International Public Health No. 4).

This book carefully presents the evidence for the eradication of one of the scourges of humanity. The triumph over this disease shows the way, argues Dr. Halfdan Mohler, Director-General of WHO, for the world community 'to attack other health problems with the same enthusiasm, optimism, and sheer hard work'.

853 **Global programme on AIDS. 1991 progress report.**
Geneva: WHO, 1992. 136p.

This is the first full-scale progress report on WHO's Global programme on AIDS. It shows how prevention and control are being addressed by national policies. WHO's main contribution is in research projects on the development of vaccines, therapeutic drugs, clinical investigation, epidemiological research, surveillance, and forecasting. A concluding chapter emphasizes early diagnosis and treatment in order to contain the spread of HIV infection.

854 **Health care: an international study. Report of the WHO international collaborative study of medical care utilization.**
Edited by Robert Kohn and Kerr L. White. Foreword by Robert F. Bridgman. London: Oxford University Press, 1976. 557p. bibliog.

In pursuing the goal of health for all, WHO by 1976 had come to the view that 'the protection and promotion of the health of individuals and populations requires an integrative approach, comprising both preventive and curative services. . .'. This large-scale expert study is a report on the use of such health care services by twelve study populations in seven countries (including the U.S., Britain, Poland, and former Yugoslavia). To avoid certain misleading international comparisons, it employs the fairer basis of the 'population centered' study. The work is primarily addressed to medical planners and administrators, scholars, and students of health care and services. Contents include: determinants of health services use (predisposing factors, morbidity factors, resource factors); use of health services (physicians, hospitals, medicines, dentistry, optometry, nurses and paramedics); and overall patterns. The authors conclude with both theoretical and practical findings.

855 **The international health regime.**
David M. Leive. In: *International regulatory regimes*, by David M. Leive. Lexington, MA: Lexington Books, 1976. vol. 1, p.1-152.

In a study concentrating on the actual practice of international organizations, the author examines the regulatory 'regime' of rules and quasi-judicial procedures within WHO that have been agreed upon to guide national health administrators in preventing the spread of communicable diseases across their borders. (A regime, then, is not a strong, central international organ empowered to direct states.) Leive concentrates on the *regulatory* regime primarily – not the whole substantive problem of world health nor the parent organization, though both receive due coverage with respect to the regime. Contents include: history, regulations, notification and publication, compliance, certification of ships, advisory processes, and domestic application. In the same volumes are comparative studies of WMO (item no. 753) and FAO (item no. 877).

856 **Issues in contemporary international health.**
Edited by Thomas A. Lambo and Stacey B. Day.   New York: Plenum Medical Books, 1990. 344p.

There are as yet no textbooks on international health. The WHO is still following the policy, laid down in 1949, that the organization should *not* seek the establishment, under its own auspices, of international research institutes. The editors recognize, however, that by 1990 physicians, educators, and health administrators can no longer treat health as a merely national problem but must place it in the context of 'global life'. Health communications, education for health, and 'biopsychosocial' approaches, including general systems theory, are now the main devices of emerging international health care delivery. Man and his environment, they write, 'are to be evaluated as interdependent parts of a united whole, a one-world'. But since their 'world perspective' is still new, they do not provide here a textbook of agreed international strategies, but rather a range of 'public choices' or 'alternative futures' that might yet *become* international policy. These are presented in the context of the WHO's Health for All – 2000 programme, which includes health policy, management, economics, education, legislation, maternity care, mental health, treatment of cancer, surgery, dentistry, and hereditary disease treatment. In the appendix are printed WHO's International Health Regulations (1969, updated to 1982)

857 **National strategies for health care organization: a world overview.**
Milton Irwin Roemer.   Ann Arbor, MI: Health Administration Press, 1985. 426p. bibliog.

A comprehensive analysis of the health care systems of all the world's nations (160 in 1985) is still beyond the capacity of a single scholar, but the author presents here a representative study of the industrialized, socialist, and developing countries, and he concludes with a survey of general health policy issues. The WHO and the U.S. government assisted him throughout. Dr. Roemer regards 'health care as a human and social right, not just a market commodity', and he devotes space to the efforts of many countries to provide health care to all by law and public policy.

858 **The Pan-American Health Organization: origins and evolution.**
Norman Howard-Jones.   Geneva: WHO, 1981. 20p. (History of International Public Health No. 5).

This brief work is a history of a typical regional organization within the WHO. The account is mostly of the roots of the Pan-American body, going back to visionary Latin Americans and cooperative U.S. physicians since at least the First General International Sanitary Convention of the American Republics in Washington in 1902. Little is said of the Pan-American Health Organization after its founding in 1949.

859 **Politics and budgeting in the World Health Organization.**
Francis W. Hoole.   Bloomington, IN: Indiana University Press, 1976. 226p. bibliog.

One approach to the scientific understanding of policy-making in international politics is to trace the quantifiable budgetary process in one of the main IOs. The author takes here the quantitative or behavioural science approach towards the WHO. He concludes that the WHO budget will probably rise to well over $1,000 million in the 1970-80 decade (compared to half that in the *two* decades of 1949-69), which will lead to a predictable strategy by policy-makers in the developed countries to slow down the growth in the WHO.

860 **Primary health care. Report [of the International Conference on Primary Health Care, Alma-Ata, U.S.S.R., 6-12 September 1978].**
WHO and UNICEF. Geneva: WHO, 1978. 49p.
A declaration came out of this conference, providing guidelines and requirements for primary health care as a human right within the scope of the International Covenant on Economic, Social, and Cultural Rights. 'The Conference strongly affirms that health, which is a state of complete physical, mental, and social well-being, and not merely the absence of disease or infirmity, is a fundamental human right, and that the attainment of the highest possible level of health is a most important world-wide social goal whose realization requires the action of many other social and economic sectors in addition to the health sector.' Practical recommendations and strategies are provided. The locale and date signify the potential for cooperation in the field of human health.

861 **The riches of the poor: a journey round the World Health Organization.**
George Mikes. London: Deutsch, 1987. 112p.
This is that rarest of works – a humorous book on the WHO. 'If an outbreak of smallpox is a tragic event, then its disappearance is a joyous one.' As brevity is the soul of wit, so humour is the light of intelligence. Mikes manages to explain what WHO is (an agency of governments), to puncture First World pretences, and to convey a good deal of information about health world-wide, including the story of the triumph over smallpox in 1979.

862 **The second ten years of the World Health Organization, 1958-1967.**
WHO. Foreword by M.G. Candau. Geneva: WHO, 1968. 413p. bibliog.
'Health is purchasable.' That is, says Director-General Candau, in the second decade of WHO it was increasingly recognized by people and governments that health is a human right and that 'without health, development has no hope of putting down its roots'. The focus by 1968 was on education, collaboration, and direct assistance to improve health in all countries. This official history covers world-wide and regional health problems, organization of health services, education, diseases under attack, progress in biology, and environmental health.

863 **Smallpox and its eradication.**
Frank Fenner, D.A. Henderson, I. Arita, Z. Jezek, and I.D. Ladnyi. Geneva: WHO, 1988. 1,460p. bibliog. (History of International Public Health No. 6).
This large-scale medical history covers a description of the disease of smallpox (illustrated), the history of the disease from ancient times to the late twentieth

century, Jenner's discovery of vaccination, and then fifteen chapters on the global eradication campaign. The book sets out a model of common action to eradicate other diseases.

864 **Toward scientifically based prevention.**
Edited by Francesco Bruno, Maria Elena Andreotti, and Mario Brunetti. Rome: U.N. Interregional Crime and Justice Research Institute, 1990. 181p. (English), 193p. (Italian). bibliog. (E.90.III.N.5).
This volume of proceedings at the United Nations' Rome institute is devoted to the *prevention* of drug abuse. Prevention is discussed with reference to the law, medicine, education, the prisons, research, policy (the 'Stop Droga' programme), and international cooperation (WHO). The Italian context is typical of the First World.

865 **The United Nations and drug abuse control.**
U.N. Department of Public Information, in consultation with U.N. Division of Narcotic Drugs. New York: United Nations, 1989. 102p. (E.90.I.3).
'It is now generally recognized that both the supply and the demand for drugs should be reduced and action should be taken to break the link between consumers and producers', writes the former Secretary-General Javier Pérez de Cuéllar. This introductory book presents an overview of the drug abuse problem and of international cooperation to reduce both demand and supply. The most recent step toward control was negotiation of the Convention against Illicit Traffic in Narcotic Drugs and Psychotropic Substances (1988), The next step, the book concludes, is for each national state to establish a comprehensive programme in cooperation with others. Like AIDS and international crime, drug trafficking transcends national borders and cultures, and hence requires cooperation.

866 **The World Health Organization.**
Peter Corrigan. Hove, England: Wayland, 1979. 96p. bibliog.
This is an elementary, illustrated introduction to the WHO. 'The policy of the WHO', begins the author, 'is that mankind should be fit and happy in body, mind, and spirit. This would help to bring universal peace to the world.' Corrigan concentrates on the battle against infectious diseases, social and occupational diseases, cancer and heart disease (the great killers of the industrialized world), and on pollution, radioactivity, accidents, natural disasters, and malnutrition. His approach is broadly international and cooperative on the basics of health.

867 **The World Health Organization: resisting Third World ideological pressures.**
John M. Starrels. Washington, DC: Heritage Foundation, U.N. Studies, 1985. 44p. bibliog.
The WHO's campaign against infant formula is seen as the entering wedge for 'regulating private enterprise'. This leads the author to a systematic attack on the WHO's Health for All by the Year 2000 – seen as an 'adjunct to the NIEO idea' – and to all of WHO's relations to the private medical and pharmaceutical sectors. The author belittles WHO's health philosophy – called 'simple decency' by one official – as 'redistribution rhetoric' closely tied to communist ideology as reflected in the

Alma-Ata conference on primary health care in 1978 (see item no. 860). Starrels concludes that Western policy should 'insist that the Organization adhere to its technical mandate' – that is, support private enterprise in medicine and allow the market to do the regulating.

868   **The World Health Organization: a study in decentralized international administration.**
Robert Berkov. Geneva: Librairie E. Droz, 1957. 173p. bibliog.

This older work of public administration could be read as a model for the decentralized U.N. system of the future. The author points out that centralization, in theory, would increase efficiency and reduce duplication of efforts; but in international relations, decentralization encounters less resistance and preserves the 'psychological aspects of support and participation'. Since an IO must provide for the 'continuous winning of consent of a great number of people', a decentralized one like the WHO may be actually more efficient. Berkov thoroughly analyses the decentralized structure and policies of the WHO, which are based on regional organizations and programmes. He concludes with reflections on the significance of WHO's form of administration for other IOs.

869   **World Health: The Magazine of the World Health Organization.**
WHO. Geneva, 1948- . bimonthly.

This official illustrated magazine of WHO is addressed to a general audience throughout the world. The topic in the January-February 1993 issue is the prevention of accidents and injuries, violence and negligence. It is published in English, French, Russian, Spanish, Arabic, and Farsi.

Food production and distribution

Food and Agricultural Organization (FAO)
International Fund for Agricultural Development (IFAD)
World Food Programme (WFP)
World Food Council (WFC)

870   **Agriculture, external trade, and international co-operation.**
U.N. Economic Commission for Latin America and the Caribbean and the Food and Agriculture Organization.   Santiago, Chile: U.N. ECLAC, 1989. 88p. (E.88.II.G.15. LC/G.1492-P).

Latin American agriculture, which is very responsive to demand, is depressed due to reduced domestic demand, linked to debt 'adjustment processes', and to reduced external demand. This short work, addressed to economists and Third World policy-makers, argues that an 'adequate strategical orientation' could reinsert Latin America into the world market. It also calls for a Latin American 'strategy of action' during the GATT talks and thereafter to improve the terms of trade for regional agricultural products.

871 **Coping with famine.**
Jean Mayer. *Foreign Affairs*, vol. 53 (October 1974), p.98-120.

As the World Food Conference of 1974 convened in Rome, this article by one of the world's leading nutrition scientists appeared in the leading American journal of foreign policy. Mayer argued that famines ought not to be unexpected but 'planned for in advance'. In the past, famines were unavoidable because means were lacking for distribution of food elsewhere on the continent or across the seas; now humanity has the technology of surveillance and transport to avert such calamities. The international agencies concerned – FAO, WHO, UNICEF, CARE, etc. – still do not have the regional or world food banks that John Boyd-Orr proposed in the 1940s (see item no. 873). Hence, responsibility falls on powerful nations that possess the food, medical supplies, and transportation to help. Mayer concludes with practical suggestions for both national and international relief operations.

872 **Famine: its causes, effects, and management.**
Edited by John R.K. Robson. Preface by Jean Mayer. New York: Gordon & Breach, 1981. 170p. bibliog.

Famines, argues Jean Mayer, are not caused simply by drought, but by an ill-organized society without strong administrative and medical structures and good transportation. A natural disaster or even a war nearby is only the last of a series of causes. The Russian famine of 1920-22 and the Bengal one of 1942-44 were typical, as were more recent ones in Biafra and the Sahel. Food rushed to such an area will not solve the problem without improvements in the organization of society. At the world level, he calls for an international convention to 'outlaw starvation as an instrument of war'. The editor has chosen scientific, developmental, and medical articles mainly in the two areas of the ecology of famine and the food supply and distribution system. All presume continued reliance on the private market for food.

873 **The Food and Agriculture Organization, 1943-48.**
John Boyd-Orr. In: *As I recall*, by John Boyd-Orr. London: MacGibbon & Kee, 1966, p.157-216.

Here is an account of the founding of FAO by its first Director-General, who had high ideals still not realized. The heart of Lord Boyd-Orr's proposals was a World Food Board to make long-term low-interest loans to states, in order to purchase food and agricultural machinery; to buy and hold surplus stocks for later resale, in order to stabilize prices; and to establish an international authority of individual experts (business people, scientists, farmers) under supervision by the U.N., in order to cooperate in economic development for the benefit of all peoples. (Boyd-Orr saw this last as a step toward 'world government.') Boyd-Orr looked upon food not as an ordinary consumption good, like cotton, but as a vital necessity to be managed as a public utility, like water. Nothing like this has ever been established. The World Food Programme (1961) is still limited to emergency and technical assistance, and the World Food Council (1974) remains an annual meeting at the level of agricultural ministers to coordinate policy.

874 **Food and nutrition policy in a changing world.**
Edited by Jean Mayer and Johanna Dwyer. New York: Oxford
University Press, 1979. 300p.
This is an abbreviated version of a five-volume report to UNICEF in 1975. The
subject is formulating food and nutrition policy in developing countries, where the
need is greatest. Eminent experts from all over the world participated. An integrated
national nutrition plan cannot be recommended, however, because of the diversity of
countries. Topics include: the macrovariables of supply, demand, and need; long-term
national planning; short-term interventions; malnutrition; and the role of the food
industry.

875 **Global food interdependence: challenge to American foreign
policy.**
Raymond F. Hopkins and Donald J. Puchala. New York: Columbia
University Press, 1980. 214p.
The United States has supplied over half of the world's grain exports since the early
1960s. American food policy, therefore, has profound effects on the alleviation of
world hunger. About 1974, the situation began to change from traditional American
generosity in feeding the world; in 1980, in response to the Soviet invasion of
Afghanistan, President Carter declared an embargo on grain shipments to the
U.S.S.R., marking the acceptance of a U.S. policy to use food as an international
weapon. The authors analyse this situation with particular reference to the unfulfilled
promises of the World Food Conference of 1974. The WFC and IFAD lack the
resources to fulfil their mandates; 'no international undertaking on food security or
grain storage exists'.

876 **International agreements in the food and health fields.**
Jean Mayer. In: *Negotiating world order; the artisanship and
architecture of global diplomacy.* Edited by Alan K. Henrikson.
Wilmington, DE: Scholarly Resources, 1986, p.3-17.
Here is a clear introduction to international cooperation in health (Red Cross, WHO,
UNICEF) and food (FAO). The author concludes with such proposals for
improvement as bringing about an agreement to renounce use of food as a weapon of
war (international or civil), and to establish an early warning system in the U.N. to
guard against famine and hence breakdowns of world health.

877 **The joint food standards program.**
David M. Leive. In: *International regulatory regimes,* by David M.
Leive. Lexington, MA: Lexington Books, 1976. vol. 2, p.373-579.
In this study of the law and practice of FAO, the author focuses on the regulatory
regime (rules and quasi-judicial processes) that has emerged in the organization and
that shows the way to similar multilateral regimes in fields where international
cooperation is reaching the intensity of that concerning food. Leive devotes his whole
second volume to the Joint FAO/WHO Food Standards Programme, conducted by the
autonomous Codex Alimentarius Commission. Covered are: the origins of the regime,
its standards, advice, 'legislation', enforcement, and verification. He concludes with
recommendations for the more widespread use of such regulation within the present
decentralized U.N. system.

878   **The multilateral approach to food security.**
Wouter Tims.   In: *The U.N. under attack*. Edited by Jeffrey Harrod
and Nico Schrijver.   Aldershot, England: Gower, 1988, p.94-110.

The author emphasizes the 'twinning of international *and* national policies to meet the challenge of hunger in the world effectively'. Adequate distribution of food to the neediest countries, stabilization of agricultural markets by international management of buffer stocks, and accumulation of emergency reserves are not enough without national programmes to increase purchasing power of the population and to create productive employment, especially in rural areas. The history of FAO, WFP, WFC, IFAD, and IDA is surveyed. Tims concludes that 'the multilateral agencies, during the past four decades, have been largely concerned with the food security of nations rather than of people'. Hence the emphasis on food production rather than distribution and consumption. Certain policies of the World Bank, he argues, show the way to meeting the needs of people.

879   **Providing food security for all.**
Mohiuddin Alamgir and Poonan Arora. Foreword by Idriss Jazairy.
New York: New York University Press for FAO, 1991. 269p. (IFAD
Studies in Rural Poverty No. 1. E.91.II.A.14).

'Give a man a fish and he will eat', goes an old Chinese proverb. 'Give a man a net and he will eat all his life.' This is the underlying philosophy at IFAD, under whose auspices this summary of 'what IFAD has learned to date about hunger and development' was produced. The authors are convinced that the eradication of hunger by the *eradication of poverty* is possible. Alamgir and Arora set their microeconomic analysis of rural poverty and food insecurity within the larger macroeconomic context that occupies the minds of most policy-makers in governments and funding agencies.

880   **Right to adequate food as a human right.**
Asbjørn Eide, Special Rapporteur.   Geneva: U.N. Centre for Human
Rights, 1989. 73p. (E.89.XIV.2).

The author was expressly charged 'to take in all relevant work being done within the United Nations system' on the human right to adequate food. He was also to relate the right to the establishment of a new international economic order (NIEO). Hence, this brief work is a comprehensive study of the right to food – or what Franklin D. Roosevelt called 'freedom from want' – within the larger context of the world struggle for economic and social justice. Covered are the issues of food and hunger, the nature of rights, the existing status of the right to food in international law, state and international obligations, and monitoring and supervision. Eide concludes with a number of recommendations to states, the U.N., specialized agencies, and NGOs in order to build consciousness of the issues and cooperate in finding mutually agreeable solutions. But he proposes no new international institution on the order of Boyd-Orr's World Food Board.

881   **The right to food: guide through applicable international law.**
Edited by Katarina Tomasevski.   Dordrecht, The Netherlands:
M. Nijhoff, 1987. 387p.

If food is a right, why does not assertion of this right lead to reform of the global distribution system? This book is a compilation of the many international legal instruments dealing with food; it also includes information on the legal force and implementation of the instruments, chosen 'to further the observance of the right to food'. Somehow, despite all the international agreements reproduced in this book, food remains a commodity, to be bought and sold for profit.

882 The story of FAO.
Gove Hambidge. New York: Van Nostrand, 1955. 303p.

This is a history of nutrition science and of efforts in the League of Nations and the United Nations to bring about international cooperation in the production and distribution of food. Special attention is given to the role of Sir John Boyd-Orr, first Director-General of FAO (1945-48), whose vision is still unfulfilled. Thereafter, the story is mostly of the growth of FAO as a technical organization, with early projects in the Middle East, Africa, Far East, Latin America, and Europe.

883 World agriculture: towards 2000; an FAO study.
Edited by Nikos Alexandratos. Rome: FAO; New York: New York University Press, 1988. 338p. bibliog.

This is a comprehensive study of agricultural production and policy perspectives in some 94 developing countries (including China) and 34 developed ones from about 1960 to 2000. 'Drawing fully on the economic and technical disciplines and field experience of FAO, the report, therefore, represents a global assessment of possible future world and country-group production, trade, and nutrition.' Several projections are encouraging. The decline in the self-sufficiency of developing countries, seen since the early 1970s, should cease by 2000. Agricultural production should be 60 per cent higher than that in 1985; average per capita caloric intake should rise by 200 to 2,620 kilocalories per day; and net cereal imports may increase by 40 million to 110 million tonnes. Similar projections are drawn region by region, decade by decade. *Sustainable* production, satisfying needs yet preserving the environment, is considered achievable. Issues of trade, adjustment, rural equity, and technology are also brought into the whole account.

884 The World Food Conference and global problem solving.
Thomas G. Weiss and Robert S. Jordan. New York: Praeger for UNITAR, 1976. 170p.

By the mid-1970s, the interdependence of states had advanced so far that both the World Food Conference (1974) and the NIEO (1974) were seen as marks of the world community's growing recognition of the necessity to come to grips with its common problems. Conference diplomacy was seized by the new states of the South to redistribute wealth and power, while the older international institutions continued to be used by states of the North to maintain the status quo. The authors treat the food conference of 1974 within this context of new world politics. Its main powers were publicity (why can't the world feed itself?) and establishment of new institutions (IFAD, 1977). They focus on the current nub of change – international bureaucracy and administration. Weiss and Jordan ask 'why [do] certain administrative processes within conferences can lead to better international cooperation and dialogue, and sometimes to the potential for a more equitable distribution of world resources'?

885 **Yearbook: Fertilizer, 1988. Yearbook: Production, 1988.**
     Yearbook: Fishery Statistics, 1988.
     Rome: Food and Agricultural Organization, 1950- . annual.
These three official yearbooks are standard references for FAO.

Intellectual property

World Intellectual Property Organization (WIPO)

886 **Global rivalry and intellectual property: developing Canadian**
     strategies.
     Edited by Murray G. Smith.   Halifax, NS: Institute for Research on
     Public Policy, 1991. 274p. bibliog.
This book is poised for final negotiations on intellectual property rights in the
Uruguay Round of the GATT talks. Canada generally supports United States policy
'to extend the reach of its domestic intellectual property laws' in a multilateral code
within GATT. Very little is said of the alternative of strengthening WIPO.

887 **Governing bodies of WIPO and the unions administered by**
     WIPO.
     World Intellectual Property Organization, Geneva.
This is the official annual report of WIPO.

888 **Intellectual property rights and U.S. competitiveness in trade.**
     Helena Stalson.   Washington, DC: National Planning Association,
     1987. 106p. bibliog. (Committee on Changing International Realities,
     Report No. 18).
The costs of R&D and the cheapness of copying are proving injurious to the rights of
inventors and authors. Not only books and records are being copied in the
international market, but electronics, legal drugs, agricultural chemicals, auto parts,
and aerospace products. Moreover, a kind of North–South divide has opened up over
whether GATT is the proper forum for negotiation (favoured by the U.S., Europe, and
other developed countries) or WIPO (favoured by the Third World). The author sees
advantages to both and urges a common approach.

889 **Intellectual property rights: global consensus, global conflict?**
     Edited by R. Michael Gadbaw and Timothy J. Richards.   Boulder,
     CO: Westview, 1988. 413p.
The global marketplace is creating a crisis for the protection of intellectual property.
Within the United States or other states, books, musical scores, and artistic works are
protected by copyright laws; new inventions by patent or trade secret laws; designs
and names by trademarks. Semiconductor designs and software are the newest

entrants into the copyright field. But in North–South relations, many developing countries pursue policies to make technology available in the domestic economy at the lowest possible price, which has led to widespread piracy of books, audio and video tapes, TV broadcasts, pharmaceuticals, and now computer chips and software. Intellectual property as a component of U.S. exports is about 27 per cent (1986 – up from 10 per cent in 1947). It is estimated that U.S. losses due to piracy (or what poor countries might call equity) amount to $60,000 million per year. This book, edited by two Washington lawyers, surveys the problem and advocates improved worldwide protection of intellectual property rights to 'enhance the competitiveness of all nations'. The main multilateral negotiating forum for this purpose is either GATT – where the goal is a code enforced by trade sanctions – or WIPO – where it is improvements to the Paris and Berne Conventions and to national laws.

International education

U.N. Educational, Scientific, and Cultural Organization (UNESCO)
United Nations University (UNU)

890   **Building a global civic culture: education for an interdependent world.**
Elise Boulding.   Syracuse, NY: Syracuse University Press, 1990.
192p. bibliog.

Vaclav Havel has defined a civic society as 'a political system based on the citizen, recognizing all his [or her] fundamental civil and human rights. . . . A civic society, based on the universality of human rights, best enables us to realize ourselves as everything we are – not only members of our nation, but members of our family, our community, our religion, our church, our professional association, our political party, our country, our supra-national communities' (Address 'On home' at Lehigh University, 26 October 1991). Elise Boulding lifts up civics from its neglected condition in the schools as the indoctrination of nationalism to an elevated position as the education appropriate to a world citizen. She recognizes that the civic culture of the West is based, not on the historically rather new nation-states, but on hundreds of ethnic groups; so the civic culture of the planet will have to be based on harmony among thousands of such groups (political geographers identify 1,300 'nations'). She foresees continued struggle between East and West and an even deeper one between North and South. 'What this book is about is how we are going to approach this complex confrontation about our future world. . . . Can we stay rooted in our own communities, retain the best of our national ways, and still develop cooperative strategies for meeting human needs everywhere. . . ?' The United Nations is part of her answer, as are the INGOs, as the new attractors of civic consciousness. This is a book for students and visionaries who will build a new world.

891   **Can scholars succeed where diplomats have failed?**
U Thant.   *Saturday Review/World*, vol. 1 (1 August 1972), p.32-34,
and (29 August 1972), p.38-39.
The former U.N. Secretary-General here describes the origins of the U.N. University,
its purposes, and its future research programme.

892   **Education between two worlds.**
Alexander Meiklejohn.   New York: Harper, 1943. 303p.
The two worlds are not those of communism and capitalism, but the old world in
which the Church had accepted the responsibility for educating the young and the
modern world in which the Church has lost that authority, yet no one short of the state
can assume it. But the contemporary state is woefully disqualified for one reason – it
is not universal.

893   **Education for global interdependence: a report with
recommendations to the Government/Academic Interface
Committee.**
American Council on Education, International Education Project.
Washington, DC: American Council on Education, 1975. 122p.
(Educational Resources Information Center No. ED113263).
This is a substantial study of the need to improve international education in the
United States. 'Nothing is more certain than that Americans will live out the
remaining years of the twentieth century enmeshed in foreign entanglements.' The
history of U.S. efforts in international education is recounted, and the need for
improvement outlined. Only six per cent of American undergraduates take a course
with international content. There are more teachers of English in Russia than students
of Russian in America. Americans are not being prepared for international business or
for leadership in the U.N. system. Specific recommendations are made for state and
federal funding for elementary, secondary, college, and adult education – in
languages, area studies, multidisciplinary problem oriented specialties, and
transnational research.

894   **Education for international cooperation and peace at the primary
school level.**
Paris: UNESCO, 1983. 138p.
This is a book for primary school teaching. It provides a guide to activities in the
classroom that will develop an international perspective.

895   **Education in world affairs: a realistic appoach to international
education.**
Kenneth Melvin.   Lexington, MA: Heath, 1970. 198p. bibliog.
Here is a powerful argument for seeking the interests and good of all nations
(*Weltpolitik*), which is conceived as a mean between seeking the interests of only one
nation (*Realpolitik*), or the common good of individuals without respect to the self-
interests of nations (*Idealpolitik*). Readers today may be surprised that such a
universal spirit once flamed and burned brightly among educators. Books like this
show the way to teaching and gathering the highest intelligence of all peoples in order

to conduct our international relations with more rationality. Melvin regards vigorous programmes of international education as the main device now to strengthen the United Nations.

896 **Essays on violence.**
Edited by J. Martin Ramirez, Robert A. Hinde, and Jo Groebel.
Seville, Spain: University of Seville, 1987. 167p.

This study complements the *Seville statement* (see item no. 917). War is not rooted in human biology. The volume includes essays on the claim that war is 'natural', on the effects of such a claim on young people, and on the 'enemy image' as a psychological antecedent to war.

897 **Fiasco at UNESCO: the smashed mirror of past illusions.**
Pierre de Senarclens. *Society*, vol. 22 (September-October 1985), p.6-14.

U.S. withdrawal from UNESCO in 1984 is here treated as symbolic of a 'crisis' affecting the future 'evolution of multilateral cooperation'. (The U.S. withdrew from the compulsory jurisdiction of the World Court similarly the next year.) The author finds that the U.S. was not alone in its criticisms of UNESCO's politicization, mismanagement, and financial irresponsibility – the U.K., Singapore, the Netherlands, Switzerland, and Japan had similar complaints. The root cause, he argues, was in the 'original design' of a liberal intellectual organization to stop wars 'in the minds of men'. The world is not yet one in culture. The attempt of the first Director-General Julian Huxley in 1948 to define a 'single world culture' based on Western science could not be accepted. Jacques Maritain called this early setback 'a manifestation of the profound spiritual distress of our days'. Hence, Senarclens analyses the ultimate failure of UNESCO to premature utopianism, neglectful of cultural divisions in the world and quixotic in attempting to temper power with considerations of humanity. By 1985, UNESCO was a crossroads of Western liberal civilization and submerged Eastern and Southern civilizations now able to react and respond. 'Peace', 'human rights' and 'development' were no longer commonly understood there. Senarclens would keep the universal organization but define its competences much more narrowly by amendment of its constitution; the alternative is the breakup of UNESCO into less than universal, regional or narrowly functional educational organizations serving like-minded national educational systems. (The real alternative is systemic U.N. reform, backed by the sovereign will of the peoples of the world.)

898 **A forum in restoration: international intellectual cooperation and America's interests in UNESCO.**
United Nations Association – USA American Panel on UNESCO, Robert T. Stafford, chairman. New York: UNA–USA, 1989. 61p. bibliog.

This is a review of U.S. policy toward UNESCO leading to and following withdrawal in 1984. It recommends seriously that the U.S. resume membership. U.S. objections to mismanagement (centralization under the Director-General, patronage), runaway budgets (10 per cent real growth in 1984-85), and politicization (Third World critique of West, duplicate disarmament campaign, support for armed 'liberation' movements, new communications order) are examined and found satisfied by reforms instituted by new Director-General Frederico Major. U.S. *interests* in participation in UNESCO's global programmes in science, education, culture, communications, and human rights are carefully identified. Re-entry, for instance, would give the U.S. 'leverage for reform'. The end of the Cold War and attrition of one-sided Third World demands over NIEO and NWICO offer a new opportunity for renewed cooperation. U.S. financial contributions ($43 million, about one-quarter of the budget) should be resumed in such a way as not to provide a 'windfall refund to the major contributor states'; it should be dedicated for 'nonrecurring expenses that help to strengthen priority programs'.

899   **The future of international education.**
       Robert M. Hutchins.   New York: UNITAR, 1970. 22p. (Lecture
       Series No. 4).

In an address given on 7 May 1970 in honour of the twenty-fifth anniversary of the United Nations, Hutchins asserted that all educational systems are now instruments of national power and hence militate against international cooperation. Yet, he argued, liberal, universal education would be useful even for national systems. That Americans regard education as an economic investment is an illusion – American universities are dedicated to preparation for jobs, and they fail at that. True education aims not at manpower but at manhood. Nations would be wise to think of education as an instrument, not to attain power, prosperity, and prestige, but to develop the full humanity of their populations. Educators should prepare students for national *and* world communities. Ultimately, the world republic of learning will become the world political republic.

900   **Higher education and the new international order.**
       Edited by Bikas C. Sanyal.   Paris: UNESCO, 1982. 242p.

Here is an analysis of the educational and social implications of the U.N. General Assembly resolution on the New International Economic Order (NIEO, 1974). Suggestions are made for each nation's contributions to the NIEO by its system of higher education.

901   **Hope and folly: the United States and UNESCO, 1945-1985.**
       William Preston, Jr., Edward S. Herman, and Herbert I. Schiller.
       Preface by Sean MacBride.   Minneapolis: University of Minnesota
       Press for the Institute for Media Analysis, 1989. 367p. bibliog.

This is a close study of the history of U.S. withdrawal from UNESCO. The authors are critical of U.S. short-sightedness, and somewhat sympathetic to the concerns behind Third World demands for a new international information order (NWICO). They argue that 'freedom of the press' was largely a cover for Western media interests, which failed to present both sides in this immensely important international controversy, and thus they demonstrated the very bias that Third World critics charged. From a U.N. perspective, its most powerful state-member became captive to narrow interests, represented by the Heritage Foundation and CBS's 'Sixty Minutes', who undid within a few years the traditional American policy of decades supporting a genuine free flow of ideas.

902 **Hope for the future.**
Amadou-Mahtar M'Bow.   Paris: UNESCO, 1984. 217p.

This collection of essays includes M'Bow's 'Reply to the general policy debate', at the General Conference on 10 November 1983, in which he defended his leadership to fulfil UNESCO's constitutional mission in such fields as peace, racism, human rights, apartheid, and disarmament.

903 **An idea and its servants: UNESCO from within.**
Richard Hoggart.   London: Chatto & Windus, 1978. 220p. bibliog.

Before the U.S. and U.K. officially withdrew from UNESCO, this former Assistant Director-General wrote a prescient analysis of its 'enclosed Byzantine system'. UNESCO is based on two 'fine fictions': (1) that an IO can be something more than its component states-members; and (2) that international civil servants can really be neutral, and not remain unconsciously 'nationals'. Hoggart tells the story of UNESCO in that inimitable style that is the fruit of an English education, and he concludes that, if UNESCO collapsed, 'the world would be poorer in expressed and – occasionally – achieved ideals'. 'Governments will not quickly learn to think and act collectively before common problems.'

904 **The idea of a world university.**
Michael Zweig. Foreword by Harold Taylor.   Carbondale, IL:
Southern Illinois University Press, 1967. 204p. bibliog.

Here is a sustained argument for the establishment of a world university in order to achieve the goals of international education. There are six broad goals to meet, Zweig argues: a broader sense of national interest in the body politic of every country; a new sense of international responsibility; improved intellectual cooperation; learning the new techniques of conflict resolution; gaining experience of diverse world cultures; and preparing intellectually and morally for the creation of lawful institutions of world order. A *world teaching university* is needed, since exchanges of students and teachers benefit too few people for too short a time, centres for the study of international relations tend to be dominated by the desire to place graduates in national governments, UNESCO has only recommendatory powers, and international academic associations have little impact on students and none on the public.

905 **Innovative methods in the Associated Schools Project.**
Paris: UNESCO, 1988. 127p.

Here is something for primary and secondary school teaching. It is a guide to principles and methods drawn from experience with 'Associated Schools' in most major nations.

906 **International education and teacher preparation.**
Betty Reardon.   *Higher Education in Europe*, vol. 9, no. 2 (1984),
p.34-39.

This is a review of the situation of international education at a low ebb during the Cold War by a leading teacher educator. The threat of nuclear war motivated many practising teachers to educate themselves and introduce international issues into the classroom. Reardon surveys various peace organizations supporting teacher education in the U.S., Canada, and Europe. The colleges and universities are still far behind, she finds.

907 **International human rights and international education.**
Thomas Buergenthal and J.B. Torney. Washington, DC: U.S.
National Commission for UNESCO, 1976. 211p.

In 1977, UNESCO recommended that international educators turn their eyes to
progress in observing human rights and hence to peace. This book is the first result in
the United States. Americans then had recently passed through the civil rights
struggle, and many remembered their past in preparing the Universal Declaration of
Human Rights and even the Declaration of Independence. 'America cannot be
America', writes an official of the U.S. Office of Education, 'without a national
system that has at its core a firm dedication to enlarging human rights and individual
liberty.' This book provides educators with fundamental documents, a history of
international education, an analysis of the international means for the protection of
human rights, an analysis of U.S. policy, surveys of students' international
knowledge, and student materials.

908 **International social science: the UNESCO experience.**
Peter Lengyel. New Brunswick, NJ: Transaction Books, 1986. 133p.
bibliog.

The author served UNESCO for thirty-one years – twenty-two of them as editor of the
International Social Science Journal. He finally was provoked to resign in 1984 after
the organization was 'despoiled' by 'breaching the bulwark of functionalism, and by
the destruction of professionalism at both the level of programming and that of
project execution'. Coming just before U.S. and U.K. withdrawals, this resignation
reflects deeper problems in UNESCO than just ideological chagrin within the Reagan
administration. Lengyel's book is a critical examination of the history of UNESCO,
culminating in the decade of 'sham revival to real collapse, 1975-1984'. He concludes
with recommendations, not for abandonment of a universal organization, but for 'two-
tier functionalism' of IGOs and NGOs. He calls for, not centralization of decision-
making in the U.N. system, but for a 'rationalized federalism'.

909 **Many voices, one world: communications and society, today and
tomorrow; towards a new, more just and more efficient world
information and communications order.**
International Commission for the Study of Communications Problems,
Sean MacBride, chairman. Foreword by Amadou-Mahtar M'Bow.
Paris: UNESCO, 1980; 2nd printing, 1983. 312p.

Here is the MacBride Commission report on the international mass media, which led
to UNESCO's proposed New World Information and Communications Order
(NWICO, 1980). Common problems discussed include: government controls,
censorship, concentration of media ownership, cultural dominance, freedom and
responsibility of the press, commercialization of the mass media, protection of
journalists, power of TNCs, technical revolution, and right to communicate.

910 **Mission of an international university.**
Alexandre Marc. *International Social Science Bulletin of UNESCO,*
vol. 4 (Spring 1952), p.225-29.

'The aim of higher education', writes Marc, 'is to create human beings worthy of the
name, regardless of all utilitarian considerations. . . . The tradition of a full thousand

years goes to prove that it is impossible to force such human beings, without maiming them, into the spiritual straightjacket of rigorous historical and geographical separatism. . . . An irresistable tendency towards union is visible in every sphere – economic, scientific, cultural, social, and even political. To regard this as a merely spiritual attitude, dismissing it with a smile as "idealistic", would be to misinterpret it. For it is not a spiritual attitude, but a historical urge to which spirit and hard fact are both lending their impetus. . . . Diversity and unity, indissolubly linked, form the hallmark and the patent of nobility of our human condition.'

911 **Most of all, they taught me happiness.**
Robert Muller. New York: Doubleday, 1978. 212p.
Muller tells the story of his experiences growing up in Strasbourg, when hatred between French and Germans was a fact of life. He laboured to abolish war and eventually rose to the post of Assistant Secretary-General of the United Nations. The autobiographical book is used as a social studies reader in many schools.

912 **The need for global education. Address on the occasion of the fortieth anniversary of the United Nations.**
Robert Muller. Dundas, Ontario: Peace Research Institute, 1984. 8p.
Muller calls for an education appropriate for a 'totally new era of history', marked by the spread of the industrial revolution all over the earth, phenomenal growth of population, and manifest interdependence between all societies. The U.N. is responding to these global crises, but the world's peoples need to be better prepared. 'Why was I not warned? Why was I not better educated?' will be the reproach hurled at teachers in decades to come.

913 **Post-World War II international relations as a component of general education in American colleges and universities.**
Washington, DC: Atlantic Council of the United States, 1989. 20p. (Available from the Council, 1616 H Street, NW, Washington, DC 20006.)
This is a syllabus for a one-semester general education course on either 'Post-World War II international relations' or 'The world since 1945'. Its central concepts are security, interdependence, international economics, and the global commons. The basic premise is the same as Thomas Jefferson's: If the people as the sovereign authority of the nation do not use their discretion wisely, the solution is not to take it away from them but 'to inform their discretion by education'.

914 **Report of the Council of the United Nations University (January-December 1985).**
United Nations General Assembly. *Official Records*, 1986. 57p. (41st sess., 31st sup. A/41/31).
Here is the first full report on the UNU programme: peace and security, global economy, hunger and poverty, social development, science and technology.

915   The rise and fall of UNESCO.

S. Nihal Singh.   Riverdale, MD: Riverdale Co., 1988. 137p.

'The crisis in Unesco is part of the crisis of the U.N. system.' The Indian author does not expect 'real reforms' in UNESCO, but if they should ever become possible, he believes the organization should 'sacrifice its intellectual pretensions and become a purely technical agency'. Singh provides a valuable Third World perspective on the problems of the major U.N. specialized agencies (WHO, ILO, FAO, and UNESCO), which he sees as being 'tilted [back] toward the West' by the threat of withdrawal and withholding of funds. UNESCO was merely 'the weakest link in the U.N. chain to attack'. To bring back the intellectuals as in the early days under Julian Huxley, and to restore debate at the highest levels on the intellectual issues that divide the modern world, Singh would revive the League of Nation's International Institute of Intellectual Cooperation (founded 1926).

916   Seeds for peace: the role of pre-school education in international understanding and education for peace.

Paris: UNESCO, 1985. 123p.

This is a book for pre-school teaching. It is a handbook of educational principles and practical suggestions based on the experience of early childhood educators from around the world.

917   The Seville statement on violence: preparing the ground for the constructing of peace.

Edited by David Adams.   Paris: UNESCO, 1989. 47p. bibliog.

A *scientific* statement that peace can be established and war abolished is here presented. It counters the scientific 'myth' that violence and war cannot be ended because they are part of our natural biology. The statement refutes five propositions: (1) that animals, like men, make war (they do not); (2) that war is part of human nature (it is part of culture); (3) that evolution selected aggressive behaviour ('dominance' also involves social bonding and affiliations); (4) that the brain is violent (no more than the hands); and (5) that war is caused by instinct (training produces soldiers and modern political leadership cultivates support for war preparations in the general populace). Suggestions for teachers are included.

918   The struggle to control UNESCO.

Lawrence S. Finkelstein.   In: *The United Nations and the world political economy: essays in honour of Leon Gordenker*. Edited by David P. Forsythe.   New York: St. Martin's 1989, p.144-64.

The struggle by the West to control UNESCO is treated here as a microcosm of the political struggle to control the U.N. Withdrawal from the one is a threat of withdrawal from the other. Finkelstein provides here a broadly political analysis. Criticisms of Israel and demands for a more open international news service (NWICO) seemed to challenge U.S. constitutional freedoms and vested interests in the communications industry. The real problem was that UNESCO, like the U.N., remained an organization of states where the United States, like the West, was increasingly reduced to the status of a minority. Attempts to institute consensus voting or non-politicized negotiations were too little or too late. Reform was abandoned for a return to unilateralism.

919 **UNESCO Chronicle.**
Paris: UNESCO, 1954- . bimonthly.

This is a 'chronicle' of the Secretariat – not a general-interest publication, nor a scientific or scholarly journal

920 **UNESCO Courier.**
Paris: UNESCO, 1946- . monthly.

Published in thirty-three languages and braille, this is the popular magazine of UNESCO. Each issue is devoted to a special topic – in January 1993 it was 'Exploring the cosmos' – and contains newsbriefs and the Director-General's comment on current concerns – e.g., 'What is culture?'

921 **UNESCO on the eve of its 40th anniversary.**
Amadou-Mahtar M'Bow. Paris: UNESCO, 1985. 216p.

During the crisis occasioned by the withdrawal of the United States and later of Great Britain and Singapore, the Director-General defended UNESCO as the 'intellectual conscience of the United Nations system'.

922 **UNESCO: structural origins of crisis and needed reforms.**
Maarten Mourik. In: *The U.N. under attack.* Edited by Jeffrey Harrod and Nico Schrijver. Aldershot, England: Gower, 1988, p.123-29.

UNESCO's difficulties are rooted in its constitution as an intergovernmental organization, which lets 'political interests prevail over the interests of international intellectual cooperation'. Every strong Director-General, argues the author, has been unable to withstand political pressures and repeatedly is made a scapegoat for national rivalries. The result of politicization is 'an absolute lack of coherence of policies, of common views, of any prevailing vision at all'. Once the problem of the Director-General is solved, the more superficial problems will disappear: NWICO, human rights *vs.* 'people's' rights, peace and disarmament. The U.S. and U.K. withdrawals (1984-85) have made reform even more difficult. Programming and medium-term plans should be made the responsibility of bodies representing member-states; the national commissions and NGOs should have strengthened roles in programming; consensus should be more relied upon; the Director-General's discretion in personnel matters should be curtailed; clear budgeting and independent auditing should be introduced.

923 **UNESCO and world politics: engaging in international relations.**
James P. Sewell. Princeton, NJ: Princeton University Press, 1975. 384p. bibliog.

Written about the same time as Richard Hoggart's account from the U.K. perspective (see item no. 903), this American history of UNESCO asks, 'whether, how, and by whom existing global relationships might be reordered or improved'? Sewell measures the effectiveness or influence of IOs in terms of how 'engaged' or involved their participants are. He finds that U.S. engagement in UNESCO slowly declined until his time of writing. (Distraction by the Cold War is not a large factor in his analysis.) Only in the last chapter does he explore the 'multilateral future'.

924 **Unilateralism, ideology, and U.S. foreign policy: the United States in and out of UNESCO.**
Roger A. Coate. Foreword by John E. Fobes. Boulder, CO: L. Rienner, 1988. 182p. bibliog.

The author treats U.S. withdrawal from UNESCO within the context of general American disenchantment with international organization. He shows, by a close diplomatic account of events in both Washington and Paris, that American policy became captive to ideologues in the Reagan administration – particularly Burton Pines, Thomas Gulick, and Owen Harries of the Heritage Foundation – who seized a moment of legitimate concerns about the organization (support for the PLO, challenge to Western news media) to advocate, not reform, but withdrawal in complete indifference to long-term U.S. interests in international cooperation. Coate concludes with practical reflections on 'multilateralism in a post-hegemonic world'.

925 **The United Nations University in the mid-eighties.**
Kathleen Newland. Tokyo: UNU, 1984. 63p.

This is a short, independent account of the UNU's programme of research, training, and communication, written by a senior researcher at the Worldwatch Institute.

926 **The United States and UNESCO. Summary [of the U.S. delegation meetings at the constituent conference of the United Nations Educational, Scientific, and Cultural Organization, Washington and London, October-November 1945].**
Luther H. Evans. Dobbs Ferry, NY: Oceana, 1971. 217p.

This is a history of the founding convention of UNESCO in 1945 by a participant. Originally, members of the Executive Board served in their *individual* capacities, not as representatives of their governments. This liberal provision was reversed by amendment in 1954, when the organization began its long slide into a diplomatic arena for the conduct of foreign policy. As in certain human rights committees, the use of individual experts could be one vital reform.

927 **The U.N., UNESCO, and the politics of knowledge.**
Clare Wells. New York: St. Martin's, 1987. 281p. bibliog.

The author, a former staff member, closely examines charges that since 1974 UNESCO has become 'politicised'. She finds that such charges reflect deeper issues, such as the real meaning of 'freedom of information', the powers granted to UNESCO to regulate education in order to construct the 'defences of peace', the regulation of science and culture, and international opposition to racial discrimination. The work is very tightly organized and written, so the busy reader is apt to find pertinent reflections immediately.

928 **U.S. withdrawal from UNESCO. Hearings [, 25-26 April and 2 May 1984].**
United States Congress, House of Representatives. Committee on Foreign Affairs, Subcommittee on Human Rights and International Organizations. 98th Cong., 2nd sess., 1984. 470p. (CIS No. H381-61. SuDocs No. Y4.F76/1:Un35/63/984-2).
Here can be found official reasoning for U.S. withdrawal. Compare Executive summary of U.S.–UNESCO policy review, Appendix 6.

929 **The world as teacher.**
Harold Taylor.   Garden City, NY: Doubleday, 1969. 322p.
Here is a masterful argument for international education, in principle and practice, by a leading American educator when President Johnson's International Education Act of 1966 was still alive. Special focus is on educating teachers for a 'world society'. Taylor brings in UNESCO and other organizations of the U.N. system at many points, but mainly he argues for inclusion of international education into the American educational system. A generation later, after the end of the Cold War, this book should prove an inspiration.

930 **World concerns and the United Nations.**
New York: United Nations, 1986. 235p. (E.86.I.8).
This illustrated book contains twenty-six model teaching units, directly usable in the classroom, at the primary, secondary, and higher levels. The lessons are about the aims and activities of the U.N.

931 **World education report.**
Paris: UNESCO, 1991. 149p.
This is the first of a series of 'global reports' from UNESCO, parallel to similar reports from other specialized agencies of the United Nations, 'on major trends and developments in fields where our common future is taking shape'. In effect, it is a global analysis of the state of education in every nation and region. The goal – reaffirmed at an international conference hosted by UNDP, UNESCO, UNICEF, and the World Bank in 1990 – is 'education for all'. This volume surveys world educational growth since 1970, continuing challenges (literacy, participation, duration of education, its content and purposes), and emerging prospects and issues (teacher requirements, assessments of learning). There is an abundance of figures, tables, and boxes for enlightenment. One is entitled; 'What education for the Information Age?'

The concept of international organization.
See item no. 736.

Science and technology

U.N. Outer Space Affairs Division

932 **High technology and the U.N.**
Jeffrey A. Hart.   In: *The United Nations and the world political economy: essays in honour of Leon Gordenker*. Edited by David P. Forsythe.   New York: St. Martin's, 1989, p.112-27.
The author surveys the U.N. agencies concerned with high technology and discusses issues particularly of information technology, transborder data flows, the proposed new international information order (NWICO), and protection of intellectual property. Hart sees potential for international standard setting as computer networks and telecommunications become more interdependent.

933 **Human rights and scientific and technological development.**
Edited by C.G. Weeramantry.   Tokyo: U.N. University Press, 1990. 222p. (E.90.III.A.3. HRSTD-1/UNUP-731).
This is an interdisciplinary and cross-cultural study on the affirmative use of science and technology for the furtherance of human rights, requested by the U.N. Human Rights Commission. Science and technology, which sometimes seem to be pursued without respect to human rights, also offer new means to extend the enjoyment of these rights to all humanity. The authors' standards for 'service to humanity' are *protection* of individuals, *access* to science and technology, and *choice* of techniques. The editor concludes that science and technology are, like human rights or telecommunications or respect for the environment, at a 'watershed in history'. They are key forces breaking down 'old concepts of sovereignty' and are 'making our planet one world'. The developing world, he argues, can take the lead in resisting the technology of the developed one, choosing and creating a more appropriate technology for the immense majority of the human race. He closes with a survey of the U.N.'s activities in the field since 1963. Compare his sequel below.

934 **The impact of technology on human rights: global case studies.**
Edited by C.G. Weeramantry.   Tokyo: UNU Press, 1993. 322p. (E.92.III.A.7. HRSTD-2/UNUP-821).
One billion people do not have enough food to sustain themselves after work (1990). The editor asks why cannot science and technology be harnessed to human rights to relieve human suffering of such magnitude? The lead essay in this volume by Jan Berting – on the historic encounter between Western scientific determinism and frustrated worldwide voluntarism – is the 'point of departure for our practical inquiries'. Other authors discuss the actual situation of science and technology in Venezuela, Thailand, Poland, Ethiopia, and Western Europe. Compare the prior volume above.

935 **Maintaining outer space for peaceful uses.**
Edited by Nandasiri Jasentuliyana. Tokyo: U.N. University Press, 1984. 333p. (GLDB-1/UNUP-537).

At a time of fear that the ABM treaty would be abrogated, and SDI lead to the militarization of space, a UNU symposium on 'maintaining outer space for peaceful uses' was held in The Hague. Participants were legal scholars, space scientists, and businesspeople from all over the earth (including U.S.A. and U.S.S.R.). They reviewed the historical background, the new field of space law, related international treaty law and regulations, and prospects for demilitarization. This is a book that is still informative, though the end of the Cold War seemed at the time beyond imaging.

936 **Outer space: a source of conflict or cooperation?**
Edited by Bhupendra Jasani. Tokyo: UNU Press in cooperation with SIPRI, 1991. 270p. (E.91.III.A.9. PGT-16/UNUP-759).

This book looks at man's recent exploitation of outer space in earth orbit as offering, on balance, more potential for peace than for war. The book clearly and exactly explains the newest high technology in space. The editor contributes an overview of space flight, remote sensing, surveillance satellites, and space weapons. Other authors discuss civilian space activities, the threat of the militarization of space, and the potential for international cooperation, particularly for arms control, remote sensing, communications, and exploration. Compare the companion volume, Marek Thee's *Military technology, military strategy, and the arms race* (1986).

937 **Proposed draft convention on the settlement of space law disputes.**
Karl-Heinz Böckstiegel. *Journal of Space Law*, vol. 12, p.136-62.

Since enforceability is the weak point of space law, like all international law, the author reviews current procedures for dispute settlement and then presents his draft convention, which provides for conciliation, arbitration, or adjudication by the ICJ or a new tribunal for space law.

938 **Science and technology and their implications for peace and security.**
U.N. Department for Disarmament Affairs. New York: United Nations, 1990. 152p. (Disarmament Topical Papers No. 2. E.90.IX.8).

Aware that hundreds of thousands of scientists are still employed in the qualitative arms race, yet hopeful that the end of the Cold War could allow very many to turn their knowledge and talents to works of peace, the U.N. held its first conference on new trends in science and technology in Sendai, Japan, in 1990. Its general themes were: (1) the inadequacy of traditional notions of national security in an interdependent world; (2) the dependence of peace and security on a more equitable distribution of existing technologies; (3) common interests that discourage unilateral action; (4) dangerous side-effects of the generally beneficial spread of science and technology (terrorism, ethnic conflict, drug trafficking); (5) the moral responsibilities of the users of technology for good or ill; (6) the need – in order to promote ethical responsibility – for more collaboration between natural scientists, social scientists, and teachers of the humanities. 'Technical assessment', argued the Under-Secretary-General for Disarmament Affairs Yasushi Akashi, leads logically to the issue of a 'code of conduct' for scientists and technologists.

939 **Space activities of the United Nations and international organizations.**
New York: United Nations, 1986- . 271p. bibliog. (E.86.I.2. A/AC.105/358).
This is a periodic review (since 1972) of the activities and resources of the U.N. (such as its Outer Space Affairs Division), of its specialized agencies (FAO), and of other competent bodies (European Space Agency) related to the peaceful use of outer space. The annex contains the texts of the Treaty on Principles Governing the Activities of the States in the Exploration and the Use of Outer Space, Including the Moon and Other Celestial Bodies (1966) and several others.

940 **The world of science and the rule of law: a study of the observance and violations of the human rights of scientists in the participating states of the Helsinki Accords.**
John Ziman, Paul Sieghart, and John Humphrey. Oxford: Oxford University Press, 1986. 343p.
This book is the result of a collaboration between a physicist, an international lawyer, and a medical scientist who examined the Helsinki Accords of 1975 as a new kind of working international law to support the fundamental freedoms or human rights on which the integrity of science depends. Thus the perspective in this book is rather different from that in other books above. Science here is to be protected from the world, rather than the world from science (and technology). One of the culminating chapters is entitled, 'One science for many nations' – a defence of freedom of scientists against the influence of state functionaries or corporate employers. This is the science that Weeramantry would enlist on the side of human rights.

Prevention of an arms race in outer space.
See item no. 683.

Pugwash – the first ten years.
See item no. 685.

Labour standards

International Labour Organization (ILO)

941 **Employment, growth, and basic needs: a one-world problem; the international basic needs strategy against chronic poverty.**
International Labour Office. Introduction by James P. Grant. New York: Praeger for Overseas Development Council, 1977. 223p.
This book is a presentation of the Basic Needs strategy for the rapid alleviation of poverty, which was endorsed at the ILO's World Employment Conference of 1976. The basic needs approach is an alternative to the New International Economic Order

(NIEO): basic needs requires domestic reforms within countries in addition to reforms in the international economic order; NIEO is concentrated on changes in the relations between countries. The approach has also been endorsed by Jan Tinbergen (*Reshaping the international order*, 1976 [q.v.]) and by Robert McNamara of the World Bank. By 1976, any notion that the Third World could extract concessions from the West on the basis of guilt for colonialism, as in the NIEO, was exposed as fatuous. This book sets out the international economic situation, the concept of basic needs, national strategies in the three 'worlds', strategy at the U.N. or in 'one world', trade adjustments, migrations of labour, technology transfer, and multinational corporations. An annex contains a declaration of basic needs principles and a programme of action.

942 **Human rights and international action: the case of freedom of association.**
Ernst B. Haas.   Stanford, CA: Stanford University Press, 1970. 184p.
This is a close study of the ILO's model procedures for the protection of human rights several years before U.S. complaints about their inadequacy led to temporary withdrawal (1977-80). The author regards functionalism as a 'second-best approach' to the protection of human rights – the very best would be the 'creation of United Nations organs with power to persuade or compel national governments to respect the rights of their citizens'. Nevertheless, Haas presents here a functionalist account of the ILO. Readers in search of more effective methods to implement human rights will find this an instructive book, since the ILO is far in advance of the U.N.

943 **The implementation procedures of the International Labor Organization.**
Ernest A. Landy.   *Santa Clara Law Review*, vol. 20 (1980), p.633-63.
'Social justice' is the ultimate objective of the ILO. Its conventions and recommendations, known as the International Labour Code, necessarily require implementation. The author argues that implementation under the ILO is enhanced by the degree of preciseness (enforceability) of the code and by the tripartite system of representation by government, business, and labour (legitimacy). Landy reviews the obligations accepted when adhering to ILO standards; the reporting, examination, and complaint procedures; and finally the relation of the ILO to the U.N. The ILO is a model for human rights implementation. With the U.S. returned (1980), Landy looked forward to even greater effectiveness.

944 **The influence of international labor standards on the world trading regime.**
Steve Charnovitz.   *International Labour Review* (Geneva), vol. 126 (1987), p.565-83.
Since the global marketplace threatens to move jobs to the cheapest labour locales, it would seem that international regulation of fair labour standards would protect workers in both developed and developing worlds. Indeed, the United States sought to put 'worker rights' on the agenda of the GATT talks about the same time as the European Parliament provided for a 'social charter' (1986). Neither effort succeeded. The author provides background for the Uruguay Round debate on worker rights. His article is addressed to trade negotiators, but general readers should find it of interest, since he includes within the 'world trading regime' GATT, ILO, treaties, national

laws, and reform proposals. Charnovitz concludes: 'At its core, the idea of fair labour standards is not protectionist. It is anti-protectionist. While workers everywhere would benefit from the further division of labour made possible by international commerce, freer trade is stymied whenever any trading partner questions the underlying fairness of the labour practices used by another. Establishing a floor for worker rights has the potential of removing one of the chief justifications for import restrictions.'

945 **The International Labour Organization: a case study on the evolution of U.N. specialized agencies.**
Victor-Yves Ghebali.   Dordrecht, The Netherlands: M. Nijhoff for the Graduate Institute of International Studies (Geneva) and Società Italiana per la Organizzazione Internazionale (Roma), 1989. 291p. bibliog. (International Organization and the Evolution of World Society, Vol. 3).

This recent study looks upon the ILO in the changed conditions of the international community since the European empires were dissolved, the bipolar system gave way to a multipolar one, science and technology became a fact of daily life, and needs for global cooperation became undeniable. Demands for a NIEO seem to mark the transition from the world in which the ILO was created to the world of a more effective U.N. Ghebali recounts the origins of the ILO, its early standard setting, and its innovations in international monitoring of state obligations and in technical cooperation. Like the World Bank and the IMF, the ILO has always reflected the values of Western liberalism; since the world is too diverse for such IOs, he particularly examines the ILO's response to socialist and developing countries. He takes up with renewed seriousness the ILO's constitutional commitment to 'social justice', now in the areas of employment, economic and social development, and protection and promotion of human rights. This book will probably be the standard on the ILO for many years.

946 **The International Labor Organization: an American view.**
Walter Galenson.   Madison, WI: University of Wisconsin Press, 1981. 351p.

The United States withdrew from the ILO in 1977 and rejoined in 1980. This book aims to explain why. Galenson recounts the history of the ILO very plainly with respect to differing views that it was a 'capitalist' organization or a front for 'creeping socialism'. He clearly describes tripartism and the rather remote participation of the U.S. government until the Soviet Union re-entered in 1954. Thereafter, the ILO was a battlefield in the Cold War. Readers in search of the political realities in the ILO – usually masked by the organization's officialese – will find it here. Galenson concludes that the U.S. will stay in the ILO only if it settles such fundamental issues as due process, the double standard, tripartism, and politicization.

947 **The International Labor Organization and the global economy: new opportunities for the United States in the 1990s.**
Economic Policy Council of the United Nations Association of the U.S.A., Ray Marshall, chairman. New York: UNA–USA, 1991. 73p. bibliog.

Here is a response to 'growing internationalization of business and markets' in the aftermath of the Cold War. This expert study argues that the U.S. has an interest in a 'predictable' and 'cooperative' new world order (25 per cent of GNP is derived from transnational economic activity). The U.S. should retake the lead in establishing, not a single universal set of labour standards, which is 'impractical', but standards 'linked' to international trade. Such standards belong in the GATT or the U.S.– Mexico Free Trade Area, since they 'recognize the different stages of development'. The authors acknowledge but skirt the issue of the 'social clause' in GATT, which would permit the use of *trade sanctions to enforce* common standards. (A dissenting member argues that the ILO should be used to develop, not common labour standards, but 'employment growth'.) The U.S. has ratified only nine of 169 ILO conventions that are legally binding. The authors conclude that, to take up leadership, the U.S. should ratify Convention No. 111 on Abolition of Forced Labour, then No. 87 on Freedom of Association and No. 98 on Right of Collective Bargaining. Then it should convene an expert working group to *link* ILO with GATT, IMF, and the World Bank. Lastly, the U.S. should create a volunteer corps of 'senior ambassadors' from business, labour, and government to give advice on a continued positive policy.

948 **The International Labour Organization as a development agency.**
Louis Emmerij. In: *The U.N. under attack*. Edited by Jeffrey Harrod and Nico Schrijver. Aldershot, England: Gower, 1988, p.111-22.

The functions of the 'old' ILO were standard setting and technical assistance. The 'new' includes the World Employment Programme, of which the author was the director. Emmerij finds that in pursuing a positive employment programme, he 'frequently had to say that organized labour was an obstacle to employment creation rather than an incentive'. He concludes that the ILO's World Employment Programme failed because the U.N. Director-General for Development and Economic Cooperation was not given the powers to coordinate all the agencies involved in development. The system's dispersion and lack of coordination 'is a reflection of national disorder in dealing with the United Nations'.

949 **Labor and hegemony.**
Robert W. Cox. *International Organization*, vol. 31 (1977), p.385-424.

At a time of U.S. withdrawal from the ILO (1977-80), this former ILO official and now prominent American political scientist analyses the incident as due to the loss of the previous 'hegemonic consensus'. Previously, Western governments, business corporations, and big labour (AFL–CIO) cooperated in the ILO against Bolshevism and subsequent international communism. But with the entry of the Third World countries into the ILO, the West seemed to be looking for other institutions in which to practise its hegemony. Cox argues that functionalism has not sustained the ILO, nor has an 'alternative counter-hegemonic base of support' in the Third World. He predicts a return to Western hegemony, but not in tripartite majority voting. The West will dominate by bureaucratic control. Hegemony (power politics) in place of genuine international cooperation prevents the ILO from confronting the deeper economic and social issues of the world – particularly the creation of employment, land reform, labour marginality, and systemic poverty. Cox exposes George Meany's anticommunism and C. Wilfred Jenks' 'vision of history . . . towards a future world government' with equal realism. But he upholds an ideal rooted in the new thinking of Antonio Gramsci: 'Some conjunction of radical forces in core and periphery', he concludes, 'would be the condition necessary for an effective challenge to or reversal of existing world social power relations.'

950 Labor and hegemony: a critique.

William A. Douglas and Roy S. Godson. *International Organization*, vol. 34 (1980), p.149-58.

The authors doubt that U.S. government, business, and labour have collaborated in an American policy to use the ILO to promote the interests of U.S. corporations abroad. Labour, particularly since the rise of serious threats to democracy from Nazism and the Communist Party after about 1935, has dissented from both government and business. The AFL–CIO was even more anti-communist than the government and criticized the Nixon–Ford détente policy. George Meany's goal was the 'non-military destruction of Soviet totalitarianism'. The AFL–CIO also fiercely criticized overseas expansion of U.S. multinational corporations, since they exported jobs. It supported a U.N. or ILO code of conduct for business.

951 Labor and hegemony: a reply.

Robert W. Cox. *International Organization*, vol. 34 (1980), p.159-76.

Professor Cox returns the focus to tripartism in the ILO. On balance, he argues, the AFL–CIO *did* support U.S. government and business in a common hegemony or 'corporative form of state'. Senator Fulbright in 1969 uncovered the role of the AFL–CIO's George P. Delany, in both the State Department and the ILO, who channelled U.S. AID money to cooperative international unions once Congress stopped the CIA. The implication remains, though Cox does not belabour it, that tripartism is an illusory form of international collaboration.

952 Organizational growth and goal structure: the case of the ILO.

Norman F. Dufty. *International Organization*, vol. 26 (1972), p.479-98.

The ILO, established after World War I, had the potential to become an 'economic counterpart' of the U.N. after World War II. (The precedent may be useful for projects after the Cold War to establish an 'economic U.N.') Since the ILO had a tripartite system of representation (of governments, businesses, and labour unions), such an enlargement would have made the world body something like a government at a stroke. In 1919, there was general agreement within the ILO that 'peace and social justice were indissolubly linked', and by 1944 the Philadelphia Declaration openly committed the organization to promotion of human rights and national economic planning in accordance with the slogan, 'Poverty anywhere constitutes a danger to prosperity everywhere'. But when the U.N. San Francisco conference of 1945 created Ecosoc, to which the specialized agencies were supposed to be subordinated, the ILO sought 'autonomy' rather than the 'apotheosis' of the new general security organization. The author traces these developments from the point of view of the theory of organizational growth. The ILO has progressed from a pressure group to a service organization to (now) a technical agency assisting nations in their economic development.

953 **The origins and evolution of the ILO and its role in the world community.**
David A. Morse. New York: Cornell University Press, 1969. 125p. bibliog.

The Director-General of the ILO (1948-70) lectured before the New York State School of Industrial and Labor Relations of Cornell University, and his thoughtful views for a general audience are reproduced here. He firmly sets the establishment of the ILO (1919) within the context of a century of conflict between capital and labour; the tripartite system of representation was designed for real effectiveness in settling this deep conflict. The ILO was not a narrow technical organization, but one mandated to promote 'lasting peace through social justice'. Its practical functions were to establish international labour standards and to collect information on labour and industrial conditions. The organization, however, within a few years went into decline, Morse admits, due to state opposition to its conventions and publications. (States withheld funds not unlike their conduct toward UNESCO or the U.N. in the next generation.) The revival with the Philadelphia Declaration of 1944 was similarly short-lived, since the new U.N. wished to avoid any taint of the League, and since communist countries backed the World Federation of Trade Unions. The Soviet Union did not join until 1954 and was not elected to the Governing Body until 1966. Morse generally skirts the problems of communist participation and of course his book appears before the U.S. withdrawal over the issue (1977-80).

954 **The origins of the International Labour Organization.**
James T. Shotwell. New York: Columbia University Press, 1934. 2 vols.

This will always be a standard history of the origins of the ILO during the Paris Peace Conference of 1919. The first volume contains Shotwell's introduction and several detailed essays; the second contains documents. Since the ILO, like the League of Nations, was more of a revolution in sovereign state conduct than the United Nations which came after it, serious readers looking for light at another revolutionary moment may want to cast their minds back to 1919.

955 **The politics of United States decision-making in United Nations specialized agencies: the case of the International Labor Organization.**
Gregory T. Kruglak. Washington, DC: University Press of America, 1980. 290p. bibliog.

U.S. withdrawal from the ILO (1977-80) was in many ways a rehearsal for withdrawal from UNESCO (1984-) and threatened withdrawal from the U.N. (1985-). The issues were similar: 'politicization', 'double standards', abuse of the United States when it was paying the largest share of the bills, lack of respect for liberty, domestic disenchantment. This study, originally a thesis at the University of Geneva, goes back to the U.S. refusal to pay its assessed dues in 1970, which was a focal point for later withdrawal. The work is a history of the ILO in the decade 1970-80, with warnings for the future.

956 **Social justice in the law of nations: the ILO impact after fifty years.**
C. Wilfred Jenks. Oxford: Oxford University Press for the Royal Institute of International Relations, 1970. 94p. bibliog.

Written about the same time as David Morse's lectures (q.v.), these lectures by his successor as Director-General take a much more ambitious view of the 'experience of the ILO to make the law more responsive to contemporary need in other fields'. Jenks saw that the ILO, especially during its long frustration by nationalism, was transforming international law from a law between states to a law reaching to individuals. He saw that the international system was weak because it lacked a legislature, could not enforce its decisions, and relied on voluntary jurisdiction. 'These are among the fundamental problems not only of world government', he wrote, 'but of all governments. . . .' The ILO, he concluded, was a 'prototype'. 'Let us look to the vitality of the law for the freedom and welfare of a world community living in peace and justice under the common law of mankind.'

957 **Trade-linked labor standards.**
Ray Marshall. In: *International trade: the changing role of the United States*. Edited by Frank Macehiarola. New York: Academic Press, 1990, p.7-78.

Here is a full exposition of less than universal 'trade-linked' labour standards, designed as a transitional arrangement to a justly ordered world economic space. Compare Economic Policy Council of the UNA–USA, *The International Labor Organization* (item no. 947).

958 **Tripartism and the ILO.**
Gregory Kruglak. In: *The United Nations and the world political economy: essays in honour of Leon Gordenker*. Edited by David P. Forsythe. New York: St. Martin's, 1989, p.179-96.

The 'tripartite' system of representation in the ILO for governments, workers, and employers holds promise for the U.N. system as a whole. The author provides a fine basic introduction to the ILO, covers challenges to the system by both the socialist and the developing blocs, and carries the story to the constitutional amendments of 1986. Kruglak looks forward to the 'trend in some socialist countries towards a lessening of state control at the enterprise level', which might lead to complete agreement on representation. (After the revolutions of 1989, the ILO might yet have a larger influence on representation in the U.N.)

959 **The United States and the International Labor Organization. Twenty-sixth report.**
Commission to Study the Organization of Peace. Louis B. Sohn, chairman; Daniel G. Partan and Paul C. Irwin, reporters. New York: Commission to Study the Organization of Peace (866 United Nations Plaza, Room 4045, New York, NY 10017), December 1979. 32p.

Appearing shortly before, and evidently influential upon, U.S. return to the ILO in early 1980, this astute legal policy paper argues that recent reforms in Conference voting should eliminate uneven practice in the Committee on Application, that politicization has declined by itself, that tripartism strengthens the U.S. when other members fail to send 'truly independent worker and employer representatives', and that fair trade as it affects labour is only treated in the ILO. But they admit that the NIEO remains an open issue, and that labour standards in developing countries are not yet settled. In short, the United States has more to gain by returning to the ILO, where it can influence developments, than by remaining isolated. Sohn, Partan, and Irwin urge U.S. ratification of the more important conventions: Forced Labour (Nos. 29 and 105), Freedom of Association (87), Right to Organize (98), Equal Remuneration (100), Discrimination (111), and others. An excellent brief history and exposition of contentious issues (e.g., supervision of standards, tripartism, competence to promote the NIEO) support the recommendations.

960 **What is the substance of tripartism in the International Labour Organization?**
H. van der Kooy. *Netherlands Yearbook of International Law*, vol. 8 (1977), p.73-106.

The author takes up the rather technical question of what are the criteria for the verification of the credentials of non-governmental delegates to the ILO? This leads him to a penetrating analysis of the representative character of the business and labour delegates. In effect, he examines the legitimacy (popular consent) of tripartism as a model for the more effective ILO or U.N. of the future. Van der Kooy finds that 'the traditional content of tripartism is based on the Western model of democracy and on an economic structure which, after 1919, has gone through fundamental changes, even in Western countries.' Hence, of his ten criteria for 'effective universality', only two are met in the ILO. The implication is that tripartism, historically, had primarily a 'domestic function'. Universality of labour laws to protect labour in the international market remains for the future.

Law of the Sea

U.N. Convention on the Law of the Sea (LOS) International Maritime Organization (IMO)

961 **Before and after.**
Arvid Pardo. *Law and Contemporary Problems*, vol. 46, no. 2 (Spring 1983), p.95-105.

The father of the Law of the Sea here denounces the legitimacy of his offspring. Pardo judges the large and complex convention by the standards of Adlai Stevenson in 1971: accommodation of interests; prevention of conflict; predictability; and promotion of common or community objectives. By each of these standards he finds the signed document wanting. 'We may perhaps conclude that the Convention, evaluated from a non-national point of view, does not effectively serve any of the functions of a law of the sea treaty enumerated by Ambassador Stevenson because of its silence, vagueness, or ambiguity on major issues.' Up to forty per cent of ocean space was acquired for national jurisdiction. The international regime for seabed mining contemplated in Part XI has 'little relationship to reality'; hence it fails to balance the extension of state sovereignty. The convention is 'fundamentally flawed: inequality between states is increased, law and order in the seas is only marginally improved, and the concept of the common heritage of mankind is ineffectively implemented.' He closes with a call for moderation from both the United States and the developing world, and for treating the 1982 convention as 'not the end, but rather the beginning, of a long process which must lead to a more rational and efficient use of our environment and towards a more just and equitable world order'.

962 Code of safety for nuclear merchant ships.

International Maritime Organization. London: IMO, 1982. 127p.

This code is typical of many IMO codes for the governance of the seas.

963 The common heritage of mankind principle in international law.

Bradley Larschan and Bonnie C. Brennan. *Columbia Journal of Transnational Law*, vol. 21 (1983), p.305-37.

The authors treat the common heritage of mankind as a new principle of international law that, like the freedom of the seas, may take decades or even centuries to be accepted within the consensus (*opinio juris*) of states. The principle has been discussed not only in the U.N. Law of the Sea conference but also in meetings of the Antarctica Treaty parties and in fora on outer space. Underlying the principle is general recognition that free trade could no longer be assumed to guarantee industrial development in poor countries, and that nature provided inexhaustible resources for economic growth. Larschan and Brennan trace the history of the principle from the Romans' *res nullius*, through Arvid Pardo's great speech in 1967 (see item no. 967), to the 'shadow' of his proposal in the actually negotiated Law of the Sea. They look forward to renegotiation of the convention on a more consensual basis.

964 Consensus and confrontation: the United States and the Law of the Sea Convention.

Edited by Jon M. Van Dyke. Honolulu: Law of the Sea Institute, University of Hawaii, 1985. 576p.

A year after the United States refused to sign the Law of the Sea Convention, a high-level retrospective workshop was held in Hawaii. Key representatives from the U.S. State Department, the developing countries (including Tommy Koh, president of the U.N. conference at its conclusion), the Soviet Union, China, the U.S. mining industry, and academics from around the world attended. They debated such issues as the status of the convention while the U.S. was not a party, whether customary law could fill the void, the issue of deep seabed mining, freedom of navigation, fishing, environmental protection, dispute resolution, enforcement, and the costs and benefits of allowing the convention to become a dead letter. The consensus was roundly against the United States, since Part XI on seabed mining would provide adequate protections for private enterprises, unilateral mining would be challenged in the ICJ, navigation rights would remain in doubt, environmental provisions will be unapplied, the benefits of dispute resolution will be lost, but most of all, since the opportunity to promote trust among nations will be lost.

965 Deepsea mining.
Edited by Judith T. Kildow.   Cambridge, MA: MIT Press, 1980.
251p. bibliog.

The most controversial part of the emerging Law of the Sea was that dealing with international exploitation of the deep seabed for the common benefit of humanity. The deep sea, like outer space, it was asserted, belonged to the 'common heritage of mankind'. Since this idea limited private profit and national freedom of the seas, and since the emerging law seemed to be both settling old problems and raising new ones, the Massachusetts Institute of Technology held an expert seminar in the winter of 1978-79 'to examine several policy issues related to deepsea mining but also more broadly to international resource mining'. The heart of the policy debate is reflected in papers from the U.S. State Department (Arthur Kobler), U.S. industry (Richard Darman), and the Third World (A.O. Adede). The editor concludes that there *is* a net strategic and economic value to the United States from manganese nodules on the Pacific seabed. But political problems, 'involving as they do national perceptions and pride', were left hanging between unilateral exploitation and international management of commonly owned resources for the benefit of all nations, especially the LDCs 'to help offset the effects of past inequitable conditions'. The experts seem to have reluctantly accepted the international regime, provided that nations with mining technologies and vested interests had 'weighted control' of the enterprise.

966 The drama of the oceans.
Elisabeth Mann Borgese.   New York: Abrams, 1975. 258p. bibliog.

This beautifully illustrated and thoughtfully written book, which appeared soon after the beginning of the third U.N. conference on the Law of the Sea, is designed to awaken broad public appreciation for the sea and its significance for man and woman. It dramatically presents the crowding of the sea by fishermen, sailors, oilmen, miners, civil engineers, architects, shore developers, and warriors. It argues for the necessity of an ocean constitution and the rule of law or else 'the oceans will surely die'. The author attempts to shape the U.N. negotiations by setting out 'the minimum requirements for rational development of ocean space and resources'. She concludes that the new organizations designed to regulate human life on the sea – partly political, partly economic, partly scientific – are the 'great laboratory' for building 'international organization in the twenty-first century'.

967 Examination of the question of the reservation exclusively for peaceful purposes of the sea-bed and of the ocean floor, and the subsoil thereof, underlying the high seas beyond the limits of present national jurisdiction, and the use of their resources in the interests of mankind.
Arvid Pardo.   United Nations, General Assembly, 1 November 1967.
75p. (Official Records, A/C.1/PV1515-16).

This is Ambassador Pardo's classic speech on the 'common heritage of mankind'. It is not merely a coinage of a new ideal, but a sustained argument about the changed realities of the seas and the necessity for the extension over them of the rule of law.

968   **Guidelines on oil spill dispersant application and environmental considerations.**
IMO/UNEP.   London: IMO, 1982. 43p.

Here, international bodies provide informed guidance to national governments and private firms trying to cope with pollution from well blowouts and tanker wrecks. 'An ounce of prevention is worth a pound of cure' is particularly true about marine pollution. Dispersants, removal, introduced bacteriological agents, and nature's ways are the main means available to man to clean up oil spills.

969   **How the Law of the Sea treaty will affect U.S. marine science.**
David A. Ross and John A. Knauss.   *Science*, vol. 217 (10 September 1982), p.1003-08.

The authors warn that, when the Law of the Sea enters into force, its articles on marine science will restrict the activities of U.S. scientists in the waters of coastal states. Some forty per cent of the ocean will fall under the new international legal regime. Getting the requisite permissions is so complicated that Ross and Knauss recommend that a 'foreign office' be established within the University National Oceanographic Laboratory System or the Joint Oceanographic Institute. The dispute settlement procedures are so lengthy and expensive as to be useless for scientists. Long-term benefits from the rule of law over the oceans are not mentioned.

970   **International Conference on the Establishment of an International Maritime Satellite System, London, 1975-76.** *Final Act, including the Convention and Operating Agreement on the International Maritime Satellite Organization (INMARSAT).*
London: Inter-governmental Maritime Consultative Organization, 1976. 102p.

INMARSAT was established in accordance with this agreement in 1976 after one year of negotiations. The ease of its establishment is a striking illustration of the ability of fifty sovereign states to cooperate in a field where the benefits are immediately obvious to all. 'The purpose of the organization is to make provision for the space segment necessary for improving maritime communications, thereby assisting in improving distress [communications] and safety of life at sea communications, efficiency and management of ships, maritime public correspondence services, and radiodetermination capabilities.'

971   **Internationalizing the seabed.**
Roderick C. Ogley.   Brookfield, VT: Gower, 1984.

Some argue that the dispute settlement provisions are the most significant part of the Law of the Sea. This author argues that the Authority for managing the exploitation of the deep seabed in the common interest (Part XI) is the most important. Ogley, an English scholar who attended most of the negotiating sessions from 1974 to 1982 as observer for the Friends World Committee for Consultation, discusses this controversial issue, or rather set of issues, historically. Who is 'mankind' in whose name the 'common heritage' should be administered? he asks. Other issues involved include: the geographical area of the common heritage, the alternatives for exploitation, the balance between private and public production, the structure of the international Authority, and, of course, dispute settlement. Ogley concludes that, even in attenuated form, the Authority is worth setting up to both regulate mining and to mine itself, for that will involve all citizens as shareholders and thus, politically, 'give us a new concept of ourselves'.

972 **The international law of the sea.**
Daniel P. O'Connell. Edited by I.A. Shearer.   Oxford: Clarendon Press, 1982. 2 vols. bibliog.

This authoritative British legal study of the stormy law of the sea appeared just before the United Nations began a third time to negotiate a modern law. The author presumes, in an old tradition of international legal publicists, that governments act from *opinio juris*, from legal conviction, and 'not from motives of power and gain'. The book is an elaborate examination of this assumption, with technical suggestions for the third Law of the Sea conference. Readers will still find this an invaluable reference for legal questions.

973 **International marine organizations: essays on structure and activities.**
Kamil A. Bekiashev and Vitali Serebriakov. Translation by V. Serebriakov.   The Hague: M. Nijhoff, 1981. 578p.

This work, translated from the Russian, is the most complete available survey of international marine organizations. The IMO is treated under its old title (to 1982), Inter-governmental Maritime Consultative Organization. INMARSAT has a section. Some sixty maritime, fisheries, and marine science organizations are fully described.

974 **The International Maritime Organization.**
Samir Mankabady. Foreword by C.P. Srivastava.   London: Croom Helm, 1984; rev. ed., 1986. 2 vols.

This work brings the IMO's extensive work in the technical and legal maritime fields to public attention. The Secretary-General in his foreword remarks that 'the International Maritime Organization has developed a well coordinated regime of international maritime technical standards for enhancing maritime safety and for protecting the marine environment from pollution by shipping'. Mankabady presents the work of the IMO and comments upon it from a legal perspective. The first chapter is entitled, 'The IMO: a law-making organization'. Topics include: rules on ship construction, cargoes and containers, seafarers, traffic and transport, navigation, protection of the environment, and accidents at sea. These volumes are comparable to those by O'Connell (see item no. 972) or Churchill (see item no. 977) on the LOS.

975 **International transfer of marine technology.**
Judith T. Kildow.   Cambridge, MA: MIT Press, 1977. 3 vols in 1. 376p.

This is a U.S.-funded study of 'more effective means for the United States to share marine science and technology with other nations'. Topics include: the political and economic background, including communications; the scientific and technical aspects of the problem, particularly in oceanography and fishing; and then a proposed U.S. programme of transfer to Mexico.

976 **The Law of the Sea.**
Elisabeth Mann Borgese. *Scientific American*, vol. 248 (March 1982), p.42-49.
This is a summary of the negotiations and the results of the third U.N. conference on the Law of the Sea. The final convention was signed by 119 nations, not including the United States, Great Britain, and West Germany. Borgese presents the basic facts about the new law in a spirit of guarded optimism.

977 **The Law of the Sea.**
Robin R. Churchill and Alan V. Lowe. Manchester: Manchester University Press, 1983; 2nd ed., 1988. 370p. bibliog.
This legal study by two leading British scholars aims to give an 'up-to-date introduction to the subject as a whole'. It explains both the 1982 convention on the Law of the Sea and the customary law which supplements it (to 1987). The authors are fully aware of the revolutionary character of the law, which reaches to individuals (who may be arrested in coastal waters on charges of illegal fishing or denied passage through archipelagos on charges of pollution). They explain the new limits on freedom of the seas because of crowding and pollution. The modern law of the sea is a synthesis of the natural law tradition and consensual positivism.

978 **The Law of the Sea.**
William Wertembaker. *New Yorker*, 1 August 1983, p.38-65; 8 August 1983, p.56-83.
This is a narrative and analytical account of the nine-year U.N. conference on the Law of the Sea. Consensus decision making was used throughout; a formal vote was taken only at the end to approve the historic document in April 1982. This is a readable and inspiring account.

979 **The Law of the Sea: a crossroads for American foreign policy.**
Leigh S. Ratiner. *Foreign Affairs*, vol. 60, no. 5 (Summer 1982), p.1006-21.
After the United States refused to sign the Law of the Sea convention on 30 April 1982 (Venezuela, Turkey, and Israel also voted no), this rather lugubrious article by one of the final U.S. negotiators appeared. The Reagan administration's 'free enterprise philosophy', Ratiner sums up, 'may have cost us a golden opportunity to convert the treaty into a better vehicle for commercial operators'. Outside the treaty, U.S. seabed miners will not be protected from risks, and other rights related to navigation and coastal jurisdiction cannot be guaranteed. The author traces the administration's review process up to the point where an alternative 'mini-treaty with our allies' seemed to offer an escape from the logic of twelve years of U.S. policy. American negotiators were then unable to change the ownership clauses or introduce weighted voting into the Seabed Authority. France and soon Japan and the Soviet Union signed the treaty, as did 130 states; Britain and West Germany abstained. Ratiner predicts that first the allies, then the Soviet bloc, and finally the United States will join the Law of the Sea, for it creates 'unchallengeable rights'.

980 Law of the Sea: the integration of the system of settlement of disputes under the draft convention as a whole.

A.O. Adede. *American Journal of International Law*, vol. 72 (1978), p.84-95.

This is a legal exposition of the several dispute settlement articles in the draft Law of the Sea as it approached its final form. Most of them related to the controversial Authority for the governance of the seabed. Others applied to the whole law, even if the Authority were never to enter into force. The author, from the U.N. Office of Legal Affairs, concludes that the draft found novel ways to encourage states to settle their disputes 'through legal channels where the principle of equality before the law prevails, as opposed to extralegal channels in which political, economic, and other [military] pressures play dominant roles'. In short, the Law of the Sea upset the traditional doctrine in international law that a state may be a judge in its own case.

981 The Law of the Sea in a nutshell.

Louis B. Sohn and Kristen Gustafson. St. Paul, MN: West, 1984. 264p.

For busy national and international officials, lawyers, and serious students, this brief, analytical, and interpretive book will be the place to go to understand the Law of the Sea (in force by 1994). Only the part (XI) relating to deep seabed mining remains controversial, holding up ratification by the United States. This book concentrates on all the other parts, which are already binding as customary international law and, for states ratifying, as treaty law. Covered are: nationality of vessels, jurisdiction of flag state, zones of national jurisdiction, internal waters and ports, territorial seas, exclusive economic zones, continental shelf, mining the seabed, protection of the environment, freedom of the seas, dispute settlement.

982 The Law of the Sea: official text of the United Nations Convention on the Law of the Sea with annexes and index; Final Act of the third United Nations conference on the Law of the Sea.

New York: United Nations, 1983. 224p. (E.83.V.5).

The *Convention*, binding on states-parties, of the Law of the Sea was signed by 119 nations, including France and the U.S.S.R., at Montego Bay, Jamaica, on 10 December 1982. It was opened for futher signatures and subject to ratification by sixty states before entering into force (1994). The *Final Act*, the official account of the proceedings but not a binding treaty, was signed by a total of 142 nations, including such states that did not sign the convention as West Germany, Italy, Japan, Switzerland, the U.K., and the U.S.A. This clearly arranged volume contains the full text of both Convention and Final Act, plus introduction, list of signatories, chronology, and index to the convention, its annexes, and resolutions. Hence, this is the place to go to find out what the Law of the Sea *is*. The then U.N. Secretary-General Javier Pérez de Cuéllar praised the law as a 'new legal order for ocean space'. The president of the U.N. conference and the chief negotiator who perfected its consensual methods of decision-making, Tommy T.B. Koh, called the law a 'comprehensive constitution for the oceans'.

983 Law, force, and diplomacy at sea.
Ken Booth. Winchester, MA: Allen & Unwin, 1985. 231p. bibliog.

This book of strategic analysis examines the Law of the Sea for its implications on naval power. Choke points in narrow straits, submarine sightings in Scandinavian waters, Cold War confrontations in every ocean are very much on the author's mind. (In 1985, the end of the Cold War could hardly be imagined.) The book is addressed to naval strategists, international lawyers supporting naval operations, and students of defence policy. Booth sees his book as neither 'hawkish' (opposed to the Law of the Sea) nor 'dovish' (assuming that naval power should go out of business). He argues that, as long as international conflict continues to explode periodically, all coastal states and especially Great Powers will need to maintain their naval defences. He supports the Law of the Sea treaty as a step toward the reliable rule of law; meanwhile, warships are still needed to 'signal' powers pursuing national advantage.

984 Negotiating by consensus: developments in technique at the United Nations conference on the Law of the Sea.
Barry Buzan. *American Journal of International Law*, vol. 75 (1981), p.324-48.

The U.N. conference (UNCLOS) pioneered *active consensus*, as opposed to *passive consensus* used in the past merely to avoid divisive voting. It was this 'major experiment in decision making by consensus', argues the author, that gives the conference its lasting significance. When state sovereignty is cherished as an ultimate defence, and weighted voting is seen as slighting smaller states, consensus may make possible a new 'era in which international negotiation appears to be the predominant mode of relations between states'. As Buzan also puts it, 'global democracy of some sort is going to be a necessary condition for dealing with planetary problems'. Here will be found a very able exposition of active consensus, especially with respect to the key role of chairpersons and to quality of output.

985 Negotiating the Law of the Sea.
James K. Sebenius. Cambridge, MA: Harvard University Press, 1984. 251p. bibliog.

This is a close study of negotiating the financial agreements in the Law of the Sea by a participant, particularly during the difficult years 1978-80. The author then reflects more broadly on reaching agreement in negotiation, which he sees as rooted in management of the 'differences' among the negotiators and in manipulation of agendas and inclusion of parties. Sebenius explains Reagan administration rejection of the convention in 1982 as due to recalculation of U.S. interests (in seabed mining and navigation) in the light of the alternative of Great Power prevalence in an anarchic marine environment.

986 Negotiating a new world order for the sea.
Tommy T.B. Koh. In: *Negotiating world order: the artisanship and architecture of global diplomacy.* Edited by Alan K. Henrikson. Wilmington, DE: Scholarly Resources, 1986, p.33-45.

Here is a clear introduction to the Law of the Sea by a principal negotiator. Koh discusses the history of 'freedom of the seas', the collapse of the old legal order, competing interests at the third U.N. conference (1973-82), the prominence given to consensus as a technique for reaching agreement, and future implications.

987 **New directions in the Law of the Sea.**
Edited by S. Houston Lay, Robin Churchill, and Myron Nordquist.
Dobbs Ferry, NY: Oceana for British Institute of International and
Comparative Law, 1973-81. 11 vols. bibliog. Continued by K.R.
Simmonds, ed., 1983, 4 vols.

Appearing as the third U.N. conference on the Law of the Sea proceeded, these
volumes collect conveniently 'all the basic documents relating to the Law of the Sea'
plus 'documentary information relevant to the present debate'. In view of the struggle
between creeping national jurisdiction and assertive international regulation, the
documents are generally divided into 'national claims to marine areas' and
'regulation of marine activities'. Negotiators, international lawyers, policy-makers,
international civil servants, scholars, and environmentalists will find this a
complement to similar strictly U.N. compendia.

988 **The New International Economic Order and the Law of the Sea.**
Arvid Pardo and Elisabeth Mann Borgese. Malta: International
Ocean Institute, 1975. 223p. (Occasional Paper No. 4).

As the new Law of the Sea began to emerge as a single negotiating text in the third
U.N. conference, the authors prepared this analysis in order to guide the process,
which was in danger of losing sight of such original goals as Ambassador Pardo's
'common heritage of mankind'. The authors affirm such principles, which they regard
as necessary and timely, as the common heritage, use but not ownership of ocean
resources, shared management, shared benefits, reservation of the seas for peaceful
purposes, and reservation for future generations. Sovereignty, they affirmed, should
not be allowed to extend all over the oceans; it should be limited to 'functional
sovereignty', that is, jurisdiction for internationally determined uses. The goal was a
'balanced international system for ocean space'. Since the 1982 convention fell far
short of these ideals, the work will still serve to guide others in the future.

989 **Ocean yearbook, 9 [1991].**
Edited by Elisabeth Mann Borgese and Norton Ginsberg (and later
Joseph R. Morgan). Chicago: University of Chicago Press, 1978- .
annual.

Under the general auspices of the International Ocean Institute of Malta, these
yearbooks continue the vision and the action of Arvid Pardo, Robert M. Hutchins,
Elisabeth Mann Borgese, the *Pacem in Maribus* convocations (1970-78) (see item
no. 991), and even Pope John XXIII, whose encyclical *Pacem in Terris* (1963)
exercised world leadership to bring about a world at peace. The *Ocean yearbook* is
designed to be a resource of facts and discussion of the immense issues of creating a
'constitution for the oceans', which means, as Borgese often writes, a 'constitution
for the world'. Each volume contains informed and inspired articles on prospects,
living resources, non-living resources, transportation and communications, marine
science and technology, environment, coastal management, military activities,
regional developments, and reports and documents; tables of statistical data can be
found throughout. The authors are not limited to those from the West. The work is
addressed to 'policymakers, students, concerned citizens, planners, conservationists,
industrialists, and fishermen'.

990 **Ordering the oceans: the making of the Law of the Sea.**
Clyde Sanger. Preface by Hugh Caradon.   Toronto: University of
Toronto Press, 1987. 225p. bibliog.

This recent history of the Law of the Sea negotiations by a Canadian journalist tells
the story with charm and liveliness (and even a few cartoons). Sanger was present
during Arvid Pardo's historic speech at the U.N. in November 1967, when he
proposed that the ancient doctrine of the freedom of the seas was outdated and should
be replaced by a new legal concept of the 'common heritage of mankind'. He carries
the story through Tommy Koh's speech at the signing ceremony in Montego Bay,
Jamaica, in December 1982, which extolled the Law of the Sea as a 'constitution for
the oceans'. General readers and sophisticated ones will find this book the most
entertaining and informative history of the law. It is divided into chapters on the
novel negotiating process of consensus, limits to national jurisdiction, rights of
passage, seabed mining, pollution control, marine scientific research, and fisheries. (It
is striking that this conference on the LOS was so successful at the very time
negotiations on the NIEO utterly failed.) 'We succeeded', explained Ambassador
Koh, 'because we did not regard our counterparts in the negotiations as the enemies
to be conquered.'

991 **Pacem in maribus.**
Edited by Elisabeth Mann Borgese.   New York: Dodd, Mead, 1972.
382p. bibliog.

The papers included here are not so technical that they are now obsolete; rather, in the
context of emerging issues before the U.N. began its third conference on the Law of
the Sea, the authors come to grips with political and economic questions that are still
unresolved. The freedom of science in its now highly professionalized state, the
making of ocean policy not on the basis of scientific recommendations but on
politicians' sense of national interests, exploring the implications of the 'common
heritage', developing the sea frontier without repeating the mistakes of the American
Wild West, containing the spread of military weapons from land to sea, organizing an
ocean authority – these are issues discussed here.

992 **Regime dynamics: the rise and fall of international regimes.**
Oran R. Young.   *International Organization*, vol. 36 (1982),
p.277-97.

The purpose of the Law of the Sea conference, the author argues in a comprehensive
article on international regimes, was to move from anarchy to 'negotiated order'.
Other types are spontaneous order (like free markets) and imposed order (as in
hegemony or conquest). Young's thoughts on 'regime transformation' would seem to
point to the future of the ocean regime, even if the Law of the Sea is very weak.
Transformation is a response to internal contradictions, shifts in external power, and
forces of technology. His thought, however, remains theoretical.

993 **The revenge of John Seldon: the draft convention on the Law of
the Sea in the light of Hugo Grotius' *mare librum*.**
John Logue.   *Grotiana*, New Series, vol. 3 (1982), p.27-56.

The recent Law of the Sea convention was not a victory for the common heritage of
mankind but for 'ocean nationalists'. John Seldon, author of *Mare clausum* (Closed
sea, 1635), was an antagonist of Hugo Grotius.

994   **Sea bed mining and the Law of the Sea.**
      Elliot Richardson.   *U.S. Department of State Bulletin*, vol. 80,
      no. 2,045 (December 1980), p.60-64.

This is an account by the chief U.S. negotiator of how close the Law of the Sea conference came to resolution of the major North–South differences over deep seabed mining. Some 120 improvements from the U.S. perspective were made in the prior negotiating text. Ambassador Richardson comments: 'The result by any standard is an unprecedented achievement for multilateral negotiation. That it was possible to find ways of accommodating such diverse and intense national interests can be accounted for only by the commitment of most participants to what they saw as an overriding and inspiring goal: the prevention of conflict and the extension of a generally agreed system of law to more than two-thirds of the Earth's surface.' He expounds the new text in detail, arguing that unilateral exploitation of the seabed will not enjoy the security for investment that the international legal regime will provide.

995   **The structure and effects of the decision process in the Seabed
      Committee and the third United Nations conference on the Law of
      the Sea.**
      Edward Miles.   *International Organization*, vol. 31 (1977),
      p.159-234.

This is a legal and political analysis of the controversial Seabed Authority in the Law of the Sea before Elliot Richardson mounted his effort to make it more acceptable to the U.S. (1980). The article is still of interest for its record of contending groups of states and its criticism of the comprehensive attempt to negotiate the entire Law of the Sea simultaneously. Miles has no appreciation for the new consensus decision-making process, which he calls 'cumbersome and inefficient'. He laments the passing of the 'good old days'.

996   **Superpower at sea: U.S. ocean policy.**
      Finn Laursen.   New York: Praeger, 1983. 209p. bibliog.

The United States has been a superpower at sea since Britain declined after World War II. The U.S. led in international negotiations to update the customary law of the sea from 1968 to 1982, when the Reagan administration, responding to domestic political pressures, refused to sign the final convention. This book, by a Danish scholar sympathetic to world order politics, is a case-study of U.S. foreign policy-making. He closely examines problems of security, offshore petroleum rights, fishing, and deep seabed mining. Laursen analyses events in these areas from four perspectives – classical realism, international interdependence, bureaucratic politics, and domestic politics. The latter, as foreign policy scholars often say, was most influential in 1982. Laursen concludes with a sustained critique of Reagan conservatives, who imagined that, in international law, states not party to a convention may pick and choose which clauses they will regard as customary. As the Law of the Sea was signed by 119 nations and as ratifications slowly came in pending the day when the convention would enter into force (1994), the situation with regard to the U.S.A. was somewhat like scenarios imagined for U.N. Charter amendment with regard to the U.S.S.R. – a working Law of the Sea, including its seabed mining enterprise, would finally induce superpowers not yet parties to join.

997 **The system for settlement of disputes under the United Nations Convention on the Law of the Sea: a drafting history and commentary.**
Andronico O. Adede.   Dordrecht, The Netherlands: M. Nijhoff, 1987. 285p.

The dispute settlement provisions in the Law of the Sea – particularly in Parts XV and XI (Section 5) – are 'one of the cornerstones of the new world order in the ocean'. Although its provisions for conciliation, arbitration, and adjudication are more flexible than in any other comparable treaty, including the Charter of the United Nations, there exists a procedure for *compulsory conciliation*, which, if it proves useful, may be another step to international compulsory jurisdiction similar to the rule of law in well-ordered states. The author explains this significant innovation by reviewing its 'legislative history'.

998 **The third United Nations conference on the Law of the Sea: what was accomplished?**
Tommy T.B. Koh.   *Law and Contemporary Problems*, vol. 46, no. 2 (Spring 1983), p. 5-9.

Here is an appreciation for the difficult accomplishments of the Law of the Sea by the final president of the U.N. conference. Koh claims that the law is 'comprehensive', though it may not have treated 'ocean space as an organic and ecological whole', as the father of the conference, Arvid Pardo, originally advocated. Koh, who here briefly introduces an expert symposium in the wake of U.S. refusal to sign the Law of the Sea, answers the critics: the law advanced the principle of equity; the 200-mile exclusive economic zone protects fisheries; the congestion in sea lanes has been regulated; oil and gas exploration is taken out of *laissez faire*; conflicting claims of coastal states have been brought into order; the marine environment is better protected; dispute settlement in some circumstances is *mandatory*; whales and dolphins are not ignored; and the controversial Part XI on seabed mining is, especially considering Resolution II, a 'fair and workable regime'.

999 **The third United Nations Law of the Sea conference: North–South bargaining on ocean issues.**
Robert L. Friedheim.   In: *Positive sum: improving North–South negotiations*. Edited by I. William Zartman.   New Brunswick, NJ: Transaction Books, 1987, p.73-114.

This retrospective scholarly paper examines the Law of the Sea conference from the viewpoint of North–South clashes. The South in effect 'won' the struggle, the author argues, since it established such features, rooted in the 'rhetoric' of the NIEO, as not recognizing first-come, first-served private or national exploitation of the deep seabed; establishing the multinational Enterprise instead; setting down production controls and mandatory technology transfers; and providing for ultimate international management in the interests of the common heritage of mankind. Friedheim's 'macroanalysis' concentrates on the parliamentary diplomacy that produced this result. He explains why so many nations and interest groups agreed on opening the negotiations, and he traces the process of the encounter along a spectrum of opinion over time (ranging from the least restrictive claims registry to the highly centralized exclusive Enterprise). Data are based on content analysis of conference records.

Freidheim concludes that, without the United States, the treaty cannot be called a success, and hence Part XI must be renegotiated.

1000   **U.S. foreign policy and the Law of the Sea.**
Ann I. Hollick.   Princeton, NJ: Princeton University Press, 1981.
496p. bibliog.

Appearing a year before conclusion of the third U.N. conference on the Law of the Sea, which, whether successful or not, the author regarded as merely another step in an 'ongoing process', this book is a substantial history of the entire process, going back to the first and second conferences (1958, 1960) and covering the issues that necessitated negotiations in a third. Hollick treats this history in 'macro' terms of the U.S. role in the prevailing international system (a middle-range sea power seeking to protect narrow resource interests in the 1930s, a superpower after 1945, and a more limited world power after the Vietnam War in 1973). She also discusses events in 'micro' terms of key individuals, interest groups, bureaucratic actors, and Congress. She sees the logic of global cooperation but is too close to national history to expect much from foresight and planning. 'Coastal states will only be driven to cooperation', she writes, 'after strictly national approaches are clearly proven to be inadequate. Thus, as in the case of Mediterranean pollution, we must expect to see near crisis situations of pollution, overfishing, or maritime accidents before states gradually move to cooperative measures.'

1001   **Who will control the seabed?**
Arvid Pardo.   *Foreign Affairs*, vol. 47, no. 1 (October 1968),
p.123-37.

Here is a restatement of Pardo's influential speech, first made in the U.N. General Assembly in the fall of 1967, proposing that the seabed beyond the continental shelves be exempted from the freedom of the seas and the claims of sovereign national states. Instead, it should be administered by the United Nations for the benefit of all nations as the common heritage of mankind.

Economic development

United Nations Development Programme (UNDP)
U.N. Economic and Social Council (Ecosoc)

1002   **Change: threat or opportunity for human progress?**
Edited by Üner Kirdar.   New York: United Nations for UNDP,
1992. 5 vols. (E.91.III.B.10).

The end of the Cold War provided the occasion in late 1990 for a conference of eminent persons from thirty-four countries to present their 'visions and long-term perspectives'. It was also the fortieth anniversary of the UNDP and its predecessors. Everyone recognized that humanity had reached a time of great threats and opportunities, as UNDP Administrator William Draper described it, in the fields of politics, economics, markets, society, and ecology. 'Peace and security', writes the editor, cannot be achieved unless international cooperation is also extended to deal with threats that stem from failures in development, from environmental degradation, and from lack of progress towards ensuring tangible human development.' Readers will find here the very best global thinking in so inclusive a format that no important topic is overlooked. The five volumes are available as a set or individually.

1003 **Change: threat or opportunity?** [Vol. 5:] **Ecological change: environment, development, and poverty linkages.**
Edited by Üner Kirdar. New York: United Nations for UNDP, 1992. 218p. (E.91.III.B.9).

This volume examines the changing ecological equilibrium in the world. Global warming, climatic change, and environmental pollution are typical of the problems. A mean must be found between preserving the environment and development to meet the basic needs of all peoples – this is now called 'sustainable development'. Natural resources should be understood as capital accumulated for the benefit of future generations; yet its depletion must not be used as a condition for suspending the economic development process. International financial investment and technology transfer need to be redirected to sustainable profit-making.

1004 **Change: threat or opportunity?** [Vol. 2:] **Economic change.**
Edited by Üner Kirdar. New York: United Nations for UNDP, 1992. 356p. (E.91.III.B.6).

The 1950s, 1960s, and 1970s made impressive economic gains for most peoples, yet the 1980s were a time of crisis, depression, and lost opportunities. The gap is widening between developing and developed countries due to declining GNP growth, reduced external financing, severe debt servicing, and losses in external trade. Despite criticism, development aid has worked satisfactorily, which bears remembering since aid is still required, particularly if it is redirected toward people-centred development, creation of new employment, and eradication of poverty. Global action is needed to prevent the debt crisis from dragging down the entire world economy. GATT is due for real reform in order to create a true free and fair trade system.

1005 **Change: threat or opportunity?** [Vol. 3:] **Market change: globalization of markets.**
Edited by Üner Kirdar. New York: United Nations for UNDP, 1992. 161p. (E.91.III.B.7).

The financial and securities markets are fundamentally changing. Borrowers are no longer confined to domestic and national markets; deregulation has led to new financial products and services; computers and satellites have wired the planet for instantaneous communications; the value of world financial exchanges exceeds trade in goods by 20 to 1. Transnational corporations rival some national governments as wielders of power; exchange rates are no longer regulated by the IMF, but are allowed to be set by speculative traders; the 'global market' is still in process of integration. The non-industrialized countries have yet to see any equitable benefits.

Functions of the U.N. System. Economic development

1006   **Change: threat or opportunity?** [Vol. 1:] **Political change.**
        Edited by Üner Kirdar.   New York: United Nations for UNDP,
        1992. 329p. (E.91.III.B.5).

The end of the Cold War promises to replace East–West tension with North–South
convergence on effective approaches to economic and social development.
Multipolarity in international politics is now a reality; but in economics, bipolarity,
the Group of 7, TNCs, and the European Community complicate the picture.

1007   **Change: threat or opportunity?** [Vol. 4:] **Social change: changes**
        in the human dimensions of development, ethics, and values.
        Edited by Üner Kirdar.   New York: United Nations for UNDP,
        1992. 145p. (E.91.III.B.8).

Population growth and especially changing age structure in the South (80 per cent of
the increase in the young population will occur in the Third World) will have
profound impacts on the realization of human potentials. Nearly 1,000 million new
jobs will be needed – more than presently exist in the developed world. The
information age is already here, and it is not unreasonable to expect that people in the
South who acquire the management capacity, specialized skills and education, and
access to new technological facilities will marshal human resources to now dimly
imaginable achievements. People are the most valuable factor of production. Future
world output will be produced more by improvements of people's capacities than by
accumulations of more capital. Development is a *cultural* concept.

1008   **Development as social transformation: reflections on the global**
        problematique.
        Herb Addo (et al.).   London: Hodder & Stoughton for U.N.
        University, 1985. 281p. (E.88.III.A.11. GPID).

Begun by Johan Galtung in 1979, this study of the global problematique examines the
crisis in the world economy, deteriorating North–South and East–West relations,
renewed threats of war, pan-Europeanism, permanent underdevelopment in the Third
World, and the green revolution. The authors offer a kind of anti-capitalist systemic
development philosophy – 'development as social transformation'. The global
probematique includes all those problems *not* being addressed by world capitalism.
The volume – like all good books of innovative thought – is far outside the pale of
economic orthodoxy, but this is the main reason why it will repay serious study.

1009   **Development for people: goals and strategies for the year 2000.**
        Edited by Khadija Haq and Üner Kirdar.   Islamabad, Pakistan:
        North–South Roundtable and UNDP Development Strategy
        Programme, 1989. 300p. bibliog. (E.89.III.B.1).

Similar to the editors' previous volume, *Managing human development* (1988) (see
item no. 1018), this collection of expert papers on North–South cooperation looks
forward to the U.N.'s Fourth Development Decade (1991-2000). There is a strong
emphasis on the human content of economic development. The chapters on global and
regional strategies include an instructive comparison of the two South Asian regional
associations – SAARC (1985) and ASEAN (1967). Missing from the volume is the
high politics at the U.N. created by the end of the East–West conflict.

1010   **Development planning in mixed economies.**
Edited by Miguel Urrutia and Setsuko Yukawa.   Tokyo: UNU Press,
1988. 359p. (E.88.III.A.6. DSDB-16/UNUP-637).

National economic planning, for the last thirty years, has not been characteristic only of the socialist countries. Many industrialized market economies adopted planning during World War II, and the practice has continued in the Marshall Plan, Colombo Plan, Alliance for Progress, and defence industries. (The Pentagon manages the largest planned economy outside the U.S.S.R.) But national planning agencies are often uninfluenced by the theories of planning taught in the universities and are unresponsive to the types of planning promoted by international agencies through their technical assistance programmes. In an effort to improve the practice, the editors sought 'to compare the philosophies, goals, methods, procedures, and implementation of economic planning in various countries'. The cases of Sri Lanka, Malaysia, Colombia, Kenya, Nigeria, Japan, and Hungary are set out.

1011   **Essays on crime and development.**
Edited by Uglješa Zvekič.   Rome: U.N. Interregional Crime and
Justice Research Institute, 1990. 377p. (Pub. No. 36. E.90.III.N.2).

'It is impossible', wrote Victor Hugo, 'for a poor man always to be honest.' Crime seems to be one of the consequences of economic underdevelopment, and then it becomes a cause of setbacks in development as scant resources are committed to crime control. The essays here deal with the causative or associative relationship between development and crime. International crime, such as border crashings, terrorism, stock market insider trading, computer virus dissemination, debt defaults, and above all, drug trafficking, is well treated by Louise I. Shelley.

1012   **For the common good: redirecting the economy toward
community, the environment, and a sustainable future.**
Herman E. Daly and John B. Cobb, Jr.   Boston: Beacon, 1989;
2nd ed., 1994. 482p.

This thoughtful book by a World Bank economist and a theologian is about a paradigm shift in economics linked to recognition of the physical limits of the ecosphere and to disappointing achievements of an unregulated economy. *Homo economicus*, motivated only by self-interest, does not seem to match *Homo sapiens*, who has feelings for others and pursues both private and public goods. Daly and Cobb describe a 'third paradigm' – after capitalism and socialism – which is related to Catholic doctrines of community and subsidiarity. They do not reject classical economics, with its core doctrine of the free market, but, in a global economy, they argue that the market must be brought into the 'service of community'. The book presents the science of economics, the alternative of economics 'for the common good', suggested U.S. policies, and the world politics of the transition. They know that their alternative economics implies granting the United Nations powers of a world government, both to solve global problems and to supervise the world market, but this reform they think will be the result of a gradual process.

1013 **Human development report, 1993.**
UNDP. Foreword by William H. Draper III.   New York: Oxford
University Press, 1993. 230p. bibliog.
This report does not measure mere increase of wealth, but the use of wealth to
improve conditions of the whole people of the earth. Its theme is that development
cooperation must include measures to improve governance, judicial systems, social
integration, and activities designed to remove obstacles to popular participation. By
1993, Egypt, South Africa, Nigeria, and Brazil were added to the list of 'failed states'
because of wide income gaps between rich and poor classes. Social upheavals and
political revolutions were predicted.

1014 **Human resources development: a neglected dimension of**
development strategy.
U.N. Ecosoc. Committee for Development Planning.   New York:
United Nations, 1988. 45p. (E.88.II.A.11. ST/ESA/208).
International debt has been one of the major causes of declining development in the
1980s, for adjustment has forced many Third World governments to reduce their
public expenditure on education and health, in order to reduce demands for imports
and thus improve their net export earnings. The above expert committee advising
Ecosoc explored a strategy of developing human resources as an alternative to the
traditional expansion of supplies of commodities. This is a succinct book for both
busy officials and students. It contains as short and authoritative a description of the
world economy as can be found anywhere.

1015 **The international economic order: essays on financial crisis and**
international public goods.
Charles Kindleberger.   Cambridge, MA: MIT Press, 1988. 237p.
In this volume of essays (the author's seventh), the international economist devotes
the second half his space to 'international public goods without international
government'. Like Herman Daly, Kindleberger knows that intervention in the free
market is 'at variance with the neo-classical version of economics'. But markets are
never free, so they occasionally get into crisis. Markets work well managing *trends*;
in *crises*, governments are needed. Whether the global market will by itself produce a
good society, 'or whether some attention to the public good, economic responsibility
perhaps, and assistance to the market to fix on standards, may not be required', is the
question addressed in this book. Contrasted with the first half, 'financial crises', the
second has all the more relevance. Readers will find this a charming, enlightening
book on the world economics of the future.

1016 **International financial cooperation: a framework for change.**
Frances Stewart and Arjun Sengupta. Edited by Salah Al-Shaikhly.
London: Pinter; Boulder, CO: Westview, 1982. 204p.
This book is typical of the North–South dialogue following the proposal of the New
International Economic Order (NIEO, 1974). Funded by UNDP, the book
concentrates on reform of the Bretton Woods system. The World Bank, IMF, and so
on are regarded as 'Western' (liberal capitalist) – hostile to Eastern (socialist) and
Southern (developing) countries. The editor contributes an historical introduction that
explains what led to the NIEO – 'the accumulation over the past twenty years of

many short-sighted policies and an overall mismanagement of the global economy'. The study identifies the main sources of dissatisfaction, especially since the collapse of the Bretton Woods system in 1971, and it discusses such areas for reform as recycling of funds from surplus to deficit countries, stabilizing the financial system, increasing aid to the poorest countries, pursuing conditionality without IMF dictates, creating an expanded international currency based on the Special Drawing Right, improving South–South financial cooperation, and establishing a world development council to manage the 'world' economy.

1017 **International institutions in trade and finance.**
Alasdair I. MacBean and P.N. Snowden. London: Allen & Unwin, 1981. 255p. bibliog.

'What we have set out to do in this book', write the British authors, 'is to examine the main institutions which influence international economic relations as continually evolving instruments of economic policy.' These institutions are the IMF, GATT, UNCTAD, international commodity agreements, OECD, E.E.C., CMEA (now defunct), and the World Bank group. Particular attention is focused on the decline of U.S. hegemony and the rise of 'increasingly assertive independent centres of economic power' in the E.C., OPEC, G-77, and UNCTAD. Since the book appeared at the beginning of the 1980s, most of its recommendations for the future do not call for any more radical reform than monetary reforms within the IMF, but many of these are still pending.

1018 **Managing human development.**
Edited by Khadija Haq and Üner Kirdar. Islamabad, Pakistan: North–South Roundtable, 1988. 294p. bibliog. (E.88.III.B.1).

The frustrations of economic development in the aftermath of the struggle over the NIEO, and the stagnation of the communist bloc on the eve of its collapse, produced this volume of new thinking on development. Financial capital, in the editors' view, is less of a problem than human capital. OPEC after 1973, for example, could not convert its windfall price gains into permanent income because of its lack of human capital, institutions, and skills. Certain former Third World countries have taken off (7 per cent growth rates) while others stagnate (3 per cent); the difference is the human skills, enterprise, and training institutions in countries like South Korea and Singapore. The expert papers here address four challenges: (1) providing education to all by 2000; (2) employing the educated; (3) amending macro-economics (GNP, savings and investments, exports and imports, national accounts) to include human factors (poverty profiles, living evaluations, distribution of income); and (4) factoring in the human costs of 'adjustment'.

1019 **Mobilizing human potential: the challenge of unemployment.**
Paul Streeten. New York: UNDP, 1989. 80p. (Policy Discussion Paper. E.89.III.B.2).

The author asks why, despite the statistical *growth* of national economies since 1945, *employment* has not kept pace and therefore threatens to decline farther. (William Draper predicts that 1,000 million new jobs will have to be created by the year 2000. That is as many as exist today in the developed world.) In a brief macro-economic book, Streeten challenges many traditional concepts that seem to block progress in the developing world – like 'unemployment', when the root problem is under-utilization of labour due to higher aspirations or to diversion into the informal sector. He asks why recommendations to supply basic needs and relieve poverty have not succeeded. He concludes that the politics must be restored to political economy.

1020 **The origins of international economic disorder: a study of United States international monetary policy from World War II to the present.**
Fred L. Block.   Berkeley: University of California Press, 1977. 282p. bibliog.

This is a 'revisionist' history in the spirit of William Appleman Williams and Gabriel and Joyce Kolko, designed to make the international economic order intelligible to ordinary people. 'The purpose of this study is to illustrate the obstacles to the contemporary efforts at international monetary reform by examining the rise and fall of the Bretton Woods system.' Block concentrates less on technical aspects than on the distribution of power. Most of his sources are American, which is not unreasonable when considering the World Bank, IMF, and GATT; the U.N. comes into the account very briefly, as with the failed ITO. Compare Richard Gardner's *Sterling–dollar diplomacy* for a more elaborate work (item no. 1057).

1021 **Overall economic perspective to the year 2000.**
U.N. Economic Commission for Europe.   New York: United Nations, 1988. 224p. bibliog. (E.88.II.E.4. ESE/EC.AD/32).

This is not a world economic perspective, but one limited to the region of Europe, though set in the context of the world economy. It aims to identify long-term economic problems – 'trends, challenges, and opportunities' – and scenarios for solution – 'long-term economic growth'. Eastern Europe and even the U.S.S.R. are brought into the picture with Western Europe. The prospect of European Union in the West gets no special emphasis. Special topics include human resources development, energy prospects, the environment, and science and technology. This is a model regional macro-economic study, though it must be updated after the revolutions of 1989.

1022 **Overall socio-economic perspective of the world economy to the year 2000.**
U.N. DIESA.   New York: United Nations, 1990. 251p. (E.90.II.C.2. ST/ESA/215).

This report 'presents an assessment of long-term trends in world economic and social developments and is intended to serve as a quantitative and qualitative framework for the preparation of the development strategy [for the Fourth Development Decade, 1991-2000]'. World economic growth has slowed (to 3.4 per cent in the late 1980s), and GNP per capita in some countries is now declining. The fall of commodity prices and hence of export earnings is a major cause of economic decline in poorer counties. Planning for the next decade is based on the Secretariat's Global Econometric Model, which projects economic growth in seventy-five countries on the basis of such macro-economic variables as share of investment in GDP and the incremental capital–output ratio. This is a book for serious world economists.

1023 **Pioneers of change: experiments in creating a humane society.**
Jeremy Seabrook.   London: New Society, Zed Books, 1993. 242p.
bibliog.

'All countries are developing countries.' This book sets out an alternative to
'accelerating global industrialism' and shows the way 'to set the world economy onto
a genuinely sustainable path'. The book is a series of interviews with winners of the
'Right Livelihood Awards' – a complement to the Nobel Prizes in the areas of peace,
sustainable development, environmental integrity, social justice, and human rights.
Founded by Jacob von Uexkull in 1980 (he made his fortune in stamps, not
dynamite), the awards honour those devoted to the 'green alternative'. This is not a
book for orthodox believers in unlimited economic growth and the expansion of
world capitalism.

1024 **The politics of international economic cooperation and
development.**
Robert W. Gregg.   In: *Politics in the United Nations system.* Edited
by Lawrence S. Finkelstein.   Durham, NC: Duke University Press,
1988, p.106-47.

This is a brief recent introduction to the complex field of international economic
cooperation. The reader must bear in mind that great changes have since taken place:
Namibia is independent, apartheid in South Africa is well on its way to extinction,
only the Palestinian issue still festers. The 'liberal international economic order',
aspired to by the West in 1944-45, is now, with the fall of communism, seemingly
universally accepted. Gregg traces the history as far as the 'stalemate' over the NIEO,
which as a 'political manifesto' remains a challenge to the U.N. system. To date, he
writes, 'the Third World coalition has pushed the cause of an authoritative, majori-
tarian U.N. as far as the realities of economic and political power will permit. . .'.

1025 **The politics of international economic relations.**
Joan E. Spero.   New York: St. Martin's, 1977; 4th ed., 1990. 404p.
bibliog.

Economics has returned to its nature as political economy. International political
economy treats the problems of interdependence in the West, dependence of the
South, and independence of the East. The author's fourth edition takes note of
Gorbachev's *perestroika*, but the revolutions of 1989 have overtaken her latest
analysis. Here readers will find a solid text on the management of international
economic relations since World War II, the link between trade and domestic politics,
the liberal and Marxist prescriptions for economic development, financial flows, trade
strategy, managing multinational corporations (MNCs), and oil interests. Spero
concludes that a NIEO will not emerge since 'the political bases are too weak and the
problems too complex'. The G-7 will continue to manage the international economy.
The most she can imagine are competing economic blocs in the Western hemisphere,
European Community, and Pacific Rim led by Japan.

1026 **Register of development activities of the United Nations system.**
U.N. Advisory Committee for the Coordination of Information
Systems. New York: ACCIS, 1987- . annual. 993p.
(GV.E.91.0.12).

Readers in search of a complete tabulation of development activities in the U.N.
system – 23,854 of them by 1990 – will find it in this large volume. Types of activity
covered include: agriculture, education, policy and planning, employment, health,
humanitarian aid, industry, trade, natural resources, population, science and
technology, social conditions, transport and communications, etc. Also given are
specific programme titles, funding sources, executing agencies, and costs. Tables are
arranged by country, region, and globe. Addressed to planners in governments, IGOs,
and NGOs, the work will satisfy the public baffled by the abundance of U.N.
development activities.

1027 **Role of free economic zones in the U.S.S.R. and Eastern Europe.**
U.N. Centre on Transnational Corporations. New York: United
Nations, 1990. 90p. (UNCTC Current Studies, Series A, No. 14.
E.90.II.A.5. ST/CTC/SER.A/14).

This short work is typical of the technical advisory function of the UNCTC. In the
first flush of optimism following the rejection of communist central planning in
Eastern Europe, the centre tried to describe the free economic zones to attract foreign
direct investment in Poland, Hungary, Bulgaria, Romania, Yugoslavia, the U.S.S.R.,
and China. The Soviet zones were designed to cater first to Soviet consumers and then
to the export market. This work describes the export-processing zones, links to
international economies, training of workers, management of enterprises, finance, and
risk. It concludes with a 'glimpse into the future', which, after the breakup of the
U.S.S.R., still reads fairly. 'The history of export processing zones and other similar
zones shows that this type of institution seldom, if ever, develops exactly according to
the original plan.'

1028 **Sharing the world's resources.**
Oscar Schachter. New York: Columbia University Press, 1977.
172p.

When the U.N. General Assembly announced the NIEO and launched a programme of
action in 1974, there was widespread agreement within the rich countries, no less than
the poor, about the principle of equitable sharing. Moreover, economic justice was
perceived as within the interests of states, since it offered a solution to recurrent
crises over oil, food, inflation, deficits, and recessions. Yet the new order was never
established. The author, a distinguished international lawyer, here examines 'the basic
normative issues raised by these demands and their practical application in
international decisions'. Besides the NIEO, Schachter also considers the 'common
heritage' of the seas, preservation of the environment, just prices or fairer terms of
trade, sovereignty over natural resources, and food security. He concludes (in 1975)
that the nations had come to no agreement on the rules of distributive justice, that is,
for the distribution of benefits and burdens. Hence, the principle would remain
unsettled or be settled by force.

1029   **Social policy in transition: adjusting to the needs of the 1990s.**
Centre for Social Development and Humanitarian Affairs (Vienna).
New York: United Nations, 1989. 132p. (E.89.IV.8. ST/CSDHA/4).
In 1968, the first international conference of ministers responsible for social welfare
was held. Subsequently, many other conferences on social policy followed: on food
(1974), population (1974, 1984), women (1975-85), employment (1976), settlements
(1976), rural development (1979), pure water (1979), children (1979), disabled
persons (1983), the aged (1982), youth (1985), drug abuse (1987), the homeless
(1987). In 1987, a second international conference of ministers was held in Vienna to
review these efforts and to plan social policy in the 1990s. Some thirty ministers and
high officials from ninety-one states attended. This is their report. The prospect of
continued and widening economic growth at the end of the 1960s has been displaced
by one of economic constriction, with all its implications for social policy. Hence, a
deliberate focus here is on 'improving standards of living with due regard to social
justice'. The report contains a review of the present world social situation and an
analysis of formal government statements about their policies toward social welfare.
For *Guiding principles for developmental social welfare policies and programmes in
the near future*, see the document E/CONF.80/10 or A/Res/42/125 or *Social
Development Newsletter* (Vienna), 25 (1988).

1030   **A study of the capacity of the United Nations development
system.**
R.G.A. Jackson.   Geneva: United Nations for UNDP, 1969.
2 vols in 1. bibliog. (E.70.I.10. DP/5).
This is the much noted – yet neglected – 'Jackson report'. It was the most serious
proposal of reform of the U.N. economic development system until, say, the
proposals of Maurice Bertrand or those of Erskine Childers and Brian Urquhart.
Jackson called for a proper 'machine' with 'capacity' to assist the Third World in its
development. His main proposal was to transform UNDP into the 'recognized central
body for consolidating and expanding cooperation with all the developing Member
States'. He proposed to subordinate the specialized agencies to UNDP 'like any
department in government'. And he sought secure and adequate financing and
'managerial talent of a quality equivalent to that found in the greatest institutions and
commercial enterprises'. Much of the detail in this now historical document is dated,
but the spirit is still infectious.

1031   **The United Nations and international business.**
Sidney S. Dell.   Durham, NC: Duke University Press for UNITAR,
1990. 191p. (E.89.III.K.ST/28).
Since negotiations began on a code of conduct for TNCs, an impression has
developed, particularly in the business community, that the U.N. is hostile to
international business. The author, an economist who has spent four decades working
at the U.N., here begins a series of UNITAR studies on the history of the economic
and social activities of the United Nations. Dell emphasizes that the U.N. reflects its
member government policies, which generally are favourable to business, and that its
regulatory activity is designed to prevent unfair competition by requiring businesses
and states to adhere to common standards. The benefits of regulation are familiar
within well-organized states. Such NGO representatives of business as the
International Chamber of Commerce have cooperated actively in the drafting of an

acceptable code of conduct. Dell chooses a range of topics of current concern in addition to the code: anti-trust action (particularly the effort to establish an ITO and the subsequent rounds of GATT talks), 'permanent sovereignty' over natural resources, technical cooperation at the UNCTC, and promoting foreign investment and cooperation (notably over preservation of the ozone layer). He prints in annexes valuable lists of concerns about TNCs and the draft of the code as of mid-1989.

1032   **The United Nations and the problem of economic development.**
Kenneth K.S. Dadzie.   In: *United Nations, divided world.* Edited by Adam Roberts and Benedict Kingsbury.   Oxford: Oxford University Press, 1988, p.139-57.

Here is a cool and informative history of U.N. involvement in economic development and a response to criticism of the U.N.'s performance in the field. Dadzie finds that the U.N. began with a rather minimal emphasis on government assistance (1945-63), turned to large-scale international intervention to achieve a 'world of economic equity and justice' (NIEO, 1974), yet also tried to make access to international resources conditional on adoption of domestic measures and policies recommended by the IMF and World Bank (1963-82), and recently has been turning back to national self-help. For the future, he argues that Maurice Bertrand's criticism of the sectoral organization of the U.N. system and of its lack of adequate negotiation structures, while true enough, does not get beyond 'mechanical flaws' to the 'quality of the international commitment to world development and . . . the political dimensions of international economic policy'. Hence, Dadzie argues against the 'dogmatism' of the prevailing theory of prices (World Bank) and of balance of payments adjustments, especially devaluation and demand compression (IMF). He challenges the idea of a single model of development as a universal norm. And he argues that attention to 'efficiency of administration' is distracting attention from the real problem of 'external policy'. What is needed is common, multinational *economic management* far beyond the U.N. share of 6 per cent of ODA or even the World Bank/IMF share of 15 per cent. 'The critical issue has been the unwillingness of the great industrial powers to match their recognition of the reality of world economic interdependence with a preparedness to share with their developing country partners the management of the global economic commons that the world's trading, monetary, and financial systems represent.'

1033   **Voting in international economic organizations.**
Stephen Zamora.   *American Journal of International Law*, vol. 74 (1980), p.566-608.

'For nations to act effectively in concert', the author argues, 'the organization through which they act must command the respect of its members, and they must abide by its decisions.' Accepted voting rules are a vital source of such respect, which makes possible ready implementation of decisions. Zamora discusses the array of possible voting rules: unanimity, vetoes, two-thirds majorities, other special majorities, weighted voting, and especially *consensus.* Voting rules are discussed in the context of recent controversies over the Common Fund for the maintenance of buffer stocks of commodities or over the International Seabed Authority of the Law of the Sea. One-nation-one-vote is more suited to organizations like UNCTAD, whose powers are limited to recommendations; weighted voting, to organizations like the World Bank, which has powers to lend money and conduct operations by executive decisions. Zamora concludes: 'Despite these reservations [that effective organizations must reflect economic realities, and that developing countries must first acquire economic power before attempting to control the organizations], international economic organizations present the most serious test of world government to date. . . . [For,] these organizations test nations' ability to limit their freedom of action in exchange for long-range economic advantages.'

1034 **World development.**
New York: UNDP, 1988-91. bimonthly. Continued by *Choices* (1992-).

This attractive, illustrated magazine aims 'to illustrate, with concrete examples, the broad scope of development assistance provided by the United Nations Development Programme', writes William H. Draper III. UNDP supports 5,300 projects worldwide in the fields of agriculture, industry, health, education, economic planning, transportation, and communications. The magazine is addressed to decision-makers, teachers, citizens, and NGOs. For readers who wonder, What does UNDP do?, this magazine will be a revelation.

The case for global economic management and U.N. system reform.
See item no. 129.

Collective management: the reform of global economic organizations.
See item no. 132.

A third generation world organization.
See item no. 164.

Beyond globalism.
See item no. 181.

An international redistribution of wealth and power.
See item no. 264.

The restructuring of the United Nations economic and social system.
See item no. 324.

International lending for development

World Bank Group: International Bank for Reconstruction and Development (IBRD) International Development Association (IDA) International Finance Corporation (IFC)

1035   **Annual report, 1991.**
International Finance Corporation.   Washington, DC: IFC, 1957- .
annual. 65p.
This is the official report of the IFC. It contains a five-year summary of operations, a
discussion of the investment climate, the year in review, investments, and financial
statements.

1036   **Between two worlds: the World Bank's next decade.**
Edited by Richard E. Feinberg.   New Brunswick, NJ: Transaction
Books for the Overseas Development Council, 1986. 184p. bibliog.
(U.S.–Third World Policy Perspectives No. 7).
The common interest of rich countries and poor ones is not a mere moral platitude. It
is a demonstrated economic fact. 'By mid-1985', writes the president of the Overseas
Development Council, 'slow growth in the developing countries was damaging the
economies and interests of both the Third World and the industrialized nations.' The
announcement of U.S. Treasury Secretary James Brady's 'plan' to settle the debt
crisis by restoring Third World growth, and the inauguration of the new World Bank
president Barber Conable in 1986, provided the occasion for this short, fundamental
analysis and set of recommendations. The editor addresses the vexing problem of the
debt crisis and discusses the Bank's competitive relationship to the Fund. He would
keep   the   Bank's   policy   to   eradicate   poverty.   Feinberg   concludes   with
recommendations in the Bank's four critical roles for the future: as coordinator,
mediator, stabilizer, and intellectual centre.

1037   **Case studies in the jurisdiction of the International Centre for
Settlement of Investment Disputes.**
W. Michael Tupman.   *International and Comparative Law
Quarterly*, vol. 35 (1986), p.813-38.
The ICSID, established in 1965, is a standing arbitral tribunal of the World Bank. To
1986, it had heard eighteen requests for arbitration and two for conciliation; five
resulted in an award on the merits, six were settled by the parties outside the tribunal,
and nine were still pending. The author discusses such cases as *Holiday
Inns/Occidental Petroleum v. Government of Morocco* from a legal point of view. He
also discusses jurisdictional issues such as multiple provisions for dispute resolution.
One of his conclusions is that 'consent to ICSID arbitration is an irrevocable legal
obligation'.

1038   **The development and future role of the International Monetary Fund and the World Bank.**
H. Onno Ruding.   In: *The U.N. under attack.* Edited by Jeffrey Harrod and Nico Schrijver.   Aldershot, England: Gower, 1988, p.57-70.

The author compares the performance of the IMF and World Bank with other U.N. institutions, gives structural reasons for the differences, answers criticisms of the Bretton Woods institutions, and discusses proposed reforms. Superior performance of Fund and Bank, he suggests, is due to their own substantial financial resources; to high-quality staff promoted for ability, not nationality; to weighted voting, leading to realistic and practical decisions; and to functional executive meetings, without public posturing and politicization. Meetings on solving the debt crisis in 1985, for instance, were not marred by North–South controversy. Ruding opposes 'reforms' to give developing countries more votes as unrealistic, alienating the industrialized nations, and not in the interest of the Third World. He also opposes eliminating conditionality on balance-of-payments assistance, for the same reasons. The IMF has only since 1982 become a development institution; it should revert, once the debt crisis is overcome, to a monetary and balance-of-payments institution. The World Bank in turn should continue to be the long-term credit institution for economic development. Unless the U.N. undergoes 'political integration', the two international financial institutions should continue independently to continue their 'financial and economic integration' of the world.

1039   **Development assistance policies and the performance of aid agencies: studies in the performance of DAC, OPEC, the regional development banks, and the World Bank group.**
Hassan M. Selim.   London: Macmillan, 1983. 531p. bibliog.

The author, a director of the Abu Dhabi Fund of the United Arab Emirates, takes up the problem of the growing gap between rich and poor nations. The problem is characterized by instability in the international monetary system, unstable prices in the commodity markets, large international transfer payments, a world recession in trade, unemployment, persistent inflation, deteriorating economic prospects in the poor regions, loss of food and grain reserves, and natural drought. Selim writes in a time of hope for the systematic reforms of the NIEO to set the goal of the 'welfare of humanity' for an 'interdependent world'. Since NIEO presupposed 'additional assistance and transfer of financial resources from rich to poor countries', he tries comprehensively 'to evaluate aid performance' by all the donor groups: OECD's Development Assistance Committee (DAC), OPEC, the World Bank group, and the regional development banks. The three basic elements of aid are examined: international finance, project appraisal and implementation, and economic development. The record is presented for the U.S.A., U.K., France, West Germany, Japan, the Netherlands, Sweden, the E.C. Commission, the several OPEC funds, the IBRD, IDA, IFC, and the African, Asian, Caribbean, and Inter-American development banks.

1040   **Economic planning for the peace.**
Ernest F. Penrose.   Princeton, NJ: Princeton University Press, 1953. 384p.

This is a contemporary history of the founding of the IBRD and IMF by the economic adviser to U.S. Ambassador John C. Winant to Great Britain from 1939 to 1947;

Penrose was, hence, a person well placed to follow the economic planning for the peace. He adds valuable light on the ill-fated third component of the new world economic institutions – the ITO, which became caught up in complicated delays until the planning almost came apart in the post-war crises of 1947-48. This history is worth recalling when contemplating radical reforms like the establishment of a world trade organization, the transformation of the World Bank into a world development authority, or the extension of the IMF into a world central bank. Penrose's thesis is 'that the economic errors of the peace were the outcome of omissions and a faulty sense of proportion in planning. . .'. He closes with balanced praise for the 'spirit of idealism' that animated Lord Keynes and the few who created the new institutions.

1041 **Elements of an international development strategy for the 1990s.**
      U.N. Ecosoc. Committee for Development Planning.   New York:
      United Nations, 1989. 89p. (E.89.IV.3. ST/ESA/214).
This brief report examines the development strategies and accomplishments of the 1980s and formulates a new strategy for the 1990s. It includes: accelerated economic growth, emphasis on human development, reduction of poverty, and preservation of the remaining environment.

1042 **Emerging from poverty: the economics that really matters.**
      Gerald M. Meier.   New York: Oxford University Press, 1984. 258p.
      bibliog.
'No society', wrote Adam Smith in 1776, 'can surely be flourishing and happy, of which the far greater part of the members are poor and miserable.' 'To economists!' declared Lord Keynes in a toast in 1944, 'who are the trustees, not of civilization, but of the possibility of civilization.' This book is a mature reflection on the interplay between economic thought and development policy from the Bretton Woods conference to the mid-1980s, when the author joined others in calling for a Bretton Woods II. The world already contains over 2,000 million people with per capita incomes below $250 a year; hunger, lack of sanitation, and illiteracy are facts of life for the great majority of the human race. This book plainly tries to think through how hard-headed economics might yet be combined with a 'warm heart'.

1043 **The future of the international monetary system: change,**
      coordination, or instability?
      Edited by Omar F. Hamouda, Robin Rowley, and Bernard M. Wolf.
      Armonk, NY: M.E. Sharpe, 1989. 223p.
Capitalism has survived other crises, but the present one at the international level – marked by massive debt, lack of hegemonic leadership, and fragility of the monetary system – raises serious questions. The editors do not expect a 'collapse of the world economy', but they find that 'almost no one anticipates that these hazards will be expeditiously resolved either by the individual acts of the principal players on the international scene or by their collaborative efforts'. Despite this pessimistic view (1988), the specialized papers included in this volume generally recommend reduction of international debt, amendment of the constitutional documents of the monetary and financial IGOs, coordination of national macro-economic policies, and 'hope' for improvements.

1044   **The future of the world economy: a United Nations study.**
Wassily Leontief.   New York: Oxford University Press, 1977. 110p.
This is an older study of alternative development strategies (1975-2000) by the
leading economist who invented input–output analysis. Leontief takes Jan
Tinbergen's advice to heart: 'No thoughtful rational choice between alternative
courses of action, in the socio-economic or in any other sphere, is possible without
systematic, detailed, and, one should add, objective understanding of the complex sets
of those direct and indirect repercussions that each of them is bound to bring about.'
Leontief's mandate from the U.N. was to show whether the development targets in
the Second Development Decade (1971-80) or in the NIEO (1974-) could be met by
the available resources. He finds that higher growth rates in developing countries,
coupled with more moderate rates in the developed ones, would *reduce by half* the
average income gap by 2000. 'The principal limits to sustained economic growth and
accelerated development are political, social, and institutional in character rather than
physical.'

1045   **The future role of the World Bank: addresses. . . .**
Edited by Edward R. Fried and Henry D. Owen.   Washington, DC:
Brookings, 1982. 91p.
At a time when the World Bank had grown into 'the largest single source by far of
publicly mobilized capital and technical assistance for development', support for the
Bank in the United States was at a low ebb and the U.S. had fallen into arrears on its
contributions to the IDA (1982). The Brookings Institution held a prestigious
conference to restore U.S. commitment. Former Bank President Robert S. McNamara,
future U.S. Secretaries of State George P. Shultz and Warren M. Christopher, current
Bank President A.W. Clausen, and other officials and bankers made major addresses.
There was interest in more private sector co-financing of World Bank projects, but
not as a substitute for continued U.S. public funding, which would maintain U.S.
leadership and leverage. 'In short, the Bank advances the general interest in a more
productive world', concluded the editors. 'This is also the interest of the United
States.'

1046   **The International Development Association: a new approach to
foreign aid.**
James H. Weaver.   New York: Praeger, 1965. 268p. bibliog.
The IDA was established in 1960 in order to provide long-term, very low-interest
('soft') loans to the neediest countries. This older work covers the history of its
founding and an analysis of some of its problems: policies, project appraisals,
increasing its resources, replenishment, and evaluation. The author concludes
glowingly that the IDA, designed to redistribute income from the rich to the poor, like
Henry Ford's paying his workers a higher wage so that they too could buy cars, will
also help the rich nations to prosper. 'If you pay them more', said Ford, 'you'll be
able to sell them more.'

1047   **The International Finance Corporation: origins, operation, and
evaluation.**
James C. Baker.   New York: Praeger, 1968. 271p. bibliog.
The IFC was founded in 1956; its purpose is to finance private enterprise projects in
member countries without government guarantees. This book covers its origins,

operations, project evaluations, and its projects (to 1968) in Latin America, Africa, the Middle East, Asia, and Europe. The author concludes that the IFC has fulfilled the expectations of its founders and has become a model for the establishment of regional development banks.

1048 **Legal and institutional factors affecting the implementation of the International Drinking Water Supply and Sanitation Decade.**
U.N. Department of Technical Cooperation for Development. New York: United Nations, 1988. 121p. (E.88.II.A.21. ST/TCD/7).
Over 1,000 million people do not have access to pure water to drink. Sanitation, on which public health depends more than on medicine, is in a primitive state throughout much of the world. This report covers slow progress throughout the little-known decade in Africa, Asia, Latin America, and the Caribbean.

1049 **Legal treatment of foreign investment: 'The World Bank Guidelines'.**
Ibrahim F.I. Shihata. Dordrecht, The Netherlands: M. Nijhoff, 1993. 468p.
Here is legal opinion that the World Bank must recognize governance issues – rule of law, political human rights – in order to implement the 'right to development'.

1050 **The lending policy of the World Bank in the 1970s: analysis and evaluation.**
Bettina Hurni. Foreword by Paul Streeten. Boulder, CO: Westview, 1980. 173p. bibliog.
This is a model history of the World Bank through about 1980. After its foundation in 1945, the Bank concentrated on economic growth and infrastructure, primarily for European reconstruction (the 'first generation'). By the time Robert McNamara became president (1968), the Bank was already shifting to poverty eradication, development, basic needs, human capital formation, and generally social welfare and distributive justice, primarily in the Third World (the 'second generation'). Hurni finds that 'the Bank has effected the mental change from economic growth as the key factor in development to the "growth with equity" strategy, with the overall goal of more distributive justice, that has been characteristic of the 1970s.'

1051 **The McNamara years at the World Bank: major policy addresses of Robert S. McNamara, 1968-1981.**
Robert S. McNamara. Foreword by Helmut Schmidt. Baltimore, MD: Johns Hopkins University Press for the World Bank, 1981. 675p.
In his thirteen years at the World Bank, Robert McNamara built it into the world's largest economic development agency. When he began, the Bank was lending about $1,000 million per year; when he retired, $12,000 million. Moreover, he presided over a fundamental redirection of the Bank from large capital projects to investment for human needs. He believed that absolute poverty could be reduced. These pages reveal how one courageous, intelligent man can transform one international organization. They show, as Helmut Schmidt writes, 'that there is no inherent

contradiction between the careful, prudent investment of scarce resources and the direct pursuit of greater social equity.'

1052 **Multinational institutions and the Third World: management, debt, and trade conflicts in the international economic order.**
Robert H. Girling.   New York: Praeger, 1985. 212p. bibliog.

The author, a Jamaican economist educated in the United States and England, has written a refreshingly clear and plain-spoken book about international economic development, particularly in the areas of debt reduction and trade. His chapters on reform contain an enlightening account of the potential roles of UNCTAD and NIEO. The debt crisis, Girling finds, is due to 'shared irresponsibilities by a cast of actors: Third World and industrial world governments searching for easy, tax-free solutions; international banks and corporations seeking high profits; development bankers seeking power and prestige; and politicians finding pots of gold to finance their careers.' His solution to the debt crisis is a four-fold strategy, initially developed for Brazil: a debt moratorium of three to five years, use of the interval to reflate domestic demand, 'countertrade' (South–South), and repayment of loans at reduced interest rates.

1053 **The political economy of international economic organization.**
Javad A. Ansari.   Boulder, CO: Rienner, 1986. 315p.

This book, originally published in England, aims to be a 'practical book' on the international economic organizations in the E.C., U.N., and, like the OECD, *not* in the U.N. But fully half of the work is devoted to UNCTAD. Ansari surveys both the literature and economic experience, and he writes a book of great compression and considered judgment. 'It is clear that EIOs [economic IOs] have a role to play in international systems not dominated by hegemons. . . . It seems unlikely . . . that the liberal economic order of the nineteenth century will be "born again" in the twenty-first century.' UNCTAD is criticized for failing, after the Ramadhan [Yom Kippur] War of 1973, to build the 'creative tension between organizational goals and systematic demands that could lead to systematic transformation'. Readers will find this an instructive work within the behaviouralist tradition of social science.

1054 **The political roles of recent World Bank presidents.**
Michael G. Schechter.   In: *The politics of the United Nations system.*
Edited by Lawrence S. Finkelstein.   Durham, NC: Duke University Press, 1988, p.350-84.

This is an introduction to the World Bank group of international financial institutions (IBRD, IFC, IDA), rendered especially vivid by concentration on the personal leadership of its presidents, including Robert S. McNamara. McNamara deliberately tried to transform the World Bank into a development agency to benefit the very poor; hence he stands as a model of the leader who would expand the power of the U.N. to meet its global challenges. One of his Congressional critics, Rep. Bill Young (R., FL), once attacked McNamara as an 'internationalist, a citizen of the world, immune from U.S. rules'. The Bank president took this as a compliment.

1055 **The politics of global economic relations.**
David H. Blake and Robert S. Walters. Englewood Cliffs, NJ:
Prentice Hall, 1976; 4th ed., 1992. 281p.

The U.S. stock market crash of 1987, the abandonment of communism in Eastern
Europe from 1989 to 1991, the single market in the European Community in 1992
were typical of events that seemed to surprise analysts of international political
economy. Actually they are quite understandable in terms of well-known forces and
trends. This short, standard text explores these trends in terms of 'liberals' and
'radicals' at a time when profound choices are being made. (The forces do not
determine events, but provide choices for free and responsible human action.) Walters
and Blake discuss 'dilemmas' in international trade, money, MNCs, aid, and
technology; they critique strategies for poor states on the periphery, U.S. economic
polity, and very weak U.N. management of the international economy.

1056 **Remaking the World Bank.**
Barend A. de Vries. Foreword by I.G. Patel. Cabin John, MD:
Seven Locks Press, 1987. 184p.

The inspiration for the creation of the World Bank came originally from the
Americans, who wanted an impartial agency to provide reconstruction loans to
Europeans, including the Russians, if they could be induced to join. The British were
mainly concerned with an international monetary clearing-house to help settle
balance-of-payments difficulties. The few developing-country representatives at
Bretton Woods prevailed in adding 'development' to the Bank's functions. Over the
years, the Bank has slowly been transformed into the world's principal development
agency, though national aid agencies still control 85 per cent of ODA. The Bank,
through the IFC, provides venture capital, and through the IDA, soft loans for
development; the general purpose has ceased to be building infrastructure and has
become building human capital for social welfare. But by the mid-1980s, the
Americans were turning away from their grown-up child. This book is an answer to
the new advocates of *laissez-faire* policies, who take the debt crisis as proof of the
credit unworthiness of poorer countries, and who wish to remedy the indebtedness of
the richest country in the world by aggressive policies designed to profit the United
States. De Vries is a thirty-year veteran of the Bank who argues cogently that the
World Bank is an invaluable common institution. It should be 'remade' only so far as
to formulate and implement a workable strategy for resolving the debt crisis; it should
deepen its collaboration with the IMF and private banks; it should strengthen the
private sector in developing countries by its lending policies; and it should expand the
capital available to the IDA and generally continue to grant LDCs a greater share in
decision-making since they are most affected by Bank programmes.

1057 **Sterling–dollar diplomacy: the origins and the prospects of our
international economic order.**
Richard N. Gardner. Oxford: Clarendon Press, 1956; New York:
McGraw-Hill, 2nd ed., 1969. 423p. bibliog.

This is the standard history of the origins of the Bretton Woods system. Gardner calls
it a 'hybrid work on the borderline of history, international relations, political science,
and even international law . . . a study of international economic diplomacy'. It is an
account, as he also writes, of 'the struggle to build a viable world economic order'
after World War II. The Bank and the Fund – however weak they were at the

beginning and however slowly they grew in subsequent decades – did end economic nationalism and committed the United States to international economic cooperation. The book explains why many things desirable in pure economic theory were not done at Bretton Woods. It puts the politics back into political economy. By the second edition, Gardner recognized that both universalism and legalism, which in the first edition he had belittled as 'errors' rooted in wartime euphoria, were the secrets of the Bank and Fund's success, for they bridged divides in the political world and brought the flexible yet sure processes of the law to the emergent world community. 'In short, these institutions', he writes, if not the agencies of world government, have certainly been instruments of a better world order.'

1058   **Towards a new Bretton Woods: challenges for the world financial and trading system.**
Gerald K. Helleiner, chairman of the Commonwealth Study Group. Foreword by Shridath S. Ramphal.   London: Commonwealth Secretariat, 1983. 147p.

After a decade of decline of the Bretton Woods system, the finance ministers of Commonwealth countries called for a study of reform. This comprehensive expert study under inter-governmental auspices reviewed the history of the system and discussed such issues as improved stabilization, international liquidity, commercial lending, debt management, long-term finance for development, and an integrated trading regime. Recommendations were made for the short, medium, and long term. So little has come of such proposals that it appears the authors' most 'pessimistic scenario' has been fulfilled.

1059   **Toward world prosperity: reshaping the global money system.**
Irving S. Friedman.   Lexington, MA: Lexington Books, 1987. 317p. bibliog.

The author, an experienced executive at both the IMF and the World Bank, boldly contradicts critics who say that the cause of the debt crisis is excessive borrowing, or that the size of the debts makes it virtually impossible to restore creditworthiness. Friedman denies that reductions of imports to improve balances of payments constitutes improvement of economic conditions. There is no shortage of world savings. His solution is to very greatly increase capital investments in poor countries by *private lenders*. Government lending (ODA) is not likely to increase despite ethical and realistic arguments, since domestic demands are so insistent. *Official institutions* at the national and international level, however, will be crucial in drawing private funds. Hence, the book looks closely at the reform of international financial institutions, calling in a climactic chapter for a 'new Bretton Woods'. Readers at the expert and general levels will find this an engaging, informative book.

1060   **The United Nations and the Bretton Woods institutions: new challenges for the 21st century. Report [of the North–South Roundtable, Bretton Woods, NH, 1-3 September 1993].**
New York: United Nations for Society for International Development, 1993. 24p.

Richard Jolly and others contribute some recent thinking about a new Bretton Woods.

1061   **U.S. policies toward the World Bank and the International Monetary Fund. A report of the panel on international financial institutions.**
Economic Policy Council of the United Nations Association–U.S.A.
New York: UNA–USA, 1982. 86p. bibliog.

At a time when the U.S. was scaling back its support of the international financial institutions, the private citizens association, UNA–USA, prepared this study of 'whether this proposed reduction would serve the national interest'. Without official aid, how would the private sector be induced to invest or lend in the poorest countries that are now beneficiaries of IDA credits? Loss of the 'carefully constructed network of multilateral economic cooperation', it was concluded, is not in 'U.S. economic and strategic interests'. Readers will find this short work very informative about the facts of U.S. contributions to international financial institutions and about the benefits to the U.S. – apart from those to developing countries.

1062   **The World Bank and the poor.**
Aart J.M. van de Laar.   Boston: M. Nijhoff for International
Institute for Social Studies (The Hague), 1980. 269p. bibliog.

Development theory by 1980 was in a state of 'disillusionment', and even the author, who had worked at the World Bank, complains of 'feeling depressed' when going through the record. Yet the Bank was in the process of shifting its fundamental policy to eradicating world poverty. Van de Laar traces the history of this shift, though he is rather doubtful. Both the World Bank and IDA are discussed, along with their bureaucracy, which resists change. He then explains what a reallocation of resources to the elimination of poverty would mean, and he critiques small-farmer projects. He concludes with reflections on the advantages of decentralization in order to better help the poor.

1063   **The World Bank: annual report, 1993.**
Washington, DC: World Bank, 1981- . annual. 252p.

This is the official annual report of the IBRD and IDA, whose purposes, respectively, are to provide 'hard' and 'soft' loans to developing countries. The two institutions also provide economic advice, technical assistance, and guidance for foreign investors. (In context, there is also mention of the IFC, MIGA, and ICSID, though these organizations have their own annual reports.) 'Poverty reduction' was the main strategy of the Bank in its 1992-93 fiscal year. Environmental management and human and social development are also foci. Private sector development (entrepreneurship, privatization, and finance) remain a large part of the Bank's work, especially with assistance to Russia's mass privatization of some 24,000 enterprises. Lending to all borrowers in 1993 amounted to $23,696 million; to the poorest countries, $9,957 million. The report is addressed to government policy-makers, yet is clear enough that students will learn from it.

1064 **The World Bank in a changing world: selected essays.**
Ibrahim F.I. Shihata. Compiled and edited by Franziska Tschofen and
Antonio R. Parra.   Dordrecht, The Netherlands: M. Nijhoff, 1991.
490p. bibliog.

The author is vice-president and general counsel of the World Bank. The volume
brings together ten essays on the Bank written from 1985 to 1991. Intended for a
general audience, the essays cover such topics as: prospects for the 1990s,
'governance' issues, human rights, the environment, involuntary resettlement, private
sector development, foreign direct investment, MIGA, and dispute settlement. Shihata
emphasizes the adaptation of legal texts to rapidly changing innovations at the Bank;
only a change in purposes would require amendment of the founding Articles of
Agreement. He sees critical challenges ahead, particularly in providing for future
generations and adapting projects to diverse local communities.

1065 **The World Bank since Bretton Woods: the origins, policies,
operations, and impact of the International Bank for
Reconstruction and Development and the other members of the
World Bank group: the International Finance Corporation, the
International Development Association, and the International
Centre for the Settlement of Investment Disputes.**
Edward S. Mason and Robert E. Asher.   Washington, DC:
Brookings Institution, 1973. 915p. bibliog.

Just before President Nixon took the United States off the gold standard and out of
the IMF for the regulation of currency convertibility, this large-scale history of the
World Bank group was completed. Here readers will find a full account of the Bank
and its affiliates written in the spirit of a great accomplishment. But in a 'final word',
Mason and Asher warn of dark events that have all come true – ODA far below the
target of 0.7 per cent of GNP, capital *exports* from the developing world, Bank
lending merely to reschedule debt, and hence loss of the Bank as a genuine
'development institution'.

International monetary stabilization

International Monetary Fund (IMF)

1066 **Banks, petrodollars, and sovereign debtors: blood from a stone?**
Edited by Penelope Hartland-Thunberg and Charles K. Ebinger.
Lexington, MA: Lexington Books for the Center for Strategic and
International Studies, Georgetown University (Washington), 1986.
193p. bibliog.

International debt, which was $150,000 million in 1975, was $900,000 million in
1985. Such debt, argue the editors of this strategic study, threatens the international
financial system and the prospects for peace and security in the developing world for

the foreseeable future. Hartland-Thunberg and Ebinger account for the crisis by going back to the first oil shock of 1973-74, when the availability of 'petrodollars' led to unwise overlending. The threat of default by debtors endangered the entire international banking system. Whether it would be met by rescheduling or require greater cooperative measures was very uncertain in the mid-1980s. The authors provide three case-studies of Mexico, Brazil, and Israel.

1067 **Developing a new international monetary system: a long-term view.**
H. Johannes Witteveen. Washington, DC: Per Jacobsson Foundation, 1983. 29p. bibliog.

The author, who has served in the Netherlands Ministry of Finance, the IMF, and international industrial and banking corporations, admits that 'the international monetary system is clearly in very unsatisfactory shape'. A 'cooperative reform effort' is needed, he says, yet governments seem unlikely to act except in crises. Witteveen finds the main obstacle in the 'illusionary . . . concept of sovereignty' in an interdependent world. Since this illusion is plainly beyond the powers of one man to dispel, he concentrates on 'lack of insight', which could be remedied and must be so before the world assembles again in a 'major conference to design or agree on a new international monetary system'. He would stabilize the international credit markets to both resolve the debt crisis and avoid overlending again in the future. In the long term, stable credit growth would support stabilization of monetary exchange rates. In time, the SDR could grow into world money. Witteveen looks upon international financial institutions, with respect to the emerging world economy, as analogous to national governments, with respect to their private national markets.

1068 **The evolution of the International Monetary Fund.**
Frank A. Southard, Jr. Princeton, NJ: International Finance Section, Department of Economics, Princeton University, 1979. 50p. bibliog. (Essays in International Finance No. 135).

By 1979, the IMF had weathered the collapse of the Bretton Woods par-value system (1971-73). The author, who served many years in the IMF, explains its survival in terms of five strategic factors: professional *esprit*, scrupulously correct relations with member countries, financial resources made available by right under gradations of conditionality, a kind of dual ('fixed but adjustable') exchange-rate policy, and wise Fund management during financial crises. Southard concludes with a rather gloomy view of the future: 'It was not easy to create the IMF and it has not been easy to develop it into a world monetary authority. It *would* be easy for the leading members to reduce it to ineffectiveness or to an institution concerned chiefly with meeting the financial needs of less developed countries.' That is, he would see it become a world central bank, and not another development agency.

1069 **The global effects of Fund-supported adjustment programs.**
Morris Goldstein. Washington, DC: IMF, 1986. 49p. bibliog. (Occasional Paper No. 42).

This is the IMF's own study of the effects of its adjustment programmes on developing countries (1973-83). The account is entirely in terms of macro-economic variables (GNP growth, share of trade, commodity composition) – not political instability. But both aggregation and interdependence are measured, and the conclusion is generally that the Fund is not indifferent to the 'general welfare'.

1070 The IMF and Third World political instability: is there a connection?

Scott R. Sidell. London: Macmillan, 1988. 82p. bibliog.

This British academic study investigates empirically, by quantitative analysis of data from the period 1969-77, the contentious question whether IMF adjustment programmes have promoted political instability in debt-ridden developing countries. Political instability is understood to include riots, strikes, demonstrations, assassinations, violence, armed attacks, civil war, and attempted and successful *coups d'état*. The author concludes that the apparent association between Fund-supported adjustment programmes and political instability is 'merely a spurious, rather than a causal relationship'. Adjustment cannot be significantly correlated, statistically, to such instability.

1071 The IMF in a changing world, 1945-85.

Margaret Garristen de Vries. Washington, DC: IMF, 1986. 226p. bibliog.

The author was a historian in the employ of the Fund; this book is a reprint edition of reflective articles she has written, often on commemorative occasions. Thus, the work is a 'minihistory' of the Fund written by an insider. Here readers will find intelligible accounts of some rather obscure yet important historical developments, like the exchange crises and changes in the world economy, 1966-71. There are month-by-month chronologies included. Looking back at forty years, de Vries concludes that the Fund had undergone a 'metamorphosis' yet has held constant its work to promote international cooperation on monetary problems; to expand trade, employment, and income; to sustain balances of payments; and to foster a liberal trade and payments regime.

1072 International capital markets. [Part I:] Exchange rate management and international capital flows. [Part II:] Systemic issues in international finance.

Morris Goldstein and David Folkerts-Landau, leaders of staff team. Washington, DC: IMF, 1993. 2 vols. bibliog. (World Economic and Financial Surveys).

Since 1988, the IMF has been producing several studies like this between annual volumes of its *World economic outlook* (see item no. 1089). This succinct two-volume issue focuses on the September 1992 European monetary crisis just before the E.C. members met at Maastricht to discuss monetary union. (Both the lira and the pound were suddenly taken out of the European Monetary System.) Systemic developments such as the single European financial market and the ECU market are also treated.

1073   **International debt and the stability of the world economy.**
William R. Cline.   Washington, DC: Institute for International
Economics, distributed by MIT Press, 1983. 134p.

The international debt crisis reached a climax in 1983, when Argentina, Brazil, and
Mexico had to suspend normal debt servicing. The Third World threatened to default
on all its debt, and the public was sceptical about rescheduling as a device to 'bail out
the banks'. Moreover, the world economy was in recession. This brief,
comprehensive analysis examines public policy on external debt. It covers the origins
of the problem, the risk of default, the prospects of continued debt, 'involuntary
lending', the adequacy of national banks and international institutions, and reform
proposals. The most technical material has been placed in footnotes and appendixes
so that non-economists, with application, can follow the explanation. Cline rejects
radical reforms. 'Despite this systemic risk, a measured policy response is the best
course.' For a more detailed, still more explanatory account, see Cline's *International
debt: systemic risk and policy response* (1984).

1074   **The International Monetary Fund: its evolution, organization,
and activities.**
A.W. Hooke.   Washington, DC: IMF, 1981; 3rd ed., 1983. 82p.

This is a short, official explanation of the IMF's organization and activities. Topics
include its regulatory function, procedures for financial assistance, conditionality,
forms of financial assistance, SDRs, and services. Readers in search of the meanings
of such technical terms as 'reserve tranche drawings', 'compensatory financing
facility', 'buffer stock financing facility', 'general arrangements to borrow',
'surveillance', and 'adjustment' will find them here. There is a section on 'reform',
but it only covers the amendments to the Articles of Agreement in 1978 replacing
gold by SDRs as the ultimate principal reserve asset of the Fund. An annex lists
current voting power.

1075   **The international monetary system and its reform: papers
prepared for the Group of Twenty-four by a United Nations
project directed by Sidney Dell, 1979-1986.**
Sidney Dell, project director.   Amsterdam: North-Holland for the
U.N., 1987. 3 vols.

The Group of 24 (G-24, 1971) is a group of developing countries particularly engaged
in negotiations within the IMF on the future of the international monetary system.
They aimed to counterbalance the Group of 10 developed countries, founded ten
years before (G-10, 1961). (The G-10 has become the *de facto* superior authority to
IMF executives.) The technical papers collected herein were written to support the G-
24. Topics include: expansion of the resources of the Bretton Woods institutions,
structural adjustment in balance of payments settlements, conditionality adapted to
adjustment, international debt, inequities affecting LDCs, South–South cooperation,
the programme of action on monetary reform, strengthening the SDR, and
establishing a stabilization account.

1076   **The international monetary system: a time of turbulence.**
Edited by Jacob S. Dreyer, Gottfried Harberler, and Thomas D.
Willett.   Washington, DC: American Enterprise Institute for Public
Policy Research, 1982. 523p.

This volume of conference papers examines the worsening international monetary
system after a decade of experimentation with flexible exchange rates. The
participants did not assume that the problem was to restore a 'global, Bretton Woods-
type system of semifixed exchange rates', even though it was admitted on all sides
that 'for twenty years the Bretton Woods system worked very well'. The learned,
somewhat technical papers seem to point to the need for a new system able to
accommodate modern mixed economies by flexible exchange rates backed by multi-
currency reserves in the IMF.

1077   **The lender-of-last-resort function in an international context.**
Jack Guttentag and Richard Herring.   Princeton, NJ: International
Finance Section, Department of Economics, 1983. 30p. bibliog.
(Essays in International Finance No. 151).

A lender of last resort is a banking institution that will provide credit under conditions
of stress. There is no world bank that is capable of performing such a function, nor is
even an international deposit insurance system likely to survive a serious crisis. The
authors warn: 'The main danger in international banking today is from a credit shock
that would wipe out most or all of the capital of major international banks.' They
imply that, if international monetary institutions are barely capable of coping with
illiquidity, a world government will be needed to guard against insolvency.

1078   **LDC debt in the 1980s: risk and reforms.**
Jeffrey Sachs.   In: *Crises in the economic and financial structure.*
Edited by Paul Wachtel.   Lexington, MA: Lexington Books, D.C.
Heath, 1982, p.197-246.

This is a close, exacting study of the LDC contribution to the international debt crisis
and of the threat from their 'sovereign default' to the international capital markets.
Sachs' theoretical model regards defaults as an imperfect 'form of insurance to debtor
countries'. International cooperation is the only way for creditors to avoid having to
pay the face value of such policies to debtors!

1079   **The lending policies of the International Monetary Fund.**
John Williamson.   Washington, DC: Institute for International
Economics, 1982. 72p. bibliog.

By the beginning of the Reagan administration, complaints against the IMF by
borrowing countries were matched by criticisms from the principal subscriber. The
Fund was said to be insensitive to the individual situations of borrowing countries; on
the other hand, it was said to be entering fields that could be perfectly handled by
commercial banks. The editor here draws on a conference of broadly representative
economists from around the globe to settle five main policy questions: the role of the
Fund, cooperation with the World Bank, design of adjustment programmes,
monitoring such programmes, and anticyclical policy. Participants generally agreed
that, except when discussing their own countries, any five economists would agree
amongst themselves on the right programme, which would be about the same as the

Fund's recommendation. 'In other words, the group concluded that the Fund is neither driven by sinister motives nor professionally incompetent in overlooking preferable adjustment strategies, but gets a bad press primarily because its job involves confronting countries with unpleasant realities.'

1080   **Organizing the world's money: the political economy of international monetary relations.**
        Benjamin J. Cohen.   New York: Basic Books, 1977. 310p.

This book on the international monetary order and on its reform is distinctive in that the author 'integrates both economic and political aspects of the problem into a single analytical framework'. Cohen sets himself the task of providing a persuasive argument to guide the international community toward a 'new constitution for the monetary system'. It will have to balance both competition and cooperation. It will have to occupy some middle ground between national autarky and international anarchy. There are four possible designs: (1) an automatic one, requiring no outside intervention, like the gold standard or flexible exchange rates; (2) hegemony of one powerful state, like the United States; (3) constant negotiation, as under the IMF and similar institutions more or less as presently constituted; and (4) supranationality, as under an IMF transformed into a world central bank. Cohen's solution is complex but consistent with current trends: (1) a regime of managed floating exchange rates; (2) an improved IMF; (3) an optimized bargaining process; (4) a multiple reserve currency standard.

1081   **Pulling together: the International Monetary Fund in a multipolar world.**
        Edited by Catherine Gwin and Richard E. Feinberg.   New Brunswick, NJ: Transaction Books for the Overseas Development Council, 1989. 174p. bibliog. (U.S.–Third World Policy Perspectives No. 13).

'As industrial and developing countries approach the last decade of this century, the need for effective international institutions remains more important that ever.' This short, authoritative work aims to resolve the controversy – now some twenty years old – about the future of the IMF. Some analysts argue that the Fund should return to its original role to ensure a stable international monetary system; eventually it should be converted into a global central bank. Others approve of the Fund's entry into economic development, while leaving the larger industrial countries to regulate their financial relations themselves; the Fund, then, would gradually merge with the World Bank. The editors argue in a succinct overview, 'Reforming the Fund', along lines of the first alternative. The IMF is needed for macro-economic management of the emerging 'one-world economy'. Immediate challenges like easing Third World debt and integrating the (former) socialist countries into the system will first have to be met. Then they would strengthen the IMF's institutional capacities in research, public debate, policy innovation, and financial resources.

1082 **The quest for economic stabilization: the International Monetary Fund and the Third World.**
Edited by Tony Killick. New York: St. Martin's, 1984. 340p. bibliog.

At a time of 'widespread questioning about the future of the Bretton Woods institutions', the editor and authors sought to evaluate the role of the IMF in protecting the stability of developing countries. The study is in two volumes. This one is on aggregate questions like the causes of disequilibrium and the actual and potential role of the IMF; the second, *The IMF and stabilization*, is a companion volume of case-studies in Latin America, Indonesia, Jamaica, and Kenya. In an effort to help the least developed countries, the authors conclude that cost-efficient reforms are needed – what they call 'real economy'. They make specific suggestions for reformed IMF policies on these lines and answer objections.

1083 **Special Drawing Rights: character and use.**
Joseph Gold. Washington, DC: IMF, 1968; 2nd ed., 1970. 91p. (Pamphlet Series No. 13).

In 1968, after a long search for a supplementary international reserve asset, the Special Drawing Right (SDR) was created. It was duly accepted by amendment of the IMF's Articles of Agreement the next year. The author, General Counsel and Director of the Legal Department of the IMF, here presents a descriptive, non-doctrinal account of the SDR. Sophisticated readers will probably find this the definitive statement. Since international law has long recognized the right of the state to regulate its own currency, Gold is impressed that the states have agreed to vest some of that power in an international organization.

1084 **The Third World and decision making in the International Monetary Fund: the quest for full and effective participation.**
Tyrone Ferguson. London: Pinter for Graduate Institute of International Studies (Geneva), 1988. 262p. bibliog.

The Fund's weighted voting rules greatly favour the developed world; the General Agreement to Borrow moved effective decision-making into the hands of the Group of 10; the United States unilaterally withdrew from the Bretton Woods system of fixed exchange rates in 1971, perhaps dooming the whole system. Originally, the IMF's Articles of Agreement provided for a code of good conduct in monetary relations and for a short-term credit facility to help member-states in difficulty to adhere to the code. The author has picked the IMF – 'the most hermetic of contemporary international organizations' – because it is the most difficult case for the present constitutional crisis over a new world economic order. Ferguson presents very fairly the claim – and the wisdom – of diverse Third World states to greater participation in the IMF.

1085 **Thoughts on an International Monetary Fund based fully on the SDR.**
Jacques J. Polak.   Washington, DC: IMF, 1979. 26p. (Pamphlet Series No. 28).

The assets of the IMF in 1979 were gold, SDRs, and member currencies (the latter ten times larger than gold, and gold four times larger than SDRs). In a pamphlet written for those familiar with IMF accounting, Polak argues for making the SDR the principal reserve asset in the international monetary system – in effect creating an international currency, and transforming the IMF into a world central bank. The SDRs on the balance sheets would be increased about eight times, and the member currencies would be reaccounted as assets for the extension of credit by the Fund. Such a reform would radically simplify the IMF. Polak argues that the world political context has so changed that an international currency, like J.M. Keynes' 'bancors', would be acceptable and presumably would settle the convertibility problem.

1086 **The unique nature of the responsibilities of the International Monetary Fund.**
Manuel Guitián.   Washington, DC: IMF, 1992. 64p. bibliog. (Pamphlet Series No. 46).

Written by an IMF official in his personal capacity, this is a pensive reflection, somewhat in the spirit of the classical political philosophers, on the need for 'internationally agreed principles and conventions to govern economic relations among politically independent nations'. The Bretton Woods regime, historically, was the first agreement to fulfil such an aspiration. Guitian sees the IMF as developing an 'international code of economic conduct'. The Fund has three evolving functions: regulation, surveillance (giving advice on national policy), and conditionality (setting standards for financial aid in conformity with the code of conduct). He sees the Fund doing for the world what the E.C. institutions are doing for Europe – developing rules for the conduct of states, when the rules are still dependent on 'discretion'. 'Now that there is a prospect', he concludes, 'for the world economic order to become fully global in geographic scope, extending the code of conduct to cover all international transactions would be most appropriate for the establishment of true universality.'

1087 **Use of the Special Drawing Right to supplement or substitute for other means of finance.**
Peter B. Kenen.   In: *International money and credit: the policy roles*. Edited by George M. von Furstenberg.   Washington, DC: IMF, 1983, p.327-60.

Here is another sophisticated study on the evolution of a world currency. The dollar is declining; the IMF's SDR has potential. The alternative is a 'basket' of floating national currencies. By the end of the petrodollar influx and the recognition of a permanent debt crisis (about 1981), the need for a more stable reserve asset was manifest. But SDRs could not be made that asset without 'drastic changes in the system as a whole'. Kenen would make the SDR the international monetary unit for *all* official transactions that affect reserves – for intervention, borrowing, etc. To do so, the SDR must first be made more attractive, substitutable, and flexible. Compare Polak, *Thoughts on an International Monetary Fund based fully on the SDR* (item no. 1085).

1088 **Voting majorities in the Fund: effects of the second amendment of the Articles.**
Joseph Gold.   Washington, DC: IMF, 1977. 77p. (Pamphlet Series No. 20).

This is a short constitutional account of the second amendment of the IMF's Articles of Agreement (effective in 1978; first amendment in 1969). The pamphlet's general interest lies in its authoritative account of reforms of the weighted voting rules in an organization of sovereign states. Generally, more decisions now require 'special majorities', and higher majorities (70-85 per cent) are often required. The effect is to institutionalize *consensus* as virtually a *rule of unanimity* in order to exercise the increased powers of the Fund. LDCs have 36 per cent of the votes and hence can veto decisions, but so can the U.S. and the E.C.

1089 **World economic outlook, October 1993.**
IMF Staff.   Washington, DC: IMF, 1980- . annual.

Unlike comparable World Bank and U.N. reports on the world economy, this handsome IMF volume is an analysis and *projection*, in the short term (one year, 1994), of standard economic indicators. Graphs are ingeniously shaded to indicate projections of current trends. Output, employment, consumer prices, real GDP, exchange rates, interest rates, current account positions, national external financing flows, external debt and debt service are typical of the indicators. Figures are given for industrial countries, developing countries, and 'countries in transition' (Eastern Europe and Russia). Special attention is given to Europe, which is experiencing delays in forming a monetary union on the basis of the ECU (European Currency Unit). 'Notwithstanding the near-term uncertainties, developments consistent with the cooperative strategy give some reason for cautious optimism that global economic performance will strengthen generally.'

International trade

General Agreement on Tariffs and Trade (GATT) International Trade Organization (ITO, proposed 1948)

1090 **An appraisal of the Havana charter in relation to U.S. foreign policy, with a definitive study of its provisions.**
James G. Fulton.   U.S. Congress, House of Representatives, Committee on Foreign Affairs. 80th Cong., 2nd sess., 1948. (Committee print. H4672).

Here is political analysis of the ITO charter as it came before Congress.

1091 **Beyond free trade.**
Robert B. Reich. *Foreign Affairs*, vol. 61 (1983), p.773-804.

The author, later Secretary of Labor in the Clinton administration, finds that a 1983 report by the President's Council of Economic Advisors makes concessions from free traders to the protectionists that reveal new realities 'beyond free trade'. 'The problem is', argues Reich, 'that the classic principle of free trade no longer offers any practical or politically compelling alternative to protectionism.' He shows this by a brief survey of the rise of new industrial powers (especially Japan) since the late 1960s, for they challenged Western governments to protect their industries and workers. By 1982, U.S. non-tariff barriers protected 34 per cent of American manufacturing; with similar percentages in West Germany and France. The 'free trade ideal' he would replace by government-managed 'transformations of capital and labor to higher value-added production'.

1092 **Canada, the GATT, and the international trade system.**
Frank Stone. Montreal: Institute for Research on Public Policy, 1984. 236p. bibliog.

'This study examines, from a Canadian perspective, the origins, structure, and operations of GATT and the other international agreements and institutions that make up the multilateral trade system.' Written after the Tokyo Round (1973-79), which generally marked a triumph for liberal principles, the book regards the multilateral trade system as a 'great advance in international cooperation over the high trade barriers, bilateralism, and discrimination in world trade that existed during the inter-war period'. Canada has particularly benefited from the system and is now comfortably within the G-7 group of developed countries. Topics include: the ITO ('what was lost'), regional trade groups (U.S.-Canada Free Trade Area), OECD, low-cost imports, GATT and UNCTAD, the generalized system of preferences, international commodity agreements, agricultural products, state trading, and the rise of protectionism.

1093 **A charter for world trade.**
Claire Wilcox. Foreword by W.L. Clayton. New York: Macmillan, 1949. 333p.

This is a contemporary account of the ITO charter just after it was signed in Havana in 1948. The book is instinct with a spirit of confidence and realism that could not be found a generation later in American writings on the GATT. As Will Clayton writes in his foreword: 'This may well prove to be the greatest step in history toward order and justice in economic relations among the members of the world community.' Claire Wilcox writes: 'The American people have come, most of them, to realize the role that they must play in world affairs. . . . We must go on, in international cooperation, from politics to economics, from finance to trade.' She provides here the actual text of the charter and a very readable account of its major chapters on employment, economic development, commercial policy (what became the GATT), restrictive business practices (cartels), commodity agreements, and the International Trade Organization.

1094   **Conflicts in principle in drafting a trade charter.**
Jacob Viner.   *Foreign Affairs*, vol. 25 (July 1947), p.612-28.
Appearing in the same issue as George Kennan's 'X' article on the 'Sources of Soviet conduct', which inaugurated the containment policy, this early article on the ITO discusses such principles as lowering trade barriers (including British Imperial preferences), non-discrimination, elimination of quantitative restrictions and quotas, accommodation of free market and centrally planned economies (not only U.S.S.R. but also Britain), and a code of trade. Viner's liberal article can be read as a corrective to more protectionist articles forty-five years later on the eve of a similar struggle to establish an ITO. 'The old schoolmen', wrote Viner theologically, 'distinguished between the grace which inspires good resolutions and that other grace which provides the will to fulfill them. There is great danger that the American supply of the latter will fall far short of the State Department's supply of the former.' He warned that, if the ITO were rejected in the new Cold War atmosphere, it would mean a 'return to the systematic economic warfare which prevailed in the 1930s'.

1095   **Current efficacy of the GATT dispute settlement process.**
Shaun A. Ingersoll.   *Texas Journal of International Law*, vol. 22 (1987), p.87-108.
In order to counter the 'growing sentiment for protectionist trade measures', the author describes improvements to the GATT dispute settlement process. 'Mistrust on the part of trading partners as to the fairness and predictability of GATT settlements', he admits, 'has undermined the Organization's ability to stimulate economic expansion.' Ingersoll surveys the history of loss of such confidence. He then rejects three 'perilous proposals' in response to the crisis: protectionism (too dependent on government); a new trade organization (too slow); and adjudication by the ICJ (too remote and suspect). His own solution is to widen use of experts in panels and to set time constraints for them; to include all forms of discrimination, especially that related to services, within GATT's competence to resolve; establish annual meetings on the ministerial level; and eliminate Council 'obstructionism'.

1096   **The deterioration of the GATT framework in international trade relations.**
Ronald I. Meltzer.   In: *Politics in the United Nations system*. Edited by Lawrence S. Finkelstein.   Durham, NC: Duke University Press, 1988, p.148-74.
GATT is not the originally planned ITO (1948). The agreement has deteriorated due to lack of a centralized political institution for the discussion of trade, formulation of uniform rules, and resolution of disputes. Over time, non-discrimination as a principle has eroded, non-tariff barriers (quotas, subsidies) have grown, and whole industries (farm products, textiles, ships, steel, autos) have been exempted. 'The framework of trade rules . . . has moved increasingly away from fixed and objective international criteria for behavior to one that is more dependent on administrative discretion by governments.' Improvement depends on 'political will, converging self-interest, and coalition formation'.

1097 **Dispute settlement in GATT: the current debate.**
Friedl Weiss. In: *The non-use of force in international law*. Edited
by W.E. Butler. Dordrecht, The Netherlands: M. Nijhoff, 1989,
p.221-47.

Since dispute settlement was on the agenda of the Uruguay Round, the author
contributes a 'synthetic overview' of debate on the issue. Weiss repeats the warning
of a former Director-General: GATT law 'is a subject matter difficult to grasp in all
its implications by those not involved with it on a day-to-day basis'. He describes the
GATT processes in a way that a practising international lawyer would appreciate. The
system, however, is 'impregnated by a hostility to legalism', since it favours
negotiation of mutually acceptable settlements. Europeans, he observes, actually
prefer 'diplomats' jurisprudence', while Americans would like more 'adjudicative
determination of rights and duties'. Reforms must bear such constitutional traditions
in mind. It is the panels that most need reform; the most radical reform would replace
them with a permanent tribunal of individual GATT experts in the law.

1098 **Economic impact of generalized trade preferences.**
Rolf J. Langhammer and Andre Sapir. Aldershot, England: Gower
for the Trade Policy Research Centre, 1987. 90p. bibliog. (Thames
Essay No. 49).

The 'Generalized System of Preferences' (GSP) is a formal derogation of the
founding principle of non-discrimination in the GATT, which has been established in
order to protect infant industries in the developing countries. A parallel device to
protect developed countries is the 'export-restraint arrangement' negotiated outside
the GATT. Such threats to the universal system have produced an impasse. The
authors are committed to trade liberalization; their focus is primarily on participation
of the developing countries in such a liberal system. But on the grounds that 'equal
treatment of unequals is unfair', poor countries demand discrimination in their favour,
like the GSP. Langhammer and Sapir conclude that both U.S. and E.C. GSP schemes
no longer have much effect when tariffs are already low; a better reform would be 'to
encourage investment in developing countries by enterprises that are engaged in a
world-wide intra-industry specialization'. The battle against protectionism should be
fought on the field of non-tariff barriers.

1099 **Economic policy and the ITO charter.**
Dean Acheson. *Department of State Bulletin*, vol. 20, no. 515
(15 May 1949), p.623-27.

In 1949, the U.S. Secretary of State was talking very much like the most advanced
supporters of the United Nations forty years later. 'We have come to realize more
clearly than ever before that foreign economic policy is not made in a political
vacuum. It is hardly possible any longer to draw a sharp dividing line between
economic affairs and political affairs.' Acheson described the international financial
institutions which the United States had led in creating in order to solve 'world
economic problems'. The 'capstone' in the arch of these was the ITO. 'The goal of
the ITO charter is the realization of higher levels of material well-being through the
expansion of world trade.' He outlined its 'detailed code of rules of fair practice to
govern' members' foreign trade policies. The reason why the charter was so long and
detailed was to make it more enforceable. The state traders were subjected to rules,
and the extreme free traders were made to compromise. The trade law in the charter,

Acheson emphasized, involved the same occasional sacrifices by the nations for the general welfare as the states made when joining the U.S. federal union. 'The character of the International Trade Organization is thus the beginning of law in the realm of world commerce and the vehicle for the growth of a spirit of mutuality and interdependence in trade relations.'

1100 The end of the ITO.

William Diebold, Jr. Princeton, NJ: International Finance Section, Department of Economics, Princeton University, October 1952. 37p. (Essays in International Finance No. 16).

This is a diplomatic account of the abandonment of the ITO – the third major organization in the Bretton Woods system. Its aim was to counter economic nationalism by an international organization to maintain free trade. The ITO would regulate tariffs, abolish quotas (quantitative restrictions), control exchanges and state trading, assist in reaching international commodity agreements, check restrictive trade practices, provide tribunals for the settlement of trade disputes, administer the regime, and generally try to maintain full employment in all countries. American politics – the 'protectionists' vs. the 'perfectionists' – largely explain its demise. The need to control war materials in case of future conflict with the Soviet Union was also at work.

1101 Fair trade: reform and realities in the international trading system.

Michael Barratt Brown. London: Zed Books, 1993. 226p.

A *free* international trading system would also be a *fair* one, but the present one is not. This informed and knowledgeable book is based on the premise that an unregulated market of profit-seekers will never – despite Adam Smith and Richard Cobden – produce a fair system. The author surveys past attempts to win a fairer deal for primary producers by commodity agreements, economic aid, central planning, counter-trade, and the NIEO. Brown's own preferred device is the 'alternative trade organization' that more closely links producers and consumers of such goods as textiles, canned fruits and jams, honey, nuts, and coffee. Measured in dollars, the volume is in millions, compared to thousands of millions for all Third World trade. But the larger trading system is in crisis, and expanded trade – not aid – is the key to opening up the Third World and Eastern Europe.

1102 GATT activities, 1992: an annual review of the work of the GATT.

Geneva: GATT, 1993.

This annual official volume is worth checking before concluding, from certain critical articles in journals of national opinion, that the GATT is declining or dead. By 1992, 111 nations adhered to the GATT, plus another 22 *de facto*, and 15 republics of the former Soviet Union pending. Some 90 per cent of world trade is accounted for by the 111 governments (only China as a great power remains outside). The report contains an overview of world trade, notices of dispute settlements, trade policy issues raised in the Council, regional trading agreements, and the like.

1103   **GATT and conflict management: a transatlantic strategy for a stronger regime.**
Edited by Reinhard Rode.   Boulder, CO: Westview, 1990. 125p.

The GATT free trade regime cannot survive without a hegemon, the editor argues. To preserve the regime, the only candidates for leadership, after the United States, are the European Community and Japan. But the E.C. is turning inwards towards its single market, and Japan continues to take profits from its very favourable balance of trade. The U.S. has been the relative loser in trade liberalization and cannot seem to overcome its huge trade deficits. This book argues that, despite these great difficulties, a trilateral strategy would uphold the 'liberal trade principle' for the benefit of all nations.

1104   **The GATT and the negotiation of international trade rules.**
Gardner Patterson.   In: *Negotiating world order: the art and architecture of global diplomacy.* Edited by Alan K. Henrikson. Wilmington, DE: Scholarly Resources, 1986, p.181-97.

This is a clear introduction to GATT – its history, principles, and future problems. Protectionist pressures in sovereign nations, a retreat from multilateral to bilateral negotiations, and sectoral approaches all threaten a flourishing though volatile free trade world system. Patterson's suggestions for reform involve dispute settlement, enforcement, rule-making, fair treatment of LDCs. Together, such reforms approach recreation of the ITO, which was finally abandoned in 1950.

1105   **The GATT and the regulation of trade barriers: regime dynamics and functions.**
Jock A. Finlayson and Mark W. Zacher.   *International Organization*, vol. 35 (1981), p.561-602.

Trade barriers are '*state* policies or practices that impede the access [that] countries enjoy to each other's markets for their exports'. GATT is at the centre of the international trade regime, which, counting other organizations that address trade barriers, includes the U.N. General Assembly, UNCTAD, and FAO. The authors set themselves the task of describing GATT's norms and functions in reducing trade barriers. The norms of the regime are: non-discrimination, liberalization, reciprocity, safeguards, development, multilateralism, and major interests. The functions are: facilitation, constraint, diffusion of influence, and promotion of interaction. GATT in its seven conferences or 'rounds' has clearly reduced trade barriers such as tariffs and non-tariff barriers. The authors explain this as due to calculations of national interest and to certain bureaucratic devices.

1106   **The GATT legal system and world trade diplomacy.**
Robert E. Hudec.   New York: Praeger, 1975. 399p.

This older legal study, prepared during the Tokyo Round of negotiations (1973-79), was designed to dispel the impression, which Third World representatives readily drew from the founding documents, that the GATT is a legal system like domestic ones. Hudec argues that 'GATT "law" is a rather unique blend of legal and diplomatic strategies'. The only way to understand it is to review its early history during the time when the ITO was under debate (1946-50). U.S. officials at the time, he recalls, thought in terms of an expanded Reciprocal Trade Agreements programme; U.K., of a broader multilateral convention establishing an international code of behaviour and an international organization to implement the code. But 'pressures of conflicting interests forced retreat at each stage of the process'. Hence, GATT rulings and dispute settlement were not at all what they appeared to be.

1107 **The General Agreement on Tariffs and Trade (GATT) and the Law of the Sea (LOS) Convention: a critical comparison of arbitration provisions.**
Thomas R. Mounteer. *International Lawyer*, vol. 21 (1987), p.989-1012.
For states to settle their disputes by arbitration requires a willingness to relinquish some measure of sovereignty for the common good. Devising trustworthy arbitral provisions in the GATT (1973-79) and the LOS (1975-82) has been time consuming, but they now exist and are quite similar. The author compares the two, explores the requirements for consultation prior to arbitration, and discusses how failure to consult triggers more formal processes of dispute resolution. Mounteer considers exceptions in the LOS to compulsory arbitration, which make its processes even more flexible, if not evasive, for states. He then reviews the scope of jurisdiction, applicable law, selection of a tribunal, remedies, and proceedings.

1108 **Globalizing the GATT: the Soviet Union's successor states, Eastern Europe, and the international trading system.**
Leah A. Haus. Washington, DC: Brookings, 1992. 141p.
Czechoslovakia was an original signatory to the GATT in 1947 yet later adopted a non-market economy. Poland, Romania, and Hungary were admitted as non-market countries in 1967, 1971, and 1973 respectively. The Soviet Union was approved for admission as an observer in 1990 before dissolving the next year. The first four countries and the successor states of the Soviet Union are reforming their economies, but they still contain large non-market sectors. The author shows that, historically, Western opposition to Eastern European participation in GATT was less related to inability to accommodate economic diversity than to fears of political sabotage. After the Cold War, the potential exists to make GATT a truly 'global' international institution whose norms and rules can maintain an open, non-discriminatory free market, with minimum governmental intervention – that is, with maximum private firm management in accordance with tariffs and prices. Haus shows, however, that such a result will depend not only on Eastern reforms but also on Western policy changes – particularly an acceptance by the United States that Western European commercial interests in Eastern Europe will require some compromise on the two principal norms of GATT – namely, non-discrimination and reciprocity – in favour of the latter.

1109 **International Trade Organization. Hearings [, 20 March–3 April 1947].**
U.S. Congress, Senate, Committee on Finance. 80th Cong., 1st sess. 676p. (S821-0-A. SuDoc: Y4.F49:In85/pt.1).
At these Senate hearings on the ITO, witnesses included William L. Clayton (State), Claire Wilcox (State), George Bronz (Treasury), Henry Dexter White (IMF), and others.

1110 **In the kingdom of the blind: a report on protectionism and the Asian–Pacific region.**
Lydia Dunn, chairperson of a study group. London: Trade Policy Research Centre, 1983. 134p. bibliog. (Special Report No. 3).

Hong Kong, Australia, New Zealand, Malaysia, Thailand, Japan, and the United States are among the Pacific countries vitally interested in trade. This study – designed to reach government ministers, business leaders, U.N. officials, experts, and the general public – argues that, to restore life to the world economy, the Asian–Pacific countries should take the lead to arrest and then reverse protectionist trends. 'What has to be done is to restore the basic elements of the GATT system, which can be succinctly described in terms of "non-discrimination", "liberalism", "stability", and "transparency".' To do this, Dunn and her colleagues propose a number of government policies – not amendment of the GATT. The book is a non-doctrinaire account of the GATT system as it actually works in international commerce, with just enough history to make the present intelligible. It also punctures many pretensions. 'At present, there are two types of charlatan. . . . The less sophisticated advocates protection. The more sophisticated recommends "concerted reflation".'

1111 **The last gasp of Gattism.**
Clyde V. Prestowitz, Jr., Alan Tonelson, and Robert W. Jerome.
Harvard Business Review, vol. 69 (March-April 1991), p.130-41.

During a suspension of the Uruguay Round, the authors unremorsefully declared all GATT negotiations dead. 'GATT's 1940s-era assumptions and principles have become largely irrelevant to the world economy of the 1990s – and to America's interests in that economy.' The U.S. is no longer available to prop up the system; attempts to eliminate non-tariff barriers to trade run into sovereign rights; non-discrimination is disadvantageous to free and democratic societies. The article is a sustained attack on free trade and 'a more international vision'. Readers will find it consistent with much recent, 'conservative' American opinion opposed to the U.N. system. The 'real debate', Prestowitz declares, should be over 'how to rebuild national economic strength'. He and the other authors offer no relief from the 'continuation of economic conflict' – from the 'competitive, anarchic nature of world politics'. They do not quite revert to the bilateral trade policies of the 1930s – they would create the ITO, but on a G-7 basis – yet they constantly return to America's great economic and military *independence*.

1112 **Linking the world: trade policies for the future.**
Edited by Khadija Haq. Islamabad, Pakistan: North–South Roundtable, 1988. 206p. bibliog.

'Over the next decade', the editor declares, 'no global economic issue is perhaps as important as the liberalization of world trade. A sustained world economic recovery depends on a progressive freeing of the world markets from the protectionism and trade constraints which became the unfortunate distinction of the 1970s.' As the Uruguay Round of GATT talks began (1986), the North–South Roundtable (an independent NGO devoted to reconciling North and South) held conferences in London on trade in goods and trade in services. This volume contains specialized papers bearing on the negotiations.

1113 **Membership and participation by the United States in the International Trade Organization. Hearings [on HJR-236, April–May 1950].**
U.S. Congress, House of Representatives, Committee on Foreign Affairs. 81st Cong., 2nd sess. 809p. (H1288-10. SuDocs: Y4.F76/1:In8/20).
These hearings reflect final negative positions of such business groups as the National Association of Manufacturers and the U.S. Chamber of Commerce. Witnesses included Dean Acheson (State), Edward H. Foley (Treasury), and representatives of American manufacturing, commerce, banking, and trade.

1114 **The new multilateralism: can the world trading system be saved?**
Miriam Camps and William Diebold, Jr.   New York: Council on Foreign Relations, 1983. 72p.
The world trading system is in trouble, just as is the larger world economic system. The authors, whose minds were formed, they admit, in the period when the ITO was being planned (1944-48), argue cogently and sympathetically 'for changing the [GATT] system so as to preserve it'. The 'old multilateralism' worked well for a decade or two; the 'new' consists of changes in rules, practices, and attitudes identified in this short treatise. Camps and Diebold make many suggestions to improve the constitution of GATT. To the pessimistic objection that governments are unable or unwilling to coordinate their policies in a new fundamental trade agreement or constitution, they reply politically that protectionist or mercantilist forces in every country are balanced or outweighed by 'people whose welfare depends to a striking degree on satisfactory relations with the rest of the world'. They also add that sheer 'fear' of a general collapse of the world economy may induce governments to summon leadership to act. But basically, the spirit animating this tough-minded little treatise is a positive regard for the 'essential public good of a strong, efficient international economic system which all countries need if they are to prosper'.

1115 **Old rules and new players: GATT in the world trading system.**
Raymond Vernon.   In: *Exploring the global economy: emerging issues in trade and investment*, by Raymond Vernon.   Cambridge, MA: Center for International Affairs, Harvard University; Lanham, MD: University Press of America, 1985, p.3-28.
With acute political sense, Professor Vernon traces here the origins of GATT (the ITO had too many 'alien ideas' like a lenient approach to the restrictive business practices of state-owned enterprises), and then he reviews its operations over the years with respect to the United States, Europe, Japan, the developing countries, and the socialist economies. Since much of world trade is conducted outside GATT rules, and since the U.S. is less and less able or willing to maintain that governmental restrictions and subsidies distort a trading system aimed at the global welfare, some revision of the GATT system is necessary, and the United States is still the only power to lead. Standing firm will allow the unravelling to continue, and unilateral adjustments of the rules with particular trading partners will generate the 'lowest common level of market access' and a 'downward spiral of restrictive action'. Vernon's third alternative is a sort of multilateral regional bargaining approach under the guise of a universal GATT system. To pursue it, he would empower the President

to negotiate such agreements rather on the model of the 1934 Congressional act empowering him to negotiate reciprocal trade agreements. Yet Vernon admits in his conclusion that even Presidential leadership will be transitory, for 'nations are no longer very manageable as economic units'.

1116 **Proposals for the expansion of world trade and employment.**
Washington, DC: U.S. Department of State, 1945. (Pub. No. 2411).
In this early U.S. position paper, the goal of the ITO was the attainment and maintenance of 'approximately full employment . . . essential to the expansion of international trade; and 'to the full realization of the objectives of all liberal international agreements'. Hence, the ITO would interpret rules and resolve conflicts. The British emphasized ITO responsibility for full employment policies.

1117 **Restructuring the GATT system.**
John H. Jackson. London: Pinter for Royal Institute for International Affairs, 1990. 121p. bibliog.
Originally, there were to be three international financial organizations: the Bank, the Fund, and the Trade Organization (ITO). The ITO, whose charter was drafted in 1948, became entangled in the breakup of wartime amity as the Soviet Union and the United States both began to withdraw their reliance on new IOs. In place of the ITO, a 'provisional' general agreement on tariffs and trade was reached by a Western group, but the GATT never became the organization aimed at full employment and equitable terms of trade originally contemplated. The above work takes a constitutional perspective on GATT with a view to a new charter for a 'world trade organization' (WTO). Jackson exactly sets his proposal into the actual negotiating context of the Uruguay Round, which concluded in 1993 with a 'concessional' WTO.

1118 **Strengthening GATT procedures for settling trade disputes.**
Ernst-Ulrich Petersmann. *World Economy*, vol. 11 (1988), p.55-89.
Confidence in international institutions is dependent on the rule of law in practice. The author, a counsellor with the GATT in Geneva, interprets the cryptic language of the General Agreement, describes the GATT dispute settlement procedures, and discusses improvements. GATT, ever since 1981 when its legal services were finally established, provides many benefits to member-states: resolution of a large number of disputes, promotion of the rule of law, economic welfare, reciprocity and equity. But delays in establishing conciliatory panels can be lengthy, some panel reports are inadequate, and implementation depends on goodwill. Petersmann considers at length the merits of a permanent international tribunal 'to extend to the field of foreign trade . . . the basic principles of democratic constitutionalism', but eventually he concludes that strengthening domestic dispute settlement procedures in the Uruguay Round is more practicable.

1119 **Towards a new international trade organization.**
Jan Pronk. In: *The U.N. under attack.* Edited by Jeffrey Harrod and Nico Schrijver. Aldershot, England: Gower, 1988, p.71-93.
The original ITO (abandoned in 1948) was to be the capstone of the Bretton Woods arch, with competence with respect to employment, economic development, investment, stabilization of commodity markets, business practices, commercial policy, and tariff concessions. GATT covered only the latter. Under GATT,

quantitative restrictions were gradually phased out, but tariff agreements could not effectively control agricultural trade, and, when extended to many new states, led to market disruptions. UNCTAD was established in 1964 largely to supply the lack of an ITO open to the socialist and developing countries and competent to negotiate economic issues. The author supports the merger of GATT and UNCTAD into a new ITO in order to meet the challenges of the world economy: breakdown of fixed exchange rates, rise of TNCs, increasing importance of developing countries in world trade, and success of regional economic cooperation and integration. Pronk implies that politically the Group of 77 in UNCTAD should take the lead in building a new consensus favouring a strong multilateral trade and economic organization, as recommended by the 1979 Brandt commission. (By 1994, the socialist bloc was no longer an obstacle.)

1120 **Trade liberalization among major world trading areas.**
John Whalley.   Cambridge, MA: MIT Press, 1985. 311p. bibliog.
This work, though highly theoretical, aims to link theory to national policy affecting global trade. The GATT and the 'unwieldy' U.N. come in as small but vital components in the whole account. Whalley utilizes a four-region model and a seven-region one (U.S., E.C., Japan, other developed countries, OPEC, NICs, and LDCs). He concludes with discussion of the implications for the GATT. He doubts that the Tokyo Round of negotiations will be the last, as critics say, 'because tariffs are really the only portion of trade protection that can be reduced through multilateral negotiations'. On the contrary, these negotiations help to 'confront the issue that protectionist policies in developing countries are significantly more restrictive than those in developed countries'. GATT is a more appropriate forum for the settlement of North–South policies than UNCTAD.

1121 **Trade policies for a better future: proposals for action.**
Group of eminent persons, Fritz Leutwiler, chairman.   Geneva: GATT, 1985. 60p.
In order to guide what became the Uruguay Round of negotiations (1986-93), the Director-General of Gatt invited seven wise men to report on 'problems facing the international trading systems'. This brief, comprehensible, and action-oriented report is the result. Readers looking for an up-to-date introduction to the GATT will find it here. The legalities and sometimes impenetrable technicalities of the GATT are left behind in order to concentrate on the principles and experience of an open multi-lateral system of trade. See expecially 'A note on the GATT', p.57-60, a *tour de force* of compression. Leutwiler and the others examine the historical situation, explain why open trade promotes the general good, and make fifteen recommendations for the negotiators.

1122 **Trade policies for a better future: the 'Leutwiler report', the GATT, and the Uruguay Round.**
GATT. Introduction by Arthur Dunkel.   Dordrecht, The Netherlands: M. Nijhoff, 1987. 174p. bibliog.
This volume contains the 'Leutwiler report' above, plus a valuable introduction by the GATT Director-General and supporting legal and technical papers by members of the group and others. Dunkel discusses several points of the report that are either at variance with international economic reality or have been ignored in the Uruguay

Round. The trade situation (addressed in recommendation 15) has further deteriorated. The reason, he finds, is 'deterioration in macro-economic policies related to budgetary and fiscal policies, exchange rate relationships, and debt and financial flows' – that is, inconsistency between trade and financial policies. Moreover, in a short-sighted effort to protect their producers and workers, governments are increasingly intervening in the world market. 'Interference in the normal patterns of supply and demand has become so blatant and widespread that in many product sectors credible world prices have ceased to exist.' Trade conflicts (wars) have escalated to the point where improved dispute resolution procedures in the GATT would be a major reform. The E.C., and NAFTA tend to 'abuse' the GATT rules permitting customs unions and free-trade areas. The proposal for greater transparency, if fundamental reforms were unnegotiable, by provision of a 'protection balance sheet' (recommendation 1) was ignored.

1123 **Trade policy in the 1980s.**
Edited by William R. Cline. Washington, DC: Institute for
International Economics, 1983. 796p.
The editor and authors, who are among the most respected economists of the United States, Europe, Japan, and the U.N. system (none from the Third World), are openly alarmist. 'World trade is in decline. Protectionist pressures are severe and increasing. The open trading system is eroding.' The volume could be read as an appeal to reason by responsible intellectuals leading to the opening of the Uruguay Round of GATT talks (1986-93). Topics include: trade policies, exchange rates, reciprocity, the 'threat' of the E.C., U.S. trade practices, the macro-economics of sales to Japan, subsidies, safeguards, labour, agriculture, textiles, steel, technology, pollution, autos, services, investments, and trade policies in the 1980s.

1124 **UNCITRAL: United Nations Commission on International Trade Law.**
New York: United Nations, 1986. 199p. (E.86.V.8).
UNCITRAL aims to harmonize and unify the law of international trade. The annexes contain the bulk of this law. It deals with international sale of goods, negotiable instruments, commercial arbitration and conciliation, transport, industrial contracts as they would be affected by the NIEO, damages, use of the SDR in place of gold as a universal unit of account for liabilities, and automatic data-processing. The book is designed for use by international lawyers, scholars, and the general public.

1125 **Unheard voices: labor and economic policy in a competitive world.**
Ray F. Marshall. New York: Basic Books, 1987. 339p. bibliog.
The author, who was Secretary of Labor in the Carter administration, regards orthodox economic analysis and policies set by business and financial interests as inadequate and unsuccessful, since they tend to ignore the needs of labour. Macro-economic policies, he holds, must be supplemented by policies supporting human resource development and full employment by regard to the labour market, control of inflation, and industrial development. 'The basic premise of this book', Marshall begins, 'is that improved U.S. economic performance and competitiveness require greater worker participation.' Labour's involvement is particularly necessary for the 'internationalization of the American economy'. American management cannot meet,

without American labour, the challenge of foreign competition, nor contribute to wiser U.S. public and private policies. The United Nations comes into his prescriptions at appropriate places – as in his suggestion that the ILO, while it cannot enforce an international minimum wage, could advance freedom of association, occupational safety and health, and freedom from discrimination and forced labour.

1126 **The United States and the International Trade Organization.**
Percy W. Bidwell and William Diebold, Jr. *International Conciliation*, vol. 449 (1949), p.185-238. bibliog.
This is a contemporary, supportive account of the ITO, with full recognition of opposition to it in Congress. The charter was drafted to prevent mass unemployment, reduce tariffs, abolish quantitative restrictions and quotas on import and exports, and practise equality of treatment in all commercial relations. Two sorts of objections were heard: (1) the charter is too weak (too long and complicated, not supportive enough of American private enterprise); (2) the charter is too strong (the ITO would interfere with domestic economic policy, and voting is not weighted sufficiently in favour of U.S. interests). The authors conclude that negotiations on the charter are exhausted. 'The choice, then, is this Charter or none at all.' Forty-five years later, the world still has none.

1127 **The United States and restoration of world trade: an analysis and appraisal of the ITO charter and the General Agreement on Tariffs and Trade.**
William A. Brown. Washington, DC: Brookings, 1950. 572p.
This is an older, substantial study of the origin and content of the ITO charter, of which the GATT was a chapter. Here readers can find a working text and a close interpretation. Brown, in discussing the draft charter, emphasizes its provisions on commercial policy, employment, economic development, commodity agreements, and restrictive business practices. The assumption running throughout Brown's account is 'that the creation of a peaceful world order requires economic cooperation among nations'. Those who would return to the establishment of the full ITO will find this an enlightening historical work.

1128 **The world trading system: law and policy of international economic relations.**
John H. Jackson. Cambridge, MA: MIT Press, 1989. 417p.
This text is an introduction to trade law and policy for policy-makers, business people, and scholars. Topics include: the GATT, national institutions (especially the U.S. Constitution and laws), implementation of GATT rules, tariff and non-tariff barriers, the two principles of non-discrimination – 'most favoured nation' and 'national treatment obligation' – competing policies, unfair trade, anti-dumping rules, subsidies, the generalized system of preferences (for developing countries), and state traders (U.S.S.R. and China). Jackson is particularly clear on the weaknesses of the GATT constitution (it isn't a constitution, nor is GATT an IO). He see advantages to a 'federal' division of powers between state governments and international authorities in an interdependent world, but most of his suggestions deal with national policies and economic diplomacy.

International trade, 1993: statistics.
See item no. 806.

Trade and development report.
See item no. 812.

International institutions in trade and finance.
See item no. 1017.

See also UNCTAD (p.393ff.).

Regional Economic Commissions

Economic Commission for Africa (ECA)
Economic Commission for Europe (ECE)
Economic Commission for Latin America and the Caribbean (ECLAC)
Economic and Social Commission for Asia and the Pacific (ESCAP)

1129   **Changing production patterns with social equity: the prime task of Latin America and Caribbean development.**
Economic Commission for Latin America and the Caribbean.
Santiago, Chile: 1990. 177p. bibliog. (ECLAC. E.90.II.G.6.
LC/G.1601-P).

The ECLAC Secretariat provides here 'a synthesized study of the main lessons left by the economic crisis of the 1980s'. It offers member-states a major proposal for the 1990s – 'the transformation of the productive structures of the region in a context of progressively greater social equity'. *Equity* is understood as distributive justice, achieved by progressive programmes of competitive industrialization and redistribution of income from growth to workers, peasants, small-business people, the poorest sectors, and underprivileged groups. The proposal is carefully set out in the context of the present situation ('the lost decade') and of the international economy and macro-economic balances. The proposal itself – to resume growth but not to neglect social equity – is discussed at length as a 'creative interaction between public and private agents'. The idea is to increase productivity and competitiveness by coordination of fiscal, monetary, trade, technological, educational, agricultural, and industrial policies. Special attention is given to linkages between the internal and external markets. Ultimately, economic integration within Latin America is a necessity.

1130 **Economic and social survey for Asia and the Pacific, 1992.**
Economic and Social Commission for Asia and the Pacific. New
York: United Nations, 1947- . annual. 2 vols. (E.93.II.F.6.
ST/ESCAP/1243/Parts I&II. 2).

The first part (volume) of this annual survey covers 'recent economic and social
developments'. The second part, 'expansion of investment and intraregional trade as a
vehicle for enhancing regional economic cooperation and development in Asia and
the Pacific'. The early 1990s reflect a steep decline in world output and trade. This
has had an effect on such social indicators as poverty, health, and nutrition. Regional
cooperation is growing: hence the emphasis in Part II on *intra*regional trade. Topics
in Part I include: world economic developments and prospects, regional development
trends, economic performance by subregions, trade and balance of payments, LDC
issues, and social development.

1131 **Economic bulletin for Asia and the Pacific [1989].**
Economic and Social Commission for Asia and the Pacific. New
York: United Nations, 1949- . semi-annual. 72p. (E.91.II.F.2.
ST/ESCAP/808).

Intended for the use of governments, this journal of the ESCAP Secretariat contains
timely, specialized articles on economic programmes and planning.

1132 **Economic bulletin for Europe, Vol. 44 [1991].**
Economic Commission for Europe. New York: United Nations,
1948- . annual. 143p. bibliog. (E.93.II.E.2. ECE/TRADE(LI)/1).

This brief annual volume continues to reflect the fact that the ECE never was divided
by the Cold War. East–West economic relations are authoritatively surveyed here.
Past issues record the historical trends, 1970-87; the 1991 issue focuses on the
transformation of centrally planned economies into market ones. The region is placed
into the context of the world economy.

1133 **Economic report for Africa, 1993.**
Economic Commission for Africa. Preface by Adebayo Adedeji.
Addis Ababa, Ethiopia: ECA, 1989- . annual. 38p.
(E/ECA/CM.17/2).

This is a survey of challenges facing Africa in the 1990s. The report was closely
studied at an Ecosoc conference of ministers responsible for economic development
and planning in May 1993. The brief, macro-economic report contains an overview,
performance analysis by subregion, examination of economic sectors (food and
agriculture, manufacturing, trade, debt), and of the social situation, and closes with an
outlook for the next year. Africa was recovering from the Gulf War, but then was
caught by the European downturn.

1134 **Economic survey of Europe in 1992-1993.**
Economic Commission for Europe. Geneva: ECE, 1947- . annual.
291p. (E.93.II.E.1. E/ECE).

After an overview and survey of Western Europe and North America, this issue of the
annual survey contains an in-depth analysis of the Eastern European countries in

transition. Topics include: their output and demand; labour markets, prices, and incomes; foreign trade and payments; macro-economic policies; market reforms; progress in privatization. It reviews developments in Eastern Europe, including Yugoslavia, the Baltic countries, and the former Soviet Union, and it records Western responses to their transition to market economies. It reports the West's aid, trade volume, financial flows, commitments to assistance, cooperative agreements, and access to markets.

1135   **Economic survey of Latin America and the Caribbean [1989].**
        Economic Commission for Latin America and the Caribbean.
        Santiago, Chile: ECLAC, 1984- . annual. 281p. bibliog. (E.90.II.G.2.
        LC/G.1741-P).

This volume covers economic trends, which by 1991 were beginning to turn upwards after three years of 'virtual stagnation'. Topics include: supply and demand, inflation, employment and wages, public finances, external trade, debt, and macro-economic policies. The Caribbean is covered separately. The international economy and exchange rate policies are treated last.

1136   **Survey of economic and social conditions in Africa, 1989-1990.**
        Economic Commission for Africa.   New York: United Nations,
        1960- . biennial. 180p. (E.93.II.K.6. E/CN.14).

The Persian Gulf crisis had the effect, for Africa, of raising crude oil prices to nearly $40/barrel before the end of 1990; at the same time, export commodity prices fell. Aggregate growth for Africa in 1990 fell to 2.6 per cent. The end of the Cold War promises to result in less economic aid to the continent. Foreign debt repayment diverts precious indigenous resources from productive investment. The hardships and disappointments are producing mass demands for participation in political processes and for fundamental reform of the development model in use since the 1960s. The editors see no reason for 'Afro-pessimism'. 'The African region has enormous untapped resources, both human and natural, and the right policies should produce eventually the right results.' The survey contains an overview of the world and the African economies, reviews changes to macro-economic policies especially for adjustment, and assesses debt, resource flows, trade, and financial policies. Economic sectors social sectors, and statistics round out the work.

1137   **Sustainable development: changing production patterns, social
        equity, and the environment.**
        Economic Commission for Latin America and the Pacific.   Santiago,
        Chile: ECLAC, 1991. 146p. bibliog. (E.91.II.G.5. LC/G.1648/
        Rev.2-P).

Complementary to the volume on *Changing production patterns with social equity* (1990) (see item no. 1129), this volume aims to bring environmental concerns more deeply into the proposal. It was timed for the U.N. Conference on the Environment and Development at Rio de Janiero in 1992. The argument is that the environment does not have to be sacrificed for economic development; that, in developing societies, environmental problems are usually associated with lack of resources rather than high levels of consumption; that concern for the environment is indivisible at every level, from the individual to the globe; that economic policies must be deliberately formulated to take account of the environment; and that international cooperation for development will be reinvigorated by shared concern for the planet.

1138   **The U.N. Economic Commission for Africa: continental development and self-reliance.**
Timothy M. Shaw.   In: *The United Nations and the world political economy: essays in honour of Leon Gordenker.* Edited by David P. Forsythe.   New York: St. Martin's, 1989, p.89-111.
African states cannot choose between independence and reductions in autonomy in order to effectively cooperate in either the O.A.U. or the U.N. The author reviews the struggles over 'inward' *vs.* 'outward' strategies for development, and in the process provides a clear introduction to the ECA. Its policies are contrasted to those of the World Bank. Since the NIEO has failed to replace the Bretton Woods system, African states for the present are reduced to 'self-reliance'.

1139   **The U.N. regional economic commissions and integration in the underdeveloped regions.**
Robert W. Gregg.   In: *International regionalism: readings.*
Boston: Little, Brown, 1968, p.304-32.
By 1968, four U.N. regional economic commissions had been established – one in Europe – the ECE – and three in developing countries – the ECLAC, ECAP, and ECA. The author credits these bodies with considerable achievements: in Europe, the ECE helped to bridge the divide of the Cold War; elsewhere, the commissions contributed to orderly decolonization; all became part of the emergent 'party system' which has kept economic issues on the U.N. agenda. Gregg attempts to measure the 'integrative output' of the three commissions in the Third World; he finds it 'modest' to 'marginal'. 'Cooperation, not federation', he concludes, 'has been the high-water mark reached by the commissions, and much of the cooperation is still in a rudimentary stage.'

World economic survey.
See item no. 814.

Agriculture, external trade and international co-operation.
See item no. 870.

Transnational corporations

U.N. Centre on Transnational Corporations (UNCTC)

1140 **Bilateral investment treaties.**
New York: United Nations, UNCTC, 1988. 194p. bibliog.
(E.88.II.A.1. ST/CTC/65).

Developed market countries, historically, have relied upon the domestic laws of host countries like themselves for the protection of their investments. But as they began to invest in developing countries, the bilateral investment treaty became attractive, both to encourage foreign direct investment and to protect those investments. Multinational treaties and customary international law are too difficult to negotiate or too uncertain in their application for such purposes. There now is a network of some 265 bilateral investment treaties (1987). This U.N. volume describes their provisions. Model treaties from Germany, the Netherlands, the United States, and the Asian–African Legal Consultative Committee are printed in annexes.

1141 **The CTC reporter.**
New York: UNCTC, 1975- . semi-annual.

This is the general interest journal of the UNCTC. Here readers will find illustrated, informative articles on the wide range of the Centre's monitoring of TNCs. Each issue closes with book reviews and bibliography.

1142 **Directory of multinationals.**
Edited by John M. Stopford.   Basingstoke, England: Macmillan;
New York: Stockton, 4th ed., 1992. 2 vols.

Company profiles on 428 major enterprises from around the globe are here provided in a consistent framework. Each multinational corporation (MNC) had consolidated sales of over $1,000 million in 1990. Together, the aggregate external sales of the 428 companies amounted to $2,173,000 million – about 47 per cent of all their sales. The profiles provide specific information on directors, products, background and current situation, five-year summaries, major shareholders, and principal subsidiaries.

1143 **Environmental aspects of the activities of transnational corporations: a survey.**
UNCTC in cooperation with UNEP. Thomas Gladwin, consultant.
New York: United Nations, 1985. 114p. (E.85.II.A.11. ST/CTC/55).

In order to develop an international code of conduct for powerful transnational corporations (TNCs), the UNCTC has conducted surveys of their impact on employment, consumer protection, toxic or hazardous products, arms production and trade, advertising, and, here, the environment. This study provides background on the concept of sustainable development, a survey of *national* regulations to protect the environment in home and host countries, TNC links to pollution, TNC environmental management policies, and the need for international cooperation especially to protect the 'global commons'.

Functions of the U.N. System. Transnational corporations

1144 **International politics in the 1970s: the search for a perspective.**
Donald J. Puchala and Stuart I. Fagan. *International Organization*,
vol. 28 (1974), p.247-66.

This is a 'reflective and interpretive essay' rather than a methodological article of
interest only to specialists. Although written during the Cold War, the authors sense
that 'international politics has changed structurally, procedurally, and substantively'
since the Cuban missile crisis. By the mid-1970s, the role of non-state actors in world
politics was very evident, and among these were IOs, MNCs, and NGOs. Puchala and
Fagan argue that these are contributing to *integrative* international processes, though
'we are nowhere near world government'. World power politics is giving way to
world welfare politics. Cosmopolitanism is overtaking nationalism.

1145 **The multinational business enterprise: what kind of international
organization?**
Louis T. Wells, Jr. *International Organization*, vol. 25 (1971),
p.447-64.

The author recognized that MNCs have the potential 'to frustrate the policies of the
traditional nation state', but whether they actually do so depends on whether decision-
making in the organization is highly centralized. If not, the various affiliates will
effectively act like national companies of the host country. Wells surveys the history
of the rise of MNCs from the beginning of the twentieth century, when books like *The
American invaders* (London, 1902) first sounded the alarm. Actually, the spread of
industrial manufacturing has been a world phenomenon, and no country or single firm
has had an imperial design. Wells concludes, rather in the spirit of his colleague
Raymond Vernon (see items 1115, 1153, 1154), that MNCs, though they appear to
challenge state sovereignty, necessarily must diversify and decentralize.

1146 **Multinational corporations and international professional
associations.**
William M. Evan. *Human Relations*, vol. 27 (1974), p.587-625.

This is a quantitative sociological study of the two types of organizations above,
which commonly cross national boundaries. The author clearly examines the effect of
such organizations on the integration of international society. He concludes with five
technical hypotheses, of which this is the first: 'Multinational ownership of
corporations and multinational leadership of international professional associations
. . . result in denser networks of inter-organizational relationships and, in turn,
contribute to a higher level of organizational and economic integration of the
international system.'

1147 **National legislation and regulations relating to transnational
corporations.**
New York: United Nations, UNCTC, 1983. Vol. II. 338p.
(E.83.II.A.7. ST/CTC/26); UNCTC, 1989. Vol. VII. 320p.
(E.89.II.A.9. ST/CTC/91).

This multi-volume reference work presents specific information on the national
legislation and regulations of every state-member of the U.N. within which TNCs
must operate. The above Vol. II (1983), a revision of Vol. I (1978), might be the best
place to start. 'The harmonization of the activities of such [transnational]

corporations', it is said in the introduction, 'with the objectives and development programmes of host countries, particularly developing countries, necessitates a fairly detailed framework of policies regarding the activities of transnational corporations.' The policies covered in the several volumes relate to: investment; monitoring and screening investors; ownership, control, and disvestment; foreign exchange control; technology transfer; restrictive business practices; fiscal incentives and taxation; export processing zones; disclosure requirements; investment guarantees; government, law, and dispute settlement.

1148 **New approaches to best-practice manufacturing: the role of transnational corporations and implications for developing countries.**
New York: United Nations, UNCTC, 1990. 76p. bibliog. (Current Studies, Series A. No. 12. E.90.II.A.13. ST/CTC/SER.A/12).
'Best-practice manufacturing' means utilizing the best available production techniques and technology, such as the automobile assembly line or, now, computer control and automation. With such new technologies come new social and international economic relations, often not foreseen. This study examines the history of such innovations in manufacturing and focuses on industries currently undergoing restructuring on an international scale – automobiles, machine tools, and computers. Policy recommendations to developing countries are made, such as focusing on training in order to facilitate the use and economy of computers.

1149 **The new code environment.**
New York: United Nations, UNCTC, 1990. 51p. bibliog. (Current Studies, Series A, No. 16. E.90.II.A.7. ST/CTC/SER.A/16).
The code of conduct for TNCs stands at an 'impasse'. This short U.N. book ably surveys the origins of demand for a code, arguing that the Cold War, as a determinant of international relations, was rivalled by decolonization and by the expansion of TNCs. Originally (in 1974), the code was inspired by criticism of TNCs, but ten years later it had been transformed into a balanced and positive device that would 'maximize the benefits of transnational business while minimizing potential conflict and negative impacts'. By 1990, macro-economic changes (especially in reaction to the collapse of the Bretton Woods system) and changing investment patterns (e.g., declines of U.S. financial hegemony) had 'metamorphosed' TNCs into the world's leading 'integrative' agent. Criticism has been replaced by competition among countries for foreign direct investment. This book still argues for the necessity of a code to govern even integrative TNCs rather in the spirit of the necessity for international law to regularize and harmonize the relations between sovereign states. 'Adoption of the United Nations Code of Conduct on TNCs would mark an important reaffirmation of a global approach to promoting growth and development through an integrated world economy. Reaching successful agreement on this framework would also symbolically shift the international community from reacting to past events to a productive search for cooperative ways to address new systemic needs.' The draft code as of 1988 is printed in an annex.

1150   **The question of a reference to international law in the United**
        Nations Code of Conduct on Transnational Corporations.
        Patrick Robinson.   New York: United Nations, UNCTC, 1986. 22p.
        (Current Studies, Series A, No. 1. E.86.II.A.5. ST/CTC/SER.A/1).
One of the difficult questions in formulating the code is, What is 'international law'
or 'international obligations', referred to in the draft code, as the *standard* of
legitimacy for both state and TNC conduct. The author explores the question from the
point of view of the developing countries. They have long had reservations about
(European, imperialist) 'international law'. Nevertheless, Robinson argues that
reference to international law, rather than to equity ('appropriate', 'just'), is in the
interests of the G-77, since that law is undergoing progressive development and is
still being applied by arbitral and adjudicative tribunals. He suggests compromise
formulae that would serve in cases of nationalization and dispute settlement.

1151   **The question of a reference to international obligations in the**
        United Nations Code of Conduct on Transnational Corporations:
        a different view.
        Detlev F. Vagts.   New York: United Nations, UNCTC, 1986. 13p.
        bibliog. (Current Studies, Series A, No. 2. E.86.II.A.11.
        ST/CTC/SER.A/2).
This work explores the above question from the perspective of the developed
countries. Vagts disputes the view of the developing and socialist countries that there
are *no* limitations on the treatment of foreign firms by states, according to customary
international law – that is, that states may expropriate foreign property without
compensation. (This Third and Second World view is known as the 'Calvo doctrine' –
that aliens are entitled to nothing more than national treatment.) Vagts concludes that
no legal reasoning can escape the familiar obligations of international law, and that
politically to attempt to restate the law of expropriation 'would be devastating to the
prospects for acceptance of the Code'.

1152   **Regional economic integration and transnational corporations in**
        the 1990s: Europe 1992, North America, and developing
        countries.
        New York: United Nations, UNCTC, 1990. 52p. bibliog. (Current
        Studies, Series A, No. 15. E.90.II.A.14. ST/CTC/SER.A/15).
While world economic integration is proceeding, there is much progress in regional
integration, notably in the European Community. TNCs are very active in such
regions. As Peter Hansen [Executive Director of UNCTC] writes, 'National
boundaries have become increasingly irrelevant in the definition of market and
production spaces, while regions rather than countries are emerging as key economic
policy arenas.' This study examines the integration programmes in Western Europe
(the Single Market in 1992), North America (U.S.–Canada Free Trade Area, precursor
to NAFTA in 1993), and among developing countries (mostly joint ventures).

1153   **Sovereignty at bay: the multinational spread of U.S. enterprises.**
        Raymond Vernon.   New York: Basic Books, 1971. 326p.
This book, the fruit of Harvard University's Multinational Enterprise Project since
1965, has had enormous influence. It was broadly informative about the sheer facts of

the spread of U.S. MNCs over the globe (to 1970). It drew conclusions rather like those twenty years later, after an interval of shock and alarm. 'The multinational enterprise as an economic institution seems capable of adding to the world's aggregate productivity and economic growth. . . . As for the distribution of benefits within the countries, it is difficult to say. . . . As a rule, the presence multinational enterprises has generated tensions in the foreign countries where they appear. . . .' Vernon doubts that socialism will raise up competitive institutions of economic expansion. He also considers the need for a 'global government' to regulate such artificial persons as MNCs. 'This simple concept lies at the heart of the many proposals for a world corporation or a U.N. corporation.' (Something like this later resurfaced in the Law of the Sea's 'Enterprise' for the development of the common heritage on the deep seabed.) But he finds such proposals 'out of joint with the times' and guilty of 'assuming the problem away'. Vernon's own solution is establishment of an 'international organization whose first order of business would be to build up ground rules' for MNCs before 'unilateral' measures are taken by uncoordinated states. In retrospect, this seems rather like the UNCTC established in 1974.

1154   **Sovereignty at bay: ten years after.**
Raymond Vernon.   In: *Exploring the global economy: emerging issues in trade and investment.*   Cambridge, MA: Center for International Affairs, Harvard University; and Lanham, MD: University Press of America, 1985, p.51-62.

The author of the 1971 bellwether (see above) complains that his book has been more often cited than understood. He admits that he did not predict the exact course of the 1973-74 oil crisis, as the exporting countries nationalized and expropriated the oligopolistic major oil companies. But his deeper contentions, reflected in the alarming title, he regards ten years later as vindicated: governments will continue to invite MNCs to help them develop; the MNCs will continue to reflect the world network; and the network remains a channel for government influence.

1155   **Tracking transnationals: United Nations Centre on Transnational Corporations.**
Richard Caplan.   *Multinational Monitor*, vol. 10, nos. 7-8 (July-August 1989), p.12-14.

This is a candid, plain-spoken introduction to the UNCTC. 'Established in 1975 in the wake of revelations about International Telephone and Telegraph's (ITT) attempts to destabilize Chile and at the height of Third World demands for the creation of a New International Economic Order, the Centre has become the focal point at the U.N. for all matters related to multinational corporations.' By the mid-1980s, the Centre still advised states to guard against corporate wrongdoing, but its relation to TNCs was much more positive, since everyone recognized that usually TNCs had positive effects on development. Caplan tries to dispel lingering suspicions.

1156   **Transnational corporations and human rights.**
Thomas E. McCarthy.   In: *U.N. law/fundamental rights: two topics in international law.* Edited by Antonio Cassese.   Alphen aan den Rijn, The Netherlands: Sijthoff & Noordhoff, 1979, p.175-95.

By 1973, of the one hundred largest economic institutions in the world, fifty were states, and fifty were transnational corporations (TNCs) whose total production exceeded all international trade. The role of TNCs in economic development is generally positive, but to control occasional negative effects, such as investment without respect to the needs of populations in less developed countries, the U.N. has attempted to draft a code of conduct for TNCs. This article reports on progress in South Africa, colonial territories, and Chile. Problems of drafting a law outside a world authority to govern private businesses operating in sovereign states are discussed.

1157 **Transnational corporations and international economic relations: recent developments and selected issues.**
New York: United Nations, UNCTC, 1989. 50p. (Current Studies, Series A, No. 11. E.89.II.A.15. ST/CTC/SER.A/11).
Foreign direct investment is increasing in the *developed* countries – in Europe, Japan, and the United States. 'The United States has once again become the world's largest home country . . . and the largest host country in terms of annual flows of foreign direct investment.' Flows to LDCs have declined. The issues selected in this study include: world-wide comparisons, Western Europe as a host region (1992), TNCs in the LDCs, and transnational banks and the debt crisis. One of the items in the latter is 'a bankruptcy law for sovereign states?'

1158 **Transnational corporations and international trade: selected issues; a technical paper.**
New York: United Nations, UNCTC, 1985. 93p. bibliog. (E.85.II.A.4. ST/CTC/54).
The issues include: transfer pricing to escape the jurisdiction of host countries, marketing of primary commodities by TNCs to the disadvantage of developing state producers, 'internalization' of markets within large TNCs, investment in 'non-traditional' manufacturing for export, the irrelevance of national or foreign ownership to the behaviour or the host economy, and disappointing foreign exchange earnings due to TNC affiliate trade with its parent company. These matters are addressed technically here by three empirical studies of transfer prices in Brazil, intra-firm trade to the U.S.A., and TNC influence on the setting of trade policy in the U.S.A.

1159 **Transnational corporations and manufacturing exports from developing countries.**
Magnus Blomström. New York: United Nations, UNCTC, 1990. 124p. bibliog. (E.90.II.A.21. ST/CTC/101).
The tigers of the Pacific Rim – South Korea, Taiwan, Hong Kong, and Singapore – are examples of developing countries that have become world competitors. This brief, knowledgeable study analyses the role of TNCs in stimulating such developing countries to become significant exporters of manufactured goods. 'This issue is particularly important', writes Peter Hansen, 'since the transfer of capital, technology, and management skills by transnational corporations to developing countries, and access to marketing and financial networks originally developed by transnational corporations, are often thought to be critical elements in the transformation of developing countries into effective world competitors.' Blomström examines the role of TNCs from the United States, Sweden, and Japan. He concludes that countries that before were fearful of TNCs now welcome them. TNCs definitely stimulated host-

country exports, but those countries' trade policies are a still more important factor, as seen in comparing different results in Latin America and Asia.

1160 **Transnational corporations and the growth of services: some conceptual and theoretical issues.**
John H. Dunning. New York: United Nations, UNCTC, 1989. 80p. bibliog. (Current Studies, Series A, No. 9. E.89.II.A.5. ST/CTC/SER.A/9).

As the world economy develops, the production and distribution of goods is being supplemented by the growth of services. The Uruguay Round of GATT was challenged by its new agenda item on services, and the UNCTC produced this up-to-date survey. In all countries, from 1965 to 1985, the share of services in GDP and the labour force was increasing. This work examines the nature of services, the competitive advantages of TNCs in services, advantages of host countries, and theories of foreign direct investment in services.

1161 **Transnational corporations and the transfer of new and emerging technologies to developing countries.**
New York: United Nations, UNCTC, 1990. 141p. bibliog. (E.90.II.A.20. ST/CTC/98).

New technologies include: electronics, telematics, biotech, genetic engineering, new materials, new and renewable energy. This study examines the role of TNCs in the transfer of such technologies and reviews policies in developing counties to increase their application and contribution to economic development.

1162 **Transnational corporations and world order: readings in international political economy.**
Edited by George Modelski. San Francisco: W.H. Freeman, 1979. 438p.

This volume of essays aims at a comprehensive view of TNCs from the vantage point of long-term world order. The sections on regulation and futures may have greatest relevance in the 1990s. Why not leave TNCs 'unfettered'? Because imperfections in the market and in host countries do not permit competition to function as an 'invisible hand'. Is there any 'global public interest' that might bring order to firms fixated on self-interest in a 'system of nation-states lacking accepted and well-established central institutions'? Yes, but so far the United Nations has not been raised to that function, for it 'has little to offer the multinational enterprise in the way of contracts or purchasing arrangements', nor does the U.N. receive from TNCs taxes or contributions in the exercise of a world fiscal power.

1163 **Transnational corporations in world development: third survey.**
New York: United Nations, UNCTC, 1983. 383p. (E.83.II.A.14. ST/CTC/46).

By the time this survey appeared (1983), the deterioration of the world economic environment had long since inclined developing countries to look more favourably on TNCs. (The first survey was in 1973; the second, in 1978.) Nationalizations of oil and fruit companies began to decline by the mid-1970s, and 'liberalization' on the basis of mutually advantageous business deals began to return. There were still concerns, however, for TNC performance requirements (export obligations, transfer of technology) and for the draft international code of conduct. This volume surveys complex, changing policies in developing countries toward TNCs.

1164   **Transnational corporations in world development: trends and prospects [1988].**
New York: United Nations, UNCTC, 1973- . quinquennial. 623p. (E.88.II.A.7. ST/CTC/89).

'The 1980s have witnessed major changes in the world production system', writes Peter Hansen, Executive Director of UNCTC, 'with TNCs being the principal forces shaping the future of technological innovation. At the same time, a more pragmatic and businesslike relationship between host governments and TNCs has emerged in the last decade. Many developing countries, burdened by debt and economic stagnation, have liberalized their policies toward TNCs, while those corporations have displayed greater sensitivity to the development and economic goals of host countries. The era of confrontation has receded and been replaced by a practical search for a meaningful and mutually beneficial accommodation of interests.' This hefty volume, replete with tables, boxes of interest, and statistics, should be a gold-mine for the widest range of readers interested in the vital contributions of TNCs to development. For an outline of its contents, see the executive summary below.

1165   **Transnational corporations in world development: trends and prospects. Executive summary.**
New York: United Nations UNCTC, 1988. 63p. (E.88.II.A.15. ST/CTC/87).

This is a succinct summary of a very large companion volume (see above), providing a comprehensive analysis of the economic, social, and legal impact of TNCs on the world economy and particularly on developing countries. Busy people may see only this trim little booklet. Topics include: trends, technological and organizational changes, trade, economic development, employment, social development, environmental protection, national policies, international cooperation and regulation (the code of conduct remains voluntary), services, and banking. One major finding is that Japan and Western Europe have emerged as the major home countries; the United States, as the major host country, partly at the expense of developing countries. Another is that TNCs have become recognized for their positive role in development, particularly for reducing debt, promoting exports of manufactures, and providing access to improved technologies.

1166   **Transnational corporations, services, and the Uruguay Round.**
Padma Mallampally.   New York: United Nations, UNCTC, 1990. 252p. (E.90.II.A.11. ST/CTC/103).

The service sector is growing at national and international levels. The Uruguay Round of the GATT talks was delayed by its controversies over services. This UNCTC study aimed to clarify the subject, which, because services are not tradable in the traditional sense, immediately opened up deeper issues of production, investment, and participation in host countries. Services covered here include: telecommunications, construction, tourism, finance, business services, and investment in relation to the emerging code of conduct.

1167 **The U.N. code of conduct for transnational corporations.**
Thomas G. Weiss.   In: *The United Nations in the world political economy: essays in honour of Leon Gordenker.* Edited by David P. Forsythe.   New York: St. Martin's, 1989, p.86-97.
This is a short, basic article on the UNCTC. 'The political will to complete the code has dissipated', Weiss concludes. For the future, he looks ahead to continued Centre effectiveness in disseminating information about TNCs and in organizing technical programmes for developing countries. TNCs have voluntarily moderated their 'excesses' and have come to accept 'unwritten rules governing their operations and behaviour'.

1168 **United Nations code of conduct on transnational corporations.**
New York: United Nations, UNCTC, 1986 (Series A, No. 4);
London: Graham & Trotman for UNCTC, 1988. 80p. bibliog.
(E.86.II.A.15. ST/CTC/SER.A/4).
'The need for a universal framework setting forth the standards of behaviour for the relations between transnational corporations and States has been recognized by both developing and developed countries', this authoritative presentation of the draft code declares. By 1986, most of the provisions of the code had been agreed to. The text is printed in an annex, with the disputed matters (principally its mode of adoption and its legal nature) in brackets. The explanatory sections cover general and political questions (such as permanent sovereignty and non-interference in internal affairs); economic, financial, and social questions (ownership and control, consumer and environmental protection); disclosure of information; treatment of TNCs in host countries; nationalization and compensation; international law; jurisdiction (state and international); cooperation; dispute settlement; and implementation (by a permanent CTC enlarged into an organizational secretariat).

1169 **University curriculum on transnational corporations.** [Vol. I:] **Economic development.** [Vol. II:] **International business.** [Vol. III:] **International law.**
New York: United Nations, UNCTC, 1991. 3 vols. bibliog.
(E.91.II.A.8 (set). ST/CTC/62).
With ten years of experience in technical assistance behind it, the UNCTC here offers model syllabuses for graduate students in the fields of economic development, international business, and international law as related to TNCs. The course is intended to guide students preparing for careers in public or private sectors. It has been designed by UNCTC experts, senior faculty members at universities in *developing* countries, and scholars of international repute. Superb bibliographies conclude each volume.

1170 **World investment report, 1992: transnational corporations as engines of growth.**
U.N. DIESA and UNCTC.   New York: United Nations, 1991- .
annual. 356p. bibliog. (E.92.II.A.19. ST/CTC/130).
The revival of economic growth can be stimulated by foreign direct investment and by the activities of TNCs. Foreign direct investment, within the U.S., E.C., and Japan,

and from them to the rest of the world, is covered briefly but informatively. The U.S. is now the major recipient of investment, while the E.C. is the major source. Data is provided on TNCs in relation to economic growth, capital formation, technology, health, education, employment, trade, environmental quality, and sustainable development. A chapter is devoted to TNCs and world 'governance'. In the conclusion, this matter is left as a challenge to 'international policy'.

Transnational relations and world politics.
See item no. 70.

Transnational corporations: a selective bibliography.
See item no. 1357.

U.N. Conference on Trade and Development (UNCTAD)

1171 **Condemned to cooperate: U.S. resource diplomacy.**
Robert L. Rothstein. *SAIS Review*, vol. 5, no. 1 (Winter-Spring 1985), p.163-77.
Besides possessive U.S. interests in foreign resources, the author argues, against the unilateralists, it also has a 'wider . . . interest in stability and prosperity in the Third World'. The danger from countries supplying scarce minerals like chromium is instability, deliberate withholding, or threats to U.S. allies in Europe or Japan. To avoid predictable North–South conflict, Rothstein argues that the United States should pursue a long-range policy of 'increasing cooperation with other producers and consumers'. Short-term policies – especially use of force to end an embargo – must not be allowed to destroy the potential for cooperation. Stockpiling remains the preferred tactic. Rothstein surveys the UNCTAD negotiations that resulted in the defeat of the Integrated Programme for Commodities and the Common Fund: '*both* sides lost a major opportunity to restructure a badly malfunctioning part of the economic system'. He concludes with practical suggestions for reformed approaches to negotiation – especially 'moving away from group vs. group confrontations'.

1172 **Creating a framework to strengthen and stabilize international commodity markets.**
Gamani Corea. In: *Negotiating world order: the artisanship and architecture of global diplomacy.* Edited by Alan K. Henrikson. Wilmington, DE: Scholarly Resources, 1986, p.167-80.
Here is a clear introduction to UNCTAD's most effective function – the negotiation of its Integrated Programme for Commodities. The Common Fund and compensatory financing have been less successful. A new consensus on trade, Corea argues, will be based on fear of inflation and of slow growth, and on repayment of debt. The North–South impasse 'is not going to persist indefinitely'.

1173 **Economic development: addressing the needs of the world's poor.**
Marvin S. Soroos. In: *Beyond sovereignty: the challenge of global policy*, by Marvin S. Soroos. Columbia, SC: University of South Carolina Press, 1986, p.195-226.

The world cannot long endure gross inequalities of rich and poor, any more than can a nation-state. This chapter clearly discusses the necessity for global economic cooperation and the making of international development policy, particularly the demand for a NIEO and the stalemated North–South dialogue. Robert McNamara's short-term 'basic needs' approach to development is contrasted with longer-term 'growth' policy. Soroos explores the political causes for non-cooperation, especially the North's felt economic independence from the South's plight. The future portends dismal South–South cooperation and coercive reductions of high fertility rates, he concludes.

1174 **Global bargaining: UNCTAD and the quest for a new international economic order.**
Robert L. Rothstein. Princeton, NJ: Princeton University Press, 1979. 286p.

Written after the NIEO had declined into a rather frustrating North–South 'dialogue', this careful study of 'bargaining' finds that such factors as power and interest among the developed countries, and unity among the developing, inhibit global negotiations. Hence, decision-making under conditions of confrontation is indecisive, neither side seriously raises questions of implementation, and strategies remain opportunistic and short-range. 'Equitable resolution of North–South conflicts' seems hardly possible 'without a long-term perspective'. Rothstein takes most of his examples from early bargaining over commodities, but he suspects the same dysfunctions will be found in negotiations over debt, trade liberalization, and transfer of technology. (In retrospect, this seems to be a study of antiquated negotiation techniques for which the new ones of conflict resolution may be more suited.) He concludes that 'major reforms' of institutions, procedures, concepts, and beliefs are necessary for progress. 'The North must recognize that the need for dependable rules cannot be met without cooperation, and that cooperation will not be given without some guarantee of consistent and increased benefits for the South; and the South must recognize that a new order must be built carefully and will not emerge more quickly by merely asserting its need.'

1175 **The history of UNCTAD, 1964-1984.**
UNCTAD Secretariat. Introduction by Gamani Corea. New York: United Nations, 1985. 294p. bibliog. (E.85.II.D.6. UNCTAD/OSG/286).

'UNCTAD is the one institution in the international system', states its Secretary-General in the introduction, 'which deals with global economic issues, not merely in narrow sectoral terms, but in terms of their interactions, and their interrelationships.' He credits UNCTAD with negotiation of 'preferential treatment for developing countries on a non-discriminatory and non-reciprocal basis' (which was at variance with the free-trade principles of the GATT), and for negotiation of the Common Fund (still a dead letter ten years later). The history will be invaluable to all students who wish to understand why the old order, reflected particularly in the GATT, must give way to the new. Covered are the philosophy and origins of UNCTAD, commodity policy, monetary stabilization and development finance, trade in manufactures, shipping, transfer of technology, state and market trade, economic cooperation among developing countries, activities on behalf of the LDCs, insurance, the arms trade, and assistance to national liberation movements (a point of criticism in the West).

1176 **The international monetary system and financial markets: recent developments and the policy challenge.**
UNCTAD Secretariat. New York: United Nations, 1985. 45p. bibliog. (E.85.II.D.5. TD/B/C.3/194/Rev.1).

Developments such as falling U.S. interest rates, failure of reserves to keep pace with trade, increased demands for conditionality before extending credit, collapse of 'voluntary' lending in the capital markets, constraints on export expansion, and difficulties of stabilization and adjustment are discussed here. Policy challenges, therefore, are to lower interest rates during recovery by the right 'mix of monetary and fiscal policies'; to improve liquidity by a substantial new SDR allocation; and to relieve adjustments by expansion of trade.

1177 **Multilateral development diplomacy in UNCTAD: the lessons of group negotiations, 1964-1984.**
Thomas G. Weiss. New York: St. Martin's, 1986. 187p. bibliog.

GATT was unacceptable to developing countries because it lacked the powers of the originally proposed ITO; UNCTAD was unacceptable to industrialized countries because it was dominated by the Group of 77. Like others on the twentieth anniversary of UNCTAD, Weiss attempts to take stock. Ultimately, his proposals for reform look rather like the old ITO. To restore the North–South 'dialogue', he argues, the present group system must give way to 'new coalitions of countries' more reflective of the diversity in the South, and in the North for that matter. Weiss argues further that negotiations must be arranged on a case-by-case basis, even though this has long been the proposal of the feared Group B. Lastly, he would reorganize the UNCTAD Secretariat into less of a 'messianic' voice of the G-77 and more of a traditional international secretariat devoted to assisting practical negotiations. Comprehensive strategies to reform the international economic order at a stroke, he concludes, are out; pragmatism is back. As one Third World observer has said, 'It is back to moderation, incremental change, and selective improvement at the pressure points. . . . It is now widely accepted that structural change will only be a gradual process and not brought about by declarations of the NIEO type.'

1178 **Proceedings of the United Nations Conference on Trade and Development, eighth session, Cartagena de Indias, Colombia, 8-25 February 1992.** *Report and annexes.*
UNCTAD. New York: United Nations, 1993. 213p. bibliog. (E.93.II.D.5. TD/364/Rev.1).

This is the official record of the most recent UNCTAD session. The meeting seems to have been businesslike. There is no hortatory final document or report.

1179 **Revitalizing development, growth, and international trade: assessment and policy options. Report [to the seventh session of UNCTAD (Geneva, 1987)].**
UNCTAD Secretariat. Foreword by K.K.S. Dadzie. New York: United Nations, 1987. 256p. bibliog. (E.87.II.D.7. TD/328/Rev.1).
This is a typical recent analysis of problems of trade and development for UNCTAD. (Cf. the first, below, in 1964.) Topics include: development in disarray, the question of debt, instability in prices of commodities, protectionism, structural adjustment in trade, and problems of LDCs.

1180 **Towards a new trade policy for development: report by the Secretary-General of the United Nations Conference on Trade and Development.**
Raúl Prebish. New York: United Nations, 1964. 125p. (64.II.B.4. E/Conf.46/3).
This is the first report to UNCTAD (1964), which led to its permanent establishment and, ten years later, to NIEO. In retrospect, the analysis may seem clearer and the times more propitious for action, which is what gives this classic report its continuing appeal. After it, UNCTAD became something like a specialized agency of the U.N., partially filling the need for an ITO. Prebish takes a broad historical and macro-economic view. The 'old order', which the Havana charter for the ITO of 1948 attempted to shore up, cannot be restored. 'It is imperative to build a new order with a view to solving the serious problems of trade and development that beset the world, especially the problems that affect the developing countries.'

1181 **UNCTAD and the South–North dialogue – the first twenty years: essays in memory of W.R. Malinowski.**
Edited by Michael Z. Cutajar. New York: Pergamon, 1985. 314p.
The 'South–North dialogue', to the leaders and workers who produced this book, reflects the fact the 'the initiative for structural change through negotiation has always started from the South'. 'North–South', the usual expression, reflects the 'trickle-down' theory of concessions and benefits from the dominant North. Here will be found an appreciation for W.R. Malinowski, a co-founder of UNCTAD; a retrospective essay by Raul Prebish, the other co-founder, entitled 'Two decades after'; and many thoughtful essays on the emergence, achievements, assessments, and prospects of the organization. Compare *The history of UNCTAD*, which also appeared in 1985 (item no. 1175).

1182 **UNCTAD, conflict and compromise: the Third World's quest for an equitable economic order through the United Nations.**
Branislav Gosovic. Leiden, The Netherlands: Sijthoff, 1972. 349p.
This is a history of UNCTAD before it undertook the revolutionary approach of the NIEO.

1183   **The United Nations Conference on Trade and Development.**
Richard N. Gardner.   *International Organization*, vol. 22 (1968),
p.99-130.
UNCTAD was established in 1964. This authoritative article written four years later
by a U.S. statesman and scholar can still serve as a generalpolitical introduction to the
negotiating forum. Gardner explains why UNCTAD took discussion on trade and
development out of Ecosoc and the Second Committee of the U.N. General Assembly
(they were too politicized by the Cold War and not representative of the emerging
Third World majority). He discusses the Prebish report (see item no. 1180), the
insolubility of the voting question (in which the countries conducting 70 per cent of
world trade were reduced to a minority of states), and the weakening of inter-agency
coordination by creation of still another agency. He concludes that 'UNCTAD has
impressed the rich countries with the problems of the poor', but he adds that poor
countries, too, share responsibilities for poverty.

1184   **The United Nations Conference on Trade and Development: an
organization betraying its mission.**
Stanley J. Michalak, Jr.   Washington, DC: Heritage Foundation,
U.N. Assessment Project Study, 1983. 78p.
Here is criticism, of a sort very influential in the United States during the 1980s, of
UNCTAD's 'struggle to replace the existing international economic system with a
new, collectivist order'. At work here is not a spirit of trying to find some middle way
between *laissez-faire* capitalism and centralized economic planning by a unitary
world state, but American isolationism manifested in an attack on such common
international institutions, like UNCTAD, that a diverse world has been able to create.
Readers may find that the text reads more rationally if the inflammatory headings
('Civil war in the United Nations') are ignored, since they convey the sense of an
'Orwellian' conspiracy. Michalak concludes that the proper course for the United
States is to leave UNCTAD.

See also NIEO (p.397ff.).

New International Economic Order (NIEO)

1185   **Changing priorities on the international agenda: the New**
International Economic Order.
Edited by Karl P. Sauvant.   Oxford: Pergamon, 1981. 319p.
The NIEO has been so controversial a proposal that the date of any volume about it
indicates something about the contents: the later the volume, the more reasonable and
dispassionate the debate. By 1981, it was possible to produce this cool, informative
book designed to reach a broad public and hence to influence debate in the U.N.
General Assembly. 'Today, we are in a process of transition', writes Karl P. Sauvant.

We are in transition from the era of colonialism to that of full participation of all peoples in the affairs of the world. Development issues are now 'high politics' at the level of heads of state and government. The book is not so much an edited volume as one co-authored. Topics include: historical and political context, perspective of the developing countries, response of the developed. An annex reprints the basic documents of the NIEO – the Declaration and Programme of Action of 1974 and the Charter of Economic Rights and Duties of States of the same year, plus statistical data.

1186 **On the creation of a new international economic order: issue linkage and the Seventh Special Session of the U.N. General Assembly.**
Branislav Gosovic and John G. Ruggie. *International Organization*, vol. 30 (1976), p.309-45.

This is an early article on the NIEO, when there was still potential for a negotiated solution. Most of the authors' attention is focused on the topics of negotiation, correlated in an elaborate table with the positions of the G-77 and the developed countries. Similar long essays in this issue of the journal by Seymour Maxwell Finger and C. Fred Bergsten recommend policies for the United States.

1187 **The Economic and Social Council and the New International Economic Order.**
Johan Kaufmann. In: *The United Nations in the world political economy: essays in honour of Leon Gordenker.* Edited by David P. Forsythe. New York: St. Martin's, 1989, p.54-66.

Ecosoc has never become a world council of economic advisers, and the Third World demand for a NIEO (1974) all but destroyed its effectiveness in Western eyes. The author fairly surveys the history of Ecosoc and considers three alternatives for the future: abolition, expansion to plenary size, or limitation. Kaufmann inclines toward Maurice Bertrand's idea that, because of the increasing need for global economic and social negotiations, Ecosoc should be transformed into an economic security council.

1188 **The Eleventh Special Session and the future of global negotiations.**
John P. Renninger and James Zech. New York: UNITAR, 1981. 57p. (Policy and Effectiveness Study No. 5).

This is an account of the attempt by the U.N. General Assembly majority to 'strengthen' central U.N. control of the system's policies, programmes, and specialized agencies in 1980, which came to naught and effectively derailed 'global negotiations' on the NIEO. The causes of the failure the authors ascribe to (1) the refusal of the North ever to accept in principle the NIEO and its programme; (2) a climate of mistrust and uncertainty; (3) inability to trade the South's energy for the North's money and finance in mutually beneficial agreements; (4) negotiation at the level of 'low politics', not involving all finance ministers or any heads of state and government. The North generally exhibited strong 'negative political will'. Renninger and Zech foresaw no future to comprehensive negotiations on trade and development unless there is a significant change in attitude by Northern governments and a significant increase in bargaining power by the South.

1189   **The First World and the Third World: essays on the New International Economic Order.**
Edited by Karl Brunner.   Rochester, NY: Research in Government Policy and Business, Graduate School of Management, University of Rochester, 1978. 272p. bibliog.

These essays, several of which first appeared in *Commentary*, generally treat NIEO from a conservative American and British perspective. The authors tend to see NIEO as an act of ingratitude for Western economic aid, now demanded as a right or even as reparations for past injustices of colonialism. Daniel Patrick Moynihan, fresh from a stint as U.S. representative at the U.N., contributes a typical essay, 'The United States in opposition'. NIEO, he argues, is the work of the 'tyranny of the majority' at the United Nations, schooled by British socialism. The Third World is not motivated by the love of liberty, and hence will not achieve equality either, he concludes. It is an open question whether such a perspective is short-sighted or reactive, for the Third World is not blameless.

1190   **Ideologies and the New International Economic Order: reflections on some recent literature.**
Robert W. Cox.   *International Organization*, vol. 33 (1979), p.257-302.

This is an able survey of the literature on NIEO to 1979. The author is particularly sensitive to more critical works of larger scope than more prestigious writing of Western academics – such as those that challenge 'the intellectual hegemony of liberal economics and its claims to an exclusive "rationality"'. Cox divides the literature into five funded networks of intellectual production: the establishment perspective ('monopolistic liberalism'), the social democratic perspective, the Third World one, the neo-mercantilist one, and the historical materialist one. Readers who are somewhat baffled by the contradictions about the highest matters in the NIEO debate might find light here.

1191   **Moving towards change: some thoughts on the New International Economic Order.**
UNESCO. Foreword by Amadou-Mahtar M'Bow.   Paris: UNESCO, 1976. 137p.

In response to the U.N. General Assembly's Declaration and Programme of Action on the Establishment of a New International Economic Order (1974), UNESCO convened a 'Panel of Counsellors . . . to hold the widest and frankest exchange of views on the major problems at present confronting the world, on the way they interact, and on how international cooperation to solve them could be arranged'. The panel's report is printed in an annex. UNESCO's contribution was to be to supplement mere economic reforms with scientific and technical advice to help developing countries make better use of their natural resources, to broaden the scope of education so that people will be involved in their economic development, to develop supportive communications and information systems, and to stimulate cultural awareness of the reforms. (By 1984, this programme would be one of those that provoked U.S. and U.K. withdrawal from the organization.)

1192   **Need for change: towards the New International Economic Order; a selection from major speeches and reports with an introduction.**
Gamani Corea.   New York: Pergamon, 1980. 278p.

The author was Secretary-General of UNCTAD from 1974 to 1980 and thus he was a key player in the drama of NIEO. This volume contains his speeches up to 1980, when he was suddenly removed from office in an action that seemed to mark frustration of the North–South dialogue. By 1976, UNCTAD had won a mandate to negotiate the NIEO; by 1980, it was well advanced toward an 'international development strategy'. Corea comments that, while the U.N. General Assembly was never able, by persuasion, to induce the developed countries to increase their development aid to the target of 0.7 per cent of their GNP (ODA by 1973 was on the order of $10,000 million per year), the OPEC countries, by withholding a resource, were able to transfer from the industrialized to the oil-producing states as much as $70,000 million – a fact which greatly influenced NIEO strategy. In retrospect, this explains the North's defensive reaction.

1193   **The New International Economic Order and the basic needs approach.**
Johan Galtung.   In: *The United Nations and a just world order*.
Edited by Richard A. Falk, Samuel S. Kim, and Saul Mendlovitz.
Boulder, CO: Westview, 1991, p.292-306.

Here is a clear comparison and critique of the two fundamental, principled approaches to international economic development: the NIEO, favoured by the Group of 77, UNCTAD, and generally the Third World; and the Basic Needs approach, favoured by the World Bank (under Robert McNamara), ILO, UNICEF, and generally the First World. Galtung concludes that the politically wise course is to insist that NIEO is meaningful only with intra-national transformations (class and political reforms), while Basic Needs is meaningful only with both material and non-material transformations (food, shelter, and human rights). He sees action to combine them in a 'third phase' of U.N. development strategy, called *self-reliance*. Regional (Third World) self-reliance needs NIEO; local self-reliance, Basic Needs; and national self-reliance, integration.

1194   **The New International Economic Order and the promotion of human rights.**
Raúl Ferrero.   New York: United Nations, 1986. 50p. bibliog.
(E.85.XIV.6. E/CN.4/Sub.2/1983/24/Rev.1).

'It must be agreed', writes the author, a U.N. Special Rapporteur, 'that the present order is a serious obstacle to the realization of the human rights and fundamental freedoms proclaimed in the Universal Declaration of Human Rights, more particularly in Article 25, which declares that everyone has the right to a standard of living adequate for the health and well-being of himself and his family.' To achieve this right is to achieve the more equitable economic order aspired to in the NIEO. The author reviews the status of NIEO by 1985 and explains the link to human rights. Ferrero particularly emphasizes the importance of integrating human rights standards into development strategies, rather as other authors would integrate environmental standards into such strategies. Just development is sustainable development.

1195   **The New International Economic Order: confrontation or cooperation between North and South?**
Edited by Karl P. Sauvant and Hajo Hasenpflug.   Boulder, CO: Westview, 1977. 474p. (Special Studies in International Economics).

The NIEO was proposed in order not to redistribute existing wealth, but to more fairly allocate new wealth, since the gap in per capita real income between developed and developing countries continues to widen. The authors – one a UNCTC officer, the other a German trade economist – have collected here a number of technical economic papers somewhat more centrist than other similar volumes from the same time. 'The main objective' of the book, Sauvant and Hasenpflug write, is 'to present, explore, and discuss various proposals and strategies aimed at [the NIEO's] establishment.' Topics include: positions of North and South, international trade and commodities, transfer of resources, technology transfer, industrialization, and self-reliance.

1196   **The New International Economic Order: the North–South debate.**
Edited by Jagdish N. Bhagwati.   Cambridge, MA: MIT Press, 1977. 390p.

This is a volume of papers by the 'most distinguished international and development economists from the developed countries' on the NIEO at the height of the controversy in 1976. The developing countries saw themselves in solidarity behind an international 'trade unionism' to wrest a greater share of the world's income from the capital-rich ones; the developed countries generally settled into policies of 'benign neglect'. The authors collected here generally found a difficulty for every solution, but they explored such substitutes for humanitarian aid as profit-sharing from seabed mining and a brain-drain tax. Topics include: resource transfers, international trade, world food problems, technology transfer, and the NIEO in general. Charles P. Kindleberger's comments are typical: 'I am deeply skeptical about the possibilities of developed and developing countries sitting down in a grand negotiation like the Congress of Vienna and putting together an elaborate bargain, with something for every country. . . . When minds do not meet, it is a mistake to agree on a form of words that papers [over] the cracks, since the paper bargain struck will not be kept.'

1197   **A new international economic order: what kind?**
Albert Fishlow.   In: *Rich and poor nations in the world economy*, by Albert Fishlow, Carlos F. Diaz-Alejandro, Richard R. Fagan, and Roger D. Hansen.   New York: McGraw-Hill for Council on Foreign Relations, 1978, p.9-83. bibliog.

This is a liberal and sympathetic view of the NIEO. For the world market to 'work', structural reforms are needed to develop a more equitable, efficient, and abundant world economy. Reform is *feasible* because it is necessary after the collapse of the Bretton Woods system and the rise of independent Third World competitors. 'Rules cannot be avoided', Fishlow writes. 'International economic relations constantly verge on neo-mercantilism.' Reform must be *global*, not regional, since the latter merely postpone the problems. Fishlow offers two principles for reform, rather at variance with the ultra-mercantilist programme of the NIEO: 'One is a joint commitment to extending and making markets more effective; the other is greater participation of developing nations in policing such markets and in making specific rules.' This rules out a centralized world development authority as proposed by Mahbub ul Haq (q.v.). He concludes with suggestions for transitional policies on trade, financial flows, and investment and technology flows. The proposals for reform are practical, Fishlow argues, if the public in every country can be made to understand the inadequacies of the status quo, and policy-makers to understand the inefficiencies of present trade and employment. This book is as profound an appreciation of the NIEO as Bedjaoui's *Towards a new international economic order* (item no. 1208).

1198 **The North–South debate: technology, basic human needs, and the New International Economic Order.**
Johan Galtung.   New York: Institute for World Order, 1980. 50p.
(WOMP Working Paper No. 12).

The author, a prominent social scientist and peace researcher, here presents 'strategies aimed at eroding the North's economic and technological dominance of the South'. Galtung sees the struggle for 'humane development' as a continuation of decolonization. His preferred strategy is a 'basic needs' approach to development, which he contrasts with the NIEO, regarded as Western capitalism in a guise that will benefit only Third World élites. Galtung argues that, if NIEO succeeds, the West will still 'end up with the better deal'; if it fails, both élites and poor will be victimized. A basic needs approach, which requires a certain conversion of Third World élites to their stewardship of the poor (intra-national reform), on the other hand, would develop economic 'self-reliance' and eventually bargaining power equal to the West's.

1199 **Policy alternatives for a new international economic order: an economic analysis.**
Edited by William R. Cline.   New York: Praeger for Overseas Development Council, 1979. 392p. bibliog.

This is a fair and full analysis of the NIEO by leading American and Canadian economists. The assumption at work here is that some sort of new international economic order is needed by *both* developing and developed countries, since trade and economic interdependence continue to link the world into one. In 1979, the volume was conceived as a contribution to North–South negotiations – the editor states that the goal was 'to identify those measures that could provide *mutual* benefits to both the developing and developed countries and to assess rigorously the possible economic effects of such measures'. Quantitative analysis has been used wherever possible. In the 1990s, the volume may be read by policy-makers and negotiators as a record of substantial past thinking on the issues. Topics covered: commodity agreements, food aid trade reform, external debt, resource transfers, world market imperfections.

1200 **Political and institutional issues of the New International Economic Order.**
Edited by Ervin Laszlo and Joel Kurtzman.   Oxford: Pergamon for UNITAR and the Centre for Economic and Social Studies of the Third World (CEESTEM, Mexico), 1981. 183p. bibliog.

Since 1977, UNITAR and CEESTEM have been producing a library on the NIEO, of which this is volume 17. (A bibliography here lists all those published to date.) NIEO, as the editors say in their introduction, 'is economic in terms of its issues, social in regard to its implications, and political in its implementation'. In this overview volume, they consider such basic questions as, Who pays? Who benefits? Is the free market a legitimate mechanism of world trade? Or is some sort of international intervention necessary to protect the poor? Do rich countries have a moral obligation to help the poor? Where is the political will? Is there enough solidarity of organized groups to move national governments on the NIEO?

1201　**Power, passions, and purpose: prospects for North–South negotiations.**
Edited by Jagdish N. Bhagwati and John G. Ruggie.　Cambridge, MA: MIT Press, 1984. 338p. bibliog.

By 1983, the North–South global negotiations were 'stalled'. This volume of specialized papers from a conference in India suggests some new approaches. 'The power had vanished [by 1983]; the passions had not subsided; the grand purpose still endured.' One step forward had resulted in two steps back. It was a time for reassessment. Bhagwati considers four types of North–South relations: Northern dominance, Northern hegemony, North–South interdependence, Southern strength through commodity power, NIEO, and global negotiations. Since the latter had proved 'ephemeral', the only alternative was for the South 'to build up its bargaining strength' rather on the model of the NICs. A recommended alternative strategy is printed in the annex.

1202　**Principles of a new international economic order: a study of international law in the making.**
Jerzy Makarczyk.　Dordrecht, The Netherlands: M. Nijhoff, 1988. 367p. bibliog.

This book of 1988 – long after the apparent defeat of the NIEO and the global negotiations – could be read as a mark of a longer-term, more mutually respectful effort to establish a just economic order throughout the world. The author aims to derive the *legal principles of a new international economic order*, which he finds rooted in the Charter of Economic Rights and Duties of States (1974), a UNITAR study on 'The progressive development of the principles and norms of international law relating to the NIEO' (1984), and an International Law Association declaration on the principles (1978). Makarczyk devotes fully half of his legal argument to the exposition of one such principle – the permanent sovereignty of a state over its wealth, natural resources, and economic activities.

1203　**Regime creation by a coalition of the weak: lessons from the NIEO and the Integrated Programme for Commodities.**
Robert L. Rothstein.　*International Studies Quarterly*, vol. 28 (1984), p.307-28.

'The attempt by the developing countries to establish a New International Economic Order (NIEO) has failed.' The author sketches various reasons for this verdict, then turns to the contribution that regime analysis makes to explaining the failure. Rothstein originally regarded the NIEO as not the attempted creation of a new regime but as a search for 'better terms within the existing regime'. In this article, he again finds that 'NIEO is not a very good example of regime-creation'. But the Integrated Programme for Commodities *was* such an attempt, which leads him to several tactical mistakes in bargaining and to a new 'mixed, indirect, and long-term strategy'. The article is apt to interest only theorists.

1204 **Regionalism in the New International Economic Order.**
Edited by Davidson Nicol, Luis Echeverria, and Aurelio Peccei.
Oxford: Pergamon for UNITAR and the Centre for Economic and
Social Studies of the Third World (CEESTEM, Mexico), 1981. 387p.

As the North–South dialogue broke down, the Club of Rome, UNITAR, and CEESTEM hosted a resourceful conference on regionalism – in effect South–South cooperation or self-reliance. The speeches and short papers collected here concern, first, regionalism historically, and second, regionalism as part of the NIEO development strategy. If the global approach is frustrated, perhaps a regional one, not only in Europe, but also in Latin America, Asia, and Africa, will make more progress, the authors hoped.

1205 **A requiem for the North–South conference.**
Jahangir Amuzegar. *Foreign Affairs*, vol. 56, no. 1 (October 1977), p.136-59.

This is an account of failed negotiations at the U.N. Conference on International Economic Cooperation (CIEC, 1975-77). In effect, the CIEC marked a way station on the road to the end of the North–South dialogue. The West made concessions ($1,000 million in a Special Action Programme to meet the needs of low-income countries, promises to underwrite the Common Fund for buffer stocks of LDC exports, pledges to increase ODA toward 0.7 per cent of GNP), but there was no agreement on the main issues of the NIEO (oil prices, indexing prices of LDC exports, debt relief, control of inflation). 'The "old" international economic order remained virtually as it was', Amuzegar concludes, 'with no radical changes yet in the relationships between the developing and the developed nations.' He traces the disappointing results to flaws in negotiation, to the very magnitude of NIEO ('characterized by equity, growth, and justice'), and to the loss of OPEC bargaining power as the oil market experienced a glut. He calls the result not the end, but 'the end of a beginning'.

1206 **Revolutionaries or bargainers? Negotiators for a new international economic order.**
Harold K. Jacobson, Dusan Sidjanski, Jeffrey Rodamar, and Alice
Hougassian-Rudovich. *World Politics*, vol. 35 (1983), p.335-67.

This article concentrates, not on the strategy for NIEO, but on its individual negotiators. They, in addition to their home governments and the formal decision-making processes of the negotiating fora, were the determinants of failure for the international economic regime. The authors interviewed eighty participants in the NIEO negotiations in Europe in 1976. The data support six conclusions: (1) The LDC negotiators, though often voting in a bloc, actually harboured a wide range of views, with only a few hostile to the West. (2) Negotiating positions were firmly grounded in national political processes. (3) LDC negotiators lacked information on a scale to match capabilities of Western states. (4) Socialist negotiators were the most emphatic about transfer of resources, the abuses of TNCs, and the faults of the E.C.'s Lomé convention. (5) Regional economic cooperation extended only to import substitution, not yet to export promotion, where real self-help lies. (6) Negotiators from the richer countries were more uniformly aware of politicization, favourable toward limiting population growth, and less negative toward TNCs. The authors predict that, if socialist ideology weakens and TNCs modify their more objectionable practices, another round of global negotiations could produce workable adjustments. 'But that hardly amounts to a revolutionary call for the overthrow of the old order.'

1207   Threat to development: pitfalls of the NIEO.
William Loehr and John P. Powelson.   Boulder, CO: Westview, 1983. 170p. bibliog.

The authors admit that the 'old' economic order is the cause for the growing gap between rich and poor nations, but they critique what is 'new' in the NIEO. They regard NIEO as a device of Third World elites to transfer resources *from the poor* in both First and Third Worlds *to the rich*. Loehr and Powelson prove this thesis by economic analysis of higher commodity prices, which would, since the poor consume a higher proportion of primary commodities, proportionately benefit the rich more than the poor; and similarly for trade reform (General System of Preferences), the code of conduct for TNCs, reform of the Bretton Woods institutions (SDRs linked to development aid), and debt relief (beneficial mainly to middle-income states). Their own solution is not an international programme like NIEO, but wiser national policies in LDCs to 'improve scientific and managerial capabilities, productivity, and trade'. This is a refreshing iconclastic book which may represent an antithesis in the reform dialectic.

1208   Towards a new international economic order.
Mohammed Bedjaoui.   New York: Holmes & Meier for UNESCO Series on New Challenges to International Law, 1979. 287p. bibliog.

Western liberals who have been looking for a Third World jurisprudence to complement the heritage of international law will find it in this book by an Algerian ambassador and legal scholar. Western policy-makers who are concerned to understand the demands of the South, rather as students sought to understand the communism of Eastern Europe by reading the works of Karl Marx, would do well to open this book. Bedjaoui sees the NIEO, in a long historical time-frame, as a continuation of the struggle for decolonization and self-determination. That struggle will radically equalize the substance and application of international law and hence create a new world economic and political order. 'The bipolar or oligarchic world relies on an "international right of confiscation", i.e., confiscation of the independence and sovereignty of satellite States. The multipolar world to be set up will involve, on the contrary, an "international right of participation", i.e., participation by all States in the formulation and application of the rules governing the relations between them.' He sees the world, under the impact of industry and democracy, as 'being rebuilt, made and unmade, in a vast and prodigious battle against inequality'. In this book, Bedjaoui traces the historical trends pointing to a NIEO, which he thinks is decades away; then he analyses the role of international law in both reforming international relations and conserving the progress made. The law, he concludes, will be *enacted* in the General Assembly – not *found* in the ICJ – since the 'Assembly is quite competent to interpret the Charter, not only its letter but also its spirit'.

1209   **Towards the New International Economic Order.** *Analytical report on developments in the field of international economic cooperation since the Sixth Special Session of the General Assembly.* Director-General for Development and International Economic Cooperation, K.K.S. Dadzie.   New York: United Nations, 1982. 73p. (E.82.II.A.7. A/S-11/5).

In view of subsequent collapse of the global negotiations, this official U.N. report remains a record of progress up to the breakdown. The principal finding, writes the Director-General, is 'that, in the future, efforts to establish the NIEO should seek to obtain global management for the world economy, which would comprise a decision-making process that is multisectoral'. (By the 1990s, this has the ring of failed socialist planning. In 1992, Secretary-General Boutros-Ghali abolished the very post of Director-General.) Nevertheless, covered here are authoritative accounts of negotiations on primary commodities, monetary and financial issues, industrialization and trade in manufactured products, TNCs, science and technology, transport, insurance, South–South cooperation, LDCs, and mobilization of domestic resources.

1210   **The United Nations and political conflict between the North and the South.** Stephen D. Krasner.   In: *The U.S., the U.N., and the management of global change.* Edited by Toby Trister Gati.   New York: New York University Press for UNA–USA, 1983, p.210-26.

Here is a clear account of the origins and politics of the NIEO. Krasner calls for a U.S. policy of 'selective engagement'. There is no hint (in 1983) of the coming end of the Cold War, when the U.S. might be able to *afford* addressing the demands for economic justice by the great majority of poor countries. Compare other articles in this volume by Sidney Weintraub, Howard Wachtel, and Ronald Meltzer.

1211   **U.S. foreign policy and the New International Economic Order: negotiating global problems, 1974-1981.** Robert K. Olson.   Boulder, CO: Westview, 1981. 168p. bibliog.

This is a judicious diplomatic history of U.S. policy toward the NIEO, from its beginning in 1974 through the virtual abandonment of the North–South dialogue in 1980, by a retired U.S. Foreign Service Officer who took part in the negotiations and then studied such global diplomatic processes at Oxford. Readers who are embittered at the United States for its unresponsiveness, or who view it as the problem to be corrected pending further progress, would do well to study closely this thoughtful and informative book. Such seemingly irrelevant incidents as the Iranian Revolution and the Soviet invasion of Afghanistan (both in late 1979) cannot be ignored for the return of the U.S. to its traditional foreign policies to maintain an open, free-market international economic order, to contain communist aggression, and to support newly emerging nations as they enter the international system. In a chapter on *preservation* of the international order, Olson explains how the negotiating strategy of the NIEO directly challenged these U.S. interests and allied the IO and E bureaus within the State Department into unwonted harmony. 'To give in to the NIEO', he remarks, 'would be as unthinkable for the United States as turning Western collective security over to Eastern Europe.' He concludes that, although the NIEO was symptomatic of real global problems, failure to negotiate any solution was rooted in the very negotiation processes and in the unreality of growth issues in a new era of limits to growth. Olson's own solution would be to start with the recommendations of the Brandt commission and follow the guidance of Gerald Barney's *Global 2000* (item no. 1321).

1212 **A view from the South: the second phase of the North-South dialogue.**
Mahbub ul Haq.   In: *The United States and the world development agenda, 1979*. Edited by Martin M. McLaughlin and Staff of the Overseas Development Council.   New York: Praeger, 1979, p.115-24.

Growing global interdependence requires international institutions for a worldwide taxation system, an international central bank, and a global planning system. Ul Haq calls for a summit conference on a 'global enterprise to meet basic needs substantially by the year 2000'. He also calls for a new Bretton Woods conference to 'establish the basic premises for a new world order'. A similar chapter by John W. Sewell deals with the central question, Can the North prosper without growth and progress in the South? The whole volume is devoted to the North–South dialogue at its climactic, if disappointing, stage. There are excellent statistical appendixes.

See also Groups (p.130ff.).

Industrial development

U.N. Industrial Development Organization (UNIDO)
U.N. Economic Commission for Europe (U.N. ECE)

1213 **Annual bulletin of steel statistics for Europe, 1991.**
Bulletin annuel de statistiques de l'acier pour l'Europe.
Ezhegodnyi biulletin evropeiskoi statistiki chernoi metallurgii.
U.N. ECE.   New York: United Nations, 1972- . annual. 94p. (E/F/R.93.II.E.6).

This is a volume of statistics on production, trade, and consumption of raw materials, iron and steel products, movements of scrap, and consumption of energy in the steel industry. Data are arranged by product and country in Western and Eastern Europe (including Russia), U.S.A., Canada, and Japan.

1214 **Annual report of UNIDO, 1992.**
Vienna: Industrial Development Board, 1985- . annual. 139p.

This official report covers policy (much constrained by the U.N. financial crisis), industrial strategy, promotion, special actions toward Africa and LDCs, evaluation, coordination within the U.N. system, administration, and finance.

1215 **Directory of development of finance institutions.**
Répertoire des établissements de financement du développement.
Guía de instituciones de financiación del desarollo.
UNIDO Industrial Investment Division.   Vienna: UNIDO, 1986.
94p. (E/F/S.86.II.B.4. ID/344).

This directory aims to assist users in the creation of new industrial investment projects in developing countries. It contains a list of some 340 development finance institutions divided into five groups: international and regional ones, industrialized, developing (265), Arab, and Islamic. The work should be especially useful to those planning joint ventures.

1216 **Industrial growth in developing countries.**
UNIDO.   In: *The New International Economic Order: confrontation or cooperation between North and South?* Edited by Karl P. Sauvant and Hajo Hasenpflug.   Boulder, CO: Westview, 1977, p.317-29.

'Historically, the industrial sector has been the most dynamic force contributing to structural change in the economic and social system.' This short survey presents the statistical facts of developing countries' progress – their average growth rates, 1955-73, consistently outstripped those of developed ones, though per capita and aggregate figures, of course, are lower.

1217 **Industry and development, 1992.**
New York: UNIDO, 1978- . semi-annual. 120p. (E.92.III.E.1.
ID/SER.M/30).

This scholarly journal 'attempts to provide a link between practitioners and theorists working on economic and related aspects of industrialization'. Its focus is on applied economics in accordance with the Lima Declaration and Plan of Action on Industrial Development and Cooperation.

1218 **Industy and development: global report, 1992/93.**
UNIDO.   New York: United Nations, 1985- . biennial. 548p.
bibliog. (E.92.III.E.4. ID/382).

This is the full-scale global report by UNIDO – equivalent to the handsomest volumes by the World Bank or the IMF. Here the focus is on the world industrial economy in the short and medium term; industrial prospects and productivity, with emphasis on human skills; structural change and employment; privatization; and a survey of a dozen selected manufacturing industries. At the time of writing, the outlook generally was dim: in 1991, for the second time in the twentieth century, after the Great Depression, global output *declined*.

1219 **Industry in a changing world. Special issue of the Industrial Development Survey for the fourth General Conference of UNIDO.**
UNIDO.   New York: United Nations, 1983. 369p. (E.83.II.B.6.
ID/CONF.5/2. ID/304).

This readable, analytical volume surveys trends in world industry and reviews progress and constraints on developing countries in achieving previous UNIDO goals.

Since 1963, the Third World's share of manufacturing value added (MVA) has risen slowly from 8.1 to 11 per cent; the Second World's rose too, from 14.6 to 25; the First World's fell from 77.3 to 64.0 per cent. 'Gradual changes in the global distribution of world MVA', UNIDO says, 'have altered many of the basic premises which have traditionally guided international industrial policy.' Policy formation has now become multipolar. The book traces such changes in the map of world industry – developing countries may acquire 15 per cent of MVA in 2000, but per capita GDP would still be one-fifth of that of developed countries – and it discusses a range of industrial strategies especially affecting manufacturing, wages, and food.

1220 **Regional industrial cooperation: experiences and perspectives of ASEAN and the Andean Pact.**
John Wong. Vienna: UNIDO, 1986. 102p. (E.85.II.B.5. ID/309).
Regional, or South–South, cooperation is now an important means for development in the Third World. This brief work examines industrial cooperation in Asia (ASEAN) and Latin America (Andean Pact). By macro-economic standards, success has been slow in coming. The author surveys obstacles to regional cooperation in the Third World. He finds that 'cooperation' (ASEAN) has worked about as well as the more ambitious 'integration' (Andean Pact) because of the diversity and low starting points of the two regions. Wong closes with practical comparisons and recommendations for the success of the two efforts.

1221 **Statistics of world trade in steel, 1992.**
Statistiques du commerce mondial de l'acier.
Statistika mirovoi torgovli staliu.
U.N. ECE. New York: United Nations, 1961- . annual. 137p.
(E/F/R.93.II.E.34).
This is a volume purely of statistics of exports of semi-finished and finished steel products from European (including Russian) and other steel-exporting countries in the world. Data are arranged by total exports per year (1980-92), by total trade between countries in the ECE region (1992), and by exporting country to regions and countries of destination (1992).

1222 **The steel market in 1992.**
U.N. ECE. New York: United Nations, 1971- . annual. 135p.
(E.93.II.E.30. ECE/STEEL/81).
This analytical volume provides a summary and outlook for the steel market; a discussion of trends in demand, supply, and prices for steel; an analysis of foreign trade and export prices; a review of production capacity and investment; and country-by-country statistics in the E.C., EFTA, and Eastern Europe (including former U.S.S.R.).

1223 **UNIDO guides to information sources.**
New York: United Nations, UNIDO Nos. 1-40, 1976-82. 88-97p.
(ID/163 - ID/269/UNIDO/LIB/SER.D/1/Rev).
These are specialized directories to information sources in some forty industries for use by those in developing countries trying to develop their own directories. Typical numbers are: meat-processing industry (1), vegetable oil industry (7), agricultural

implements and machinery industry (8), fertilizer industry (21), dairy product manufacturing industry (23), non-conventional sources of energy (30), and the like.

Human rights

U.N. General Assembly and Economic and Social Council
U.N. Commission on Human Rights
International Bill of Human Rights

1224 **The constitution of rights: human dignity and American values.**
Edited by Michael J. Meyer and William A. Parent. Ithaca, NY: Cornell University Press, 1992. 248p.

Readers who prefer to approach international human rights through U.S. constitutionalism and its more familiar concepts will find this an excellent book. The U.N. Covenants are brought in at several points, mainly to show their consistency with the Constitution, and to indicate their potential to make a reality of human dignity.

1225 **The diplomacy of human rights.**
Edited by David D. Newsom. Lanham, MD: University Press of America for Institute for the Study of Diplomacy, Georgetown University, 1986. 240p. bibliog.

This is a practical book of U.S. diplomacy to protect or promote human rights in other countries in accordance with settled American foreign policy. U.S. diplomatic tools include access to foreign leaders and their people, public statements, U.S. legislation (e.g., on immigration), country reports to Congress on observance of human rights abroad, U.S. assistance programmes, consultation with allies and friendly governments, participation in the World Bank and other multilateral lending institutions, leadership in international organizations like the U.N., and cooperation with private NGOs. Such policies encounter many difficulties, not the least of which is that, as Newsom explains, the United States must become 'judge and jury of another country's internal struggle'. Case-studies cover Iran, Korea, Indonesia, Brazil, Argentina, South Africa, the Soviet Union, Romania, and the Helsinki process. (Central America and the Philippines, objects of traditional American diplomacy in the Reagan administration, are omitted.)

1226 **The ethnic question: conflicts, development, and human rights.**
Rodolfo Stavenhagen. Tokyo: UNU Press, 1990. 185p.
(E.90.III.A.9).

Just before the Yugoslav federation broke up into 'ethnic conflict', this comprehensive analysis appeared. There are some 183 states-members of the United Nations; but, according to political geographers, there exist 1,300 'nations'. Anthropologists find even more ethnic groups and cultures. With the end of the Cold War, long-suppressed ethnic conflict may become a comparable problem of world politics. The League of Nations began to deal with the problem in its effort to protect minorities; the United Nations takes the more universal approach of human rights. The author sheds real light on the nature of 'nation-states' (the states are prior), and he discusses the struggle between state and nation and, now, between both and the international system. Stavenhagen argues that states cannot develop and modernize if they are divided by ethnic conflict. He concludes with suggestions for education and cultural policy to relieve such divisions, yet, to preserve diversity, he would guarantee the rights of groups. Not the Melting Pot but the Human Mosaic is the middle way between atomized individuals and the never existent pure race.

1227 **Human rights: a compilation of international instruments.** [Vol. I, Parts 1 and 2:] **Universal instruments.** [Vol. II:] **Regional instruments.**
New York: United Nations, 1994. 3 vols. (E.94.XIV.1. ST/HR/1/Rev.5).

To understand what human rights *are*, one must study the 'instruments' – the standard-setting declarations, recommendations, principles, and rules; and the binding treaties, conventions, protocols, and covenants. (The latter are binding only for those states that ratify the particular treaties, etc.) This basic reference work prints the text of the now ninety-five universal instruments (forty-five binding), including twelve of the more important ILO conventions and four UNESCO conventions and one declaration). The second 'volume' (actually the third) is valuable for comparative purposes, giving the regional instruments of the O.A.S., Council of Europe, O.A.U., and CSCE. The European Convention for the Protection of Human Rights and Fundamental Freedoms, which belongs to the Council of Europe (not the European Community), reflects a greater degree of political consensus and hence is legally much stronger than the comparable International Covenant on Civil and Political Rights of the U.N. Only Asia has not yet produced a regional charter of human rights.

1228 **Human rights: an agenda for the next century.**
Edited by Louis Henkin and John L. Hargrove. Washington, DC: American Society of International Law, 1994. 524p. (Studies in Transnational Legal Policy, No. 26).

The end of the Cold War and the convening of the Vienna Conference on Human Rights in 1993 provided the opportunity for the experts whose papers are collected in this volume to try to define the human rights issues that will emerge as the superpower conflict dissipates. The editor warns that the next round of opposition to human rights, evident already at Vienna, will rally around the banner of 'cultural relativism', which has overtaken the old one of 'national sovereignty'. Three tasks are ahead, Professor Henkin foresees: (1) strengthening human rights standards in the face of ethnic conflict, massive refugee flows, and difficulties in establishing and maintaining democracy; (2) making a reality of such established principles as the rights of women, economic and social rights, the rights of children, and the non-derogability of rights even in times of emergency; and (3) implementing and enforcing the rights, especially by moving toward enforcement on individuals. He closes with a call for renewed U.S. leadership.

1229 **Human rights and American foreign policy.**
Edited by Donald P. Kommers and Gilburt D. Loescher.   Notre
Dame, IN: University of Notre Dame Press, 1979. 333p. bibliog.
In the first flush of surprise and enthusiasm at the human rights policy of the Carter
administration, this volume of expert papers explores such problems as the conflict
between traditional individual rights and the newly claimed rights of groups; the
conflicting ideologies of First and Third Worlds; human rights in the Second World
(notably the Helsinki process); monitoring human rights by IGOs and NGOs;
American foreign policy respecting human rights from the perspectives of, first, the
executive branch and, second, the legislature (by the architect of the policy,
Minnesota Representative Donald M. Fraser); and finally more specialized problems
of U.S. 'anti-radical bias' and of humanitarian intervention. A.H. Robertson, the
leading interpreter of the European Community and the Council of Europe to
Americans, contributes a 'global assessment'.

1230 **Human rights and American foreign policy: the Carter and
Reagan experiences.**
A. Glenn Mower, Jr.   Westport, CT: Greenwood, 1987. 167p.
bibliog. (Studies in Human Rights, No. 7).
The United States began to make the defence of human rights part of its foreign
policy under the leadership of President Jimmy Carter. It tried to abandon economic
and social rights under President Ronald Reagan, but human rights in general could
not be shaken. This book is a history and comparison of the two administrations'
human rights policies. It includes two case-studies of how each treated South Africa
and South Korea. The author concludes that, by 1986, human rights had proved their
'staying power' in American foreign policy, had been 'institutionalized' within the
State Department, and had become an 'active, positive concern' in U.S. relations with
other countries. Mower considers such evidence of the policy's success as reduced
disappearances in Argentina and Chile, but his fundamental view is that human rights
are on the U.S. agenda not because they always succeed, but because they are akin to
the liberties and fundamental political values of the American people. Since the
United Nations has very limited powers to protect human rights on its own, readers
will be impressed at how one great sovereign power has taken up this cause.

1231 **Human rights and international relations.**
R.J. Vincent.   Cambridge: Cambridge University Press for Royal
Institute of International Affairs, 1986. 186p.
This book 'is written by a student of international relations who takes human rights
seriously, not by an advocate of human rights whose conviction makes him oblivious
to his environment'. The author honours the late Hedley Bull, yet he cannot be
regarded simply as a 'realist'. Vincent explains the origins of human rights and
accepts their full range – that is, the civil and political rights (or claims to 'security')
and the economic, social, and cultural ones ('subsistence'). He traces their impact on
international politics in East–West and North–South relations and in the emerging
'world society'. He makes a policy recommendation that *subsistence rights* should
have priority over the others, not because of their association with the ideologies of
East or South, but because 'the suffering of the starving and malnourished [is] the
worst offence to human rights in contemporary world society'. In effect, he argues
that international cooperation for economic development is the least ideologically

divisive policy. He concludes that the international law of human rights can be seen as a 'progression away from the primitiveness of tribal attachment to the state and towards a situation in which individuals treat each other in their capacities as human beings'. Or it can also be seen as legitimating and consolidating the historic states as guardians of human diversity.

1232 Human rights and the American tradition.
Arthur M. Schlesinger. *Foreign Affairs*, vol. 57 (1978), p.503-26.

The prominent American historian finds human rights rooted in the humanitarianism of the last four centuries. Until the idea of equality spread, the rich and powerful had little notion of the dignity of the poor. The United States was founded on 'inalienable rights', so the Carter administration was making no innovation in undertaking the mission of shining 'the beacon of human rights to an unregenerate world'. Schlesinger makes clear that it was *Realpolitik* from the onset of the Cold War to Henry Kissinger's diplomacy that was uncharacteristic in the American tradition. When Carter wrote in *Why not the best?* (1975) that 'our government's foreign policy has not exemplified any commitment to moral principles', he was restoring an ideal. The human rights campaign in the new administration could not escape many inconsistencies and provocations to Soviet adversaries, but by 1978 it was 'institutionalized'. Schlesinger wonders if the next step might be to ratify 'those toothless wonders, the U.N. conventions and covenants' then before the Senate. He closes with some gentle gibes at the American Historical Association for its silence over Soviet persecution of historians Amalrik, Medvedev, Solzhenitsyn, and Moroz.

1233 Human rights and the future international community.
John G. Ruggie. *Daedalus*, vol. 112, no. 4 (Fall 1983), p.93-110.

International human rights law, writes Louis Henkin, 'serves no patent, particular national interest. It is essentially ideological, idealistic, humanitarian; its true and deep purpose is to improve the lot of individual men and women everywhere . . . a unique and revolutionary purpose for international law.' Ruggie examines whether such a revolution is occurring in the international community. If so, it would be moving away from the 'Hobbesian floor' of power politics to the 'Kantian ceiling' of a world federal republic. Ruggie finds that, in the normative order, human rights have provided a new standard of *legitimacy*, to which most states pay lip-service, and a few actually restrain their behaviour. As institutions, the U.N. Human Rights Committee is weaker than the European Court of Human Rights, but both do exercise new authority in *domestic* areas, though to a weaker degree than the nuclear NPT regime. As for emerging world society, human rights claims so far have been made against national societies, as the only ones with the power to relieve abuses (as well as to cause them). Hence, 'world society constitutes not a framework within which moral claims can be met, but a vocabulary within which they may be articulated.' In short, there has not been revolution but 'rule-governed change'; not a transformation to cosmopolican society, but a 'new domain' within which the sovereign state system continues to 'reproduce itself'. In the European Community, a revolution is occurring; in the world, anarchy remains the reality.

1234 Human rights and the United Nations: the great adventure.
John T.P. Humphrey.   Dobbs Ferry, NY: Transnational Publishers, 1984. 350p.

This is a history of human rights negotiations by a Canadian who contributed to the drafting of the Universal Declaration and later served as first director of the Human Rights Division (now Centre) of the U.N. Humphrey carries the story from 1946 to 1966. Readers who prefer a narrative account, filled with living people, to the analytical and legal works of most writing on human rights, will find this history engaging.

1235 Human rights and U.S. foreign policy: Congress reconsidered.
David P. Forsythe.   Gainesville, FL: University of Florida Press, 1988. 224p. bibliog.

Congress, reflecting the values of the American people, is the branch of the U.S. government least persuaded by the late 1980s of the usefulness of the United Nations. Yet from 1973 through at least to the first year of the Carter administration in 1977, Congress virtually made human rights a U.S. foreign policy interest, where they remain. The author provides a political, rather than legal, analysis of U.S. human rights policy; he traces Congress's role; he analyses Congressional effects on the President's conduct of diplomacy and on world politics. The last chapter is entitled, 'The wisdom of Congressional action'. Forsythe does not consider the matter of Congressional opposition to ratification of international human rights treaties, for which the book below by Kaufman, *Human rights treaties and the Senate* (item no. 1250), fills the gap.

1236 Human rights and world politics.
David P. Forsythe.   Lincoln, NB: University of Nebraska Press, 1983; 2nd ed., 1989. 316p.

This is an introduction to human rights for the university student and general reader by a leading and far-seeing political scientist. Forsythe's main focus is on the political process of making and implementing rules, so he postpones the philosophy of human rights to a later chapter. He attempts a synthesis of human rights as a 'visionary ideal and legal ideology' within anarchic world politics. Human rights, he concludes, 'signifies a major effort at defining new standards of legitimacy and hence a new push for systematic change in world politics'. In the long run, a commitment to human rights will not injure, but strengthen every government. Moreover, human rights are in the air as an ideal, and people and private organizations demand them as the guarantees of their dignity.

1237 Human rights and world public order: the basic policies of an international law of human dignity.
Myres S. McDougal, Harold D. Lasswell, and Lung-chu Chen.   New Haven, CT: Yale University Press, 1980. 1,016p.

'[T]he contemporary world arena', argue the authors, 'exhibits an increasingly viable constitutive process of authoritative decision which, though it has not yet achieved that high stability in expectations about authority and in degree of control over constituent members that characterizes the internal processes of certain national communities, still offers in more than rudimentary form all the basic features essential to the effective making and application of law on a global scale.' That is, world government is lacking, but there is sufficient 'world community' and 'comprehensive transnational social processes' to establish a 'global bill of human rights'. The authors aim in the book to formulate model 'public order policies' and 'global constitutive processes of authoritative decision' that might guide leaders of national governments and 'citizens of the larger community of humankind' to finally establish a 'world civic order'. This is a work of jurisprudence in the 'law as process' school. Human rights are not described philosophically, but are defined as they emerge from public demands, claims, and concerns about wrongs or 'deprivations'. All human rights are variants on a demand for *respect*, they conclude. In their final, climactic chapter on the future public and civic order, they never discuss the necessity for *government* to maintain order, but rather emphasize all the freedoms and claims to be enjoyed under such order.

1238 **Human rights at the United Nations, 1955-85: the question of bias.**
Jack Donnelly. *International Studies Quarterly*, vol. 32 (1988), p.275-303.
'I find that there is considerable bias, and argue that it is one of the most important impediments to increasing the effectiveness of the United Nations' human rights work. There is, however, evidence of a modest but significant decline in bias in the eighties. The problem, therefore, would seem to be real, but neither fatal nor incurable.'

1239 **Human rights fact sheets.**
Geneva: U.N. Centre for Human Rights, 1987- . (To order, inquire at either the Geneva or New York offices of the Centre for Human Rights.)
These short booklets, available free and distributed world-wide, are very informative on selected topics:
No. 1: Human rights machinery;
No. 2: The International Bill of Rights;
No. 3: Advisory services and technical assistance in the field of human rights;
No. 4: Methods of combating torture;
No. 5: Programme of action for the Second Decade to Combat Racism and Racial Discrimination;
No. 6: Enforced or involuntary disappearances;
No. 7: Communications procedures;
No. 8: World Public Information Campaign for Human Rights;
No. 9: The rights of indigenous peoples;
No. 10: The rights of the child.
No. 11: Summary or arbitrary executions;
No. 12: The Committee on the Elimination of Racial Discrimination;
No. 13: International humanitarian law and human rights;
No. 14: Contemporary forms of slavery;
No. 15: Civil and political rights: the Human Rights Committee;
No. 16: The Committee on Economic, Social, and Cultural Rights;
No. 17: The Committee against Torture;
No. 18: Minority rights;
No. 19: National institutions for the promotion and protection of human rights.

1240 **Human rights: improving U.N. mechanisms for compliance.**
Joseph Preston Baratta. Washington, DC: Center for U.N. Reform
Education, 1990. 109p. bibliog. (Monograph No. 8).
This is a review of the origins of human rights and of the International Bill of Human
Rights. In 1990, there were sixty-eight instruments (declarations, conventions,
covenants, charters), including twenty-two binding treaties. The United States led in
creating the human rights 'order' after World War II, but since the Bricker
amendment controversy in the 1950s, U.S. leadership has foundered. U.N.
implementation mechanisms are contrasted with those of the ILO, European
Convention on Human Rights, and American Convention on Human Rights.
Recommendations for improvement of compliance include: integrating the law;
improving co-ordination; exposing bias; increasing use of individual experts in
supervisory committees; granting the right of individual petition; increasing NGO
access; creating a High Commissioner for Human Rights; upgrading the Commission
on Human Rights to a Council; and establishing a World Court of Human Rights.

1241 **Human rights in a changing world.**
Antonio Cassese. Philadelphia: Temple University Press, 1990.
245p. bibliog.
Readers who are baffled by the elegant structure of international human rights law
and the daily reality of persecutions and violence against people will be helped by
this book. It is not another edition of specialized essays like so many volumes on
human rights, but a sustained philosophical musing on the subject, rooted in world
literature and the noblest tradition of the law, yet constantly drawn back to the
realities of the 1990s. It culminates with several chapters on 'human rights in a
gradually unifying world'. Cassese argues that we are misguided if we yield to
passive anguish in the face of life's evils, or if we assume naïvely that human rights
will triumph in place of a world religion. He regards human rights 'as a *new ethos*, as
an extremely important set of *secular, humanitarian precepts*, unencumbered by
myth, though based on the main ideals of traditional religion (taken both from the
West and the East), with a backbone of ideas borrowed from Western philosophy.' By
elevating individuals to the status of 'subjects' of international law, like states, the
states themselves have accepted limitations on their sovereign freedom of action.
Human rights law, then, represents the beginning of a law of the *Gemeinschaft* or
community of states and peoples. To ensure *universal* respect for the dignity of the
human person, it will finally be necessary to establish a 'supra-national (yet
democratic) authority'.

1242 **Human rights in international law: legal and policy issues.**
Edited by Theodor Meron. Oxford: Clarendon Press, 1984. 2 vols.
bibliog.
This is a standard textbook on human rights, especially written for teaching. Human
rights must be taught, argues Professor Louis B. Sohn as the editor recounts, not only
because their theory goes to the 'essence of the law', and because they are already
useful in practice, 'but because it is a part of general education which people ought to
have'. Law students will read this book, but general readers, who are searching for an
exact introduction to the subject, will also find it worth an investment of time. Topics
include: U.S. constitutionalism as a principal human rights system; the nature of
rights; civil rights; political rights; economic, social, and cultural rights; human rights
and the ILO; race, sex, and religious discrimination; human rights in armed conflict;

the U.N. system for the implementation and supervision of human rights; the NGO contribution; the Inter-American system; and the European Convention on Human Rights.

1243 **Human rights in the world community.**
Edited by Richard P. Claude and Burns Weston.   Philadelphia:
University of Pennsylvania Press, 1989; 2nd ed., 1992. 463p. bibliog.

This is an illustrated teaching text aimed not at law students alone but at college and graduate students as well. The editors provide for each chapter a careful introduction, notes, questions for reflection and discussion, a bibliography, and a most unusual and welcome 'filmography' to bring the issues of human rights home in our visual culture. The text consists of the more enduring articles that have previously appeared in the scholarly press. The volume is broadly divided into 'issues' and 'action'. Topics of the six chapters are: overview: political and civil rights; economic, social, and cultural rights, plus the third generation of rights of peoples; international implementation; national implementation; and non-governmental approaches to implementation. The editors in their overview treat human rights as a 'challenge to state sovereignty', an 'agenda for preferred world policy', a 'standard for assessing national behavior', and a 'populist worldwide movement influencing international relations'.

1244 **Human rights in the world community: a call for U.S. leadership.**
U.S. House of Representatives, Committee on Foreign Affairs,
Subcommittee on International Organizations and Movements.
Report. 93rd Cong., 2nd sess. 1974. 54p. (CIS No. H382-11. SuDocs
No. Y4.F76/1:H88/3).

This is the briefer 'Fraser report' – the source for the Carter administration's human rights policy three years later. It is a report on public testimony and correspondence during the subcommittee's August-December 1973 hearings. Part I examines U.S. consideration of human rights violations in other countries; Part II, human rights protection by U.N. and regional organizations. For the full record of the testimony from the State Department, current and former officials, Representatives and Senators from Congress, international lawyers, and human rights activists, see *International protection of human rights: the work of international organizations and the role of U.S. foreign policy. Hearings,* 93rd Cong., 1st sess., August-December 1973. 987p. (CIS No. H381-26. SuDocs No. Y4.F76/1:H88/4).

1245 **Human rights: questions and answers.**
New York: United Nations, 1987. 54p. (DPI/919).

What are human rights? What is the Universal Declaration of Human Rights? Can an individual file a complaint with the United Nations for a violation of a right protected by a U.N. treaty? These are some of the basic questions answered in this informative booklet. For readers just becoming familiar with the U.N.'s approach to human rights, this short work will acquaint them with the public posture, without revealing the political complications.

1246 **Human rights sourcebook.**
Edited by Albert P. Blaustein, Roger S. Clark, and Jay A. Sigler.
New York: Paragon House for Washington Institute for Values in
Public Policy, 1987. 970p. bibliog.

This is a 'one volume compilation of the *official* texts of *all* the fundamental human
rights documents'. Here the reader can find the relevant articles of the U.N. Charter
and the International Bill of Rights; the other U.N. instruments; the ILO and
UNESCO main instruments; the procedures of the U.N., ILO, and UNESCO; the
regional conventions; the laws of war; the CSCE and Helsinki Accords; key passages
in national constitutions guaranteeing the rights of the individual against the state;
important legislation and judicial decisions; and revolutionary documents, such as
the U.S. Declaration of Independence and the Declaration of Charter 77 in
Czechoslovakia (1977).

1247 **Human rights: status of international instruments and chart of
ratifications as of 31 January 1993.**
New York: United Nations, 1993. 336p. (E.87.XIV.2.Rev.8.
ST/HR/5).

This volume, a companion to *A compilation of international instruments* (see item
no. 1228), contains a record of the ratifications and the often very important
reservations of states to each of the twenty-two main conventions of human rights
law. A handy, fold-out chart of ratifications, regularly updated, can be found in the
inside pocket of the back cover.

1248 **Human rights: the International Bill of Human Rights.**
New York: United Nations, 1988. 42p. (DPI/925).

The International Bill of Human Rights consists of the Universal Declaration of
Human Rights (1948), the International Covenant on Civil and Political Rights and its
Optional Protocol (1966; in force, 1976), and the International Covenant on
Economic, Social, and Cultural Rights (1966; in force, 1976). These four documents
are conveniently reprinted in this booklet. U.N. Secretary-General Javier Pérez de
Cuéllar provides needed perspective: 'The realization of human rights and
fundamental freedoms proclaimed in the International Bill of Human Rights is a
dynamic process. As is evident in today's world, a great deal remains to be
accomplished.'

1249 **Human rights: their implementation and supervision by the
United Nations.**
Louis B. Sohn. In: *Human rights in international law: legal and
policy issues.* Edited by Theodor Meron. Oxford: Clarendon Press,
1984, p.369-94.

This is a brief exposition of the U.N. procedures for the implementation of human
rights by a legal scholar who is well aware of what more effective measures would be
if the world community would support them. Sohn contrasts national and
international measures of implementation. He explains the periodic reporting systems
in the U.N., procedures for dealing with inter-state complaints, the even more
restricted procedures for dealing with private communications about state violations,
and conflicts between the various procedures unique to each treaty. He concludes by

raising the questions whether human rights are really enforceable under international law, and why are existing procedures so ineffective?

1250 **Human rights treaties and the Senate: a history of opposition.**
Natalie H. Kaufman.   Chapel Hill, NC: University of North Carolina Press, 1990. 256p. bibliog.

The U.N. Charter was approved for ratification in 1945 by the U.S. Senate *without reservations*. But with the coming of the Cold War and the introduction of the Bricker amendment in 1951, the Senate developed a hostility to human rights treaties that hardly changed through debate on the Genocide Convention in 1986 or treaties still pending in the 1990s. The main objections are that the international treaties would erode American civil and political rights, would abridge states' rights within the federal system, and would advance the United Nations towards world government. When postponement failed, the Senate has had recourse to debilitating reservations. This timely history traces current U.S. opposition to human rights treaties to the legacy of the 1950s. Readers who wonder why the United States, with probably the best record on human rights of any country in the world, continually resists ratification of treaties agreed to by a majority of states will find the reasons here. The author argues that opposition has been essentially 'political' – reservations being a 'legalistic strategy in an essentially political game'. But acceptance, too, would be political in both domestic and international senses, for she concludes that non-ratification conveys the symbolism of U.S. supremacy, while ratification would support the international human rights movement and even give domestic groups the standards 'to advance the implementation of human rights within the United States'.

1251 **An inquiry into the legitimacy of humanitarian intervention.**
Tom J. Farer.   In: *Law and force in the new world order*. Edited by Lori F. Damrosch and David J. Scheffer.   Boulder, CO: Westview, 1991, p.185-201.

The end of the Cold War has created an opportunity for the international community to restrain national governments from the most brutal treatment of their own citizens, despite the traditional prohibition of intervention into a state's domestic affairs. American international lawyers, led by Professor Anthony D'Amato, argue that genocide, slavery, and widespread torture justify humanitarian intervention. The author contrasts their views with those of most British and European lawyers, who fear that such an innovation could lead to the unravelling of the rudimentary structure of international law. Farer prefers U.N. multilateral intervention but would accept state intervention. U.S. interventions in Grenada and Panama were not a response to genocide, slavery, or torture, but future legitimate occasions are conceivable.

1252 **The international dimensions of human rights.**
Edited by Karel Vasak.   Paris: UNESCO, 1982. 2 vols. bibliog.

This large work is a legal treatise for the teaching of human rights. The editor has not sought authors who either regard human rights as solely a matter of domestic jurisdiction, and hence without effect on absolute national sovereignty, or treat them as limiting national sovereignty, since the individual is increasingly regarded as a subject of international law like the state. The volumes reflect current indecision about so fundamental a matter, and they exhibit that tolerance which is of the very essence of human rights. Here the reader will find authoritative accounts of such topics as: the legal reality of human rights; historical foundations; fundamental principles (self-determination, equality, non-discrimination); the *positive* international law of human rights; the liberal and socialist list of rights; derogation *vs.* preservation of human rights in emergencies (underdevelopment, catastrophes, war); universal institutions (U.N., ILO, UNESCO); humanitarian law; and regional institutions (Council of Europe, O.A.S., Arab League, O.A.U., the Soviet bloc, and Asia).

1253 The internationalization of human rights.
David P. Forsythe. Lexington, MA: Lexington Books, 1991. 201p. bibliog.

Until the Universal Declaration of Human Rights in 1948, the bills of rights (called natural or civil rights) that citizens could rely upon for protection from their governments were national. The author, a political scientist with a lively sense of history ('I am using empiricism to arrive at norms'), argues in this book that human rights have acquired an international political character. That is why the *New York Times* could editorialize in 1989 that 'no dictatorship . . . could plausibly argue that human rights were purely an internal matter'. Forsythe knows that the new international regime does not formally negate state sovereignty nor, as in Europe, establish an international court of justice and a common authority to enforce human rights. Yet something new has arisen under the sun.

1254 The international protection of human rights.
Edited by David Evan T. Luard. New York: Praeger, 1967. 384p.

This older volume of specialized chapters fills a gap between the early international activity on behalf of human rights, immediately after World War II, and the renewed activity in anticipation of the end of the Cold War, beginning in the mid-1970s with the entry into force of the two Covenants and President Carter's human rights policy. Here one will find thoughtful retrospectives and expert articles on the Commission on Human Rights, the European Convention on Human Rights, the promotion of human rights by the U.N. General Assembly and Security Council, the role of NGOs, the model of the ILO, and the issue of 'domestic jurisdiction'.

1255 The lawful rights of mankind: an introduction to the international legal code of human rights.
Paul Sieghart. Oxford: Oxford University Press, 1985. 252p. bibliog.

The International Bill of Rights is usually said, in the United Nations context, to consist of the Universal Declaration of Human Rights, the International Covenant on Civil and Political Rights, its Optional Protocol, and the International Covenant of Economic, Social, and Cultural rights. The author takes a broader, more human point of view and includes within the international legal code of human rights *nine* instruments: the U.N. Charter, the Universal Declaration, the two International Covenants and Optional Protocol, the European Convention on Human Rights and its Protocols, the European Social Charter, the American Declaration of the Rights and Duties of Man, the American Convention on Human Rights, and the African Charter on Human and People's Rights. (When an Asian Charter is negotiated, it will be a tenth instrument.) Sieghart presents here a magisterial introduction for general readers to the new code. The book also complements his more learned reference work, *The international law of human rights* (1984). This is not a book of the philosophy of human rights, but of human rights *law* – what the law now is, not what people think it ought to be. He argues that *individuals*, under the international code, now have *rights against the states that exercise power over them*; and that states are obliged to respect these individual rights since the *legitimacy of government* depends on the *legality* of its acts.

1256 **Manual on human rights reporting.**
New York: United Nations, 1991. 203p. bibliog. (E.91.XIV.1. HR/PUB/91/1).
Addressed to government officials for preparing and submitting reports required for the implementation of international human rights treaties, this manual provides general guidance and then six specific chapters on the major treaties: the two Covenants, the International Convention on the Elimination of All Forms of Racial Discrimination, the International Convention on the Suppression and Punishment of the Crime of Apartheid, the Convention on the Elimination of All Forms of Discrimination against Women, and the Convention against Torture and Other Cruel, Inhuman, or Degrading Treatment or Punishment. It is not addressed to NGOs (though there is brief mention of them), nor to individuals; however, NGOs, individuals, and scholars will find the work helpful in understanding the existing reporting system.

1257 **New directions in human rights.**
Edited by Ellen L. Lutz, Hurst Hannum, and Kathryn Burke.
Philadelphia: University of Pennsylvania Press, 1989. 246p.
The 'new directions' evident to human rights lawyers in 1989, before the Cold War officially ended and before the sudden hopes for a new world order were dashed by the rise of long-suppressed ethnic and national conflicts, included: new norms and procedures (minority group rights, rights of women, an Asian human rights organization); protecting human rights in armed conflict; implementing international norms in domestic areas of jurisdiction (notably in the U.S.); and redressing past abuses of human rights. The final essay celebrates the 'creative and dynamic' leadership of law professor Frank Newman, who showed how one individual could influence the shape of international human rights law and actually help people caught in massive abuses, as in Chile. The essay contains a rare and informative critique of the U.N.'s disappointing 1503 procedure.

1258 **The obligation to implement the Covenant in domestic law.**
Oscar Schachter. In: The *International Bill of Rights: the Covenant of Civil and Political Rights*. Edited by Louis Henkin. New York: Columbia University Press, 1981, p.311-31.
This essay was written after President Carter sent the International Covenant on Civil and Political Rights to the Senate for ratification with recommended reservations to the effect that U.S. national law would not have to be modified on adherence to the treaty. The author here methodically dispels this illusion. In the process, he explains the primary means of implementation of international law. Article 2 plainly requires states-parties 'to adopt such legislation or other measures as may be necessary to give effect to the rights', and it enjoins them to grant judicial remedies to individuals who seek to exercise and vindicate their rights. 'Rights are thus brought from the lofty plane of international principles', concludes Schachter, 'to enforceable law in concrete cases.'

1259   **Official records of the Human Rights Committee.** [Vol. I:]
1982-84. [Vol. II:] **1985-86.** [Vol. III:] **1987-88.**
New York: United Nations, 1993. 307p. (E.93.XIV.3. CCPR/7).

The Human Rights Committee monitors compliance with the International Covenant
on Civil and Political Rights. These volumes contain consideration of reports
submitted by states-parties, documents, and matter published in yearbooks.

1260   **Peace as a human right.**
Philip Alston.   *Bulletin of Peace Proposals*, vol. 11 (December
1980), p.319-30.

The 'third generation' of human rights – after, first, political and civil rights, and,
second, economic, social, and cultural ones – were called by 1980 'solidarity rights'
or rights of peoples (as opposed to those of individuals). They included the right to
development and the right to peace, which is the subject of this instructive article.
Alston sees the new rights as rooted in the breakdown of the Bretton Woods and
United Nations systems as the superpowers seemed to be moving inexorably toward
World War III. 'Solidarity' would unite humanity since 'integration' was failing. He
prefers to call 'peace' a 'synthetic' rather than a 'new' right, and hence it should
enjoy the same protection and promotion as the other rights.

1261   **People matter: views on international human rights policy.**
Theo C. van Boven. Edited by Hans Thoolen.   Amsterdam:
Meulenhoff, 1982. 186p. bibliog.

Theo van Boven was Director of the U.N. Division of Human Rights from 1977 to
1982. He was the very type of an international public servant who struggles
vigourously for the human rights of people against, necessarily, their governments.
(The new High Commissioner for Human rights (1993), some may expect, will have
to have some of his qualities, or avoid his mistakes.) Van Boven was an open critic of
Argentina over the *desaparecidos* [those who have 'disappeared'], and he defended
the 'right to development' at a time when the NIEO was anathema in the North. This
book is an edition of his courageous speeches published by his friends within weeks
of his dismissal.

1262   **The politics of efficacy: the United nations and human rights.**
David P. Forsythe.   In: *Politics in the United Nations system.* Edited
by Lawrence S. Finkelstein.   Durham, NC: Duke University Press,
1988, p.246-73.

'Cosmopolitan human rights standards', mentioned in the Charter and first defined in
the Universal Declaration of Human Rights of 1948, have continued to expand
despite the Cold War. There has been a slow movement toward global institutions
that recognize the individual, in addition to the state, as a 'subject' of international
law. The Commission on Human Rights, for example, 'has become the world's first
intergovernmental body that regularly challenges sovereign nations to explain abusive
treatment of their own citizens'. Forsythe finds the political leadership to advance
human rights in Western industrial democracies (first the U.S., then Europe), then in
truly non-aligned Third World states. He treats the present international institutions
for the *protection* of human rights at length. Light for improvement can be found in
the European convention and ILO practice.

1263 **The politics of human rights.**
Edited by Paula R. Newberg. New York: New York University
Press for UNA–USA, 1980. 287p. bibliog. (Policy Studies Book).
This is another volume of essays written in response to the Congressional and
Presidential initiatives after 1974 that put human rights on the agenda of American
foreign policy. The approach here is not legalistic nor immediately focused on
national policy, but philosophical, in the tradition of long-range statesmanship. Here
one will find discussions of citizenship, the American debate about the U.S. place in
international life, and the relation between the individual and the state. The papers
then become more specific, ending with one on the statistical analysis of human rights
violations which may have had some influence on the State Department's *Country
reports* or Amnesty International's annual volumes.

1264 **Population and human rights.**
U.N. DIESA. New York: United Nations, 1990. 240p. bibliog.
(E.91.XIII.8. ST/ESA/SER.R/107).
This is a report on the third experts' meeting on population and human rights
(previous ones: 1974 and 1981). 'The purpose of the meeting was to assess the
current status of the relationship of fertility, mortality, and population growth to
human rights concerns and to recommend such actions as might be called for.' The
meeting was pursuant to the World Population Plan of Action. By 1989, there was
increasing concern to protect the individual from the side-effects of advances in
science and technology, whose contributions to medicine and public health have made
the population explosion possible. Topics discussed include population trends,
contraception, abortion, new bio-technologies, AIDS, terminal illness, euthanasia, and
'intergenerational equity'. Recommendations emphasized non-coercive family
planning, safeguards in medically assisted reproduction, and equitable governmental
social policy toward the ageing population. The report takes only 22 pages; the bulk
contains the expert papers.

1265 **The power of legitimacy among nations.**
Thomas M. Franck. New York: Oxford University Press, 1990.
303p.
It is said that states observe human rights law not because the law is enforced by a
superior sovereign, but because states recognize the 'legitimacy' of the law. What is
legitimacy? In an argument very much addressed to other legal scholars, Franck finds
legitimacy rooted in the evolving world community. It would be equivalent to *justice*,
if that community were united under a single set of moral principles. 'That [world]
community would have few rules', he argues, 'if the validity of each rule depended
on shared perceptions of justice.'

1266 **The quest for self-determination.**
Dov Ronen. New Haven, CT: Yale University Press, 1979.
144p.
Historically, there have been five forms of the idea of self-determination: nationalism,
class interests, minority rights, decolonization, and ethnic conflict. The latter is
especially relevant for secession movements after 1989. 'The outcome of ethnic
quests for self-determination will probably not be complete secession', Ronen writes,
'but . . . a new type of federation in which the wider economic entity provides a

framework for sociopolitically independent entities.' (This is not too far from Kropotkin's and Bakunin's 'anarchical federalism' of the last century.)

1267 **The rights of man today.**
Louis Henkin.   Boulder, CO: Westview, 1978. 173p.

This is a volume of lectures, whose grace and naturalness will be appreciated by readers seeking an introduction to the subject of human rights. The author takes a leaf from Thomas Paine's *The rights of man* (1792) to treat human rights as a resurgence of such principles as constitutionalism, the sovereignty of the people, and civil rights as delegations of power to a representative government returned as guarantees of freedom. Henkin sees human rights as 'above and beyond nations'.

1268 **The rights of peoples.**
Edited by James Crawford.   Oxford: Clarendon Press, 1988. 236p. bibliog.

One of the complaints of the United States, on withdrawing from UNESCO in 1984, was that it supported 'rights of peoples'. This third generation of rights was seen as growing out of the second generation of economic and social rights, which the Reagan administration also disputed. The rights of people include the 'right to self-determination', the 'right to development', the 'right to permanent sovereignty over natural resources', and the 'right to peace'. The editor does not regard the eighteenth century, which gave us the liberal individual rights, as closing the age of prophecy, but he asks if such novelties are not 'a new range of State rights in disguise'? He also asks if individual rights have any meaning apart from the security and sustenance of the communities in which individuals dwell. Hence, the conclusion is that peoples' rights are a link between the evolving non-statist human rights order and the older inter-state order, as well as a link between liberal, individual rights and socialist, economic ones. (In federalist terms, they are the rights of national peoples in their rudimentary legal status of world citizens.)

1269 **The right of self-determination: historical and current development on the basis of United Nations instruments.**
Sub-commission on the Prevention of Discrimination and Protection of Minorities. Aureliu Cristescu, rapporteur.   New York: United Nations, 1981. 125p. (E.80.XIV.3).

The principle of 'equal rights and self-determination of peoples' (U.N. Charter, Article 1(2)) has been interpreted in an increasingly progressive spirit since Woodrow Wilson's time, and it now can be taken as the transposition of human rights to the collective level as the premier 'right of peoples'. Hence, international intervention is increasingly permitted to protect such a right.

1270 **Selected decisions under the Optional Protocol.**
International Covenant on Civil and Political Rights. Human Rights Committee.   New York: United Nations, 1989. 246p. (E.89.XIV.1. CCPR/C/OP/2).

A year after the International Covenant on Civil and Political Rights entered into force (1976), the Human Rights Committee (not to be confused with the U.N. Commission on Human Rights) began its supervisory work under the Optional

Protocol, which permits *individuals* who claim to be victims of violations of the human rights *by a state-party to the Protocol* to send communications to the Committee. In effect, the Optional Protocol guarantees the right of petition. (States not parties to the Protocol, however, do not consent to receiving, via the Committee, such petitions. The Committee's powers, moreover, extend only to communication to the state concerned and, in extreme and persistent cases, publication.) This volume and the one before it (1984) document the historic and pioneering cases of such international petitions for redress of grievances.

1271 **Self-determination in the new world order.**
Morton H. Helprin, David J. Scheffer, and Patricia L. Small.
Washington, DC: Carnegie Endowment for International Peace, 1992.
178p. bibliog.

'Self-determination' – a term introduced to world politics by Woodrow Wilson – after the Cold War became the principle invoked by states seceding from federations or by ethnic groups aiming at sovereignty of their own in the Soviet Union, Yugoslavia, Czechoslovakia, and even Canada. The United Nations, in accordance with Article 2(7) of the charter, historically did not intervene in civil wars of self-determination, as in Nigeria in 1967 or Pakistan in 1971. But by the 1990s, the world community had developed to the point where 'national sovereignty' could no longer convincingly be invoked as a bar to intervention by a powerful state or a coalition of states under U.N. auspices. By the early 1990s, there were active movements in more than sixty countries to achieve independence, autonomy, or greater rights. The book is an examination of the confusion about the right of self-determination and a prescription for proper U.S. and U.N. policies. The authors establish standards for evaluating claims to self-determination. They argue against policies of aloofness or blind support for an existing government, in favour of 'early action to promote resolution', which in the Yugoslav case would mean seeking some new 'federated system'. Some of the U.S. devices are monitoring, diplomatic intervention, and economic sanctions, but the authors prefer that U.N. oversight and ultimately U.N. military enforcement be brought into play. U.S. leadership to bring about a 'new world order' will require, they conclude, an active U.S. foreign policy, mid-way between isolationism and the interventionism of the Cold War. The legitimate course is cooperation with the United Nations.

1272 **A short history of United Nations documents on human rights.**
Louis B. Sohn. In: *The United Nations and human rights: eighteenth report of the Commission to Study the Organization of Peace.* Dobbs Ferry, NY: Oceana, 1968, p.39-186.

This is an excellent short history of the basic U.N. documents on human rights – the U.N. Charter (1945), the Universal Declaration of Human Rights (1948), and the two Covenants (signed 1966; in force 1976). Sohn's history covers the formative period from 1945 to 1967. Sohn is especially helpful in explaining why the U.N. was vested with powers to 'promote respect for human rights', why the declaration of principles was separated from the binding convention to enforce the rights, and why the covenants were divided into one on traditional liberal, civil and political rights, and a second on socialist, economic, social, and cultural ones. He particularly explains why the system of implementation under the committee provided for in the Covenant on Civil and Political Rights was so very much weaker than the court provided in the European Convention on Human Rights and Fundamental Freedoms. With a view to the future, he discusses the necessity, if more than two conventions on human rights were negotiated (there are now twenty-two binding treaties among ninety-five instruments), for a 'cumulative effect' and for 'priorities among implementation procedures' in order to avoid possible conflicts of law. 'In each case the individual should have the benefit of the instrument which gives him greater protection against governmental interference with his rights.' On the other hand, recourse to the U.N. Human Rights Committee is clearly made a last resort, after prior recourse to domestic remedies and other institutions, like the ILO or European Court of Human Rights.

1273   **Sovereignty and human rights in contemporary international law.**
W. Michael Reisman.   *American Journal of International Law*, vol. 84 (1990), p.866-76.

This is a particularly clear and authoritative analysis of sovereignty. Sovereignty has passed through several incarnations: as the locus of power when medieval Christendom broke up, as the authority of dynastic kings, as the consent of the people. The sovereignty of the people was recognized as the source of political legitimacy by the American and French Revolutions, but not until the end of World War II was it recognized in international law. The Universal Declaration of Human rights provided in Article 21(3): 'The will of the people shall be the basis of the authority of government. . .'. Today, an aggressor or a usurper who claims to be exercising the sovereignty of the state will no longer be recognized under international law, though cases like Kampuchea are still exceptions to the rule. The Soviet invasion of Afghanistan or the Iraqi agression against Kuwait, on the other hand, have been rejected because of the rule. Abuse of human rights, as in the Chinese government's massacre in Tiananmen Square, Reisman interprets as a 'violation of Chinese sovereignty'. He knows that fair elections are the only way to determine the 'wishes of the people', so he predicts much forward and back motion while sovereignty is 'updated' or *actualisée* by reference to human rights. 'Centralized institutions' at the world level will ultimately be required. Pending so remote a U.N. reform, Reisman calls for implementation of existing procedures for redressing violations of individuals' human rights.

1274   **Status of the individual and contemporary international law: promotion, protection, and restoration of human rights at national, regional, and international levels.**
Erica-Irene A. Daes, special rapporteur.   New York: United Nations; Geneva: Centre for Human Rights, 1992. 68p. bibliog. (E.91.XIV.3).

After a review of municipal law as compared with international law, and of international law particularly in the era of human rights and the Nuremberg Principles, the author concludes that, while the status of the individual as a subject of international law remains controversial, it has been theoretically and practically demonstrated that 'the individual is a bearer of international rights and responsibilities'. She shows that the sovereignty of the state is giving way again, as when natural law was recognized (up to the middle of the nineteenth century), to the rights of the individual. The U.N. is his or her protector. Readers in search of succinct statement of the new doctrine will find it here.

1275   **The U.N. and human rights: more than a whimper, less than a roar.**
Tom J. Farer.   In: *United Nations, divided world.* Edited by Adam Roberts and Benedict Kingsbury.   Oxford: Oxford University Press, 1988, p.95-138.

Here is a highly informative article on the history, standards, and implementation (protection and promotion) of human rights by the U.N. system. It contains a rare clear diagram of the non-centralized system of commissions, sub-commissions, committees, working groups, special rapporteurs, centres, subsidiary bodies, and trust funds. The author draws particular attention to the slow progress of the 1503 procedure, which permits *individuals* and NGOs to charge states with abuse of their human rights and fundamental freedoms. Future progress, Farer concludes, will depend on the 'not always comfortable coalition of liberal and socialist ideologies'. He adds: 'Despite all the horror that surrounds us, I believe . . . that we are in a new era.'

1276   **The U.N. Commission on Human rights.**
Howard Tolley, Jr.   Boulder, CO: Westview, 1987. 300p. bibliog.

The U.N. Charter did not include an international bill of rights. But it provided in Article 68 for the Commission on Human Rights, which was duly established in 1946. Over the next two decades, led by Western liberal states, the commission concentrated on fashioning and promoting human rights law, starting with the Universal Declaration on Human Rights; after about 1967, as a Third World majority emerged, it shifted to enforcement activities and to running controversy ofer a 'third generation' of human rights. (The first and second generations were political and economic rights, enshrined in the two covenants.) This book is an excellent history of the commission from 1947 to 1986. The author judiciously concludes: 'During its first forty years, the Commission has contributed to the inadequate but nevertheless incremental growth of supranational authority capable of scrutinizing practices that had previously been exclusively within governments' sovereign jurisdiction.'

1277   **UNESCO procedure for dealing with human rights violations.**
Philip Alston.   *Santa Clara Law Review*, vol. 20 (1980), p.665-96.

A new procedure of 1978 allows individuals, groups, NGOs, and states to petition UNESCO on alleged violations of human rights, provided that the petitioner is either a victim or a witness. Decision 3.3 of the UNESCO Executive Board promises to remedy some of the U.N.'s less effective procedures, particularly the Optional Protocol and the 1503 procedure. The author surveys the role of UNESCO in protecting and promoting human rights, examines the new communications procedure, and discusses problems that may affect its success. The applicable rights are itemized, and the practical conduct of a petition is described. This is not the first provision to grant the individual the right of petition to an international authority for a redress of grievances against a states, but it is another. Alston argues that victims will best be served by a 'diversity of approaches'.

1278   **United Nations action in the field of human rights.**
New York: United Nations, 1988. 359p. (E.88.XIV.2.
ST/HR/2/Rev.3).

This is an official history and exposition of the activities of the United Nations in the field of human rights. It is divided into two parts: first, the constitutional measures available (e.g., the human rights clauses of the Charter, measures to put a stop to violations); second, actual procedures taken and existing (e.g., the handling of communications concerning human rights, the 1503 procedure). Persons new to the field must not expect the international protection and promotion of human rights to be a simple matter; sophisticated readers will find this large volume a model of compactness and exactitude. Individuals seeking a redress of grievances will find this work one of the few guides available. A short section deals with 'Improving the capacity of the United Nations system to take urgent action in cases of serious violations of human rights'.

1279   **The United Nations and human rights: a critical appraisal.**
Edited by Philip Alston.   Oxford: Clarendon Press, 1992. 765p.
bibliog.

Prepared in time for the 1993 World Conference on Human Rights in Vienna, this substantial volume examines what its agenda called an evaluation of the 'effectiveness of the methods and mechanisms used by the United Nations in the field of human rights' and the formulation of 'concrete recommendations for improving' that effectiveness. Here readers will find specialized chapters on the U.N. General Assembly, Ecosoc, Commission on Human Rights, Sub-commission on Prevention of Discrimination and Protection of Minorities, Commission on the Status of Women, Security Council, Committee of the Elimination of Racial Descrimination, Human Rights Committee, Committee on the Elimination of Discrimination against Women, Committee on Economic, Social, and Cultural Rights, Committee against Torture, the U.N. Secretariat, and the ILO. The final chapter is on the most important future problem of 'human rights co-ordination within the U.N. system'. Its author, Klaus T. Samson, makes many pertinent suggestions for a decentralized system without a supreme authority; one of them, supporting a suggestion by Theodor Meron, is 'bringing together in a single body responsibility for supervising the implementation of a number of conventions'.

1280   **United Nations and human rights: a critical appraisal.**
Theo C. van Boven.   In: *U.N. law/fundamental rights: two topics in international law.* Edited by Antonio Cassese.   Alphen aan den Rijn, The Netherlands: Sijthoff & Noordhoff, 1979, p.119-35.

The author surveys U.N. action in the field of human rights through its phases of standard setting, promotion, and protection. He answers criticisms that the U.N. neglects unjust social and economic structures at the root of most human rights violations, is selective and biased (condemnations of Israel but not of Uganda, Chile but not Guatemala), anti-democratic (pro-socialist), and too slow to really help people. The root cause, which no state seems to wish to remedy, is 'lack of authority' in the world organization. Van Boven concludes with modest proposals to keep open 'channels of communication'.

1281　**The United Nations and human rights, 1945-1985.**
　　　David P. Forsythe.　*Political Science Quarterly*, vol. 100 (1985),
　　　p.249-69.

This is a rapid overview of U.N. involvement in human rights up to the point when some sort of 'U.N. supervision' was operating. In an observant political analysis, Forsythe finds five factors responsible for the change: states' policies (sometimes cancelling to the benefit of genuinely cosmopolitan policy); NGO activism; the Secretary-General's patient leadership; uninstructed individuals on the various expert supervisory committees; and world public opinion. The significance of the change in the short term is rather small; in the long term, it is 'socializing' states toward the cosmopolitan U.N. standards, and it is dispensing the 'stamp of legitimacy' on those who conform. In the long term, moreover, Forsythe predicts the greatest effect will be felt by authoritarian (non-Marxist) states – a prediction that ten years later seems to have come true even for the Marxist states.

1282　**The United States, the United Nations, and human rights: the**
　　　Eleanor Roosevelt and Jimmy Carter eras.
　　　A. Glenn Mower, Jr.　Westport, CT: Greenwood, 1979. 215p.
　　　bibliog. (Studies in Human Rights, No. 4).

This earlier work (compare Mower's *Human rights and American foreign policy,* item no. 1230), is an examination of the precedent of American leadership in the cause of human rights under Eleanor Roosevelt – the moving spirit behind the Universal Declaration of Human Rights in 1948 – for the Carter administration after 1976. In the process, the author thoroughly compares the views of 'realists' and 'idealists' for the conduct of American foreign policy, and he himself necessarily and practically comes to a rather 'mixed' view. Mower concludes, in the midst of the Carter presidency, that the human rights policy had resulted in the freeing of some political prisoners in other lands, that human rights had become institutionalized in Congress and the executive branch, and that it was firmly seated in international organizations like the U.N.

1283　**Universal human rights in theory and practice.**
　　　Jack Donnelly.　Ithaca, NY: Cornell University Press, 1989. 295p.
　　　bibliog.

This is a largely philosophical (Donnelly would say theoretical) account of human rights. The author admits that human rights are historically conditioned – there is no eternal list of such innate human characteristics, like that of the five physical senses. Yet they are 'strong', if not radical, universal moral and political freedoms and entitlements, which do not require us to accept the claims of radical cultural relativists. The rights to life, liberty, and security of person are fully deserving of respect in Islamic countries or in traditional India or China. Freedoms of speech and assembly are a bit more relative. Readers who are puzzled about the nature of 'rights', will find this an informed and reflective account. In the last part of the book, Donnelly sets out the international and regional human rights regimes, which students will find broadly informative. He concludes realistically that, 'in an international system where government is national rather than global, human rights are by definition principally a national matter.'

1284   **U.S. ratification of the human rights treaties, with or without reservations?**
Edited by Richard B. Lillich.   Charlottesville: University Press of Virginia, for the International Human Rights Law Group, 1981. 202p. bibliog.

In 1978, President Carter sent to the Senate four major human rights treaties, breaking a long hiatus: the International Covenant on Civil and Political Rights (minus its Optional Protocol); the International Covenant on Economic, Social, and Cultural Rights; the International Convention on the Elimination of All Forms of Racial Discrimination; and the American Convention on Human Rights. However, he also sent a number of declarations, understandings, and reservations, which on their face seemed to negate the effect of the treaties should they become part of the supreme law of the land. One declaration (legally not as strong as a reservation) for each treaty provided that it was 'not self-executing', and hence not directly enforceable in U.S. courts without specific national enabling legislation. This volume of legal essays examines the question whether the 'reservations' (including the declarations and understandings) evaded the legal obligations to bring U.S. law into conformity with the international treaties, or were a 'political' device, of little technical or long-term significance, designed to break the tradition of Senate opposition and thus finally bring the United States fully into the international human rights order. Most of the professors present at a conference on the subject took the first alternative; representatives of the Carter State Department took the second. It is significant that the Genocide Convention was not ratified until similar reservations were added in 1986. Similarly, reservations made possible ratification of the Covenant on Civil and Political Rights in 1993. But haunting memories of the Senate battle over reservations to the League of Nations Covenant in 1919-20 continue to rankle.

1285   **The Vienna Declaration and Programme of Action, June 1993.**
World Conference on Human Rights. Opening statement by U.N. Secretary-General Boutros Boutros-Ghali.   New York: United Nations, 1993. 71p. (DPI/1394).

In 1993, representatives of 171 states and of some 800 NGOs gathered in Vienna to recommit the peoples of the world to the strengthening of human rights. 'The Vienna Declaration and Programme of Action, which is presented in this booklet in its entirety, marks the culmination of a long process of review and debate over the current status of human rights machinery in the world. It also marks the beginning of a renewed effort to strengthen and further implement the body of human rights instruments that have been painstakingly constructed on the foundation of the Universal Declaration of Human Rights since 1948.' Two of the convention's major recommendations were to establish a Special Rapporteur on Violence against Women and also to establish a High Commissioner for Human Rights. The Secretary-General in his opening address saw human rights as both 'absolute timeless injunctions; and 'a moment in the development of history'. He did not see a conflict between human rights and national sovereignty – understood as legitimate power – but he warned against 'a cynical approach according to which the international dimension of human rights is nothing more than an ideological cover for the *Realpolitik* of States'. Use of 'sovereignty' as a cover for domestic abuses would be, he argued, 'condemned by history'. For the improvement of respect for human rights, he emphasized their universality, guarantees, and democracy. He particularly emphasized the link between sustainable development and promotion of democracy.

1286 **Yearbook of the Human Rights Committee, 1983-1984.**
New York: United Nations, 1991. 2 vols. (E.88.XIV.8. CCPR/4).
The Human Rights Committee monitors compliance with the International Covenant on Civil and Political Rights. This annual volume contains its summary records and reports of states-parties under Article 40, which requires such reports. (Reports under Article 41, which permits states to complain about one another, are rarely published. Individual petitions under the Optional Protocol are never published here.)

1287 **Yearbook on human rights for 1988.**
New York: United Nations, 1992. 150p. (E.92.XIV.2).
This annual volume, in Part I, reports the work of the U.N. General Assembly, Ecosoc, Commission on Human Rights, and Sub-commission on Prevention of Discrimination and Protection of Minorities. In Part II, the activities of the various supervisory committees (e.g., the Human Rights Committee) are reported. In Part III, national compliance (reported by themselves) with international treaties is reported.

Monitoring human rights violations in the 1980s.
See item no. 375.

Non-governmental organizations at the United Nations.
See item no. 377.

The role of international nongovernmental organizations in the implementation of human rights.
See item no. 379.

Sisyphus endures: the international human rights NGO.
See item no. 380.

Humanitarian good offices in international law.
See item no. 447.

International human rights and international education.
See item no. 907.

Human rights and scientific and technological development.
See item no. 933.

Women's rights

U.N. Decade for Women: Equality, Development, Peace (1975-85)
Convention on the Elimination of All Forms of Discrimination against Women (CEDAW)
U.N. Centre for Social Development and Humanitarian Affairs (U.N. CSDHA, Vienna)

1288 **Compendium of statistics and indicators on the situation of women, 1986. Recueil de statistiques et d'indicateurs sur la situation des femmes.**
U.N. DIESA. New York: United Nations, 1989. 592p. (Social Statistics and Indicators, Series K, No. 5. E/F.88.XVII.6. ST/ESA/STAT/SER.K/5).
This large volume of statistical data is one of the fruits of the U.N. Decade for Women: Equality, Development, Peace (1975-85). It is the database for the World Plan of Action. Topics covered: population composition, households and families, economic participation (including women not 'economically active'), national and household income and expenditure, education, health, housing, political participation, criminal justice. Data are given per country.

1289 **Compendium of international conventions concerning the status of women.**
U.N. Centre for Social Development and Humanitarian Affairs (U.N. CSDHA, Vienna). New York: United Nations, 1988. 186p. (E.88.IV.3. ST/SCDHA/3).
There are four U.N. conventions specifically dealing with the rights of women, and four similar ILO conventions. An additional fourteen contain relevant provisions. Probably the most important of the first group is the Convention on the Elimination of All Forms of Discrimination against Women. This volume contains the text of all these conventions for quick reference; lists of parties and statements of all-important *reservations* are appended.

1290 **The Nairobi foreward-looking strategies for the advancement of women.** *As adopted by the World Conference to Review and Appraise the Achievements of the United Nations Decade for Women: Equality, Development, and Peace, Nairobi, Kenya, 15-26 July 1985.*
New York: United Nations, 1989. 89p. (DPI/926-09859).
Here are recommendations adopted by consensus by 157 nations represented at the final conference of the U.N. Decade for Women. They are addressed to governments, international and regional organizations, NGOs, men, and women in a 'spirit of solidarity'. The *strategies* include changing national laws to recognize women's

equality and their rights, admitting women to participation in policy-making and to management in economic development, allowing them full access to development programmes, monitoring progress and gathering statistics (very important for the next stage), recognizing women's informal and invisible economic contributions (especially in the calculation of GNP), educating children, women, and men 'to redress the imbalance imposed by centuries of discrimination'. (All are normative – none obligatory.) The strategies were conceived within the 'context of the broader goals and objectives of a new international economic order' (NIEO). Significant dissents by the United States and other developed countries were made to the fundamental documents and the programmes of action for the implementation of the recommendations by the year 2000 (paragraph 35). The U.N. Commission on the Status of Women monitors progress.

1291 **Statistics and indicators on women in Africa, 1986.**
Statistiques et indicateurs sur les femmes en Afrique.
U.N. DIESA. New York: United Nations, 1989. 225p. (Social Statistics and Indicators, Series K, No. 7. E/F.89.XV.11. ST/ESA/STAT/SER.K/7).

These statistics have been drawn from the *Compendium* above (item no. 1288) 'to provide a convenient reference for analysts, planners, and policy-makers specifically concerned with the African region in the context of the United Nations Programme of Action for African Economic Recovery and Development, 1986-1990'.

1292 **Staying alive: women, ecology, and development.**
Vandana Shiva. Foreword by Rajni Kothari. London: Zed Books, 1988. 224p.

It may be, as Rajni Kothari says in his foreword, that this book sometimes falls short of seeing 'that the struggle for femininity is a struggle for a certain basic principle of perceiving life, a philosophy of being . . . that can serve not just women but all human beings'. But readers who wonder why the natural environment continues to be systematically destroyed will find a coherent and impassioned answer here. The author regards both Western science and economic development as 'patriarchies' bent only on private profit and the conquest of nature. Shiva is particularly acute in her analysis of the assumptions of recent official development aid. Even the U.N. Decade for Women (1975-85) is exposed as based on the error, not of women's inadequate 'participation' in 'development', but on their *enforced and asymmetric participation*. The bulk of the book is an exposition of the 'feminist principle' in nature and of Indian women's quietly heroic efforts to preserve the environment against 'development'.

1293 **Women, households, and change.**
Edited by Eleonora Masini and Susan Stratigos. Prologue by Elise Boulding. Tokyo: UNU Press, 1991. 241p. (E.91.III.A.3. HGA-3/ UNUP-766).

One of the major discoveries of the Women's Decade was that women who work in households without pay are not considered in the 'labour force' according to orthodox economics. This book is a sensitive report on an international project on Households, Gender, and Age supported by the U.N. University. Its purpose was 'to provide material that would change the way policy makers approached development planning

433

by providing a more realistic picture of the people and resources involved'. It includes case-studies from Colombia, Brazil, Argentina, Chile, Sri Lanka, Kenya, and China. Development has an entirely different aspect when looked at from the perspective of women. Under 'development', lower-class women experience a change for the worse, as men leave for the cities and women stay back to care for their children. The fewer middle-class and upper-class women enjoy the benefits of modernization – education, better jobs, fertility control – but unemployment will hit all women first. Women everywhere work 'two jobs'. The implication is that, if women were effectively brought into the development process, poverty would be ended and the old social order of patriarchy overthrown.

1294 **Women in development: a progress report on the World Bank initiative.**
Barbara Herz and Götz Schreiber. Washington, DC: World Bank, 1990. 32p.

After the Women's Decade (1975-85), the World Bank launched an 'initiative to integrate attention to women in development through its analytical work and lending'. In effect, the Bank began to remedy the invisibility of women in economic accounting. By 1989, it is reported, one out five Bank projects assisted women. This brief work defines women's contributions to development and discusses lending operations with attention to women. Thirteen cases illustrate the projects.

1295 **Women in the world economy: an INSTRAW study.**
Susan P. Joekes. New York: Oxford University Press, 1987. 161p. bibliog.

Since 1983, the U.N. International Research and Training Institute for the Advancement of Women (INSTRAW) has been studying the 'interlinkages between the macro- and micro-levels of the economy and their impact on the role and position of women'. The *Forward-looking strategies* agreed to at Nairobi in 1985 (see item no. 1290) gave impetus to the work. This study, based on technical papers, is the first analysis of the interlinkages between women and international economy. It passes over national research findings and social and cultural implications for the 'restrictive approach of traditional economic analysis'. The author is fully aware of women's unpaid contribution to the economy, but she does monitor the sexual division of labour by measuring women's participation in the labour force, partly because statistics exist, partly because focus on that participation 'opens up to women an area where a broader range of skills can be developed than in family and household labor'. Policy-makers will find this a most serious book.

1296 **Women of the Mediterranean.**
Edited by Monique Gadant. Translated by A.M. Berrett. London: Zed Books, 1986. 196p.

Third World women want change, but not necessarily to become like women of the First World. 'Corsican women dream of leaving Corsica; but they do not want to become Frenchwomen.' Women, who have barely been admitted to the development process, are now beginning to fully realize the potentialities of their economic liberation. This is a book about 'the ways in which feminist ideologies are articulated with the various social realities' in such countries as Turkey, Lebanon, Palestine, Iran, Egypt, Tunisia, Algeria, Spain, Corsica, southern France, Yugoslavia, and south

Italy. Rossana Rossanda contributes the concluding chapter on whether feminism and machismo can ever unite in what Herbert Marcuse called 'androgynous' culture.

1297 **The work of CEDAW: reports of the Committee on the [Elimination of Discrimination against Women (CEDAW).**
[Vol. 1:] **1982-85.** [Vol. II:] **1986-87.**
U.N. CSDHA.   New York: United Nations, 1989-90. 744p.
(E.89.IV.4. ST/CSDHA/5); 502p. (E.90.IV.4. ST/CSDHA/5/Corr.1).
CEDAW is the monitoring body for the Convention on the Elimination of All Forms of Discrimination against Women (signed in 1979; in force, 1981). These volumes are the public record of the committee. The intention is 'to make this international treaty a living instrument'. (As of 1989, forty-five states were parties to the convention, including the U.K., but not the U.S.A.) By its second session (1983), CEDAW reviewed its first reports from states-parties, one of which was the U.S.S.R. Readers who wish to follow the committee's work will have to turn to the country of interest within the volume containing that country's report.

1298 **1989 World survey on the role of women in development.**
U.N. CSDHA.   New York: United Nations, 1984- . quinquennial.
397p. bibliog. (E.89.IV.2. ST/CSDHA/6).
This analytical volume, like the *Compendium of statistics* (item no. 1288), is also a fruit of the Women's Decade. The first survey (1984) concentrated on women's contribution to agriculture; this update provides an overview plus five sectoral analyses: on households (effect of the debt crisis), agriculture, industry, services, and the informal sector. The main trend is a 'differential' hardship for women, yet it is admitted that the data, which are incomplete, are not always negative. 'Rather, there is a complex interrelationship between economic changes, public economic policy, pre-existing inequalities, and advancement of women.' The issues emerging in the medium term are women's participation in economic decision-making, maintenance of of both economic role and family life, and involvement in preservation of the environment.

1299 **The world's women, 1970-1990: trends and statistics.**
U.N. DIESA, CSDHA, UNICEF, UNFPA, UNIFEM.   New York: United Nations, 1991. 120p. bibliog. (Social Statistics and Indicators, Series K, No. 8. E.90.XVII.3. ST/ESA/STAT/SER.K/8).
This is still another statistical and analytical volume growing out of the Women's Decade. The difference is that this one is not as spare as the *Compendium* (item no. 1288), nor as bureaucratic as the *World survey* (item no. 1298). This volume, very attractively laid out, is designed to communicate to busy people what will be useful to know to advance the cause of women. 'It provides concerned women and men with information they can use to inform people everywhere about how much women contribute to economic life, political life, and family life, and to support appeals to persuade public and private decision makers to change policies that are unfair to women.' Here the chapters are not sectoral but more related to women's actual lives: families, leadership, education, health, childbearing, housing, and women's work and the economy.

Preservation of the environment

U.N. Environment Programme (UNEP)
U.N. Economic Commission for Europe (U.N. ECE)
U.N. Conference on Environment and Development (UNCED, 1992)
Commission on Sustainable Development (CSD)

1300 **Acid rain: an issue in Canadian-American relations.**
John E. Carroll.   Washington, DC: National Planning Association
for Canadian–American Committee and C.D. Howe Institute, 1982.
80p. bibliog. (Report No. 194).

Acid rain is an international problem for the United States and Canada. The author
finds that 84 per cent of the SO_2 emissions and 92 per cent of the NO_x emissions were
caused by U.S. powerplants, smelters, and motor vehicles. He reviews the polariza-
tion of the two federal governments, then proposes a 'basic bilateral agreement' that
has some of the elements of the judgement of Solomon. That these two friendly
developed countries could not solve this mutual problem during the 1980s indicates
the difficulty of cooperation to preserve the environment.

1301 **ACCIS Guide to United Nations Information Sources.**
Advisory Committee for the Co-ordination of Information Systems
(ACCIS) in collaboration with the Programme Activity Centre of the
International Environmental Information System (INFOTERRA
PAC) of the United Nations Environment Programme (UNEP).
New York: United Nations, 1988. 141p. (GV.E.87.O.6).

This reference work helps the U.N. to function as a focus for environmental concerns
of states, international organizations, NGOs, and citizens. The guide contains sources
of information on the environment within thirty-four organizations of the U.N. system
(Administrative Committee on Coordination to World Tourism Organization) and
within selected non-U.N. organizations (World Wide Fund for Nature). Sources are
classified as comprehensive, agricultural, aquatic, atmospheric, demographic, energy,
human settlements, industrial, transportation, natural resources, pollution, and
statistical. For instance, here one can find out where to get information about the
Global Environment Monitoring System (GEMS), which has set up a regional
environmental information network in support of global strategies of preventive and
remedial action.

1302 **Agenda 21: Programme of Action for Sustainable Development.**
Rio Declaration on Environment and Development.
Statement of Forest Principles.
United Nations. Foreword by Maurice Strong.   New York: United
Nations, 1993. 294p. (E.93.I.11).

The Rio Declaration is a short statement of twenty-seven principles to guide nation-
states and peoples toward sustainable development. Agenda 21 is a much longer

programme of action. The Statement of Forest Principles is a preliminary to final agreement on a treaty. (All that is missing here is the text of the Climate Treaty and the Biodiversity Treaty. All five constitute what are called the Rio documents.) The documents were agreed to by more than 178 governments. Except for the two treaties, the documents are legally not binding, but, like the Universal Declaration of Human Rights and the various programmes to protect and promote human rights, they represent international consensus and will surely guide voluntary action. Agenda 21 is particularly worth close attention for practical action. It consists of four sections: social and economic dimensions; conservation and management of resources for development; strengthening the role of major groups; and means of implementation. Maurice Strong calls the process that Agenda 21 inaugurates a 'second industrial revolution', an 'ecological revolution that is essential in order to shift the world onto a new pathway to a more secure, sustainable, and equitable future'.

1303   **Agenda 21, Rio Declaration, and Forest Principles.**
New York: United Nations, 1992. 1 vol. (E.92.I.16.
A/CONF.151/4(Parts I-IV); A/CONF.151/5; A/CONF.151/6).
This is the unabridged text of the above three Rio documents as of April 1992, one month before UNCED. It is now an historical document, but readers who must refer to the internationally agreed text will find it here.

1304   **Annual report of the Executive Director, 1991.**
United Nations Environment Programme.   Nairobi, Kenya: UNEP, 1992. 213p.
This is the official annual report of UNEP, including financial and project information. In 1991, UNEP spent $3 million preparing for UNCED. It also established a U.N. Centre for Urgent Environmental Assistance and, with the cooperation of UNDP and the World Bank, the Global Environment Facility.

1305   **Building a sustainable society.**
Lester Brown.   New York: Norton for Worldwatch Institute, 1981. 433p.
'We have not inherited the earth from our fathers', is one of Lester Brown's sayings; 'we are borrowing it from our children.' The idea of a sustainable economy was not new in the Brundtland report (1987) (item no. 153). It had been talked about for years in books like this one. Readers will find this book by one of the founders of the environmental movement engaging and informative. The first half describes the crisis of disappearing cropland, biological species, and fossil fuels under the pressure of growing population; the second, the solutions of a 'gradual awakening', conservation, solar energy, 'simpler life styles among the affluent', leadership during the transition, the contributions of corporations, religions, universities, and the public, and the new importance of *equity* as economic growth settles into steady state. Brown brings in U.N. agencies at many points.

1306   **Chainsaws in tropical forests: a manual.**
FAO/ILO.   Rome: FAO, 1980. 96p. (Training Series No. 2).
As part of their educational and training activities – and typical of technology transfer to developing countries – the FAO and ILO here provide the complete guide to

cutting down the rainforests with chainsaws! The presentation is entirely technical, without the slightest mention of the value of rainforests to biodiversity, climate, or sustainable development.

1307   **Climate crisis: the societal impacts associated with the 1982-83 worldwide climate anomalies. The Lugano report.**
Edited by Michael Glantz, Richard Katz, and Maria Krenz.   Nairobi, Kenya: UNEP; Boulder, CO: National Center for Atmospheric Research, 1987. 105p. maps. (E.87.III.D.9).

El Niño is a periodic shift in the ocean currents off Peru which in 1972-73 destroyed the anchoveta fishery. It is typical of droughts, floods, and other climate anomalies that are not well understood and hence contribute to fears about the still-larger phenomenon of global warming. This report is based on expert papers presented at a converence in Lugano, Switzerland, in 1985. No strict causal connections were found, but a 'baseline' was established for further climate studies, and certain 'hypothesized teleconnections' were proposed.

1308   **Code of conduct on accidental pollution of transboundary inland waters.**
New York: United Nations, 1990. 50p. (E.90.II.E.28).

Addressed to industrial engineers and environmentalists, this booklet contains definitions and measures to prevent, control, and clean up accidental water pollution.

1309   **In defence of the earth: the basic texts on the environment – Founex, Stockholm, Cocoyoc.**
Nairobi: UNEP, 1981. 119p. (Executive Series No. 1).

This is a valuable reprint edition of three fundamental documents for the U.N.'s approach to 'environmental management', dating from 1971, 1972, and 1974 respectively. There is a hint here that linking development to preservation of the environment might be an alternative strategy to the more confrontational NIEO, for cooperation on the environment would solve a largely Northern problem, while enabling the South to avoid the mistakes and distortions of development in the past. Twenty years later, the seeds planted in these documents were producing a rich harvest.

1310   **In defense of Earth: international protection of the biosphere.**
Lynton K. Caldwell.   Bloomington, IN: Indiana University Press, 1972. 295p.

This book is typical of the environmental movement at the time of the first U.N. conference on the environment at Stockholm in 1972. The book s broadly philosophical and hence may state principles that twenty years later had come to be taken for granted. The ecology movement is not the work of governments, but of people. The idea of the 'biosphere' was developed by a Russian geologist (V.I. Vernadsky) and a French palaeontologist (Pierre Teilhard de Chardin), who understood life in the long term. The movement is something of a successor to Marxism, for it is based on science, yet is inspired by a religious conviction to accept moral responsibility to shape history.

1311 **The diplomacy of acid rain: the North American experience in global perspective.**
John Roberts. In: *Negotiating world order: the artisanship and architecture of global diplomacy.* Edited by Alan K. Henrikson. Wilmington, DE: Scholarly Resources, 1986, p.19-32.
This is a clear introduction to environmental policy, using the Canadian effort to move the United States to undertake long-term planning (not punitive regulation) to stop the industrial emissions that cause acid rain. The International Joint Commission, established in 1909 to settle disputes in U.S.–Canadian boundary waters, is seen as a model for a new kind of environmental management system throughout the world.

1312 **The Earth Summit's Agenda for Change: a plain language version of Agenda 21 and the other Rio agreements.**
Michael Keating. Geneva: Centre for Our Common Future, 1993. 70p. (Available in English, French, German, Italian, and Russian. Centre, 52 rue des Paquis, 1201 Geneva, Switzerland.)
This attractive and informative booklet is ideal for bringing the problems, the solutions, and the joy of the U.N. Conference on Environment and Development to the public. It reprints the Rio Declaration on Environment and Development, whose twenty-seven principles will guide humanity for years to come. It also sketches the background and the content, often with clear diagrams and tables, of the other four Rio documents: Agenda 21, the Convention on Climate Change, the Convention on Biological Diversity, and the Statement on Forest Conservation. The whole world over the last half century is its oyster. Readers will not find here the nation-state held up as the supreme reality. The world is beginning to discover a political voice. As W.H. Linder, executive director of the centre, says, 'By attempting, at times more successfully than at others, to bring all sectors of society into its deliberative and decision-making functions, [the Rio conference] became the first international experiment in democratizing inter-governmental decision-making.'

1313 **The Earth Summit: the United Nations Conference on Environment and Development (UNCED).**
Stanley P. Johnson, introduction and commentary. London: Graham & Trotman and M. Nijhoff, 1993. 532p. (International Environmental Law Series).
This is an interpretive edition of Agenda 21, with invaluable introductions. The full text of all five documents is printed here, including the Rio Declaration, the Convention on Climate Change, the Convention on Biological Diversity, and the Statement of Forest Principles. The general introduction is a history of UNCED from the beginning of the preparatory process (1988) to the ongoing negotiating process (1992-). 'Did we really save the Earth at Rio?' asks the commentator. Whether history will judge Rio a turning-point depends on whether the problems it so dramatically marked out – climate, biodiversity, forests, finance, economic development, elimination of poverty – are solved by international cooperation in the future. As Maurice Strong, Secretary-General of the conference said in his closing speech, 'The New World Order, Mr. President, must unite us all in a global partnership, which, of course, has to respect national sovereignty as a basic tenet, but must also recognize the transcending sovereignty of nature, of our only one Earth.'

1314   **'East–West' diplomacy for environment in the United Nations: the high-level meeting within the framework of the ECE on the protection of the environment.**
Evgeny Chossudovsky.   New York: UNITAR, 1990. 256p. bibliog. (E.88.XV.ST.26).

In 1979, one month before the Soviet invasion of Afghanistan, a high-level meeting on a 1976 Soviet proposal to improve cooperation for the protection of the environment and the development of transport and energy was held at U.N. ECE headquarters in Vienna. In an atmosphere of renewed Cold War, progress was slow, but in 1985 the CSCE parties did conclude a convention to reduce sulphur emissions. The author recounts the tangled diplomatic history of this initiative, which he hoped would serve as a 'model of conference diplomacy' on mutual environmental problems even during times of great suspicion and hostility. With the end of the Cold War, the precedent could have greater applications.

1315   **The economics of coming spaceship Earth.**
Kenneth E. Boulding.   In: *Environmental quality in a growing economy*. Edited by Henry Jarrett.   Baltimore, MD: Johns Hopkins University Press for Resources for the Future, 1966. Reprinted in: *Sanctuary: Journal of the Massachusetts Audubon Society*, vol. 27 (February-March 1988), p.11-13.

This is a classic of ecological thinking, environmental law, and action. The 'closed earth', like a spaceship, requires different economic principles. Success of the economy cannot be measured by production from infinite reserves, consumption, and disposal into infinite reservoirs, but by 'the nature, extent, quality, and complexity of the total capital stock, including in this the state of the human bodies and minds in the system'. Not throughput but stock maintenance is the new measure. Not income but capital is the objective. And if capital is fixed, is not conservation a necessity?

1316   **Energy 2000: a global strategy for sustainable development. A report for the World Commission on Environment and Development.**
Advisory Panel on Energy, Enrique Iglesias, chairman.   London: Zed Books, 1987. 76p. bibliog.

This is a contribution to what became the Brundtland report, *Our common future* (1987) (item no. 153). Iglesias provides a thorough critique of energy supply and consumption, which are generaly non-sustainable. In developed countries, cheap fuels promote waste; in developing, use of wood destroys the forests on which the future depends. He suggests alternative 'strategies to negotiate predictable world oil prices, at levels high enough to encourage efficiency measures; to reduce the use of fossil fuels wherever possible, and use them in environmentally favourable conversion systems; stabilize the woodfuel resource base in developing countries; increase the role of renewables substantially; and make nuclear energy an acceptable source of power'. In 1985, this must have seemed utopian; ten years later, it was self-evident.

1317 **The environment in international relations.**
Caroline Thomas.   London: Royal Institute of International Affairs,
1992. 291p.

Chatham House's previous studies of the environment had focused on oil extraction and other energy issues. This book, in a new departure, focuses on preservation of the environment. The author asks a pertinent question – why have threats to the environment rather suddenly achieved a 'high diplomatic profile', when the issues have been studied for years and the even greater threat from nuclear arms did not similarly produce 'meaningful global action'? Thomas argues that enhanced appreciation for the environment 'derives largely from the activities of NGOs who took advantage of the political space provided by the fortuitous ending of the Cold War'. She traces the historical placement of the environmental cause on the international political, economic, and security agendas. Case-studies on global warming, ozone depletion, and deforestation are included. Thomas does not expect 'radical reform' of the international system; but 'limited cooperation is possible'. If the nuclear threat would not 'trigger global cooperation', why would that of environmental destruction?

1318 **Forging international agreement: strengthening intergovernmental institutions for environment and development.**
Lee A. Kimball.   Washington, DC: World Resources Institute, 1992.
84p.

More than a preparatory report for the U.N. Conference on Environment and Development at Rio de Janeiro, this booklet is an informal and shrewd analysis of the 'political ecology' of the U.N. system, with recommendations for its strengthening along the lines of the UNA–USA's *A successor vision* (item no. 163). 'The opportunities today – with the end of the Cold War – permit a new diplomacy to flourish. Superpower competition may be replaced by a common vision of global well-being and the potential peace dividend to realize it. The necessity for international cooperation has never been more apparent.' Recommendations are more ambitious than the establishment of the Commission on Sustainable Development at Rio; hence, they remain pertinent for the future. Special attention is given to monitoring and assessment, environmental management, strategic planning, accountability, and international development assistance. Valuable appendixes are included on the U.N. system, financial estimates to achieve ideals, chronologies, and reform.

1319 **Global outlook, 2000: an economic, social, and environmental
perspective.**
New York: United Nations, 1990. 340p. (E.90.II.C.3.
ST/ESA/215/Rev.1).

This recent U.N. study concentrates on long-term trends of sustainable development – that is, economic growth linked to preservation of the environment. Comparable studies of the world economy by the World Bank or IMF still do not account for environmental costs and concentrate on medium- or short-term trends. Here, it is found that world economic growth has slowed in the last thirty years and by 1990 was in a 'state of fundamental disequilibrium'. By 2000, assuming no major policy changes and continued deterioration of the environment, the world economy will exhibit great contrasts of 'economic advance and decline, of structural change and stagnation'. The study establishes a baseline scenario of continued current policies, then explores six alternative scenarios, the most optimistic of which – if savings are mobilized, investment stimulated, and trade liberalized – could substantially reduce debt and increase the growth of developing countries by one percentage point.

1320   **The global partnership for environment and development: a guide to Agenda 21.**
        UNCED. Foreword by Maurice Strong.   Geneva: UNCED, 1992.
        116p. (E.92.I.15).

Although this short work is somewhat outdated with the completion of UNCED, it can still serve as an introduction for the general reader to Agenda 21. It conveys basic facts and the spirit of the historic conference. After chapters on a prosperous world, a just world, a habitable world, it concludes with one on a 'peoples' world' – affirming the contributions that women, children, indigenous people, farmers, union workers, businesspeople, scientists, technologists, and NGOs can make to a better world.

1321   **The Global 2000 report to the President: entering the twenty-first century.**
        U.S.. Council on Environmental Quality and Department of State,
        Gerald O. Barney, study director.   Washington, DC: U.S. GPO,
        1980-81. 3 vols.

Barney was a member of the *Limits to growth* project (1972), which first warned against unsustainable economic growth. The *Global 2000* report is a classic analysis of the economic, demographic, minable, agricultural, and environmental future of all nations. World population is certain to increase to 12,000 million within the twenty-first century, even assuming drastic declines in human fertility, guided by revised teachings of the world's religions. Virtually all of the increase will occur in the South – leaving 1,000 million in the North in relative affluence. This is a formula for a disaster to humanity as great as general nuclear war. Barney outlines alternative strategies to save the human species – the human family – culminating with fundamental U.N. reform.

1322   **The historical roots of our ecological crisis.**
        Lynn White, Jr.   *Science*, vol. 155 (1967), p.1203-07. Reprinted in:
        Sanctuary: Journal of the Massachusetts Audubon Society, vol. 27
        (February-March 1988), p.3-6.

This is another classic of ecological thinking, environmental law, and action. White finds the roots of Western man's attitude that nature exists to be exploited in the Christian doctrine that man is made in the image of God and hence shares his transcendence. He also sees it rooted in Christian destruction of pagan animism, which had seen spirits in every place, plant, and animal. He doubts that 'more science and technology' is a solution to the ecological crisis – what is needed is a 'new religion' or a rethinking of the old one. St. Francis, whose humility 'set up a democracy for all God's creatures', should be the patron saint of ecologists.

1323 **International environmental policy: emergence and dimensions.**
Lynton K. Caldwell. Durham, NC: Duke University Press, 1984; 2nd ed., 1990. 460p.

'This book is a comprehensive survey of the world-wide movement for protection of the human environment. It is therefore also a history and chronology of international cooperation on environmental issues.' Partly history, partly policy analysis, the book is instead 'an account of the emergence of a new configuration in international policy'. The many U.N. agencies are thoroughly incorporated into the account. This is probably as complete an account as can be found of the environmental movement before the Rio conference in 1992. Caldwell concludes with a chapter on 'Defense of Earth in a divided world'. He argues that means are lacking to adequately protect the environment, monitor implementation of agreements, and assist countries faced with socio-ecological collapse. He prefers a decentralized system of voluntary cooperation: 'The biosphere is too large, too diverse, and too complex to be "managed" by any centralized coordinating authority.'

1324 **Managing planet earth: perspectives on population, ecology, and the law.**
Miguel A. Santos. New York: Bergin & Garvey, 1990. 172p. bibliog.

This book, by a biologist, examines the 'international ecological crisis' scientifically; it aims to define equilibrium or 'stability' naturally, socially, and politically. The author is fully aware of the problem of international anarchy for preservation of the environment. 'The interaction between present-day nations is a paradox', he writes and later repeats, 'for one cannot have environmental order, stability, and sovereign nations within a larger sovereign environment.' In his last chapter, Santos comes to the opposite conclusion to Caldwell above, drawing out at some length the shape of a 'World Environmental Authority'. He is quite confident that a world authority is within the wit of man to create in order to solve common environmental problems. Present international law is 'horizontal', he concludes, as on the surface of a sphere. But the biosphere has depth; a law appropriate to it would be 'vertical', developed by a 'seventh organ of the United Nations'.

1325 **Microbial technologies to overcome environmental problems of persistent pollutants.**
Edited by Martin Alexander. Nairobi: UNEP, 1987. 132p. (E.86.III.D.2).

Five million chemicals are known to man. About 53,500 are of commerical value; of these, some 35,660 chemicals, drugs, and pesticides are little understood for toxicity. Their presence in the environment clearly must have ill-effects on health. 'This book provides state-of-the-art and up-to-date scientific information on the microbial degradation of persistent pollutants, as one possible means of minimizing risks associated with their accumulation and biotransformation in the biosphere.'

1326 **Nations of the earth report: United Nations Conference on Environment and Development. National reports summaries.**
UNCED.   Geneva: United Nations, 1992-93. 3 vols. (E.92.I.17-19. A/CONF.151/PC/8 and Add.1).

Here can be found country reports, from Afghanistan to Zimbabwe, in preparation for the U.N. Conference on Environment and Development. Each nation was asked to state its problem areas, capacity-building initiatives, priorities, financial arrangements, preferred environmentally sound technologies, record on international cooperation, and expectations from UNCED. The U.K. report is in vol. I; the U.S., in vol. III. There are unabridged reports in the U.N. conference document cited above. These volumes are a 'quick reference compendium'.

1327 **One earth, many nations: the international system and problems of the global environment.**
Jeffrey Laurenti and Francesca Lyman.   New York: UNA–USA, 1990. 64p. bibliog.

Written in cooperation with the Sierra Club for young and general readers, this is a survey of U.S. and U.N. agencies, atmospheric problems (ozone depletion and global warming), transboundary problems (acid rain, hazardous wastes, driftnet fishing), sustainable development, and more effective international institutions.

1328 **Only one world: our own to make and to keep.**
Gerard Piel. Foreword by Maurice Strong.   New York: W.H. Freeman for the René Dubois Centre and the United Nations, 1992. 367p. bibliog. (Vox Populi Series, No. 1. E.92.I.5).

The publisher of *Scientific American* here presents a broad scientific and political account of the interaction between natural and social systems in time for the Rio conference on the environment in 1992. Matters covered are: biology and humanity, the biosphere, the human condition, energy, the agricultural revolution, industrial revolution, and human development. Piel's argument is that a sustainable future requires a 'new partnership' between the developing and the industrialized worlds a joint stewardship over both environmental and economic growth.

1329 **Pollution: keeping house on a planetary scale.**
Marvin S. Soroos.   In: *Beyond sovereignty: the challenge of global policy*, by Marvin S. Soroos.   Columbia, SC: University of South Carolina Press, 1986, p.294-322.

Pollution respects no national frontiers. The author discusses environmental degradation as a global and regional problem, to which the international community responded with the Stockholm conference on the human environment in 1972 and the founding of UNEP. (He wrote before the Rio conference of 1992.) UNEP's Global Monitoring System is described, as are the programmes of the IMO, the Convention on the Prevention of Marine Pollution, the Law of the Sea, the Limited Test Ban (precursor of the Comprehensive Test Ban), and other international policies.

1330 **Rational use of water and its treatment in the chemical industry.**
U.N. ECE. New York: United Nations, 1991. 146p. (E.91.II.E.3.
ECE/CHEM/78).

'Rational' use means sustainable use. 'The goal is to discharge water with chemical-physical and biological characteristics that will not have a detrimental impact on the environment, or better yet, that can be reused.' This thorough study, which should be of interest to engineers, ministers of industry, and conservationists, examines rational use of water and disposal of waste water in the chemical industry of Europe. Specific suggestions are made for such selected sectors as petroleum, dyestuffs, fertilizers, pulp and paper, and man-made fibres.

1331 **Recommendations on the transport of dangerous goods.**
New York: United Nations, 1957; 7th ed., 1991. 515p. (E.91.VII.2.
ST/SG/AC.10/1/Rev.7).

Dangerous goods include explosives, gases, flammable liquids, flammable solids, oxidizing substances, poisons, pathogens, radioactive materials, and corrosive chemicals. This international guide provides recommendations for the safe transport and storage of such goods. Uniformity in the classification, packing, labelling, and testing of dangerous materials will assist customs regulators and promote free trade. Here is another instance of functional integration.

1332 **Should trees have standing? Toward legal rights for natural objects.**
Christopher D. Stone. Los Altos, CA: W. Kaufmann, 1974.
Reprinted in: *Sanctuary: Journal of the Massachusetts Audubon Society*, vol. 27 (February-March 1988), p.14-16.

This is another classic of ecological thinking, environmental law, and action. The inanimate environment, flora, and fauna – like children, corporations, and national states – should have *rights* as persons recognized in law, the author argues. The expansion of rights is a mark of man's moral development. The forests, oceans, fish, and birds – as dumb and helpless as a child – deserve our sympathy and legal protection, for the realization of their potentialities fulfill life for all.

1333 **State of the world, 1993: a Worldwatch Institute report on progress toward a sustainable society.**
Lester R. Brown, Christopher Flavin, and Sandra Postel. New York and London: Norton for Worldwatch Institute, 1984- . annual. 256p.

This is a highly regarded annual report on the earth's environment, very broadly understood to include food production, preservation of nature, sustainable economic development, even global military security and world peace. It is now selling 300,000 copies per year, translated into twenty-six languages, and used by policy-makers, scholars, teachers, and activists the world over. The 1993 edition has a section on U.N. reform.

1334   **The state of the world environment, 1991.**
UNEP. Preface by M.K. Tolba.   Nairobi: UNEP, 1989- . biennial.
48p. bibliog. (E.91.III.D.8. UNEP/GC.16/9).

Since 1988, UNEP has been publishing two sorts of state-of-the-world report: in even years, a social report; in odd years, as above, a physical one. In 1991, the focus was on air quality, biodiversity, shared water resources, and the marine environment. The context throughout is the plight of the developing world, where burgeoning population is making extreme demands on the environment. Readers in search of accurate data with respect to specific environmental treaties and programmes will find them here.

1335   **State of transboundary air pollution: 1992 update.**
U.N. ECE.   New York: United Nations, 1993. 104p. (Air Pollution Studies No. 9. E.93.II.E.25. ECE/EB.AIR/33).

Since the Convention on Long-range Transboundary Air Pollution was signed in 1979, the ECE has been monitoring SO_2, NO_x, NH_3, CO_2, and volatile organic compounds emitted into the air. The area monitored includes Western and Eastern Europe, the U.S.A., and Canada. Tables show data from 1980 to 2005. National policies are fully covered, as is the rather smaller international activity.

1336   **Strengthening global environmental governance.**
Hilary French.   In: *State of the world, 1992*. Edited by Lester Brown.
New York: Norton for Worldwatch Institute, 1992, p.155-73.

Appearing in time to have some influence on the U.N. Conference on Environment and Development in 1992 (the Earth Summit), this informative article surveyed the climactic round of international negotiations on environmental treaties, especially the ones on biodiversity and global warming. Over 150 environmental treaties have been adopted since 1872 – most since 1970. The author argues further for 'international governance', since sovereign 'borders are routinely breached by pollution, financial flows, refugees, and other forces'. French finds that, on balance, the Law of the Sea Convention (1982) and, even more, the Montreal Protocol on ozone depletion (1987) are positive steps forward. But she emphasizes political conditions – like a profitable substitute for CFCs or public will to do something about acid rain or NGO monitoring of compliance – behind their success. She concludes with suggestions for 'radical' reform of the sprawling U.N. system, modelled on the Hague Declaration of seventeen heads of state in 1989, or the Stockholm Initiative in 1991, which calls for a world summit on global governance in 1995.

1337   **Sustainable energy developments in Europe and North America.**
U.N. ECE.   New York: United Nations, 1991. 217p. (ECE Energy Series No. 6. E.91.II.E.2. GE.91-30023/2790B).

Europe and North America now consume seventy per cent of world energy. Projections are for the ratio to fall to sixty per cent by 2010. The ECE was asked, Is this trend 'sustainable' in Europe and North America? The study concludes that, if energy and environmental policies are integrated and managed carefully, the crossover into unsustainable usage will occur at some time after 2010. Market 'adjustments' to correct 'imperfections', technological breakthroughs in efficiency (like superconductivity), and finally 'decoupling economic growth and energy demand' will allow 'market forces' to be preserved until that date. Thereafter, international cooperation and management will become unavoidable.

1338 The tragedy of the commons.
Garrett Hardin. *Science*, vol. 162 (1968), p.1243-48. Reprinted in: *Sanctuary: Journal of the Massachusetts Audubon Society*, vol. 27 (February-March 1988), p.7-10.

This is a fourth classic of ecological thinking, environmental law, and action. The whole habitable or cultivable earth is the 'commons'; the age-old habits of free and unlimited exploitation of the land bring 'tragedy' or ruin. 'Freedom in a commons brings ruin to all', Hardin writes. Since conscience will not preserve the environment, coercion (law) must. The rule of law is the foundation of civil freedom. Hence the plethora of environmental laws since 1968.

1339 The United Nations and ecosystem issues: institutionalizing the global interest.
Donald J. Puchala.   In: *Politics in the United Nations system*. Edited by Lawrence S. Finkelstein.   Durham, NC: Duke University Press, 1988, p.214-45.

Ecosystem issues are understood broadly to include food (earliest to arise), population, and the environment. The link to economic development is recognized in anticipation of the concept of 'sustainable development' at the centre of the Brundtland report (1987) (see item no. 153). All these larger environmental issues beyond the capacity of individual sovereign states to solve have been termed the *global problematique*. Puchala reviews the history and settled principles of the U.N. response (like shared responsibility for poor countries). Why the U.N. moved into this area, he explains, goes back to the emergence of new leadership in Northern Europe and the Third World, their organization of dramatic international conferences (of which the Stockholm conference on the environment in 1972 was typical), a resourceful U.N. response emphasizing agreements on declarations and programmes of action rather than confrontation, contributions by Western intellectuals, and U.S. and Soviet inability to expand the Cold War into the area. Today, there is general agreement about the *problematique*, if not its *resolution*.

1340 Vital signs, 1992: the trends that are shaping our future.
Lester R. Brown, Christopher Flavin, and Hal Kane.   New York and London: Norton for Worldwatch Institute, 1992- . annual. 131p.

This is a new annual volume complementing *State of the world* (item no. 1333). Trends measured include those relating to: food, agricultural resources, energy, atmosphere, economy, society, and armed forces. The aim is to supply environmental and social information missing from the usual economic measures and trends. For example, U.N. FAO data on the oceanic fish catch are augmented here with discussion of the sustainable stocks, preservation of habitats, pollution, and national and international laws. The book is conveniently divided into two parts: one of historical global data (text on one page, graphs on the other); a second on important trends for which data are yet unavailable (like annual loss of plant and animal species).

1341 A world at risk.

Lester R. Brown, Christopher Flavin, and Sandra Postel. In: *State of the world, 1989*. New York and London: Norton for Worldwatch Institute, 1989, p.3-20.

Articles in this annual volume have become a major source of public information on the environmental crisis. This article not only covers global warming and declining food production; it also reviews awakening public consciousness and stirring international cooperation. In 1989, the Cold War was ending, and the authors declared: 'Protecting the biosphere is a new channel for the vast energies now directed to the cold war rivalry.' They would strengthen the U.N. as the only way to preserve national governments.

1342 The World Bank and the environment, fiscal 1993.

Washington, DC: World Bank, 1990- . annual. 193p. bibliog.

One year after UNCED, the World Bank issued this substantial report on its 'transition' to improved environmental concerns in its sectoral work. Funds and personnel have already been redirected to improving environmental aspects of its projects. Four objectives are sought: (1) assisting countries in their environmental stewardship; (2) assessing and mitigating adverse impacts of Bank-financed projects; (3) building on the positive synergies between development and the environment; (4) assessing global environmental challenges. A typical project in area 2 is one to rehabilitate Morocco's historic cities (medinas) of Fez, Meknes, and Rabat-Sale, which had been passed by in unplanned urban development. The volume is filled with such examples.

1343 World public order of the environment: towards an international ecological law and organization.

Jan Schneider. Foreword by Myres McDougal and J. Alan Beesley, Q.C. Toronto: University of Toronto Press, 1979. 319p.

This is a work of jurisprudence for the environment – understood not merely as the mineral, plant, and animal environment, but also as the human local, national, and world political environment. For, after all, what is the 'environment'? 'The protection and preservation of the earth–space environment is essentially a public order problem', begins the author, 'in the sense that it affects the whole global community and its multiple and interpenetrating component communities.' Schneider treats such familiar problems as access to resources, regulation of use, and development of resources, but he does not shrink from the implications for government of managing resources that extend over all the planet. His notions of 'custodianship' over coastal waters – which has been granted to coastal states, he says, by 'delegation of powers' from the unorganized 'world community' – is the root he finds for the emerging 'international ecological law'. States do not assume such powers by virtue of their sovereignty: the powers are delegated to them by the world community. (This novel doctrine is the reverse of the usual democratic one, by which the people, as sovereigns, are said to delegate powers to the state.) Schneider is aware that the logic of environmentalism points to 'world government' or 'federation', but he regards this as matter 'for political philosophers extending way beyond the aspirations of the present inquiry'.

On the problems of 'the global problematique'.
See item no. 59.

Our common future.
See item no. 153.

Consolidated list of products whose consumption and/or sale have been banned, withdrawn, severely restricted or not approved by governments.
See item no. 849.

Sustainable development: changing production patterns, social equity, and the environment.
See item no. 1137.

Environmental aspects of the activities of transnational corporations.
See item no. 1143.

Bibliographies

1344 **Bibliographie de la Cour internationale de Justice, 1992.**
Bibliography of the International Court of Justice.
La Haye: C.I.J., 1947- . annual. 113p. (F/E.ICJ/637).
This annual work covers establishment of the international judicial system, organization of the Court, jurisdiction, procedure, cases brought before the Court (ninety to 1992), and writings referring to the Court.

1345 **Documents of international organizations: a bibliographic**
handbook covering the United Nations and other
intergovernmental organizations.
Compiled by Theodore D. Dimitrov.   London: International
University Publications; Chicago: American Library Association,
1973. 301p.
Prepared at the U.N. Library in Geneva, this is not a guide to the documents, but a handbook for librarians to manage the documents in order to guide others to the documents. It is, in short, a contribution to library science.

1346 **Guide to the United Nations Organization, documentation, and**
publishing: for students, researchers, librarians.
Peter I. Hajnal.   Dobbs Ferry, NY: Oceana, 1978. 450p. bibliog.
This reference work is an explanatory guide to the structure, functions, and evolution of the United Nations system as related to its voluminous publications. Librarians will be its primary users, but students and researchers trying to find their way into the system may also try it.

1347 Human rights: a topical bibliography.
Compiled by Center for the Study of Human Rights, Columbia University; J.Paul Martin, project director; Louis Henkin, advisor. Boulder, CO: Westview, 1983. 297p. bibliog.

Addressed to the broadest audience, this bibliography is divided into more than 150 categories so that teachers, students, and specialists can quickly find relevant materials in English.

1348 Human rights bibliography: United Nations documents and publications, 1980-1990.
Compiled by U.N. Library in cooperation with the Centre for Human Rights, Geneva. New York: United Nations, 1993. 5 vols. 2,048p. (GV.E.92.O.16).

'The present bibliography, published on the occasion of this [Vienna] Conference [on Human Rights], is conceived as a means of encouraging a broader understanding and wider knowledge of this universal aspiration for the freedom and progress of man, for prosperity and for peace.' The first volume is arranged by categories now standard: human rights; civil and political rights and the administration of justice; economic, social, and cultural rights; self-determination of peoples; non-discrimination; rights of individuals and particular groups; right to development; violations of and threats to the enjoyment of human rights; role and work of the U.N. system; work of other organizations and institutions for the promotion and protection of human rights. The other volumes contain author and subject indexes.

1349 The international organizations and world order dictionary.
Compiled by Sheikh Rustum Ali. Santa Barbara, CA: ABC-Clio, 1992. 283p.

This is a ready-reference guide to commonly used terms in international organization (300 entries).

1350 The Law of the Sea: a bibliography on the Law of the Sea, 1968-1988; two decades of law-making, state practice, and doctrine.
Compiled by Office for Ocean Affairs and the Law of the Sea. New York: United Nations, 1991. 472p. (E/F.91.V.7).

This is a guide to English and French books and periodical articles on the 'revolution' of the Law of the Sea, from the General Assembly's first positive response to Arvid Pardo's speech on the common heritage of mankind to the Preparatory Commission's first registration of a group of 'pioneer investors' in the new deep seabed regime established by the Convention on the Law of the Sea. Entries are arranged by categories in the law. In 1993, a multilingual supplement was published in Chinese, German, Italian, Russian, Spanish, and Arabic.

1351   **The Law of the Sea: a select bibliography, 1992.**
Compiled by U.N. Division for Ocean Affairs and the Law of the
Sea.   New York: United Nations, 1985- . annual. 61p. (E.93.V.12.
LOS/LIB/8).
This annual publication lists works under categories related to the Convention on the
Law of the Sea: e.g., general, territorial sea, exclusive economic zone, etc.

1352   **Multilateral negotiations and third-party roles: an annotated
bibliography. UNESCO Yearbook on peace and conflict studies,
1984.**
Compiled by International Peace Academy.   Paris: UNESCO, 1986,
p.181-207.
This work includes general studies, art of negotiation, third-party roles, negotiation
simulation, and audiovisual sources.

1353   **The New International Economic Order: a bibliography.**
Compiled by Tawfique Nawaz.   Westport, CT: Greenwood, 1980.
163p.
This work encompasses general literature on the NIEO, North–South negotiations
(commodities, trade, money and finance, transfer of technology, and TNCs), South–
South economic cooperation among developing countries, legal and policy aspects,
socialist countries, and international organizations.

1354   **Peace and world order studies: a curriculum guide.**
Edited by Daniel C. Thomas and Michael T. Klare.   Boulder, CO:
Westview for Five College Program in Peace and World Security
Studies, 1989. 5th ed. 666p.
This is a very successful guide (first published in 1973) to teaching and curricula in
the general field of world order. The U.N. is not here assumed as a given, but rather is
a consequence, among others, of a broad debate about the values universally desired
in a preferred world (peace, social justice, economic well-being, ecological balance,
democratic participation). Also debated are global problems, human rights, international law, non-violence, social movements, conflict resolution, women, religion
and ethics, the media, education, and revolution. The work concentrates on
contemporary popular and scholarly literature.

1355   **Peaceful settlement of disputes between states: a selective
bibliography.**
Compiled by Dag Hammarskjöld Library.   New York: United
Nations, 1991. 209p. (E.91.I.49).
This guide lists books, monographs, chapters in monographs, and articles arranged by
subject. Part I contains references to material published before the founding of the
U.N. in 1945; Part II, from 1945 to 1979; Part III, 1980 to 1991. It complements the
Handbook on the peaceful settlement of disputes between states (1991).

1356   **Strengthening the United Nations: a bibliography on U.N. reform and world federalism.**
Compiled by Joseph Preston Baratta.   Westport, CT: Greenwood, 1987. 351p.

This is a survey of the literature (from seventy-five countries) on the founding of the United Nations and on subsequent efforts to amend the Charter or to replace the U.N. with a constitutionally limited, popularly representative world federal government. Critical works pro and con especially have been sought. Topics include: Atlantic union of democracies, League of Nations, United Nations, international control of atomic energy, universal federation, European federation, world order, diplomacy of the Cold War, peace movement, international education, films, journals, and archives.

1357   **Transnational corporations: a selective bibliography, 1988-90.**
Compiled by UNCTC.   New York: United Nations, 2nd ed., 1991. 617p. (E.91.II.A.10. ST/CTC/116).

This very large bibliography contains virtually every technical, national, and international work on the subject of TNCs published between 1988 and 1990. (An earlier edition listed those from 1983 to 1987.) Topics include: general studies; foreign direct investment; enterprises; TNCs in specific economic sectors and in specific countries; economic issues; political, social and environmental issues; international law and policy; national law and policy; contracts; labour; technical assistance; and references.

1358   **United Nations documents index.** [After 1979:] **UNDOC: current index.**
Compiled by Dag Hammarskjöld Library.   New York: United Nations, 1950- . monthly, with annual cumulations. (ST/LIB/SER.E/1).

U.N. documents and official records are indexed here by subject, author, title, document symbol, and (in the case of publications) sales number. Readers are advised to become familiar with the U.N. document symbol, which is Theseus's key to the labyrinth. After 1990, the index was made available on CD-ROM, which is much easier to use.

1359   **United Nations publications catalogue, 1994-95.**
New York and Geneva: United Nations, 1994. 200p.

Updated biennially, this catalogue lists and annotates all the currently in-print U.N. publications. General categories include: reference, political science, social science, law, environment, economics, education, and electronic products. (It is not a guide to U.N. documents and official records, for which one must go to a U.N. depository library, found in many large cities.) To order publications for sale, contact:

U.N. Publications, Sales Section
2 United Nations Plaza
Room DC2-853, Dept. 007C
New York, NY 10017
Tel.: 212-963-8302
       800-253-9646
Fax: 212-963-3489
E-mail: UNPubsatUNHQ3@UN.ORG

Bibliographies

U.N. Publications, Sales Office and Bookshop
CH-1211 Geneva 10
Switerland
Tel.: 41-22-917-2614 Orders
       41-22-917-2613 Inquiries
       41-22-917-2615 Subscriptions
       41-22-917-2606 Accounts, trade
Fax: 41-22-917-0027

1360 **World bibliography of international documents.**
      [Vol. I:] International organizations, activities, structure, policies,
      documents control; [Vol. II:] Politics and world affairs,
      periodicals, conferences, indexes.
      Compiled by Theodore D. Dimitrov.   Pleasantville, NY: UNIFO
      Publishers, 1981. 2 vols. bibliog.

Prepared at the U.N. Library in Geneva and following two world symposia on
international documentation in 1972 and 1980, this is an authoritative, multilingual
guide to literature on the intergovernmental organizations and to their bibliographical
control in libraries. Readers will find here titles of books and periodicals on the whole
range of organizations within the U.N. system up to 1979.

Indexes

There follow two indexes: authors (personal and corporate); and subjects. A few references are to pages in the Introduction and take the form: p.xi, xx-xxi. Otherwise, the numbers refer to bibliographical entries and not to pages. Individual index entries are arranged in alphabetical sequence.

Index of Authors

Holmes, Kim R. 191
Hooke, A. W. 1074
Hoole, Frances W. 859
Hopkins, Raymond F. 875
Hopkinson, Nicholas 237
Horton, Philip C. 843
Hougassian-Rudovich, Alice
1206
Howard-Jones, Norman
858
Howe, Josephine 642
Howell, David 225
Hudec, Robert E. 1106
Hudson, Richard 130
Hufbauer, Gary C. 614
Hugo, Victor 1011
Hume, Cameron R. 574
Humphrey, John 940
Humphrey, John T. P. 1234
Hunter, Martin 492
Hurni, Bettina 1050
Hurwitz, Leon 743
Hutchins, Robert M. 242,
899, 989
Huxley, Julian 382, 915
Huzzard, Ron 713

I

Iglesias, Enrique 1316
Iklé, Fred C. 435
Ilan, Amitzur 452
Independent Advisory
Group on U.N.
Financing 262
Independent Commission on
International
Development Issues
133
Ingersoll, Shaun A. 1095
Ireland, Timothy P. 183
Irwin, Paul C. 959

J

Jackson, John H. 1117,
1128
Jackson, R. G. A. 1030
Jackson, Richard L. 367,
636, 1030
Jackson, Robert H. 633

Jacobson, Herold K. 656,
734, 744, 745, 837,
1206
James, Alan 581
Jarrett, Henry 1315
Jarvin, Sigvard 493
Jasani, Bhupendra 936
Jasentuliyana, Nandasiri 935
Jazairy, Idriss 879
Jenks, C. Wilfred p.xiii, xvii,
80, 261, 276, 521, 949,
956
Jennings, A. 39
Jennings, Robert 492
Jensen, Kenneth M. 32
Jerome, Robert W. 1111
Jervis, Robert 49, 290
Jessup, Philip C. 102, 109,
110, 274, 337, 348
Ježek, Z. 863
Jiménez de Aréchaga,
Eduardo 531
Joekes, Susan P. 1295
Johansen, Robert C. 137,
601
Johnson, D. H. N. 269, 483
Johnson, Stanley P. 1313
Johnston, Douglas M. 103,
245, 524
Jolly, Richard 658, 1060
Jonah, James 124, 596
Jordan, Robert S. 303, 308,
310, 743, 884
Jordan, William 357
Jose, James R. 567
Joyner, Christopher 277
Junker, Abbo 475

K

Kampelman, Max 618
Kant, Immanuel 74, 98, 242
Kane, Hal 1340
Kapur, Ashok 717
Karns, Margaret P. 207
Kassebaum, Nancy 163
Kassis, Antoine 497
Katz, Milton 523
Katz, Richard 1307
Kaufman, Natalie H. 1250
Kaufmann, Johan 267, 362,
1187

Kay, David A. 334
Keating, Michael 1312
Keatinge, Patrick 726
Kebbon, Niklas 532
Keeny, Spurgeon M. 647
Kelen, Emery 779
Kelman, Herbert C. 389, 430
Kenen, Peter B. 1087
Kennan, George F. 180, 187,
1094
Kennedy, Edward 729
Kennedy, John F. 424, 675,
733
Kennedy, Paul 65
Keohane, D. 716
Keohane, Robert O. 29, 57,
70, 716, 740
Kerameus, K. D. 473
Kerwin, Gregory 106
Keynes, John Maynard
1040, 1042, 1085
Khan, Rahmatullah 490
Kihl, Young W. 821
Kildow, Judith T. 965, 975
Killick, Tony 1082
Kim, Samuel S. 15, 66, 116,
137, 257, 1193
Kimball, Lee A. 1318
Kindleberger, Charles 1015,
1196
Kingsbury, Benedict 3, 22,
114, 127, 235, 314,
1032, 1275
Kingué, Michel Doo 16, 162
Kirdar, Üner 27, 1002-1007,
1009, 1018
Kirgis, Frederic L. 466, 530
Kirkpatrick, Jeane 200, 360
Kissinger, Henry 452, 1232
Klare, Michael T. 1354
Knauss, John A. 969
Koenderman, Tony 625
Koh, Tommy T. B. 982, 986,
990, 998
Kohn, Robert 854
Kolb, Deborah 458
Kolko, Gabriel and Joyce
1020
Kolosovsky, Andrei I. 222
Kommers, Donald P. 1229
Koojimans, Peter H. 530
Kotaite, Assad 825
Kothari, Rajni 48, 1292

459

Krasner, Stephen D. 51, 368, 1210
Krass, Allan S. 709, 712
Kratochwil, Friedrich 90, 414, 742
Krause, Keith R. 74
Krauthammer, Charles 74, 178
Krenz, Maria 1307
Kriesberg, Louis 373, 432
Kruglak, Gregory T. 955, 958
Krushchev, Nikita 308
Kuczyński, Janusz 781
Kumaris, Brahma 75
Kurtzman, Joel 1200

L

de Lacharrière, Guy Ladreit 477
Lachs, Manfred 392, 454
Ladnyi, I. D. 363
Lall, Arthur S. 288, 439, 443, 460
Lambo, Thomas A. 856
Lande, Gabriella Rosner 263, 270
Landy, Ernest A. 943
Lange, David 401
Langhammer, Rolf J. 1098
Larschan, Bradley 963
Lasswell, Harold D. 91, 1237
Laszlo, Ervin 42, 1200
Laurenti, Jeffrey 1327
Laursen, Finn 996
Lauterpacht, Hersch 92, 269, 496, 512
Lawson, Ruth C. 538
Lay, S. Houston 987
Leach, James A. 186
Leary, Virginia 376
Ledogar, Robert 774
Lee, Dwight E. 284
Lee, John M. 629
Lefever, Ernest 592
Leigh, Monroe 339
Leive, David M. 753, 835, 855, 877
Lent, John A. 844
Leontief, Wassily 1044

Lester, Sean 306
Leurdyk, Dick A. 4442
Leutwiler, Fritz 1121
Lichenstein, Charles M. 168
Lie, Trygve 299, 306, 313, 316, 317, 448, 466
Lillich, Richard B. 1284
Lincoln, Abraham 523
Linder, W. H. 1312
Lissitzyn, Oliver 110, 344
Liu, F. T. 598, 599
Lockhart, Charles 431
Lodge, Henry Cabot 355, 361, 545
Loeb, Benjamin S. 692
Loehr, William 1207
Loescher, Gilburt D. 755, 756, 764, 1229
Logue, John 993
Lowe, Alan V. 977
Luard, Evan 3, 41, 71, 72, 243, 388, 739, 1254
Luck, Edward C. 215, 648
Lukashuk, Igor I. 166
Lutz, Ellen L. 1257
Lyman, Francesca 1327
Lysén, Göran 672

M(a)c

MacBean, Alasdair I. 1017
MacBride, Sean 909
McCarthy, Thomas E. 1156
McCloy, John J. 674, 682, 703
McDermott, Anthony 573
McDonald, John W. 432, 437, 440
MacDonald, Maryellen 120
Macdonald, R. St. J. 103, 245, 396, 524, 541
McDougal, Myres S. 91, 118, 1237, 1343
McDougall, Gay J. 466
McDowell, Eleanor C. 339
McGrew, Anthony G. 716
McHenry, Donald 359
McKinlay, John 575, 610
McLaughlin, Martin M. 1212

McNamara, Robert S. 134, 163, 192, 941, 1045, 1050, 1051, 1173, 1193
McNeill, John H. 676
MacPherson, Bryan F. 641
McWhinney, Edward p.xvii, 117, 342, 505, 518, 820

M

Macehiarola, Frank 957
Mahajan, Harpreet 414
Makarczyk, Jerzy 392, 1202
Malitza, Mircea 443
Major, Frederico 898
Malinowski, W. R. 1181
Mallampally, Padma 1166
Mandela, Nelson 615
Mangone, Gerald 251
Mankabady, Samir 974
Mapel, David R. 68
Marc, Alexandre 910
Marcuse, Herbert 1296
Maritain, Jacques 897
Marks, Leonard H. 834
Marshall, Ray F. 947, 957, 1125
Marsteller, Thomas F., Jr. 467
Martin, J. Paul 1347
Martin, Laurence 228, 231
Martinez, Larry 828
Masini, Eleonora 1293
Mason, Edward S. 1065
Mason, Paul E. 467
Mautner-Markhof, Frances 441
Mayer, Jean 871, 872, 874, 876
Mayne, Richard 542
Mazrui, Ali A. 176, 559
M'Bow, Amadou-Mahtar 902, 909, 921, 1191
Meagher, Robert F. 264, 265
Meany, George 949, 950
Meier, Gerald M. 1042
Meiklejohn, Alexander 892
Melman, Seymour 661, 682
Meltzer, Ronald I. 160, 1096, 1210

Melvin, Kenneth 895
Mendlovitz, Saul H. 15, 35, 37, 66, 67, 90, 116, 137, 257, 555, 1193
Meredith, Christopher 713
Merkle, Melanie L. 168
Meron, Theodor 1242, 1249, 1279
Merrills, John G. 403
Metzl, Jamie 777
Meyer, Michael J. 1224
Michalak, Stanley J., Jr. 1184
Mikes, George 861
Miles, Edward 995
Miller, Linda B. 560
Miller, Lynn H. 43
Mills, Susan R. 565
Miluwa, Tiyanjana 550
Mingst, Karen A. 207
Mitchel, C. R. 462
Mitrany, David 34, 40, 76, 735
Modelski, George 1162
Mohler, Halfdan 852
Monahan, Laila 765
Monnet, Jean 542
Moore, John N. 595, 780
Moore, Margaret 780
Morgan, Joseph R. 989
Morgenthau, Hans p.xvii, 79, 187
Morris, Ellis 710
Morrison, Fred L. 529
Morrison, Philip 667
Morse, David A. 953, 956
Morse, Edward L. 56
Mortimer, Robert A. 369
Mosler, Hermann 517
Mounteer, Thomas R. 1107
Mourik, Maarten 922
Moynihan, Daniel P. 185, 189, 198, 1189
Mowrer, A. Glenn, Jr. 1230, 1282
Müller, Joachim W. 155
Muller, Robert 10, 151, 911, 912
Murphy, John F. 113, 426
Murray, James N., Jr. 336
Mushakoji, Kinhide 411
Muther, Jeannette B. 244

Myers, Robert, Jr. 49
Mykletun, I. Jostein 735
Myrdal, Alva 668

N

Nanda, Ved P. 762
Narasimham, C. V. 18
Nardin, Terry 68, 98
National Conference of Catholic Bishops 131
Nawaz, Tawfique 1353
Nelson, Richard W. 466
Nerfin, Marc 15, 137
Newberg, Paula R. 1263
Newcombe, Hanna 122
Newland, Kathleen 925
Newman, Frank 1257
Newsom, David D. 1225
Nicholas, Herbert G. 19
Nicol, Davidson 293, 324, 1204
Nixon, Richard 950, 1065
Nkrumah, Kwame 559
Noam, Eli M. 840
Nordquist, Myron 987
Northedge, F. S. 406
Notter, Harley 248
Nye, Joseph S. 57, 70, 74, 140, 548, 551, 553, 714, 720, 723, 730
Nyerere, Julius 134

O

O'Connell, Daniel P. 972
Ogata, Shijuro 262
Ogley, Roderick C. 971
Olson, Robert K. 1211
Onuf, Nicholas 88
Oppenheim, Lassa 92
Orfila, Alejandro 547
Osakwe, Christopher 84
Osgood, Charles E. 386, 704
Osmańczyk, Edmund Jan 4
Ostrower, Gary 259
Ostrowski, Krzystan 124
Otunnu, Olara 124
Owen, Henry D. 1045

P

Palme, Olof 135, 729
von Pagenhardt, Robert 629
Pardo, Arvid 961, 967, 988, 989, 998, 1001
Parent, William A. 1224
Park, William W. 488
Parker, Peter 472
Parker School of Foreign and Comparative Law 481
Parra, Antonio R. 1064
Parsons, Anthony 234, 235
Parton, Daniel G. 789, 959
Patchen, Martin 471
Patel, I. G. 1056
Patterson, Gardner 1104
Paulsson, Jan 488
Pearson, Lester 590
Peccei, Aurelio 1204
Pechota, Vratislav 504
Pelcovits, Nathan 584
Penrose, Ernest F. 1040
Pérez de Cuéllar, Javier 12, 55, 295, 296, 314, 317, 448, 982, 1248
Perkins, John A. 197
Petersmann, Ernst-Ulrich 1118
Peterson, M. J. 272
Petrovsky, Vladimir 123
Pfaltzgraff, Robert L. 36
Pickering, Thomas 124
Piel, Gerald 1328
Pilon, Juliana G. 168
Pines, Burton 178, 924
Pitt, David 312
Plano. Jack C. 24
Pogany, Istvan 533
Polak, Jacques J. 1085, 1087
Pool, Ithiel de Sola 840
Postel, Sandra 1333, 1341
Powell, Jon T. 833
Powelson, John P. 1207
Powers, Averill L. 136
Prebish, Raúl 1180, 1181, 1183
Preston, William, Jr. 901
Prestowitz, Clyde V., Jr. 1111

Princen, Thomas 457
Probst, Raymond R. 449
Pronk, Jan 1119
Prott, Lyndel V. 511
Pruitt, Dean 453
Puchala, Donald J. 875, 1144, 1339

Q

Quester, George H. 720

R

Ramachandran, Arcot 802
Raman, K. Venkata 394, 468, 580, 609
Ramcharan, Bertrand G. 147, 351, 382, 447, 456
Raiffa, Howard 429
Ramírez, J. Martín 896
Ramphal, Shridath S. 50, 134, 174, 1058
Raskin, Marcus 663
Ratiner, Leigh S. 979
Reagan, Ronald 391, 713
Reardon, Betty 137, 906
Redfern, Alan 492
Reich, Robert B. 1091
Reichart, John 184
Reicher, Harry 282
Reid, Escott 203
Reisinger, William R. 744
Reisman, W. Michael 108, 118, 529, 604, 1273
Reiss, Michael 733
Renninger, John P. 323, 324, 356, 1188
Renwick, Robin 611
Rhinelander, John B. 676
Richards, Timothy J. 889
Richardson, Elliot 163, 360, 648, 994
Riggs, Robert E. 24, 115, 735
Rikhye, Indar Jit 566, 576, 591, 592, 596
Riphagen, Willem 530
Rivlin, Benjamin 301, 359

Roberts, Adam 3, 22, 114, 127, 235, 314, 1032, 1275
Roberts, John 1311
Robertson, A. H. 1229
Robinson, Patrick 1150
Robson, John R. K. 872
Rocha, Ruth 783
Roche, Douglas 123
Rodamar, Jeffrey 1206
Rode, Reinhard 1103
Rodley, Nigel S. 375
Roemer, Milton Irwin 857
Rogers, Barbara 624
Rogers, William D. 200
Rogge, John R. 767
Rohatyn, Felix G. 213
Rohn, Peter H. 119
Rohrlick, Paul 414
Rolin, Henri 513
Roling, Bert V. A. 112
Ronen, Dov 1266
Roosevelt, Franklin D. p.xi, 301
Roosevelt, Eleanor 1282
Rosenau, James N. 73
Rosenbaum, Eli 297
Ross, David A. 969
Ross, John A. 791
Rossanda, Rossana 1296
Rossene, Shabti 519, 524
Rotblat, Joseph 685, 726
Roth, Otavio 783
Rothstein, Robert L. 370, 1171, 1174, 1203
Rovine, Arthur W. 306
Rowley, Robin 1043
Royal Institute of International Affairs 255
Rozenan, James N. 46
Rubin, Jeffrey Z. 453
Rubino-Sammartino, Mauro 485
Ruding, H. Onno 1038
Ruggie, John Gerard 59, 246, 742, 1186, 1201, 1233
Ruloff, Dieter 188
Rusk, Dean 499
Russell, Ruth B. 204, 244
Russett, Bruce 627, 646
Rutkowski, Anthony M. 836

S

Sachs, Jeffrey 1078
Sachs, Moshe Y. 14
Sagan, Carl 729
Saltzman, Arnold A. 296
Salvatore, Dominick 798
Samson, Klaus T. 1279
Sanders, Pieter 476
Sandole, Dennis 462
Sanger, Clyde 990
Santos, Miguel A. 1324
Sanyal, Bikas C. 900
Sapir, André 1098
Sathirathai, Surakiart 537
Saunders, Robert J. 841
Sauvant, Karl P. 364, 365, 1185, 1195
Sawyer, Jack 430
Sayegh, Fayez A. 534
Scanlon, John A. 755, 756
Schacter, Oscar 94, 103, 598, 602, 605, 1028, 1258
Scharf, Michael P. 635
Schear, James A. 730
Schechter, Michael G. 1054
Scheffer, David J. 96, 166, 200, 292, 515, 604, 605, 676, 1251, 1271
Scheinman, Lawrence 721
Scheinman, Ronald 756
Scheman, L. Ronald 535
Schiffer, Robert L. 298
Schiller, Herbert I. 901
Schlesinger, Arthur M. 1232
Schmalberger, Thomas 680, 686
Schmidt, Helmut 163, 1051
Schneider, Jan 1343
Schoettle, Enid C. D. 731
Schott, Jeffrey J. 614
Schreiber, Götz 1294
Schrijver, Nico 107, 174, 748, 878, 922, 948, 1038, 1119
Schultz, George P. 1045
Schwartzenberger, Georg 101, 495
Schwebel, Stephen M. 84, 271, 316, 348, 486
Scott, Andrew M. 61
Scott, Gary 509

Index of Subjects

466

B

Balance of payments 1032, 1038, 1056, 1060, 1071, 1075, 1130

Balance of power p.xii, xiii, xvii, 36, 58, 63, 65, 74, 105, 183, 244, 258, 290, 349, 649, 730, 757

Bangladesh 322, 394, 447, 461

Basic needs 153, 382, 397, 401, 657, 658, 774, 878, 941, 1003, 1019, 1050, 1051, 1173
    Alternative to NIEO 941, 1193, 1198

Behaviourism 36, 734, 859, 1053

Bernadotte, Folke (biography) 452

Biafra 464, 537, 549, 872

Bias 3, 5, 462, 901, 1229, 1238, 1240, 1280

Bilateral diplomacy p.xiii, 39, 124, 439, 505, 530, 644, 665, 673, 684, 691, 709, 743, 825, 826, 1006, 1092, 1104, 1111, 1140, 1300
    See also Multilateralism

Binding triad 125, 130, 175, 201

Biodiversity Treaty 1302, 1306, 1312, 1313, 1336

Birth control (family planning) 770, 771, 774, 789, 792, 794, 1264, 1293

Bloc politics 38, 47, 60
    See also Groups, Parties

Bosnia 563, 564, 595

Brandt report 133, 152

Brazil 162, 288, 714, 717, 722, 728, 732, 848, 1013, 1052, 1066, 1073, 1158, 1225, 1293

Bretton Woods system 133, 181, 255, 368, 631, 1020, 1024, 1038, 1040, 1042, 1056, 1057, 1065, 1084, 1086, 1099, 1100, 1117, 1119, 1149, 1197, 1260
    New Bretton Woods (reform) 129, 134, 157, 163, 1016, 1038, 1042, 1043, 1058, 1059, 1060, 1067, 1075, 1076, 1080, 1138, 1207, 1212
    See also International financial organizations

Brezhnev doctrine 166, 604

British policy 224-237, 308, 570, 619, 686, 693, 716, 718, 848, 897, 979, 996, 1039, 1116, 1297
    In medium term, challenge is to reinforce the system of collective security 225
    British politics in 18th century is like U.N. politics today 41, 84, 273

Bruntland report 134, 153, 1339

Buddhist Eightfold Path 321, 322, 401

Budget p.xix-xxiii, 6, 8, 20, 23, 28, 127, 155, 168, 170, 202, 209, 265, 828, 859, 898, 922, 1122
    Reduction of national military budgets (peace dividend) 657, 658, 687, 688

Buffer stocks (stockpiling) 875, 878, 1033, 1171, 1205

Bulgaria 1027

Bunche, Ralph (biography) 359, 452, 464

Bureaucracy 36, 142, 162, 178, 239, 309, 312, 324, 355, 361, 377, 437, 734, 743, 884, 949, 996, 1000, 1062, 1105, 1211
    Manipulation will escape majority rule 949
    See also Administration

Business, international 73, 94, 188, 362, 371, 381, 429, 469, 474, 481, 734, 806, 868, 893, 947, 1031, 1113, 1156, 1169, 1320
    See also Transnational corporations

C

Cambodia (Kampuchea) 295, 391, 407, 447, 539, 563, 564, 569, 618, 630, 760, 777, 1273

Canada 123, 124, 180, 383, 579, 580, 582, 619, 722, 733, 832, 906, 1092, 1271, 1300, 1311

Capitalism, world 31, 45, 523, 734, 736, 892, 946, 949, 950, 951, 1008, 1012, 1017, 1023, 1043, 1091, 1184, 1198
    Global *problematique* includes all problems not addressed by world capitalism 1008
    See also Global market

Central America 466, 543, 552, 1225
    See also Nicaragua

Centralization 25, 223, 325, 604, 898, 1145, 1197, 1273

Charter 2, 5, 24, 62, 79, 114, 238, 244, 253, 254, 274, 292, 531, 628, 690, 742, 1246, 1255, 1272
    Based on assumptions even more untrue in 1991 than in 1945 200, 232
    Beginning to function as designed 148, 162, 225, 235, 304, 391
    Comparison with U.S. Constitution 206

Community, world
  See World community
Comprehensive test ban
  (CTB) 131, 424, 432,
  449, 643, 656, 660,
  669, 670, 675, 676,
  680, 684, 686, 692,
  710, 712, 724, 726,
  727, 1329
  Would increase states'
    confidence in
    international security
    686, 709
Compulsory jurisdiction 92,
  121, 172, 343, 344,
  345, 349, 393, 396,
  405, 419, 426, 495,
  505, 506, 508, 509,
  510, 512, 514, 516,
  519, 527, 528, 530,
  532, 826, 897, 956,
  997, 998, 1107
  Problem is political and
    psycholgical 521
  See also International
    Court of Justice
Computer and data networks
  831, 832, 836, 840,
  845, 932, 1005, 1011,
  1124, 1148, 1161
Conciliation and
  consultation 177, 281,
  283, 317, 385, 387,
  395, 396, 398, 403,
  406, 408, 409, 413,
  414, 415, 419, 426,
  447, 450, 469-473, 503,
  511, 525, 535, 540,
  609, 632, 826, 836,
  937, 997, 1037, 1107,
  1118, 1124
  Standing Consultative
    Commissions in SALT
    I 676, 690
  International conciliation
    and mediation service
    158, 389, 395, 396,
    417, 446, 465, 467,
    484
Conference diplomacy 7, 39,
  59, 267, 361, 368, 439,
  884, 1314, 1339
  See also Multilateralism

Conference on Security and
  Cooperation in Europe
  (CSCE) 52, 124, 195,
  216, 445, 578, 610,
  654, 694, 703, 1227,
  1246, 1314
  NATO merged into CSCE
    182
Confidence 362, 422, 483,
  511, 521, 527, 532,
  550, 630, 686, 704,
  709, 1093, 1095, 1118
  Necessary for creation of
    lasting peace 630
  See also Trust
Confidence-building
  measures 384, 552,
  578, 654, 655, 673,
  678, 679, 690, 701, 721
Conflict
  Opposite of cooperation
    60
  Synonym for politics 60,
    271, 545
  Types short of invasion
    likely in the future 148
  See also Disputes
Conflict resolution p. xv, 16,
  32, 60, 71, 73, 79, 139,
  148, 306, 381, 385-428,
  432, 462, 465, 471,
  475, 551, 552, 578,
  582, 745, 821, 826,
  904, 1174, 1354
  Domestic models 430,
    434, 437, 451, 458,
    459, 472
  Facilitated 418
  International facilitating
    service 389
  See also Peaceful
    settlement,
    Peacemaking,
    Preventive diplomacy,
    Early warning
Congo 204, 282, 400, 549,
  563, 593
Consensus p.xvi, 25, 30, 38,
  52, 55, 74, 84, 98, 116,
  120, 127, 148, 154,
  163, 179, 186, 257,
  283, 287, 363, 394,
  415, 427, 459, 493,

  556, 567, 590, 733,
  747, 769, 772, 889,
  918, 922, 949, 963,
  978, 982, 984, 986,
  995, 1088, 1119, 1172,
  1227, 1290, 1302
  Defined 609
  Interim form of majority
    rule 84, 269, 271, 274,
    279, 283
  Consensus (majority rule),
    rather than consent
    (sovereignty), is the
    legal basis of obligation
    269, 271, 275, 276,
    279, 609, 963, 984,
    1033, 1302
  Is an escape from state
    insistence on
    sovereignty and
    rejection of weighted
    voting 984
  Way out from
    unacceptability of
    weighted voting and
    irremovability of veto
    276
  Midway between
    traditional diplomacy
    and national
    parliamentary
    procedure 274, 403
  Transition between
    exchange of
    ambassadors and
    enactment of law in a
    world legislature 274
  Opinio juris (legal
    conviction): 963
  Basis for political reforms
    163
  Genuine and fake 271
  Harder for Congress,
    states, and public to
    monitor and control
    363
  Negotiation of consensus
    is prime U.N. function
    74, 127, 128, 163, 164,
    190, 193, 200, 270,
    276, 281, 287, 362,
    403, 426, 609, 612,
    984

Principle on which peace
and solidarity rest
270
Virtual rule of unanimity
by higher majorities in
IMF 1088
See also Majority rule,
Voting, Veto, Decision
making
Consent p.xvi, 94, 97, 101,
415, 506, 521, 574,
598, 623, 868, 960
Source of legitimacy 30,
275, 279, 1037, 1272
Required for effective
action 55, 94, 415, 468,
562
Giving way to majority
procedures 55
Giving way to consensus
275
Necessity of evolution of
U.N. into a world state
256
Constitutional crisis, world
See World constitutional
crisis
Conventions 117, 353, 388,
1086, 1227, 1240,
1272, 1289
See also Treaties
Convergence 46, 176, 218,
367, 492, 840, 1006,
1096
Conversion of military
industry to civilian 136,
192, 216, 326, 651,
658, 699, 814, 815
Cooperation
See International
cooperation
Cosmopolitanism 68, 194,
196, 765, 1144, 1233,
1262
State policies cancel to
benefit of cosmopolitan
policy 1281
Council of Europe 425, 450,
1227, 1229, 1252
See also European
Convention on Human
Rights, European
Community

Crime, international 233,
354, 376, 638, 639,
776, 848, 850, 865,
1011, 1288
Cuban missile crisis 311,
322, 400, 404, 431,
546, 661, 1144
Culture 87, 747, 811, 833,
890, 897, 898, 904,
909, 910, 917, 920,
927, 1007, 1191, 1226
Development is a cultural
concept 1007
Cultural relativism is
opposed to human
rights 1228, 1283
See also UNESCO
Custom 32, 68, 81, 82, 85,
95, 98, 100, 115, 117,
245, 271, 277, 279,
388, 604, 612, 636,
964, 981, 996
Develops international
law: 103
Cannot keep pace with
international society 101
Heritage of colonialism
116
See also Praxis
Cyprus 394, 399, 440, 447,
448, 632
Czechoslovakia 322, 1108,
1246, 1271

D

Dangerous goods 1331
Debt crisis 52, 129, 133,
213, 216, 619, 621,
699, 807, 808, 813,
815, 831, 844, 870,
1004, 1011, 1014,
1036, 1038, 1043,
1052, 1056, 1060,
1065, 1066, 1067,
1073, 1075, 1078,
1081, 1087, 1089,
1122, 1133, 1135,
1157, 1164, 1165,
1172, 1174, 1179,
1199, 1205, 1207,
1298, 1319

Decentralization p.xvii, 3,
25, 33, 57, 62, 72, 73,
94, 98, 164, 171, 309,
340, 396, 604, 868,
877, 908, 1062, 1145,
1275, 1279, 1323
Pluralistic world view is
now accepted by most
scholars 389
Decentralization encounters
less resistance and
continuously wins
consent 868
Decision-making 36, 51, 61,
71, 91, 116, 118, 142,
154, 174, 187, 208,
229, 276, 283, 286,
288, 325, 355, 361,
362, 363, 368, 429,
609, 667, 734, 736,
742, 745, 769, 824,
836, 908, 954, 978,
982, 995, 1056, 1084,
1145, 1174, 1206,
1209, 1298, 1299,
1312
See also Consensus
Decolonization p.xii, 1, 7, 8,
14, 20, 21, 28, 80, 112,
114, 126, 141, 142,
158, 171, 204, 218,
223, 232, 245, 256,
270, 327-336, 341, 342,
359, 427, 518, 531,
541, 556, 559, 608,
742, 765, 941, 945,
1139, 1149, 1185,
1198, 1266
Eclipsed security issues at
U.N. (1954-64) 331
Model for cooperative
solutions in world
community 332
Continued in struggle for
economic development
1198, 1208
See also Trusteeship
Council
Defence 32, 94, 96, 101,
108, 121, 215, 292,
387, 416, 535, 539,
604, 605, 629, 646,
648, 653, 667, 688,

Chemical 187, 643, 646, 647, 648, 650, 673, 680, 690, 705, 706, 710, 711
Biological 187, 673, 691, 705, 711
Qualitative 136, 657, 678
Environmental 673, 683, 695, 705, 710
Food as a weapon 872, 875, 876
General treaties will be necessary if superpowers disarm to level where they could be threatened by middle powers 648, 698, 727
See also Arms control, Effective international control, Non-proliferation
Disaster relief 28, 53, 76, 165, 382, 632, 768, 866
Disease, epidemic 59, 223, 795, 846, 851, 852, 853, 855, 860, 862, 866
Smallpox eradication 852, 861, 863
See also AIDS, Health
Disputes
Defined 413, 419
Distinction between legal and political disputes 343, 419, 505, 510, 512, 517, 518, 519, 522
Listed 60, 404, 414, 417, 425, 455, 536, 550, 551, 552, 560, 826
Intensified by U.N. 149
Franco-German 542
See also War, Conflict resolution
Dispute settlement
See Peaceful settlement of disputes, Conflict resolution
Division of labour, international 59, 382, 944, 1196

Domestic conflict 36, 53, 69, 382, 394, 397, 401, 432, 560
International war is decreasing, but domestic conflict threatening international peace and security is increasing 432, 607, 615, 618
Civil war 69, 606, 723, 760, 876, 1271
Domestic jurisdiction (Article 2.7) p.xiv, 43, 141, 146, 162, 206, 215, 228, 231, 295, 368, 387, 417, 419, 506, 513, 593, 595, 602, 615, 617, 620, 640, 641, 689, 757, 889, 941, 996, 1025, 1126, 1233, 1251, 1252, 1253, 1254, 1257
Hard to distinguish from international affairs 43, 368, 397
See also Humanitarian intervention
Dominican Republic 149, 322, 567, 579, 622
Double standards 145, 168, 946, 955
See also Bias
Drug abuse, trafficking, and control 7, 14, 28, 46, 124, 182, 233, 641, 739, 774, 808, 848, 850, 864, 865, 938, 1011, 1029
Dumbarton Oaks conference (1944) 240, 248, 253, 255
New Dumbarton Oaks 182

E

Early warning 121, 145, 295, 317, 382, 384, 417, 426, 445, 577, 667, 671, 775, 876
See also Global watch, Fact-finding

East–West relations 29, 192, 268, 328, 340, 370, 391, 402, 403, 483, 552, 593, 654, 674, 685, 698, 710, 726, 890, 1006, 1008, 1025, 1132, 1231, 1314
See also Cold War
Ecology (and movement) 33, 48, 150, 257, 1003, 1008, 1012, 1023, 1292, 1302, 1305, 1310, 1318, 1323
Classics 1315, 1322, 1332, 1338
Contribution of people, not governments 1310
Successor to Marxism 1310
Economic and Social Council (Ecosoc) 132, 163, 164, 167, 244, 254, 323-326, 425, 952, 1183, 1187, 1279, 1287
Reform 323, 324, 325, 1187
Economic cooperation 55, 95, 129, 158, 160, 171, 204, 216, 195, 356, 365, 542, 741, 743, 825, 1013, 1024, 1057, 1066, 1071, 1078, 1089, 1127, 1171, 1174
Required for peaceful world order 1127
See also International cooperation, Economic management
Economic development p.xii, xvi, xvii, 1, 7, 8, 11, 14, 21, 22, 24, 27, 28, 33, 41, 42, 48, 49, 53, 107, 122, 124, 132, 133, 134, 150, 152, 153, 159, 162, 172, 177, 218, 232, 256, 288, 298, 301, 304, 321, 365, 410, 630, 657, 660, 687, 688, 689, 734, 737, 739, 775, 795, 798, 807, 812, 813, 814, 815, 828, 829, 841, 945,

Economic development
contd.
952, 963, 998,
1002-1034, 1038, 1039,
1041, 1052, 1054,
1055, 1056, 1062,
1063, 1071, 1081,
1082, 1093, 1119,
1127, 1129, 1133,
1164, 1165, 1169,
1173, 1216, 1218,
1288, 1290, 1313
'No society can be
flourishing and happy
whose greater part are
poor and miserable'
1042, 1046
Undercut by arms race
664
Foundation of world
peace: 293
People-centred 1004,
1007, 1009, 1013,
1018, 1021, 1041,
1050, 1320
People are the most
valuable factor of
production 1007
All countries are
developing countries
1023
Right to development
1049, 1260, 1261, 1268
Without health,
development has no
roots 862
Six stages from national
development to
ecological balance 257
Rural development 808,
809, 1029
Feminist perspective
1292, 1293
Homo economicus does
not match *Homo
sapiens,* who pursues
both private and public
goods 1012
Eighty percent of budgets
of U.N. system are
devoted to economic
and social development
323

U.N. projects (23,854)
1026
World development
authority 1040,
1197
Economic organizations
present most serious
test of world
government to date
1033
Economic management,
global 129, 132, 133,
141, 149, 150, 152,
156, 160, 181, 188,
208, 213, 218, 233,
236, 264, 295, 368,
832, 841, 873, 889,
965, 988, 999, 1007,
1009, 1016, 1025,
1030, 1032, 1055,
1086, 1209, 1309,
1337
Depends on prior building
of consensus by
negotiations at U.N.
164, 1032
Ecosoc is not working
well 323, 325
Economic United Nations
p.xvi, 127, 155, 164,
324, 362, 952, 1318
Economic well-being 319,
412, 1039, 1069, 1099,
1144, 1318
World order value 35, 37,
43, 66, 67, 91, 137,
144, 176, 555, 1354
Education, national 35, 44,
75, 77, 174, 380, 592,
737, 783, 795, 803,
811, 818, 844, 856,
862, 864, 893, 897,
900, 913, 927, 929,
931, 1007, 1014, 1018,
1026, 1034, 1170,
1191, 1242, 1288,
1299
Instrument of national
power: 899
Education for all 931
See also International
education, Knowledge
system

Effective international
control (complement of
general and complete
disarmament) p.xv,
135, 424, 644, 656,
657, 661, 666, 668,
674, 678, 685, 699,
702, 708
Egypt 534, 572, 580, 588,
1013, 1296
Electoral assistance 656,
603, 630, 1273
Élites and élitism 37, 48, 71,
91, 215, 319, 370, 397,
511, 556, 612, 722,
734, 774, 1198, 1207
See also Participation of
people
Embargo
See Sanctions
Energy (including oil and
nuclear power) 28, 42,
44, 59, 133, 153, 159,
182, 210, 326, 366,
513, 716, 718, 729,
732, 739, 740, 743,
801, 817, 962, 996,
998, 1021, 1025, 1028,
1136, 1154, 1161,
1201, 1205, 1213,
1301, 1317, 1328,
1337, 1340
Collective policies needed
because market is not
free 368
Enforcement 17, 93, 94, 114,
115, 121, 162, 173,
186, 191, 195, 204,
215, 225, 234, 236,
244, 258, 292, 295,
304, 356, 398, 415,
563, 604-629, 663, 877,
937, 942, 956, 964,
1099, 1104, 1249,
1258, 1272
Necessity for deterrence
and coercion 627
Penalty to secure
obedience to law
611
On states and individuals
177, 616, 617, 956,
1228

476

Forests 87, 1302, 1306,
1312, 1313, 1316,
1317, 1332
See also Deforestation
Four Policemen 240, 248,
723
See also Veto
Fourth World (LDCs) 45
France 183, 287, 542, 570,
619, 671, 686, 708,
714, 722, 911, 979,
1039, 1296
Freedom 27, 75, 120, 189,
261, 268, 479, 781,
825, 831, 833, 838,
840, 843, 901, 907,
909, 918, 927, 940,
955, 956, 1055, 1125,
1189, 1230, 1237, 1267
To be fully enjoyed by all,
freedom must be
subject to some legal
limitations 820, 829,
833
Freedom in a commons
brings ruin to all 1338
Freedom from want 880
See also Human rights,
Ideology
Freedom of the seas 92, 101,
964, 977, 981, 986
Superseded by common
heritage of mankind
963, 990, 1001
Free markets 168, 181, 186,
208, 213, 326, 365,
492, 775, 812, 831,
868, 872, 888, 992,
1005, 1010, 1012,
1015, 1094, 1101,
1108, 1132, 1134,
1197, 1200, 1211, 1337
Immoral 48
Liberal regime 368
Markets work well
managing trends; in
crises, governments are
needed 1015
In a global economy,
markets must be
brought into the service
of community 1012
See also Global market

Free trade 182, 186, 208,
409, 744, 812, 944,
963, 1004, 1071, 1091,
1098, 1099, 1101,
1103, 1104, 1111,
1112, 1119, 1121,
1174, 1319, 1331
Promotes the general
good 1121
See also GATT,
Protectionism
Functionalism 24, 29, 33,
40, 76, 97, 101, 142,
146, 149, 174, 229,
306, 377, 535, 541,
548, 551, 553, 734,
735, 736, 744, 745,
746, 748, 766, 772,
897, 908, 942, 949,
988, 1038, 1331
Defined 735
Political approach taken
by U.N. and E.C.
76
Neofunctionalism 34, 149,
735
Critique 41
Alternative of regional
federation 535
See also International
cooperation
Future 51, 91, 117, 123, 126,
141, 142, 143, 144,
146, 147, 153, 159,
187, 189, 190, 191,
208, 210, 252, 280,
286, 300, 303, 337,
340, 345, 357, 380,
393, 396, 438, 482,
499, 511, 516, 530,
532, 563, 566, 580,
591, 592, 632, 642,
662, 670, 675, 856,
883, 890, 899, 923,
955, 960, 986, 988,
1007, 1015, 1021,
1022, 1027, 1036,
1045, 1064, 1066,
1068, 1075, 1089,
1104, 1112, 1121,
1167, 1252, 1272,
1318, 1319, 1328,
1340

Sovereign nations cannot
control their future
542
Law in accordance with
the standards of the
future 636
Global 2000 report 1321

G

Game theory 32, 36, 42, 71,
429, 436, 668, 677
General Agreement on
Tariffs and Trade
(GATT) 29, 52, 129,
132, 133, 207, 211,
430, 477, 734, 746,
806, 807, 812, 870,
886, 888, 889, 944,
947, 1017, 1058,
1090-1128, 1160,
1177
Deteriorating 55, 181,
1111, 1115
Thriving 1102
Negotiation preferred over
legalism 1097, 1106,
1118
Escape clauses 149
Dispute settlement 1095,
1096, 1097, 1102,
1107, 1118, 1122
Reform 1004, 1097, 1098,
1101, 1104, 1108,
1114, 1115, 1117,
1122
See also Trade
General Assembly 6, 21, 23,
171, 227, 253, 266-282,
398, 628, 1105, 1279,
1287
Annual issues 8
Legislative capacity 84,
88, 92, 93, 97, 100,
106, 107, 114, 115,
116, 117, 122, 160,
172, 244, 266, 269,
270, 271, 274, 275,
277, 279, 280, 303,
351, 352, 376, 439,
454, 507, 519, 524,
532, 607, 1208

N

Namibia (South West
Africa) 272, 279, 295,
327, 391, 407, 456,
462, 507, 522, 562,
563, 601, 621, 630,
1024
Nationalism 49, 50, 63, 71,
105, 112, 191, 195,
221, 223, 225, 329,
362, 402, 428, 524,
541, 556, 757, 890,
956, 987, 993, 1080,
1144, 1184, 1226,
1266
Economic nationalism
1057, 1092, 1094,
1100, 1111
Colonial nationalism was
main factor for
decolonization 329, 548
Thirteen hundred nations
1226
See also Ethnic conflict
Nationalization of TNC
property 1150, 1151,
1154, 1163, 1168
National liberation wars 168,
604, 898, 1175
National missions and
ambassadors to the
U.N. 212, 303, 355-361
Missions are 'in' the
Secretariat 357
National security p.xiv, 41,
56, 124, 135, 191, 205,
207, 215, 228, 368,
386, 524, 647, 662,
718
See also Security
NATO 17, 25, 52, 62, 108,
124, 140, 161, 195,
203, 211, 215, 231,
245, 247, 254, 258,
423, 535, 538, 554,
578, 662, 698, 1211
Reasons for alliance 183,
184
Not a mere alliance but an
emerging Atlantic and
even global collective
security order 544

To be merged into CSCE
182, 184, 203, 706
See also Warsaw Pact,
Regional organization,
CSCE
Negotiation 32, 52, 133,
159, 267, 395, 396,
398, 403, 406, 413,
415, 419, 426, 429-443,
454, 460, 499, 505,
516, 525, 592, 615,
632, 652, 673, 677,
681, 686, 749, 826,
970, 1097, 1121, 1174,
1352
Pre-negotiation 433, 436,
437, 465, 467
Prior to peacekeeping 574
Domestic 430, 434, 437
More important than
passing resolutions 72
Pace increasing,
effectiveness
decreasing 441
Failure over NIEO 1188
U.N. to become forum for
negotiation of
consensus 74, 127, 128,
163, 164, 190, 193,
270, 362, 402, 426,
629, 666, 673, 918,
984, 985, 1032, 1080,
1177, 1187, 1196
Negotiating world order
52, 1127
See also Peaceful
settlement, Diplomacy,
Consensus
Neo-colonialism 88, 332,
366
Neo-mercantilism 1190,
1197
Netherlands 1039, 1140
Neutrality 92, 308, 449, 462,
665
New International Economic
Order (NIEO) p.xv, 50,
70, 129, 133, 144, 159,
160, 171, 174, 178,
265, 271, 324, 328,
341, 351, 364, 365,
368, 369, 370, 374,
746, 748, 829, 830,

868, 880 884, 898, 900,
941, 945, 959, 988,
990, 999, 1016, 1024,
1025, 1028, 1032,
1039, 1044, 1052,
1084, 1101, 1124,
1138, 1155, 1173,
1174, 1177, 1180,
1182, 1185-1212, 1261,
1290, 1309, 1353
Right to adequate
standard of living 1194
Economic in issues, social
in implications,
political in
implementation 1200,
1205
Needed by both North and
South in interdependent
world 1199, 1202,
1212, 1309
Continuation of struggle
for decolonization
1198, 1208
Based on guilt for
colonialism 941
OPEC oil embargo, which
transferred $70,000
million from First to
Third World, was
model 1192
Threat to replace liberal
market regime with
U.N. authority: 368
Ultra-mercantilist
programme 1197
Will benefit only Third
World élites; alternative
of basic needs strategy
would benefit all in
South 1198
Magnitude and difficulties
of negotiation explain
failure 1174, 1188,
1196, 1201, 1205,
1206, 1211
Comprehensive strategies
like NIEO are out;
pragmatism is back
1178
Alternative strategy is to
preserve the
environment 1309

Peace enforcement units
121, 186, 304, 578,
623
See also Standing U.N.
military forces
Peaceful coexistence 35,
117, 204, 245, 303,
391, 417, 698
Peaceful settlement of
disputes p.xii, xv, 5, 7,
8, 17, 24, 32, 60, 79,
92, 93, 94, 95, 119,
135, 138, 141, 147,
158, 172, 177, 193,
197, 205, 220, 235,
252, 289, 314, 337,
344, 347, 385-428,
429-560, 657, 663, 690,
889, 937, 964, 980,
981, 994, 1064, 1097,
1355
U.N. worsens disputes
149
Draft general treaty on the
peaceful settlement of
disputes 395, 398, 484,
495
Developed legal systems
include dispute
settlement, prevention
of conflict, duties,
rights, and equitable
goals 410
See also Conflict
resolution, Preventive
diplomacy
Peacekeeping p.xii, 1, 6, 9,
13, 16, 20, 21, 23, 34,
53, 72, 74, 121, 123,
124, 139, 162, 173,
186, 204, 210, 215,
220, 225, 228, 231,
232, 256, 291, 292,
295, 301, 303, 305,
307, 320, 359, 384,
400, 401, 417, 427,
446, 531, 552, 561-603,
628, 631, 643, 671
Defined 562, 563, 566,
569, 576, 590, 598
The projection of non-
violence onto the
military plane 590

Based on non-use of force
562, 569, 598, 599,
601, 602, 605
Classic (traditional) 590,
596
Palliative compared to
national restraint on
war power 425, 627
U Thant's legal deference
to Egypt on withdrawal
of UNEF I 321, 322,
589, 590
Carter report on reserves
and training 154, 569
Improvements in training,
equipment, logistics,
finance, and authority
154, 304, 569, 577, 627
Expansion after 1989 566,
569, 596, 601, 603,
610, 616, 623, 627,
629, 690
U.N. command 623, 627
If dependent on U.S.
security interests, U.N.
would be converted
into an agency of
national foreign policy
141
Gliding into enforcement
or war 191, 195, 227,
304, 563, 593, 603,
610, 616, 623, 627, 629
Transitional to world
marshals or true
international police
569, 601, 616
Non-U.N. peacekeeping
forces 227, 533, 564,
568, 569, 570, 573,
575, 581, 587
Arab Deterrent Force 533
Inter-American Peace
Force 567
Multinational Force 533,
564, 570, 573, 575, 584
Multilateral Force and
Observers 572, 575,
584
ONUC 561, 565, 571,
593, 600, 602
UNDOF 574, 575, 584,
588

UNEF I 561, 575, 585,
588, 590, 600, 602
UNEF II 572, 575, 580,
584, 588, 590
UNFICYP 561, 571, 600,
602, 632
UNIFIL 533, 570, 574,
575, 580, 583, 584,
588, 594
UNIIMOG 574
UNIPOM 600
UNMOGIP 600, 602
UNOGIL 600
UNSCOB 600, 602
UNSF 600
UNTAC 563, 569, 574
UNTAG 562, 569, 574
UNTEA 561, 569, 571
UNTSO 574, 588, 600,
602
UNYOM 600, 602
U.S. Sinai Field Mission
572
Peace-loving states 608
Peace-making p.xi, 11, 21,
121, 124, 173, 191,
195, 398, 403, 417,
419, 421, 464, 576,
577, 578, 631
See also Peaceful
settlement of
disputes
Peace messenger initiative
75
Perestroika (reform) 219,
223, 416, 1025
Persian Gulf War 96, 123,
170, 219, 227, 234,
326, 494, 605, 620,
646, 655, 711, 797,
1133, 1136
An American action
licensed by the U.N.
228
Lessons for U.N. 145,
148, 191, 234, 292,
295, 610, 627
Prototype of future
collective security 53,
189, 195
Peru 1307
Philanthropy 70
Philippines 539, 1225

494

Power *contd.*
International organizations have no power 57, 201
Law-making powers of U.N. 84, 88, 94, 100, 128, 130, 269, 279, 280, 350, 351, 352, 376, 607
Temporary exercise of sovereign powers by U.N. 330, 569, 630
Power of one courageous man 307, 425, 1051, 1054, 1257
See also Sovereignty
Power politics 32, 33, 34, 39, 56, 65, 79, 81, 103, 187, 224, 241, 245, 286, 302, 305, 318, 456, 462, 509, 554, 604, 828 949, 972, 1233
Challenge of China 288
Cycles 65
Current substitute for international legislation 97
Counter-productive 33
Beyond power politics 54, 187, 218, 293, 341, 397, 535
Giving way to welfare politics 1144
Abandoned by Hans Morgenthau 79, 187
See also Realism, Balance of power, Deterrence
Praxis, practice, pragmatism 54, 65, 85, 104, 113, 126, 188, 195, 199, 227, 242, 252, 267, 271, 273, 276, 279, 283, 293, 325, 339, 351, 352, 353, 377, 382, 385, 386, 393, 394, 402, 414, 418, 421, 426, 429, 433, 437, 440, 443, 446, 449, 459, 461, 464, 481, 482, 516, 519, 573, 590, 598, 603, 604, 609, 628, 629,

642, 657, 665, 675, 679, 689, 741, 742, 828, 854, 855, 871, 924, 953, 1028, 1038, 1053, 1121, 1177, 1220, 1262, 1302
See also Transition, Custom
Preliminary draft of a world constitution 555
Prevention of conflict and war 65, 139, 173, 177, 220, 390, 410, 623, 673, 680, 683, 684, 994, 1301
Preventive diplomacy p.xii, xv, 53, 121, 139, 162, 192, 195, 225, 234, 252, 293, 295, 307, 314, 317, 382-384, 410, 417, 465, 578, 629
See also Global watch, Early warning, Fact-finding, Secretariat
Principles of international law 38, 51, 55, 68, 79, 95, 101, 103, 104, 106, 108, 113, 114, 117, 148, 274, 290, 345, 382, 392, 413, 496, 520, 521, 633, 833, 835, 963, 1086, 1202, 1227, 1258, 1272, 1302, 1310, 1312
Procedure 273, 281, 283, 285, 286, 289, 338, 363, 393, 394, 405, 418, 468, 482, 492, 519, 520, 554, 641, 734, 835, 1257, 1273, 1277, 1278, 1344
Process theory of law 59, 91, 94, 102, 115, 118, 279, 341, 342, 518, 542, 824, 1237
See also Positivism
Projects of economic development 1026, 1034, 1045, 1047, 1051, 1062, 1064, 1215, 1294, 1342
Proliferation
See Non-proliferation

Propaganda 39, 61, 514, 692, 742, 833
Prosperity 137, 479, 699
See also Economic well-being
Protectionism 38, 221, 809, 944, 1091, 1094, 1095, 1098, 1100, 1104, 1110, 1112, 1114, 1120, 1122, 1123
See also Free trade
Psychology of international relations 409, 431, 441, 471, 542, 749, 781, 869, 896
See also Motives
Publicists, international legal 32, 85, 94, 117, 200, 352, 606, 972
Public opinion 38, 53, 73, 75, 150, 186, 200, 249, 250, 293, 302, 311, 360, 378, 380, 385, 388, 468, 499, 558, 601, 617, 636, 648, 660, 663, 685, 693, 705, 713, 734, 743, 762, 884, 904, 1244, 1281
Ultimate third party 454
See also Political will
Pugwash conferences 685, 726

Q

Quakers (Society of Friends) 463
Quantitative methods 36, 44, 60, 65, 188, 319, 340, 366, 425, 658, 734, 744, 767, 770, 771, 778, 797, 812, 859, 999, 1022, 1070, 1146, 1199
See also Statistics
Queen in Parliament, source of law 84
Quiet diplomacy 16, 39, 317, 425
See also Good offices, Conciliation, Secretary-General

Normal to adjustment of balance of power 31, 63, 228, 604

Transformative war at critical historical periods 65

Causes 36, 105, 124, 334, 409, 428, 608, 896

Not rooted in human biology 896, 917

Wars since 1945 60, 78, 112, 234, 290, 388, 404, 414, 417, 425, 432, 455, 536, 550, 551, 552, 560, 608, 695

Threat of world war 131, 140, 196, 198, 228, 295, 311, 387, 401, 411, 442, 465, 581, 646, 652, 664, 666, 668, 685, 692, 693, 695, 727, 906, 1008, 1260, 1317, 1321

Limited nuclear war 646

Civil war 69, 606, 723, 760, 876, 1271

Waged by U.N. 192, 205, 258, 397, 563, 608, 610

Reduction of threat 386, 581, 644, 653, 654, 666, 667, 680, 681, 684, 694, 704, 745

Danger reduced by Security Council 220, 293, 317

Sanctions an alternative 614

Regional organization no solution 541, 554, 606

No third world war before U.N. reform 141, 256, 690

Law of war 92, 449, 636, 665, 1246

Abolition 136, 140, 177, 189, 244, 250, 295, 387, 401, 428, 517, 521, 598, 629, 633, 638, 656, 684, 693, 726, 897, 911, 917

See also Peace

War crimes 296, 297, 637, 641

War of position by disadvantaged 47

Warsaw Pact 108, 124, 161, 184, 423, 538, 544, 698, 706

Water, pure 59, 87, 774, 873, 1029, 1048, 1330

Weighted voting 20, 122, 125, 127, 157, 276, 281, 355, 362, 747, 751, 965, 979, 984, 1033, 1038, 1074, 1084, 1088, 1126

Weighted votes of superpowers in areas like atomic testing or outer space where other states are unready to enter 279

See also Representation

Whales and dolphins, protection 998

Wisdom 17, 20, 31, 38, 42, 141, 178, 180, 197, 206, 242, 249, 293, 314, 399, 415, 492, 675, 689, 717, 720, 780, 827, 1068, 1084, 1121, 1191, 1193, 1207, 1235, 1315, 1322, 1338

General wisdom of statesmen in a world without strong central authority 406

Withdrawal from U.N. 50, 86, 168, 178, 247, 266, 748, 918, 955, 1184

From Bretton Woods 1084

From IAEA 746

From ICJ 342, 343, 345, 349, 505, 514, 528, 529

From ILO 746, 942, 946, 949, 953, 955, 959

From NPT 722

From UNESCO 50, 746, 747, 838, 843, 844, 897, 898, 901, 903, 908, 915, 918, 921, 922, 924, 928, 955, 1268

Women's rights 28, 141, 310, 326, 374, 737, 772, 798, 803, 1029, 1228, 1256, 1257, 1279, 1285, 1288-1299, 1320, 1354

World Bank 38, 115, 129, 132, 133, 207, 211, 255, 362, 619, 738, 746, 789, 841, 878, 931, 945, 947, 1016, 1017, 1032, 1033, 1035-1065, 1077, 1138, 1193, 1294, 1319, 1342

Cold War reasons for non-coordination with U.N. are now out of date 631

Economic stabilization programmes 631

Long-term credit institution for economic development 1038, 1045, 1051, 1054, 1056, 1065

World development authority 1040, 1197

World citizenship 35, 45, 46, 73, 128, 137, 142, 159, 175, 257, 322, 422, 890, 1054, 1237, 1263, 1268

World community p.xv, xvii, xviii, 15, 24, 33, 35, 36, 57, 63, 64, 68, 69, 71, 74, 89, 90, 91, 95, 112, 118, 126, 128, 131, 141, 144, 150, 157, 166, 188, 189, 193, 205, 216, 219, 221, 223, 236, 256, 267, 280, 299, 303, 332, 344, 381, 388, 402, 404, 408, 443, 512, 518, 524, 542, 560, 586, 607, 608, 614, 618, 653, 675, 735, 762, 766, 776, 807, 852, 884, 899, 956, 1012, 1057, 1093, 1149, 1237, 1241, 1244, 1265, 1343

Still weaker than local sovereignty 141

World Meteorological Organization (WMO) 746, 753, 754

World order 15, 31, 32, 33, 35, 37, 38, 43, 52, 63, 65, 66, 67, 68, 83, 91, 98, 114, 137, 159, 175, 194, 196, 199, 201, 205, 251, 252, 272, 309, 342, 345, 363, 514, 544, 553, 554, 595, 669, 719, 753, 830, 904, 961, 996, 1024, 1057, 1127, 1162, 1354, 1356

Defined 35, 554, 555

Contending approaches 35

See also Peace, Justice, Economic well-being, Environmental preservation, Participation, Maintenance of international peace and security, New world order

World Order Models Project (WOMP) 37, 91, 144, 176

World peace through world law (Clark–Sohn plan) 122, 143, 175, 177, 187, 242, 290, 480, 708

World politics 29-79, 137, 152, 179, 194, 226, 303, 318, 340, 369, 378, 402, 408, 431, 672, 718, 735, 745, 781, 859, 884, 913, 923, 1012, 1085, 1235, 1246, 1312

Similar to British politics before rise of disciplined political parties 41, 84, 273

Contemporary interest groups 155, 362-370

Should be guided by primacy of human values 216

Primacy of law over politics 220

Place of U.N. 72, 272, 301, 336

U.N. is used to pursue self-interests rather than settle conflicts 138

New paradigm in place of state-centric one 70, 1144

War, which was necessary for the unification of the modern state, is not tolerable for the evolution of the U.N. 141, 256, 401

Absolutism, which was checked by development of democratic institutions in the formation of the modern state, is not tolerable for the evolution of the U.N. 274

World politics is an absurdity until all human beings are members of one world state 404

World weather 97, 739, 753, 842

Y

Yemen 534, 797

Youth 770, 771, 772, 781, 785, 793, 892, 896, 1007, 1029

Agents for development, rather than passive recipients 772

On the threshold of historical transformation 781

Yugoslavia 190, 227, 228, 231, 297, 564, 618, 1027, 1134, 1226, 1271, 1296

Z

Zimbabwe
See Rhodesia

Zionism 178, 185, 265